Web Design:
The Complete Reference

About the Author ...

Thomas Powell has been professionally involved in the Internet community since 1987. His career began with network support at UCLA's PICnet, followed by several years at CERFnet. In 1994, he founded Powell Internet Consulting, LLC (www.pint.com), a firm specializing in advanced Web design and development.

Powell is the author of three other Web Development books: *Web Site Engineering* (with Dominique Cutts and David Jones), *HTML Programmer's Reference* (with Dan Whitworth), and *HTML: The Complete Reference*. He has written extensively about the Web and development technologies for *NetGuide, Internet Week, Interactive Age, Communications Week,* and *Network World*.

Mr. Powell teaches Web publishing classes through the Information Technologies program at UCSD Extension. He holds a B.S. in Math Applied Science from UCLA and an M.S. in Computer Science from UCSD.

Web Design:
The Complete Reference

Thomas A. Powell

Osborne/**McGraw-Hill**

Berkeley New York St. Louis San Francisco
Auckland Bogotá Hamburg London Madrid
Mexico City Milan Montreal New Delhi Panama City
Paris São Paulo Singapore Sydney
Tokyo Toronto

Osborne/**McGraw-Hill**
2600 Tenth Street
Berkeley, California 94710
U.S.A.

For information on translations or book distributors outside the U.S.A., or to arrange bulk purchase discounts for sales promotions, premiums, or fund-raisers, please contact Osborne/**McGraw-Hill** at the above address.

Web Design: The Complete Reference

1234567890 AGM AGM 019876543210

ISBN 0-07-212297-8

Publisher
Brandon A. Nordin

Associate Publisher and Editor-in-Chief
Scott Rogers

Acquisitions Editor
Megg Bonar

Project Editor
Mark Karmendy

Acquisitions Coordinator
Stephane Thomas

Technical Editor
Tony Arguelles

Copy Editor
Dennis Weaver

Proofreader
John Gildersleeve

Indexer
Rebecca Plunkett

Computer Designers
Jani Beckwith
Jim Kussow

Illustrators
Michael Mueller
Robert Hansen
Beth Young

Series Design
Peter Hancik

This book was composed with Corel VENTURA ™ Publisher.

Contents at a Glance

Contents

Part I

Core Web Design Issues

Part II

Site Organization and Navigation

Part III

Elements of Page Design

Part IV

Technology and Web Design

Part V

Future Directions

15   The Future of Web Design 713

Part VI

Appendixes

A   Core Web Site Design Principles 735

Acknowledgments

The struggle to publish this book has been nearly Herculean at times. Without the assistance and encouragement of many others, it would certainly not have come to pass. First, thanks to the folks at Osborne/McGraw-Hill, including Megg Bonar, Stephane Thomas, and Mark Karmendy, who put up with extraordinary delays related to the difficulty of pulling this book off. Technical editing by Alan Herrick , Daisy Bhonsle, and Maytal Dahan helped ferret out inconsistencies. Great thanks again to Dan Whitworth, who despite jury duty and other complications of real life, managed to help get everything together. Other staff members at PINT—particularly Francesca Weisser, Eric Raether, Rob McFarlane, Jason Zimmerman, Cory Ducker, David Snow, Meredith Hodge, Nikos Ioannou, Regina Montoya, Patrick Fischer, Rueben Poon, Anh Tran, Lina Pei, Dave Andrews, and many others—provided valuable help with the editing, examples, and the immense workload that putting out a book takes. Staffers from my other businesses, particularly Joe Lima, also lent a helpful hand on numerous occasions. Business associates, including Tony Rihan, Rodolfo Garcia-Muriel, and Jim Tam, also provided support with my other business affairs, enabling me to take care of this monster project.

My family and friends, particularly Sylvia Cheung and Diana Powell, were always there rooting me on to finish. Finally, I would like to thank Harvey Stern, Jim Brown, the staff of UCSD Extension, Bill Griswold, the staff of the UCSD Computer Science

Department, Lee Schlesinger of *ITWorld*, Christine Burns of *Network World*, and all my students, past and present, for helping spread and expand knowledge about Web design and publishing.

Thomas A. Powell
April 2000

Introduction

A design book without color pictures! Who would have thought it could be published? Yet that's actually what I set out to do. There are plenty of design books out there that provide color screen snapshots of cool sites with short discussions on interesting aspects. Given the fluid nature of the Web, those interesting sites have changed by the time the ink on the book has dried, leaving only a paper record of what the site used to be like. Unfortunately, what is left on paper only provides a limited idea of the good and bad qualities of the site. They don't tell you about the nasty e-mails from users confused by navigation or locked out because they didn't have the latest browser. They don't show you the programming error messages thrown when users do something unpredictable, the speed at which their pages load, or the size the screen must be for the design to work. Even so, I turn to these books often as they provide a great deal of visual inspiration. Still, they tell only half the story. This book will try to tell the other half.

Don't worry—I do speak from experience. This book isn't going to wallow in obtuse theory or get hung up on nitty-gritty technical issues of building pages. Instead, I will try to discuss important theory, as well as the practical rules of thumb and technical gotchas that my firm has picked up in the practice of building or redesigning nearly 150 sites over the past few years. Not everything has worked, and some designs have failed miserably. I have learned a great deal, both from my own mistakes and from those made by others. Experience is a good teacher, and it will teach you that truly excellent sites are hard to execute; on the Web, a very fine balance has to be struck between designer wants and user needs, between form and function, and between uniqueness and consistency, all the while respecting what is reasonably possible to execute in the chaotic medium of the Web.

Web design is a mixture of art and science, inspiration and execution, and, ultimately, of frustration and elation. You may solve the visual aspect of the site, only to find that the site is difficult to implement. Web design is all-encompassing; how things are done behind the scenes is just as important as how it looks up front. With the rise of e-commerce, Web sites are beginning to exhibit more software qualities as they focus more and more on task. Usability is now a paramount concern. Progressive site designers will accept this trend and seek to better understand their medium and their users.

As you read this book, you won't always agree with what I have to say. You may even find that some ideas contradict others. That's okay. Part of being a good designer is being able to question why and how things are done. There's room for plenty of opinions. After all, the conventions of the Web change all the time. Unfortunately, I won't be able to show what's cool or provide a step-by-step process of what visuals will appeal to users. This is highly opinion-driven, and the trends change so fast. There is only one way for the designer to pick this up: browse and use a large number of sites, particularly the popular and the cutting-edge ones. Try to find the common patterns and isolate what makes a site tick. I hope that after reading the book, you will know what to look for, and understand the theory and practice behind why a site works. If I've done that much, this will book will be 50 percent of what you need to make great Web sites. The rest will be up to you and your creativity. So get out there and show the Web what you can do!

Using This Book

This book relies heavily on a Web component found at http://www.webdesignref.com. This site contains all the examples in the book, as well as demos related to topics presented. The demos presented will tend to focus on the Demo Corporation—purveyors of fine fictitious, futuristic goods, such as robots, personal space vehicles, and living domes. A complete execution of the site can be found, of course, at http://www.democompany.com. The downside of this approach is that it may seem to suggest a single way to approach site design for readers who can't see beyond a particular style of execution. However, the only purpose here is to make sure the examples match what is discussed in the book. Using various sites from around the Web may better profile different design styles, but it also runs the certain risk of the sites changing and not staying consistent with the good design ideas presented. The Web site will also be used to provide links to articles and resources that update the ideas presented in the book. Downloads for suggested tools can also be found at the support site.

The text assumes that readers are fairly fluent in core HTML technologies like HTML and CSS, have passing familiarity with JavaScript, and can use basic graphics-manipulation tools, such as Photoshop. Readers who are interested in learning these subjects in greater depth should consider the companion book, *HTML: The Complete Reference* (www.htmlref.com), also by this author. The two books together provide a complete discussion of both theory and execution of sites not specifically tied in to using a particular visual or Web page design tool. Tutorial books on various editors and tools can of course be utilized in conjunction with either book.

Undoubtedly, bugs will be found in the code presented, and design theories may change as trends shift. Readers are encouraged to send information about fixes, oversights, and new ideas directly to the author at tpowell@pint.com. These suggestions and comments will certainly be seriously considered for a second edition of this book.

Thomas A. Powell
tpowell@pint.com
April 2000

The Complete Reference

Web Design

Part I

Core Web Design Issues

The Complete Reference

Web Design

Chapter 1

What Is Web Design?

A ny discussion of Web design often quickly gets off track because what people mean by the expression varies so dramatically. While everyone has some sense of what Web design is, nobody seems to be able to define it exactly. Certain components, such as visual design or programming, are generally included in any discussion, but their importance in the construction of sites varies from individual to individual, as well as from site to site. Beyond visuals and technology considerations, many point to the creation and organization of content in Web sites as the most important aspect of Web design. Finally, with the rise of e-commerce, consideration of business issues has become an important component in a successful site design.

Depending on the particular project, all of these disciplines, as well as other subdisciplines representing the intersection of these major facets of Web design, may be required. With influences from library science, graphic design, programming, client/server technology, user interface design, usability, and a variety of others, Web design is truly a multidisciplinary field.

The Web Design Pyramid

While we could include influences from literally dozens of fields, the four primary aspects of Web design are content, technology, visuals, and economics. The primary purpose of content is to inform or perhaps persuade users. The point of using technology on a Web site is to implement the function of the site. The visuals provide the form for the site. Lastly, for most sites we need to consider the economic ramifications of building the site. If there is no clear purpose or benefit for the site, sites generally are not built. Of course, the amount of influence of each particular aspect of Web sites varies based on the type of site being built. A personal home page generally doesn't have the economic considerations of a shopping site. An intranet for a manufacturing company may not have the visual considerations of a public Web site promoting an action movie, and so on. Because the requisite mix of disciplines varies so dramatically with the nature of the site being built, it is a difficult task to discuss Web design as a unified whole.

It is useful to think of Web sites metaphorically as pyramids, as shown in Figure 1-1. Content provides the bricks we use to build the pyramid, but the foundation rests solidly on both visuals and technology, with a heavy reliance on economics to make our project worth doing. As Web designers, we try to architect our sites carefully, but construction is difficult. The shifting sands of Web technology make it challenging to build our site; it requires teamwork and a firm understanding of the Web medium. Even if we are experts able to construct a beautiful and functional Web site, our users may look at our beautiful construction with puzzlement. Designers, or their employers, often spend more time considering their own needs and wants than those of the site's visitors. Our conceptual Web pyramids may become too much like brick-and-mortar pyramids—impenetrable tombs that leave us wondering if our users can even find the door. Do they even understand the point of the site? While

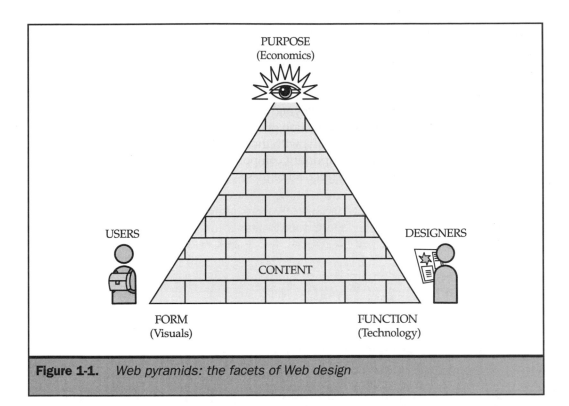

Figure 1-1. *Web pyramids: the facets of Web design*

Web development challenges aren't quite on the level of those faced by the ancient Egyptians, building a functional, pleasing Web site that can stand the test of Internet time is certainly not easy.

Building Web Sites

Building a Web site can be very difficult. While some of the core technologies like HTML are easy enough to master, developers seem to make numerous mistakes. The chief reasons for this are a lack of developer experience, a poorly defined process, and unrealistic schedules. Because of time constraints or inexperience, designers tend to start from one extreme or another, and then jump right to implementation without considering the preceding steps. For example, some Web professionals start out building the site from the visuals. The design process consists of mocking up site pages in a visual design tool and then figuring out what to do from there. The resulting sites often consist of image-heavy pages that look like online glossy brochures. Today's visually driven sites are often built entirely in Macromedia Flash (www.macromedia.com/flash) and resemble movie intros without a film to introduce. While the site's logo may spin and bounce to a looped beat, there usually is little purpose to the site itself other than to show off the creator's visual skills. For a portfolio site, this may be the intent, but what about other types of sites? Sites for which the visuals were developed first generally are difficult to update, lack any major technology beyond glitzy effects, lack function, and tend to be slow to download. Many people have termed such sites brochureware or introware since the function of the sites is little beyond what a paper brochure, fancy software, or video introduction would consist of. An example of such as site is shown in Figure 1-2.

Of course, on the opposite side of the spectrum are those who start implementing a site with a focus directly on technology. While these sites may use the latest and greatest programming facilities, they often do not have a cohesive design. Any visuals used seem tacked on and the interface is often very confusing. Sometimes such sites practice "Christmas tree" design. Once the function is completed, the developer

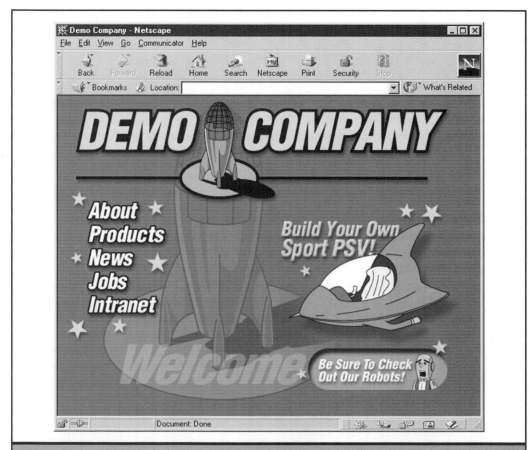

Figure 1-2. *Visuals first result in "brochureware" or "introware"*

decides to decorate the page like a Christmas tree—with a variety of colored balls, clip art, and animated GIFs hung on the page in a fruitless attempt to make the page more appealing. In this case, visual design takes a backseat to technology. Here again, as in the case of the visuals-first site, technology is used more to show off what the developer can do than to provide what the user wants. Heavy use of Java applets and plug-ins, and requirements that browsers support the latest addition to DHTML, XML, or CSS are sure signs the page is driven by technology first. Technology-first sites tend to practice exclusionary design, use the latest browser innovations, and often lack support for the function of the site. An example of a technology-first site is shown in Figure 1-3.

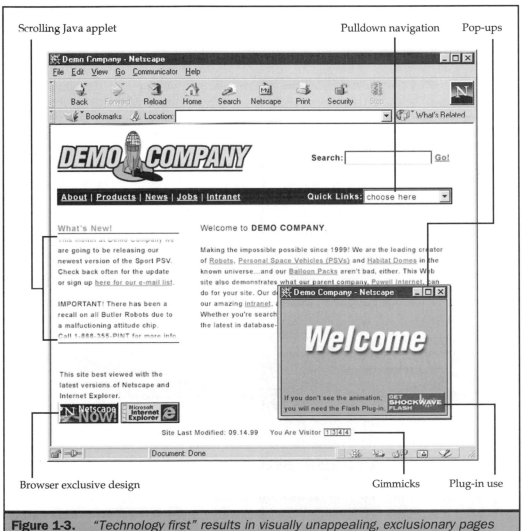

Figure 1-3. *"Technology first" results in visually unappealing, exclusionary pages*

Web Development Process Model

Technology and visuals provide the base of the Web design pyramid; both are necessary and must relate directly to the purpose of the site. Instead of implementing first and asking questions later, it makes more sense to discuss the purpose of the site and then determine how to accomplish any defined goals. This deductive or "top-down" approach to Web site development is fairly well understood. First, it is important to consider the purpose of the site. Before building a site, you should carefully define the problem the site may be addressing or any goals you are trying to achieve. A clear understanding of the purpose will reduce the risk of the project failing and help determine if it is even reasonable to do the site at all. After determining the goal(s) of the site, a specification should be created. The specification will note all the requirements for the site and consider the audience very carefully. Next, a design for the site should be produced. The design may include both technical and visual prototypes. Once the design is finalized, the site should be implemented and tested. Eventually, all the pieces of the site, including the content, should be integrated and further tested. Only then should the site be released, with various fixes and modifications to be made once users begin to provide feedback. Many disciplines such as software engineering have defined a process model similar to the one described, the most famous being the *waterfall* approach, which describes the software life cycle from project planning to eventual release and maintenance. The process is split into a variety of steps that help guide the developer from general requirements to specific implementation. An example of the stages in the waterfall process is shown here:

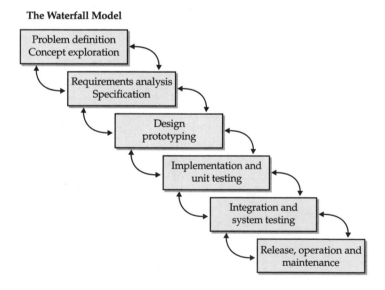

Note that the number of steps in the process model, and their names, varies from developer to developer. Furthermore, the basic waterfall is not the only model in use;

numerous other process models such as modified waterfall, spiral, joint application design (JAD), and others could also be used. Always remember that the ultimate purpose of a process model is to help guide the development of the site. An ideal model will help the Web developer deal with the complexity of the site, minimize any risks of project failure, be able to handle changes encountered during the project, provide feedback for management, and be fast and easy to follow. A pretty tall order, especially considering that most Web developers are not skilled in formal software engineering principles, and the Web development field is not even a decade old. Chapter 2 will discuss the Web development process in more depth.

Building for Users

As already noted, a common mistake made in Web development is that, far too often, sites are built more for designers and their needs than for the site's actual users. A process model won't guarantee a good site if designers ignore the needs of their users. Always remember this important tenet of Web design:

Rule: YOU are NOT the USER.

What you understand is not what a user will understand. As a designer, you have intimate knowledge of a Web site. You understand where information is. You understand how to install plug-ins. You have the optimal screen resolution, browser setup, etc. Accept the fact that many users will not necessarily have intimate knowledge of the site you have so carefully crafted. They may not even have the same interests as you.

Given the importance of the users' interests and desires, it might seem appropriate to simply ask the users to design the site the way they want. This seems to be a good idea until you consider another basic Web design tenet:

Rule: USERS are NOT DESIGNERS.

Not everyone is or should be a Web designer. Just as it would seem foolish to let moviegoers attempt to direct a major motion picture on the basis of their having viewed numerous movies, we should not expect users to be able to design Web sites just because they have browsed a multitude of sites. Users often have unrealistic requirements and expectations for sites. Users will not think carefully about the individual components of a Web site. In summary, users are not going to have the sophisticated understanding of the Web that a designer will have.

That said, the key to successful, usable Web site design is always trying to think from the point of view of the user. *User-centered design* is the term given to design that always puts the user first. But what can we say about users? Is there a typical user? Does there exist a "Joe Average Internet" for whom we should design our sites? Probably not, but we certainly should consider average traits such as reaction times, memory, and other cognitive or physical abilities as we design sites. An overview of cognitive science helps us understand basic user capabilities and is discussed further in Chapter 3. Remember, however, that while users may have similar basic characteristics, they are also individuals. What may seem easy to one user will be hard for another. Sites that are built for a "common" user may not meet the needs of all users. Power users may find the site restrictive while novice users find it too difficult. Users are individuals with certain shared capacities and characteristics. Sites should take account of the relevant differences while focusing on the commonalities, as stated by the following Web design tenet:

> **Rule: Design for the common user, but account for differences.**

Utility and Usability

Great Web sites are truly useful to their users. Usefulness can be thought of as a combination of utility and usability[1]. *Utility* describes the site's functionality that hopefully meets a user's need. *Usability* describes the user's ability to manipulate the site's features in order to accomplish a particular goal. Consider a site that provides online banking facilities: It could be said that it has great utility if it provides all the features like balance checking, transfer, bill payment, and so on that the user would come to expect. However, the site itself may be an utter failure because the function provided is so confusing that the site is effectively unusable. Clearly if a site does not function properly, either because of designer mistakes or poor design choices that make it difficult to use, it is not a great site. Usable sites will be efficient, easy to learn, and help users accomplish their goals in a satisfactory and error-free manner. A detailed discussion of usability is presented in Chapter 3.

From Paper to Software

The growing importance of usability in Web design is directly related to the movement from a Web-as-print paradigm to a Web-as-software paradigm. In the early days, the functionality provided by a Web site was relatively simple. Most sites were just an electronic form of a print product like a brochure, catalog, or magazine. Even if the site suffered from severe usability problems, the worst the user could do was get lost or maybe make mistakes while filling out a form. Today's Web sites, however, come in many forms, ranging from simple "brochureware" sites to complex Web-based applications, as shown in Figure 1-4. The resulting variety and complexity have put a premium on usability as a key element of site design.

---

[1]Grudin, J. (1992) Utility and Usability: Research issues and development contexts. *Interacting with Computers* 4,2 (August), 209-217.
Nielsen, Jakob *Usability Engineering*, Academic Press, Chestnut Hill, MA, 1993

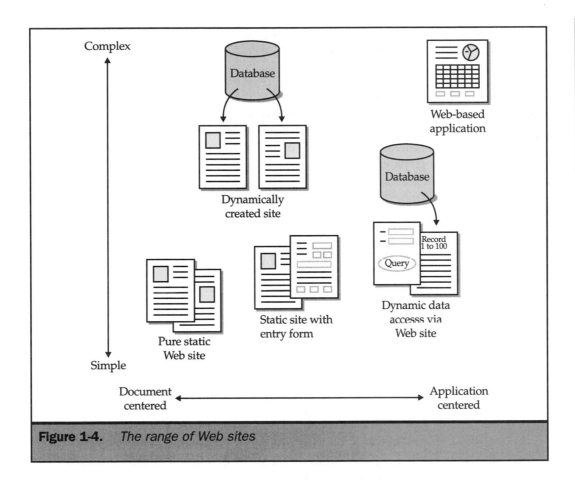

Figure 1-4.   *The range of Web sites*

Like software, a Web site should only be considered excellent if it is useful, usable, correct, and pleasing. The meaning of each of these considerations is somewhat subjective, except in the case of correctness. For a site to be well designed, its execution must be excellent. This means that the site must not break in any way. The HTML must be correct and the images saved properly so that the page renders as the designer intended. Any interactive elements, whether in the form of client-side scripts in JavaScript or server-executed CGI programs, must function properly and not result in error messages. The navigation of the site must work at all times. Broken links accompanied by the all too common "404: Not Found" message are not the signs of a well-executed site. While execution seems like an obvious requirement for excellence, too many sites exhibit execution problems to let this consideration go unmentioned:

Rule: A site's execution must be close to flawless.

The problem with execution is due to the following factors: technology shifts, lack of developer experience, aggressive time lines, lack of methodology, and no consideration for medium restrictions. While many of these issues can be addressed with methodology as discussed in Chapter 2, developing for the Web can be difficult compared to traditional software because the tools shift so rapidly. A site developed in one technology often must be redone in another in a matter of months. Consider that in the past few years HTML has been through three major revisions, and numerous proprietary features have been introduced by browser vendors. Technologies like JavaScript change even more frequently. The difficulties created by specification shifts are compounded by browser vendors who continually introduce new browser versions at a frenetic pace, each filled with its share of bugs. Developers need to understand the core technologies of the Web before building sites. HTML, cascading style sheets (CSS), and the other core Web technologies are discussed in Chapter 13. Yet even if the site is built properly, it is often not delivered to the user efficiently. Designers should understand network, server, and protocol issues that may affect Web design. These issues are discussed in Chapter 14. A Web designer who ignores technical and medium effects is like the print designer who will not admit that ink bleeds on paper—a Web designer must know and respect the medium, which includes everything from browsers and bandwidth to programming and protocols.

Rule: Know and respect the Web and Internet medium constraints.

The Web's GUI Heritage

Many Web sites provide interesting functionality including online shopping, electronic banking, software download, gaming, chat, and so on. Such complex Web sites do not just provide content, but allow people to interact or manipulate content just like traditional software. However, Web sites are not identical to traditional software. While both may be built using similar programming technologies, Web sites are distributed differently, must be quickly learnable, lack an install/uninstall barrier, must be very content focused, and must integrate marketing more directly. Furthermore, the Web often has more complex time considerations and distribution considerations than regular software. Consider a site like superbowl.com and you'll understand what is meant by timeliness and distributions issues.

While in many ways Web sites are different than traditional software, they still rely on basic *graphical user interface* (GUI) design components: windows, icons, menus, and a pointer. The use of the various GUI widgets such as menus and input fields is presented in Chapter 12. Because users are experienced with GUI objects from traditional software, they will expect them to work in a similar fashion on the Web. In short, Web sites utilize a modified graphical user interface. While some GUI design conventions such as double clicking and dragging don't make much sense within

Web sites, there is no reason that Web sites shouldn't build on what people already understand. This can be summed up in the following principle:

Rule: Web sites should respect GUI principles where appropriate.

Traditionally, Windows and Mac applications have employed design guidelines so that users do not have to relearn interface concepts from one software package to another. Does Web design have similar rules? Not really, particularly considering that no single organization—not even the World Wide Web Consortium (www.w3.org)—has the ability to dictate standards that all users and firms will follow. Maybe someday this will change. However that may be, there already exists today a body of design ideas that are both useful and commonly held. These concepts are less abstract hard-and-fast rules than shared conventions grounded in cumulative experience. (To use an analogy from the world of jurisprudence, they are more like common law than Roman law.) These conventions are based on several factors such as tradition, social forces, technology, common sense, and even random chance. A good example of these unacknowledged conventions is link color. Through experience, Web users come to understand that something that is blue, particularly when underlined, is clickable. Changing link colors to something else is generally considered to cause usability problems. Users expect to see blue link text; when a new color is used they may become confused and have a frustrating experience.

Similarly, we probably wouldn't want to use blue as a text color for nonlinked text as users might become confused. While there might be some situations where link color changing would be considered acceptable, breaking with convention could result in unnecessary user frustration. The search for these common design concepts and an overview of the major conventions of GUI design is discussed throughout this book.

Content Focus

Web sites tend to be much more content-focused than traditional software. The intersection between a site and its content often becomes very blurry. Content is what makes up a Web site. It provides the bricks for our virtual pyramid. Content might be text, two-dimensional images, three-dimensional images, animation, audio, video, or the interplay of any number of these content forms. Original, quality content is the most valuable commodity of the Web. Users look for useful content and consume it voraciously once they find it. While pleasing navigational graphics or sophisticated-looking design may encourage users to begin browsing a site, it certainly won't keep them there. Eventually users will begin to explore the site with the intention of doing something useful or finding some valuable content. If there is nothing of use, they will eventually leave. However, even if there is quality content, it really doesn't matter if the user can't find it.

Users need help to find their way though a site. A clear site structure as discussed in Chapter 4 helps, but good navigation requires more than structure. Meaningful link names, logical grouping of buttons, clear page titles, and consistent navigational elements as discussed in Chapters 5 and 6 also influence "wayfinding." While navigation design is certainly important, designers often spend too much time trying to organize a site in such a logical way they miss the point of navigation. The best Web designs are often those that employ simple or subtle navigation. Keep in mind that users do not come to your site to marvel at your ingenious navigation. Site visitors use navigation to move around the site in search of some desired nugget of information. The navigation is simply the way they do it. If the navigation is truly ingenious, they literally won't notice it. Remember, from the user's perspective the focus is not on the moving or the doing, but hopefully on the result they achieve or the content they find. Hence the following rule:

Rule: Navigation is only a means to an end result.

In fact, despite all the discussion about site structure and navigation ideas, it is doubtful that users really put a great emphasis on their location within a site. Users do not form flow charts in their minds and spend time mapping complex organizational relationships. For users, the only time their location within a site really matters is when they can't find what they are looking for. As long as users feel they are making their way to an end result in a satisfactory fashion, the navigation is appropriate. Of course, because of user differences it will be impossible to engineer perfect navigation. Users will need wayfinding assistance such as a search engine, a site map, a site index, or even a help system to aid them on their way to their goal. These navigational aids are discussed in Chapters 7 and 8.

Looks Matter

While a great Web site has to function well and be easy to navigate, these features are not always immediately recognizable. A site's visual design is often the first thing noticed. Like it or not, on the Web, looks do matter. While it may not be possible to force good taste or predict trends, we know that good Web design is closely related to how people perceive the look of the site. First impressions count heavily online. Looking at Figure 1-5, a user without any previous knowledge of the two sites would probably assume that the second (front) site was much better and more worth exploring than the first.

The look of the site may certainly influence a user's opinion of the site. The good-looking site is often assumed to be "better" than the bad-looking one, at least on first blush. Thus:

Rule: Visuals will heavily influence the user's initial perception of a site's value.

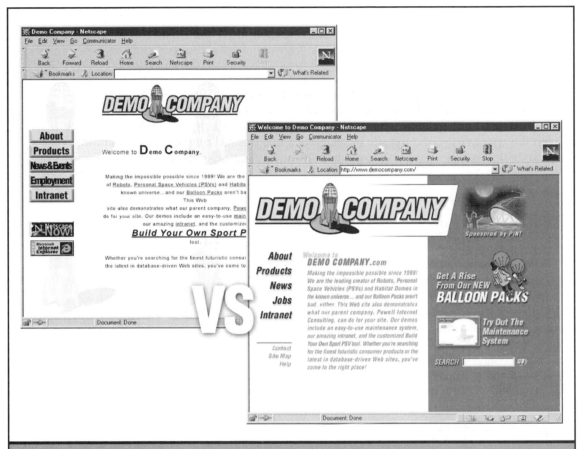

Figure 1-5.   *Which site is "better"? Which site is more trustworthy?*

The issue of looks may also be important in gaining the user's trust, which is so crucial in online transactions. Consider which site you would purchase from if you knew little about each firm. Remember that trust isn't solely related to the look of a site and will be heavily influenced by previous knowledge, endorsements from third parties, or reputation of the firm beyond the Web.

The Take-away Value

While looks matter at first, users will probably come to focus less on the site's visuals as they continue to use the site. When a user exits a site, they leave with what might be called a take-away value, a basic feeling of how successful the site visit was. In general, this feeling is positive, negative, or neutral to some degree. Consider first the case when a user really hates a site. What caused it? Did the user find the site difficult to use? Was the site slow? Was the execution of the site poor and did it result in errors? Was the site ugly? There could be any number of reasons a person might leave with a negative take-away value. While initially the user might be disproportionately influenced by visual design, the final impression will be influenced by a more balanced combination of visuals, content, technology, and usability. The take-away value also will be heavily related to whether or not the user was successful in accomplishing their goals during the visit. Thus, although visuals may play a dominant role in first impressions, the final impression is much more complicated, as summed up in the following design rule:

> **Rule: The site's take-away value is influenced by visuals, content, technology, usability, and goal accomplishment.**

While the take-away value includes more than just a user's opinion of a site's look, never underestimate the importance of visuals on the Web. Colors, backgrounds, text use, imagery, and page layout all can be used to improve a page's presentation. Consider the sites shown in Figure 1-6. One site lacks graphics and layout while the other has them.

Discounting the visually impaired user, or a user browsing from an environment that is unable to display graphics, the site with visuals is bound to seem more interesting. Don't take this previous statement as an opinion, but look for yourself. Do not focus on the particular look of the visual site or any implied download. Just consider which appears more appealing in the abstract sense. Even visual-design curmudgeons concerned more with content, function, or superfast downloads should heed the pleasing visual-design requirement, lest their sites repeat history. If graphics are not important, why isn't Gopher—the leading information system of the Internet in the early 1990s—used any longer to any significant degree? Gopher was easy, it had linking, and it had a great wealth of content. However, it wasn't terribly visual and was quickly superseded by the Web. While there are still the radical few that view the Web as overly embellished with buttons, backgrounds, and all forms of graphical elements—without such elements, many sites would be bland and unmotivating.

Web pages can be developed for both aesthetics and use. Within a site, pages may have very different purposes and thus require different looks. Of course, making things too different will disrupt usability, so designers should consider using consistent page layout and length, as discussed in Chapter 9, to improve use. Text layout will also greatly affect a page's usability. While in the past technical limitations on the Web have limited text control, newer technologies like cascading style sheets (CSS) should provide more control. Web typography principles and technologies are discussed in Chapter 10. Lastly, graphics, color, and background usage can greatly influence a user's experience. For example, when misused, graphics can slow a Web visit to a crawl. Yet even when using low-bandwidth visual design principles, things can go

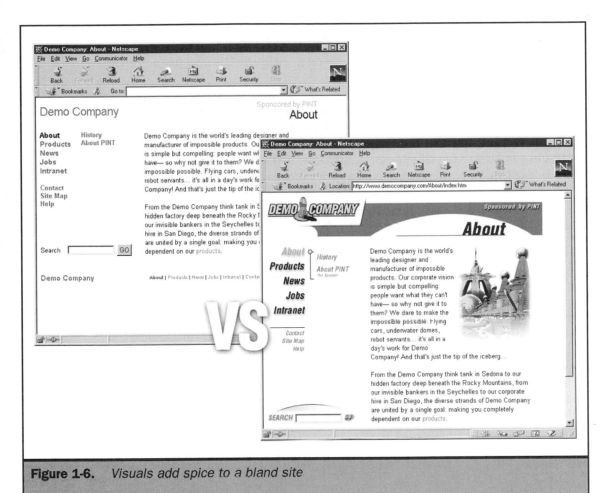

Figure 1-6.   *Visuals add spice to a bland site*

wrong—colors or images may not reproduce properly, or may influence the user in an unforeseen way. Colors, images, and backgrounds are discussed in Chapter 11.

While the look of a site may heavily influence a user's opinion about it, be careful not to focus only on the visuals. A user may like or dislike a site and its visuals for a variety of reasons, ranging from simple taste to interest in the content being presented. If you are not interested in snowboarding, you might consider a snowboard site only slightly visually pleasing, in the same way that someone else may find your site on rose gardens uninteresting. Looks matter, but what is good looking to one person could be awful to another. Furthermore, even if the graphics are pleasing in themselves, if they are poorly implemented or slow to download, the user may still dislike them. Remember the pyramid analogy: you can't just focus on one aspect of the construction.

The Form and Function Balance

A key problem with Web design is that sites often do not balance form and function. Under the influence of modernism, many designers have long held that the form of something should follow its function. Consider that form is one base of our Web design pyramid, while function is the other. Function without form would be boring. While the site may work, it won't inspire the user. Conversely, even if the form is impressive, if the function is limited the user will be disappointed. There needs to be a clear and continuous relationship between form and function. Put simply, the form of a site should directly relate to its purpose. If the site is marketing-driven, it might be very visual and even incorporate heavy amounts of multimedia if it helps to accomplish our goals. However, if the site is clearly a task-based one, such as an online banking site, it might have a much more utilitarian form. Of course, to determine the appropriate form for a site assumes that the function of the site is clearly defined. Unfortunately, for many Web sites the ultimate function of the site isn't always clearly understood. Even worse, development of form and function for the site are not always clearly related.

It is likely that there will be a continual struggle between the form (art) and the function (technology), despite the fact that the only side the designer should be on is that of the users. Form and function do not always have to fight; they complement each other much of the time. A nice-looking design makes a functional site much better, while great functionality will make up for a deficiency in look and feel over time. Consider the look and feel of the most heavily traveled sites on the Web such as portals like Yahoo! or Excite, or even large e-commerce sites. While these sites are often similar, each has a distinct look, while none focuses too heavily on either look or technology. However, despite the potential for balance, some designers feel that GUI principles adopted for the Web are too restrictive and remove too much of the creative or marketing element from Web design. If all sites are consistent in how they operate, how will the site be memorable and help build the brand identity of the company? The consistency that is key to usability flies in the face of marketing, which wants to create differences between sites—inconsistency is the marketing way to get attention. However, what should be different? Consider a real-world clothing store: Should the racks, doorknobs, cash registers, and fitting rooms be different from those in other stores, or should the focus be on the clothes? The obvious answer is that while all the components of the store will add to its memorability, the clothes are the key. The Web is no different. The focus should not be on the GUI widgets—they are just interface. The focus should be on the content and task at hand. Far too often, however, designers attempt to build memorability for their site by making the interface unusual.

Rule: Do not invent interfaces to build brand.

Branding solely with buttons is nearly impossible. Consider that users will see dozens, hundreds, or even thousands of sites over the course of a year. How likely are they to remember the shape, color, or action of your site's buttons? The user is not there to admire your buttons; they visit the site to accomplish some goal. Web designers should never forget this.

What Is Good Web Design?

Even if we can agree that the development of Web sites requires many talents and a balance between form, function, content, and purpose, it is difficult to pinpoint what is meant by good Web design. If you believe that a Web project has four aspects that are often at odds with each other, as illustrated by the pyramid, it is not hard to guess that what is considered appropriate design will vary from project to project, and even from person to person. This is common sense. In software development, the design challenges for a video game are very different from those of a corporate client/server application. This does not change suddenly for the Web. The design issues for marketing sites built to support a well-known name brand are very different from an intranet. Despite the obviousness of this statement, many turn to guides claiming knowledge of how to build "killer," "cool," or "sizzling" sites, then blindly apply these ideas to their sites. While many of the ideas are correct for the sites described, obviously not all sites will have the same issues as those that the killer rules were derived from. What is cool or clever for one site may be an absolute disaster for another. A great example is the *splash page* shown in Figure 1-7. A splash page is the term used to describe an entry page to a site—one that comes before the actual home or core page of the site.

A splash page is often used to set tone for the site and may consist of an interesting animation. A splash page may also serve to warn users about what technologies are required to view the site. What is interesting is that while in many cases the splash page can be used to lure users in, it can just as easily constitute a barrier. For example, in a site geared towards engineers the use of the splash page actually caused more than a quarter of the users to leave the site without actually passing the splash page, according to the site's log files. After talking to users about why they wouldn't use the site, it turned out that, for the information-hungry, the splash page served as a barrier, an unwanted annoyance, simply a page to click through to get what they wanted. In this case the use of a splash page was downright dangerous. However, for those looking to be entertained it could serve as a great lure or a setup for a wonderful experience. Just like a movie without opening credits, some entertainment sites would be incomplete without a splash page. This simple example illustrates the most dangerous problem in Web design, namely, assuming there is only one form of good Web design:

Rule: There is no form of "correct" Web design that fits every site.

So is that it? Can we say absolutely nothing else about Web design? Hardly, but if you approach Web design as a set of absolute rules to follow you will be frustrated and disappointed all the time. Proclamations like "never use frames" or "always keep page

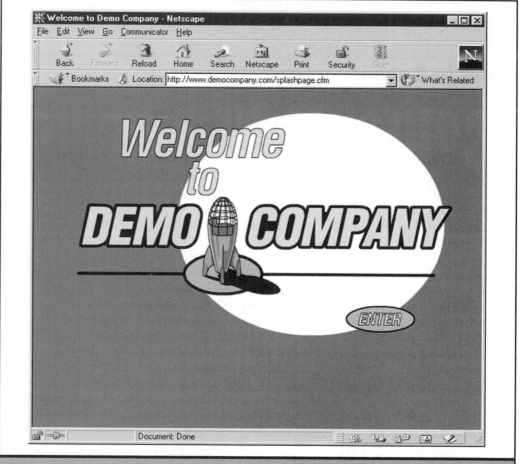

Figure 1-7.   *Example of a splash page*

sizes at 50KB or less" seem harmless enough, but without careful understanding of their motivation, designers are bound to misuse them. Consider for example the 50KB page size rule of thumb. This is clearly suggested because of Web access speed. Users consistently complain about long download times on Web sites. While this is true for modem users accessing graphics-laden Web sites, would this problem hold for people viewing intranet pages within a company, or those who have cable modems or other forms of high-speed access? Certainly not. However, despite this observation, it is common to find design principles like image color reduction, breaking images into many small pieces, and so on in sites designed for high-speed environments. Rules can be good, but understanding their motivation and application is better. Always strive to understand the motivations behind the design rules presented rather than blindly applying them. This will serve you particularly well once you start to see that many of the rules will be at odds with each other.

Web Site Evaluation

While it seems difficult to put our finger on what good Web design is, it certainly isn't hard to point out that which is not well done. Many sites and books can describe what "sucks" or what is poorly designed. The problem with this approach to Web design is that while it identifies what you shouldn't do, it generally avoids answering the tough question: What should you do instead? Most of the bad-design problems are well known: slow pages, gratuitous use of graphics, overly animated pages, sites continually under construction, confusing links, garish backgrounds, hard-to-read text, slow download speeds—and the list goes on and on. It will be important during the discussion to point out what not to do, but spending too much time discussing bad Web design may not be fruitful, particularly when you consider the truth that there is no accounting for bad taste. Many Web site evaluations seem to focus more on the designer's lack of good judgment or taste than on positive ways to fix the site.

When evaluating a Web site, consider reversing the design process. In a sense you could call this "walking up and down the waterfall." First, test the site's implementation. Is the site delivered well? Is the HTML valid? Are the images saved properly? Do the scripts work? Next, consider the visual and navigation design. Do you understand the navigation? Are there broken links? Is it easy to find what you are looking for? Next, make sure you considered why the site was built and for whom. What is the purpose of the site? What kind of users would use this site? What goals would these users have? Now, with your design hypothesis, walk back down the waterfall. Does the visual design make sense now? How about the navigation? Does the site's execution make sense given the audience? Evaluation of a site should be performed very carefully and opinions formed primarily after looking at all site considerations. A detailed discussion of site evaluation is given in Appendix B. While designers will often have to evaluate sites, remember that designers are not users. We may still have to solicit direct feedback from users to truly verify or correct our beliefs.

In Search of Web Design

So what exactly is Web design? It is a very user-centered multidisciplinary design pursuit that includes influences from visual arts, technology, content, and purpose. Purpose may even include economic considerations such as the cost of the site versus its benefit. Because Web design is so multidisciplinary, it is often very appropriate to pull ideas and theories from related fields. Indeed, we've been doing that even in the very first pages of this book. However, some people take this approach a little too exclusively, and so end up engaging in a form of Web "metaphor madness." Based on what field of expertise the designer had previous to the Web, or what communication medium they are most familiar with, the designer attempts to graft all the rules of one medium into the other. Statements like "the Web is very similar to print" or "Web sites are pretty much just software" are common. While it is true that the Web borrows heavily from other mediums, there are significant differences. True, the medium is very different than print because more function is provided—not unlike software. However, delivery issues and content effects make Web sites different from traditional software applications as well.

While the Web isn't exactly something old, we shouldn't say the medium is totally different either. There are plenty of people who do that as well. The Web is so revolutionary, they say, that none of the rules of old hold. This is complete nonsense. Despite the proclamations of pundits, historically new media forms have always adopted various conventions from each other as well as inventing new ones of their own. Furthermore, no new form really has completely eliminated any other. Radio, magazines, television, and so on all continue to exist despite emerging technologies and new media forms. The Web certainly isn't all new, so new that we throw out any valuable concepts we learned before, but it does have its own principles. We should strive to understand other media design concepts and modify them to fit the Web.

What You See Is What You Want

An overriding design principle is always required to sum up the others. For graphic user interface design, it was "What you see is what you get" or WYSIWYG. A great focus was placed on allowing the user to ensure that what they did onscreen was what they expected, and what hopefully appeared on paper if the screen was output. On the Web, this slogan doesn't fit. First, the desire to transfer exactly what is on screen to paper is inappropriate. In some cases, the screen may be made purposefully simpler than the printer output. The user doesn't want exactly what appears on-screen. Second, users want to control their Web experience a great deal. Users don't always want to "get" a particular experience; they often want to form their own. Web site personalization is a prime consequence of this desire. Even if users are receiving a controlled or common experience, they certainly don't want to feel that they are. The user needs to feel that they are in control of the Web experience. The user wants to direct the action. Nothing is more frustrating than being forced down a path. Control of the overall experience is in the hands of the designer, but within the site the user must feel they are guiding the action. This yields the following Web principle:

Rule: Control should be given or at least appear to be given to the user.

The last design principle points to the tension between user and designer for control. Designers may need to be in control to influence outcomes and keep the user from making mistakes, but the user should be considered a partner. If their site experience is controlled, the user shouldn't know it. Most of the time the power of control is shifting back to the user. Consider that the vast wealth of information available on the Internet itself has put a great deal of control back in the user's hands. No longer are users limited to the interactive content that was worthy enough to be mass-produced on CD-ROM. Today, they can easily hunt down the most obscure topic and probably find numerous sites devoted to it. Because of this focus on the user's desires, the concept of WYWSIWYG should be modified to the following slogan:

Slogan: What you see is what you want (WYSIWYW).

"What you see is what you want" is a user-focused slogan that places the user in control of what they want to see and how they want to see it. If a user wants to see their site on a cell phone, so be it. If they want to print the site, it's no problem. If they want to navigate using a directed search or just want to browse, it's all up to them. It seems pretty obvious that many customer-driven sites already practice the WYSIWYW principle. The only major problem with the principle is that it lacks an easily pronounceable acronym! Regardless of the adoption of the exact concept, there is no guarantee that even the basic ideas behind WYSIWYW will continue to be important in Web design. The Web doesn't sit still. Innovation occurs at a frantic pace, and the distance between a "cobweb" and a bleeding-edge site is short. As times change, the design principles presented in this book should be questioned, lest they become too restrictive or even inappropriate for the current Web environment.

Summary

Web design is a multidisciplinary pursuit that consists of four primary components: content, form, function, and purpose. However, agreement as to exactly how these components mix together varies from person to person as well as project to project. While good Web design is hard to define, there is certainly an understanding of what not to do. The field has a great deal to learn from other disciplines, particularly from the intersection of graphical interface design and traditional print design. Yet borrowing heavily from other disciplines can also cause problems, because the Web is a unique medium. Its fusion of media forms, its unpredictable delivery environment, and the extreme variability that results from its acute sensitivity to societal and technological influences makes it an extremely challenging medium to work in. However, if the designer keeps the user in mind at all times, many of the most serious design errors can be avoided. Furthermore, designers should respect the restrictions of the medium, as well as any emerging conventions, regardless of what users may think they want. While the development process may be challenging, following even a basic Web site development methodology can be extremely helpful. The next chapter will introduce the basic process that is often followed when building sites.

The
Complete
Reference

Web Design

Chapter 2

The Web Design Process

Building a great Web site can be challenging. With so many different components ranging from visual design to database integration, there is plenty of room for things to go wrong. In order to minimize the risk of a Web project failing, we need a process to guide us. Unfortunately, many Web designers seem to utilize what might be called the "NIKE" method of Web development—they just do it, often with little forethought and planning. The process of building a site this way is not methodical at all. The site's goals tend to be loosely defined, the process more intuitive than procedural, and the end result highly unpredictable. Sites developed this way are like plants. They grow organically—occasionally into a beautiful flower, but most often into a tangled mess. Complex Web sites require careful planning. A process or methodology should always be employed to help guide our Web design and development efforts.

The Need for Process

Today a crisis similar to the "software crisis" of the late 1960s exists in Web development. A few years ago most Web sites were little more than digital brochures, and were often termed "brochureware." Creating such a site didn't require a great deal of planning—often, simply developing an interface and then populating the site with content worked adequately. Today sites are becoming much larger and more complex. With the introduction of e-commerce and dynamic pages, sites have clearly moved away from brochureware to full-fledged software applications. However, many developers have yet to adopt a robust site-building methodology and often continue to rely on ad hoc methods.

Note *The "software crisis" refers to a time in the software development field when increasing hardware capabilities allowed for significantly more complex programs to be built. However, building and maintaining the new programs was challenging because little methodology had been used in the past, thus resulting in experts stating a crisis was occurring because of numerous project failures. Methodology such as structured or top-down design was introduced to combat this crisis.*

Evidence of the crisis in Web development practices is everywhere. Unlike the in-house client/server software projects of the past, the dirty laundry of many failed Web projects is often aired for all to see. The number of pages that seem to be forever under construction or coming soon suggests how poorly planned many Web sites are. Unfortunately, the yellow-and-black construction signs and animated jackhammers rarely are removed. Some sites have been in a state of construction for years judging by their content or date of last modification. Like some form of online ghost town, these half-dead sites are cluttered with old content, old-style HTML, dated technologies, broken links, and malfunctioning scripts. Don't discount some of these problems as mere typos or slight oversights. A broken link is a catastrophic failure. Imagine if a software program had menus that just didn't go anywhere!

Why sites exhibit problems certainly varies. Some sites may deteriorate simply because the site's builders got bored or moved on. Other sites may fall apart because the site wasn't considered useful or funding was withdrawn. Still other sites probably just couldn't be completed because the site's complexity overwhelmed the developer. Sometimes the developer may just not have understood the tools they were working with, or was not well enough versed in medium restrictions. Why development projects fail varies, but the numerous dead sites on the Web suggest that they are risky.

Ad Hoc Web Process

Often the way a Web site is built is simple: implement the site, perform a brief visual test in a browser, and then release it to the world. This is similar to the "by the seat of your pants" code and test process used in small software projects. Not surprisingly, the problems encountered in Web sites that are built using these informal methods are often numerous. Today's approach to the Web is so fast that the process almost boils down to two steps: implement and then release. Notice that many Web design tools encourage this design-on-the-fly approach. Some tools encourage the developer to immediately begin mocking up an interface and later use wizards to add functionality, while others can create huge amounts of code but consider adding the interface later on. There is no doubt that the speedy approach to development, given the time demands of the Web, is important. However, releasing a shoddy, poorly thought-out site may backfire when the user becomes frustrated with the site's problems.

In the software industry, most professionals tend to agree that such informal or "design as you go along" methods are only good for small projects, generally with only one programmer, and where future maintenance is not expected to be great. Often, programs built with such little planning exhibit convoluted programming logic—often called "spaghetti code," which is very difficult to maintain because nobody besides the initial developer can untangle the mess. Even the initial developer may forget the meaning of the code over time. Web sites exhibit similar patterns. Small Web sites that have expected short life spans might be built by one person using little methodology, and inspection of the site's underlying HTML, JavaScript, and navigation structure tends to show that "spaghetti code" is being served, this time with a side dish of "tossed HTML markup salad."

Planning can certainly help offset some of the problems that may be encountered during a Web development project. Unfortunately, in the ad hoc Web process planning is often limited to a few brief meetings, a brief but incomplete collection of potential content, and maybe a hastily conceived flow diagram. The amount of time spent planning is generally negligible next to the amount of time spent during implementation in this case. Of course, it is always possible to plan too much and suffer from a form of "analysis paralysis," which keeps a site from ever getting built, but this is relatively uncommon. Always consider the amount of planning to be proportional to the complexity of the project. The key to dealing with project management challenges is to create a formal process by which to plan, implement, test, and deploy a site in a structured manner.

Basic Web Process Model

To help reduce the difficulty in constructing sites, we should adopt a *process model* that describes the various phases involved in Web site development. Each step can then be carefully performed by the developer, using guidelines and documentation along the way that tell the developer how to do things and ensure that each step is carried out properly. An ideal process model for the Web would help the developer address the complexity of the site, minimize the risk of project failure, deal with the near certainty of change during the project, and deliver the site quickly with adequate feedback for management during the process. Of course, the ideal process model would also have to be easy to learn and execute. This is a pretty tall order, and it is unlikely that any single process model is always going to fit the particular requirements of a project.

The most basic process model used in Web site development should be familiar to most people—at least in spirit, as it is deductive. The basic model starts with the big picture and narrows down to the specific steps necessary to complete the site. In software engineering this model is often called the *waterfall model*, or sometimes the *software lifecycle model*, because it describes the phases in the lifetime of software. Each stage in the waterfall model proceeds one after another until conclusion. The model starts first with a planning stage, then a design phase, then implementation and testing, and ends with a maintenance phase. The phases may appear to be distinct steps, but the progress from one stage to another may not always be obvious. Furthermore, progress isn't always towards a conclusion, and occasionally previous steps may be revisited if the project encounters unforeseen changes. The actual number of steps and their names varies from person to person, but a general idea of the waterfall model is shown in Figure 2-1.

> **Note**   *While this model of Web development is probably the most common one, it seems that many Web designers think they invented a special form of it; then they publish it on their Web site as their patent-pending design process. There really isn't anything new here, whether there are five steps or seven steps or the names are complex sounding or simple. Always remember that what matters is whether the model helps the site's production and improves the final result.*

The good thing about the pure waterfall approach is that it makes developers plan everything up front. That is also its biggest weakness. In a Web project there is often a great deal of uncertainty as to what is required to accomplish a project, particularly if the developer has not had a great deal of Web development experience. Another problem with this process model is that each step is supposed to be distinct, but the

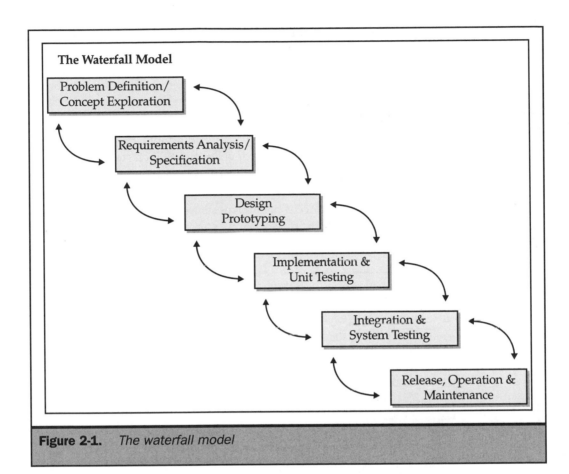

Figure 2-1.   *The waterfall model*

reality is that in Web development, like software, steps tend to overlap, influence previous and future steps, and often have to be repeated. Unfortunately, the waterfall approach can be fairly rigid and may require the developer to stop the project if too many changes occur and redo many steps. In short, the process doesn't deal well with change. However, the waterfall model for site design continues to be very popular because it is both easy to understand and easy to follow. Furthermore, the distinct steps in the process appeal to management as they can be easily monitored and serve as project milestones.

Modified Waterfall

One important aspect of the waterfall model is that it forces planning up front. However, because of all the steps required in the process, many developers tend to rush through the early stages and end up repeating them again later on or building a site based upon flawed ideas. The process is so rigid that it doesn't support much exploration and may cause unnecessary risk. One possible improvement is to spend more time in the first few stages of the waterfall and iterate a few times, exploring the goals and requirements of the site before entering into the design and implementation phase. Because of the cyclical nature of this process, it has been dubbed the modified waterfall with whirlpool to relate to the small whirlpools that are often found before a waterfall in nature. When you approach a project with a high degree of uncertainty, the modified waterfall with whirlpool approach, as illustrated in Figure 2-2, is a good idea.

Joint Application Development

The last software development process model that makes sense for Web site development is called joint application design, or JAD. It is also called evolutionary prototyping because it involves evolving a prototype site to its final form in a series of steps. Rather than

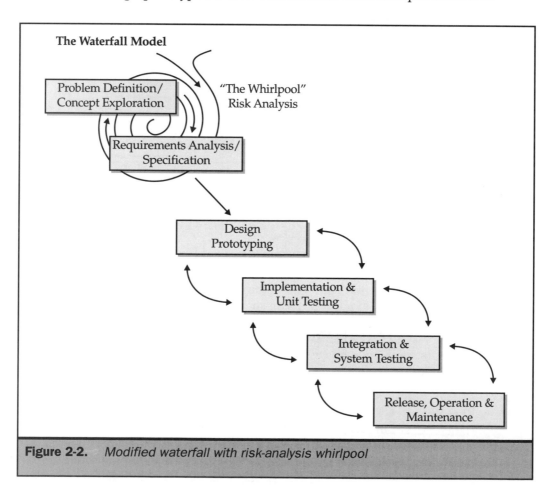

Figure 2-2. *Modified waterfall with risk-analysis whirlpool*

creating a mock site to test a theory, a prototype is built and shown to the user. The user then provides direct feedback that is used to guide the next version of the prototype, and so on until the final form is developed. The basic concept of JAD is shown in Figure 2-3.

Many aspects of the JAD process model seem appropriate for Web development, particularly when it is difficult to determine the specifics of the project. The process is very incremental as compared to the large release approach of the waterfall model, so it also appears to be faster. However, JAD can have some serious drawbacks. First, letting users see an unfinished site could harm the relationship between the users and developer. Even when users want to actively participate in guiding the project, we must always remember that users are not designers. As stated in Chapter 1, this

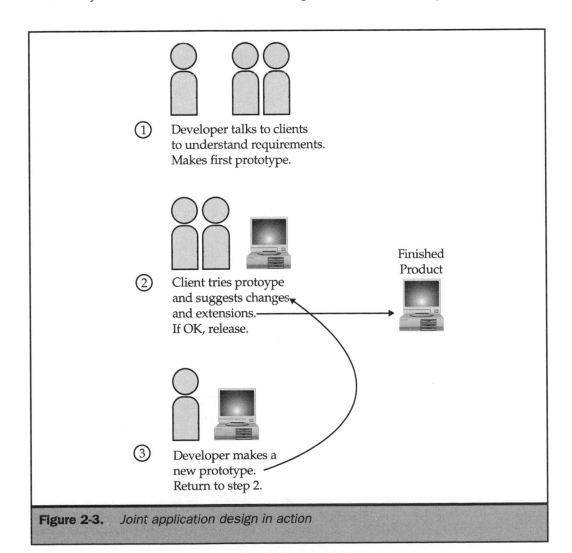

Figure 2-3. *Joint application design in action*

guiding Web design principle should always be remembered as users may steer development off course with unrealistic demands. Projects run in a JAD style are also difficult to budget for since the number of revisions can't be predicted. If users are fickle, costs can quickly spiral out of control. Remember that the core concept behind JAD is to build the wrong site numerous times until the correct site falls out. Despite its drawbacks, JAD has its place in Web development, particularly in maintenance projects. However, for initial project development JAD is best left to experienced developers—particularly those who are capable of communicating with users well.

A few possible candidates for guiding a Web project have been discussed. Numerous others exist and might serve a developer equally well. Remember that the act of building a site is to clearly identify a problem to solve or goal to reach and then attempt to arrive at an outcome in a consistent and enlightened manner. Site development should be approached critically and deliberately rather than casually or passively. While a critical approach doesn't necessarily rule out chance or sudden inspiration, it does offer the opportunity to direct it. Designers should not look at the use of Web site engineering concepts as limiting factors, but rather as something that can guide design.

Approaching a Web Site Project

In theory, Web site engineering process models make sense, but do they work in practice? The answer is a resounding yes. However, site development rarely works in a consistent manner because of the newness of the field, the significant time constraints, and the ever-changing nature of Web projects. Developers should always proceed with caution. To guide development, a process model should be adopted at the start of the project. If the site is brand new or the addition is very complex, the waterfall model or the modified waterfall with whirlpool model should be adopted. If the project is a maintenance project, is relatively simple, or has many unknown factors, joint application design may make sense. Regardless of the project, the first step is always the same: set the overall goal for the project.

Goals and Problems

Many Web site projects ultimately fail because they lack clear goals. In the first few years of Web design, many corporate sites were built purely to show that the firm had a site. Somehow, without a site the firm would not be progressive or a market leader, and competitors with sites were somehow a threat. Many times, the resulting site provided little benefit because it wasn't really designed for a reason other than to provide a presence for the company. As familiarity with the Web has grown, the reasons for having Web sites have become clearer. Today, site goals have become important and are usually clearly articulated up front. However, don't assume that logic rules the Web—a great number of site development projects continue to be driven by pure fancy and often react more to perceived threats than to solve real problems.

Coming up with a goal for a Web site isn't difficult; the problem is refining it. Be wary of vague goals like "provide better customer service" or "make more money by opening up an online market." This may serve as a good sound bite or mission statement for a project, but details are required. Good goal statements might include something like:

■ Build a customer-support site that will improve customer satisfaction by providing 24/7 access to common questions and result in a 25-percent decrease in telephone support.

■ Create an online car-parts store that will sell at least $10,000/month of product directly to the consumer.

■ Develop a Japanese food restaurant site that will inform potential customers of critical information such as hours, menu, atmosphere, and prices and encourage them to order by phone or visit the location.

Notice that two of the three goal statements had measurable goals. This is very important as it provides a way to easily determine success or failure as well as assign a realistic budget to the project. The third goal statement did not provide an obviously measurable goal. This can be dangerous because it is difficult to convince others that the site is successful, or to even place a value on the site. In the case of the restaurant informational site, a goal for number of viewers of the site or a way to measure customer visits using a coupon would help. Consider a revised goal statement like:

■ Develop a Japanese food restaurant site that will inform 300 potential customers per month of critical information such as hours, menu, atmosphere, and prices and encourage them to order by phone or visit the location.

The simple addition of a particular number of visitors makes the goal statement work. By stating a number of desired visitors, the restaurant owner could compare the cost of placing advertisements in print or on the radio vs. the cost of running the site to provide the same effective inquiry rate.

Brainstorming

Generally, coming up with a goal statement is fairly straightforward. The largest problem is keeping the statement concise and realistic. In many Web projects there is a desire to include everything in the site. Remember, the site can't be everything to everyone; there must be a specific audience and set of tasks in mind. To determine goals, a brainstorming session is often required. The purpose of a brainstorming session is simply to bring out as many possible ideas about the site as possible. A white board is useful during a brainstorming session to quickly write down or modify any possible ideas for the site.

Oftentimes, brainstorming sessions get off track because participants jump ahead or bring too much philosophy about site design to the table. In such a case, it is best to focus the group by talking about site issues they should all agree on. Attempt to find a common design philosophy by having people discuss what they don't want to see in the site. Getting meeting participants to agree they don't want the site to be slow, difficult to use, and so on is usually easy. Once you obtain a sense of a common goal in the group, even if it is just that they all believe that the site shouldn't be slow, future exploration and statements of what the site should do seem to go more smoothly.

When conducting a project to redo a site, be careful not to run brainstorm meetings by berating the existing site unless no participant in the project has any ownership stake in the site. A surefire way to derail a site overhaul project is to get the original designers on the defensive because of criticism of their work. Remember, people have to build sites, so building a positive team is very important.

Narrowing the Goal

During the brainstorming session, all ideas are great. The point of the session is to develop what might be called the *wish list*. A wish list is a document that describes all possible ideas for inclusion in a site regardless of price, feasibility, or applicability. It is important not to stifle any ideas during brainstorming lest it take away the creative aspect of site development. However, eventually the wish list will have to be narrowed down to what is reasonable and appropriate for the site. This can be a significant challenge with a site with many possible goals. Consider, for example, a corporate site that contains product information, investor information, press releases, job postings, and technical-support sections. Each person with ownership stakes in a particular section will think their section is most important. Everyone literally wants a big link to their section to be on the home page. Getting compromise with so many stakeholders can be challenging!

One possibility for narrowing the goal is to use small sheets of papers or a deck of 3 × 5 cards. Have each one of the ideas written on a card and put them in a large pile. Now go around the room and have each person pull out one card at a time to include in the site based upon importance. Of course, make sure to limit the number of cards pulled from the pile. Hopefully, performing a procedure like this will allow the most important ideas to surface. Unfortunately, depending on the group, this exercise may fail—particularly if the participants place a great deal of ownership in their respective areas.

Audience

The best way to narrow a goal is to make sure that the audience is always considered. What a brainstorming group wants vs. what a user wants doesn't always correspond. The first thing to do is to accurately describe the site's audience and its reason for visiting the site. However, don't look for a generic Joe Enduser with AOL and a 56K modem who happened on your site by chance. It is unlikely such a user could be identified for most sites, and most users will probably have a particularly goal in mind. Consider first what kind of people your end users are. Consider asking some basic questions about the site's users, such as:

- Where are they located?
- How old are they?
- What is their gender?
- What language do they speak?
- How technically proficient are they?
- What kind of connection would they have to the Internet?
- What kind of computer would they use?
- What kind of browser would they probably use?

Next, consider what the users are doing at the site:

- How did they get to the site?
- What do the users want to accomplish at the site?
- When will they visit the site?
- How long will they stay during a particular visit?
- From what page(s) will they leave the site?
- When will they return to the site, if ever?

While you might be able to describe the user from these questions, you should quickly determine that your site would probably not have one single type of user with a single goal. For most sites, there are many types of users, each with different characteristics and goals.

User Profiling

The best way to understand users is to actually talk to them. If at all possible, you should interview users directly to verify any guess you may have about their wants and characteristics. A survey may also be appropriate, but live interviews provide the possibility to explore ideas beyond predetermined questions. Unfortunately, interviewing or even surveying users can be very time-consuming, and it is not possible to account for every single type of user characteristic or desire. From user interviews, surveys, or even just thinking about users generically, you should attempt to create stereotypical but detailed profiles of common users. Consider developing at least three named users. For most sites, consider that the three stereotypical users should correspond roughly to an inexperienced user, a user who has Web experience but doesn't visit your site often, and a power user who understands the Web and may visit the site frequently. Most sites will have these classes of users, with the intermediate infrequent visitor most often being the largest group. Make sure to assign percentages to each of the generic groups so that you account for each with appropriate weight. Now name each person. You may want to name each after a particular real user you interviewed, or use generic names like Bob Beginner, Irene Intermediate, and Paul Poweruser. Now work up very specific profiles for each stereotypical user using the questions from the previous section. Try to make sure that the answers correspond roughly to the average answers for each group. So, if there were a few intermediate users interviewed that had fast connections, but most have slow connections, assume the more common case. Chapter 3 discusses the concept of general user characteristics vs. individual traits in more detail.

Once your profiles for each generic site visitor are complete, you should begin to create visit scenarios. What exactly would Bob Beginner do when he visits your site? What are the tasks he wishes to perform? What is his goal? Scenario planning should help you focus on what each user will actually want to do. From this exercise, you may find that your goal statements are not in line with what the users are probably interested in doing. If so, you are still in the risk-analysis whirlpool. Return to the initial step and modify the goal statement based on your new information.

Requirements

Based on the goals of the site and what the audience is like, the site's requirements should begin to present themselves. What kind of content will be required? What kind of look should the site have? What types of programs will have to be built? How many servers will be required to service the site's visitors? What kind of restrictions will users place on the site in terms of bandwidth, screen-size, browser, and so on? Requirements will begin to show site costs and potential implementation problems. The requirements will suggest how many developers are required and show what content is lacking. If the requirements seem excessive vs. the potential gain, it is time to revisit the goal stage or question if the audience was accurately defined. The first three steps of the process may be repeated numerous times until a site plan or specification is thrown out of the whirlpool.

The Site Plan

Once a goal, audience, and site requirements have been discussed and documented, a formal site plan should be drawn up. The site plan should contain the following sections:

- **Short goal statement** This section would contain a brief discussion to explain the overall purpose of the site and its basic success measurements.

- **Detailed goal discussion**   This section would discuss the site's goals in detail and provide measurable goals to verify the benefit of the site.

- **Audience discussion**   This section would profile the users that would visit the site. The section would describe both audience characteristics and the tasks the audience would try to accomplish at the site.

- **Use scenario discussion**   This section discusses the various task visit scenarios for the site's users. Start first with how the user will arrive at the site and then follow the visit to its conclusion. This section may also include a discussion of conclusion measurements such as number of downloads, page accesses per visit, form being filled out, and so on as they relate to the detailed goal discussion.

- **Content requirements**   The content-requirements section should provide a laundry list of all text, images, and other media required in the site. A matrix showing the required content, form, existence, and potential owner or creator is useful as it shows how much content may be outstanding. A simple matrix is shown in Table 2-1.

- **Technical requirements**   This section should provide an overview of the types of technology the site will employ, such as HTML, JavaScript, CGI, Java, plug-ins, and so on. The technology requirements should directly relate to the user's capabilities. More information of technical considerations can be found in Chapter 13.

Content Name	Description	Content Type	Content Format	Exists?	Owner
Butler Robot Press Release	Press release for new Butler 7 series robot that ran in *Robots Today*	Text	Microsoft Word	Yes	Jennifer Tuggle
Software Agreement Form	Brief description of legal liability of using trial robot personality software	Text	Paper	Yes	John P. Lawyer
Handheld Supercomputer Screen Shot	Picture of the new Demo Company Cray-9000 handheld palm-size computer	Image	GIF	No	Pascal Wirth
Welcome from President Message	Brief introduction letter from President to welcome user to site	Text	Microsoft Word	No	President's Executive Assistant

Table 2-1.   *Content Matrix*

■ **Visual requirements**   The visual requirements section should outline basic considerations for interface design. The section should indicate in broad strokes how the site should relate to any existing marketing materials and provide an indication of user constraints for graphic and multimedia use such as screen size, color depth, bandwidth, and so on. The section may outline some specifics such as font or color use, but many of the details of the site's visuals will be determined later in the development process.

■ **Delivery requirements**   This section should indicate the delivery requirements, particularly any hosting considerations. A basic discussion of how many users will visit the site, how many pages will be consumed on a typical page, and the size of a typical page should be included in this section. Even if these are just guesses, it is possible to then provide a brief analysis of server and bandwidth required to deliver the site.

■ **Site structure diagram**   This section should provide a site structure or flow diagram detailing the various sections within a site. Appropriate labels for sections and general ideas for each section should be developed based on the various user scenarios explored in earlier project phases. Organization of the various sections of the site is important and may have to be refined over time. Selecting a site architecture is discussed in Chapter 4, but in general, a site diagram will look something like the one shown in Figure 2-4.

■ **Staffing**   This section should detail the resources required to execute the site. Measurements can be in simple man-hours and should relate to each of the four staffing areas: content, technology, visual design, and management.

■ **Time line**   The time line should show how the project will proceed using the staffing estimates from the preceding section combined with the typical waterfall process outlined earlier in the chapter.

■ **Budget**   A budget is primarily determined from the staffing requirements and the delivery requirements. However, marketing costs or other issues such as content licensing could be addressed in the budget.

The actual organization and content of the site plan is up to the developer. Remember, the purpose of the plan is to communicate the site's goals to the various people working on the project and help guide the project towards a positive conclusion. Don't skip writing the plan even though it may seem daunting, as without such a document you can only develop a project in an evolutionary or JAD fashion. Furthermore, it will be nearly impossible to obtain any realistic bids from outside vendors on a Web site without a specification. However, a finished plan doesn't allow you to immediately proceed to implementation. Once the specification is developed, it should be questioned one last time. The completed specification may reveal unrealistic estimates that will throw you back in the whirlpool of questioning initial goals or audience. If not, it may be time to actually continue the process and fall over the waterfall into the design and prototyping stage.

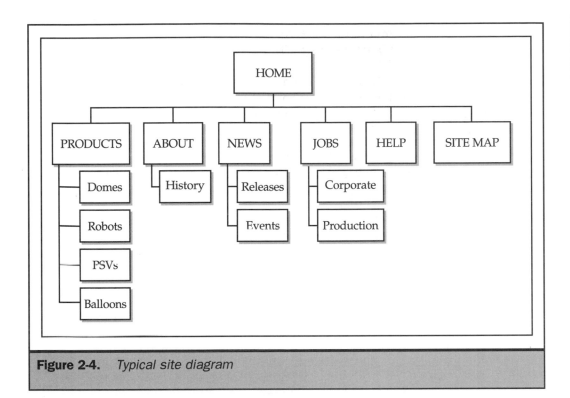

Figure 2-4.   *Typical site diagram*

Design Phase Dissected

The design or prototyping stage is the most fun for most Web designers, as it starts to bring form to the project. During this phase, both technical and visual prototypes should be developed. However, before prototypes are built, consider collecting as much content as possible. The content itself will influence the site and help guide its form. If the content is written in a very serious tone but the visuals are fun and carefree, the site will seem very strange to the user. Seeing the content up front would avoid the designer not integrating the design and content. Also consider that content collection can be one of the slowest aspects of site design. Many participants in a Web project are quick to attend brainstorming meetings but are difficult to find once their content contributions are required. Lack of content is by far the biggest problem in Web projects. Deal with this potential problem early.

Suggestion: Always collect content before design if at all possible.

Block Comps

Design should proceed top-down. Consider first how the user will enter the site and conclude with how they will leave. In most cases, this means designing the home page first, followed by subsection pages, and finally form or content pages.

Rule: Visual Design should proceed in a top-down fashion from home page to sub section pages and finally content pages.

First consider creating page mockups on paper in a block form, as shown in Figure 2-5.
The block comp allows designers to focus on the types of objects and their organization in the page without worrying too much about precise placement and detail. The block-sectioning approach will also help the designer to consider making templates for pages, which will make it easier to implement them later on. Make sure to create your block comps within the constraints of a Web browser window. The influence of the browser's borders can be a significant factor. Pages to print for sketching page-block comps can be found at www.webdesignref.com./chapter2/. Once the home page (chapter 2) block comp has been built, flesh out the other types of pages in the site in a similar fashion. Once a complete scenario has been detailed in this abstract sense, make sure that the path through the blocked screen is logical. If so, move on to the next phase.

Screen and Paper Comps

The next phase of design is the paper or screen prototyping phase. In this phase, the designer can either sketch or create a digital composite that shows a much more detailed example of a typical page in the site. Make sure that, whether you do the composite on paper or screen, a browser window is assumed and that screen

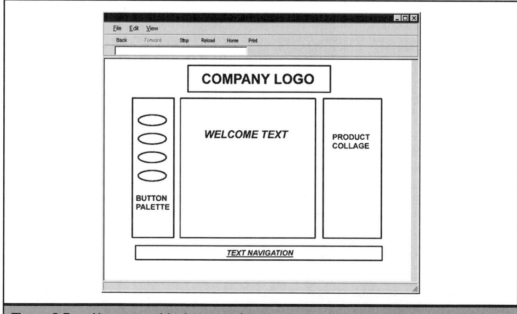

Figure 2-5.   *Homepage block composite*

dimensions are considered. A piece of paper with a browser window outline as used in the block comp stage can be used for sketches.

Suggestion: Always consider the bordering effect of the browser window when developing visual composites.

Sketch the various buttons, headings, and features within the page. Make sure to provide some indication of text in the page—either a form of "greeked" text or real content, if possible.

Many designers appear to use only lorem ipsum or greeking text within screen composites. While this approach does bring focus to the designed page elements, if real content is available, use it, as it more closely simulates what the final result will be like.

The comping stage provides the most room for creativity, but designers are warned to be creative within the constraints of what is possible on the Web and what visual requirements were presented in the design specification. Thinking about file size, color support, and HTML layout capabilities may seem limiting, but it avoids the designer coming up with a page that looks visually stunning but is nearly impossible to implement. In particular, resist the urge to become so artistic as to reinvent an organization's look in a Web site. Remember, the site plan will have spelled out visual requirements, including marketing constraints. The difficult balance between form, function, purpose, and content, as discussed in Chapter 1, should become readily apparent as designers grapple with satisfying their creative urges within the constraints of Web technology, user capabilities, and site requirements. A typical paper comp is shown in Figure 2-6.

In the case of a digital prototype, create a single image that shows the entire intended screen, including all buttons, images, and text. Save the image as a GIF or JPEG and load it into the Web browser to test how it would look within a typical environment. At this stage, resist the urge to fully implement your page design with HTML. You may end up having to scrap the design, and it would be wasteful to implement yet.

Once your paper or digital prototype is complete, it should be tested with users. Ask a few users to indicate which sections on the screen are clickable and what buttons they would select in order to accomplish a particular task. Make sure to show the prototype to more than one user, as individual taste may be a significant factor in prototype acceptance. If the user has too many negative comments about the page, consider going completely back to the drawing board. During prototyping, you can't get too attached your children, so to speak. If you do, the site will no longer be user focused, but developer focused. Remember the following design rule:

Rule: Don't marry your design prototypes. Listen to your users and refine your designs.

Once you come up with an acceptable home-page design, continue the process with subpages and content pages. A typical subpage composite is shown in Figure 2-7.

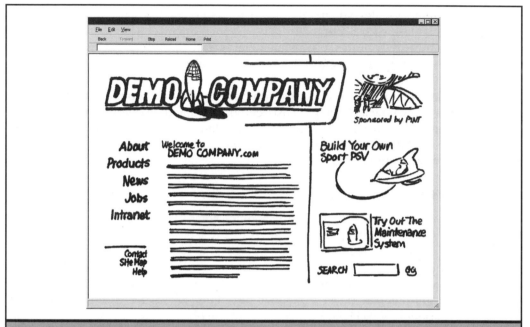

Figure 2-6. Paper composite for Demo Company site home page

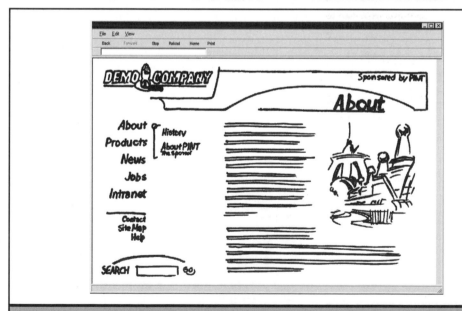

Figure 2-7. Subpage paper composite for Demo Company

In highly interactive sites, you may have to develop prototype pages for each step within a particular task such as purchasing or download. Prototype pages for such pages may have to be more fully fleshed out and include form-field labels and other details to be truly useful. A sample paper composit for a more interactive page is shown in Figure 2-8.

While not all sites will require technical prototypes, highly interactive sites should consider developing not only interface prototypes but working proof of concept prototypes that show how technological aspects such as database query, personalization, e-commerce, and so on, work. Unfortunately, what tends to happen is that technical prototypes are not built until a nearly complete interface is put in place, which may result in a heavy amount of rework.

The Mock Site

After all design prototypes have been finalized, it is time to create what might be called the mock or alpha site. Implementation of the mock site starts first by cutting a digital comp into its pieces and assembling the pages using HTML and, potentially, cascading style sheets. Try assembling the site in templates so that the entire site can be quickly assembled. However, do not put the content in place during this phase. Use greeking text on most pages unless real text is required for testing scenarios. Once the mock site is assembled, the site should be fully navigable but contain no content and only canned

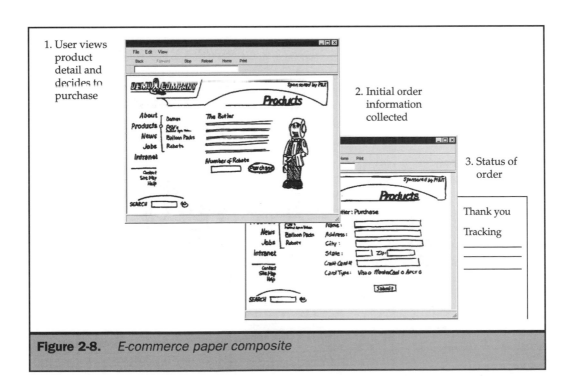

Figure 2-8.   *E-commerce paper composite*

interactivity. A sample mock site can be found at www.webdesignref.com/mocksite. At this point, it is a good idea to have a few users try the mock site. Observe if the site is easy to navigate and responsive. Have users attempt to complete real tasks with faked results in place. If the users have difficulty performing the tasks, you may have to consider scrapping the design and returning to a previous step in the development process. Generally, this won't happen unless the site was overdesigned or little user feedback was considered up until this point.

Beta Site Implementation

Once the mock site is acceptable, it is time to actually implement the real site. Real content should be placed in pages, and back-end components and interactive elements should be integrated with the final visual design. Implementation and technology considerations are too numerous to discuss here, but are presented individually in Chapters 10–13. While implementation would seem to be the most time-consuming aspect of a project, in reality, if all the components have been collected and prototypes built previous to this stage, the actual site implementation might occur relatively rapidly.

Testing

For most developers, testing is probably the least favorite aspect of the Web development process. After all the hard work of specification, design, and implementation, most people are ready to just launch the site. Resist the urge. Testing is key to a positive user takeaway value. Don't force your users to test your site after its release. If they encounter bugs with what is considered a production site, they won't be forgiving. Always remember the following design rule:

> **Rule: Sites always have bugs, so test your site well.**

Unfortunately, testing on the Web is generally relegated to a quick look at the site using a few browsers and maybe checking the links in the site. Bugs will exist in Web sites, no matter what. Unfortunately, most developers consider that if the site looks right, it is right. Remember from Chapter 1 that site design doesn't just include visual design: you must test all the other aspects of site design as well, as summarized by the design rule presented here:

> **Rule: Testing should address all aspects of a site, including content, visuals, function, and purpose.**

Appendix B discusses evaluation and testing of sites in detail, particularly completed sites, but the basic aspects of Web testing are overviewed here.

Visual Acceptance Testing

Visual acceptance testing ensures the site looks the way it was intended. View each of the pages in the site and make sure that they are consistent in layout, color, and style.

Look at the site under different browsers, resolutions, and viewing environments equivalent to those of a real user. Browse the site very quickly and see if the layouts jump slightly. Consider looking at the pages while squinting to notice abstract irregularities in layout. Visual acceptance testing may also require each page to be printed. Remember not to focus on print testing pages that are designed for online consumption.

Functionality Testing

Functionality testing and visual testing do overlap in the sense that the most basic function of a page is to simply render onscreen. However, most sites contain at least basic functions such as navigation. Make sure to check every link in a site and rectify any broken links. Broken links should be considered catastrophic functional errors. Make sure to test all interactive elements such as forms or shopping carts. Use both realistic test situations as well as extreme cases. Try to break your forms by providing obviously bad data. Remember: users won't think as you do, so prepare for the unexpected.

Content Proofing

The content details of a site are very important. Make sure content is all in place and that word usage is consistent. Check details like product names, copyright dates, and trademarks. And always remember to check the spelling! Clients and users may often regard an entire site as being poor just on the basis of one small typo; the importance of this cannot be stressed enough. The best way to perform this test is to print each page and literally read every single line for accuracy.

System and Browser Compatibility Testing

Hopefully, system and browser restrictions have been respected during development, but this must be verified during testing. Make sure to browse the site with the same types of systems and browsers the site's users will have. Unfortunately it often seems that designers check compatibility on systems far more powerful than the typical user's. The project plan should have detailed browser requirements, so make sure the site works under the specified browsers.

Delivery Testing

Check to make sure the site is delivered adequately. Try browsing the site under real user conditions. If the site was designed for AOL modem users, set up an AOL account and a modem to test delivery speed. To simulate site traffic, consider using testing software to create virtual users clicking on the site. This will simulate how the site will react under real conditions. Make sure that you test the site on the actual production server to be used or a system equivalent to it. Be careful not to underestimate delivery influences. The whole project may be derailed if this was not adequately thought about during specification. For further information on delivery conditions, see Chapter 14.

User Acceptance Testing

User acceptance testing should be performed after the site appears to work correctly. In software, this form of testing is often called *beta* testing. Let the users actually try the working site and comment on it one last time. Do not perform this type of testing until the more obvious bugs have been rectified, as stated by the following design rule:

Rule: User test is the most important form of testing and should be performed last.

User testing is the most important form of testing because it most closely simulates real use. If problems are uncovered during this phase of testing, you may not be able to correct them right away. If the problems are not dramatic, you may still release the site and correct the problems later. However, if any significant issues are uncovered, it is wise to delay release until they can be corrected.

Release and Beyond

Once the site is ready to be released, don't relax—you are not done. In fact, your work has just begun. It is now time to observe the site in action. Does the site meet user expectations? Were the site development goals satisfied? Are any small corrections required? The bottom line is that the site must live on. New features will be required. Upgrades to deal with technology changes are inevitable. Visual changes to meet marketing demands are very likely. The initial development signifies the start of a continual development process most call *maintenance*. Once over the waterfall, it is time to climb back to the top, as stated in the following design rule:

Rule: Site development is an ongoing process—plan, design, develop, release, repeat.

Welcome to the Real World

While the site development process appears to be a very straightforward cycle, it doesn't always go so smoothly. There are just too many variables to account for in the real world. For example, consider the effects of building a site for another person such as boss or client. If someone else is paying for a site to be built, you may still need to indulge their desires regardless of whether the requests conform to what the user wants. Make sure you attempt to persuade others that decisions should always be made with the user in mind. Try to show the benefits of design theories rather than preach rules. Be prepared to show examples of your ideas that are fully fleshed out. However, accept that they often may be shot down.

Note   *Experienced designers often will create a variety of site comps to guide discussion, similar to a book of haircuts for customers that can't verbalize what they want.*

Most Web projects tend to have political problems. Don't expect everyone to agree. Departments in a company will wrestle for control, often with battle lines being drawn between the marketing department and the technology groups. To stir up even more trouble, there may be numerous self-proclaimed Web experts nearby ready to give advice. Don't be surprised when someone's brother's friend turns out to be a Web "expert" who claims you can build the whole site with Microsoft FrontPage wizards in one hour. The only way to combat political problems is to be patient and attempt to educate. Not everyone will understand the purpose of the site; without a clear specification in place, developers may find themselves in a precarious position open to attack from all sides.

Always remember that the purpose of following a process model like the one discussed in this chapter is to minimize the problems that occur during a Web project. However, a process model won't account for every real-world problem, particularly people issues. Experience is the only teacher for dealing with many problems. Developers lacking experience in Web projects are always encouraged to roll with the punches and consider all obstacles learning experiences.

Summary

Building a modern Web site can be challenging, so site builders should adopt a methodology or process model to guide the development process and hopefully minimize risk, manage complexity, and generally improve the end result. Software engineering process models such as the modified waterfall can be applied easily to most Web projects. However, occasionally because of a lack of project management experience or clear goal statements, a prototype-driven or joint application process should be employed. While a prototype-based approach would seem to easily fit with the organic nature of many sites, it can produce needless risk and result in building the wrong site numerous times, before building the right one. Planning during the early stages of a site's development minimizes risk and should improve the end result. A design document that usually includes site goals, audience and task analysis, content requirements, site structure, technical requirements, and management considerations should always be developed. The design document guides the production of the Web site. During the design phase of site production, use block diagrams, paper mock-ups, storyboards, and even mock sites to reduce the likelihood of having to redesign the site later on. If a plan is well thought out and the design phase prototypes built, implementation should proceed rapidly and require little rework. However, once finished, be careful not to rush the site online—adequate testing is required. Overtime maintenance will be required, and continued vigilance will be required or your finely crafted site will begin to degrade.

Chapter 3

Designing for Users

As discussed in Chapter 1, Web sites are often developed from one particular philosophical reference point. Sometimes this point of reference is content centered; other times, it is technology centered. Even more frequently, it is visually centered. However, the real emphasis when building sites should always be the user. Keeping the user in mind and always trying to meet their needs is the key focus of user-centered design. Understanding user needs isn't easy. While users share common capabilities such as memory or reaction time, each user is still a distinct individual. Sites should be built for common user capabilities, rather than the extreme novice or power user. Sites should be accessible to all, and still be able to account for the differences exhibited by individuals. Usability is concerned with understanding how easy a Web site is to use. Building a usable Web site is challenging because what is usable to one person may be problematic for another. The likelihood of building a user-centered site is greatly improved through user interviews, testing, or even iterative design. Always be wary, though, of falling into the user trap. While a site should always be built for users, the desires of the site's creators must also be met, even though these may be somewhat at odds with the desires of the site's users. The fine balance of power between user and designer is not easily achieved.

Usability

Everyone has a vague idea of what it means to be usable. People will talk at length about how Web sites are supposedly user friendly, intuitive to use, or simply "usable." What, exactly, does it mean for something to be usable? First, consider the idea of utility. Two e-commerce sites selling books offer the same basic features. Both allow the user to search or browse for books, read information on books, purchase books, and track their orders. If both sites have basically the same features, they have the same utility—meaning they can do the same thing. Given that the sites have a few basic functions, you may find it easier to perform the same task on one site than the other. In this case, we can say that one site is more usable than the other. Unfortunately, is difficult to agree on what is usable. Plenty of people have attempted to characterize what usability is. Consider the following definition adopted from an ISO standard definition of usability.

> **Definition: Usability is the extent to which a site can be used by a specified group of users to achieve specified goals with effectiveness, efficiency, and satisfaction in a specified context of use.**

Consider each piece of the definition. First, note that we should limit the group of users when talking about usability. Recall that usability will vary greatly depending on the user.

Next, usability should be related to a task. You should not consider a site to be usable in some general sense. Instead, discuss usability within the context of performing some task, such as finding a telephone number for contact, purchasing a product, and so on. Usability is then defined by the effectiveness, efficiency, and satisfaction the user experiences trying to achieve these goals. Effectiveness describes whether or not the user is able to actually achieve their goals. If a user is unable to, or only partially able to, complete a task they set out to perform at a site, the site really isn't usable.

Next, usability is related to efficiency. If the user makes a great number of mistakes or has to do things in a roundabout way when they visit a site, the site isn't terribly usable. Last, the user must be satisfied with the performance of the task.

Many other definitions of usability exist. Some usability professionals suggest that usability can be concretely defined. Maybe it could be computed as some combination of the completion time for a typical visit and the number of errors made during the visit. From the user's point of view, that might not mean much; a user might just be concerned with how satisfied they were after performing a task. Many usability experts such as Jakob Nielsen (www.useit.com) tend to have similar definitions more in line with the ISO one. For example, Nielsen suggests that the following five ideas determine the usability of a site:

- Learnability
- Rememberability
- Efficiency of use
- Reliability in use
- User satisfaction

By this definition, a site is usable if it is easy to learn, easy to remember how to use, efficient to use (doesn't require a lot of work on the part of the user), reliable in that it works correctly and helps users perform tasks correctly, and the user is generally satisfied using the site. This still seems fuzzy in some ways, and conflicts arise easily in usability. For example, a site that is easily learnable by a novice user may be laborious to use for a power user. Because people are different and come with different levels of capabilities and Web knowledge, not everyone is going to agree on what is supposedly usable. A site that is easy to one user may be hard for another.

Rule: There is no absolute idea of what constitutes a usable site. Usability will vary as much as the users accessing the site.

Even without considering user differences, we may find that usability varies depending on how a single user interacts with a site. Usability also often depends on the medium of consumption; textual content viewed on the screen may be more usable in a large size, but when it is consumed on paper it might be better smaller. If you have tried to read large amounts of small content online you know it can be difficult. People tend to find that it is much easier to read the same information on paper. Some experts have suggested that people read much more slowly onscreen and tend to scan more than read content online. In this case the medium of consumption, screen vs. print, has affected the perceived usability of the content. In the case of the Web, the medium, which includes networks, browsers, screen sizes, and technologies like HTML, often contributes in a large way to usability problems. Throughout this book, the mantra of "know thy medium" should be repeated over and over.

Rule: Usability depends on the medium of consumption.

What is considered usable often varies between sites. An entertainment site would have different usability constraints than a commercial one. Furthermore, the user's familiarity with a site—as well as how often and what they plan on using the site for—will affect how they feel about its user friendliness. Consider how people may feel about the usability of a site that they have never been to before and are only marginally interested in vs. one that they frequently visit or must use. They may be much more forgiving of errors in the site they need to use or have come to use vs. the one they are just casually interested in. In short, a "throwaway" single-time-visit site has different usability constraints than a site a user relies on day to day.

Rule: Usability depends on the type of site as well as the user's familiarity with it.

This last idea might seem a tad unusual, but it shouldn't. People often come to believe inefficient ways of doing things are perfectly acceptable. Be careful about getting too scientific when talking about usability (measuring page clicks, mouse travel, errors rates, and the like). How the user "feels" about the experience when they come away—their satisfaction with the site or the task performed—is really the most important thing. For some people, how they feel may not always be logical, or even one hundred percent related to what happened during the site visit. Consider how many people gain satisfaction from performing difficult tasks; they may feel that way about some sites as well. Also consider how people let organizations that they are familiar with outside the Web get away with things at their sites that a new company can't, simply because they trust the name brand of the older firm. On the other hand, don't assume that the occasionally illogical user can be used as an excuse to produce a site that is hard to use. A site that requires the user to learn a new way of doing things, is inflexible, results in errors, or just doesn't work will generally result in poor user satisfaction. Improve usability, and users will be happier.

Rule: Usability and user satisfaction are directly related.

To understand how to make something usable, you must understand users. The next few sections will discuss usability in light of user capabilities and tendencies. The conclusion of the chapter will revisit these subjects and present a few rules of thumb that can be applied during Web site design to improve a site's usability.

Who Are Web Users?

Site designers often make the common mistake of oversimplifying or completely ignoring the capabilities and desires of users. In some cases, statements about designing the site with a particular browser or bandwidth in mind replace any serious thought of the user. Don't design your site for Netscape—design for people who happen to use the Netscape browser. Always remember the following very important Web design rule.

Rule: Browsers do not use sites, people do.

Fortunately, most designers don't go to the extreme of completely forgetting the user, but often they do oversimplify who the site's users are. Far too often, sites are built for some elusive stereotypical Web user—the 14.4-Kbps modem user accessing via AOL. This user is just a nameless person cruising the Internet to be enticed into visiting the site and performing whatever task the designer desires. The reality is that users are not automatons with consistent capabilities and desires, but individuals with a wide range of physical capabilities, needs, wants, expectations, and goals. Real Web users have bad days or can't always figure sites out, just like the rest of us.

Suggestion: There are no generic people. Always try to envision a real person visiting your site.

While it may not be possible to create a perfect stereotypical user to design Web sites for, there are some general things that can be said about users. The first thing is to think about how today's typical user interacts with a Web site. Until alternative browsing environments such as cell phones become commonplace, you almost certainly imagine a user of your site sitting at desk or table with a computer. They sit at most a few feet from a monitor, and generally use a keyboard and a mouse to interact with a Web site shown on the monitor. Primarily, they are using their eyes to access the information on the screen, though sound may also come into play. The stimulus from the site is filtered, and choice items may be consumed or, more accurately, committed to short- or long-term memory. The information they consume then may cause them to react by making a choice such as clicking a link, or entering data into a form. This simplified view of a user interacting with a site is shown in Figure 3-1.

Abstractly, you can describe how people tend to react to the world around them, including Web sites in the following way. First, they encounter some sensation that is stored into memory. Then they try to understand the sensation, which is filtered both consciously and unconsciously. Information from past experiences may be called into action, influencing how they perceive things and possibly helping them decide what to do. From this perception, the user may form an action—or possibly an inaction—that will later result in more sensations to be interpreted. This simplified action/reaction/action loop is shown here:

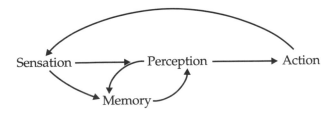

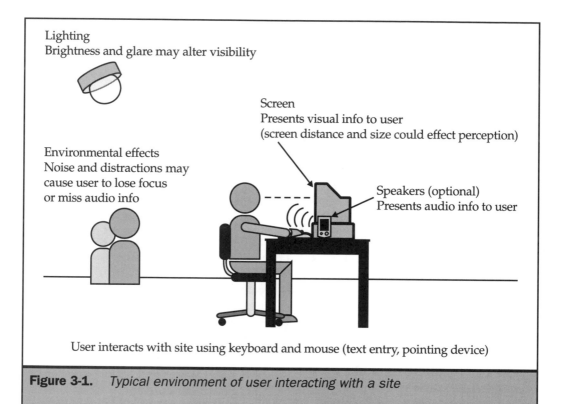

Figure 3-1.   *Typical environment of user interacting with a site*

Do not think that people can be simplified down to a formula where a stimulus is provided that results in an action. People are more complicated than that. People are capable of learning things, and information they encounter is committed to memory that can be used to modify what they do. Furthermore, people aren't perfect. Problems may occur, such as not remembering things properly. Different people perceive stimuli differently. Not everyone sees color quite the same way. Regardless of the simplification, the model does force designers to consider how people interact with the world—which includes their Web site. Common user characteristics such as sensation and memory need to be well considered, at least in a general sense, when building sites.

Common User Characteristics

There are no generic people, but people tend to have similar physical characteristics. Most people tend see about the same, are capable of remembering things, and react to stimuli about the same way. However, remember that people are individuals. There will be some users who will be able to see much better or worse than others. There will be people who can memorize hundreds of links and be able to quickly filter them, and others who will be overwhelmed when presented with more than two choices. There will also be a few users who react much faster or slower to information. However, as with all aspects of Web design, we should aim first for the common user and make sure to account for differences. Let's first consider common user characteristics such as vision, memory, and stimulus reaction.

Vision

The first aspect to consider about users is how they receive information from a Web site. The primary way most users consume data from Web sites is visually. They look at a screen and consume information in the form of text, color, graphics, or animation. The user's ability to see is obviously very important. Consider, for example, a user with poor eyesight. Unless the text is very large and the contrast between foreground and background elements very distinct, they may not be able to effectively interact with the content of the site. Unfortunately, many sites seem to assume that users have nearly superhuman vision, as text is sized very small or a minor degree of contrast is used between foreground and background elements. A simple example of some of contrast and sizing problems can be found at http://www.webdesignref.com/chapter3/visionissues.htm.

In order to avoid troublesome color combinations, designers should be aware of how color is perceived by the human eye. Three factors affect how color is perceived:

- **Hue**   The degree to which a color is similar to the basic colors such as red, green, and blue, or some combination of these colors.

- **Vaule**   The degree to which a color differs from achromatic (white, gray, or black).

- **Lightness**   The degree to which a color appears lighter or darker than another under the same viewing conditions.

Users with vision that is somewhat color deficient are often unable to differentiate between colors of similar hue when those colors are of the same lightness and saturation. For example, someone with the most common color deficiency—red-green color blindness—has trouble distinguishing between red and green when the red and green are close in saturation and lightness. Such color-vision issues can be troublesome when you consider the difficulty in distinguishing between red and green traffic lights. Does the color-deficient user really know when to stop or go? Consider on the Web, if links are similar in hue, lightness, and saturation, how difficult it might be for someone to determine what links have been clicked on and which have not.

Web page designers can avoid vision issues for users if they follow a few simple rules. First, make sure not to use text or graphic combinations that have a similar hue. Instead of using light blue on dark blue use blue on yellow or white instead.

Suggestion: Avoid using text, graphics, and backgrounds of similar hue.

It is possible to get in trouble when using colored text on backgrounds with similar saturation. For example, instead of using a grayish blue text on a rose-colored background, where both colors are close to achromatic gray, use white text on a rose background or vice versa.

Suggestion: Avoid combining text, graphics, and backgrounds of similar saturation.

The most obvious problem is when contrast is not great enough. Designers need to consider that dark text on a dark background or bright text on a bright background just may not be readable on all monitors or by people with color or vision deficiency. Instead of using a light-blue text on a pale-yellow background, use blue text on white background. Or, black text on a white background is always a safe bet. You could consider that yellow and black contrast very well; therefore, they are used on road signs that are very important to read. However, before changing your Web site to this color combination, consider that design shouldn't be thrown completely out the window just because of usability concerns.

Rule: Keep contrast high. Avoid using text, graphics, and background of similar lightness.

A very important use of color in a Web page is link color. In general, you should really avoid modifying link colors at all. However, if you do modify link colors, make sure to avoid using link-state colors of similar hue, similar saturation, or similar lightness to the background or to one another. For example, avoid links that change from red to pink. For some reason, designers seem to favor such types of combinations. Instead, consider using links that change from dark blue to pink, similar to the normal link state. Be careful with the background color as it may interfere with link readability, depending on link state. Because of this, white is a good background color. However, if a sacrifice has to be made with color contrast, make the visited state color the one with the contrast problem since these are links the user would generally be less interested in.

Links, as well as normal text, often have problems with backgrounds. In particular, avoid patterned backgrounds with multiple hues, saturations, or lightness. Common backgrounds like speckles or texture patterns tend to make poor backgrounds; instead, choose a subtle pattern or simple color.

Suggestion: Avoid using busy background tiles.

To make pages more readable, and to deal with users who might have some color or vision deficiency, Web designers should make sure colors that are meant to distinguish items are significantly different in two areas (e.g., hue and lightness). If this rule is followed, users color deficient in one area (e.g., red-green hue) can still distinguish the item by another attribute such as its lightness or saturation.

Rule: Make sure colors that are meant to distinguish items like links are significantly different in two ways, such as hue and lightness.

Memory

Memory is critical to a user being able to utilize a site. If the user is unable to remember anything about a site as they browse it, they will become hopelessly lost since they will not be able to recall if they have been someplace before. However, a user's memory is far from perfect, and they don't consciously spend time trying to memorize things. Users tend to always follow a simple rule: try to do minimal work for maximal gain. Simple human nature suggests that a user is not going to spend a great deal of time to figure something out unless there is a potentially good payoff.

Rule: Users try to maximize gain and minimize work.

Of course, what is considered a good payoff will vary from person to person. Consider that some people like to solve complex puzzles just for personal satisfaction. For them, the payoff is an intense feeling of accomplishment from solving a puzzle. However, let's assume that users are generally not going to exhibit such behavior; rather, they will only work hard if they know they need to or if there is a really good payoff that will result. If you want a blunt or somewhat negative way to remember this idea, just assume users are lazy! More general rules of thumb about how users tend to act will be presented later in the chapter. The previous rule is simply presented to tie in with a few ideas about memory.

Now, assuming users will not like or will even avoid Web sites that require them to work too hard, forcing them to memorize things is not a good idea. To illustrate this idea in practice, consider the interface of an automated telephone-banking system. When you call the bank, you are prompted for your account number and then read a list of items and corresponding keys to press, "Press 1 for balance, press 2 for transfer, press 3 for payments..." If you have encountered such a system and you are unfamiliar with all the choices, use can be difficult. You may find that you will try to remember a choice presented in your mind until all the choices have been presented. If too many choices are presented, you might not be able to recall the range of choices or you might even forget which item you chose and have to listen to the choices again. Now if the same information is presented on a small text menu, it would be much easier to find the item. You would just look over the list and pick the appropriate one. The voice example requires you to recall the choices, which is very difficult. In general we always consider that it is easier for users to recognize choices than it is easy for them to recall them. Because users may make mistakes and then tend to favor easier-to-use systems, we should always try to rely on recognition over recall.

Rule: Recognition is easier than recall, so don't force users to memorize information.

There are plenty of examples of how recognition is easier than recall. Students generally consider a multiple-choice test to be easier than a fill-in test. You must study, of course, for each, assuming the tests are created correctly—but the amount of memorization required is much higher for the fill-in test. The multiple-choice test doesn't require the depth of memory because you will hopefully see the answer and recognize it even if not perfectly using a relatively minimal amount of recall.

It turns out that many of the rules and suggestions presented in this book ultimately are related to this idea of recognition being easier than recall. For example, consider the idea of modifying link color that will be discussed further in Chapter 6. If we turn off link coloring so that links never look visited, we are forcing the user to recall if they have selected a certain link before. If the links do change color, users simply have to recognize the different color to know they have been there before.

> **Rule: Do not make visited links the same style or color as unvisited ones, as it forces the user to memorize where they have been.**

Another important aspect of memory to consider is that it isn't perfect. Users are not going to memorize things easily, and often users will have only partial memory or flawed memory of something. Just as in real life, repetition will lead to improved memory. For example, frequent users or power users may actually even rely on memorization of the location of objects on the screen, but most users will have only vague memories of link choices or how pages are organized. However, when people are memorizing things, it is known that image memory is one of our most robust forms of memory. It is far easier to retrieve pictures or even words or ideas that evoke pictures than it is to retrieve abstract ideas without visual cues from memory. Consider that it is often far easier to remember a person's face or a location that you have visited than it is to remember a name. Given that users will generally find it easier to remember visuals, it would be wise to make pages that should be remembered visually different from the rest. For example, in site navigation, a home page serves as a safe zone for a user. Using a distinct image or a different color is important to make the home page memorable. However, do not assume the user to have perfect memory. Don't make the home page only subtly different from the other pages or expect the user to notice or memorize text items on the page to distinguish it from other pages.

> **Suggestion: Since it is easier to remember visuals, make pages that should be remembered visually different from the rest.**

Another aspect of memory that is important to the usability of Web pages is the amount of information a person can recall from short-term memory. Let's return to the automated-phone-banking-system example. When the user was read the choices, they had to memorize them. If too many choices were presented, they might forget an item. This is an example of short-term working memory. In a sense, we need a little scratch space in our brain to remember something for a few moments. This memory does not hold a great number of items and is highly volatile. Cognitive scientists have long been interested in short-term memory and have conducted many experiments where participants are presented random objects or words and asked to quickly look at them or to make choices from them to test short-term memory. What is found is that participants are able to recall a range of seven items, plus or minus two, from short-term memory. What this means is that when given 5–9 items, the user will be able to recall all the items for a short period of time and choose from them fairly equally.

The implication of users being able to remember quickly 7 (±2) items on Web design is profound if you think about it. If you present a user with a set of links, shouldn't you limit the choices to 5–9? Well you better—if you want the user to choose from the choices evenly. For example, if you present a list of dozens of what may appear to be randomly ordered links to a user, you will find they will have a tough time picking from them. You may notice that users will tend to favor extremes. In practice, the author has seen this happen on Web sites. A large music site that I was consulted about faced a problem in that bands listed on the site having names beginning with A or Z had a much higher download rate than anything else. What was happening was that users had little knowledge of the bands, so they would scan the lists and—unless something jumped out at them—they tended to choose the first or last items in the list to see what happened. They really couldn't memorize the names of the bands that were interesting as they went along—there were just too many of them. If you want users to easily choose from a list of things that are equally important, you should limit your set of choices to between 5–9 items.

Suggestion: Limit groups of similar choices such as links to 5–9 items.

However, do not go overboard with the 5–9-items idea. Some designers might be tempted to use this rule to suggest that pages should have only 5–9 links on them. However, this could be rather limiting if you have a lot of content. Users can focus on items progressively. Consider, for example, being presented 5–9 distinctly different clusters of links on a page. Maybe the clusters are labeled and colored so the user chooses a cluster after looking at each. Once in the cluster, there are 5–9 links. In this sense, we could imagine there might be as many as 81 links on a screen and the user would still be able to use them easily. When looking at well-designed pages with numerous links, you hopefully will see fewer than 100 links and notice that the clustering used an organization method, such as alphabetical, to avoid memorization.

Memory rules of thumb can be also be applied to clicks. It appears that users are able to remember about three pages presented sequentially. Anything more than that and there tend to be gaps in memory. For example, as a user clicks through dozens of pages, they will probably remember a variety of pages but not all sequentially. The memorable pages may be visually different enough to trigger recall. In Chapter 5 we will talk about these pages serving as landmarks in a site. However, if you want the user to remember a path, they tend to only remember about three page views sequentially—and maybe less if the pages look nearly identical. Because of this, you should not expect a user to memorize a sequence or path longer than three items without consistent use.

Suggestion: Aim for memorization of only three items or pages sequentially.

This is by no means a complete discussion of memory, but it does serve to remind Web designers that, in order to make a site easy to use, we need to limit the amount of memorization going on. The less effort the user has to expend trying to recall what sequence of buttons they pressed or what choices they may have seen, the better.

Response and Reaction Times

If you have watched people browse around Web sites, it is obvious that some people are faster than others. Some users appear to cut quickly through page content, make choices rapidly, and are frustrated with even the slightest download delay. Others struggle to keep up and seem to have the patience of Job when it comes to waiting for pages to load. However, over time you'll come to find that people's patience for Web page loading will go away, particularly as their frequency of use increases. Consider, for example, how long it takes for users to become annoyed at an automated teller machine that has not returned their money to them. The entire transaction may only take a few seconds, but customers are quickly annoyed. But when automated tellers first came out, a wait of even 30 seconds to a minute seemed tolerable compared to waiting in a long bank line.

Tip *Users tend to be more patient with something they are unfamiliar with or that is a novelty.*

We see this idea on the Web all the time. Sites that could be considered single-visit sites like movie-promotion sites or designer portfolios seem to get away with huge download times. These sites could be termed single-visit or "throwaway" sites since the user is unlikely to return. Splash pages, excessive animations, and long downloads are less annoying to a user who hasn't seen them before, but patience wears thin on return visitation. Consider that even when a splash page has a "skip intro" button, a return visitor will still be frustrated with having to even make such a choice. The very fast loading design of successful, heavy-frequent-use sites such as portals or e-commerce sites shows that patience wears thin. The needs and desires of the first-time visitor, who in some sense could be considered a novice user of the site, are different than the frequent or expert user of a site. However, users do not have infinite patience, and they are getting more and more impatient as they get used to what facilities the Web, or a particular site, provides. In general we find the following rule to hold.

Rule: The amount of time a user will wait is proportional to the payoff.

The better the payoff, the longer the user will wait. Users who get something for free or who are stealing some desirable piece of software or music seem to be willing to wait an eternity. Consider some users who illegally download songs from the Internet with a modem. They'll literally spend hours downloading songs when they could have gone out, worked at a near-minimum-wage job, and earned enough to purchase the entire CD in a similar period of time. Of course, this imbalance will certainly change with the increase in bandwidth—much to the annoyance of the music industry. The Web design issue to consider from the previous tip and this last example is that if you are going to expect a user to wait for a page to load, there'd better be something useful there.

The exact times users will wait will vary based on the individual user, their personality, and the potential benefit of waiting. However, there are some things we can say about response and reaction times for users in general. Some usability experts (Jakob Nielsen, www.useit.com) relate that studies about response times report similar results. Common response times and user reactions are summarized in Table 3-1.

When it comes to the Web, there is generally little chance of going too fast for the user. Most of the time, it takes more than a few seconds even on a fast connection to download something. However, be careful once something like a Java applet or Flash file is downloaded. If the user has a faster processor than you, the program may end up

Time Elapsed	Probable User Reaction
0.1 second	When something operates this fast or faster, it appears instantaneous or nearly instantaneous to the user. Unfortunately, due to bandwidth and technology constraints, few Web pages will exhibit this level of responsiveness in the near future.
1.0 second	When something reacts in around a second, there is no major potential for interrupt. The user is relatively engaged and not easily distracted from what is happening on the screen.
10 seconds	This is suggested to be the limit for keeping the user's attention focused on the page. Some feedback showing that progress is being made is required, though browser feedback such as a progress bar may be adequate. However, do not expect that the user may not look to do something else if they become bored.
> 10 seconds	With a delay this long, the user may actually go about other business, look at sites in other windows, talk on the phone, etc. If you want the user to continue to pay attention, you will have to give them constant feedback about progress made, and you should try to give them some sense of when the page will be finished. Consider when you are downloading software how the browser tries to let users know how much time is left before the download is completed.

Table 3-1. *Response Time and User Reactions*

running much faster on their system than expected, so much so that the user might not be able to keep up. On occasion, you may notice how scrolling marquees written in Java used in some Web pages appear to travel at a rate only a superhuman could read.

Tip	*Be careful with overly fast response times of downloaded objects.*

In most cases, a Web site will probably not outpace the user; in fact, it may be much too slow for their liking. Because users may get impatient, you need to make sure that they are given some indication of the progress being made. The browser itself actually gives a great deal of feedback about the progress being made. When loading a page, a browser will generally convert a cursor to a wait indicator such as an hour glass, spin or pulsate a logo (generally in the upper-right corner of the screen), provide a progress meter towards the bottom of the screen, and display messages about objects being loaded in the status bar at the bottom of the screen. The Web designer will hopefully design their pages to provide even more feedback. For example, the designer may build their page so text loads first or pieces of the page are loaded one at a time. Often, users will cut images up into multiple pieces so the user will see a bit load at a time. Also, designers often use images that load in a progressive fashion from an unclear one to a sharp one so that the user is able to get a general sense of a complete fuzzy picture early on and watch its loading progress, if necessary. Figure 3-2 illustrates all these progress indicators in action.

For page loads that only take 10–20 seconds, the feedback given by the browser as well as through incremental loading of a page should be enough to let the user know something is going on. However, when loading takes longer, you should give the user more information. For example, many sites that use binary technologies like Flash use a special loading page complete with a status bar showing progress. Such progress meters can also be created using technologies like JavaScript. However, don't bother with a progress bar or other forms of feedback unless load times are around 30 seconds or more.

Rule: When response times such as page loads take more than 30 seconds, try to provide your own feedback to the user such as a load-time progress bar.

If you are building a static site, there are some simple tricks to let the user know about a longer wait for an object. Consider a very large image download. Besides interlacing the image or making it progressive, as discussed in Chapter 11, it is possible to use a trick with the **LOWSRC** attribute. For example, you could load a low-resolution version of an image first, or even a graphic message stating the image is loading, like so:

```
<IMG SRC="hirezpicture.jpg" LOWSRC="lowrezpicture.jpg" HEIGHT="1000"
WIDTH="1000">
```

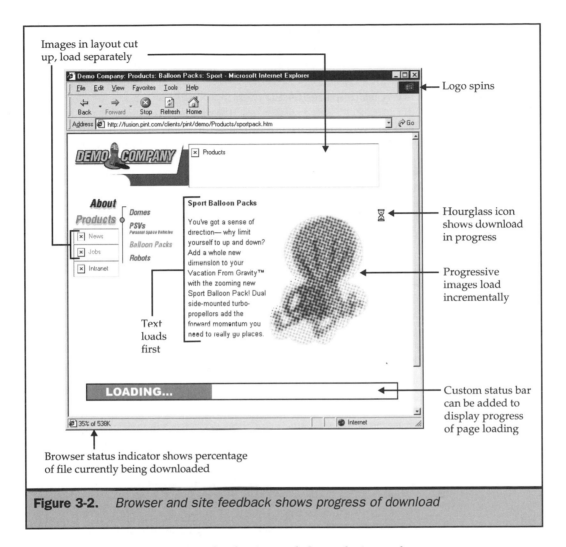

Figure 3-2.   *Browser and site feedback shows progress of download*

Or, you might have a message display instead. Some designers have even experimented using the **ALT** attribute of an image to show file size or a loading message, like so:

```
<IMG SRC="hirezpicture.jpg" ALT="Loading picture of Mars (800K)"
HEIGHT="1000" WIDTH="1000">
```

Of course, it is probably better to reserve the **ALT** text for its primary purpose— providing an alternative rendering for users without images. Another HTML or CSS trick that can be used to let a user know about a long download is to use a background image with a message on it that says a page is loading, which is eventually covered up by content that is being downloaded as shown in Figure 3-3.

When attempting to create a site that appears responsive to a user, remember that time is what matters the most. How users actually perceive a page loading will not necessarily equate to the bytes delivered. A user who isn't paying for bandwidth isn't going to care if 1K or 100MB is delivered as long as it appears fast to them.

Rule: Time matters more to a user than bytes delivered.

Because time is so important to a user, it is important to take advantage of every second. Consider that the general way a user navigates the Web is that they look at a page scan to find an appropriate link, click, and then wait for the page. Once the page loads, they then look at the page to find the next link or spend time consuming the content. Notice the time is split between user "think time" and download time. The reality is that for most users, the think time for navigation pages is pretty small compared to the wait time. For content pages, however, the user may spend a great deal of time looking at the page. One way to improve responsiveness would be to take advantage of the thinking time by downloading information to be used later on. This could be called preloading or precaching. Assuming you are able to preload most or all of the next thing to be looked at by the user during the think time, the next page-load time could be significantly reduced. Somewhat like the magician who has the result of a trick set up in advance, downloading during idle moments can produce a nearly mystical appearance of speed.

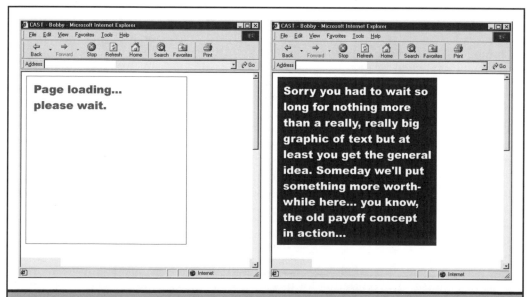

Figure 3-3.   *Backgrounds that are covered up can contain loading messages*

Suggestion: Improve Web page response time by taking advantage of user "think time" with preloading.

A variety of browser-accelerator tools have been built in an attempt to improve Web responsiveness by preloading pages linked from the current page. The only problem with this approach is that many pages have so many outbound links it is difficult for the browser to predict the page the user will load next. The best way to improve the odds of caching the correct "next page" is to look at the common paths users take through a site by examining a log file and then putting in code to preload pages along these paths. However, this just improves the odds. The only time you can really guarantee that preloading will improve things is when the user is navigating a linear progression of pages.

Suggestion: Use preloading on a linear progression of pages.

To see a demonstration of preloading a linear progression of pages, see http://www.webdesignref.com/chapter3/preloaddemo.htm.

The responsiveness of a Web site is a key aspect to a user's feeling of the site's usability. Beyond loading of pages, consider that time is important to a user even after a page has loaded. For example, if a page loads quickly but the user can't figure out what is going on in the page in around one minute, they can become just as frustrated as waiting for a simple page to download. Consider aiming for what might be called the "one-minute Web page." A one-minute Web page is one where the user gets the gist of the page in around one minute and can decide after that if they want to consume the content more seriously or not.

Tip	*Aim for a one-minute limit for the user to determine the basic gist of a page's content or purpose after loading.*

Dealing with Stimulus

Users are constantly being bombarded by stimuli from our sites. The text, the links, the graphics, animation, even sound all create a cacophony of information that the user tries to distill meaning from. Because of the continual stimulation, we need to filter out some of the data, and we do this both unconsciously and consciously. Three primary ways it is thought that people filter sensation data include thresholds, an idea often dubbed the cocktail-party effect, and sensory adaptation.

Thresholds

Rather than deal with every minute change that happens, we tend only to notice something that exceeds a particular threshold. For example, if on a Web page an object moves very slowly—say a pixel every few seconds—we may not notice at first because the speed of its movement is below our absolute threshold. However, over time we may notice the movement. Thresholds are tough to predict. Depending on the user's psychological state, they may be able to detect something under normal conditions, but if they are tired or distracted they may not be able to notice the difference between two similar but different colors or fonts that have been used to separate navigation forms.

When designing pages, designers should always consider thresholds. Thresholds suggest making objects or pages noticeably different from each other because if they are too similar, the user will have to work too hard to understand their difference. For example, consider if link and text color in a page are too similar. The user may have to carefully inspect underlined text to make sure that it is a link and not just underlined text, because text colors are only subtly different. In other words, they might not always be sure what's a link and what isn't without putting in at least some degree of effort. Designers should strive not to force the user to spend time and effort trying to interpret the differences between objects on a page, as it is both frustrating and takes time away from the main goal of getting the user to consume the content or perform a task. Consider the threshold effect when trying to differentiate objects on a page.

Suggestion: Make page elements obviously different if they are different.

Things need to be just different enough for the user to notice. If the designer is too subtle, however, the user may not be able to tell. And if you go overboard, the design may backfire. It would be easy enough to always put site buttons in bright colors and content in dark colors, but this could be annoying to the user. The next two ideas show how users tend to filter out information when being bombarded with excessive stimuli.

Cocktail-Party Effect

The cocktail-party effect describes how people are able to concentrate on important data when being bombarded by nonessential stimuli. People at a cocktail party can concentrate on their own conversation despite being in a room filled with numerous other conversations. Don't dismiss the other conversations as background noise. If the listener stopped and focused on another conversation, they probably could hear certain parts of it. However, the threshold effect is also in play during a cocktail party. If the person you are trying to listen to speaks too softly, the proximity of other conversations is too close, or the volume of other conversations too loud, you will be overwhelmed by the outside stimuli.

Web page designers should consider that, like in a cocktail-party conversation, the user might want to concentrate on only a small portion of the information on a page. The rest is background noise that has to be filtered out. If there is too much going on, the user will not be able to effectively concentrate on what they want and will become frustrated. Because of this, we should try to section things off just like a cocktail party so the user can effectively concentrate. A good site has lots of choices but provides the visitors the ability to focus on what they want to see. Towards this end, we might consider grouping similar items together and separating groups of items with a lot of white space. Also, within text, we might draw important points in a bullet-point form or with a pull quote, or highlight them with a background color. Always strive to limit noise, namely competing objects on a page. If not, then like at the cocktail party that gets too loud, the user won't be able to filter out information that isn't important to them.

> **Suggestion: Limit page noise and segment page objects so that they don't compete so much visually that the user is unable to focus on what they are interested in.**

Thresholds and the cocktail-party effect present a balance between having too little difference and too much. Don't become so concerned with trying to get an absolutely perfect balance of stimuli—just try to get it about right. You may consider erring in favor of a little much since people are very adaptable, as shown by the next cognitive-science idea.

Sensory Adaptation

Sensory adaptation occurs when a user becomes so used to a particular stimulus that they no longer respond to it—at least not consciously. Consider the watch on your wrist. You probably don't notice it normally, except that you just thought about it. Take the watch and put it on your other wrist and you'll notice it for a while, but eventually you'll get used to it. That's sensory adaptation. Life is filled with things that people adapt to: the ticking of an alarm clock, the clothes you wear, the loudness of the music coming from your car stereo, and so on. Life on the Web is no different. Users adapt to Web stimuli quickly. That continually animated GIF that grabbed the user's attention once or twice quickly fades into the background. Probably the most interesting sensory adaptation is the rise of so-called "banner blindness." People are becoming so used to the shape and location of banners that they are just tuning them out. Experiments as well as click rate show that people don't look at banners terribly attentively. Animation added to the mix improved things, but it too has succumbed to sensory adaptation. Rich banner ads complete with sound and complex interaction are being experimented with to see if we can regain user attention. The bottom line is that the user will decide what they want to focus on. Designers may want users to focus on something such as a banner ad or a download button, but in order to grab their attention they will have to continue coming up with new tricks as users will adapt to stimuli over time— particularly if they are related to things users aren't terribly interested in.

> **Rule: Sensory adaptation does occur on the Web. If you want a user's full attention, you'll have to vary things significantly and often.**

Sensory adaptation suggests that the numerous fonts, animations, and colored regions on a page may go unnoticed over time. This doesn't mean that we should completely avoid using things to stimulate the user, but we should not be so reliant on them as they lose strength with use. Sensory adaptation really suggests that in order to get users' full attention, we have to "wake them up" with something different. A little bit of surprise can be useful to make the user pay attention. However, be careful with this idea. In general, the user will want to peacefully go about their business and will expect pages to look and act consistently. We shouldn't disturb them, but should let them focus on the task or content at hand. If you bombard the user all the time, they will feel uncomfortable because of the lack of consistency, and they may become so annoyed that they leave.

Movement Capabilities

Once the user has absorbed information they have been provided, they will eventually react to it and make some choice. While someday voice interfaces may become commonplace, today's Web sites are generally manipulated using the keyboard or mouse. Because of this, we should always attempt to minimize user efforts using these devices. Few sites consider that users may prefer using the keyboard or arrow keys, instead of a mouse, to move through choices in a page. While many form pages are optimized for quick navigation via the keyboard, other pages may not be.

Rule: Try to optimize keyboard access for all pages in a site, not just form pages.

Consider also the work a user performs moving their mouse around the screen. Moving the pointer around the screen takes effort, and a button or link press may take up to a few seconds if a user has to move a long distance or focus on clicking a very small button. In fact, the time it takes a user to press a button is governed by something called Fitts' law (Fitts, 1954). Fitts' law basically states that the smaller the button to press and the farther away it is, the longer it will take to perform the action. This seems logical if you consider that a user will either tend to overshoot small click targets because they moved too fast and have to correct, or else they will take extra time to clock the button more carefully.

Fitts' law would suggest that to improve speed of use and thus efficiency, we should first bring things closer together. First we might consider reducing the amount of mouse travel between successive clicks. Notice how efficient a wizard-style interface is, since when clicking Next the successive Next button tends to be directly under or very close to the current mouse position. There is no reason we couldn't apply this to navigation elements. Try to keep successively clicked buttons close together. Navigation bars tend to encourage following this plan, anyway.

Rule: Minimize mouse travel distance between successive choices.

However, with the Web we can't always be sure that the user will press another button within the page as their next choice. In fact, quite often the user may move to a browser button such as the Back button rather than rely on an internal-site Back button nearby. Given some users' preference for the browser Back button, designers should try to minimize the mouse travel to the Back button. The question is, travel from where? We should assume that the user will probably hover over the navigation bar or near the scroll bars most of the time. While we can't decrease the distance from the scroll bars, which will tend to be far away from the Back button in the upper left of the screen, there is no reason that we should not consider putting primary navigation buttons on the left or top portions of the screen since this will minimize the distance from a primary selection area and the heavily used Back button, thus reducing mouse travel and increasing the speed at which the site can be used.

> **Rule: Minimize mouse travel between primary-page hover locations and the browser's Back button.**

Fitts' law would also suggest that we make clicking targets larger, particularly if they are far away. Some designers find this design suggestion troublesome because it would suggest making big huge buttons, which would take up a great deal of screen real estate as well as potentially making the site look like it was designed primarily for novice users. Big buttons also bring too much attention to the interface. However, buttons should be made big enough for the user to mouse to them relatively quickly— and spaced out well enough so they are able to click on them without accidentally pressing an adjacent choice.

> **Rule: Make clickable regions large enough for users to move to them quickly and press them accurately.**

Understanding general user capabilities is not all that we need to consider when discussing what ideas affect usable Web design. We must also consider the world the user inhabits and the user's general and unique characteristics and experiences.

The User's World

People truly are the centers of their own universe, in the sense that they perceive everything initially from their own point of view. Consider the idea of how a user might perceive the Web site shown in Figure 3-4. The user lives in the real world.

They are affected by their environment, from the physical conditions of their location, to the noise around them, to the visual quality of monitor they are using. From their world, they access your Web site via the medium of the Internet and the Web that includes things like network connections, servers, browsers, and so on. Once on the Web they navigate about and visit sites, where they first notice the presentation of the site. If they decide to actually interact with a site, they finally begin to consume or react to the content presented.

Note *The presentation and navigation layers could be interchanged considering that a user's ability to navigate Web space is greatly affected by the way it is presented.*

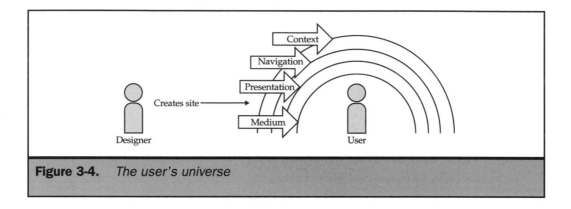

Figure 3-4. *The user's universe*

Suggestion: Always remember that you need to bring a site into the user's world, not the other way around.

The previous suggestion is an important one. Designers often believe that a user is coming to their site where they have set the rules. That may be true, but how the user tends to interpret things is based on their own viewpoint. Each user will have different opinions, capabilities, environment, and experiences that will influence how they interpret the site. A fine balance between what the user thinks and wants and what the designer thinks and wants has to be struck. This will be discussed in more depth later in this chapter.

User Environments

The user is heavily influenced by what could be called their environment of consumption. For example, consider a user in a public place such as an airport using a public Internet kiosk to remotely access their email. The user is standing up, it might be crowded and noisy, and they are waiting to dash off to the plane. Because of their environment, the user may not be tolerant of long waits, excessive menus, or anything that slows down their task at hand. Furthermore, due to the noise, they may not be able to always hear sound cues. Last, because they are standing up, the amount of time they might spend during the whole online session will certainly be significantly less than their normal session from an office. When designing for users, always think about where the user is accessing the site. Table 3-2 details some of the possibilities.

The environment will greatly affect the user's view of what is usable. For example, consider that color combinations that contrast acceptably indoors might be troublesome outdoors. Content must consider the environment of consumption.

Rule: Account for the characteristics of the probable environment in which the user will access a site.

Location	Characteristics
Office	Generally computer-based access Single user Relatively quiet Should be primarily work or task focused, at least during primary work hours Often high speed
Home office or bedroom	Generally computer-based access Single user Noise level variable, but often quiet Purpose may be work or play Access could be anytime Speed of access varies dramatically from modem to high speed
Home living room	Access may be from set-top box or video-game console Distance from device may be larger Use may be less input oriented (reduced typing) Noise level variable May be group-oriented access or single user Access probably more entertainment related Printing may not be an end result
Cybercafe	Probably computer-based access Cost may influence usage Noise level variable Use is probably entertainment or research oriented Speed of access probably high May be group oriented or single user Security or privacy may be a concern
Public kiosk	Cost may influence usage Noise level variable User may be standing Use will be less input oriented (reduced typing) Use is probably task oriented-particularly access to communication such as email or limited to very important information Access to location-related information may be a high priority Security or privacy may be a concern

Table 3-2. *Common User Environments Characteristics*

Location	Characteristics
Car	Probably noncomputer-based access (PDA or smart phone) Use will be less input oriented (reduced typing) Focus will not be primarily on the access if user is the driver Use is probably task oriented or limited to very important information Access to location-related information may be a high priority Speed and quality of access is probably low
Mass transit or plane	Probably noncomputer-based access (PDA or smart phone) or using a laptop User may be standing or sitting Use could be entertainment or work Access to location or time-sensitive information may be a high priority Speed and quality of access is probably low Security or privacy may be a concern
Outside	Probably noncomputer-based access (PDA or smart phone) Screen glare could be a significant problem Use will be less input oriented (reduced typing) User may standing or moving Noise level variable Use is probably task oriented or limited to very important information Access to location-related information may be a high priority Speed and quality of access is probably low

Table 3-2.   *Common User Environments Characteristics* (continued)

General Types of Users

There are three types of general users in the sense of knowledge of how to use a Web site: novices, intermediates, and experts or power users. A novice user is one who may have little knowledge of a site, or even how the Web works. A novice user will need extra assistance and may prefer extra clicks with extra feedback to accomplish a simple task. An example of an interface idea tuned to novices would be a wizard that automates some common task. Conversely, power users are those users who understand the Web or a site very well. Power users should be considered in two distinct categories: frequent and infrequent visitors to the site. A power user who frequently visits a site will utilize advanced features of a site such as sophisticated searching, may directly form their own URLs, and may memorize the position of objects within the site. A power user who is an infrequent visitor to a site may not be familiar with the site's structure, but will expect certain facilities, such as search, to be available to navigate a site. Power users will need relatively little handholding and will desire to click less and consume more. Obviously, the distance between a power user and novice user is great. A site geared too much towards one audience or another will certainly annoy—the power user if the site has been dumbed down, or the novice user if the site is geared mostly towards power users.

The third group of users, the infrequent intermediate user, is actually the largest category of users on the Web. Most users are infrequent intermediate users because they pretty much understand how the Web works, but they may not know how to navigate in a very efficient manner. Furthermore, the infrequent intermediate user doesn't continually revisit the site; if they do, they will probably eventually become an advanced user. Because site usage tends to be dominated by intermediate users, you may consider designing the site around the knowledge and capabilities of these users. However, that may lock out novice users and bore or restrict advanced users. The best approach to building a site for basic user groups is to build a site that provides features that cater to all users. Software applications do this, so there is no reason a Web site cannot. A software application provides keyboard shortcuts and customization features, such as customizable interfaces for power users, at the same time providing icon and menu systems utilized by intermediate and novice users. Help systems and wizards are also provided, which are mostly geared towards the novice user. A Web site could provide features like a clean URL system, advanced search facility, and personalization features for an advanced user. A site with consistent navigation bars that have button labels similar to other sites (About, Products, Careers, etc.) is very friendly to novice and intermediate users, and it can also have dynamically built "bread crumb" style navigation lines, popular with advanced users. Last, a Web site could provide help systems, maps, and alternative forms of access such as simple text links for the novice.

Suggestion: Aim to create an adaptive Web site that meets the requirements of novices, intermediates, and advanced users.

In a perfect world, there is no reason that a Web site can't be built to meet the needs of all general-user groups. However, time and cost constraints may limit the number of features that can be added to some Web sites. In this case, it is probably best to aim for the largest group of users: the intermediate. Because this may lock out some novice users unable to figure the site out, some might argue that you should aim for the lowest common denominator in a user. The problem with this is if you start building only for the complete novice, you can quickly alienate users who know what they are doing.

Suggestion: Design for the intermediate user if an adaptive Web interface is not possible.

Even if an adaptive interface is built, consider that we are talking only about meeting the basic needs of general users. Real users can be a much different situation. No matter how hard we try, there is bound to be a user who doesn't understand or like the site we have built.

 Remember there will always be real users who don't like or get a site, no matter how good it is.

Users are individuals with different tastes and opinions. They will have different experiences, capabilities, personalities, age, gender issues, and cultural issues. Some individuals may have disabilities that prohibit them from using a Web site that most users find easy to use. Users bring what they know from the real world and from other Web sites to your site. They bring concepts of the real world, such as navigation. They may expect to use navigational metaphors from the real world. However, they may also bring knowledge of how Web sites work because they have visited many other sites. Knowledge of how traditional software applications work may also be brought into play. Remember from early in the chapter, a user brings the site into their world—they don't visit the universe of your Web site.

Rule: Users bring past experiences with the world, software, and the Web to your site. Make sure your site meets their expectations.

You need to make sure that your site acts like other sites or software a user has used and meets their general expectations. Remember the rule of consistency: if you do things different from everybody else, you can't rely on past knowledge and you force the user to learn something new. Of course, the challenge with real users is that expectations will vary greatly based on their experience. However, try to understand that there are some common conventions from GUI design or Web sites that users are probably familiar with.

GUI Conventions

Graphical user interface (GUI) design has long followed a variety of standards developed by operating-system vendors such as Microsoft and Apple, or industry groups like OSF. These conventions are obvious in most software applications. Consider the screen snapshot of a recent version of Microsoft Word shown in Figure 3-5.

Notice that in the interface there are common menus like File, Edit, View, and Help. Many applications have these menus. These primary menus are always located at the top of the screen, and the Help menu is always the far-right menu. The Close box is always in the upper-right corner, and other window controls such as Minimize and Maximize are as well. The primary toolbar in software applications tends to be at the top of the application, and the bottom of the screen is reserved for less important controls and status messages. The functions of the application can generally be performed in multiple ways, such as using push-button icons, text menus, keyboard shortcuts, and wizards.

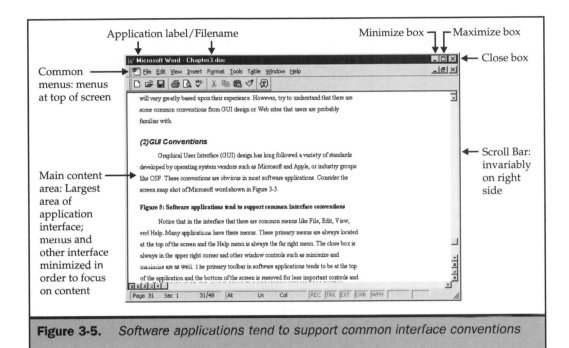

Figure 3-5.   *Software applications tend to support common interface conventions*

GUI conventions are very useful to understand, particularly when designing forms and other interactive elements of a site. Chapter 12 discusses the use of GUI widgets and provides a brief discussion of the difference between Web and GUI interfaces. The Web has not been able to develop conventions that are as well understood as those for software applications. There are two main reasons for this. First, software applications are often defined significantly by the operating system they are written for. Microsoft has great influence on how applications written for Windows should work. Apple can dictate conventions for Macintosh software. Second, the ability to author and distribute software applications is restricted to a much smaller group of people than in Web design. Many Web designers lack any formal understanding of GUI conventions and may actually shun them in favor of artistic freedom.

Web Conventions

While Web sites may not exactly follow GUI usability conventions, they do have a loose set of conventions. Straying from the way that most Web sites work is a dangerous idea. Consider the idea that most users will probably spend most of their time at other sites. Unless you happen to be running an important day-to-day use site like an internal site, or a heavily trafficked site like Amazon, or a portal like Yahoo, you will probably not be able to introduce any conventions of your own. In fact, if users come to expect that a company logo in the upper left-hand corner of the screen will return them to the home page, you had better do this in your site. If you don't do this, you may surprise the user, which could cause a negative reaction. Forcing the user to learn a new idea also could cause a negative feeling in the user.

> **Rule: Do not stray from the common interface conventions established by heavily used sites.**

Web conventions, unfortunately, are difficult to pinpoint. A few are well known and are summarized in Table 3-3.

Figure 3-6 illustrates some of the common Web conventions used in a page within the DemoCompany site.

Convention	Description
Upper left-hand corner logo signals home page return	Users tend to expect a corporate logo to return them to the home page. Most sites put this in the upper left-hand corner. An explicit Home button as well as a ToolTip is a good idea.
Text links are repeated at the bottom of a page	Most sites like to repeat text navigation at the bottom of a page, particularly if top or side navigation is a graphical form.
Back-to-top link used on long pages	While sites will provide text navigation to move to the next page, a back-to-top link or arrow is generally included at the bottom of the page to quickly jump the user up the page.
Special print forms used for heavily printed pages	Increasingly, sites are providing special printer-friendly versions either in a stripped HTML form or even in an Acrobat form. This is most commonly found on sites that distribute large volumes of content.
Clickable items are blue and underlined	Fight it all you want, but most text links are blue and underlined. While many users may be able to understand nonunderlined links or different colors, the best way to signify that something is pressable is making it blue and underlined. Be careful creating logos or other content that is blue, as users may actually try to click on it.

Table 3-3.   *Some Common Web Conventions*

Convention	Description
Secondary navigation elements such as site map or search are presented separately from sectional navigation	Because they are navigation aids, most sites have tended to put less emphasis on links to site maps, site indexes, help systems, and even search facilities. However, given the rise in popularity of search features, content-rich sites may especially emphasize search facilities.

Table 3-3.   *Some Common Web Conventions* (continued)

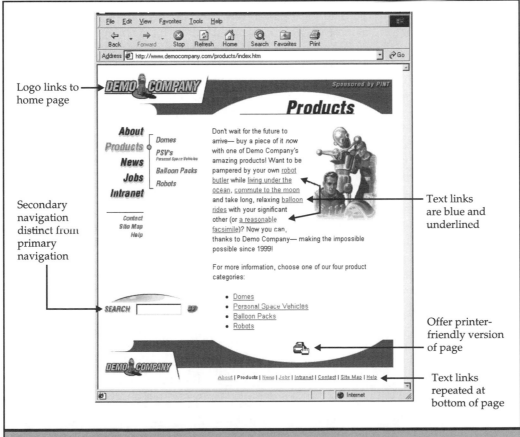

Figure 3-6.   *Web conventions in practice*

The problem with Web conventions is that they are moving targets. New conventions may be invented and sweep across the Web like fads. Consider how frames were very popular in the past. Splash pages also used to be popular, but have somewhat fallen out of favor. Conventions are not always well considered, and may often have more to do with novelty than usability. However, don't use this as an excuse to attempt to invent new conventions or avoid them. The best way to keep up with current conventions is to simply browse the well-trafficked e-commerce and content sites often and look for common features. If users are exposed to features there, such as one-click ordering, it isn't going to be difficult to explain to them how it works on your site. Don't assume that everyone understands common conventions or that all users will be able to use current conventions. Some users will have special needs.

Accessibility

There is no way to account for all the small differences between people. In fact, we only aim to create sites that *most* people like. This may lead us to stereotype groups of users into categories like casual female surfers under 18 and so on, but this may be a compromise we have to make. Yet, from this admission, don't go out and build a site catering to the largest demographic group of users hitting your site. Try to please as many distinct groups as possible by making your site as accessible as possible. Don't forget that some people may have difficulty if you assume they have perfect physical and technical capabilities.

Providing accessibility for people that may have deficiencies such as vision, hearing, or other physical capabilities isn't just a nice idea anymore—it may actually be required for some organizations—particularly government agencies, or those that could incur serious liability if they did not account for all users. For example, consider Section 508 of the 1986 Federal Rehabilitation Act. One of the most interesting aspects of Section 508 is that the federal government must include solutions for employees with disabilities when awarding contract proposals. This would also eventually apply to systems such as intranets, extranets, and most likely public Web sites. Also consider the 1992 Americans with Disabilities Act (ADA), which states that firms with 15 or more employees provide reasonable accommodation for employees with disabilities. This could apply to intranets or extranet creation! But don't assume that making a Web site accessible is something that has to be done because of some law or to avoid future litigation. In reality, if a site addresses accessibility concerns, it could result in the creation of a much better Web site for everyone. Very often, creating systems that are accessible to all users also creates benefits for all users, regardless of capability. Consider that so-called talking books, initially considered for the blind, fostered books on tape. Also consider that easy ramps to access buildings, and curb cutouts made for wheelchairs, make walking easier for all and tends to reduce the number of people falling flat on their face after crossing the street or severely twisting their ankles as they step off the curb.

The W3C (www.w3.org) has long advocated designing sites for good accessibility and promotes the Web Accessibility Initiative (www.w3.org/wai). The WAI is not only concerned with creating sites that are accessible to people with disabilities, but also with making sites that are accessible simply by anyone who might be operating in a different environment than what a designer may consider "normal." Remember that users will not necessarily be using a fast connection and a large monitor like you do—or if you aren't using a fast connection with the latest and greatest, your users just might be! From the W3C guides, you should always consider that users may have different operating constraints:

- They may not be able to see, hear, or move easily, or may not be able to process some types of information easily (or even at all).

- They may have difficulty reading or comprehending text because of language knowledge.

- They may not be able to use a keyboard or mouse because of access method (e.g., cell phone) or physical disability.

- They may have a less than ideal access environment such as a text-only screen, a small screen, a screen without color, or a slow Internet connection.

- They may be accessing the site in a nonstandard environment where they may be affected by environment considerations, like accessing the Web in a noisy cybercafe or as they drive a car.

- They may have an older browser, a nonstandard browser or operating system, or use an alternative form of user interface such as voice access.

To deal with these issues, the W3C has issued a few suggestions to improve the accessibility of a site. These are summarized here:

- **Provide equivalent alternatives to auditory and visual content.** In other words, don't rely solely on one form of communication. If you use picture buttons, provide text links. If audio is used, provide a text transcript of the message, and so on.

- **Don't rely on color alone.** As discussed earlier in the chapter, not everyone will be able to view colors properly, so if color alone is used to convey information such as what text is links, people who cannot differentiate between certain colors and users with devices that lack color or even visual displays will not be able to figure out what is being presented. You need to consider avoiding color combinations with similar hues or those without enough contrast—particularly if they are to be viewed on monochrome displays or by people with different types of color-vision deficits.

- **Use markup and style sheets, and do so properly.** Basically, make sure to use HTML for structure and CSS for presentation. Particularly avoid using proprietary markup or presentation elements, and avoid using technology that may not render the same way in different browsers. Chapter 13 discusses this in more depth.

- **Clarify natural language usage.** Make sure to define terms and use markup that indicates acroymns, definitions, quotations, and so on. In other words, use more logical markup. Furthermore, make sure to clearly indicate the language being used in the document so that a browser may be able to switch to another language.

- **Create tables that transform gracefully.** In short, in the future when CSS works, don't use tables for layout—use them for presenting tabular data such as a spreadsheet. When tables are used, provide a clear caption, column and read headings, and other indicators on the meaning of cell contents.

- **Ensure that pages featuring new technologies transform gracefully.** This is a key idea discussed throughout the book. Basically, make sure that if you are going to push the limit of design that any new technologies degrade gracefully under older browsers. For example, if you are relying on JavaScript, does the page still work without it on?

- **Ensure user control of time-sensitive content changes.** Make sure that moving, blinking, scrolling, or autoupdating objects or pages may be paused or stopped by the user. Besides being highly annoying, such distractions may actually make it difficult for users to focus on the site.

- **Ensure direct accessibility of embedded user interfaces.** If you use an interface within the page—for example, a Java applet that has its own internal interface— make sure that it, too, is accessible.

- **Design for device independence.** Try to build interfaces that can work under multiple devices, including different screen sizes, different viewing devices (cell phone vs. computer), and using different manipulation devices like keyboard only or mouse and keyboard. A particularly important consideration is just making sure that a site doesn't rely solely on the mouse for navigation. Some users may find mouse movement difficult, and power users may actually prefer to use the keyboard for navigation.

- **Use interim solutions.** Because not all browsers will support the same technologies or standards completely, make sure to provide alternatives in the short term for noncompliant browsers.

- **Use W3C technologies and guidelines.** A somewhat self-evident but occasionally troublesome suggestion. Of course you should always try to follow the W3C guidelines, at least in spirit. However, be careful as many W3C guidelines are no more than proposed ideas and browsers may lack significant or consistent support for a defined specification.

- **Provide context and orientation information.** In some sense, this just means try to explain things or provide instructions for complex areas. You should try to design pages so that the meaning of links is clear through the use of ToolTips or scope notes, as discussed in Chapter 6. Furthermore, forms should be designed that explain what is required, as discussed in Chapter 12. In the most basic way, a site should provide a help system.

■ **Provide clear navigation mechanisms.** Basically, you should provide obvious navigation that is easy to understand and in a consistent location on the screen. Navigational aids such as search engines, site maps, and site indexes (as discussed in Chapters 7 and 8) should also be provided.

■ **Ensure that documents are clear and simple.** Yet another fairly obvious suggestion, but powerful nonetheless, is that simplicity will lead to greater accessibility. Given that not everyone will be able to read a language well, and usability is directly related to simplicity and consistency, try to make your documents simple.

Besides manual inspection of a site, it is easy enough to evaluate it for accessibility using a tool such as Bobby (www.cast.org/bobby), as shown in Figure 3-7. Bobby will analyze a Web page and see if it meets certain basic accessibility criteria such as the use of **ALT** text.

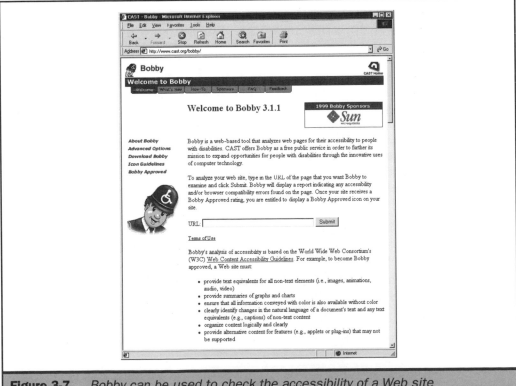

Figure 3-7.   *Bobby can be used to check the accessibility of a Web site*

Building a Usable Site

One of the keys to usable Web site development is to develop an early focus on the users of the application. Remember that the user's goal is not to use computers or to use your Web site. The user's goal is to accomplish some task—purchase a product, find a bill-payment center, register a complaint, and so on. You should try to make direct contact with users, and you must listen to them. Do not fall into the trap of thinking that you should just simply ask users what they want and they will design your site for you. Users are not designers, and they make illogical or unrealistic requests. Because of this, you may be tempted to implement your own idea of a great site instead, without regard for user requests. However, the core idea of user-centered design is to always remember we are designing for users and not ourselves. Recall again the following very important Web design rules.

Rule: You are NOT the user.

Rule: Users are NOT designers.

As you design the site, consider the general characteristics of users, such as vision, memory, and sensory reaction (presented earlier in the chapter). Also recall that users really do prefer usable sites, since they attempt to minimize effort and maximize gain at all times. A site that is hard to use with little payoff is not going to be visited often, but if the site is easy to use or the payoff for learning the site is great, the user will investigate. Beyond basic characteristics and tendencies, you should consider that users are individuals. In a broad sense, we might view users in several categories such as novices, intermediates, and power users. However, even within these groups users are very different and may have vastly different tastes and capabilities. The best way to account for the possibility of variation is to talk to users directly. You might consider interviewing them or giving a survey. Whatever you do, make sure to let the user talk—and listen to them. While this may seem like JAD (Joint Application Design), we will try to avoid letting the user control the project; rather, they will be used as a source of ideas and a way to verify the execution of implemented features. From interviews, you should build a profile of stereotypical types of users. While this may seem to be a bad idea, consider that unless you have a very small audience, it is virtually impossible to build a site that will conform perfectly to every taste preference and task requirement every possible user might have. Even if it were possible, it would be prohibitively expensive.

From your discussions with users, build a prototype site, or just a set of simple diagrams on paper of how pages might look, and test them out with users. Make sure you test your site with users as early as possible in the development cycle so as not to build a site that users can't figure out.

Suggestion: Perform user testing early and often.

There are many ways to verify usability. Tests might include:

- Casual observation of users
- Surveys and interviews
- Focus groups
- Lab testing
- Heuristic evaluations by developers or usability experts

The results of the tests can include more quantitative measurements such as the number of mistakes made during a task, the amount of mouse travel, the time it takes to perform a task, and so on. Tests will certainly also have to include qualitative measures where the users indicate what features they liked or didn't like. Before you don a white coat and rent lab time in a room with a two-way mirror to observe users, consider that formal testing may be overkill for most sites just because of the sheer cost and trouble of performing user tests in a formal fashion. Simple observations might do the trick, and opinions tend to be free from many users, though not always well founded. Collect a few users, or even your friends and neighbors, and sit them down at the site. Try to have them perform a few tasks. What's interesting is that even an informal test will uncover the major problems with a site. However, informal tests only work if you let them. Designers seem far too proud of their sites and tend to act as copilots trying to show a user the interesting aspects of a site. Talking too much during a test or guiding the user in any way keeps the user from making his or her own decisions and may actually steer the user away from mistakes.

Suggestion: When performing even an informal usability test, avoid talking too much or guiding the user.

Before running off to round up your friends to ask them what they think, consider looking at a site and trying to see if it follows some basic usability guidelines that could be defined from the ideas presented earlier in the Chapter. Table 3-4 presents some ideas you should look for when judging the usability of a site.

When evaluating a site, the rules of thumb here cover the basic aspects of usability. However, don't assume that just because the site meets most of these basic ideas that it is a good site. There are plenty of other ways for a site to fall down. For example, a site might not contain excellent content, its technology may be unreliable, or its graphics may be hideous to look at. Appendix B presents a more in-depth evaluation procedure that accounts for many other aspects of Web design. Remember that usability isn't the only part of a positive Web experience.

Guideline	Explanation
Be consistent.	Consistency is the key to an easy-to-use interface. If something is consistent, the user only has to learn it once. Within your own site, don't change the position of buttons or the way things act.
Don't violate user's expectations, and make sure to follow Web and GUI conventions.	Consistency can go beyond the contents of a site. Users will have expectations about how things works shaped by visits to other sites. Make sure your site is consistent with what they expect. In short, follow any conventions used in GUI or site design that the user is used to.
Support the ways people use Web pages.	Users use the Web pages in a few basic ways. They load a page, they unload a page, they print the page, they save the page either by bookmarking the address or saving the file to a local drive, and they read the page or they interact with the page (such as fill-in forms or manipulating content objects within the page). Similar to the previous guideline, make sure users can do all the things they expect. If users expect to print or bookmark a page and they can't, they may consider the site unusable.
Use surprise properly and sparingly.	Occasionally, being inconsistent is useful. If you want to "wake a user up," it might be OK to dramatically change the way a page looks or acts. Just make sure you don't do this often since users may not become comfortable with the site, and may even become frustrated with the ever-changing interface.
Simplify the site and individual pages as much as possible.	Simplicity makes it easy for users to understand a site. Try to pare a site or page down to its bare essentials. Look at statistical logs to determine what pages are not needed from a site. On a page level, remove clutter from layouts and try to reduce visual noise.
Rely on recognition, not recall.	Memorization is difficult. Don't expect the user to memorize the structure of your site or the position of your buttons. Minimize what the user has to remember by exposing available choices. Even something as simple as hiding a menu when it isn't in use increases the cognitive load on a user since they have to memorize what items are on what menus.

Table 3-4.   *Common Web Usability Guidelines*

Guideline	Explanation
Do not assume users will read instructions.	You may not get a chance to hold a training class for every user who visits your site. Generally, users will only read help files when they are in trouble. Try to make sure that they don't need to be trained. Avoid introducing features in a site that would require training or documentation for proper use.
Try to prevent or correct errors.	Don't let users make mistakes that are unnecessary. For example, validate form entries and limit users to doing only what they should. Don't provide a choice that is not easily undone by the user. If errors do occur, let the user know about the error and its possible solution.
Provide feedback.	Let users know what's happening. Don't be imprecise with feedback. If there is going to be a delay, let them how long it is going to take. If an error has occurred, provide a clear error message.
Support different interaction styles.	Try to provide multiple ways of doing the same thing to deal with different approaches to problems. For example, some users may prefer to use a site map over a search engine when looking for something. Don't limit users, and try to account for a range of interaction styles from novice users to power users.
Minimize mouse travel and keystrokes.	Typing and moving the mouse around the screen is work for the user, so try to minimize it. This means successive button choices should be nearby. Try to minimize the distance from primary navigation to the Back button, which is certainly the most commonly pressed button in a browser. This may suggest navigation should be towards the top of the screen.
Consider medium of consumption.	Make sure to understand where the user will consume the content—onscreen or on paper. If users print pages to consume them, shouldn't the usability test be performed on the paper document as well?
Consider environment of use.	If known, consider where a user will interact with a page. Where the user interacts with a page will affect how usable they perceive it. For example, relying on sound in a noisy environment isn't a wise idea.
Focus on speed.	Users dread slow-loading sites. Make sure pages are fast loading by practicing the idea of minimal design. This doesn't mean eliminating graphics, just that a page should be no slower than it needs to be to deliver its message.

Table 3-4.   *Common Web Usability Guidelines* (continued)

Usability Above All Else

One problem with usability discussions is that it is easy to use usability concerns as a way to squash any other reasonable idea. For example, some people have gone so far as to discuss how banner ads contribute to poor site usability because they are animated or increase the download time. However, consider that with the banner ads the site may not be economically viable. Pleasing graphics also are a common target for usability experts. It is interesting to note how boring most usability gurus' sites actually are. Consider that while a site without much graphics may be usable, it won't do much to improve the brand identity of the organization running the site; in fact, without graphics, it may undermine brand identity built through other mediums. In some situations, it may be important to let the user wait to see the corporate logo and new advertising look. Advanced technology also is a common enemy of good site usability. The truth is that while advanced technology may lock out some users, what is provided may be worth it. If we always designed for the lowest common denominator, we'd still have the equivalent of Gopher on the Web. Don't let usability completely stifle innovation. Usability is certainly very important, but there are often other considerations in a Web site's design. Always remember that while we design for users, we are ultimately in control of our site.

> **Suggestion: Do not use usability concerns as a way to avoid or eliminate visual, technical, or economic aspects of a site.**

Who's in Control of the Experience?

While it is true that we must give the people what they want, the masters of sites—meaning those who pay for them—may have desires that are not congruent with the desires of the site's users. Do not become a slave to the user; remember that in some sense we are the masters of our own sites. How we want to treat our visitors is going to influence greatly how they feel about visiting our sites. Do you want to be a dictator, forcing the user to download certain plug-ins or resize a window? Conversely, you could be very democratic and let users pick their own path through your site. You may even allow users to modify content on the site or influence other users with indicators of link popularity. Last, you could aim for a middle ground and maybe act as a benevolent dictator, trying to help the user along the way and giving them freedom within certain constraints, but always trying to guide them along.

The issue of control during a site visit is somewhat an unwritten contract between the site user and the developer. There is give and take in the relationship. Consider that while one of the main tenets of user-centered design is to put the user in control, users are imperfect like everyone else; if we give them complete control, they may make serious errors. Developers will want to keep users from making mistakes. However, the role of the benevolent dictator of the online experience is difficult. If you control things too much and the user notices that they can't resize their window or press certain buttons, they may become angry or frustrated. The key is to provide an illusion of control. Users can do everything they need to do and nothing more. People need to feel like they are in control, but the control should have limits. Good interfaces exhibit this control. Consider, for example, the famous adventure game Myst. In Myst, the user can click on objects onscreen and move in a direction simply by clicking in the appropriate direction. The interface is very simple and also very restrictive, though game players rarely notice this. In Myst, as in many well-designed video games, the progression is very controlled by the game designer, but the illusion of control is always preserved. A great Web site would follow the cue of a video game by trying to guide someone to a conclusion like purchasing a product, but in a manner that the user doesn't really notice.

The best example of the balance of control in an experience is probably Las Vegas. Casinos create a complete experience of visiting an ancient land, tropical paradise, or foreign country. A gimmick outside the casino like an exploding volcano or pirate battle attracts hordes of visitors. Hopefully, some of these visitors step onto the nearby conveyor belt to be quickly whisked into the casino. Inside, they attempt to create a pleasant environment by controlling the temperature, lighting, and oxygen levels. The passage of time becomes difficult to determine since windows are few and tinted, and clocks are nonexistent. Assistance is plentiful from dealers and waitresses who will provide free drinks. If you get hungry, cheap food is nearby at an all-you-can-eat buffet. Want to stay overnight? Rooms are reasonably priced, and if you spend enough at the tables they might even be free. But when you come to your senses as your wallet begins to empty, notice how difficult it is to find the exit! Good Las Vegas casinos practice the ultimate in experience design, second only (maybe) to Disneyland. The experience is always controlled; the point is to maximize the money the casino takes in. If you step out of line, get irate and loud when you lose, or try to do something to win back control in gambling by card counting, you'll find that you are quickly escorted outside. The experience is fun and you can win, but know that the control is there and the house always has the edge. It's pure math. If you plan on running a commercial site in particular, learn from Las Vegas.

Suggestion: Practice "Las Vegas" Web design. Provide the user with a pleasant experience complete with perks and the illusion of unlimited choices, but control the situation strictly at all times.

Summary

Usability is about the aspects of a site that aren't always noticeable but yet seriously influence the ease in which a user is able to accomplish a task using the site. Usable Web sites should be easy to learn, easy to use, easy to remember, result in few errors, and be satisfying to the user. While some ways to improve usability such as consistency and simplicity of design are easy to predict, sometimes it is difficult to satisfy the needs of every user. Remember that while users may have similar base capabilities such as vision and memory, which are used when accessing a site, and that users can be broadly grouped into three categories—novice, intermediate, and advanced—users are also individuals. As individuals, users will have unique capabilities, characteristics, opinions, and experiences that they will bring to bear when visiting your site. You probably won't be able to accommodate every user's unique requirements, but if you attempt to create an adaptive interface that can be used by the three broad categories of users and make sure to test your site carefully with real users, you stand a good chance of making a site that is usable by most users. Be careful not to lock users out, particularly those who may be disabled or slightly different from your common user. A site should always be built to meet the needs of its users within the constraints or the desires of its creators. However, never use the quest for a usable site as a way to avoid difficult problems or as an excuse not to use graphics or technology, or introduce new features that a user might want. An overzealous Web professional waving the usability banner can easily stifle innovation. Balance is always the key to great Web design. The next chapter will begin to explain how to structure and design sites that have the user's needs in mind.

The
Complete
Reference

**Web
Design**

Part II

Site Organization and Navigation

The
Complete
Reference

Chapter 4

Site Types and
Architectures

Just as there are many types of software—from games to business applications—there are many types of Web sites. Sites can be categorized generally in categories like intranet or extranet sites, as well as specific genre sites like commercial or personal home page. Each type of site will have different design constraints related to the site's purpose. Organizing the site appropriately will help the site achieve its purpose. Numerous site structures—from simple linear organizations to complex mixed hierarchies—exist. Heuristics from cognitive science and traditional GUI conventions provide some clues as to which structures work well. However, the structure of a well-designed site isn't always apparent to the user—nor should it be.

General Web Site Types

There are three general categories of Web sites: *public Web sites*, *extranets*, and *intranets*.

Definition: A public Web site, an Internet Web site, an external Web site, or simply a Web site is one that is not explicitly restricted to a particular class of users.

An external Web site is, in a sense, a public place available to anyone on the Internet at large to visit. Not every user in the world may want to visit the site—the site shouldn't be designed for such a wide range of users—but there is no set limitation as to who can visit the site. At the opposite end of the spectrum would be an intranet Web site, generally called simply an intranet. An intranet site is generally very private, and is often only available to users on a particular private network.

Definition: An intranet Web site is a site that is private to a particular organization, generally run within a private network rather than on the Internet at large.

In between an external Web site or intranet would be a semiprivate site, generally termed an extranet.

Definition: An extranet site is a Web site that is available to a limited class of users, but is available via the public Internet.

An example of an extranet would be a site catering to company partners or resellers. Limiting access to an extranet site might range from simple "security by obscurity" such as not using a well-known address or Web server port number to pages restricted by password or IP address of the visiting browser.

The major difference between the three basic forms of site is audience. Public Web sites are completely open, while intranets and extranets are more exclusive. The more private the site, the greater understanding the designer will have about its potential users. As mentioned in Chapters 2 and 3, understanding a site's users is crucial when designing a site. Consider that for a private intranet, a designer may actually be able to physically meet each and every potential user of the site. They may know the capabilities of each user, from their sophistication as computer users to the equipment or browser they use. On the opposite end of the spectrum is the public Web site. Designers of public sites often know very little about their users. They may rarely get to interact with their users directly, and often will have little knowledge about the range of user capabilities. The design considerations will vary dramatically between the general Web sites, as illustrated in the following table:

	Intranets	**Extranets**	**Public Sites**
Info About Users	High	Medium	Low
Capacity Planning	Possible	Usually possible	Difficult to impossible
Bandwidth	High	Varies	Varies greatly
Ability to Set Technology	Yes	Sometimes	Rarely

This table illustrates general characteristics of these types of sites, but designers should always strive to understand their audience and plan whenever possible.

Interactive vs. Static Sites

Another way to classify sites is if they are *interactive* or *static*.

Definition: An interactive site is one where the users of the site are able to interact directly with the content on the site or with other users of the site.

To some degree, all sites have some interactivity in that users can choose how they want to browse content. Truly interactive sites allow users to manipulate the content itself, and in some cases even add their own content. A site that allows a user to post technical-support questions for other users to view would be considered interactive, while a site that only allowed users to browse preexisting answers to questions would be considered static.

Definition: A static site is one where content is relatively fixed in that the user is unable to affect the look or scope of the data they view. In short, the visitor has minimal ability to interact with the site's content other than choosing the order in which to view content.

Accessing a static site is like reading a paper magazine. A user can choose to flip back and forth between pages and read articles in a different order, but the presentation is relatively rigid and there is really no ability to do anything with the content other than read it. Like print, once an absolutely static site is posted it doesn't change over time and users can't modify the way the site looks or acts. However, most sites aren't absolutely static; changes are made to pages over time.

Dynamic Sites

While at a given moment the content of many Web sites appears relatively static, most often it is in a state of gradual change. The more frequently the site changes, the more dynamic it could be thought to be. The content of most sites is being updated all the time. Often a small statement with the date of the last change is put on a page to show how fresh its content is. For example,

Document Last Modified: January 5, 2000

might be found on the bottom of the page. Often this is just a text line that is modified by the developer. While the last modification date varies from page to page, sites may also exhibit more consistent update statements. For example, some sites include statements about the current day, week, month, or year in the page design to indicate how often the page is changing. However, in many cases the pages are basically static in that they are created ahead of time for the user and change very little.

> **Definition: A dynamically generated site is one where the pages of the site are generated at request or view time for the user.**

The benefit of a dynamically generated site is that the pages can be created based upon user browsing conditions or desires. For example, a static site has only one form of presentation that all users must deal with, while a dynamic site may have multiple forms optimized for different browsers or bandwidth levels.

The benefit of a dynamically generated site should be obvious since it presents content the way the user probably wants it. A site that is targeted to specific users and allows them to determine exactly what they want to see is often termed a *personalized page*. Examples of personalized pages are becoming more common; the most familiar are probably the personal start pages such as myYahoo (my.yahoo.com) that are common to most large consumer Web sites.

> **Definition: A personalized site is one where content is directly geared towards a particular user, and the user generally can explicitly determine the content, look, or technology contained within a page.**

The downside is that dynamically generated sites are significantly more complicated to create and often are very server intensive, as each page must be generated for the user when they visit. Dynamically generated sites often use a database to store site content. In these sites, pages are constructed from content merged into page templates at request time to create the final page for delivery. In contrast, a static Web is relatively simple because it acts just like a strict file server. Pages are requested and delivered to users with little computational overhead. A comparison between static and dynamically generated sites is shown in Figure 4-1.

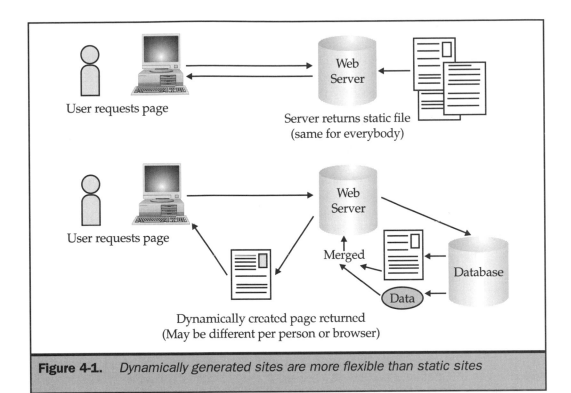

Figure 4-1. *Dynamically generated sites are more flexible than static sites*

Site Structure

There are two structural aspects to any Web site—logical structure and physical structure. A logical structure will describe documents that are related to other documents. The logical structure defines the links between documents. However, the logical location of documents within a site may not relate to the actual physical location of a document. A physical structure describes where a document actually lives, showing, for example, the document's directory path on a Web server or its location in a database.

> **Premise: A Web site's logical structure is more important to a user than its physical structure.**

Users generally will not care where information originates, from a file-system point of view, as long as they can find it on the site. A user doesn't need to know what disk drives contain what data and how you have decided to organize your file tree. For example, a particular file might live in a deep directory on a file system with a path like D:\WebSite\DemoCompany\Assets\Product\RobotButler\ index.htm. However, from a user perspective they might just see a URL like http://www.democompany.com/RobotButler/. Resist the urge to expose paths to users. As the maintainer of the site, you will have to have explicit knowledge of the site's physical structure, but a user should not have to.

Rule: Do not expose physical site file structure, when possible.

The benefit of not showing real paths should be clear. By abstracting away paths, you are free to change the location of files freely as long as they map to the appropriate URL known to users. Fortunately, all modern Web servers support mapping facilities to create virtual paths, so there is no requirement to directly mimic your logical structure in a physical file system.

Rule: A site's logical document structure does not have to map to directly match physical structure.

From a programming point of view, consider your site's URLs as your public interface. Every URL exposed is a potential address to access your site that will have to be maintained. If you are able to avoid exposing all URLs, using anything from frames to dynamic pages, you increase your ability to change the implementation of the site underneath without worrying about users noticing.

Logical Site Organization Models

There are four main logical organizational forms used in Web sites: *linear*, *grid*, *hierarchy*, and *web*. Variations on some of the schemas are also common, as are combinations of each within a larger site. Choosing the correct site organization is important in making a site usable. For example, an online sales pitch would benefit from a linear form where slide 2 follows slide 1. In some sense the user is almost forced to see the content in the order the designer wants. If the presentation were organized in another fashion, such as a tree form, it might encourage users to access slides out of order, possibly reducing the impact of the sales pitch. Other information, such as technical-support questions, might be better suited to a nonsequential access form, because forcing the user to wade through pages of needless information would be extremely frustrating. The goal is to pick the most appropriate organization form for the content so complex content can be made clear.

Linear

A *linear* form is the most familiar of all site structures because traditional print media tend to follow this style of organization. For example, books are generally written so that one page follows another in a linear order. Presenting information in a linear fashion is often very useful when discussing a step-by-step procedure, but there are times when supplementary information may be required. Linear forms can be modified slightly to provide more flexibility, but will eventually degenerate into a grid, hierarchical, or pure web form when extended too much.

BASIC LINEAR A *pure linear* organization facilitates an orderly progression through a body of information, as shown by the illustration here.

Pure linear

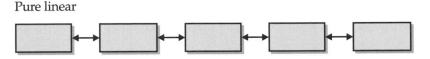

On the Web, this form might be good for a presentation like a "slide show" to give new visitors an overview of the company and its products. By using a controlled sequential organization like a linear form, the designer can ensure that the user receives the information in the intended order.

The linear style of organization provides a great deal of predictability in that the designer knows exactly where the user will go next. Because of this knowledge, it may be possible to *preload* or *precache* the next bit of information to improve perceived performance of the site. For example, while the user is reading the information on one screen, the images for the next screen can be loaded into the browser's cache. When the user advances to the next screen, the page is loaded from the cache, giving the user the illusion that the page downloads very quickly. Preloading is not a viable solution unless the user's next path can be anticipated, as is the case with a linear organization.

Because there is really no choice but to move forward or back, a user may find a linear form to be very restrictive. Because of this, it is often important to let a user know how far they are in a linear structure and what is previous and behind the current page being viewed. Indicating a user is on a page in a series could be as simple as putting a label on the page like "Page X of Y" where X is the current page number and Y is the total number of pages. This is helpful because a page-number concept is somewhat foreign to the Web, and this type label does not address previous and next pages in the sequence structures like the one shown here.

BUTLER
ROBOT
BACK   NEXT
[Trainer]   [Page 4 of 10]   [Security]

A pure forward linear form is somewhat difficult to implement on a Web site because of the browser's backtrack feature though it is possible. It is generally assumed that all linear forms are bidirectional.

LINEAR WITH ALTERNATIVES   While a liner organization is useful to present information in a predetermined order, it may provide little room for the user to interact with the information. A *linear with alternatives* organization simulates interactivity by providing two or more choices out of a page, which eventually end up pointing the user back to another page within sequence as illustrated here.

Linear with alternatives

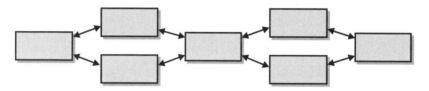

The uses for this form are numerous. Imagine a quiz Web site that prompts the user for a Yes or No answer to a question on each page, and advances the user to the next page based on the answer. Though it might appear to the user that there is some back-end technology at work, in reality the two tracks are already established and the user is just presented with an illusion of interactivity. A health-care site might use a general health quiz to attract people's interest. The quiz might begin with a question such as, "Do you smoke?" Users who answer "yes" advance to a page that describes the hazards of smoking while users who answer "no" see a message congratulating them on their to decision to abstain from cigarettes. Regardless of their answers to the first question, both users advance to question 2. Though the pages are static and there is no dynamic generation of pages, to the user it appears that there is some interactivity. Despite its appearance of choice, the linear with alternatives structure preserves the general linear path through a document collection. Unfortunately, the multiple path possibilities make preloading of pages more difficult with this form of site.

LINEAR WITH OPTIONS   A *linear with options* structure is good when the general path must be preserved, but slight variations must also be accommodated, such as skipping particular pages. This type of hypertext organization might be useful for an online survey where some users might skip certain inapplicable questions. Given that linear with options often generally provides a way to skip ahead in a linear structure, this organization is often called linear with skip-aheads. An example of this structure in action might be a bicycle presentation. While some core pages may be common to all bikes, certain pages may be skipped based on a user's particular interest in mountain bikes or road bikes. In paper documentation, a survey that asks the taker to skip to a particular question based on some criterion matches the linear-with-options form. The basic idea of this site structure is shown below.

Linear with options

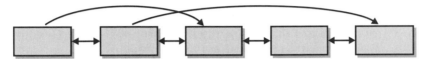

Again, this organization simulates an intelligent system even though it is often nothing more than static files in a well-thought-out hypertext structure.

LINEAR WITH SIDE TRIPS   A *linear with side trips* site organization allows controlled diversions. Although the user might take a short side trip, the structure forces the user back to the main path, preserving the original flow. Perhaps an article about frogs is presented in a linear fashion. A hyperlink on a particular word such as lily pad would lead to a tangential page with the definition of the word and maybe a short series of pages discussing how frogs and lily pads are related. Eventually the side trip dead-ends or returns the viewer back to the main path. A side trip to a linear progression is like a sidebar to a magazine article. Rather than distracting the user too much from the main path, this bit of information enhances the experience. Making the side note part of the main linear progression would dilute the continuity of the primary message. However, when many side trips are added into the linear progression, the structure begins to look like the common tree or hierarchy form discussed later in the chapter.

Linear with side trips

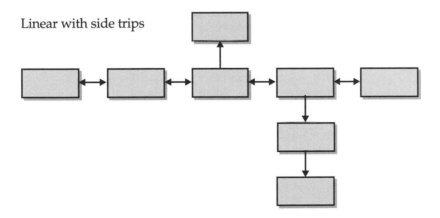

Grid

A *grid* is a dual linear structure that presents both a horizontal and a vertical relationship between items. Because a grid has a spatial organization, it is good for collections of related items; however, a pure grid structure is (so far) uncommon on the Web. When designed properly, a grid provides horizontal and vertical orientation so the user may not feel lost within the site. For example, items in a clothing catalog might be organized into categories like shirts, pants, and jackets. Another way to organize information would be by price. A grid style would allow a user to look across a price as well as within a particular line of clothing very easily.

Grid

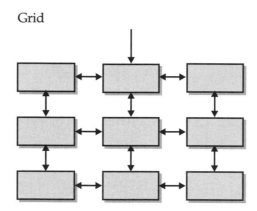

While a grid structure is highly regular and may be easy for a user to navigate, not many types of information are uniform enough to lend themselves well to this organization style. One notable exception is product catalogs.

Hierarchy

The most common hypertext structure on the Web is the tree or hierarchy form. While a hierarchy may not provide the spatial structure of a grid or the predictability and control of a linear structure, the hierarchy is very important because it can be modified to hide or expose as much information as is necessary. Hierarchies start with a root page that is often the home page of the site or section. The home or root page of the site tree serves as a "landmark" page and as such often looks much different than other pages in the site. Site landmarks such as home pages are key to successful user navigation. This is further discussed in the next chapter. From the home page, various choices are presented. As the user clicks deeper into the site, the choices tend to get more and more specific until eventually a destination, or leaf page, in the tree is reached. Because of this, trees tend to be described by their depth and breadth.

Narrow Trees

A *narrow tree* presents only a few choices but may require many mouse clicks to get to the final destination; this organization emphasizes depth over breadth.

Narrow hierarchy

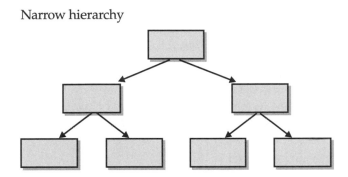

A narrow tree may require the user to make many choices to reach a leaf page, but for some sites this is a very effective way of quickly funneling users into the correct category. For example, a Web site for an employment service generally has two main audiences: job seekers and employers looking to hire. Making this distinction obvious on the home page and requiring the user to choose a category facilitates quick and easy access to relevant sections of the site. Expanding the top-level choices to include the specific options for job seekers and for employers could be distracting. Using a narrow hierarchy as a means of progressive disclosure can help keep the user focused. However, it may increase the number of clicks required for the user to get to the ultimate destination. It is important to balance these two factors and to avoid putting up unnecessary barriers between the user and the information they desire. One way to understand if a site hierarchy is too narrow is when there are many pages that are purely navigational beyond the home page. Remember that users want "payoff"— clicking endlessly through pages provides little more than frustration.

Wide Trees

A *wide tree* or *wide hierarchy* is based on a breadth of choices. Its main disadvantage is that it may present too many options as pages have numerous choices emanating from them.

Wide hierarchy

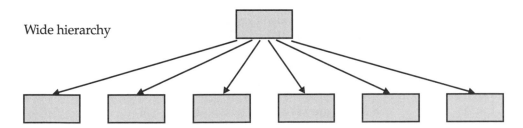

While the user only has to click once or twice to reach the content, the time spent hunting through all the initial choices may be counterproductive. Many people think that everything important must go on the home page. However, if everything gets a link from the home page, then the hierarchy is not preserved and information may lose its effectiveness—in some sense becoming lost in a crowd. Choosing the appropriate balance between site depth and breadth will be discussed later in the chapter.

Web Trees

The reality of the Web is that the typical pure-tree structures are rarely used. In a pure tree, there are no cross-links, and backtracking is often required to reach other parts of the tree. Consider if a user is at page A in the structure below; to reach page B, they have to back up two levels and then proceed forward.

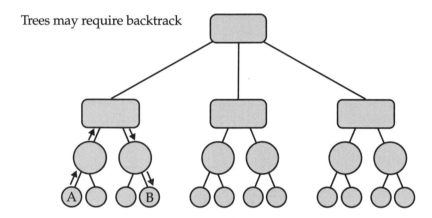

Trees may require backtrack

While on the Web backtracking is possible using the browser's Back button, links are often added to pages so that users who reach a page not through its primary path can navigate the site. In many cases, pages are cross-linked using a navigation bar or explicit back-links to help users quickly navigate the site structure. Consider the site diagram shown in Figure 4-2.

It would be common to create a navigation bar for a site that contained the main sections of the site such as Home, About, Products, News, and Contact, like so.

With such a navigation bar, it would be much easier to jump from section to section without a significant degree of backtracking. However, the site diagram would be much more complex and look something like the one in Figure 4-3.

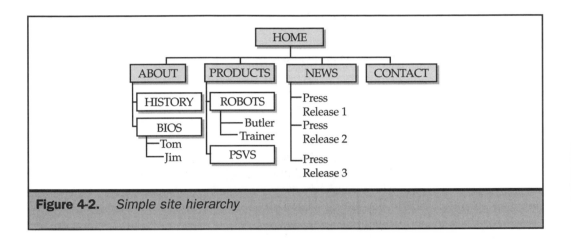

Figure 4-2.   *Simple site hierarchy*

The back- and cross-links within the site increase the complexity greatly. In this case, consider that only main section pages are cross-linked. Imagine if the whole site were linked this way.

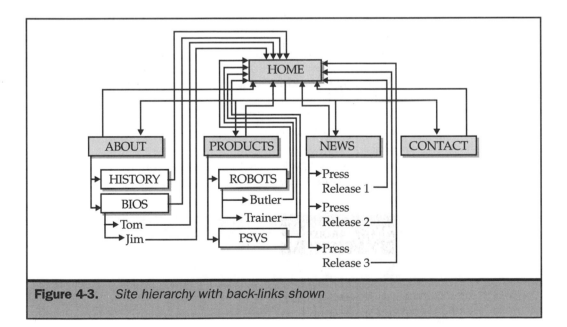

Figure 4-3.   *Site hierarchy with back-links shown*

Full Mesh

A site that links every page to every other page could be considered to exhibit a structured called a *full mesh*. The illustration below shows a full mesh for a site with five pages.

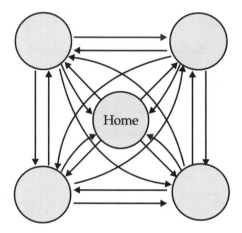

In a full mesh, the number of links is equal to the number of pages × (number of pages − 1). This means for a 5-page site, there are 20 links. For a 10-page site, there are 90 links. For a 100-page site, there are 9,900 links (100 × 99), and for a 1,000-page site, there are nearly one million links! A full mesh doesn't really work out that well from a usability perspective when you consider the 7 +/- 2 discussion presented in Chapter 3. If we aim for a maximum of nine links per page we can only consider a site with at most ten pages in a full-mesh style. In reality, as discussed in the previous section, most sites tend to use a partial mesh style with cross-links to only the most important pages.

Mixed Forms

While a wide tree may present too much, too narrow a hierarchy will hide too much information. A linear approach may provide too little user control, while a pure Web approach provides too much. In some cases, there will be a need to augment the hierarchy to allow choices to bubble up to the top. This structure is called a *mixed form* or a *mixed hierarchy*, as the tree is the dominant form of the structure. A mixed form is probably the most common form of site organization used on the Web. Linear devices, skips, and even grids may be contained within a mixed form. Consider a site that contains Download Now or similar buttons that skip deep into a site structure. This is somewhat like a linear-with-skips structure. Other sites may contain linear tours available only from certain pages in the site. Though spatial organization is not as pronounced as in other site structures, a hierarchy is still generally evident in most mixed sites.

Mixed hierarchy

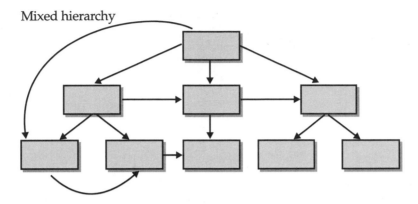

One common mixed style is the use of a linear structure to enter a site with a tree once the real home page is reached. Sites that have splash pages or tours leading up to a central page that a user can explore from use this type of structure. A structural diagram of this form is shown here.

Tree with linear entry

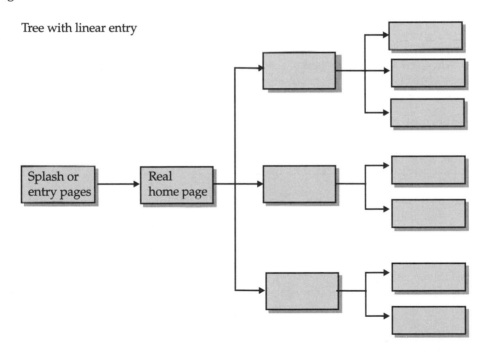

Another style, which is not really unique, is termed the *hub and spoke* structure. Many sites consist of main pages called hubs and then subpages that are reached via spokes. To visit other pages in the site, the user is forced to return to the hub page. Many portals use this style to encourage page revisits. However, there is really no difference between the hub-and-spoke model and a typical tree as shown in Figure 4-4.

The only benefit of thinking about hub-and-spoke is that it may provide an easy way to visualize a site. For example, some site-mapping tools present site diagrams in

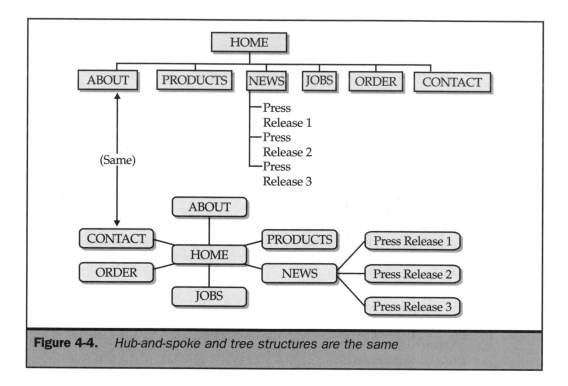

Figure 4-4. *Hub-and-spoke and tree structures are the same*

this style because they are easier to lay out than a tree structure. See Figure 4-5 for an example of a hub-and-spoke visualization of a site.

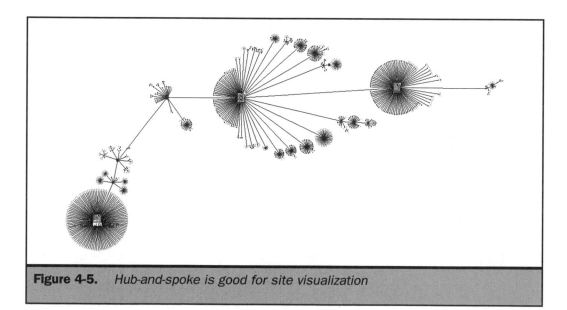

Figure 4-5. *Hub-and-spoke is good for site visualization*

Web Style

When too many cross-links, skip-aheads, and other augmentations are made to a structured documentation collection, the form will become unclear to the user. When a collection of documents appears to have no discernible structure, it is called a *pure web* as shown in the illustration here.

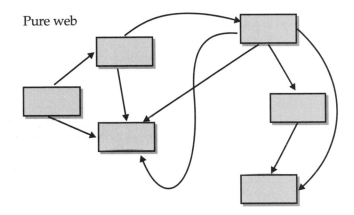

Pure web

A pure-web structure can be difficult to use because it lacks a clear spatial orientation. Though information can be accessed quickly if the correct choice is made, it may be difficult to orient oneself in a Web site with an unclear structure. If a site's structure is unclear or unfamiliar to the user, they may resort to a home-page-based navigation, always returning to a top level when beginning a new task. Yet the benefit of a less structured form is that it provides a great deal of expressiveness. For example, a technical paper might provide links to related diagrams, supporting statements, and papers, and even excerpts from outside resources. The organization of the site may not easily fit any one of the more structured forms. While some might argue that the confusing pure web structure may cause the user to lose focus and make it difficult for participants to form a mental map of the site, this may actually not be a problem when the information or task is properly designed.

Users and Site Structures

While a linear structure may be easier for users to comprehend than a mixed tree or pure web, users do not necessarily memorize the layout of the site or visualize a flowchart in their head as they move around. In some sense, information structure may not matter if the user's focus can be retained. Whether something is back, next, or up from a current page in the site should not be the user's focus. The main point is what the user is doing, or what content they are consuming. If users are content and accomplishing their goals, they really aren't lost. When organizing a site, always attempt to retain the perspective of the user visiting the site. Many, if not most, of the visitors will be relatively unfamiliar with the site and its structure. Don't assume that the organization will be clear to them, and remember that underlying organization may not have to be clear if the site is providing satisfactory utility to the user.

Consider that a user really goes through three phases upon reaching a site. Phase 1 is entry to the site. In phase 2, the user moves around the site, which could be termed the "visit phase." Phase 3 is the conclusion to the visit, where the user exits from the site either happy to have reached a successful conclusion or potentially unhappy or neutral—having failed or given up on their task. Figure 4-6 shows a conceptual overview of how this might work for a site with a single entry point and single primary conclusion page, such as an order-confirmation message in an e-commerce site.

In reality, sites are generally not so simple. Often there are many entry points to a site, and many exit points as well. During the visit, users may make a variety of moves both towards and away from their eventual conclusion. They are probably also not completely aware of the underlying site structure of the visit and are happy as long as they feel they are making progress towards the goal state. Figure 4-7 shows a conceptual overview of a site's structure and possible user paths through the site structure.

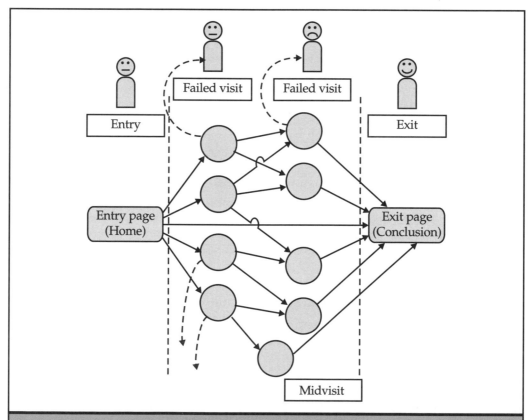

Figure 4-6.   *Simple site structure from a user perspective*

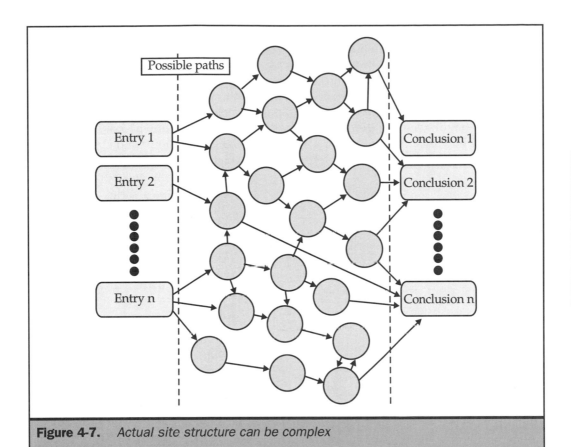

Figure 4-7. *Actual site structure can be complex*

Even though users may not focus heavily on site structure, don't throw out logical information structuring like linear, grids, and hierarchies in favor of a pure Web structure that gives up spatial information. Remember that people are spatially oriented and prefer to navigate in terms of location. Web sites are locations. People generally talk about "visiting" sites, not about reading them. Furthermore, these structures help us organize a site whether the user notices the underlying structure or not.

Porous, Semiporous, and Solid Site Structure

The previous discussion suggests that entry and exit are really the key milestones for the user. Therefore, another way to categorize Web sites would be on the number of entry points to a site. Using exit points isn't realistic since every page in a site can be considered an exit if the user just decides to quit. When a site exposes all documents with public URLs, it could be said to exhibit a "porous" structure. A porous site does not force users to enter through common points such as the home page, major section pages, and so on. Most users will probably enter through such pages, but theoretically any URL, however deep in the site structure, could be an entry point. In contrast, a site with a "solid" structure would be one that severely limits the entry points to the site to a few URLs or even a single URL. Figure 4-8 presents a graphical representation of porous, semiporous, and solid site structures.

The advantage of a solid site structure is that it does not expose all the inner workings of the site. By hiding such information, the underlying site content can be changed easily. Another advantage of a solid site is that by forcing users to enter

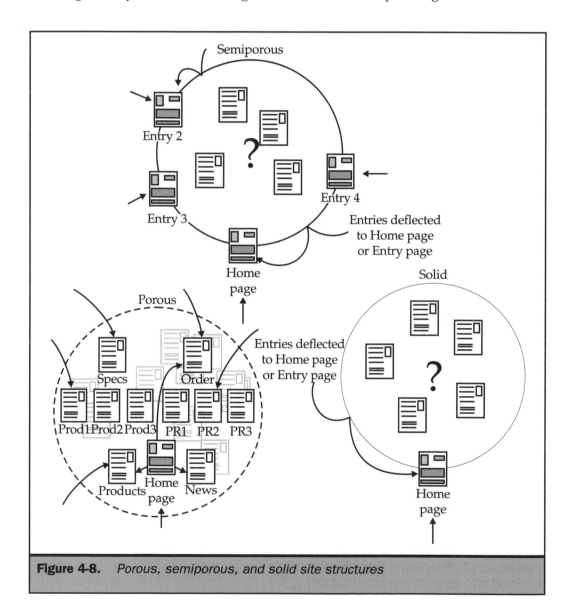

Figure 4-8.   *Porous, semiporous, and solid site structures*

through known points, their experience can be controlled much better. Users entering through known points can be exposed to important announcements, setup tasks can be performed more easily, and they can be oriented to the site in a consistent manner. However, the downside is that the user will not be able to directly enter any particular URL in the site. Power users may be extremely frustrated by the inability to save their place within a large structure.

The table below summarizes the basic pros and cons of the two site forms:

Site Type	Pros	Cons
Porous form	+ Puts user in control + Allows the user to enter any URL directly or enter by bookmark	– Decreases ability to change deep pages without addressing outside linking – Does not easily provide a common entry point for announcement, setup, or orientation information
Solid form	+ Does not expose site structure, making modification and maintenance easier + Forces user to enter through known points + Makes tracking of users more predictable	– Removes user from control – May limit the effectiveness of outside search engines

Deep vs. Shallow Sites

Another way to characterize sites would be the number of clicks required to reach a destination. Consider the choice between a narrow tree and a wide-tree structure. A narrow tree would require the user to click numerous times to reach pages deep in the site. A wide tree would require fewer clicks, but would require the user to look among numerous links for the one that interests them. Obviously, a balance between link breadth and site depth is the best choice. Various Web studies suggest that users prefer sites that require fewer clicks and are more satisfied with a wide selection of choices. A good rule of thumb is to consider aiming for a depth of three clicks before the user hits the content they are looking for.

Suggestion: Aim for a site-click depth of three.

The three-click suggestion makes sense when considering the limited number of locations for different navigation bars on pages, traditional GUI conventions, and memory limitations of users. Inspection of Web site access logs should back up the three-click rule. In fact, many sites seem to exhibit bailouts in only one or two clicks.

Of course, reducing a site's depth to three clicks or fewer is not always possible. Remember that progress towards an end goal must be made and shown to the user within three clicks (and hopefully every click).

> **Suggestion: Aim for positive feedback indicating progress towards a destination every click, with a maximum of three clicks without feedback.**

Consider, however, that by making a shallower site by putting numerous links on the pages, the design may inadvertently favor extremes. Anecdotally, when faced with many choices users may focus on extremes when making a choice. The phone book serves as a good example of trying to stand out from many competing choices. For example, in alphabetical listings of nonpreferential choices, observationally the letter A and Z sections tend to be selected the most. Near the center around M is also a common choice. Notice how in the Plumbing section of the phone book how many firms have names like AAA Plumbing or Z-1 plumbing. To combat the effects of first choice and last choice in a large listing such as the phone book, bolding, color, and display-style advertisements are used to help choices stand out from the crowd. Similarly, Web designers try to remedy this by calling even more attention to certain areas with larger sizes, bolder color, animation, or blinking—the digital equivalent of shouting. While at first these persuasion techniques may work, they may also cancel each other out or leave the user feeling overstimulated and annoyed. Remember, over time a user will become accustomed to any extra stimulation and the attention-grabbing techniques lose their power. As discussed in Chapter 3, this is a known phenomenon from cognitive science called *sensory adaptation*. Ideally, there should be just enough choices for users to give each choice equal weight when deciding what to do.

Now consider the 7 +/- 2 idea for optimal short-term memory recall of choices. Given that 5–9 choices is too few for more sites, consider instead 5–9 clusters. Each of the clusters of links will use a different attractive technique like a color, animation, or graphic. With a maximum of 5–9 clusters and 5–9 items per cluster, a page could hold anywhere from 25–81 links.

> **Suggestion: Even for wide-site structures, consider a range of 25–81 links per page when page links are ideally clustered.**

Unfortunately, with dozens of links users are bound to make mistakes, and important links may be lost in the clutter. Because of this potential for user mistakes, many sites favor a redundant link approach where numerous links lead to the same conclusions. Convention suggests that the number of links to a particular page is proportional to its importance.

> **Premise: The more important the page, the more redundant links should be provided to it.**

Consider how many links in a site point to a home page, or to software download pages, or to a purchase page, and it becomes apparent that redundant links are commonplace within most sites. Given users' interest in clicking, increasing the number of links pointing to successful conclusions just increases the odds of the user hitting the right link. Be careful not to add too many redundant links, though, lest the users feel they are being pushed towards a particular page. Again, the control issue becomes apparent. If nearly every link in a page pushes a user towards a particular conclusion, the user may feel frustrated with the lack of control.

> **Suggestion: Redundant links in a site should be no more than 10–20 percent of a page's total exit links.**

Despite the suggestion that users are better able to deal with flat site structures, many sites completely avoid building sites this way. Certainly some of the reason could be attributed to developers being unaware of the idea, but many times the rules of thumb are avoided on purpose. Consider a site whose revenue is primarily from banner advertisements. For such a site, the more banners viewed by the user per visit, the better. In the advertising-driven site owner's mind, a site that gets the user quickly to their destination is one that takes money out of its own pocket. Many banner-driven sites favor hub-and-spoke site design or deep-tree structures in an attempt to force the user to click through numerous pages and view banners. Of course, there is a limit to the "click more, view more ads" approach in that an unsatisfied user won't continue to click if they get frustrated. However, consider that in some situations site designers will design to reduce clicks to the lowest tolerance level without overly confusing a user with too many choices. In other situations, they will want to increase clicks to the maximum tolerance level without frustrating the user. Oftentimes the specific type of site being built drives the type structure used.

Specific Types of Web Sites

There are numerous ways to characterize sites, including their audience, their frequency of change, or the structure. However, these characterizations may seem too abstract at times. There are numerous genres of sites that use these abstract forms. A short discussion of site types is useful if only to classify and gain a respect for the differences between different sites. We'll focus only on public sites, but characterizations of private intranet sites could also be made. One very general way to categorize sites would be as commercial, entertainment, informational, navigational, artistic, or personal. The general goals, audience, and features of each type of site vary dramatically. Because of this, be cautious not to apply the same design philosophy to each form.

Commercial Sites

Commercial sites are those sites that are built primarily to support the business of some organization. Generally, the primary audience of a commercial site is potential and current customers of the organization. A secondary audience often includes potential and current investors, potential employees, and interested third parties such as the news media or even competitors. Given such an audience mix, common purposes for commercial sites include:

- **Basic information distribution**   The site is used to disseminate information about products and services provided by the organization. Other basic information provided generally includes how to contact the firm via methods other than the Web.

- **Support**   Portions of the site might be built to provide information to help existing customers effectively use products or services provided by the organization.

- **Investor relations**   A public company or one seeking outside investment might build a site or a section within a site to disseminate information about the current financial situation of the company as well as future opportunities for investment.

- **Public relations**   Many firms use their Web sites to distribute information to various news-gathering organizations as well as provide general goodwill information to the community.

- **Employee recruiting**   A Web site is often used to post information about employment opportunities and benefits of working for a company.

- **E-commerce**   A growing number of commercial Web sites allow a visitor, whether an end consumer or a business partner like a reseller, to conduct business directly on the Web site. Common facilities supported by e-commerce sites include transactions like ordering, order-status inquiries, and account-balance inquiries.

Look at all the potential purposes of a commercial site, and you'll see the following premise follows directly.

Premise: The overriding purpose of any commercial site is to serve the user in a way that hopefully benefits the company either directly or indirectly.

Given this premise, consider that the purpose of information dissemination is to try to get people to purchase a product or service from the company. Whether the method is a direct approach trying to persuade the user or an indirect approach of providing helpful information that hopefully builds a trusting relationship between the organization and the potential customer, the end desired result is always the same—try to encourage a business transaction to take place.

Informational

Informational sites are different from commercial sites in the general purpose of information distribution. Government, educational, news, nonprofit organizations, religious groups, or various social-oriented sites are often considered informational sites. While the sites may be driven by some commercial factors, the primary purpose of the site may be to inform for reasons beyond causing a transaction to happen. Understanding the audience mix of an informational site is difficult since it depends highly on the type of information being provided. About all that can be said is that the audience of the site is someone who has an interest or requirement to view the information provided.

The purpose of the informational sites varies dramatically. A site at a university for a class might try to help educate visitors on a certain topic like American history. An informational site for some particular religious, social, or political group might have a primary purpose of trying to convince people to join or donate something to the organization. News sites might have a primary purpose of trying to inform people of current events in a helpful manner so that people rely on the resource enough that the news sites can sell their visitors' attention. A government site might have a purpose of trying to inform citizens of various law changes, convince them to join civil or military service, or even get them to vote a particular way. The crossover between commercial and informational sites can be great, but always remember that the main difference is that commercial sites are much more economy driven than informational sites. Informational sites may be built to meet design criteria that may not make fiscal sense. A commercial site always has an underlying goal of trying to increase the profits of the firm, and its purpose is often more predictable.

Entertainment

Entertainment sites are generally commercial, but they bear special consideration. The purpose of an entertainment site is simply to entertain the site's visitors. In some sense they are usually selling entertainment. In other words, they are trying to sell an enjoyable experience. While commercial sites such as e-commerce sites do want the site visitor to have a positive or even entertaining experience, entertainment is really a secondary objective. While a site selling clothes might have a jungle-explorer theme and entertain the visitor with tales of visiting far-off lands, the bottom line is that the experience is to help sell clothes. If the clothes don't sell, the site doesn't work. In the case of an entertainment site, the purpose is to sell the experience itself.

Creating an entertaining experience—whether it be visiting a Web site, playing a video game, or watching a movie—isn't something that is easily engineered. Keeping the viewer occupied and happy can be difficult and isn't always as formulaic as people might believe. For example, Hollywood continually struggles to understand why some blockbuster movies bomb while an unknown independent movie succeeds. Novelty is about the only thing that seems to continually sell. If a story is too much like something a person has experienced before, it often seems boring or formulaic. Web sites that are built to entertain are often required to break with convention to be successful.

Premise: Entertainment sites may find novelty or surprise more useful than structure or consistency.

Navigational

A navigational site is one whose focus is on helping people find their way on the Internet. These sites are called *portals* since the sites serve as major hubs pointing to other destinations.

> **Definition: A portal is a site that is generally a primary starting point for a user's online journey and serves to help people find information. Portals often attempt to provide as much information and serve as many tasks for the user as possible to encourage them to stay or to at least continually revisit the site.**

Navigational sites would also include search engines or site directories—that coincidentally are often the backbone of many portal sites.

Community

A community site is one whose purpose is to create a central location for members or a particular community to congregate and interact. Visitors come to the site, which is often very informational in nature, not just to find content that is interesting to them but also to interact with other like-minded individuals. Community sites are very interactive and are often dynamically generated and personalized. The content of a community site varies as greatly as that of an informational site. Some communities may be very general in their membership, focusing on a broad demographic such as women in general. Other communities may be very focused and target a select group of individuals such as Asian American college students in southern California. Community sites and informational or commercial sites often cross over. The main distinction between pure information or commercial sites and community sites is simply the ability for a site's visitors to interact with each other. If over time the ability to interact with other site visitors becomes commonplace, the special distinction of community sites will be lost.

Artistic

An artistic site is a site that is purely the expression of the individual or artist. The purpose of the site would be to inspire, enlighten, or entertain its viewers. In some cases, the site may simply be the product of the artist just trying to express his or her feelings. They may not really care what the viewer thinks of the site. As long as the site makes the artist happy, it is successful. Artistic sites may be user driven only in that they encourage thought and may go out of their way to avoid convention or logic.

Personal

Similar to an artistic site, a personal site—often called a personal home page or just a home page—is often an expression of its creator. Personal pages may be built to inform friends or family, or they might just be built to try to learn a new skill like HTML. Some personal pages appear to be literal shrines to their creators in some vain attempt to become famous through the Web. Other personal pages are mere résumé sites, useful to point potential employers during job searches. In some sense the purpose of the personal page is to personify the individual on the Web. Unfortunately, this can be a rather dangerous concept. While it would seem obvious not to post your credit card number, social security number, bank account numbers, and so on to your personal page, the degree of details posted on many personal pages is frightening. Many people post intimate details of their lives, from pictures of friends and family to literally their daily diary. While such online exhibitionism might seem harmless, consider the possibility of stalking or profiling. Users should consider that stating all your likes and dislikes online in the form of a personal page is a direct-marketer's dream. Profiles are easy to build from such information and may result in highly targeted and potentially intrusive junk mail and junk email. Consider that posting a personal Web page isn't too different than posting information on a local bulletin board in a town square. You never know who is going to look at the information and what they might do with it.

Like artistic sites, personal pages will not be discussed to any major degree in this book, because often their main purpose is just to make their creators happy. However, you would do well to consider that many personal sites could certainly improve their look, structure, usability, or technology.

Picking a Site Structure

The idea of picking the correct structure for a Web site by organizing information into a collection of pages is often called *information architecture*. Choosing the correct structure for a site is complex and can be influenced by many factors. For example, the data itself may suggest a particular method of organization. This could be considered a bottom-up approach. For example, a slide show really should be organized in a linear fashion since the logical order of the presentation would be lost if the information was presented in another form such as a tree.

Another way to consider organizing information would be more top-down, based upon the use of the data. Consider who is using the site and how the data it provides is consumed. For example, linear structures will provide little control for the user and limited expressiveness, but will be very predictable. Novice users will prefer simple structures such as linear structures or deep trees since the choices to be made in such structures are relatively easy.

> **Premise: Novice users prefer sites with predictable structure and may put up with extra clicks or a lack of control to achieve a comfortable balance.**

Of course a power user will often find a site with a very rigid structure or one that requires a large number of clicks to be very restrictive. Spatial feedback is not as important to the power user as control or flexibility of navigation.

> **Premise: Power users or frequent site users want control and will favor structures that provide more navigation choices.**

Each site structure style has its own pros and cons. Figure 4-9 shows the relationship between the expressiveness and predictability of the different site structures. While linear is very predictable, it provides a limited relational view. While a pure web form is very expressive, it can be confusing. The hierarchy and mixed structures share the middle ground. When building sites that are not dynamic, aiming for the middle ground is the best bet. It is no wonder that most sites tend to exhibit some form of hierarchy.

Proper information design is key to the development of a successful Web site. If a site has great content and a great interface but poor information architecture, it may be relatively useless. If the user cannot easily find the information, the site loses its effectiveness. Most sites now use a mixed-hierarchy approach that is familiar to many Web users. Depending on the goals of the site, however, several types of structures might be combined. For example, while the overall structure of a site might be a hierarchy, a pure linear structure could be used to provide an introduction to the company, and a narrow hierarchy could be used in the technical-support section.

The key point of site structure is to make the site easier for the user to navigate. Always remember that users are not going to intimately understand the underlying site structure—nor should they have to. Remember that from the user's point of view, they enter the site, then move around the site trying to accomplish their goal, and then they eventually leave. Users will not care about structure as long as they achieve what they want in a positive way. So, any structure that we choose for a site should help

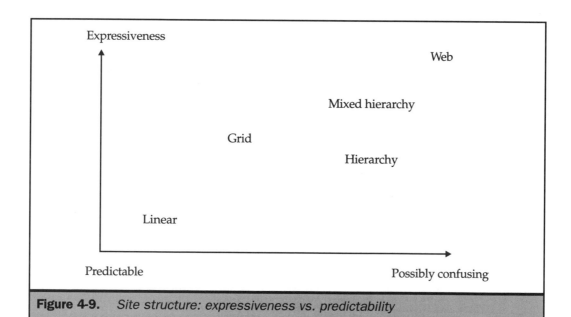

Figure 4-9.   *Site structure: expressiveness vs. predictability*

users navigate around and improve their likelihood of success. The next chapter focuses on site navigation and organization.

Summary

One way to categorize Web sites is by their audience. Public Web sites tend to have loosely defined audiences while the audience of a private intranet may be extremely well understood. Audience considerations greatly affect the design considerations of a site. Another way to categorize a site is by its main purpose. Commerce pages have much different considerations than entertainment pages. Designers should always be careful not to apply the same design criteria to a site regardless of audience or purpose. However, despite audience or purpose, most sites share similar organizations. Some sites have simple architectures like a linear progression of pages, while others exhibit complex hierarchies or mixed forms. When building the site's structure, always consider cognitive science issues and attempt to balance click depth with link breadth. Designers should understand that the logical organization of the site and the physical organization do not have to match. In fact, the structure of the site is often more useful to the designer than to the user. While structure can improve a site's organization, users may not always be aware of a site's form as they navigate towards desired content or attempt to complete a particular task.

Chapter 5

Navigation Theory and Practice

Navigation is the science, or art, of getting people or things from one place to another. We navigate the real world when we take a trip to a far-off land or just try to walk down the hall to get a glass of water. While the Web is not a physical place, users utilize navigational cues to move around the information space. Many ideas from real-world navigation can be adapted to the Web. However, site designers are cautioned to remember that the Web is not the real world: direct translation doesn't always work. Web navigation should help the user understand where they are, where they can go, and how they can get somewhere else. The visibility, labeling, and placement of navigational elements go a long way towards making things clear to the user. Since navigation is such a complex subject, this chapter will introduce the basic theory and illustrate use through navigation markets, button placement, and the use of common navigation extensions such as frames. The following chapters will discuss the nuances of links and navigational aids such as search engines and site maps.

Navigation

In real life, we often need to get from point A to point B. Maybe we need to pick up a package at the post office, drop off our dry cleaning, or just get out for some fresh air. We want to reach our intended destination quickly and efficiently, and not get lost on the way. That's the focus of navigation. Navigation is concerned with helping people find their way.

When navigating, people often ask the following questions:

- Where am I?
- Where can I go?
- How do I get where I want to go?

They also tend to ask secondary questions that are related to the primary questions. For example, lost people often ask:

- Have I been here before?

    or

- How can I get back to someplace I was?

Sometimes if a trip is long, or simply if the individual is a child in the back seat of a car, they may ask:

- How long will it take to get there?

All these questions are valid. Unfortunately, on the Web it isn't always easy to answer these questions with any precision. Always remember that, at least in its current form, the Web lacks the physicality of the real world. In fact, given the lack of physicality, exact location on the Web may not be as important as you think; the user may be much more concerned about possible future directions and a general sense of how to get where they are going. Some experts suggest that, in fact, users act somewhat like animals foraging for food when navigating the Web. The user, as the information omnivore, sniffs out the scent of the information they are looking for or the task they are trying to complete. Once on the trail, they keep on it until the scent dies. If they begin to get lost, they back up until the scent is strong again. If they get completely lost, they may quickly retreat to a known safe place such as a home page. The idea of information foraging suggests that exact location may not be quite as important as the user feeling they are on the right track and knowing basically where they are. Good navigation should always try to answer the user's navigation questions by providing cues to show the user they are on the right path. This is done by using navigational aids such as URLs, page labels, landmark pages, and navigation bars.

Where Am I?

It is often difficult for a user to know where they are on the Web since it lacks central points of reference. In the world of naval navigation, longitude and latitude can be used to chart a course. However, these concepts rely on a finite earth and assumptions to start measuring things from Greenwich, England and the earth's equator, respectively. Does the Web contain an absolute center? Let's say Yahoo! is the center of the Web. How many clicks are we away from Yahoo! at any given moment? The answer is both one click and many, at the same time. It really depends on if you allow people to access something directly or if they must follow a path. The point of this discussion is that location and distance on the Web aren't terribly precise most of the time. A URL will give a precise location, but oftentimes it says little about a document's location relative to other documents, and URLs are not always understood by users. Users may instead come to rely not only on URLs, but page labels, colors, and even document styles to understand where they are.

Precise Location on the Web: URLs

Today, the URL (Uniform Resource Locator) defines location on the Web. A user's browser may identify the current page as http://www.democompany.com/products/trainer.htm. Like it or not, the URL precisely answers the user's "Where am I?" question. Unfortunately, the answer may not be useful or understood by the user. Consider the previous URL. This address states that the user is accessing a page called trainer.htm in the products directory on a machine named www.democompany.com. Of course, this address may not tell us much as far as our location relative to other pages. Relationships with pages, both within and outside a Web site, are not easy to judge from a URL. For example, this page may be a single click away from a page on a server in a foreign country halfway around the world. For example, consider if there is a link off the last page to http://www.robotparts.co.nz/robots/bodyparts.htm, a fictitious robot parts vendor in New Zealand. Users will glean some information from a URL like this one, such as basic physical location as in a geographic domain, a server name, and maybe a directory or document name. However, don't expect the URLs to always help determine where people are. Many dynamically generated sites have URLs like

```
http://www.robotsforsale.com/store/showprod.cfm?&DID=7&User_ID=6185
1&st=1985&st2=-78872300&st3=211170630&CATID=3&ObjectGroup_ID=18
```

This is not exactly something the user is going to be easily able to use to tell where they are! While it won't always be possible, you should always strive to make URLs easy to understand.

Rule: Use simple and memorable URLs to improve navigation.

Because the URL shows location, you should not hide it unless you are trying to avoid direct outside linking. Some sites utilize frames, which will not show the URL of the document being viewed, or may even open windows without a location bar. Because users may look to the URL to understand where they are, you should consider not hiding the URL unless you are trying to avoid deep linking or a porous site structure, as discussed in Chapter 4.

Rule: Do not hide URLs—complex or simple—unless you are trying to keep people from direct linking.

Page and Site Labels

Beyond the exact location of a URL, users may get a somewhat less precise location through a page label. Most pages contain a page label that may indicate the contents of the page as well as provide some sense of location within a site. Generally, the page label is located at the top of the page and is set off on its own. Designers should make sure to make page labels look different than navigation or content. Generally, this means labels are either larger, are in a different font or color, or are grouped alone. The position of page labels should also be consistent from page to page.

Rule: Use consistent and explicit page labels for all pages in a site.

Consider that it is not only important to indicate the particular page a user is on, but potentially the site they are within as well. The most common way to do this is to use the corporate or organization logo or name throughout the site. The position of the site label varies, but probably the most common location is the upper-left corner of the screen. Given that this is the primary scan path of the user, it will reinforce to the user that they are indeed on the same site. Some sites put it on the right, but Web conventions appear to favor the upper left, which is consistent with the location of program icons in the title bar of most software applications. Compare the title bar of this common word-processing application to the Web site shown here.

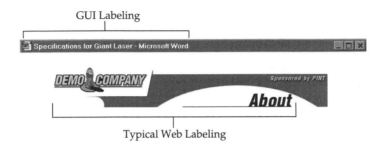

Notice that while the Web site does lack the typical Minimize, Maximize, and Close boxes of a GUI application, it has an icon showing the current site as well as a label showing the current document. Of course, the Web site is highly stylized compared to the application, but the labeling tends to be consistent.

Regardless of the position of the site label, it should always have the defined action of returning the user back to the home page of the site. Think of this as a panic button for the lost user—an instant way to get back to the main page. Many users will know this Web convention, but you should also consider using the **TITLE** attribute so that when the mouse passes over the logo, it indicates that it will return them to the site home page. This idea is discussed in detail in the next chapter. Also, remember that you do not have to limit yourself to only a logo to return home. Many sites provide more explicit Back to Home buttons elsewhere within the page, particularly at the bottom.

> **Rule: Sitewide labeling icons or words such as the organization name or logo should always return a user to the home page of the site when clicked.**

Another way to indicate location is through an implied page label. When using graphical buttons, the current button will be indicated with a different style. Sometimes designers will make the selected state of the button bright in order to let users know they are on that particular page. However, this is the role of the page label itself, not the selected button statement. In fact, this button should no longer be selectable. Putting it in a bright color would suggest that it is more important than other buttons, rather than less. This common mistake is illustrated in Figure 5-1.

Also, recall that the convention of a typical graphical user interface is to gray out a selection that is no longer selectable, and the user will expect buttons to act this way.

> **Suggestion: Button states should be considered a secondary form of page label, and the selected state should always be subdued, not prominent.**

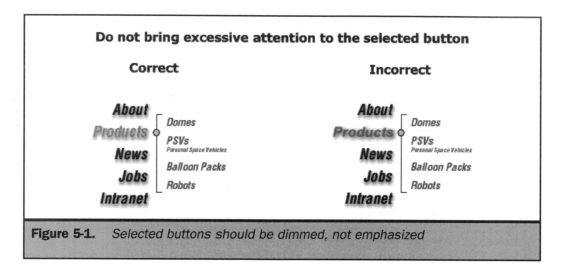

Figure 5-1.   *Selected buttons should be dimmed, not emphasized*

A more advanced form of page labeling adds in more information about location. This style could often be called a *depth gauge* since it shows the user's depth in the site, as shown here.

Home > Products > Robots > **Trainer**

Notice in this case that the first three links in the label are selectable while the fourth is bold, showing that it is the current page we are on. Some people like to use the pipe symbol rather than the greater than sign.

Home | Products | Robots | **Trainer**

The choice of separator may seem subtle, but notice that the first style suggests progression. In fact, many people mistakenly view this form of page label as path information. While it is true that it shows a path from the home page, in this case, to the Trainer robot, this is not necessarily how the user ended up at this page. Because of this confusion, some people may refer to this form of page labeling as a path indicator, but depth gauge seems more accurate as it really shows the distance from the main page—not path.

The last way to label a page is not a common technique, but it is easy to implement. Consider that the browser status bar normally does not display any information unless the user is rolling on a link. During the default time, it could display the current page label as well as URL information. Consider putting information about the current page as well as its URL in the status bar so the user can see it when they are focusing towards the bottom of the page. Using a short script within the **<BODY>** tag triggered by the **onLoad** event is an easy way to set this up. If the browser doesn't understand JavaScript, it will simply ignore this statement:

```
<BODY onLoad="window.defaultStatus='Current page: Robot Trainer
(http://www.democompany.com/products/robot/trainer.htm)';return true;">
```

The only downside to the default status bar message is that it may be overlooked by the user, or the user may not easily notice that it changes between the default message and the URL destinations when the mouse passes over links. More information about using the status bar for link information will be presented in Chapter 6. All the forms of page labeling, including the status bar message, are shown in action in Figure 5-2.

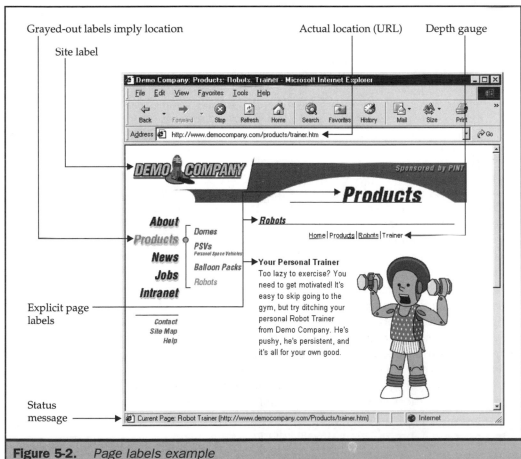

Figure 5-2. *Page labels example*

SITE ORGANIZATION AND NAVIGATION

Page and Site Style and Location

Another way to let the users know where they are is by the look of the page relative to other pages. This form of feedback is not exact, but will give the user a relative idea of where they are in a site.

Many sites use color-coding to imply location. Using this method, each section of the site has a different primary color for its buttons and graphic flourishes. For example, the site may use red for products, green for investor relations, blue for technical support, and so on. Each page in the section would use this primary color to reinforce where the user is. The only limitation to the use of color to identify location is that the colors of each section must be different enough to be noticeable to all users. Given that people may perceive color differently or have limited color-viewing environments, you may be limited to primary colors like black, red, yellow, green, cyan, blue, and magenta. Even if you push it and add in colors like orange, you may find that you are limited to around ten or twelve colors. Because of significant difference required between colors, sites with many different sections may find this approach limiting.

Suggestion: When using color-coding to imply section location, make sure the colors used are significantly different from each other.

Some designers despise the color-coding approach to section identification because it often results in a garish rainbow-style site, particularly if the buttons on the Navigation palette are colored to represent their section. Despite this criticism, this design style is very commonly used.

Another approach to implying location is through theme. Consider how in the real world many neighborhoods may utilize a theme like trees (Elm St., Birch St., Pine St.) or planets (Venus Ct., Neptune Way, Mars Place) for street names to bind the various locations together. They may also use thematic street signs or other flourishes to distinguish the neighborhood from adjacent ones. Web sites can use theme as well. Some sites may use certain forms of illustration or pictures on all pages within a section as a device to let people know they are in the same section. For example, in the products section they may have a picture of a salesperson on all the pages, in the investor-relations area a picture of a broker watching a stock ticker, in the tech-support area a picture of technical support operator, and so on. The theme concept works well, but oftentimes designers go crazy with the theme and begin naming sections "Tech Support Garage" or even "The Garage" instead of just "Technical Support." If you're not careful, it is easy to take the theme so far it becomes a metaphor-based design. This may work out in some cases, but consider what happens if the user just doesn't get it. In general, metaphors tend to be difficult to pull off.

Suggestion: Do not go so overboard with theme-based location hints that you fall into a designer-defined metaphor.

Like color, the key to using thematic hints to indicate location is making sure that the hints or page styles are different enough for the user to notice. This can be difficult because usability suggests that pages be consistent in form. Variation should be just noticeably different, but not so different the each page is considered unique. This is particularly important if we are to take advantage of landmark pages, discussed further on in the "Landmarks" section

Where Have I Been?

When you get lost, you might worry about how to get back to where you once were. Also, if you feel that you are traveling around in circles, you may wonder if you have already seen this page or the current links. One important aspect of letting the users know where they have been is changing link colors once a link has been visited. This is often called *breadcrumbing*, after the famous fairy tale Hansel and Gretel where the children drop bread crumbs to find their way back out of the forest. Typically, unvisited links are blue while visited links are purple. Because a user may rely on the link colors to understand if they have tried a choice or not in the past, it is unwise to modify link colors. This could be almost as detrimental to a site visitor as the forest animals eating all the childrens' breadcrumbs. An in-depth discussion of link colors and their effect on navigation can be found in Chapter 6.

History

Besides coloring links, a Web browser also keeps track of where users have been using a mechanism called history. The reference to each page visited is stored in a browser's history list, and the user can use the Back and Forward buttons to traverse the entries in the list. In this sense, the Back and Forward are really temporal back and forward. Some sites use link labels like "Back" on the site and utilize a JavaScript to provide the same function as the history mechanism, as shown here:

```
<A HREF="javascript:window.history.back()">Back</A>
```

Using a script like this is not a good idea since the page the back link will send the user to will vary based on where they just came from. Users do not expect a site link to act like a browser Back button. Despite the poor label, a user would expect a link labeled Back to send the user to a page one back in the site structure, not perform a back using the browser history—which may even send them outside the site. Except in a few cases when using complex framed sites, designers should not use the history mechanism with normal site links.

Suggestion: Do not attempt to mimic the browser history mechanism with links.

To avoid any unnecessary confusion about the meaning of back links, designers are always encouraged to explicitly label their back links. For example, "Back to Products" or "Back to Robot Butler" is always preferred to simply "Back."

Rule: Avoid links named simply "Back." Always explicitly indicate where a back link will go.

Do not underestimate the user's focus on the history. Certainly the favorite button of a novice user is the Back button. When some novice users become lost, they like to hit on the Back button faster than a hungry monkey hitting some food dispenser bar in a behavioral study. While certainly users should instead try to use the browser's "Go" menu to quickly traverse the history list, the reliance on the Back button should not be overlooked. For example, some sites use redirection to send users to another page or even site. The reason for the redirection might be browser detection or even just a desire to redirect a user from a misspelled URL or to deal with an outdated URL. Regardless of the reason, the method employed often has no delay and creates a page that the user is unable to back out of using the standard Back button.

Looped pages due to redirection can be highly annoying to a user who has to shut down his or her browser, open a new window, or figure out how to use the Go menu to jump over the redirection page.

The reason for the loop often has to do with the misuse of the **<META>** tag. Using a script like the following can minimize this problem in JavaScript-aware browsers.

```
<!DOCTYPE HTML PUBLIC "-//W3C//DTD HTML 4.0 Transitional//EN">
<HTML>
<HEAD>
<SCRIPT LANGUAGE="JavaScript1.1">
<!--
location.replace("redirectpage.html");
//-->
</SCRIPT>
<NOSCRIPT>
<META HTTP-EQUIV="Refresh" CONTENT="0; URL=redirectpage.html">
</NOSCRIPT>
</HEAD>
<BODY>
This page has moved <A href="redirectpage.html">to URL here</A>.
</BODY>
</HTML>
```

Rule: Avoid creating pages that cannot be backed out of easily using the browser Back button.

Indicating Past Visits with Cookies

Probably the most advanced form of indicating to a user they have visited a site before is using a cookie.

Definition: A *cookie* is a small bit of textual information handed out by a site that is stored on the user's system.

In some sense, a cookie is like a laundry ticket. When you visit a site, you are given a cookie that is then saved on your system, assuming you allow it. Any preferences you set could be stored to the cookie and reread every time you visit the same site. The basic use of cookies is to save state information in order to provide advanced Web facilities such as site personalization. A full discussion of programming cookies for user tracking is beyond the scope of this book. For now, just consider that a cookie can be used to track a user and could provide some assistance in navigation.

Using cookies, a site could potentially track users and let them know they are coming back to a site or to a particular page by putting a "Welcome Back" message on the screen, or even putting information in the page indicating the last time the user visited the particular page. Of course, users may not allow cookies or trust any messages built from cookie data particularly, because the end site could trick the user and issue Welcome Back messages when the user really hadn't been there before. The idea here would be to try to build a false sense of security in the users by making them think they had already done business with the site sometime in the past. In some cases, the user might question their memory and actually fall for such a ruse.

Beyond link color, there is really little information to let users know they have been some place before. A user's own memory—both short term and long term—is the main way people know they have been someplace before. Given the imprecise nature of human memory, the user probably won't be able to remember specifics such as a document's URL or content precisely, but they may remember general characteristics of a page or site. For example, the user may be able to remember the site's or page's color or even layout, particularly if it is significantly different from other sites they have visited. Pages that are easily remembered like this could be considered landmark pages.

Landmarks

In the offline world, we utilize many techniques to find our way—probably the most basic is the landmark. A *landmark* is a prominent identifying feature of a landscape, basically something unique enough that it is easily noticed and remembered. People use landmarks as points of reference for navigation all the time. For example, when giving someone directions you might say "my house is just past the flagpole" or "turn right when you get to the Burger Shack." Since we use a landmark to fix our position relative to other objects, a landmark must be easily identifiable and memorable.

On the Web, users tend to identify two major landmarks. The first is the page they enter the Web with: this could be called the user's home page or start page. Oftentimes, this page is set to the user's personal home page, corporation home page, or a portal page such as Yahoo! This landmark doesn't change very often. However, the second form of landmark on the Web is a little more transitory. When a user enters a site for exploration, the home page of the site is often used as a temporary landmark. The key to a landmark is that the page must look different enough from other pages visited for the user to identify it as a landmark. If it looks too similar, the user may not be able to recall if the page he or she is currently on is the landmark or not.

However, don't go overboard with the idea of using differences to improve memorability. Consider an actual site that used a randomization script to make its home page look significantly different every time the page was loaded. The idea was to make the site look dynamic. However, during a site visit, users who became lost often returned to the home page to begin again, but in this case, home wasn't how they left it. The randomization caused disorientation. The comfortable landmark of the site's home page changed and the users were confused as to where they were. Even worse, the URL bar in the browser had been hidden, and many users truly had no idea where they were and just gave up. Landmarks must be different, but they also must be stable if they are to be used as points of reference for the lost visitor.

Rule: Users remember their start page as a permanent landmark and the home page of a visited Web site as a semipermanent landmark. Because of this, these pages should be stable in their presentation but look noticeably different than other pages visited.

Where Can I Go?

Oftentimes, the most important question the user has is, "Where can I go?" The various links and labels on a page indicate the places that the user can go. The user will generally select a destination by the choices presented to them, unless they have some previous knowledge of some potential destination or have been to the site before and bypass what is shown. Presentation of the various choices available to the user is important. The first thing to consider is to make sure the choices available are obvious. Some sites aim to hide choices behind pull-down menus or offscreen with some slide-off menu. Consider that users may not notice such choices, so they are less likely to be selected.

Suggestion: Don't hide a destination choice from a user unless the link is less important or clutter forces sacrifices.

Placing Navigation

The position of navigation elements is not only a question of taste; it also brings up numerous usability issues. On a screen there are really only five general areas for navigational elements in a Web page: top, bottom, left, right, and center. Each of these locations has its pros and cons.

Top Navigation

Many sites put navigation choices towards the top of the screen. This makes sense given that it is fairly likely that all the navigation choices will show up immediately.

Also, traditionally in graphical user interfaces, the top of the screen is home to the primary menus of a program, so why not on a Web site? Given the most common scanning direction of a typical Web page of left to right and top to bottom, this is a good location for navigation.

The downside of this form of top navigation can be subtle. However, the most obvious navigation problem is that the user may scroll the navigational elements off the screen as they travel down the page. When the user hits the bottom of the page, they may be ready to move on, but with a top-only form of navigation they would have to scroll back up to the top of the page in order to continue. To combat this problem many sites adopt one or more of the following solutions.

Fix Navigational Elements in Top Portion of the Screen

Generally, this is accomplished with frames, which results in some usability problems discussed in the "Frame Problems" section later in this chapter. It is also possible to use DHTML to do create a floating Navigation palette that sticks to the top of screens, but this is only supported in the more recent browsers.

Use a Back-to-Top Link

Some sites use a back-to-top link that jumps the user back to the top of the page where the Navigation palette is. This has the downside of requiring an extra click before the user can navigate away from the page. The upside to a back-to-top link is that the user may just simply want to return to the top of the page. This type of link avoids a great deal of scrolling. The opposite go-to-bottom link is not common because the user has no idea really what is at the bottom, so why would they want to go there? In the case of the top-of-page link, the user has been to the top or knows the navigation to be there so they have reason to select the link. One downside to the go-to-top link is that some users may be surprised that the link scrolls the page up. Using a good label like "Return to top of page" or simply "Top of page" is suggested vs. the shorter "Top." Some designers prefer to use upward-pointing arrows.

Top

Back to Top

Return to top of page

In such a case, make sure that at least the **ALT** or **TITLE** text reveals the purpose of the link. Creating usable links is discussed in depth in Chapter 6.

Provide Text Links at Bottom of Page

Text links that mimic the top links are often added to a page, usually below a horizontal rule. Often, the text links are separated by brackets ([ ]) or pipe symbols (|)to make them more obviously navigation links, as shown here.

About | Products | News | Jobs | Intranet | Contact | Site Map | Help

The style of navigation of mimicking top links on the bottom of a page is often termed a *header-footer design*. This form is so common that users tired of waiting for a page's graphical buttons to load will quickly scroll to the bottom of the page to utilize the backup text links.

Another aspect of top navigation that can be troublesome is that labeling and site branding, such as a corporate logo, can be lost among the navigation elements. For example, look at the navigation bar here:

![DEMO COMPANY News: Press Releases | About | Products | News | Jobs](image)

Notice how the logo, the page label indicating location, and the buttons all compete for user attention. With top navigation, you make sure not to let your buttons drown out the rest of the information presented at the top of the page. Consider the use of menu bars within typical software applications—generally they are very thin and take up no more than about 10 percent of the vertical screen real estate. However, in many Web sites the navigation bars can get quite large, making it less likely that the user will see much content without having to scroll, and potentially putting more focus on navigation than content.

 When using top navigation, be careful not to overwhelm page labeling and site-identity information with navigational elements.

Bottom Navigation

In most cases, bottom navigation doesn't seem to make much sense, as it would probably force scrolling. This is because navigation elements would probably not show up in the first screen region unless page content was limited, or the user had a very tall screen. Of course, using frames, it is possible to fix navigation at the bottom of the screen that stays onscreen. This will be discussed later in the "Frames" section. However, even without frames, an upside of placing navigation at the bottom of the screen is that it leaves the top free for page labeling and corporate branding.

A potential problem with navigation placed at the bottom of a page is that the navigation is not in the primary scan path of the user. However, if the user did scan the whole page, they would eventually reach the bottom of the page where the navigation resides just as they were ready to move to the next page. Because of this usage pattern, many sites provide text links on the bottom of the page (as mentioned in the previous section). However, putting the primary navigation forms, such as a graphical button, at the bottom of the screen is not suggested and does not fit with where traditional software places controls.

> **Suggestion: Avoid placing primary navigation at the bottom of the screen. Reserve this area for secondary or reinforcement navigation.**

Left Navigation

The left portion of a page is a very common position for navigation elements. Since English and other Western-language readers will scan information left to right, this puts the navigation directly in the reading path of the user. Also, the left of the screen is a common location for navigation in many programs and has also become somewhat of a convention in Web design. Even in print design, left-side navigation is common—for example, consider how most tables of contents read.

The main problem with left-side navigation is that it can get in the way of content and may reduce the amount of available screen space for content. Consider that a navigation bar on the left of the page creates a type of "navigation fence" that the user must jump over to read content. This can serve both as a distraction as well as a positive limiting region for the page. Consider also that left navigation creates a margin for content that would be absent without a navigation bar. The other problem is that the navigation bar consumes precious screen real estate that limits how much content can be shown on a typical page. Say, for example, the user has a limited screen resolution like 640 pixels by 480 pixels. Given browser chrome and the fact that the user may not immediately maximize their browser to take up the full screen, there may be as little as 570–580 pixels available for content. Even with a liberal assumption of 600 pixels for content, there still may be little room for content once the buttons are added in, as shown in Figure 5-3.

> **Tip** *When using left navigation, make sure to reformat content to fit a narrow screen.*

Unfortunately, it may be impossible to reformat all content to deal with left-navigation screen limitations. There are only three approaches to this problem, as discussed next.

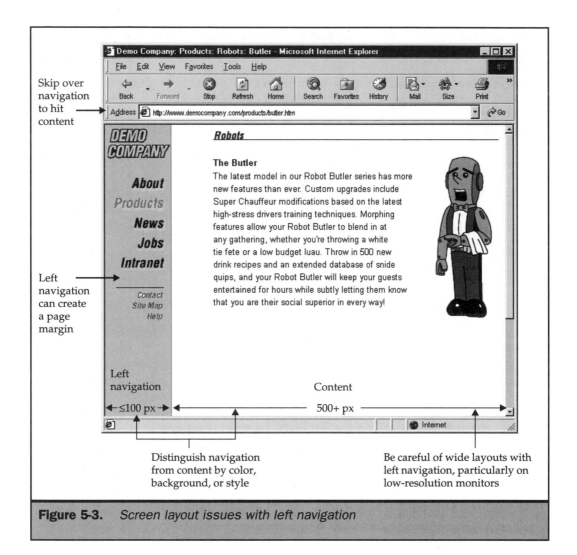

Figure 5-3.   *Screen layout issues with left navigation*

Let User Scroll if Necessary

While the number of low-resolution systems is rapidly diminishing on the desktop, with the rise of Web appliances and mobile access this may change dramatically in the future. Users are not comfortable with left-to-right scrolling, and site designers should not format content so that it forces this.

Open New Window for Wide Content

Many sites opt to open a window without left navigation when users need to view wide content such as a table that can't be reformatted and requires the full screen width at low resolution. Removing the navigation and letting content go full screen is also common with sites that format content for printing. While opening a new window does have drawbacks, it may be a necessary workaround in a limited-resolution environment. There are two ways to open a new window for the wide content. The first relies on the use of the **TARGET** attribute in HTML, while the other uses JavaScript. To open a new window using HTML, simply set the **TARGET** attribute on a link to **_blank** as shown here:

```
<A HREF="widepage.htm" TARGET="_blank">Product Table (new window)</A>
```

Of course, it might be a good idea to let the user know you are about to open a new window by explicitly stating this. The downside to the HTML approach is that while it would generally work, it does create a window with full browser controls. Many designers prefer to open a special window to display wide content. For example, the HTML here shows how a JavaScript could be used to create a link that opens a special maximized window:

```
<!DOCTYPE HTML PUBLIC "-//W3C//DTD HTML 4.0 Transitional//EN">
<HTML>
<HEAD>
<TITLE>Window Opener</TITLE>
<SCRIPT LANGUAGE="JavaScript">
<!--
function createWindow(filename,width, height){

NewWindow = window.open(filename, "","toolbar=0, location=0,
directories=0,status=0,menubar=0,scrollbars=1,
resizable=1,copyhistory=0,width="+width+",height="+height);
}
//-->
</SCRIPT>
</HEAD>
<BODY>
<TABLE WIDTH="100%">
<TR>
<TD WIDTH="100" BGCOLOR="yellow">
  Navigation buttons in this column
</TD>
<TD>
<H2>Text links are going to open a new window</H2>
<HR>
<A HREF="http://www.yahoo.com"
```

```
onClick="createWindow('http://www.yahoo.com', 640,460); return
false">Yahoo!</A>
</TD>
</TR>
</TABLE>
</BODY>
</HTML>
```

Weblink: *http://www.webdesignref.com/chapter5/windowcreator.htm.*

In this case, we pass the desired size of the window to the **createWindow** function. We gave it something equivalent to about the maximum resolution under 640 × 480. Consider that we only use 460 because the window taskbar may take up some room. It is also possible to use JavaScript to sense for screen resolution and open up to the size of the screen. It is even possible to go to full screen and take over the entire desktop, but this is not suggested.

The main downside to using new windows without browser chrome and navigation is that some users may be confused by the new window and not know how to use or close the window. Because of this potential confusion, an explicit Close button or even a frameset should be used to indicate the use of an external window. Some sites even use this approach when opening links to outside sites. Figure 5-4 shows some examples of how this might work.

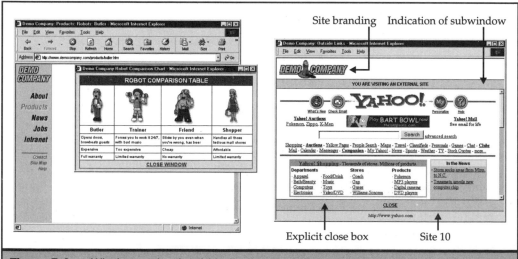

Figure 5-4. *Window style should indicate secondary window*

Hide Left Navigation

Some sites have begun to use dynamic HTML to hide left navigation and only show it if required. This form of slide or pull-out navigation does save screen real estate, but exchanges the space issues for usability problems related to hiding the navigation from the user. By hiding the navigation, we have limited the users' capability to understand the range of choices they have without explicitly pulling out the navigation. On the other hand, a slide-out navigation does place the majority of the focus on the content. The JavaScript and HTML shown here demonstrate how to use this form of navigation:

```
<!DOCTYPE HTML PUBLIC "-//W3C//DTD HTML 4.0 Transitional//EN">
<HTML>
<HEAD>
<TITLE>Hidden Left Menu Demo</TITLE>
<STYLE>
<!--

#iemenu,
#netscapemenu    {font-weight: bold;
                  font-size: 12px;
                  font-family: Verdana, Sans-serif;
                  line-height:20px;
                  position:absolute;
                  left:-75px;
                  width:85px;
                  top:10px;
                  border:1.5px solid black;
                  background-color: #ffff99;
                  layer-background-color:#ffff99;}
.menulinks       {color: black; text-decoration: none;}

-->
</STYLE>
</HEAD>
<BODY>
<SCRIPT>
<!--
function generateLinks() {

var menuitems=new Array()
var menulinks=new Array()
// Add menu titles here
menuitems[0]="Home"
menuitems[1]="About"
```

```
menuitems[2]="Products"
menuitems[3]="News"
menuitems[4]="Jobs"

//Add corresponding menu links here
menulinks[0]="http://www.democompany.com/";
menulinks[1]="http://www.democompany.com/about/index.htm";
menulinks[2]="http://www.democompany.com/products/index.htm";
menulinks[3]="http://www.democompany.com/news/index.cfm";
menulinks[4]="http://www.democompany.com/jobs/index.htm";

for (i=0;i<=menuitems.length-1;i++)
document.write('  <A HREF='+menulinks[i]+'
CLASS="menulinks">'+menuitems[i]+'</A><BR>');

}

/ * output the menu */
if (document.all)
{
  document.write('<DIV ID="iemenu" STYLE="left:-75"
onMouseover="show()" onMouseout="hide()">')
  generateLinks();
  document.write('</DIV>');
}
else if (document.layers) {
  document.write('<LAYER ID="netscapemenu" onMouseover="show()"
onMouseout="hide()">');
  generateLinks();
  document.write('</LAYER>');
 }
else
 generateLinks();

//-->
</SCRIPT>

<SCRIPT LANGUAGE="JavaScript1.2">
<!--
/* Deal with Netscape resize bug */
function regenerate(){ window.location.reload() }

function NetscapeRegenerate() {
```

```
   if (document.layers)
     setTimeout("window.onresize=regenerate",400)
}
window.onload=NetscapeRegenerate;
/* end Netscape resize bug code */

if (document.all) {
  menu=document.all.iemenu.style;
  rightboundary=0;
  leftboundary=-75;
}
else {
  menu=document.layers.netscapemenu;
  rightboundary=70;
  leftboundary=10;
}

function show() {
if (window.hidemenu)
   clearInterval(hidemenu);
   showmenu=setInterval("doshow()",50);
}

function doshow() {
if (document.all&&menu.pixelLeft<rightboundary)
   menu.pixelLeft+=5;
else if(document.layers&&menu.left<rightboundary)
   menu.left+=5;
else if (window.doshow)
   clearInterval(doshow)
}

function hide() {
 clearInterval(showmenu)
 hidemenu=setInterval("dohide()",50)
}

function dohide() {
  if (document.all&&menu.pixelLeft>leftboundary)
    menu.pixelLeft-=5;
  else if(document.layers&&menu.left>leftboundary)
    menu.left-=5;
  else if (window.dohide)
```

```
        clearInterval(dohide);
}
// -->
</SCRIPT>

<H2 ALIGN="CENTER">Hide Left Navigation Demo</H2>
<HR>
<P>Put your site content here</P>

</BODY>
</HTML>
```

Tip   *Weblink: http://www.webdesignref.com/chapter5/dynamicleftnav.htm.*

The code presented does, unfortunately, have to deal with some Netscape-specific issues such as the use of the **<LAYER>** tag. Hopefully, workarounds like this will no longer be necessary in the future. Changing the code to fit your site design is just a matter of positioning the objects and adding your own labels and links to the arrays defined in the generateLinks() function. A rendering of this example showing the hidden menu as well as the exposed menu is shown in Figure 5-5.

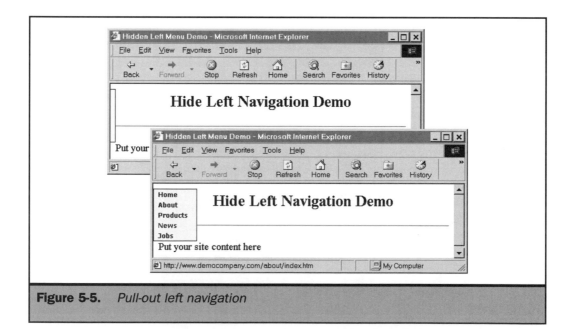

Figure 5-5.   *Pull-out left navigation*

Right Navigation

Recently, placing navigational elements on the right has become popular. Some argue that right navigation places the navigation out of the way of the content and allows the user to immediately dive in and read the content. Right-navigation supporters also note that the navigation buttons will be near the scroll bar, thus limiting mouse travel for the user.

Despite its potential upside, right navigation has some potentially serious drawbacks. First, consider a simple question. Where exactly is the right? Depending on a user's monitor and browser size, the distance from the left to the right of the screen may vary greatly. On a very large monitor, the navigation could be very far from the left edge of the screen and the mouse travel between the navigational elements and the users' favorite button—the Back button—could be extreme. Also, with such a flexible right side, screen design will have to be very flexible. Because of this, some designers opt to create an artificial right margin for right-focused navigation. Generally, they tend to make this margin somewhere between 600 and 700 pixels so that the entire page ends up being around 800 pixels wide, which is approximately equivalent to the width of standard letter-size paper on most monitors. This would be acceptable, but it does not really obtain the second benefit of right navigation on all monitors: being close to the scroll bars. Sure, it is closer than left navigation, but it still may be a long ways away on a huge monitor. Figure 5-6 illustrates some of the basic problems and benefits of right-oriented navigation.

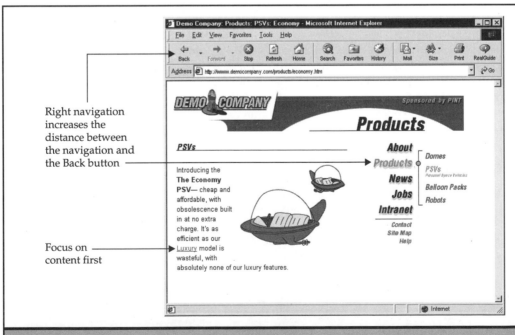

Right navigation increases the distance between the navigation and the Back button

Focus on content first

Figure 5-6.   *Right navigation can be problematic*

Probably the biggest reason not to consider using right navigation is simple convention. Graphical user interfaces tend not to favor right navigation, and most Web sites do not either. While left-style navigation may not be optimal in some people's opinion, right navigation is certainly not standard. Consider this well before literally switching the position of a site's doorknob! Does this mean never use right navigation? Not quite, but certainly don't put your primary site-navigation elements there unless convention changes. Some sites have already started to put advertisements, cross-links, and secondary forms of the navigation on the right.

Suggestion: Avoid placing primary navigation on the far right of the screen.

Navigation in the Center

The last choice for navigational elements within a window is the center. Generally, putting heavy navigational elements such as graphical buttons or image maps in the center of the page is only used on the home page. Navigation-in-the-center designs tend to be heavy and don't leave much room for content since the navigation is in the user's primary focus region. However, for home pages, this may not be a problem. Considering that the main purpose for a home page is to help the user decide where to go, putting a site's initial navigation in the middle makes sense. This design also allows a home page to be visually different from subpages, making it easier to establish it as a landmark page.

Suggestion: Home pages or other landmark pages should consider using center-oriented navigation to distinguish themselves from other pages in a site.

Subpages should stay away from using center-oriented navigation regions other than simple text links. Content should appear in the center of the screen so that the only navigational elements presented there would be cross-links within content. There is one final choice for navigation elements, and that is outside the current window. A discussion of frames and subwindows, often called *remotes*, is presented later in this chapter in the "Subwindows" section.

Consistency of Navigation

Regardless of which position is selected for navigation—or even if literally all the positions are used, just with different types of navigation—everything must be consistent. If primary navigation is on the top and secondary navigation is on the left, then keep it there. Variation of navigation may be possible between landmark and other pages, but in general the following Web design rule should always be considered.

Rule: Placement of navigation should be consistent within a page layout.

The importance of the stability of navigation cannot be understated. It is known from numerous studies that consistency is key to usability, and navigation that jumps around the screen may confuse or disorient the user. Consider that even if the placement of navigation is basically the same, subtle jumping may still occur. The easiest way to spot this is to do a "fast browse" of a site. To perform a fast browse, quickly click between screens and notice if the navigation moves or you have to move your mouse greatly to reach the next choice in a navigation bar.

The number and position of elements within a navigation region should also be stable from screen to screen. Many sites add and remove buttons from navigational regions as the user moves around. Imagine if an application like your favorite word processor suddenly added primary menu items or deleted them as you worked. Do not even be tempted to remove a navigation choice just because it is the one the user selected; instead, make it unselectable or gray it out. Simply removing it will cause all the buttons to shift. Consider the menu choices shown in Figure 5-7. Notice how removing an item as it is selected from the navigation changes the size of the region, breaking the stability, as well as how the menus may not obviously be the same.

Look carefully and you'll see that one of the menus actually has a slight button change in it. Users will find the movement of buttons and addition of choices in this manner highly disorienting.

> **Rule: Navigation should be consistent, and elements should exhibit stability in position, order, and contents.**

The previous rule doesn't preclude the ability to add navigational elements. However, if we do so, we must certainly let the user know we are about to do that and make it obvious what was added. For example, consider a tree navigational control. In a tree control, the user can expand or contract navigation to show or hide navigational choices. However, this control indicates that navigation will change and attempts to differentiate added navigational items. For example, consider the unexpanded and expanded tree control shown in Figure 5-8. Once expanded, the exposed navigational choices are indicated by indentation as well as a different style.

Tree controls are by no means perfect. Oftentimes the tree control will expand too far down or to the right. In fact, after expanding three or four levels, most tree controls for most sites get somewhat unwieldy.

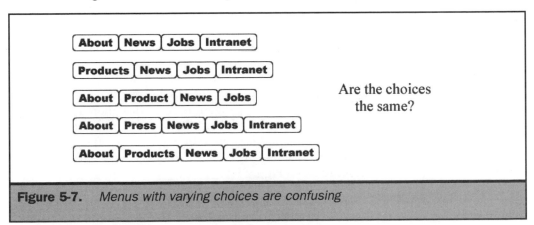

Figure 5-7.   *Menus with varying choices are confusing*

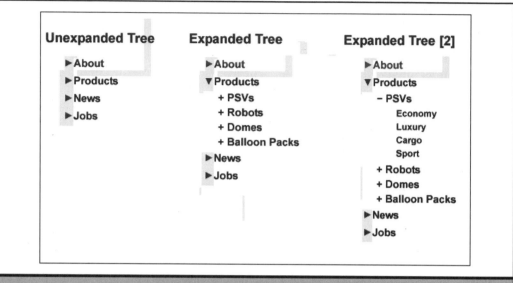

Figure 5-8.   *Tree navigation allows navigation flexibility*

Navigation Meaning by Screen Position

Besides using an expandable/collapsible-style navigation device, designers often opt to show new navigational choices in other regions of the screen. For example, many sites follow the convention of placing the primary site or section navigation across the top of the screen with backup text links across the bottom and secondary navigation along the left. A third level of navigation can be added in a tree fashion on the left, or, to a limited degree, towards the center of the screen if it is limited in its scope and does not interfere with the content. What's interesting to see is that, while using the different positions of the screen equals a different form of navigation approach, it is difficult to go beyond three or four levels of site navigation.

> **Suggestion: When separating navigation choices by position onscreen, understand that four locations is a hard barrier.**

Usually this common navigation form includes text links backing up the primary navigation. Because of the common position of navigation, some designers refer to this approach as TLB or "top-left-bottom" navigation. In this form, the primary navigation is laid across the top of the page, with secondary navigation along the left side of the page. Generally the subnavigation is also less prominent than the primary navigation. A simple TLB block diagram is shown in Figure 5-9.

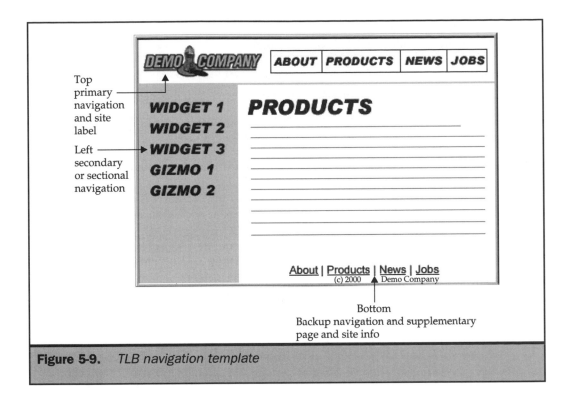

Figure 5-9. *TLB navigation template*

The TLB approach to setting navigation meaning by screen position makes good sense if you consider the user's scan path. If the user looks first to the top of the screen, they will read across the primary navigation choices. Once they return to the left to begin looking down the screen, they will see secondary choices. If they scroll the page to look through the content or choices, they will eventually reach the bottom of the page where they are greeted with the text form of the main navigation. TLB design may not seem creative to many designers, but it is a convention and it does work.

Navigation and Scrolling

A contentious issue for some is whether or not pages should scroll, particularly when navigational elements are involved. Nonscrolling advocates feel that keeping pages a fixed size makes things consistent and thus more predictable for the user. This may be true considering that with variable page sizes, users really don't have any idea of the volume of information they are about to receive after a typical button click. Of course, there are numerous drawbacks to the fixed-page-length concept. The page size discussion is discussed thoroughly in Chapter 9. For now, consider that pages that are just used to navigate to other pages probably shouldn't scroll. You should always strive to minimize the user's effort in selecting the next page, and scrolling offscreen to see choices both adds movement and forces the user to recall any choices not visible. This idea leads to the following Web design suggestion.

Suggestion: Navigation-oriented pages should fit vertically within the screen whenever possible, as should primary navigation in all other types of pages.

This rule suggests, in particular, that pages that are simply pages that lead to others should focus on the screen region that does not scroll, or that they be, as they say, "above the fold." It is impossible to guess an exact height that is available, because browsers have different amounts of surrounding chrome, and users may minimize their browser window at their own discretion. However, using scripting, it is possible to determine screen height on page load, as discussed in Chapter 9, but the user is always free to change things at will. In all cases—particularly when dealing with low screen resolutions such 640 × 480—designers should always be conservative in their estimates. Many sites fit the entire navigation within the first 300 pixels regardless of screen resolution. The first screen is considered the prime screen real estate, as any navigation outside this region may require the user to scroll to activate it.

Navigation and Mouse Travel

Besides striving to limit scrolling to navigational elements, designers should always attempt to limit mouse travel between navigational choices. First, always consider the distance from the navigation elements and the Back button, which is the most frequently used browser button. While advanced users may use a right-click or a similar navigational shortcut to avoid moving the pointer to the upper-left corner of the screen, many users will not do this. Therefore, the distance between navigation items and the Back button should be minimized when possible as mentioned in the discussion of movement and usability presented in Chapter 30.

Suggestion: Minimize the distance between primary site navigation buttons and the Back button.

This mouse distance idea generalizes when you consider the user clicks a navigation choice and then makes another choice. The choice may be either the Back button or another button within the screen if the user is going to stay within the site. If they are moving away from the site, they may move to invoke a window to type a new URL or move to the address bar to do the same thing. If the user chooses another button on the screen, it would be wise to limit the amount of mouse travel the user must make between subsequent choices. If this distance is limited, with the next choice appearing close to the button just pressed, navigation will appear effortless. Recall the rule from Chapter 30.

Rule: Minimize mouse travel distance between successive choices.

Limiting mouse distance isn't just a commonsense method to improve navigation. Consider again Fitts' law, as discussed in Chapter 3, which indicates the speed to which a user can click on a button is inversely proportional to its size and its distance away from the current mouse position. Basically, if the button is small, the user can't get to it to quickly if it is far away. If you keep buttons big and right next to the previous selection, Fitt's law says the user will be able to use the interface quickly. If you consider how easy it would be to press big red buttons that appear right next to each other, you can see Fitt's law may state the obvious. Then why are small buttons jumping up all over Web pages? To deal with the effects of Fitt's law, bring choices closer together and make choices that are farther away larger. Notice that many interfaces, such as installers and Wizard-style interfaces, already limit mouse travel by making the screens similar, and the next button to click is right near the position of the last one clicked.

Frames

One navigation device that can be used to improve stability and possibly reduce scrolling—and maybe even mouse travel—is the frame. Frames, unfortunately, have somewhat of a bad name on the Web, primarily due to some early implementation problems and some vocal critics such as usability expert Jakob Nielsen. The reality of frames is that they are generally misused, but actually do have some redeeming features that should be considered before dismissing them out of hand.

The biggest problem with frames is a misunderstanding of their purpose. Many designers accidentally use frames as a page layout tool. The truth is that frames are navigation devices. The idea of a frame is to divide the screen into multiple regions, panes, or windows. The benefit of breaking the browser window into multiple independent regions is that it allows the viewer to see more than one document at a time. In fact, consider that even using a simple two-frame design as shown in Figure 5-10, there are actually three documents being used—a document setting up the frames, a document for the left frame, and a document for the right frame.

The benefits of using frames can be great. First, using frames, it is possible to fix navigation onscreen at all times. Whether navigation buttons are placed in a frame at the top, left, bottom, or even right of the screen, the buttons can be fixed to never scroll away.

> **Tip**   *Weblink: A demonstration of this can be found online at http://www.webdesignref.com/chapter5/framesfixednav.htm.*

Another benefit of frames is that they can create an appearance of speed. Consider the case of the fixed navigation shown in the previous example. If you click on the various links in the navigation bar, notice that only the right portion of the screen updates while the left stays onscreen. Because there is less screen repainting, the site appears fast to the user. If the frameset is much larger, the illusion is more noticeable.

> **Tip**   *Weblink: A demo of this can be found at http://www.webdesignref.com/chapter5/framespeed.htm.*

Frames also provide the benefit of allowing multiple documents to be shown within the window at once. For example, if you want to compare various items, it

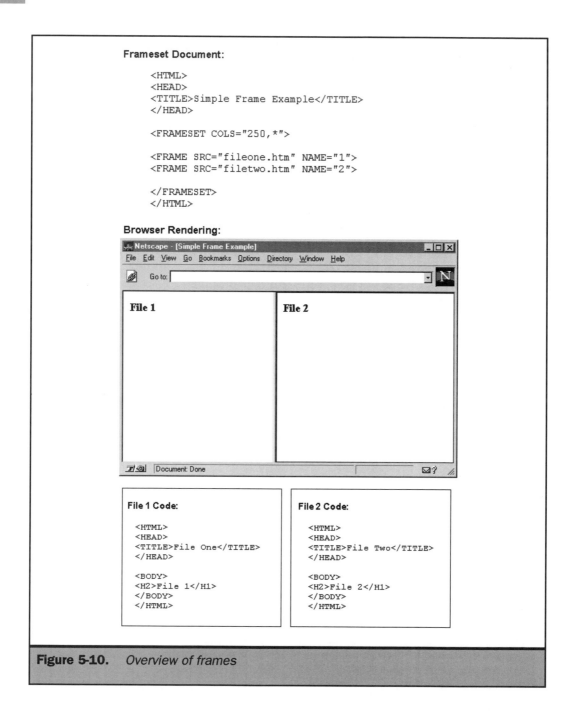

Figure 5-10. *Overview of frames*

might be possible to build a framed environment so the user could click on buttons and bring up pages with products to compare, as shown in Figure 5-11. This example also suggests that using frames can result in very complex navigation.

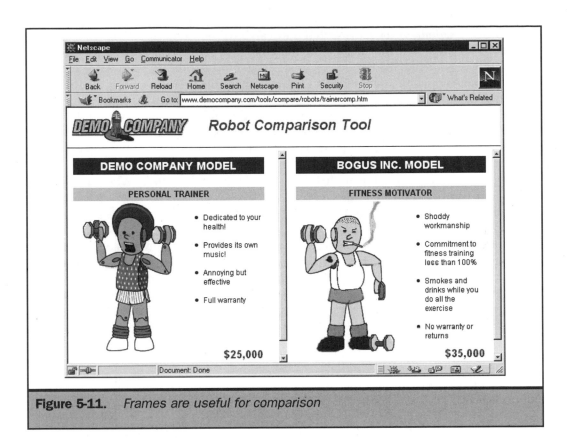

Figure 5-11.   *Frames are useful for comparison*

Frame Problems

Admittedly, frames have some serious drawbacks that should be considered before being used. First, understand that frames upset the basic page metaphor of the Web. On most Web sites, a single URL is equivalent to a single document. Click a link or enter a new URL and you get a brand new full screen worth of data. A framed site doesn't follow the "one URL equals one document" model of the Web, or at least it doesn't appear to. In fact, in most framed environments, the URL will appear to stay the same. Revisit the example at http://www.webdesignref.com/chapter5/ framesfixednav.htm and notice the URL never changes, no matter what link you select. This can be a serious problem when you consider that the user may use the URL to determine their location.

Because the URL does not change in framed environment, the user may find it difficult to bookmark interior pages. This may be by design, as mentioned in Chapter 4 when discussing solid site architectures. However, if the user feels they should be able to bookmark a particular press release, for example, and find that what they have bookmarked is a top-level page, they may become frustrated. Even advanced users who are able to open a framed page in a new window and bookmark the deep URL will be annoyed that what they have bookmarked does not include all the page elements, such as navigation.

Another problem with frames is that they can be difficult to print. To print a framed page, the user must know to click in the framed region before printing. Many sites that use frames do not make the various regions of the frames obvious, so the user may have problems knowing what region to click into in order to print.

Lastly, many designers have found out the hard way that search engines do not work well with frame designs, and may not be able to index site contents or follow links. Because of this limitation alone, some designers have abandoned frames altogether. This is unfortunate since it is possible to deal with most of the problems presented. In fact, the real problem with frames is that they are difficult to implement properly—particularly if you want to address all their shortcomings. When using frames, it is easy to screw up your site.

While frames can be difficult for some users, people, as both designers and users, are becoming more used to frames; some common forms of frame have begun to appear. Furthermore, it is possible to get around many of the limitations of frames mentioned in the previous section, such as bookmarking and fixed URLs. Unfortunately, the solution often comes at the expense of frame benefits such as screen refresh, or with an increased reliance on scripting. Improvement in Web browsers will also solve some frame problems. Already, Internet Explorer provides much better support for printing and bookmarking frames. However, despite all the potential advances in frame technology, the main problem continues to be sloppy execution.

Using Frames

This section will discuss frame use as well as some techniques to avoid problems. However, for a full discussion of frame syntax, readers are directed to the companion book *HTML: The Complete Reference*. The first thing to consider is to know if you even need to use frames. Remember, frames are navigation devices, so you should only be using them when you are trying to create regions such as control bars that load other portions of the screen—not when you are attempting to create some sophisticated layout.

Suggestion: Avoid using frames for layout. Use them for navigation.

If it makes sense to use frames, stick to the styles shown in Figure 5-12. Hopefully, a user will have encountered one of these common styles; thus, many of the negative effects of not knowing what will update when things are clicked will be alleviated by plain experience.

The common feature of all these frame layouts is that the little regions control the big regions. This makes sense considering navigation should always be smaller than the content presented. Also, the regions tend to control regions that are adjacent or below them.

Suggestion: When using frames, make smaller frames control larger adjacent frames.

Besides the two-, three-, and four-frame layouts, many designers opt for a fixed-frame layout style similar to a picture frame, with the content fixed in the middle of the screen. This is often done more for its dramatic layout than navigation. Unfortunately,

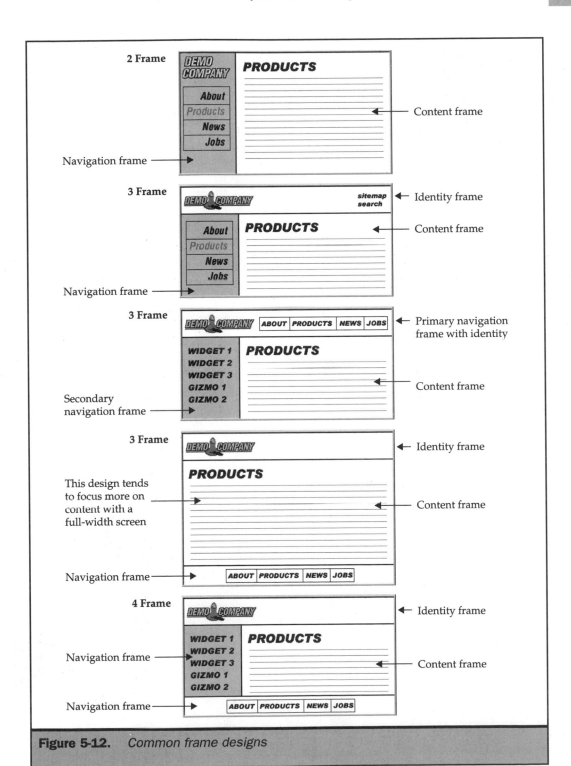

Figure 5-12.   *Common frame designs*

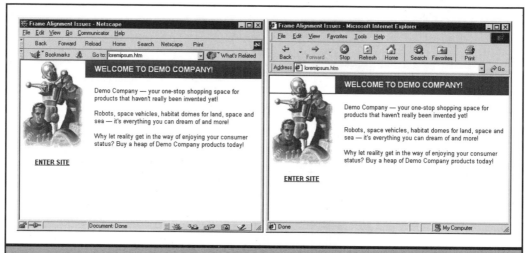

Figure 5-13. *Complex frame use may exhibit layout problems*

despite the potential for a unique layout coding, such a design can be problematic—particularly given subtle layout problems with frames under the various browsers. Figure 5-13 shows an example of a fixed-page frame design. Notice the subtle offset between the two browser screens. While future browsers may solve such problems, do not underestimate the not so subtle frame-rendering differences in browsers.

Microsoft Internet Explorer supports the **<IFRAME>** tag that could make a layout like the one shown in Figure 5-13 quite simple. It is possible to also create a similar layout using CSS in conjunction with JavaScript. Hopefully, over time, less reliance on frames for layout will be possible.

Printing Frames

The best suggestion with printing frames is to make a design obvious enough so a user knows what region of the screen is in what frame. Hopefully, a user will be able to pick up on the problem and click into the region when printing. Consider that it is also possible to add a Print button to a framed page, like the one shown in Figure 5-14.

The Print Page button could then be used to either open a new page without frames or to invoke a Print dialog box immediately using a scripting language. The following script demonstrates how the Print button is added:

```
<SCRIPT LANGUAGE="JAVASCRIPT">
<!--

if (window.print)
 {
```

```
   document.write('<A HREF="javascript:window.print()">');
   document.write('<img src="../images/printer.gif" width="110"
height="40" border="0" align="right"></A>');
 }
else
 {
   document.write('<A
HREF="javascript:window.top.location=window.location">');
   document.write('<img src="../images/printer.gif" width="110:
height="40" border="0" align="right"></A>');
 }

// -->
</SCRIPT>
```

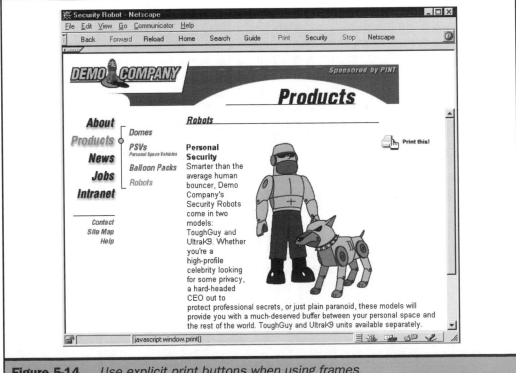

Figure 5-14.   *Use explicit print buttons when using frames*

Bookmarking Issues

Because frames show the URL of the frameset document and not the actual contents, it is often difficult for the user to bookmark the page. First, consider that you may not want people to bookmark some pages. Many complex e-commerce sites frame internal pages on purpose, because they are often dynamically generated and may have very difficult URLs.

However, often users will try to bookmark a framed page, and the browser will not show the correct page. For example, as shown in Figure 5-15, often when the user bookmarks the page on the left, leaves, and then returns they see the initial frameset on the right. Notice how the URL is the same in both the screens.

Fortunately, some of the newer browsers like Internet Explorer 5 are able to deal with frame bookmarking problems and will not exhibit this problem. Of course, a more sophisticated user will figure out how to bookmark just the framed page regardless of browser support. Unfortunately, they will find that they lose any contextual information, such as navigation, when they return, and that they have inadvertently created an orphan page where the user is unable to navigate without splicing the URL, as shown in Figure 5-16.

There are two approaches to get around the frame bookmark problem. The first is to create multiple framesets, each with a different URL that is a bookmarkable. The problem with this approach is that you lose the reduced screen-refresh benefit of frames, and you are forced to create multiple documents.

A better approach to the bookmarking problem is to use a scripting language to detect if the user is entering in an unframed page and dynamically rebuild the

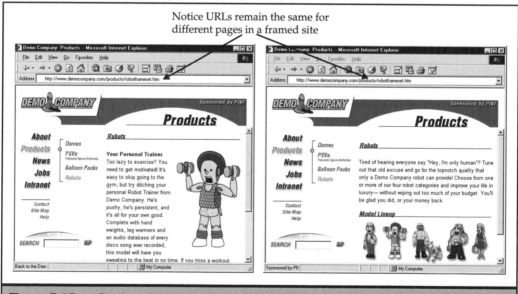

Figure 5-15.   *Bookmarking framesets may be difficult because URL is fixed*

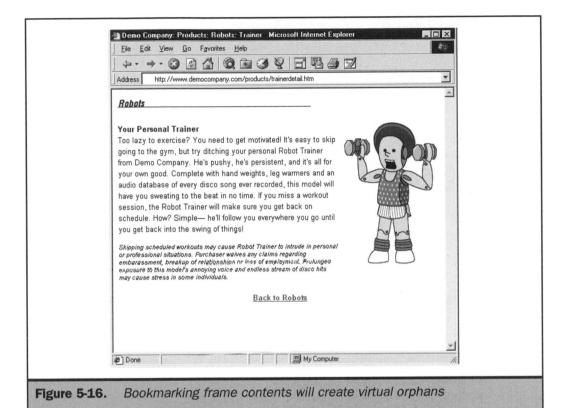

Figure 5-16. *Bookmarking frame contents will create virtual orphans*

appropriate frameset if necessary. For example, if you define your frameset for a section of the site with the file frameset.htm, you can use JavaScript to see if a page is within a frameset defined by that file. If it isn't, you can then set the location to be the initial frameset document. The script here shows how this might be done. Just place it within the **<HEAD>** tag of all the framed documents.

```
<SCRIPT>
<!--
 var containingwindow =
top.location.pathname.substring((top.location.pathname.lastIndexOf(
"/"))+1).
toLowerCase();

  if (containingwindow!="frameset.htm")

    top.location.replace("frameset.htm");
```

```
//-->
</SCRIPT>
```

This script will not work if the user has gone deep into a frameset, as the regenerated frameset will point to the initial document in the frameset. What we would have to do instead is dynamically generate the frameset itself based on the page that was not within its frames. The following files illustrate how this is done. Make sure that you run this example from a live Web server. If you don't, it generally won't work because the URL will not be formed normally.

File: frameset.htm

```
<!DOCTYPE HTML PUBLIC "-//W3C//DTD HTML 4.0 Transitional//EN">
<HTML>
<HEAD>
<TITLE>Dynamic Frames Demo</TITLE>
</HEAD>
<SCRIPT>
<!--
function getPage() {
    return unescape(
window.location.search.substring(window.location.search.
indexOf("=")+1));
    }

  document.write('<FRAMESET COLS="100,*">');
  document.write('<FRAME SRC="controls.htm" NAME="controls">');
  if (window.location.search=="")
    document.write('<FRAME NAME="display" SRC="page1.htm">');
  else
    document.write('<FRAME NAME="display" SRC="'+getPage()+' ">');
  document.write("</FRAMESET>");
// -->
</SCRIPT>
</HTML>
```

File: controls.htm

```
<!DOCTYPE HTML PUBLIC "-//W3C//DTD HTML 4.0 Transitional//EN">
<HTML>
<HEAD>
```

```
<TITLE>Control Frame</TITLE>
</HEAD>
<BODY>
<A HREF="page1.htm" TARGET="display">Page 1</A><BR>
<A HREF="page2.htm" TARGET="display">Page 2</A><BR>
<A HREF="page3.htm" TARGET="display">Page 3</A><BR>
</BODY>
</HTML>
```

File: Page1.htm

```
<!DOCTYPE HTML PUBLIC "-//W3C//DTD HTML 4.0 Transitional//EN">
<HTML>
<HEAD>
<TITLE>Page 1</TITLE>
<SCRIPT>
<!--
var container = "frameset.htm";
  var wname =
top.location.pathname.substring((top.location.pathname.
lastIndexOf("/"))+1).toLowerCase();
  if (wname!=container)
    parent.location.replace(container +
"?display="+escape(this.location));
// -->
</SCRIPT>
</HEAD>
<BODY>
<H1 ALIGN="center">Page 1</H1>
</BODY>
</HTML>
```

The other files, page2.htm and page3.htm, are exactly the same as page1.htm.
Just change their titles and headings so you can tell the difference. The key to this
demonstration is trying to bookmark an individual framed page. Select a framed page
like page1.htm and directly bookmark it. Now, when you return to the page, it should
automatically generate the surrounding frameset so the page is not orphaned. The
only downside to this technique, which can also be accomplished using a server-side
technology, is that it causes an extra round-trip to the server to rebuild the frameset.

Tip | *Weblink: For a live example of the dynamic frameset, see
http://www.webdesignref.com/chapter5/dynamicframes.htm.*

Layout Issues

When using frames for layout or for navigation, it is important not to be too restrictive. Many designers turn off frame borders, turn off scrolling for all frames but the content frame, and restrict resizing of the frames by the user. While this may create a nice-looking layout, consider what happens for a user whose screen isn't large enough to hold the frameset in its entirety. If you are not using screen resolution sensing, you should be careful when turning off frame resizing and scrolling. About the only time you may consider doing this is if you set the size of a navigation frame exactly equal to the minimum size of its buttons.

Suggestion: Do not turn off frame resizing and scrolling unless resolution is very well accounted for.

Frame borders are another issue. Keeping the borders on a framed environment may make it more obvious where the frames are, but could result in a less than optimal layout, as shown by the examples in Figure 5-17.

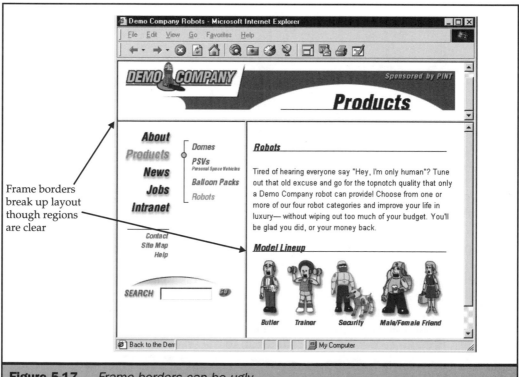

Figure 5-17. *Frame borders can be ugly*

However, if the user will have to resize frames, it is a good idea to keep the frames borders on.

Frame Busting

A common problem with frames is where a frameset starts to appear within an existing frameset. Sometimes this is done on purpose by outside sites trying to capture the user. Other times, it is simply a mistake, and the frames begin to appear within themselves. This developer mistake could be dubbed the "Russian dolls problem" after the famous Russian dolls that contain smaller and smaller identical dolls inside. Both examples are shown in Figure 5-18.

While one example is simple designer error, you may wonder how to keep users from framing your site. A simple way if you are not using frames in your own site is just to write your HTML to make sure that every link in your site has its **TARGET** attribute set to **_top** as shown here:

```
<A HREF="robots.htm" TARGET="_top">Robots</A>
```

With this approach, any time a user is within a frameset, the next link loaded will load over the top of the existing frameset. This idea is often called "frame busting."

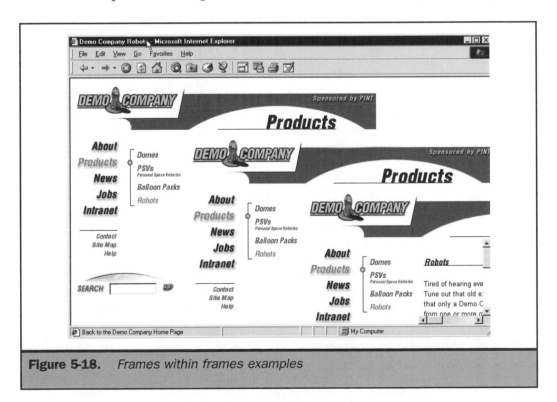

Figure 5-18.   *Frames within frames examples*

SITE ORGANIZATION AND NAVIGATION

Another approach is to use a short JavaScript to detect if the page is framed and then bust out of the frames. This could be used even within a frameset document of your own, so you can use frames in your own site safely.

```
<SCRIPT LANGUAGE="JavaScript">
<!--
if (window != top) top.location.href = location.href;
// -->
</SCRIPT>
```

However, be careful with frame busting. While it may be true that the extra real estate gained will improve the layout, the user may want the framed environment. Consider that maybe the user was just taking a side trip to your site and wanted the other site's navigation around yours in order to return easily to the old site. Again the control issue rears its head. You could certainly write the script to check with the user whether or not they want to kill the frames, but this may also annoy the user.

```
<SCRIPT LANGUAGE="JavaScript">
<!--
if (window != top)
 if (confirm("Remove framing document?"))
   top.location.href = location.href;
// -->
</SCRIPT>
```

<NOFRAMES>

A potentially serious problem with frames is that all browsers do not support frames. Very old browsers such as early versions of Netscape or Mosaic, as well as browsers found on network appliances or handheld devices, generally have limitations associated with frame pages. Furthermore, many search engines will not index sites with frames. This could severely limit the site's ability to be listed with public search engines, as discussed in Chapter 7. If frames are used, make sure that at least some content is presented using the **<NOFRAMES>** tag within a frameset document. Users without frame support, as well as search engines, will be able to see this content, while typical users will see the framed site, as illustrated in Figure 5-19.

Of course, dealing with both frame and nonframe supporting browsers may mean creating two versions of every page. Though this can be done dynamically, it may be expensive. However, before simply creating a **<NOFRAMES>** page that tells users to upgrade their browser, consider that the numerous users who seem to dislike frames with a serious passion might appreciate an unframed site.

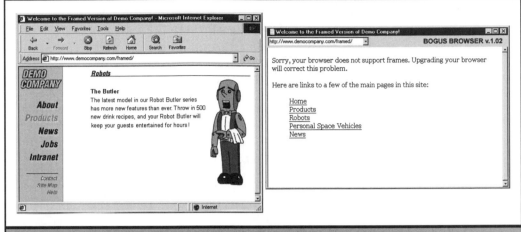

Figure 5-19.   *Users who don't support frames see a much different site*

Subwindows

Another navigation scheme less popular than frames is the idea of a "remote." Basically, a remote is a small subwindow that is detached from the browser and can be used to load content into the main window. An example of a remote is shown in Figure 5-20.

In some sense, a remote is like a frame in that it is always available—it is just not attached to the main window. Remotes could also be considered equivalent to a tear-off menu. Creating a remote is fairly easy—just name a window and then create a smaller secondary or remote window with links that target the main window. For example, the file remotetester.htm launches the remote, while remote.htm contains the links with the **TARGET** attributes set to the main window.

File: remotetester.htm

```
<!DOCTYPE HTML PUBLIC "-//W3C//DTD HTML 4.0
Transitional//EN"><HTML>
<HEAD>
<TITLE>Remote Tester</TITLE>
<SCRIPT LANGUAGE="JAVASCRIPT">
<!--
window.name = "mainwindow";

function spawn()
```

```
  {
    remotewindow=window.open("remote.htm", "remote",
"toolbar=0,location=0,directories=0,status=0,menubar=0,resizable=1,
copyhistory=0,width=200,height=400", false);
  }
// -->
</SCRIPT>
</HEAD>
<BODY BGCOLOR="#FFFFFF">
<H2 ALIGN="center">Remote Tester</H2>
<HR>
<P>
<A HREF="javascript:spawn()">Spawn Remote</A>
</P>
</BODY>
</HTML>
```

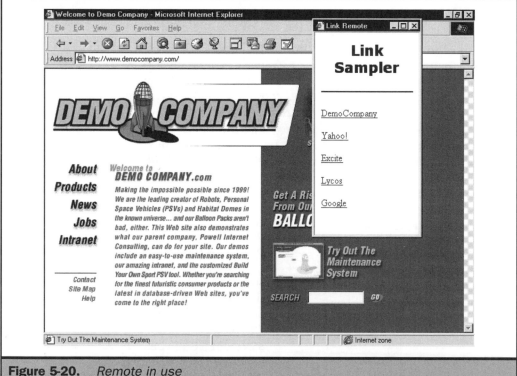

Figure 5-20.   *Remote in use*

File: remote.htm

```
<!DOCTYPE HTML PUBLIC "-//W3C//DTD HTML 4.0 Transitional//EN">
<HTML>
<HEAD>
<TITLE>Link Remote</TITLE>
</HEAD>
<BODY BGCOLOR="#000000" TEXT="#FFFFFF" LINK="#FFFF33"
VLINK="#FF0000" ALINK="#FF0000">
<H2 ALIGN="center"><FONT COLOR="#FF6600" FACE="Verdana, Arial,
Helvetica, sans-serif">Link Sampler</FONT></H2>
<HR>
<A HREF="http://www.democompany.com/"
TARGET="mainwindow">DemoCompany</A><BR>
<A HREF="http://www.yahoo.com/" TARGET="mainwindow">Yahoo!</A><BR>
<A HREF="http://www.excite.com" TARGET="mainwindow">Excite</A><BR>
<A HREF="http://www.lycos.com" TARGET="mainwindow">Lycos</A><BR>
<A HREF="http://www.google.com" TARGET="mainwindow">Google</A><BR>
</BODY>
</HTML>
```

The main problem with remotes is that they can get lost. Some people set their operating environment to automatically lower windows. This could make it easy to "lose" the remote behind the main window. Another problem could be that the remote just gets in the way. On a small screen, the remote might always be hovering over content since there would be no place to put it. Remotes are interesting for frequently used sites, but other sites should consider only using them in an optional manner.

Suggestion: Do not make a remote the mandatory form of navigation.

Bookmarking

Bookmarking is an important aspect of navigation. Oftentimes, the user will bookmark a page to return to it in the future. In some browsers, the user may even bookmark the page so that it is downloaded for offline viewing or is checked on a regular basis automatically for changes. Traditionally, designers could do little to affect bookmarking other than make it difficult for a user to bookmark a page by using a frame. However, under Internet Explorer 5 and beyond, it is possible to somewhat customize bookmarks, or as they are called in Microsoft parlance, "favorites."

The simplest customization is to create a custom icon to be associated with a bookmark. First, create a small icon you wish users to see, using a tool like IconForge (http://www.cursorarts.com). The icon file must be saved as the .ico type and must be the dimensions 16 pixels by 16 pixels; otherwise, the browser will ignore it. Next, copy the icon to the root directory of your Web server handling pages for a particular domain (e.g., www.democompany.com/favicon.ico). Internet Explorer will automatically use this icon anytime a user sets a favorite or quick link for your site.

 Some people express the concern that a potential privacy risk occurs with a standard bookmark file. Consider that a request for a standard graphic like favicon.ico can be filtered from a log file and used to indicate that the user has bookmarked the page.

It is possible to set a favorite on a page-by-page basis using the HTML **<LINK>** tag, for example:

```
<LINK REL="SHORTCUT ICON"
      HREF="http://www.democompany.com/icons/robot.ico">
```

Most users will utilize a browser's bookmarking menu, but it is possible to add your own custom button so that a user can automatically add the page to their favorites list. The following script shows how you can add a text link that when pressed invokes a dialog box to add the current page to the Favorites menu:

```
<SCRIPT>
<!--
if ((navigator.appVersion.indexOf("MSIE") > 0) &&
(parseInt(navigator.appVersion) >= 4)) {
   document.write("<U><SPAN STYLE='color:blue;cursor:hand;'
   onclick='window.external.AddFavorite(location.href,
   document.title);'>Add this page to your favorites</SPAN></U>");
}
//-->
</SCRIPT>
```

One important consideration with bookmarking is making sure to deal with dynamic data. For example, consider if you have a special URL where you store the latest press release at http://www.democompany.com/latestnews. After a particular item is no longer the latest item, it is moved to an archive and replaced by a new item. Imagine the user's frustration if they bookmark a particular piece of content only to have it change. If you have variable data, you may consider creating a special bookmark button on a page that spawns a new window, using JavaScript as shown by the small modification to the previous script shown here:

```
<SCRIPT>
<!--
archivelocation='http://final-url-goes-here';
```

```
if ((navigator.appVersion.indexOf("MSIE") > 0) &&
(parseInt(navigator.appVersion) >= 4)) {
    document.write("<U><SPAN STYLE='color:blue;cursor:hand;'
    onclick='window.external.AddFavorite(archivelocation,
    document.title);'>Add this page to your favorites</SPAN></U>");
}
//-->
</SCRIPT>
```

Always consider if a page could be an entry point to a site. If it can be, make sure that it is easily bookmarked.

Navigation No-No's

Before concluding this chapter, let's take a look a brief list of navigational no-no's, some of which we have touched on already. None of these problems will completely ruin a site's navigation, but all can frustrate the user greatly.

Back-Button Hijacking

The user's favorite browser button, particularly the novice user, is the Back button. Unfortunately, some sites turn this off through the use of redirection. Be careful of making special pages that just redirect a user to another page instantly. Oftentimes, this is done because of sensing for a particular browser using JavaScript. It is much wiser instead to sense the browser on the server side and build the page to fit. With this model, the user will be able to back out of the page as if it were a regular page.

Pop-Up Windows

Many sites have begun to spawn windows as users begin to leave a site. Oftentimes, these windows contain advertisements for other sites or attempt somehow to keep the user from leaving. Very unscrupulous designers might even attempt to override the user and send them back to the site they are trying to leave. Don't beg. Just let users go if they want to.

Unique Navigation

Users navigate the Web all day, and they don't have a great deal of patience for sites that deviate too much from the norm. Some designers bemoan the rise of navigation sameness that results when people utilize existing conventions. They argue that site navigation has begun to look so similar that users can't tell the difference between sites, and that there is little room for creative flexibility. However, the consistency of site navigation plays to usability. Users have come to understand designs like Amazon or Yahoo! Why deviate too far from such designs when you can reap the benefit of previous user experience? People know how these sites work, just as they understand basic Web conventions such as blue as link color and GUI conventions. Further, consider that most word processors and spreadsheets work the same, so why shouldn't most e-commerce sites follow suit? Remember, you aren't selling navigation to the user!

Heavily Branded Buttons

Overemphasis on navigation elements over content is often due to the designer's attempt to "brand with the buttons" and make the navigation be the design. The idea here is to attempt to build brand through a visually distinctive navigation look. A distinctive-looking button may be memorable to a user, but the odds are against it. Consider the last time you really sat and admired buttons in an elevator. Well, maybe as a designer you might, but ask the person in the elevator with you what they think, and they may consider you a little odd. Again, remember that users use navigation only to accomplish a task they have set out to perform.

Reliance on Back Button

If you rely primarily on the Back button for navigation—particularly on content pages—you may create an orphan page lacking outgoing links. If a user has followed a particular path through the site, the Back button will work fine. However, users may not enter the site the way you think. Consider if the user bookmarks this page and returns another day—the Back button won't get them out

Making Users Work too Hard

Like it or not, people can be somewhat lazy, and will generally prefer sites that don't require much effort to use. This becomes more and more important as the user continues to use the site. The buttons should be placed obviously and be legible. Don't force the user to strain visually, mentally, or physically to use your navigation. Users should not have to recall information about buttons to choose—they should simply have to recognize the choices. Lastly, don't make the user work physically to move around the site. Navigation should always be as effortless as possible. Once again, consider checking the amount of mouse travel by focusing carefully on the distance between subsequent choices.

Rule: Limit scrolling and mouse travel in navigation as much as possible.

Also, consider measuring the number of clicks it takes to reach a destination page. We often consider three to be the maximum number of clicks, but you should not focus solely on clicks; it may be more the page-load time, often due to the network round-trip time, that frustrates the user. Consider limiting your navigation depth to three page loads.

Rule: Consider a maximum of three page loads before a result.

It is easy to build bad navigation, but it is sometimes hard for designers to detect what is bad. The reason is that, as a designer, you are probably going to know how to navigate your own site. Take to heart any complaints you receive from users about site navigation problems. If you suspect a problem, conduct a quick site evaluation focusing on navigation, as discussed in Appendix B.

Summary

In the real world people take different approaches to navigation, depending on the circumstance. For example, people act differently during a museum visit, a park visit, a store visit, or looking for a friend's house. Depending on the task at hand, the navigation techniques vary. Regardless of the site type, the goal of navigation should be simply to help the user find their way. Good navigation should help a user answer location questions such as "Where am I?", "Where can I go?", "How do I get where I want to go?", "Have I been here before?", and "How can I get back to someplace I was?" The use of page labels, URLs, landmark pages, page style, and color can help users identify location. Navigation elements can be added to help users make choices about future destinations. However, the placement and stability of navigation items should be well thought out. While advanced techniques such as hidden menus, frames, and remotes could address some problems, the problems they introduce should be considered before implementation. Lastly, always remember that navigation is a means to an end, not the end itself. Generally, a user is not going to marvel at the beauty of your navigation system; in fact, they probably consider your site a small stop on a much larger journey they are taking on the Web. Sites should not focus on bringing undue attention to their navigation. In fact, if the user notices it too much, we are probably not doing a good job. The next chapters discuss the use of various navigational elements such as links and search engines, and navigational aids such as site maps.

SITE ORGANIZATION AND NAVIGATION

The Complete Reference

Web Design

Chapter 6

Linking: Text, Buttons, Icons, and Graphics

avigation through Web sites is accomplished by selecting links that relate pages to each other. Though the Web follows a relatively simple linking model, the form of links within Web pages varies from HTML text links within body copy to visually rich graphical buttons. Each type of link form has various pros and cons that a designer should be aware of. Particular attention should be paid to making links easily understandable for the user, as poor link usage is a sure way to an unusable site. Proper use and maintenance of links can be difficult, and link problems can easily occur.

The Basic Web Linking Model

The Web's hypertext linking model is relatively simple. Links are traditionally unidirectional, and without building in any special programming will cause a single page to load. The primary way to add links to the Web is using HTML's **<A>** or "anchor" element. Use the **<A>** element to enclose content that will trigger a link and then specify the destination of the link using the **HREF** attribute as shown here:

```
<A HREF="URL of document to load">linked content</A>
```

The **HREF** attribute would be set to the URL (Uniform Resource Locator) of the page to load when the link is activated.

A common way to categorize links is by the address or URL of the document to load. We could describe links to be *internal*, meaning they connect to another page or URL within the site. On the other hand, we could describe a link as being *external* if it connects to a page outside the current site. Internal links would also include *intrapage* links. These are links that jump a user around a single file. An example of an intrapage link is the common "back to top" link that is frequently found in lengthy pages.

Structured Links vs. Unstructured Links

Within Web sites, there tend to be two types of links: those that are consistent and those that are not. For example, consider links within a navigation bar. These links tend to be fairly consistent in position, style, and even destination from page to page. We could call these links *structured* links because their use often fits very closely with the hierarchical structure common to most Web sites. Structured links are beneficial to users who are on a planned mission to find something or accomplish a particular task.

Unstructured links, on the other hand, are those that may appear somewhat random to the user. For example, contextual links within the body of text could be considered *unstructured* links. If I were suddenly to suggest in the middle of a sentence that you see the Robot Butler at http://www.democompany.com/products/butler.htm (as indeed I just did), you'd get a firsthand example of how baffling an unstructured link might appear to a user who encounters one on a Web page. Why, exactly, did I give you a link to the Robot Butler then and there, inviting you to drop the thread of my argument entirely? Unstructured links do not necessarily follow the structure of a Web site and may jump across a site structure or outside a site at any time. However, do not assume that unstructured links should never be used. On the contrary: a site with only consistent navigation links will feel stale. Consider adding a few contextual jumps and exploration links to your pages—primarily to important words and phrases within body text. These tangential links might just encourage a visitor to stay and look around. Not everyone is going to be on a precise mission; letting people wander a bit can be useful.

> **Suggestion: Occasionally provide some unstructured links within document text to promote exploration and thought.**

Be careful with unstructured links, however; as discussed in the previous chapter, logical navigation within a site is central to its usability. Links that appear random to the visitor and numerous cross-links may confuse the user just as easily as delight them.

Static vs. Dynamic Linking

Another way to categorize links on a Web site is in terms of how they are created. Are the links permanently pointing to the same content, or are the links created dynamically based upon content? We call these two link types *static* links and *dynamic* links.

> **Definition: A static link is one where the destination file is hard-coded into the anchor by the document author.**

Most Web sites use predominantly static links. The downside to these types of links is that the meaning of a link may change based upon user desire or context. A dynamic link that could change based upon environment might be better suited to a more interactive Web.

> **Definition: A dynamic link does not have a fixed destination. Instead, the destination document is computed at page-view time according to the environment and needs of the viewer.**

Dynamic links offer two significant advantages over static links. First, dynamic links react to user conditions so they may present different destinations based upon user skill, browser capabilities, user preference, or other environment conditions. Second, dynamic links provide the potential for improved maintenance. A common problem with Web sites is the numerous broken links encountered. A site where links are dynamically determined could avoid this problem since links could be automatically recalculated as pages are added or removed. As discussed later in this chapter, dynamic links could remove the major burden Web designers face in maintaining sites.

A Taxonomy of Link Forms

Links on the Web come in many forms, ranging from basic HTML text links to complex images with irregularly shaped hotspots (called *image maps*). Each form of link has its use and will be examined in turn. Considering the numerous forms that links can take, designers are strongly cautioned to make linked content obvious. Remember: running a mouse all over the screen in an attempt to find the active click regions is generally a tedious or even frustrating task for users. After each form of link is discussed, the techniques for ensuring usable links will be presented.

Text Links

The most basic form of link in a Web page is the *text* link as specified by plain text within an **<A>** tag, as shown here:

```
<A HREF=http://www.democompany.com>Visit Demo Company –
                Makers of the Robot Butler</A>
```

These forms of links are very versatile; they are used both for primary navigation links and as contextual links within large amounts of body copy. Figure 6-1 shows these two forms of links.

A common position for text links within a site is the bottom of a page, as shown in Figure 6-2. These backup links are often used to mimic the links on top of a page or provide alternative link forms in place of heavy graphical link forms such as image maps. Many advanced users instinctively scroll down to the bottom of slow-loading, graphical-laden pages looking for text links to use instead.

Suggestion: Always provide textual links at the bottom of pages when using long pages or pages with graphical buttons.

Text links are very useful because they are very lightweight; their download time is minimal. It is easy to update them or even make them completely dynamic.

The major downside to text links is that they are often difficult to spot, particularly when designers change link feedback such as color or underlining (discussed later in the chapter). While fixed navigation links may be relatively easy to spot, text links buried within content will become nearly invisible when link decoration is modified dramatically. Discussion of link color and decoration for usability is presented later in this chapter.

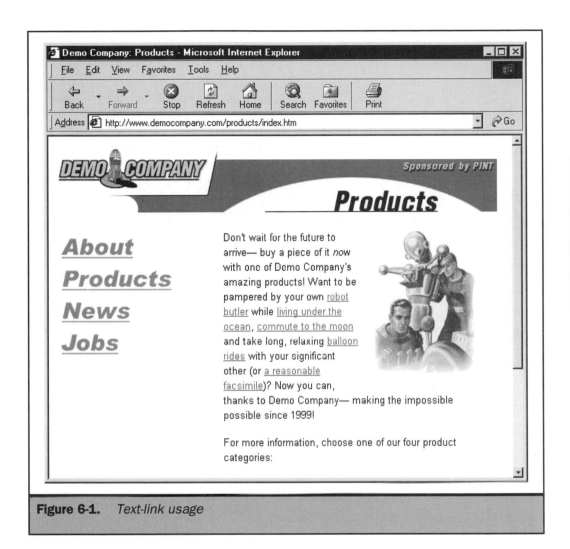

Figure 6-1.   *Text-link usage*

Graphic Text Links

Because text links are rather simple and may not support the marketing goals of Web sites, some designers opt to use graphic text links. Up until the release of 4.0-generation browsers, the only way to accurately control text appearance on the Web was to make

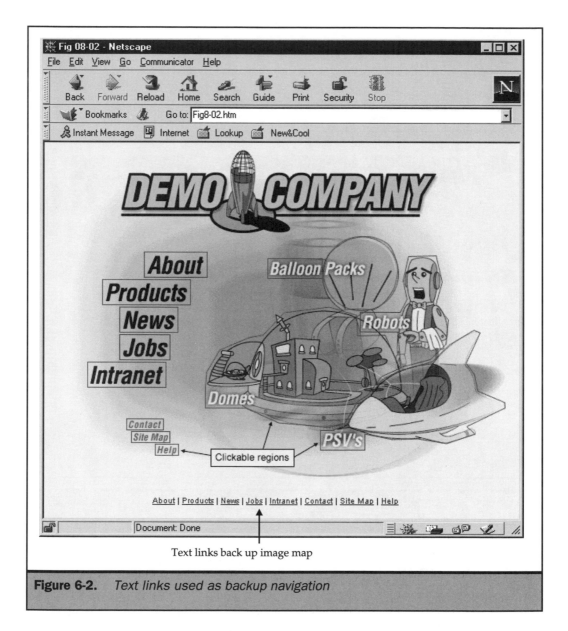

Figure 6-2. *Text links used as backup navigation*

an image out of graphics. For significant navigation links, designers would often create graphical text buttons.

To ensure that these graphic text items appear pressable, designers often choose a different font for the text buttons, change their color, increase their size, set the text away from other content or use an effect such as a drop shadow. Figure 6-3 shows a variety of examples of text treatments used to make graphic text buttons.

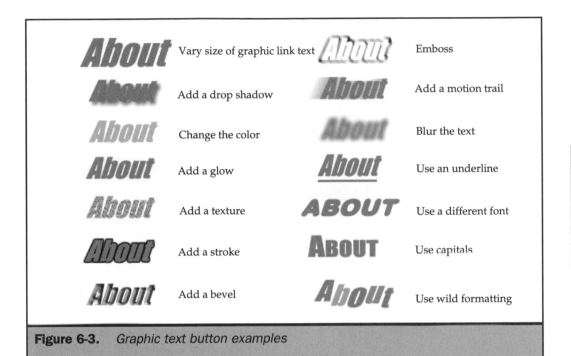

Figure 6-3.   *Graphic text button examples*

A major downside of graphic text buttons is that even when optimized they can result in significant download times, particularly when combined with rollover states. No matter how much optimization is employed, the word "About" in plain text will always be smaller than a GIF image containing it. Furthermore, image buttons may limit accessibility in many cases. Without alternative text, they cannot be translated to nonvisual environments; even within a graphics environment, they may not change to fit the resolution of the viewing environment.

Creating Styled Text Links Using Fireworks

As a short demonstration of graphic button creation, we'll create a small navigation bar using a popular image-editing program, Macromedia Fireworks (www.macromedia.com/fireworks).

Among professional graphic designers, Adobe Photoshop (www.adobe.com) is probably the leading image-editing program, but using Fireworks 3 it is easy to create buttons and all matter of Web-site graphics. The purpose of this demo is to show the basic approach people take when creating graphic buttons.

Using Fireworks 3 (or later), create a small document around 250 pixels high by 200 pixels wide.

Select the Text tool, which looks like this, from the Tool palette on the left.

In the Text Tool dialog box, add some text for the various buttons. In this case, we added About, Products, News, and Jobs. We selected a 36-point Impact font with a red-orange color (#CC3300) for the text, as shown here.

After inserting the text into the document, select the Fireworks text box with the arrow and then choose Effect from the Window menu.

Select Shadow and Glow from the drop-down menu in the Effect window and then select Drop Shadow. Adjust the degree of the shadow effect to make the text look as if it is sitting above the page. When done with restraint, this will make the text stand out from the normal text in the page and look more pressable. The final dialog boxes to complete the effect are shown in Figure 6-4.z

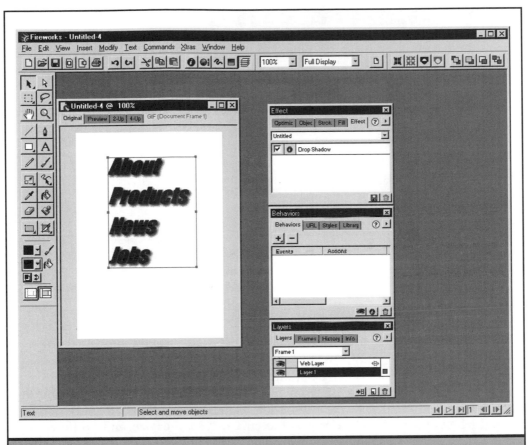

Figure 6-4.   *Creating text drop shadows in Fireworks*

At this point the text images can be directly exported, either as a single image or as individual slices. Using Fireworks, it is also possible to make the graphic text into buttons.

First, use the Arrow tool to select the text box already in the document.

From the Insert menu, select Hotspot to add a hotspot on top of the text box.

Size the hotspot region, which should be colored light blue, over the text to make it active, then set the destination URL and **ALT** text as shown here.

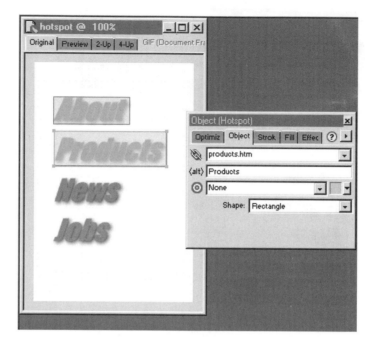

Note that using a single text region with hotspots will create an image map. It is possible to create each button separately and make each a button. The process is similar and will be used when making the buttons in Fireworks later on in this chapter.

No matter the graphics tool used, always remember as you make your graphic text buttons to make sure to make the buttons look significantly different than the body text or page labels used in the site. Using a different color, a larger size, and a different style like oblique or effects like drop shadows will help users understand that these graphical text elements are clickable.

Creating Stylized Text Buttons in CSS

The major downside to graphic buttons is that they take time to download. With the rise of cascading style sheets, it is now possible to create appealing text links without a graphics editor. To create drop-shadowed links like the previous section, we could create two words of slightly different color and offset them from each other. The HTML markup sample below shows how this could be performed:

```
<!DOCTYPE HTML PUBLIC "-//W3C//DTD HTML 4.0 Transitional//EN">
<HTML>
<HEAD>
<TITLE>CSS Styled Text Links</TITLE>
<SCRIPT>
```

```
<!--
(document.layers || document.all) ? css=true : css=false;
//-->
</SCRIPT>
<STYLE>
<!--
.dropshadow {position: relative;
left: 50px;
   font-size: 30px;
   font-family: Impact;
   font-style: oblique;
   color: black;
   font-weight: bold;
   letter-spacing: 2px;}
 .buttontext {position: relative;
top: -35px;
left: 46px;
      font-size: 30px;
      font-family: Impact;
      font-style: oblique;
      color: #CC3300;
      font-weight: bold;
      letter-spacing: 2px;}
A {text-decoration: none;}
A:hover {text-decoration: underline;}
-->
</STYLE>
</HEAD>
<BODY>
<A HREF="about.htm">
<SCRIPT>
<!--
if (css)
   document.write('<DIV CLASS="dropshadow"> About </DIV>');
//-->
</SCRIPT>
<DIV CLASS="buttontext"> About </DIV>
</A>
</BODY>
</HTML>
```

Note   *Weblink: You can find this code online at http://www.webdesignref/chapter6/ csstextlinks.htm.*

Note that this code relies heavily on CSS. A nonstyle-sheet-aware browser would output the text link About twice, so we need to use JavaScript to detect for a 4.0-generation or better browser before adding in the second text line. Even in CSS-aware browsers, the results may not be consistent. Figure 6-5 shows the result in Internet Explorer 4, Netscape 4, and Netscape 3 under Windows.

CSS2 defines the text-shadow property that could be used to create drop shadows. To create a special drop-shadow class, you might define a CSS rule like this:

```
.dropshadow    {text-shadow: black 0.2em 0.2em}
```

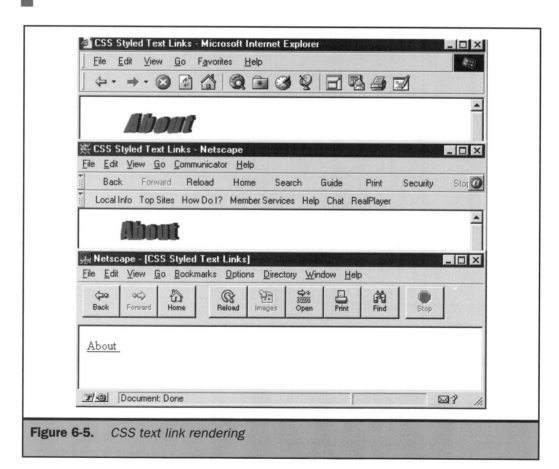

Figure 6-5.   *CSS text link rendering*

This will place a small black shadow to the right and below an object. Setting values to negative could change the shadow to appear on the left or above an object. It is also possible to set a blur value:

```
H1 { text-shadow: red 4px 4px 5px}
```

This specifies that all **<H1>** elements should have a 4-pixel shadow to the right and below with a 5-pixel blur radius. While text shadow would certainly simplify the creation of drop shadows in CSS, 4.X- and early 5.X-generation browsers do not support it.

Buttons

Stylizing a link to make it look like a button is a good way to improve the usability of site links. It is possible to make both custom buttons with graphics or utilize HTML form buttons. For example, putting a stroke around a button and giving it some relief is an easy way to make a region look pressable. There is a variety of button styles that can be employed, as shown in Figure 6-6.

Creating Buttons in Fireworks

With a tool such as Photoshop or Fireworks, it is fairly straightforward to create graphic push buttons.

The following demonstration will again use Macromedia's Fireworks.

From within your sample document, select the New Button command from the Insert menu.

In the Button dialog box, draw a rectangle using the Rectangle tool from the main Tool palette. The Rectangle Tool icon is shown here.

Double-click on the tool to reveal options to draw a rectangle with rounded corners. In this example, draw a rectangle with a 60 value for the corners.

Set the background color for the button to whatever color you desire. In this example, we used #FFCC00.

Now make the button look pressable by selecting Effect from the Window menu.

From the Effect dialog box, select Bevel and Emboss from the pull-down menu. Now tune the values to create the size of the bevel for the menu.

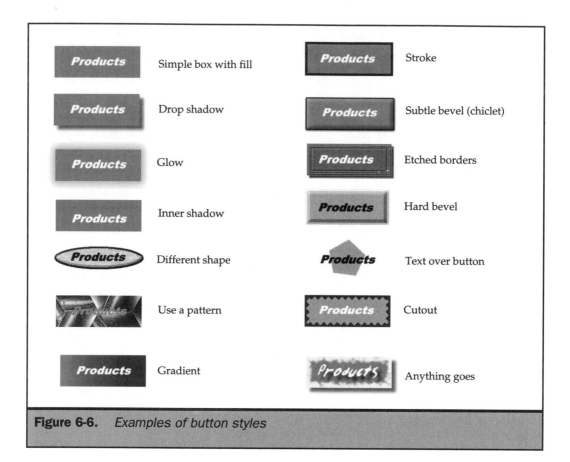

Figure 6-6. *Examples of button styles*

Once the button has been created, add some white text to the button for its label. You should have something similar to the screen shown in Figure 6-7.

Once a single button is made, just replicate it and change the label text. Fireworks supports numerous effects that can be used on buttons, and even allows easy creation of multiple-state buttons called *rollovers*. These are discussed later in this chapter.

Creating Buttons Using HTML

Like graphic text links, graphic buttons do incur download and can be difficult to update. The upside is that they are often more visually appealing than standard links. With more advanced HTML and CSS, it is possible to create lightweight buttons of your own.

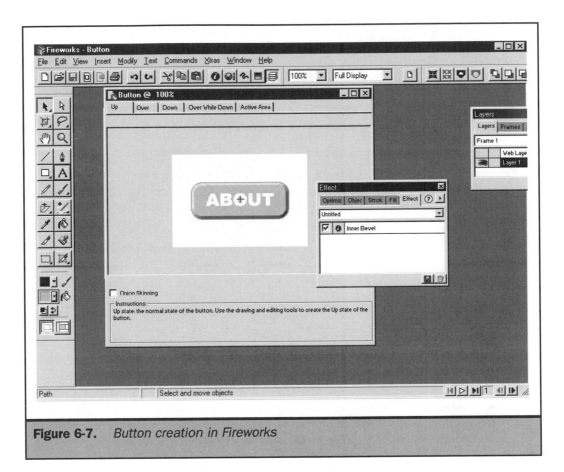

Figure 6-7.   *Button creation in Fireworks*

The easiest way to create buttons in HTML is using colored table cells. Setting the table cells to a background color, and potentially even turning the border on, can create very nice text-style buttons like this:

While this may look like a button, it really isn't since only the text is clickable. This is yet another reason to keep the underlining on. To create the button shown here, use the following markup:

```
<!DOCTYPE HTML PUBLIC "-//W3C//DTD HTML 4.0 Transitional//EN">
<HTML>
<HEAD>
<TITLE>HTML Table Buttons</TITLE>
</HEAD>
<BODY LINK="black" VLINK="black" ALINK="white">
<TABLE BORDER="1" BORDERCOLOR="black">
<TR>
<TD BGCOLOR="#CC3300">
 
<FONT FACE="Verdana,Helvetica,sans-serif" SIZE="+2">
<A HREF="products.htm">Products</A>
</FONT>
 
</TD>
</TR>
</TABLE>
</BODY>
</HTML>
```

Note   *Weblink: See this code online at http://www.webdesignref.com/chapter6/ htmltablebuttons.htm.*

Note   *Some older browsers (notably Netscape 2) will allow you to set the font color but not the table color. Be careful when using white text on colored table cells if these browsers are used, as the button text may not show at all if the background of the page itself is white.*

It is also possible to create simple buttons using the form **<INPUT>** element:

```
<FORM>
  <INPUT TYPE="BUTTON" VALUE="Yahoo!"
onClick="location='http://www.yahoo.com'">
</FORM>
```

Unfortunately this particular example will only work in a JavaScript-aware browser when the script is turned on. With a Submit button, it is possible to deal with any browser type:

```
<FORM METHOD="GET"
                ACTION="http://www.yahoo.com">
<INPUT TYPE="SUBMIT" VALUE="Yahoo!">
</FORM>
```

Note	*While this will work, it has a drawback. As in the case of a form submission, the code will append a question mark to the URL it attempts to call. Unlike an actual form submission, however, no parameters are passed, so the question mark is not followed by the typical string of trailing words and symbols. The unusual appearance of the resulting URL may confuse the user.*

Given the appearance of form buttons, along with a user's belief they are related to some form such as an order form, designers are warned not to use form buttons to trigger links.

Creating Buttons Using CSS

Using CSS, it is possible to create all manner of simple buttons. Later, we'll see that combined with a little JavaScript it is even possible to make the buttons act like buttons. The markup shown here creates a simple button with a drop shadow:

```
<!DOCTYPE HTML PUBLIC "-//W3C//DTD HTML 4.0 Transitional//EN">
<HTML>
<HEAD>
<TITLE>CSS Buttons</TITLE>
<STYLE>
<!--
.dropshadow {position: relative;
             left: 52px;
             top: 5px;
             font-size: 30px;
             font-family: Impact;
             font-style: oblique;
             background-color: black;
             font-weight: bold;
             letter-spacing: 2px;
             height: 30px;
             width: 100px;}

.buttontext {position: relative;
             top: -35px;
             left: 46px;
             font-size: 30px;
             font-family: Impact;
             font-style: oblique;
             background-color: #CC3300;
             color: white;
             font-weight: bold;
```

```
                        letter-spacing: 2px;
                        height: 30px;
                        width: 100px;}
A {text-decoration: none; cursor: hand;}
-->
</STYLE>
</HEAD>
<BODY>
<BR><BR>
<A HREF="about.htm">
<DIV CLASS="dropshadow">   </DIV>
<DIV CLASS="buttontext">  About  </DIV>
</A>
</BODY>
</HTML>
```

Note　　*Weblink: You can find this code online at http://www.webdesignref.com/chapter6/cssbuttons.htm.*

With CSS border properties, it is easy to create all manner of clickable regions that have bevels, color, or even patterned backgrounds, as shown by this example:

```
<!DOCTYPE HTML PUBLIC "-//W3C//DTD HTML 4.0 Transitional//EN">
<HTML>
<HEAD>
<TITLE>CSS Buttons 2</TITLE>
<STYLE>
<!--
.button    {border-style: inset;
            border-color: #0066FF;
            background-color: #CC3300;
            background-image: url("blueswirls.gif");
            width: 80px;
            text-align: center;}

A.buttontext {color: white;
              text-decoration: none;
              font: bold 12pt Verdana;
              cursor: hand;}
-->
```

```
</STYLE>
</HEAD>
<BODY>
<A HREF="about.htm" CLASS="buttontext">
<DIV CLASS="button">About</DIV></A>
</BODY>
</HTML>
```

 Weblink: *You can find this online at http://www.webdesignref.com/chapter6/ cssbuttons2.htm.*

Under Internet Explorer, the previous markup produces this style of button.

Unfortunately, because of the bugs in many browsers' CSS implementation, this example does not work properly in Netscape. Even within Explorer, setting the width explicitly is not the best approach since it does not allow the text to easily scale. Hopefully, however, the demos suggest that in the near future creating stylized push buttons will no longer require as much image manipulation.

Icons

An icon is a small picture used on a screen to represent some action or content. Icons can be used alone or with words. By themselves, icons can save space. A very visual icon can often say more in a few pixels than even a few words can. Consider the following icons and their equivalent words.

 HOME

 E-MAIL

 PRINT

An icon also can just as easily become as decipherable as ancient Egyptian hieroglyphics. Consider the meaning of the following common Windows system icons:

**Icons Without
Labels**   **Match with Meaning**

Internet options   World time

Add/Remove programs   Tools

Regional settings   Directory assistance

ODBC data sources (32 bit)

Without labels, it is very difficult to decipher the meanings of icons unless the
idea is very simple. Without their associated text labels, it is somewhat difficult to
understand some icons. The icon of the earth may be well understood, but its meaning
within the context of a page might vary from a button to access some multinational
corporation's global home page to a link about geography. A label brings clarity to
the meaning of an icon. Consider the same icons now with their labels. They are far
easier to deal with.

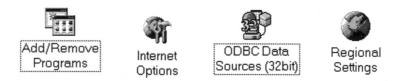

Unfortunately, with their labels showing, icons lose their space advantage.
With the **TITLE** attribute, as discussed later in this chapter, it is possible to hide
icon labels until a user puts the pointer over the icon. However, site designers should
try to show labels wherever possible to avoid users having to explore a button to
determine what it means.

Regardless of label usage, icons may retain some advantages over text links. Icons
are often easier for users to recognize than words. Even when icons are difficult for
people to decipher, people may still be able to recall their meaning over time more
easily than words. Remember how people often remember faces but not names?
Consider the Paste icon common to many desktop applications.

Does the clipboard really say "paste," when you think about it? Can you even tell this is a clipboard at such a small size? Over time, it may not matter what icons represent—simply that the user knows that when they press the picture of the magnifying glass over the paper, they get a print preview. In this sense, many common desktop icons have become somewhat idiomatic to the user. As the Web grows, some icons will certainly become commonplace and their meaning fairly well understood. Most of these icons will probably owe some heritage to desktop applications, but some may be new. Table 6-1 presents a few common icons used on the Web and their typical meanings.

Note *The particular style for the icon is inconsequential. Consider the shape to be the primary focus of the icon.*

This is not a complete list of icons, nor will all Web users always understand these icons, though most should find them familiar, particularly when combined with text labels. If you desire to make your own icons, it is possible to use any image manipulation program, but icon creation tools such as AX-Icons (http://www.axialis.com/axicons/) may make the process easier.

Be careful not to fall into the trap of assuming that icons make it possible to provide perfectly transparent site navigation without relying on the user to actually read anything. While it may be true that users don't have to be able to read to decipher an icon, consider what happens next. If an illiterate user or non-native speaker can decipher an icon's meaning, they still will typically end up at content that they may not be able to consume because of their language skills. In summary, don't think that use of icons will solve all localization issues. As discussed in Chapter 3, usability makes interface design somewhat tricky.

Image Maps

Many visual Web interfaces use image maps or large images with clickable regions called hotspots. Image maps are very popular because they afford the designer the ability to make arbitrary click shapes. In the case of buttons or icons, the clicking region is square or rectangular. With an image map, rectangles, circles, and arbitrary polygon shapes are possible.

Task Icon

Email (send email or contact)

Print

Post (message to discussion board)

Discuss or chat

Make a comment

Contact

Download or save

Bookmark

Access shopping cart

Edit

Delete

Close

Attach

Table 6-1. *Common Icons Found on Web Sites*

Navigation Icon

Home

Back

Forward

Up (top of page or back up a level)

Help

Search

Something within (next level)

Content Icon

Audio

Video

Picture attachment

Picture blowup

Acrobat file

New information

"Cool" information

SITE ORGANIZATION AND NAVIGATION

Table 6-1.   *Common Icons Found on Web Sites* (continued)

Image maps as defined in HTML come in two forms: client-side and server-side. Server-side image maps are defined by the inclusion of the **ISMAP** attribute and a link to a map file on a remote server, as illustrated by this simple example:

```
<A HREF="shapes.map">
<IMG SRC="shapes.gif" ISMAP BORDER="0" WIDTH="400" HEIGHT="200">
</A>
```

The map file would contain coordinates indicating the hotspots as well as the URL to fetch when a particular hotspot is selected. A sample map file might look like this:

```
rect rectangle.htm 6,50 140,143
circle circle.htm 195,100 144,86
poly polygon.htm 256,120 306,52 333,58 336,0 386,
73 372,119 322,172 256,120 256,119 256,119 258,118

default defaultreg.htm
```

The problem with server-side image maps is twofold. First, decoding where a user should go based on where they clicked requires a visit to the server, where the server interprets the map file. The network round-trip could slow the user down. Second, as the user mouses over the various parts of the image, coordinates—rather than a URL—are shown in the status bar.

Coordinates of the pointer position are less-than-ideal feedback for users who often consult the URL for information about link destination. Fortunately, server-side image maps are primarily a thing of the past. All modern browsers support client-side image maps. A client-side image is defined using the **USEMAP** attribute for the **<IMG>** element. The **USEMAP** is set to reference a **<MAP>** element somewhere else in the file that indicates the hotspots in the image. The following simple example illustrates the HTML markup required for a basic client-side image map:

```
<!DOCTYPE HTML PUBLIC "-//W3C//DTD HTML 4.0 Transitional//EN">
<HTML>
<HEAD>
<TITLE>Client-side Imagemap</TITLE>
</HEAD>
<BODY>
<H1 ALIGN="CENTER">Client-side Imagemap Test</H1>
```

```
<DIV ALIGN="CENTER">
<IMG SRC="shapes.gif" USEMAP="#shapes" BORDER="0" WIDTH="400"
    HEIGHT="200">
</DIV>

<MAP NAME="shapes">
<AREA SHAPE="RECT" COORDS="6,50,140,143"
      HREF="rectangle.htm" ALT="Rectangle">
<AREA SHAPE="CIRCLE" COORDS="195,100,50"
      HREF="circle.htm" ALT="Circle">
<AREA SHAPE="POLY"
      COORDS="255,122,306,53,334,62,338,0,388,
              77,374,116,323,171,255,122"
    HREF="polygon.htm" ALT="Polygon">
<AREA SHAPE="DEFAULT" HREF="defaultreg.htm">
</MAP>

</BODY>
</HTML>
```

Note *Weblink: See this code online at www.webdesignref.com/chapter6/clientsidemap.htm.*

Despite the daunting markup involved in specifying active regions in an image, creating an image map doesn't have to be difficult. A variety of image-mapping tools exists for creating maps. Popular editors such as Macromedia's Dreamweaver provide simple editing of image maps, as shown in Figure 6-8.

Before defining an image map, make sure you are not going to modify the image. If you resize an image or move things around, the hotspots will not be adjusted and may not relate. Making an image map is generally the last part of a layout.

The primary benefit of image maps is that they allow irregular hotspots, which can be used to create interesting interfaces such as the one shown in Figure 6-9. In this example, rolling over the various parts on the robot reveals information about its features.

Note *Weblink: See this code online at http://www.democompany.com/products/buddy.htm.*

A secondary benefit of image maps is that they may reduce the number of requests to a server. Designers will often cut up menu bars into multiple images, particularly when trying to create rollover images. A second-generation rollover script using image maps will be discussed later in this chapter. Always remember that file size isn't

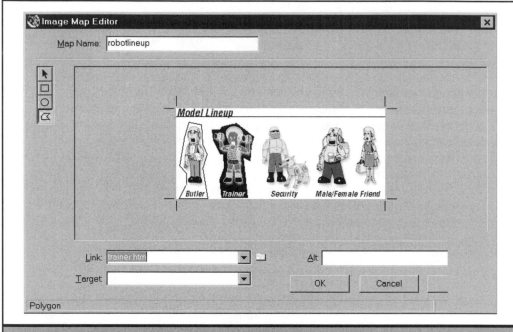

Figure 6-8. *Drawing an image map using Dreamweaver*

everything; with a page laden with many small changes, the increased number of connections to a server may slow page loading significantly. Because a single image map may include many hotspots, a large navigation bar with multiple image requests can be reduced to a single request—although the resulting image map may be quite large.

The main problem with image maps is that they tend to encourage very lush layouts that may result in significant download time. Furthermore, image maps tend to be less accessible than standard link forms, particularly for nonvisual-rendering environments. Because of this, designers are always encouraged to provide secondary navigation links for image maps as shown in Figure 6-10.

> **Suggestion: When using image maps, always provide a secondary navigation form such as text links.**

Other Link Forms

Besides text links, buttons, and image maps, there are many other objects that can trigger a page load or action. The most common are a special form of advertising

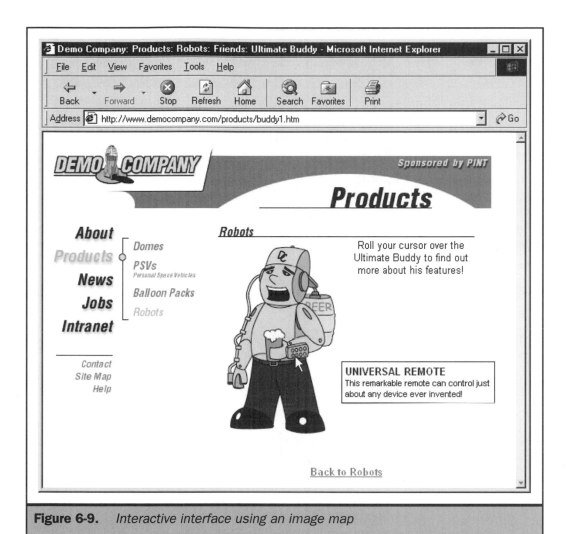

Figure 6-9.   *Interactive interface using an image map*

button called a banner ad and modified form elements. However, with the rise of HTML 4.0, it will be possible to make anything trigger a page load.

Banners

Given the commercial nature of many Web sites, banner ads are frequently found. Banner ads come in many sizes and are often animated. Clicking on the ad will generally take the user to the advertiser's site. The effectiveness of the advertisement is often measured by its click-through rate, meaning the percentage of people who see the

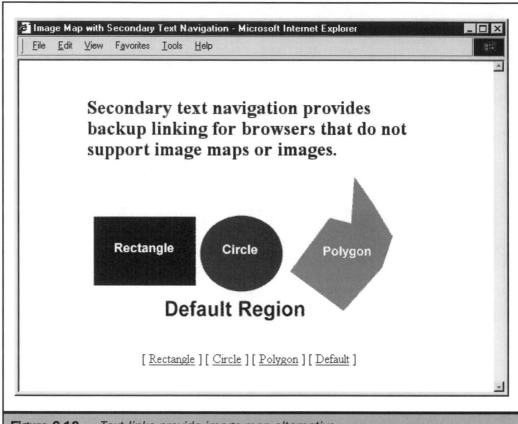

Figure 6-10.   *Text links provide image-map alternative*

ad vs. those who actually click on it. Unfortunately, over the years, the click-through rate for banners has plummeted. Some experts attribute this to a phenomenon dubbed "banner blindness." Basically, banner blindness suggests that users have become so accustomed to the size, shape, and placement of banners that they can easily ignore them. Because of this, designers are warned to avoid making nonadvertising links in a similar style.

Tip   *Avoid making your buttons similar in size or style to banner advertisements.*

Regardless of your particular take on the usefulness of banners, they are a common link form, and it is important to understand their conventions. The Internet Advertising Bureau (www.iab.net) specifies the standard banner sizes shown in Table 6-2.

Banner Type	Size in Pixels
Full banner	468 x 60
Full banner with vertical navigation bar	392 x 72
Half banner	334 x 60
Square banner	125 x 125
Vertical banner	120 x 240
Button #1	120 x 90
Button #2	120 x 60
Micro button	88 x 31

Table 6-2.   *Common Banner Sizes*

SITE ORGANIZATION AND NAVIGATION

Banner forms other than those shown in the table may be available, depending on the site. Furthermore, the size of the banner in kilobytes and the possibility for animation may vary from site to site. For example, the banner network LinkExchange (www.linkexchange.com) had a limit of 10KB for banner ads and seven seconds of animation without looping at the time of this book's writing. Make sure to check the specifications of your banner network before creating banners.

Using GUI Widgets for Link Triggering

Many sites have come to rely on using various form widgets for navigation in a site. Probably the most common form element used to trigger links is the pull-down menu. Many sites utilize a pull-down menu as a quick-jump facility to move from page to page.

While the pull-down has become commonplace and appears to be fairly well understood by users, the use of other form elements for navigation purposes should be avoided. In particular, neither radio buttons nor check boxes should ever be used in this manner. However, the use of generic form buttons, while not encouraged, is acceptable, though be aware that it may suggest to the user a function other than page loading. A full discussion with code and solutions to command problems using GUI widgets is presented in Chapter 12.

Hotspots Everywhere?

With the introduction of HTML 4, it is now possible to make nearly every HTML element clickable using the **onClick** core event handler and attaching it to JavaScript. For example, try the following HTML markup with a small JavaScript attached to the **onClick** attribute:

```
<P onClick="location='http://www.yahoo.com'">
Is this a link? Maybe or maybe not.</P>
```

If you are using Internet Explorer 4 or better, clicking the paragraph will actually load a new page. However, if your scripting support is off or you are using an older browser, nothing will happen. Regardless of browser support, the potential for problems should be obvious. With the ability to make anything clickable, the possibility of confusing the user becomes great. The next section deals with how to ensure it is obvious what is clickable in a page and what is not.

Link Implementation Issues: Usability, Feedback, and Support

No matter what link form or combination of link forms a site employs, when it comes to the actual implementation of links on a site, certain interface design considerations will always apply: Links should enhance rather than detract from a site's overall usability. They should provide adequate feedback to the user about what they signify, and they should be an adequately supported feature of the site rather than being left to bear the entire burden of site navigation on their own. The next section addresses these general implementation issues by taking up a series of specific topics that relate to them: link usability, rollovers, user expectations, the use of scope notes, and, finally, keyboard support for links.

Usable Links

Like it or not, users expect links to be blue and underlined. Furthermore, they expect buttons to literally look pressable, which often means using hackneyed effects like bevels or drop shadows. Unfortunately, some designers do not find these conventions conducive to appealing layout and often just downright ignore them. Before breaking rules in favor of look, it is important to understand the usability of links. Always remember that it won't matter how good the site looks if the user can't figure it out.

Link Colors

The default link colors on the Web are blue for nonvisited links, red for links that are being activated (pressed), and purple for visited links. It is also possible under the CSS2 specification to modify the color of a link when a pointing device is hovering over or about to select a link.

Link colors can easily be overridden using HTML or CSS. Changing link colors in HTML requires modifying attributes for the **<BODY>** element, while CSS relies on pseudo class rules for the **<A>** element. Table 6-3 shows the link types, colors, and modification syntax.

Some consideration of the position of the CSS rules for link colors should be made. The order of definition within a global or linked style sheet should be unvisited, visited, hover, and, finally, active. Any other order may produce incorrect results considering that cascade will cause style rules to be potentially overriding.

Changing link colors significantly from their blue/red/purple settings is dangerous. For better or worse, users have come to understand that blue is the color of links and purple is the color of links they have already pressed. Changing link color is important so that users know where they have been. This is often called "bread crumbing" in the spirit of Hansel and Gretel, where the children drop bread crumbs to find their way out of the forest. Unfortunately, site designers occasionally feel that it is useful to override bread

Link Type	Standard Color	HTML Tag	CSS Pseudo Class Rule
Unvisited	Blue	<BODY LINK="*colorvalue*">	A:link {color: *colorvalue*}
Visited	Purple	<BODY VLINK="*colorvalue*">	A:visited {color: *colorvalue*}
Hover	N/A	N/A	A: hover {color: *colorvalue*}
Active	Red	<BODY ALINK="*colorvalue*">	A:active {color: *colorvalue*}

Table 6-3.   *Link Types and Colors*

crumbing for marketing reasons. The idea might be that if the user can't tell they have been to a certain page before, they might be encouraged to revisit. While it might seem a good idea at first to encourage multiple page views, consider the frustration of a user going around in circles revisiting pages they already saw before.

Rule: Never completely remove visited link indication.

Another reason for changing link colors might be for aesthetics. The blue or purple color combination just might not fit with corporate colors. Of course, once changed, the visited links may look better to some, but the end user might not recognize links or know which links they have visited before.

Rule: Avoid changing link colors.

If link colors must be changed for some reason, always make sure there is a great contrast between unvisited and visited links. Also, make sure that link colors contrast enough with background colors to easily be seen. Poor color choices can make a site difficult to use for most people and impossible for those with any vision impairment. For a more in-depth discussion of color use on the Web, see Chapter 11.

Link Decoration

Under common browsers, links are often indicated not only by color but also by underlining. The second form of feedback is useful particularly when users are not sensitive to color changes. Because of this, designers should be sensitive to the use of underlines in design. The HTML **<U>** tag and the CSS **text-decoration** property both can be used to create underlines like so:

```
<U>This looks like a link</U><BR>
<SPAN STYLE="text-decoration: underline">
This also looks like a link</SPAN>
```

Unfortunately, this type of text can confuse the user who attempts to click on it thinking that it is a link, which inspires the following design rule.

Rule: Avoid underlining nonlinked text in Web documents— use italics or bold instead.

While underlining is useful to provide a second form of link feedback beyond color, a page filled with underlined text often does not look terribly pleasing. Because of this, many people opt to turn off link underlining in a browser preference. Users who do this should not be a primary concern, but they do provide an additional reason not to alter link color significantly. However, with CSS, it is now possible for designers to turn off text-link decoration themselves using the **text-decoration** property as shown by the following rule:

```
A    {text-decoration: none}
```

Of course, this could make it very difficult for users to determine what is linked text. Another form of feedback should be added to linked text, such as changing its font family, size, style, or background color. For example, with underlines turned off, linked text could be indicated by using slightly larger text, bold text, italic text, a varied text style such as small caps, changing background colors, or even changing the font family in use. As discussed in Chapter 10, when using text it is important to set up a clear type hierarchy and provide enough of a difference between font size, style, and family for a user to clearly distinguish differences. When the changes are subtle, the link text will look too similar to the normal text and confuse the user. Table 6-4 presents the methods for distinguishing links when the underlining is turned off and the style rule to implement them.

While many designers find underlining less than pleasing, users do understand underlined text as links. So be careful when changing link appearance.

> **Suggestion: Avoid automatically turning off link underlining. If you do, add another link indicator form.**

Link Feedback: Cursors

Often, browsers will indicate that something is a link or is pressable by changing the cursor. In most GUI systems, the typical cursor is an arrow or pointer that changes to a

Link Indication	CSS Rule
Larger text	A {text-decoration: none; font-size: larger;}
Bold	A {text-decoration: none; font-weight: bold;}
Italic	A {text-decoration: none; font-style: italic;}
Small caps	A {text-decoration: none; font-variant: small-caps;}
Background color	A {text-decoration: none; background-color: yellow;}
Different font	A {text-decoration: none; font-family: cursive;}

Table 6-4.   *Other Forms of Link Indication Using CSS*

hand when something can be clicked or an I-beam when something can be typed into (such as a form field). CSS2 and CSS3 introduce the ability to change the cursor for an element using the **cursor** property.

For example, to set the cursor when a user moves over any **<B>** tag to make it appear pressable, use a style rule like the following:

```
<B STYLE="cursor: hand">Can you press me?</B>
```

CSS2 defines a variety of cursors, as shown in Table 6-5.

The CSS3 specification proposes a variety of new cursor property values, as shown in Table 6-6.

Typical renderings for these cursor values were not possible since no browser supported these values at the time of this book's writing.

Custom Cursors

In theory, CSS2 defines the ability to define a custom cursor. On a Windows system, cursors are defined using a .cur file, which is a 32 × 32 or smaller bitmap—generally with 16 colors. Cursors are also occasionally animated, and in this case may have .ani file extension. According to the CSS2 specification, a browser should retrieve a cursor file from a specified URL—similar to retrieving a font. The property takes a list of cursor values separated by commas. So the CSS rule

```
#specialcursor    {cursor: url("robot.cur"),
                   url("robot.csr"), default;}
```

would specify to set the cursor to either robot.cur, robot.csr, or the default cursor when the user's mouse passes over the element whose **ID** attribute is set to **specialcursor**.

At the time of this writing, no browsers support downloadable cursors natively. However, Comet Systems (www.cometsystems.com) supports both an ActiveX control as well as a Netscape plug-in that can provide similar functionality—including support for animated cursors.

CURSOR TRACKING IN JAVASCRIPT   While it may not be possible in many browsers to set the cursor shape, it is fairly easy to attach a small GIF or JPEG image to a cursor using JavaScript and style sheets and have it follow the cursor around the screen. Various effects, including an animated image that literally chases the cursor, are possible. The JavaScript presented here shows a simple example of how to make a custom cursor under Internet Explorer 4.X and beyond:

```
<!DOCTYPE HTML PUBLIC "-//W3C//DTD HTML 4.0 Transitional//EN">
<HTML>
<HEAD>
<TITLE>JavaScript Cursor Demo</TITLE>
</HEAD>
<BODY>
<SCRIPT LANGUAGE="JavaScript1.2">
<!--
function MainMouseEvent(e) {
   customcursor.left=event.clientX + document.body.scrollLeft;
   customcursor.top=event.clientY + document.body.scrollTop; }

function Initialize() {
   customcursor=document.all.cursorlayer.style;
   document.onmousemove = MainMouseEvent; }

var IE = (document.all) ? true:false;  // make sure IE
if (IE) {
  document.writeln('<DIV ID="cursorlayer"
  STYLE="position:absolute; ');
  document.writeln('top:-32; left:-32; width:32; height:32">');
  document.writeln('<IMG NAME="cursorimg" SRC="yourcursor.gif"');
  document.writeln(' border=0>');
  document.writeln('</DIV>');

  window.onload = Initialize;}
//-->
</SCRIPT>


<BR><BR>Insert your page content here.<BR><BR>

</BODY>
</HTML>
```

Note   *Weblink: See this code online at http://www.webdesignref.com/chapter6/ customcursor.htm.*

To use the code, simply create a cursor that is 32 pixels by 32 pixels, save it as a GIF image, and substitute the text that reads "yourcursor.gif" for your cursor's filename. The image should then track the cursor as you move around the screen.

While it is possible to create a cross-browser version of this cursor code, Netscape 4.X–generation browsers are so buggy that correctly written code to implement custom

CSS Cursor Property Value	Description	Typical Rendering
auto	The browser determines the cursor to display based on the current context.	N/A
crosshair	A simple crosshair generally resembles a plus symbol.	
default	The browser's default cursor generally is an arrow.	
move	This indicates something is to be moved; usually rendered as four arrows together.	
e-resize	This indicates resizing as an arrow pointing east (to the right).	
ne-resize	This indicates resizing as an arrow pointing northeast (to the top right).	
nw-resize	This indicates resizing as an arrow pointing northwest (to the top left).	
n-resize	This indicates resizing as an arrow pointing north (up).	
se-resize	This indicates resizing as an arrow pointing southeast (down to the right).	
sw-resize	This indicates resizing as an arrow pointing southwest (down to the left).	
s-resize	This indicates resizing as an arrow pointing south (down).	
w-resize	This indicates resizing as an arrow pointing west (to the left).	
text	This indicates text that may be selected or entered; generally rendered as an I-bar.	
Wait	This indicates that the page is busy; generally rendered as a watch or hourglass.	
Help	This indicates that Help is available; the cursor is often rendered as a question mark or a balloon.	

Table 6-5. *CSS2 Cursors and Typical Renderings*

CSS 3 Cursor Property	Meaning
Copy	Indicates something is to be copied. Could be rendered as an arrow with a small plus sign next to it.
Alias	Indicates an alias or shortcut to something. Often rendered as an arrow with a small curved arrow next to it.
Context menu	This cursor shows a context menu, usually selected with a secondary mouse button available for the object. Often rendered as an arrow with a small menu graphic next to it.
Cell	Indicates that a cell or set of cells may be selected. Should be rendered as a thick plus sign.
Grab	Indicates that the object could be grabbed. Should be rendered as an open hand.
Grabbing	Indicates that the object has been grabbed. Should be rendered as a closed hand.
Spinning	Indicates that the program is performing a task. Similar to the **wait** property, but the user may still be able to interact with the program. A variety of renderings, including a spinning beach ball, are possible.
Count up	Indicates that the system is performing a counting up operation. Could be rendered as finger counting.
Count down	Indicates that the program is performing a count down operation. Like count up, could be rendered as a finger.
Count up-down	Indicates that the program is alternately counting up and then counting down.

Table 6-6.   *CSS3 Cursor Properties*

cursors may still cause the browser to lock. Rather than tempt fate, the code given will degrade gracefully in Netscape browsers and will simply not render a custom cursor.

Always remember that changing the cursor should be limited to situations where it adds value. Subtle changes may be nice; a fairly common change is to change the finger pointer to an opposite-direction arrow using a style rule, as shown in this short example:

```
<!DOCTYPE HTML PUBLIC "-//W3C//DTD HTML 4.0 Transitional//EN">
<HTML>
```

```
<HEAD>
<TITLE>Subtle Cursor Change</TITLE>
<STYLE TYPE="text/css">
<!--
A:hover {cursor:ne-resize;}
-->
</STYLE>
</HEAD>
<BODY>
<A HREF="http://www.yahoo.com">Yahoo</A>
</BODY>
</HTML>
```

However, be aware that, like changing link color, changing the cursor may leave some users confused about what is and what is not a link.

Links and Ellipses

In graphical interfaces, ellipses (...) are often used to indicate that something more will happen when a user selects a particular command—particularly that more input is required. However, this idea does not translate well to the Web. Consider that nearly all links have something behind them, and the user expects this. Probably the only time you should use ellipses is when the page will simply open another page that contains a large number of choices and little content. Today, few sites uses ellipses except when occasionally when using teaser excerpts that lead to more information, as shown here.

Gravity Defeated

Today the DemoCorporation announced that gravity has been defeated.

Dr. R. Smart boasted that his anti-Newton drive would turn the

Personal space craft industry on its head. [More...]

Conventions may change, but for now ellipses should be avoided.

Suggestion: Avoid using ellipses in links, as they are generally redundant.

Rollovers

A very common link feedback mechanism is called the *rollover*. A rollover link is a link that activates in some fashion, usually with a color or shape change when the user's mouse is positioned over it. While the use of rollovers is so common on the Web that they have become clichéd, they can be useful to provide more feedback to a user, add a little spice to a page, and, in very well-done cases, provide more information about link purpose.

The simplest way to make a rollover link is to activate text links using the CSS2 **A:hover** pseudoclass in a **<STYLE>** tag, as shown here:

```
<STYLE>
<!--
A:hover {color: #FF0000}
-->
</STYLE>
```

In this case, any text link will turn red when the user places their mouse over the linked text. Using a style sheet rule, it is possible to change the link to show a variety of changes, such as text size or style. Designers are cautioned to avoid too dramatic a roll effect, as the browser may have to repaint the page in a very obvious way as the user rolls on the link.

It is also possible to create basic text rollovers for graphical buttons using JavaScript. These types of rollovers work basically like this. Create a regular graphic button, then create an activated version of the button about the same size. Next, add a JavaScript that swaps the normal image button for its activated image when the user's mouse passes over it and changes it back to the normal state when the user passes off the button. The JavaScript code is relatively simple to write, and only requires that the images be loaded in first and that support for the images object be determined. The following code illustrates the basic rollover:

```
<!DOCTYPE HTML PUBLIC "-//W3C//DTD HTML 4.0 Transitional//EN">
<HTML>
<HEAD>
<TITLE>Simple Rollover</TITLE>
<SCRIPT LANGUAGE ="JavaScript">
<!--
/* Preload the images */

  if (document.images)          {
    abouton = new Image(85, 48);
    abouton.src = "images/abouton.gif";
    aboutoff = new Image(85, 48);
    aboutoff.src = "images/about.gif";
  }

function On(imgName) {
        if (document.images) {
```

```
        imgOn = eval(imgName + "on.src");
        document [imgName].src = imgOn;
        }
}

function Off(imgName) {
        if (document.images) {
        imgOff = eval(imgName + "off.src");
        document [imgName].src = imgOff;
        }
}
// -->
</SCRIPT>
</HEAD>
<BODY>

<A HREF="About/index.htm"
   onMouseover="On('about')"
   onMouseout="Off('about')">
<IMG SRC="images/about.gif"
    WIDTH="85" HEIGHT="48" BORDER="0" ALT="About" NAME="about"></A>
<BR>

</BODY>
</HTML>
```

Note   *Weblink: See this code online at http://www.webdesignref.com/chapter6/rollover.htm.*

To use the code, simply add in a new **<IMG>** tag with proper **HEIGHT** and **WIDTH** attributes. Make sure to name your **<IMG>** element. Then add in the preloading code to load the on state for the image. So to add another button for a Products button, you would add

```
producton = new Image(85, 48);
producton.src = "images/producton.gif";
productoff = new Image(85, 48);
productoff.src = "images/product.gif";
```

in the preloading section of the JavaScript. Within the **<BODY>**, add another link to an image like this:

```
<A HREF="products/index.htm"
   onMouseover="On('products')"
   onMouseout="Off('products')">
<IMG SRC="images/product.gif"
     WIDTH="85" HEIGHT="48" BORDER="0" ALT="Products"
NAME="products"></A><BR>
```

The script should work in Netscape 3.0 versions and beyond and Internet Explorer 4.0 versions and beyond. The only problem with using the script is making sure to name the images properly. If you are not interested in adding this type of script by hand to your document, many Web editors, including Macromedia Dreamweaver, support the addition of such scripts, and its often just a matter of running a command like "Insert Rollover Image" and selecting the appropriate image states. Figure 6-11 shows the Dreamweaver dialog box using the same data from the previous example.

Creating Rollovers in Fireworks

Even creating the various rollover images is easy using Fireworks. Just follow these steps:

1. With a document open, pull down the Insert menu and select New Button.

2. Now create a simple graphic button similar to the process discussed previously in the section "Creating Buttons in Fireworks" earlier in this chapter. Once you are finished, your dialog box might look something like this.

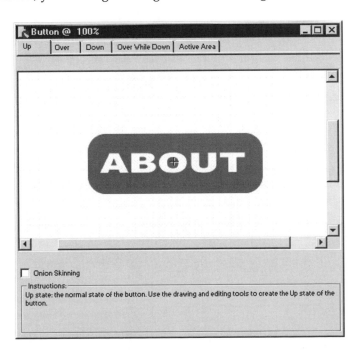

SITE ORGANIZATION AND NAVIGATION

3. Once you have the button created, select the tab in the current dialog box labeled Over. This will allow you to specify the image that should be used when a mouse passes over the button.

4. Press the button labeled Copy Up Graphic. This should make a duplicate of the normal button in the window.

5. Modify the color or style of the button for the over state. You should have a dialog box that looks similar to the one shown here.

6. Close the New button dialog box by selecting the Close box in the upper-right corner of the dialog box.

7. Back in the main window, select the new button, and you should focus the Object palette. If not, access the Object palette from the Window menu.

8. From the Object palette, select the button labeled Link Wizard.

9. Within the Link Wizard, select the tab labeled Link and specify the URL the button should link to and any **ALT** text. Press the OK button to finish up.

10. Preview your rollover by selecting Preview in Browser from the File menu.

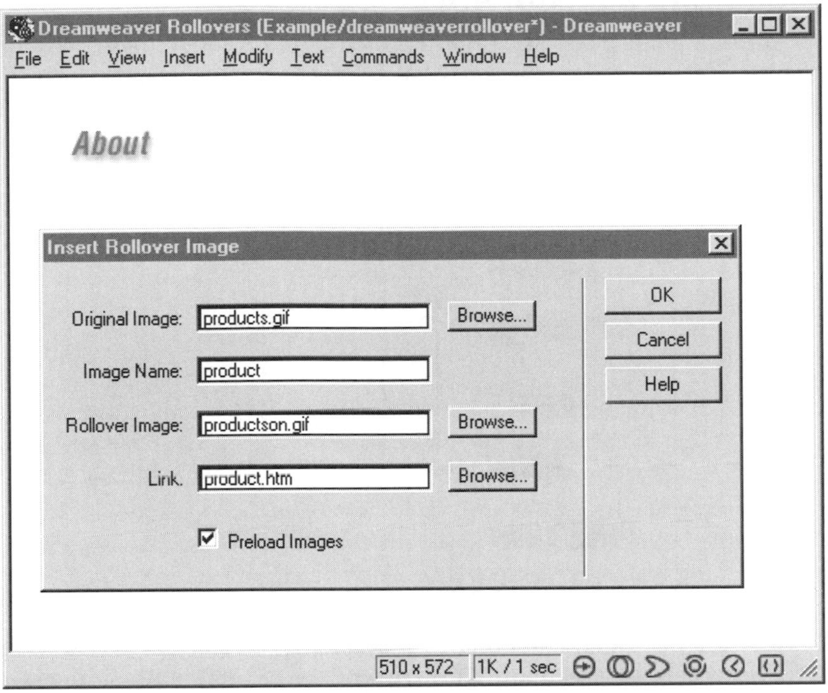

Figure 6-11. *Dreamweaver Rollover dialog box*

Once you have mastered making a single rollover button in Fireworks, it is easy enough to duplicate the rollover and change the text and reset the link using the Link Wizard. Once you are finished, you can even export the entire layout—including HTML and JavaScript—to have a page filled with numerous rollovers.

The major downside of graphic rollover buttons is that they require two or more separate images for each rollover button. So, given a navigation bar with eight buttons, a total of sixteen images have to be downloaded. Given the multiple connections to the server, rollovers can certainly cause a major download delay. Fortunately, with the rise of style sheets, it is possible to create lightweight rollovers using the hover property as well as using positioning.

Second-Generation Image Rollovers

With CSS positioning, it is possible to create a menu of graphic rollover buttons using only two images. Create one large image of all buttons in their on state and one large image of all buttons in their off state, as shown here:

All off   All on

About   *About*

Products   *Products*

News   *News*

Jobs   *Jobs*

Intranet   *Intranet*

In this case, we named these all.gif and allon.gif. Next, create an image map for the image. Now we can use positioning CSS properties to put the two images in the document right on top of each other—except the allon.gif image will be hidden. Next we'll write a script so that as the user passes over the image, a portion of the allon.gif will be revealed. The key is using a clipping path to cut out the area of the image we want to show. Since we used an image map on top of the image, we have the clipping paths already. The code and markup below illustrates this idea:

```
<!DOCTYPE HTML PUBLIC "-//W3C//DTD HTML 4.0 Transitional//EN">
<HTML>
<HEAD>
<TITLE>Rollovers Generation 2</TITLE>
<STYLE TYPE="text/css">
<!--
 #menu {position: relative }
 #menuoff {position: absolute;
          top: 0; left: 0; }
 #menuon {position: absolute;
          top: 0; left: 0;
          visibility: hidden;}
-->
</STYLE>
```

```
<SCRIPT>
<!--
IE4 = (document.all) ? 1 : 0;
NS4 = (document.layers) ? 1 : 0;
ver4 = (IE4 || NS4) ? 1 : 0;


function clipRegion(left,top,right,bottom)
 {
   this.left = left;
   this.top = top;
   this.right = right;
   this.bottom = bottom;
}


if (ver4) {
    /* create clipping regions */

             var cliparray = new Array();

   cliparray[0] = new clipRegion(5,138,83,164);
   cliparray[1] = new clipRegion(4,107,83,133);
   cliparray[2] = new clipRegion(3,77,83,102);
   cliparray[3] = new clipRegion(2,49,83,73);
   cliparray[4] = new clipRegion(23,19,84,43);


   }


function rollover(region,turnon)
 {
   if (!ver4)
     return;

   if (IE4)
     currentbutton = document.all.menuon.style;
   else
     currentbutton = document.menu.document.menuon;

   if (!turnon)
     {
```

```
        currentbutton.visibility = "hidden";
        return;
      }


   if (NS4)
     {
             currentbutton.clip.top = cliparray[region].top;
             currentbutton.clip.right = cliparray[region].right;
             currentbutton.clip.bottom = cliparray[region].bottom;
             currentbutton.clip.left = cliparray[region].left;
        }
   else
      currentbutton.clip = "rect(" + cliparray[region].top + " " +
cliparray[region].right + " " + cliparray[region].bottom + " " +
cliparray[region].left + ")";
      currentbutton.visibility = "visible"
      }

//-->
</SCRIPT>
</HEAD>

<BODY BGCOLOR="#FFFFFF">

<DIV ID="menu">
 <DIV ID="menuoff">
  <IMG SRC="images/all.gif" WIDTH="85" HEIGHT="168"
      BORDER="0" USEMAP="#buttons">
</DIV>
<DIV ID="menuon">
   <SCRIPT>
   <!--
    document.write('<img src="images/allon.gif" width="85"
            height="168" border="0" usemap="#buttons">');
   //-->
   </SCRIPT>
</DIV>
</DIV>

<MAP NAME="buttons">
```

```
    <AREA SHAPE="rect" COORDS="5,138,83,164" HREF="intranet.htm"
ALT="Intranet"
 onMouseover="rollover(0,true)" onMouseout="rollover(0,false)">
<AREA SHAPE="rect" COORDS="4,107,83,133" HREF="jobs.htm" ALT="Jobs"
onMouseover="rollover(1,true)" onMouseout="rollover(1,false)">
<AREA SHAPE="rect" COORDS="3,77,83,102" HREF="news.htm" ALT="News"
onMouseover="rollover(2,true)" onMouseout="rollover(2,false)">
<AREA SHAPE="rect" COORDS="2,49,83,73" HREF="products.htm"
        ALT="Products"
  onMouseover="rollover(3,true)" onMouseout="rollover(3,false)">
  <AREA SHAPE="rect" COORDS="23,19,84,43" HREF="about.htm"
        ALT="About"
  onMouseover="rollover(4,true)" onMouseout="rollover(4,false)">
</MAP>
</BODY>
</HTML>
```

Note   *Weblink: See this code online at http://www.webdesignref.com/chapter6/rollover2.htm.*

Adopting this code for your site should be relatively easy. First, make the two images. Then set up the image map. Next, add the positioning using the **<DIV>** elements and the style properties provided. If you view the page at this point, you should see only the off state image showing. Now add in the JavaScript. The only change would be setting the various clipping regions, which is this part of the code:

```
cliparray[0] = new clipRegion(5,138,83,164);
    cliparray[1] = new clipRegion(4,107,83,133);
    cliparray[2] = new clipRegion(3,77,83,102);
    cliparray[3] = new clipRegion(2,49,83,73);
    cliparray[4] = new clipRegion(23,19,84,43);
```

Just change the coordinates on the right to match your image-map coordinates and add more **cliparray[ ]** entries like so:

```
cliparray[5] = new clipRegion(28,19,84,20);
```

Now, in the image map, just change the various **<AREA>** elements to have

```
onMouseover="rollover(5,true)" onMouseout="rollover(5,false)">
```

and you should be in business. The only downside to this script is that it works only in 4.X-generation and better browsers. It will, however, degrade gracefully in older browsers. You just won't see the rollover effect.

 At the time of this writing, no WYSIWYG editors supported easy creation of this second-generation rollover code. Hopefully this will change in the near future.

CSS-Only Rollovers

When using CSS-styled push buttons, it is possible to create rollover effects as well. The **A:hover** pseudoclass may useful to create simple rollovers such as changing color, as shown by these style rules:

```
A        {color: blue;}
A:hover  {color: red;}
```

Another common style is adding underlines only when a user mouses over a link, which is accomplished with these two basic CSS rules:

```
A        {text-decoration: none;}
A:hover  {text-decoration: underline;}
```

However, for complex CSS buttons, this **A:hover** pseudoclass may not be enough. Using JavaScript, it is possible to modify the style of a region dynamically. The short example here shows how to make a simple rollover in CSS with some JavaScript. Note that this currently only works in Internet Explorer browsers.

```
<!DOCTYPE HTML PUBLIC "-//W3C//DTD HTML 4.0 Transitional//EN">
<HTML>
<HEAD>
<TITLE>CSS Rollover Buttons</TITLE>
<STYLE>
<!--
  #mybutton    {border-style: inset;
                border-color: #ff6633;
                background-color: #CC3300;
                width: 80px;
                text-align: center;}
  A.buttontext {color: white;
text-decoration: none;
     font: bold 12pt Verdana;
```

```
        cursor: hand;}
  .buttonover  {color: yellow;
     text-decoration: underline;
     font: bold 12pt Verdana;
     cursor: hand;}
-->
</STYLE>
</HEAD>
<BODY>
<A HREF="about.htm" CLASS="buttontext"
onMouseover="this.className='buttonover';
     mybutton.style.background='#FF6633'"
onMouseout="this.className='buttontext;
     mybutton.style.background='#CC3300'">
<DIV ID="mybutton">
About
</DIV></A>
</BODY>
</HTML>
```

Note *Weblink: See this code online at http://www.webdesignref.com/chapter6/
cssrollovers.htm.*

Using Rollovers

No matter the form, designers should attempt to use rollovers correctly. The most
common mistake made is not considering how many states a rollover button should
have. Buttons have four possible states. The first state is the normal or unselected
state. Some people call this the "up" state. This is the form of the button when it is
not pressed, but can be pressed. The second state is the selected state. In this state, the
button cannot be pressed because either it is not available in the current context or it is
currently selected. Generally, buttons in the selected state are grayed out or subdued in
look. A third state is the over state, which is often termed the active state. This is the
state when the user passes their mouse over the button before deciding to select it. A
fourth possible state is called the press state or mouse down state. This state occurs
when the user actually presses the button. An example of all these states for a graphical
button is shown in Figure 6-12.

Notice that these states are the same as the link states—*unvisited, active, visited,* and
the new state, *hover.* Despite this, many sites lack all the states for their buttons. The
main reason for this is that for graphical buttons, each extra state causes more images
to be downloaded. Because of this, consider the following design suggestion.

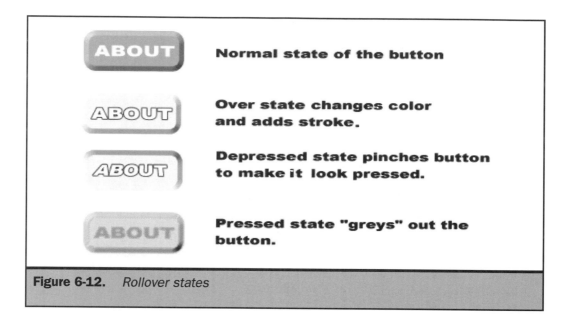

Figure 6-12.   *Rollover states*

Suggestion: Graphical buttons should have at minimum an unselected and selected state. Over states and press states should be considered optional.

When download is not a consideration because you are using CSS-based buttons or bandwidth is plentiful, always include all states for buttons.

When used properly, rollovers are useful because they further let the user know that the object is active. Most of the time, rollovers are somewhat gimmicky—just making text glow or a button change shape. However, in some situations rollovers can be used to let a user know what is about to load by revealing some descriptive text. When used in this fashion, a rollover effect can actually make buttons more usable.

Understanding User Expectations

For users, possibly one of the most annoying aspects of using a Web site beyond slow-loading pages is choosing a page and then not getting the information expected. From a user's perspective, each link represents a door, and the link label is supposed to indicate what is beyond each door. When users aren't sure what is behind a link, they are forced to try the link—and potentially return back if it wasn't what they were looking for. At first this might sound somewhat fun—almost like exploring—but after awhile it can become very frustrating.

Site designers should always strive to let the user know what they will see when they press a link. When faced with a link, the user might ask the questions shown next. A few suggestions about how to deal with these questions are presented, along with illustrated examples.

■ What kind of content does this link load?

Suggestion: Provide good labels indicating the form of the content. Consider using icons to show content types.

Datasheet – robot235.pdf (Adobe Acrobat Format)

 Robot Datasheet

■ Where will the link take them?

Suggestion: Make sure to indicate if the link will jump them within a page, within a site, or to an external site. Don't hide the URL, in case the user can deduce the answer from it.

Use up-down arrows for intrapage jumps.

^ Back to top

v Spec Sheet

Label external links as such or use an icon:

DemoCompany Partners (outside link)

DemoCompany ☞

Suggestion: Indicate an external link by exposing the URL or using an icon. Indicate file size if triggering a download.

Leave all other links alone so the user assumes they are normal internal site links:

About Demo Company

■ Will it mean a long download?

Specification.pdf (854K)

■ Will it cost money?

Suggestion: Use an icon or symbols, or issue an Alert dialog before the link.

<u>$ sign-up today $</u>

<u>Specification</u> **(payment required)**

■ Is the linked content fresh?

Suggestion: Add the last modification date where necessary or use a New icon.

<u>Printer drivers</u> (1/5/99)

`NEW` <u>Specifications</u>

■ Is the content potentially offensive?

Suggestion: Use an alert, or warn with an obvious label if content is potentially offensive.

<u>Red light district (21 and up only)</u>

The key to most of these questions is to label a link properly. While links themselves sometimes have to be short—using the **TITLE** attribute—a text rollover or extra scope-notes information can be provided to the user. The status bar also presents a venue for informing the user of a link's destination. Each of these approaches will be discussed in turn.

Using Scope Notes

One of the best ways to let users know about the meaning of a link, beyond good labeling, is through the use of *scope notes*. Scope notes provide a description of what a link means as well as other contextual information. Consider a link label like About. We could add scope notes to clarify the meaning of the label as shown here:

```
About
```

> Information about DemoCompany including corporate history,
> press releases, and self congratulating biographies.

Make sure to set your scope notes in a smaller font or a different style so as not to overwhelm the primary link.

It is possible to provide further benefit with scope notes by providing skip-ahead links within the description text, like so;

> About
>
> Information about DemoCompany including <u>corporate history</u>,
> <u>press releases</u>, and self congratulating <u>biographies</u>.

The only major downside to scope notes is that they may clutter up a layout or take focus away from important items on a page. In some sense, the scope notes are like help information. They really are the most useful to those who are looking for more information. Because of these potential drawbacks, many designers decide to hide scope notes and only reveal them when a user passes over or invokes a link.

In general, you should avoid putting skip-ahead links in scope notes that are revealed. It is very annoying for a user to try to ensure their mouse does not make the scope note disappear as the user moves to click on the newly revealed link. So, if you are including skip-ahead links in your rollovers, make sure to ensure the scope note stays revealed once the user passes their mouse over it.

TITLE Attribute

The simplest form of revealed scope note is the ToolTip information provided by the **TITLE** attribute. Set the **TITLE** attribute for a link to any desired text as shown here:

```
<A HREF="about.htm" TITLE="Information about DemoCompany including
corporate history, press releases, and self congratulating
biographies.">About</A>
```

When the user holds their mouse over the link, the extra link information should appear. The link titles should provide more information about what the link will do, but should not be so verbose as to be ignored. Try to make link titles short and scannable—maybe 10–15 words, or around 60–80 characters maximum.

Note   *Be careful with long link titles, as some older browsers will not wrap title information and scope information could be clipped.*

When using graphical text buttons there may be some question as to whether **ALT** or **TITLE** attribute text will show. Depending on the browser, you may find the results vary. Consider making the **TITLE** and **ALT** attribute information the same, if necessary.

Rollover Messages

It is possible using rollovers to reveal text or imagery someplace else on the screen as the user mouses over a link. A script can be written to reveal a scope note as well as change the state of the link. The following markup and JavaScript illustrates how this would work using graphics:

```
<!DOCTYPE HTML PUBLIC "-//W3C//DTD HTML 4.0 Transitional//EN">
<HTML>
<HEAD>
<TITLE>Targeted Rollovers</TITLE>
<SCRIPT LANGUAGE="JavaScript">
<!--

if (document.images)
  {
      abouton = new Image(147, 29);
      abouton.src = "abouton.gif"
      aboutoff = new Image(147, 29);
      aboutoff.src = "about.gif"

      blank = new Image(130, 127);
      blank.src = "blank.gif"

      description1 = new Image(130, 127);
      description1.src = "description.gif"
  }

function On(imgName,description) {
        if (document.images) {
        imgOn = eval(imgName + "on.src");
        document.images[imgName].src = imgOn;
        document.images.descriptionregion.src= description.src;
```

```
        }
}

function Off(imgName) {
if (document.images) {
        imgOff = eval(imgName + "off.src");
        document.images[imgName].src = imgOff;
        document.images.descriptionregion.src= "blank.gif";
        }
}

// -->
</SCRIPT>
</HEAD>

<BODY>

<A HREF="about.htm"
onMouseover="On('about',description1);
window.status='Company'; return true"
onMouseout="Off('about');">
<IMG SRC="about.gif" BORDER="0" ALT="About" NAME="about"
WIDTH="159" HEIGHT="57"></A>
   
<A HREF="">
<IMG SRC="blank.gif" NAME="descriptionregion" WIDTH="328"
HEIGHT="84" BORDER="0" ALT=""></A>

</BODY>
</HTML>
```

| Note | *Weblink: See this code online at http://www.webdesignref.com/chapter6/
targetedrollovers.htm.*

Figure 6-13 shows the rollover code in action.

Generally, designers are encouraged to use rollovers that reveal extra information, but always remember that, like multiple-state rollovers, rollover messages can be

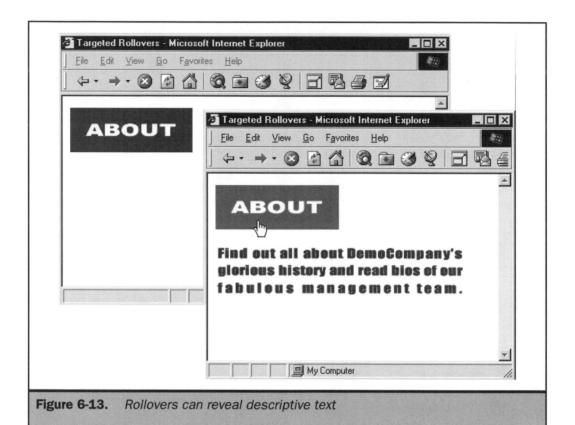

Figure 6-13. *Rollovers can reveal descriptive text*

troublesome because they require numerous images. Fortunately, using style sheets, lightweight rollover messages can be built. The code below illustrates how this might be accomplished:

```
<!DOCTYPE HTML PUBLIC "-//W3C//DTD HTML 4.0 Transitional//EN">
<HTML>
<HEAD>
<TITLE>CSS Target Rollovers</TITLE>
<STYLE>
<!--
#buttons    {position: absolute;
             top: 10px;
             background-color: yellow;
             width: 20%;}
```

```
#blankdescription {position: absolute;
        top: 10px;
        left: 40%;
        background-color: orange;}

#aboutdescription {position: absolute;
        top: 10px;
        left: 40%;
        background-color: orange;
        visibility: hidden;}

#productsdescription {position: absolute;
        top: 10px;
        left: 40%;
        background-color: orange;
        visibility: hidden;}
-->
</STYLE>
<SCRIPT>
<!--
var IE4 = (document.all) ? true : false;
var NS4 = (document.layers) ? true : false;

function changeVisibility(id, showflag)
 {
   if (NS4)    {
      var str = (showflag) ? 'show' : 'hide';
      eval("document." + id).visibility = str;
    }
   else    {
      var str = (showflag) ? 'visible' : 'hidden';
      eval("document.all." + id).style.visibility = str;
    }
}

//-->
</SCRIPT>
</HEAD>

<BODY>

<DIV ID="buttons">
```

```
<A HREF="about.htm"
onMouseover="changeVisibility('blankdescription', false);
             changeVisibility('aboutdescription',true)"
onMouseout="changeVisibility('blankdescription', true);
             changeVisibility('aboutdescription',false)">About</A>
<BR>
<A HREF="products.htm"
onMouseover="changeVisibility('blankdescription', false);
             changeVisibility('productsdescription',true)"
onMouseout="changeVisibility('blankdescription', true);
        changeVisibility('productsdescription',false)">Products</A>

</DIV>

<!-- Description text follows -->
<DIV ID="blankdescription">

</DIV>

<DIV ID="aboutdescription">
Discover the history and management behind the DemoCompany.
</DIV>

<DIV ID="productsdescription">
If you like our domes, you'll love our robots!
</DIV>
</BODY>
</HTML>
```

 Weblink: *See this code online at http://www.webdesignref.com/chapter6/ csstargetedrollovers.htm.*

Note *This code only works under 4.X generation browsers, and does not degrade gracefully because it relies not only on JavaScript but also on style sheets.*

Status-Bar Messages

It is possible to show link results in the status bar at the bottom of the browser window. Generally, a browser will display the destination URL in the status bar, but it is possible to customize this using a short JavaScript. In all versions of JavaScript, you can manipulate the status property of the window object, which defines the whole browser window. You could then trigger a message when a user passes their mouse over the link, using the core HTML 4.0 **onMouseover** attribute. A script that illustrates this is shown here:

```
<!DOCTYPE HTML PUBLIC "-//W3C//DTD HTML 4.0 Transitional//EN">
<HTML>
<HEAD>
<TITLE>Status Bar Link Messages</TITLE>
</HEAD>
<BODY>
<H2>Status Bar Link Messages</H2>
<A HREF="http://www.democompany.com/"
   onMouseover="window.status='Visit DemoCompany home of the
 Robot Butler! '; return true;"
   onMouseout="window.status='';return true;">Demo Company</A><BR>

<A HREF="http://www.yahoo.com/"
   onMouseover="window.status='Have you been to Yahoo! today?';
return true;"
   onMouseout="window.status='';return true;">Yahoo!</A><BR>
</BODY>
</HTML>
```

> **Note**   *Weblink: See this code online at http://www.webdesignref.com/chapter6/statusbar.htm.*

> **Note**   *The **onMouseover** code must return true; otherwise, the message will not display.*

In the previous example, just change the string in the single quotes to the appropriate message text to display.

Consider the potential downside to providing messages to the user in the status bar. First, the user may not look in this location. Second, if the user does look here, they may be expecting URL information in order to make a determination of link destination. Far too often, the status information shown here repeats the basic text-link information. This could be particularly troublesome for outside links where the user may want to know the URL before they decide to click the link, or for links to other content forms. With outside links, consider using a status-message style like the one shown here:

```
<A HREF="http://www.yahoo.com/"
   onMouseover="window.status='Have you been to Yahoo! (www.yahoo.com)
today? '; return true;"
   onMouseout="window.status='';return true;">Yahoo!</A>
```

When linking to another content form, the status bar may also be used to let the user know the format of the content, as shown in the example here:

```
<A HREF="robotdatasheet.pdf"
    onMouseover="window.status='Adobe Acrobat Format'; return true;"
    onMouseout="window.status='';return true;">Robot Butler Datasheet</A>
```

In this example, an icon or even an indication in the label that the linked content is in Acrobat format is better than solely relying on the status bar.

Suggestion: When using status-bar messages, consider providing URL information with the text when linking externally.

In many ways, providing status-bar messages is redundant considering the same information could be provided in a **TITLE** attribute, as shown here:

```
<A HREF="http://www.yahoo.com/"
    TITLE="Have you been to Yahoo! (www.yahoo.com) today?">Yahoo!</A>
```

In this particular example, the ToolTip will even show the destination URL directly where the user's mouse is focused, as well as in the user's status bar. The only real upside to the status-bar message is that it will work on older JavaScript-aware browsers, while the **TITLE** attribute only works in HTML 4.0–compliant browsers.

Keyboard Support for Links

Designers should always strive to make sites usable and accessible by all. Consider that some users may find the mouse difficult to use or prefer to use a keyboard. Links should be easily invoked using keyboard commands. Most browsers support tabbing of links, and some already support accelerator keys.

The HTML 4.0 specification adds the **ACCESSKEY** attribute to the **<A>** tag as well as to various form elements. With this attribute, it is possible to set a key to invoke an anchor without requiring a pointing device to select the link. The link is activated with the combination of the accelerator key, usually ALT, and the key specified by the attribute. So,

```
<A HREF="http://www.yahoo.com" ACCESSKEY="Y">Yahoo!</A>
```

makes a link to Yahoo!, which can be activated by pressing ALT-Y. So far, only Internet Explorer 4.X and beyond appear to be supporting this upgrade to link access.

While adding keyboard access to a Web page would seem a dramatic improvement, HTML authors are cautioned to be aware of access-key bindings in the browsing environment. Assuming that both the major browsers support the **ACCESSKEY** attribute, authors would be cautioned to stay away from accelerators using the keys in Table 6-7.

One other problem with accelerator keys is how to show them in the page. Generally in software, the letter of the accelerator key is indicated by underlining. Of course, links are generally underlined in browsers, so this approach is not feasible. It is possible with style sheets to change link direction, so underlining the first letter is possible, but then the user may be disoriented because they expect links to be fully underlined. Another approach to indicating the accelerator key might be to set the access key letter of a text link in bold or slightly larger size. Designers are encouraged to adopt whatever notation becomes standard on Web pages.

It is possible to use the **TABINDEX** attribute of the **<A>** tag to define the order that links will be tabbed through in a browser that supports keyboard navigation. The value of **TABINDEX** is typically a positive number. A browser will tab through links with increasing **TABINDEX** values, but will generally skip over those with negative values. So, **<A HREF="about.htm" TABINDEX="1">** sets this anchor to be the first thing tabbed to. If the **TABINDEX** attribute is undefined, the browser will tend to tab through links in the order in which they are found within an HTML document.

Key	Description
F	File menu
E	Edit menu
C	Communicator menu (Netscape only)
V	View menu
G	Go menu
A	Favorites menu (Internet Explorer Only)
H	Help

Table 6-7. *Reserved Accelerator Keys*

Advanced Web Linking Models

Today, the Web exhibits a very simple linking model; however, that may change in the future. HTML 4.0 introduces the **<LINK>** element, which can be used to define linking relationships between documents. The most common way that the **<LINK>** element is used is when associating a style sheet to a Web page, as shown in this example:

```
<LINK REL="STYLESHEET" HREF="corporate.css">
```

A **<LINK>** element like this is found in the **<HEAD>** of an HTML document.

It is possible, however, to specify any arbitrary relationship using the **REL** attributes. For example, using **<LINK>** we might define which document is likely to be clicked next, like so:

```
<LINK REL="NEXT" HREF="nextpage.htm">
```

Some browsers such as WebTV might use this as a cue to preload a page. All sorts of other relationships, such as home pages, copyright, links to owners, and so on, can be specified. However, until browsers support more link types, the simple linking model will have to suffice.

Link Maintenance

Even when links are used correctly within a site and a user understands the meaning of each link perfectly, links will require maintenance. One approach is to not let broken links enter a site in the first place. A site that uses dynamic links can avoid broken links, because as pages are added all links are adjusted. However, most sites do not employ dynamic links, so invariably, over time, content changes and internal links may break. More commonly, links to external sites will break as other sites move their pages without considering outside linkage. Ferreting out the broken links within a site can be tedious, but doing so should be a top priority. A broken link should be considered a serious problem. Users clicking on a broken link are on the road to nowhere, eventually to receive the now infamous "404 Not Found" message or something similar. Imagine if a menu on a software application triggered a message saying "Sorry spell check not found." Such oversights would not be tolerated within software and should be considered the same level of problem within a site.

Rule: Broken links should be considered catastrophic failure.

Fortunately, identifying and fixing broken links isn't terribly difficult. Armed with a tool like LinkBot (www.linkbot.com) or Coast WebMaster (www.coast.com), finding broken links is a more simple matter. However, consider that if you have external links within a site, even constant monitoring isn't going to keep broken links out of the site at all times. To account for the unforeseen broken link, consider installing a custom 404 page. Then, put information such as link to a site map or a method to contact the site's administrator in the custom error page. An example custom 404 page is shown in Figure 6-14.

Note   *Installation of a custom 404 error page depends on the server being utilized.*

Redirection Pages

Rather than show errors, many sites prefer to redirect users to new pages. If the content at a URL such as http://www.democompany.com/movedon.htm has moved to a new location, it is best to install a page that points people to the new page or even quickly

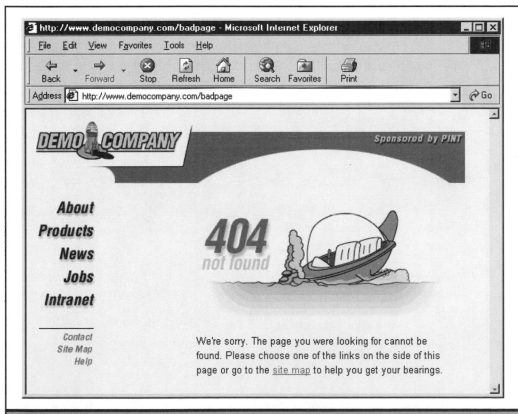

Figure 6-14.   *Custom 404 pages can fit with a site design*

redirects them there. The URL previously given will do just that. Some site maintainers prefer to send people directly to the new page while others will install a temporary page informing visitors of the page change, like the one shown in Figure 6-15.

Sending people directly to the new page may be seamless, but it does take some control away from the user. For example, if the user requests a particular page on, say robotic dogs, and a redirect takes them to a different page, they will become very frustrated. Always make sure that the new page is related to the moved page.

Redirection and 404s

Some sites prefer to send users directly to the home page of the site if they request a page that no longer exists. This is not a recommended approach as it may confuse

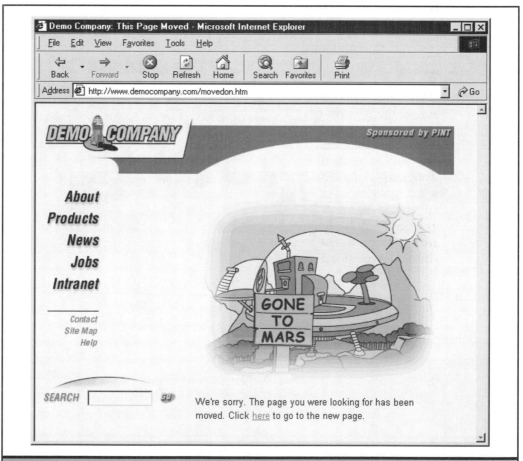

Figure 6-15.   *"Page Moved" example page*

users. Errors are inevitable, and users will make them. A goal of a site designer should be to soften the blow and help users avoid making errors—not take control away from them. Furthermore, instant redirection for bad page requests will not encourage a site maintainer to address the reason behind the errors.

Suggestion: Avoid automatic redirects for 404 errors.

Maintaining site links can be a great deal of work. Custom error pages and redirection pages can help, but Web managers will have to be ever vigilant in link monitoring. Good Web sites should make sure to watch log files for referring sites. Furthermore, consider visiting a search engine and doing a reverse search. Specifically, search for sites that link to yours and make sure they are up-to-date on any significant site changes made. Making sure that other sites link to you correctly may be a great deal of work, but it is all part of being a good Web citizen. More about maintaining links and sites can be found in Chapter 14.

Summary

Making sure that users understand what links do is an integral part of developing a usable site. There are many ways to add links in a Web site, including text links, buttons, image maps, and even arbitrary hotspots. Designers should respect common link conventions such as color, underlining, and URL feedback. However, it is possible to change link styles in an aesthetically pleasing manner using both images and, more recently, CSS properties. Rollovers and other dynamic facilities can be added to links to further improve navigation and create dynamic Web sites. Links can also be difficult to maintain, and site designers are encouraged to account for broken links and moved pages. Yet, even when links are used correctly, there are sure to be users who will have difficulty navigating your site. For those users, special facilities such as search engines and site maps should be provided, and these are discussed in the next two chapters.

Chapter 7

Search and Design

Many users will find traditional navigation an inefficient way to find what they are looking for. Often, a user knows something exists and just needs to find it within a site. Search appeals to power users, frequent visitors, and the plain impatient, who are all looking to find a result quickly. A well-executed search facility is one major advantage a Web site has over printed media, as it gives users great control over a site's content, allowing them to filter it to just what they want to see. Larger Web sites, especially those with complex data, must provide search facilities—and may consider making it the central navigation method. Searching facilities, however, must be designed with the user in mind. Give careful consideration to how users expect search to work, the type of search required, the design of the search page, the help system, and the types of search result listings before adding search to a site.

Webwide Search

Designers must be especially careful not to fall into the familiar trap of exactly imitating search on the Web at large. The needs of Webwide searching are very different than those of a single site, or even a group of controlled sites. Unfortunately, users often expect site search facilities to act similarly to public search engines like Lycos. Public search engines have to deal with the nearly impossible task of gathering and indexing the enormous and ever-changing Web filled with documents that are often purposely filled with misleading information. Then, from all this information, the user is supposed to quickly and easily retrieve a useful result using a simple query. In summary—finding a needle in a haystack is a much easier task than searching the Web. Regardless of the difficulty, users do rely on public search engines a great deal. Designers should consider a user's experience with Webwide search engines, since users will generally understand the functionality of these engines and reference that knowledge when they use a local search engine. The following sections will explore the components of Web searching and explore some of the problems encountered.

Web Searching Overview

The requirements for Webwide searching are daunting. Users expect to be able to quickly type in a simple search phrase at a global search engine like AltaVista (http://www.altavista.com) and end up with a realistic result. Consider walking into a public library and expecting to find a particular passage in a book in a few seconds and you'll understand the near futility of instant search gratification. When searching, users are often overwhelmed with too much information, are shown irrelevant information, or do not get anything at all! Despite this frustration, users keep pounding away at search engines hoping to get a good result in a few minutes.

Many of the problems with search-engine usage have to do with users not searching correctly. Searching really should only be used when looking for known items or for very specific topics. Consider searching for a generic phrase like "hamburgers." Search engines may not necessarily pull up sites about hamburgers or even large hamburger restaurant chains. In fact, testing this query in some search engines resulted in numerous links to pages about Hamburg, Germany, as well as recipe sites for personal home pages and pages that appeared to have absolutely nothing to do with hamburgers. The problem is you haven't been specific enough. Consider searching for something like "White Castle Slyders"—a regionally famous hamburger in the United States—you may find a more useful list of results.

When looking for general information on a subject, users hopefully turn to a directory rather than a search engine. The main difference between a search engine and a directory is that a directory usually involves some human editing and usually contains a very limited number of links. Yahoo is probably the most famous directory around, but it now provides search-engine features as well. In fact, most of the search engines have begun to offer directory links as well as searching. Some popular directories like www.about.com or www.dmoz.org are organized by individuals who are responsible for a particular type of content. The benefit of a directory is that it limits links to the "good sites" and may even provide reviews of sites.

> **Definition: A Web directory is a human-edited and organized collection of site links and associated information such as descriptions and reviews.**

In comparison to a directory, a search engine is more like the phone directory that you can only search. This is similar to calling your information service and asking for a phone number, except you ask for something related to a particular topic. Consider using a phone information service such as 411 in the United States and asking for the phone number of a "Chinese restaurant" rather than asking about a particular Chinese restaurant. If you ask for a particular restaurant, chances are you're going to get a good result. However, when asking for general information you'll be very lucky if the operator actually spends some time to give you a particular restaurant they know about, or even returns one that looks reputable based upon its ad in the print directory. In many cases, directory assistance might just give you the first one or even a random one from a list. Search engines tend to act the same way. They are good at returning specific answers, but results vary otherwise. Search engines always attempt to be comprehensive and may list numerous sites with no regard to content quality or freshness. Search engines are primarily automated in the collection and organization of links, though today some human editing is being introduced because of the increasing amount of search-engine trickery going on.

> **Definition: A search engine is an automated collector and organizer of site information that users can run queries against.**

How Users Search

Before getting into the theory of how search engines work and how to utilize both external and local search engines to improve site design, consider first how people actually use search facilities. People search for a variety of reasons. A big reason to search is when they are looking for something known to exist. An example of known item searching is when a user is looking for a particular part like RBA-4456. In this case, it is usually fairly easy for the person to locate the item in question assuming that the search facility has seen it before—particularly if the item is fairly unique. Oftentimes, however, the user may not know if the item they are searching for exists or not—in fact, they might just be searching to see if such an item exists. A query like "Robot shops" is a more general search where the user might be looking for the existence of a shop that could repair their robot. Other times, a user may be simply be performing an exploratory search to get a sense for the extent of something. For example, a query for "Robot Butler" may be done not only for the existence of such a device but to see the extent of sites offering information on a metallic servant. Hopefully, known-item searching is what users would generally use search engines for, but, oddly, existence and exploratory searching are commonly employed.

Regardless of the reason for a search, users go through four basic steps.

1. Formulate a Query

Depending on the search facility being used, the query formed by the user may vary greatly. A simple query might only include keywords like "Robot Butler." More complex queries might include Boolean queries like "Robot AND Butler." Many search engines utilize queries filled with symbols, such as "+Robot +Butler –Jeeves." The search facility may even support a natural-language interface where the user can ask something like "Where can I buy a robot butler?" The query formulation might not only include the selection of various search words, but also refinement of search criteria such as indicating the areas to search, a date range to query, data types to search, and so on. Users may also at this point specify how they would like their results returned—say, ten at a time, sorted by last update, and so on. However, further criteria beyond keywords is usually part of an advanced search and is often performed only by more experienced users.

2. Execute the Search and Wait for the Result

The second step of searching usually consists of a simple button click, followed by a short wait for network round-trip time plus time required for the search engine to run the query and list the result. While there isn't much going on interactively during this phase, don't ignore it. The user views this as a discrete step in the process and will not wait around forever for results to appear.

3. Review the Results

Once the results have been listed onscreen, the user will peruse them to see if there is anything interesting in the list. During the review stage, the user will rely greatly on supplementary information such as relevancy ranking and description of the results, including summaries, modification dates, and file sizes. During the review stage, the user may sort or filter the results in order to help them determine what to do. However, making a decision on results will depend highly on what is actually returned by the query. Results will vary from the so-called negative result that contains no matches. Another extreme case would be a huge volume of data returned or even every document in a collection. Most cases will be somewhere in between no documents and all documents in the search space.

4. Decide What to Do with the Result

Based on the results, the user decides what to do. For example, if there are no results, the user may search again with a new query, or may simply give up. If the search didn't appear to provide the correct answer, they may also search again. When the search provides too many results, the user may try to refine the search. Maybe the user selects a few of the choices in the search results to examine. While there may be numerous variations, basically the user decides either to explore some of the results, redo or refine the search, or just quit.

This basic overview is important to keep in mind when designing a search facility. Later in the chapter we'll present theory and practical design suggestions that deal with each step the user takes during the search process. However, before doing this we'll present an overview of how search engines function.

How Search Engines Work

So how to search engines work? First, a large number of pages are gathered off the Web using a process often called *spidering*. Next, the collected pages are indexed to determine what they are about. Finally, a search page is built so that users can enter queries in and see what pages are related to their queries. The best analogy for the process is that the search engine builds as big a haystack as possible, then tries to organize the haystack somehow, and finally lets the user try to find the proverbial needle in the resulting haystack of information by entering a query on a search page.

Gathering Pages

Every day the Web is growing by leaps and bounds. The true size of the Web is unknown, and it will undoubtedly increase even as you read this sentence. At any given moment numerous documents are added and similar numbers of documents are removed. Gathering all the pages and keeping things up-to-date is certainly a significant chore. Users always want to know which search engine covers the most of the Web, but the truth is that today even the largest search engines only index maybe a third of the documents online. Some only index a few percent. This may change in the future, but for now be happy that not everything is indexed. The resulting mess of information to wade through would be even worse.

Most search engines use programs called spiders, robots, or gathers to collect pages of the Web for indexing. We'll use the term "spider" to mean any program that is used to gather Web pages. Spiders start with a certain number of URLs, either submitted by people looking to get listed or built by forming URLs from domain names listed in the domain name registry. As the spider visits the various addresses in the list, it saves the pages or portions of the pages for analysis and looks for links to follow. For example, if a spider was visiting the URL http://www.democompany.com, it might see links emanating from this page and then decide to follow them. Not all search engines necessarily index pages deeply into a site, but most tend to follow links—particularly from pages that are well linked themselves or contain a great deal of content.

Indexing Pages

The next step search engines take is attempting to determine what a page is about. This is usually called *indexing*. The method each search engine uses varies, but basically an indexer looks at various components of a page, including possibly its **<TITLE>**, the contents of its **<META>** tags, comment text, link titles, text in headings, and body text. From this information it will try to distill the meaning of the page. Each aspect of a page might have different relevance, and within the actual text, the position or frequency of different words will be taken into account as well. However, not all content within a page matters to a search engine. For example, *stop words* are words that a search engine ignores, normally because they are assumed to be so common as to carry little useful information. Examples of stop words might be "the," "a," "an," etc. Most search engines have some stop words, but some engines like AltaVista claim to even index common stop words like "the."

While the use of stop words may improve a search engine by limiting the size of the index file and focusing it on more content words, it may not match how users think about queries. Novice users may be feel "The Best Butler Robot" is a better query than "Best Butler Robot." Sometimes the stop word may be important to the search. Consider searching for a song title like "Rock the Town." "The" is an integral part of the term and without it many other songs may come up. However, if the search were "Rock the Casbah", it would be easier to throw out the noise word "the" given that "Rock" and "Casbah" probably rarely occur near each other except in this song title. Deciding what stop words should be used can be very problematic given the unlimited topic domain of the Web.

Once a page has been analyzed for the various keywords, it is ranked relative to other pages with similar keywords and stored in a database. Ranking is the very secret part of search-engine operation. How a particular search engine decides one page should be higher than another is what search engine promotion specialists are always trying to figure out.

Providing a Search Mechanism

The final aspect of a search engine is the search page itself. A search page is the interface the user makes their query from, and it generally contains a primary query text box as well as other search fields for advanced users who may want to modify a query. For example, consider the interface for Northern Light (www.northernlight.com) shown in Figure 7-1.

The degree of complexity of the search page varies greatly in public search engines. Consider the difference between HotBot's advanced search form and Goto.com's basic interface as shown in Figure 7-2.

The users enter queries as simple as natural-language queries like "Why is the sky blue?" as encouraged by sites like www.ask.com, to complex Boolean expressions and other filters. Once queried, the search engine will retrieve the pages that meet the criteria and present them on a result page. Figure 7-3 shows a result page for the search engine Google (www.google.com).

From the result page, the user can pick some results to explore, further refine the search with a new query, or just give up and try another method to locate what they were hunting for. The general function of search engines is illustrated in Figure 7-4.

Understanding what people expect Webwide search engines to do is important, because users will bring their past experiences with searching to bear when using your

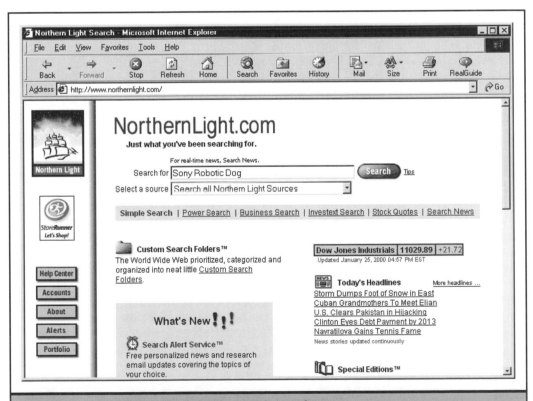

Figure 7-1.   *Northern Light's basic search interface*

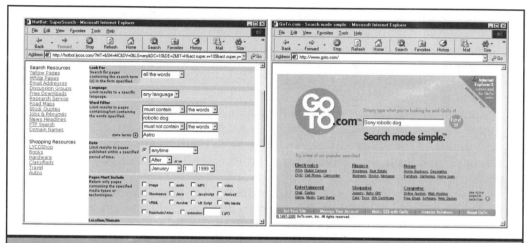

Figure 7-2.   Search interfaces may vary by audience type

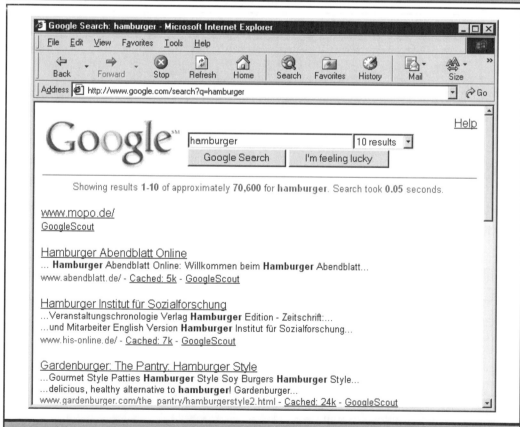

Figure 7-3.   Google's result page is clean and simple

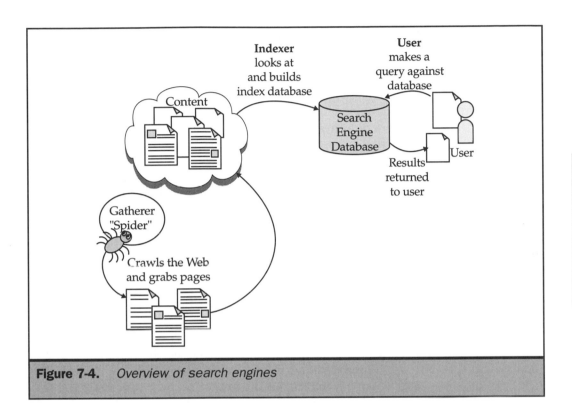

Figure 7-4.   *Overview of search engines*

local site search. Labeling, form layout, and result pages should somewhat mimic what users have come to expect from the public search engines. However, be careful not to directly imitate what public engines do. Public search engines aren't always terribly accurate; they are often geared towards the needs of advertisers and the demands of dealing with the numerous tricks people employ to try to improve their site's ranking. Hopefully, nobody within an organization is going to be resorting to literal trickery to skew page rankings within a local search. Local search engines can be built with trust in mind and should be more accurate.

> **Rule: Utilize past user experience with search engines by using similar layout and labeling in local search-facility design, but avoid imitating aspects of public search engines that deal with the uncontrollable nature of public Web sites.**

Before we discuss adding local search, let's briefly turn our attention to how designers try to utilize search engines and other facilities to promote and drive traffic to their site. This is by no means a complete discussion of a topic that literally changes on a weekly basis. Readers looking for more up-to-date information are directed to the numerous search engine sites that exist on the Web, especially Search Engine Watch (www.searchenginewatch.com).

Search-Engine Promotion

Site owners always want to be number one in search engines. Consider if you are a small travel agent. You probably would love it if people would go to a search engine, type **travel**, and have a link to your site show up as the first one. You'd get a large number of visits for sure. Unfortunately, there are probably a lot of other people who would like to be number one, and being ranked 4,036th isn't going be worth much. In fact, if you are outside the first 20 sites or so returned you probably aren't going to get many clicks at all. Because of this, page designers are always trying to determine how search engines categorize pages, and building their page with keywords in such a way to get a high ranking. In some ways, this idea is similar to how people name their company something like AAATravel in order to get listed first in the phone book. Unfortunately, consider how many travel agents in the world want their site to be in the top ten in search engines, and you'll see a potential problem. The Web is not as geographically specific as the phone book. Consider if there were a single phone book for the United States. There would probably be dozen of pages filled with companies, all starting with AAA. The Web already has this problem, and that's one of the reasons you get so many results when you run a query for a competitive industry like discount travel.

The war to be first in the search engine has an obvious final chapter—the rise of pay for position. Consider that the tricks to be at the top of the search-engine list spread rapidly. For common search phrases, it is nearly impossible to stay at the top of the list for long since other sites use the same search-engine promotion techniques. Already search engines such as Goto (www.goto.com) are opting to push people to the top of the list that are willing to pay for position. Priority placement is also being made for banner ads triggered to correspond to particular search phrases. Just like with the phone book, naming your company AAATravel might put you at the top of the line listings, but readers may opt to look at the large display ads. Search engines will eventually adopt the same model. Furthermore, as end users become more sophisticated, they will begin to rely more on directory listings for generic topics and use search engines only for very specific or complex lookups. The eventual outcome of the search-engine war will almost certainly be a return to traditional models of information retrieval methods used in other advertising forms where you pay for audience relevancy and position. For now, designers should consider not taking advantage of search-engine positioning tricks, regardless of their long-term viability, very foolish.

Adding to the Engines

Getting a site's pages gathered by a search engine is the first step in making a site findable on the Web. The easiest way to do this is simply to tell search engines that your site exists. Most search engines will allow you to add a URL to be indexed. For example, Lycos allows you to add a site for gathering by using a simple form (http://www.lycos.com/addasite.html). Of course, adding your site to every single search engine could be a tedious task, so many vendors (http://www.submit-it.com) are eager to provide developers with a way to bulk submit to numerous search engines. Most Web site promotion software such as WebPosition Gold (http://www.webposition.com/) also includes automated submission utilities.

A big question is, How many search engines should you submit your site to? Some people favor only adding few links to the important top ten engines, especially Yahoo! Numerous studies, as well as this author's experience, suggest that big search sites, particularly Yahoo, account for most search-engine-referring traffic. However, some site-promotion experts feel this is not correct, and believe it is best to create as many links to sites as possible. In fact, a whole class of link sites called "Free For All" links or FFA sites (not to be confused with anything related to the Future Farmers of America) have sprung up to service people who believe that "all links should lead to me" works. The reality is that most of these link services are pretty much worthless and often generate worthless traffic and spam messages. Further, consider that even if you do get back links and email, it is mostly from people who are doing the same thing you're doing—trying to get links.

Robot Exclusion

Before getting too involved putting yourself in every search engine, consider that it isn't always a good idea to have a robot index your entire site, regardless if it is your own internal search engine or a public search engine. First, consider that some pages such as programs in your cgi-bin directory don't need to be indexed. Second, many pages may be transitory, and having them indexed may result in users seeing 404 errors if they enter from a search engine. Lastly, you may just not want people to enter on every single page—particularly those deep within a site. So-called "deep linking" can be confusing for users entering from public search engines. Consider that because these users start out deep in a site, they are not exposed to the home- or entry-page information that is often used to orient site visitors.

Probably the most troublesome aspect of search engines and automated site gathering tools such as offline browsers is that they can be used to stage a denial-of-service attack on a site. The basic idea of most spiders is to read pages and follow pages as fast as they can. Consider if you tell a spider to crawl a single site as fast as it possibly can. All the requests to the crawled server may very quickly overwhelm it, causing the site to be unable to fulfill requests—thus denying services to legitimate site visitors. Fortunately, most people are not malicious in spidering, but understand that it does happen inadvertently when a spider keeps reindexing the same dynamically generated page.

Robots.txt

To deal with limiting robot access, the Robot Exclusion protocol was adopted. The basic idea is to use a special file called robots.txt that should be found in the root directory of a Web site. For example, if a spider was indexing http://www.democompany.com, it would first look for a file at http://www.democompany.com/robots.txt. If it finds a file, it would analyze the file first before proceeding to index the site.

If you have a site like http://www.bigfakehostingvendor.com/~customer, you will find that many spiders will ignore a robots.txt file with a URL of http://www.bigfakehostingvendor.com/~customer/robots.txt. Unfortunately, you will have to ask the vendor to place an entry for you in their robots.txt file.

The basic format of the robots.txt file is a listing of the particular spider or user agent you are looking to limit and statements including which directory paths to disallow. For example,

```
User-agent: *
Disallow: /cgi-bin/
Disallow: /temp/
Disallow: /archive/
```

In this case, we have denied access for all robots to the cgi-bin directory, the temp directory, and an archive directory—possibly where we would move files that are very old but still might need to be online. You should be very careful with what you put in your robots.txt. Consider the file

```
User-agent: *
Disallow: /cgi-bin/
Disallow: /images/
Disallow: /subscribers-only/
Disallow: /resellers.html
```

In this file, a special subscribers-only and resellers file has been disallowed for indexing. However, you have just let people know this is sensitive. For example, if you have content that is hidden unless someone pays to receive a URL via e-mail, you will certainly not want to list it in the robots.txt file. Just letting people know the file or directory exists is a problem. Consider that malicious visitors will actually look carefully at a robots.txt file to see just what it is you don't want people to see. That's very easy to do: just type in the URL like so, **http://www.companytolookat.com/robots.txt.**

Be aware that the robot-exclusion standard assumes that spidering programs will abide by it. A malicious spider will, of course, simply ignore this file, and you may be forced to set up your server to block particular IP addresses or user agents if someone has decided to attack your site.

Robot Control with <META>

An alternative method to the robots.txt file that is useful particularly for those users who have no access to the root directory of their domain is to use a **<META>** tag to control indexing. To disallow indexing of a particular page, use a **<META>** tag like

```
<META NAME="robots" CONTENT="noindex">
```

in the **<HEAD>** section of the HTML. You can also inform a spider not to follow any links coming out of the page:

```
<META NAME="robots" CONTENT="noindex, nofollow">
```

When using this type of exclusion, just make sure not to confuse the robot with contradictory information like

```
<META NAME="robots" CONTENT="index, noindex">
```

or

```
<META NAME="robots" CONTENT="index, nofollow, follow ">
```

as the spider may either ignore the information entirely or maybe even index anyway. The other downside to the **<META>** tag approach is fewer of the public search engines support it than robots.txt.

Optimizing for Search Engines

Optimizing your site for a search engine is not difficult. The first thing to do is to start to think like a search engine—in other words, don't really think at all. Search engines literally look at pages and make educated guesses about what pages are about by following a set of rules to try to understand what the page is about. For example, search engines look for word frequency, **<META>** tags, and a variety of other things. However, they really can't tell the difference between a page about the Miami Dolphins football team and a dolphin show in Miami. The reason is that search engines generally rely on keyword matching in conjunction with some heuristics such as the placement of words in a page or the number of linking sites. So if a designer knows what a search engine is looking for, it is easy enough to optimize a page for the search engine to rank it highly. The next few sections provide a brief overview of some of the things search engines look for as well as some tricks people have employed to improve their search ranking.

<Meta> Tags

Many search engines look at the **<META>** tags for keywords and descriptions of a page's content. A **<META>** tag like

```
<META NAME="Keywords" CONTENT=" Butler-1000, Robot butler, Robot
butler specifications, where to buy a robot butler, Metallic Man
Servant, Demo Company, robot, butler">
```

could be used in our example page about robot butlers. Notice how the content started first with the most specific keywords and phrases and ended with generic keywords. This should play into how most users approach search engines.

Once a search engine looks at the **<META>** tag, it may rate one site higher than another based upon the frequency of keywords in the **CONTENT** attribute. Because of this, some designers load their **<META>** tags with redundant keywords:

```
<META NAME="Keywords" CONTENT=" Robot butler, Robot butler, Robot
butler, Robot butler, Robot butler, Robot butler, Robot butler,
Robot butler, Robot butler, Robot butler">
```

However, many search engines consider this to be keyword loading and may drop the page from their index. If the keyword loading is a little less obvious and combinations of words and phrases are repeated like so

```
<META NAME="Keywords" CONTENT=" Robot butler, Butler-1000, Metallic
Man Servant, Robot butler, Butler-1000, Metallic Man Servant, Robot
butler, Butler-1000, Metallic Man Servant, Robot butler,
Butler-1000, Metallic Man Servant ">
```

the search engine may not consider this improper. An even better approach is to make sure the pattern of repeating words isn't quite as obvious as it varies its order as shown here.

```
<META NAME="Keywords" CONTENT=" Butler-1000, Robot butler, Metallic
Man Servant, Robot butler, Butler-1000, robot, Robot butler,
Democompany, Metallic Man Servant, Butler-1000, robot, butler,
Robot butler, Butler-1000">
```

However, be aware that search engines may still notice the heavy use of certain words or phrases and consider this spamming, potentially reducing the page's ranking or dropping it from the index completely.

Search engines also look at the description value for the **<META>** tag. For example,

```
<META NAME="Description" CONTENT="The DemoCompany Robot Butler is
the most outstanding metallic man servant on the market. The
Butler-1000 comes complete with multiple personalities and voice
modules including the ever-popular faux-British accent.">
```

would be included on the robot-butler page and could be examined by the search engine as well as returned by the search engine on the results page. Because it may be output for the user to see, provide some valuable information in the description that will help the user determine if they want to visit your site. Preferably, keep the description to a sentence or two, and at most three or four sentences.

Titles and File Naming

One important aspect of search-engine ranking is making sure your page has a very good title. For example,

```
<TITLE>Robot Butler</TITLE>
```

is a bad title as far as search-engine ranking goes. A better title might be

```
<TITLE>Butler-1000: Specification of Demo Company's Robot Butler,
the leading metallic man servant on the market</TITLE>
```

Remember that people also look at page titles, and they are used for bookmarking, so a really long title may be more for search engines than for users.

The name of a file can also be important for search engines. Rather than naming a file "butler.htm", use "butler1000_robot_butler.htm" Consider that if you have a good domain name and directory structure, you may create a URL that almost makes sense. Consider, for example, if we named our server democompany.com as well as www.democompany.com. We may have a URL like

```
http://democompany.com/products/robots/butler1000_robot_butler.htm
```

Notice how this almost includes the same information as the title. This provides a secondary benefit of letting the user know where they are, rather than resorting to cryptic URLs like

```
http://democompany.com/products.exe?prod=robots&mod=butler1000
```

Relevant Text Content

One of the best ways to get indexed is to have the keywords and phrases actually within the content of the page. Many search engines will look at text within a page, particularly if it is either towards the top of the page or within heading tags like **<H1>** or **<H2>**. Search engines may also look at the contents of link text. Thus,

```
<A HREF="specifications.htm">Specifications</A>
```

is not as search-engine friendly as

```
<A HREF="specifications.htm">Robot Butler Specification</A>
```

One problem with the fact that search engines focus on page text is that often designers create home pages that are primarily graphic. Search engines may have little to go on besides the **<META>** tag and page title and thus rank the page lower. Consider first using the **ALT** attribute for the **<IMG>** tag to provide some extra information. For example,

```
<IMG SRC="robot.gif" ALT="Butler-1000: Demo Company's industry
leading robot butler">
```

Of course, putting the actual text in the page would be better. Some designers resort to either making text very small, in a color similar to the background, or both so that users won't see it but search engines will hopefully pick it up. For example,

```
<FONT SIZE="1" COLOR="white">The Demo Company Butler1000 is the
best robot butler. The Democompany Butler1000 is the best robot
butler. The Democompany Butler1000 is the best robot butler.</FONT>
```

Be careful with the small or invisible text trick. Many search engines will consider this to be spamming and may drop the page from the search engine.

Links and Entry Points

Another aspect of search-engine ranking has to do with the number of links leaving a page as well as the number of pages that link to a page. Landmark pages such as home pages tend to have a lot of outgoing and incoming links. Search engines would prefer to rank landmark pages highly, so it is important that key pages in your site have links to them from nearly every page. Some search engines also favor sites that have many sites pointing to them. Because of this, people are already starting to create sites solely for the purpose of pointing to other sites.

Another approach to improving search-engine ranking is to submit many pages in a site, or even off a site to a search engine. All of these entry pages, often called *doorway pages*, point to important content within your site. Unfortunately for many users, doorway pages are more like decoy pages, as they can be loaded with false content to attract the visitor and nearly always eventually deposit the user at a page they didn't really want to see. The problem with search-engine promotion is that the distance from simple logical keyword loading and various tricks is a short one—particularly if designers obsess with top-ten ranking.

Tricky Business

The tricks employed by search-engine specialists are numerous and change all the time. Many ideas are simple add-ons to normal Web design techniques. For example, many designers rely on invisible pixel shims to force layout. Search-engine promoters say why not put **ALT** attributes on these images to improve things. Imagine

```
<IMG SRC="pixel.gif" ALT="robot butler robot butler robot butler">
```

all over your page. Then pity the user who pauses on top of one of these invisible pixels only to have a ToolTip pop up screaming about whatever the page is promoting. Spamming pages with invisible text, small text, and multiple images, or just loading the **<META>** or **<TITLE>** tags, are not the most sophisticated tricks, but they often work.

Other tricks include the infamous "bait and switch," where a special search-engine page is created and then posted to a search engine. Once the ranking is high, the bait page is replaced with a real page built for users. A more complicated version of this could be dubbed "feeding the dogs." In the "feeding the dogs" scenario, you write a program that senses when a search engine hits the site and "feed" the engine the page it wants to see. Like a ravenous dog, it gobbles up the food with no idea it just ate the equivalent of informational pig snouts. As real users hit the site, they aren't served the dog food, but get the real site.

Detecting search engines vs. regular users isn't terribly difficult since the engines identify themselves and come from consistent IP addresses. In reality, "feeding the dogs" is just a modified form of browser detection. Search engines can do little to combat this approach since they would have to consider eliminating dynamically built pages—which is impossible given their growing importance—or not informing sites that they are search engines while indexing. A few search engines have already begun to provide a link to a page that shows what was indexed so users can determine if they are being shown something different than what a search engine indexed.

The problem with all the search-engine promotion business is that it tempts the designer to stop building pages for users and start building them for search engines. This is just another form of designing more for your own needs than for your users.

> **Rule: Do not design pages solely to attract search engines as, ultimately, pages are for people.**

One of the most interesting aspects about search engines is that many large organizations don't rely greatly on them for driving traffic. In fact, for many corporations, unless you type their name in directly, you'll be hard-pressed to find them in a search engine. However, despite what appears to be a major oversight on their part, these sites continue to get huge amounts of traffic. According to studies such as the GVU Internet Survey, people type in URLs directly quite often. How are they finding out about sites? Search engines aren't the only way to drive traffic. There are many ways to get users to visit your site. One increasingly popular way to attract visitors is to rely on things outside the Internet. Television, radio, print, billboard, direct mail, and a variety of other venues are being used to spread the address of the latest Web site. While somewhat off topic, we'll discuss very briefly some of the other online techniques beyond search engines used to drive traffic.

Banner Ads

Advertising also exists on the Internet as well. Banner advertisements are used on sites ranging from personal home pages to huge portal sites. Banners are just small images that advertise a particular site, product, or service. Their size varies greatly from microbuttons to full-size banners. The Internet Advertising Bureau (www.iab.net) provides specifications for banner sizes.

There are two primary aspects to promotion with banners. First, you have to get the banners out there in front of the right people. Then you have to get people to click them. If you run your own sites, you may find that you can run your own banner campaigns. However, mostly you want to drive traffic to your site from other places. One way is to swap banners with another site. There are numerous reciprocal banner-swapping programs like LinkExchange (www.linkexchange.com) online. However, you may find you need to book ads on particular sites. Sites can be contacted directly, but there are also large pay-for-banner networks such as DoubleClick (www.doubleclick.com) that are capable of running an ad across many sites or even targeting ads to a particular domain such as a college campus.

The second aspect of using banners, getting people to click them, is a difficult task. Studies show that many users appear to suffer from a form of "banner blindness," where they ignore anything that has similar dimensions as a banner. The banner itself is simply a linked image, as already discussed in Chapter 6. However, we'll quickly present some basic information about how banners can be improved. Click-rates studies suggest that color and animation help attract some users. Text also has been shown to help, particularly when the text looks clickable. Some have found that using a text link below a banner is useful to increase click rates.

[Click for Futuristic Products]

As with search-engine promotion, some people have resorted to tricking users to click by making banners look like GUI widgets.

> **Bad Banner Survey**   _ □ ✕
>
> **Do you hate banners that look like form**   ○ Yes   ○ No | Vote Now! |
> **or GUI items?**

Some unscrupulous banner designers even resort to making ads appear very much like site navigation, as shown here. Notice how hard it would be for novice users to determine if this wasn't part of the site.

Be careful: most legitimate banner networks won't allow such banners, and users may become very annoyed at being tricked.

Probably the biggest problem with banner ads is that very little can be said in a small strip of graphics. Rich banner ads that allow the user to search, shop, or even play a game show some promise, but like search engines, banners shouldn't be considered the only way to attract visitors to a site.

Other Online Promotion Techniques

Beyond banners, there are numerous other online promotion techniques that can be used to drive traffic. A few are listed here. This is by no means a complete list, and is solely meant to stir designers to think of the numerous ways beyond search engines that users come to find sites.

EMAIL Very targeted emails have been shown to be highly effective ways to reach customers. Unfortunately, people often send email in a mass untargeted fashion. When this is done without the recipient's permission, it is termed _spamming_. Spam mail is, of course, both annoying and illegal. Opt-in emails that are sent only to people who ask for something are much better, but you must make sure that users really know they have opted to receive email. Unfortunately, some users filling out forms will not notice that they are being subscribed to an opt-in mail list. This could lead to trouble later on.

NEWSGROUP POSTING Some people find that small advertisements posted to USENET newsgroups are helpful. In general, less aggressive forms of promotion such as simply being active in a group related to your site is a more effective way to promote a site from within USENET.

CONTESTS Sites have already begun to experiment with driving traffic with various forms of sweepstakes and contests. Users often must visit sites or pages a certain number of times in order to qualify for contests. One downside to using contests is that they often attract groups of people looking solely to win something. Many sites on the Internet are built to show users where all the contests are online. Another troublesome aspect of contests is that they often have legal restrictions. Some states and countries do not allow certain types of contests, so it is a good idea to check with a special online contest agency before running one.

FREEBIES   Like contests, various forms of freebies certainly help attract users. Give a user a chance to collect special points redeemable for goods or services and you find users are willing to jump through hoops. Consider in the real world how well freebie promotions like frequent-flyer miles have worked. Of course, giving away points or even small prizes like t-shirts is no comparison to giving the user cold, hard cash.

PAY FOR CLICKS AND AFFILIATE PROGRAMS   Some sites have already begun to experiment with pay-for-click models. It is possible to pay users to visit your site as well as pay other sites to drive traffic to your site. Some sites rely simply on paying referring sites for each user coming to their site regardless of how it happens.

Affiliate programs take the pay-for-click model farther—to be more of a pay for result or even share the profits with others. The best way to understand affiliate programs is with an example. Our example DemoCompany could consider setting up an affiliate program for other sites to sell their robots. Affiliate sites would provide pages and links to promote DemoCompany robots. However, the actual transaction itself would eventually take place via a DemoCompany server. In an affiliate program, the referring site would get a portion of the transaction. Affiliate programs have been used by many large organizations such as Amazon, and affiliate networks like Be Free (www.befree.com) have sprung up to service this market. Probably the most significant downside to affiliate-style marketing is that some users consider it to have a similar feeling as multilevel marketing schemes—particularly when it is done in a less than professional manner.

GOOD DOMAIN NAMES   A large mistake designers seem to make is underestimating their site's name when it comes to traffic generation and retention. Never underestimate the power of a short memorable or already known domain. How many sites that are very popular are named 123-travel-for-less.com, www.thisisaridiculouslylongdomain.com, or, even worse, are outside of a common domain space like .com. Notice how most of the popular sites have domains that are less than 10 characters, and many are as few as 3–6 characters. Words that are easy to remember and spell, like Amazon, are more common than hard-to-pronounce or difficult-to-spell domain names. Even generic domains for a particular product or service are turning out to be useful. For example, some users simply guess domains like books.com when looking for books.

PREVIOUS KNOWLEDGE   The truth is that very often people will come to the Web with previous knowledge of something. Ask users about books on the Internet and they'll probably mention Amazon, but many people had already heard of Barnes and

Noble from everyday life. Notice that many of the most popular properties on the Web actually have long-standing associated real-world equivalents that are either named the same or are utilized to push the fledgling Web property. Already the major television networks and print conglomerates command a great deal of Web traffic. Just because the Web is open, don't think that it immediately turns normal marketing on its head.

How users find their way to a site can't always be determined. Many factors may influence a user to go to a particular site. This book only touches on these subjects to show how global search position is just a small part of site-traffic generation. Interested readers should visit sites like http://www.wilsonweb.com/ for more information on site promotion.

SITE ORGANIZATION AND NAVIGATION

The Need for Local Search

Once a user has made it to your site, they may find a local search a helpful mechanism to navigate the content found there. However, not every site actually needs an internal search engine. The amount of data in a site, and the type of data, influence the need for a search engine. Sites with only a dozen or so pages may find a search provides little benefit over strict browsing or navigational aids such as site maps (discussed in Chapter 8). However, if a site is larger than 100 pages, a search engine is almost always needed. Regardless of the size of a site, if it is filled with complex data—particularly if it is regular in its structure—search will be very useful. Data such as part numbers, product catalogs, and other structured data sets such as a list of locations lend themselves well to search.

> **Rule: If a site is filled with regularly formatted data, very complex-to-digest data, or contains more than 100 pages, include a local search engine.**

Besides data types, the types of visitors and tasks performed at the site also influence the need for a search engine. If the site caters to power users, it should include a search engine. Power users often use search engines to bypass hierarchical navigation schemes. If the site has a significant percentage of return or frequent visitors, a search also makes sense. A user who returns to a site has knowledge of the existence of a particular product, so why should they be forced to browse for it? Return visitors who know the part number of a particular part they are looking for will just want to enter it in a search field and go directly to it.

> **Rule: If a site caters to power users or frequent-return visitors, provide a search facility.**

The Process of Adding a Search Facility

The following eight steps summarize the process of adding a search facility to a site.

Step 1: Decide what to index.

Do you want to index every document in a site or only certain documents? Oftentimes it is only a part index, technical support database, or other area that a user wants to search. Don't just index everything because you can.

Step 2: Decide how you want to index the information.

Once you have determined what you should index, then you need to determine how it will be indexed. Should the search engine just create a free-text index of the document set where every non-stop word is recorded, or would it be better to create a special search-term vocabulary and relate search terms to particular pages in the site?

Step 3: Select a search engine.

It is very important not to select the search engine until you've figured out the volume and type of information you wish to search as well as how it will be indexed. There are numerous search engines available, both free and commercially. Search engines can be installed locally on your system or can be outsourced to third parties who will run the search facility for you. For pointers to some search engines and services, see http://www.searchtools.com.

Step 4: Design the search interface.

Design the search screen to account for the types of searches the user may perform. Often, searches are separated into basic and advanced forms. The search interface should be integrated into the site, should meet the search needs of the users, and should fit the type of data being searched.

Step 5: Design the result pages.

Make sure to consider building pages that deal with positive results when a query is successful, as well as negative results when nothing is returned.

Step 6: Index the data.

During this step, the search engine is used to crawl all or part of the site and build an index. You may actually be forced to manipulate the index by hand to create optimal queries.

Step 7: Integrate the search engine with the search interface.

This step involves making the search interface access the index. Generally, this is just a matter of setting the **ACTION** attribute of the <FORM> tag used to implement the search form. Integrating the result page is a little more difficult, but is often a matter of taking the designed result page and making it into a special template the search engine can read.

Step 8: Test and monitor.

A key aspect of implementing a search engine is making sure to test that it gives back the correct results for important queries. Search engines should also be monitored and common queries identified. Users also should be allowed to rate the value of the individual search results so that refinements can be made.

The focus of the next few pages is not on how to actually create an index, which will vary greatly by the data being indexed as well as the search engine being used, but to show how to design the various aspects of a search interface.

Designing the Search Interface

Assuming that a search facility is needed, a designer should first and foremost consider what the user wants to search for. Far too often, search engines are added to a site and set to index everything using a free-text search. As with a Webwide search site, users pound their heads as they search for a particular part number like KF-456 only to be shown every single document the part number occurs in, ranging from press releases to technical notes. To the user, the ordering of the documents seems almost arbitrary, and the most important document isn't first in the list. What's interesting is why this form of search was used. Designers assume that since public search engines work like this, so should their local search engine. This seems like a good idea—users are familiar with formulating search strings at public sites and bring this knowledge with them to your site. However, global search engines are not very accurate for a variety of reasons, including numerous sites trying to get to the top of lists. Public search engine results don't always seem to make sense, and the ordering often has to do with sheer luck, in some cases, rather than accuracy. Consider that in your own site, if you want a particular page to be shown when a user types in "Robot Butler," you can do that. Remember, as mentioned earlier, when building a local search facility, copy the style, syntax, and interface of public Web search engines, but don't imitate their imprecise functionality.

The main advantage of local searching is that you can utilize controlled vocabularies to deal with what users will probably want to search for. Besides relating keywords with certain pages in a more precise manner, you may even suggest common queries for users to run. Remember, local search engines provide designers with a much greater degree of control than public search engines.

Accessing Search

A big question is how users will get to a search facility. Some sites create a special button labeled search that when selected takes the user to a special search page. Other sites utilize a search field within all pages. A comparison of the two approaches is shown in Figure 7-5.

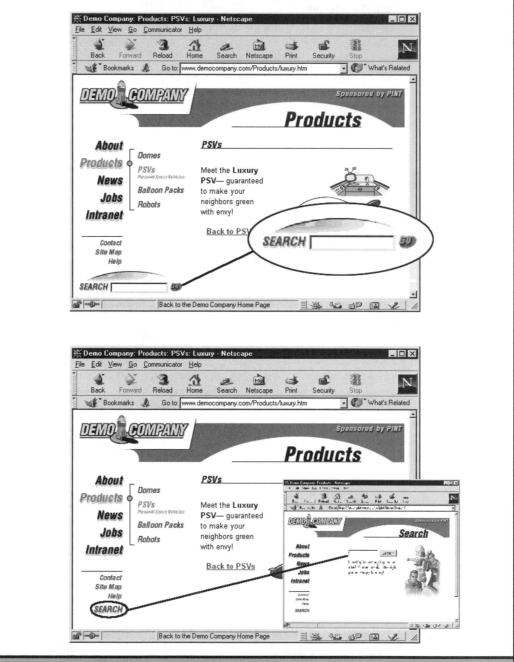

Figure 7-5. *In-page search vs. a special search page*

While putting the search directly on the page eliminates one click for the user, a search field within a content page must be very basic. There still may be a need for a special search page if more complex queries are to be formed. It really isn't possible to put advanced search mechanisms within every page, as it tends to make the search facility too prominent and takes away from the page's primary purpose of delivering content. So the question is really to expose a simple search facility on content pages or provide it on a special search page. Regardless of the choice, search should be easily found from every page in a site.

Suggestion: When search is available in a site, include a search button or field on all pages.

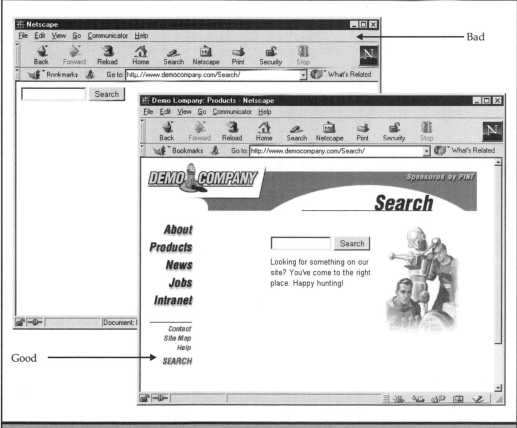

Figure 7-6.   *Search pages should resemble other pages in a site*

Designing a Basic Search Interface

The search facility of a site should look the same as the rest of the site. Oftentimes it is not the same because it is added by technical staff, who don't set up the search templates to match the site's look and feel. Users who utilize such search engines may feel they have left the site if the look changes greatly. Look at the two search facilities shown in Figure 7-6, and the need for integration becomes obvious.

> **Rule: A search form as well as the result pages must match the look and feel of a site.**

Also, the search form should fit the type of data being searched. For example, if users are searching for objects that are colored, shouldn't the search form provide a way to specify by color? The example search interface in Figure 7-7 for searching for

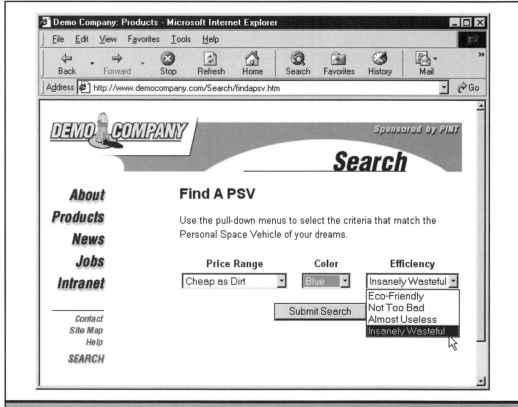

Figure 7-7.   *Search forms vary based on content being searched*

personal space vehicles shows how search forms should match the content that is being searched.

Consider the golden rule of designing a search facility for a site—the more we know about what users are looking for, the better able we'll be to help them find it. One way to do this is to analyze what people search for by looking at the queries they enter. Regardless of how we figure out what users search for, we need to help users narrow down things properly. For example, if we are searching for names, try to help people enter last names or first names into individual text boxes rather than just letting them type names into a single text box. If part numbers are being searched in a range from 1–10,000, then let people know that is the range, limit them to the range, and alert them if they are out of range. A ToolTip set using the **TITLE** attribute in HTML or a simple JavaScript is an easy way to let people know about ranges without explicitly printing them onscreen. A few search forms that fit the data being searched are shown here.

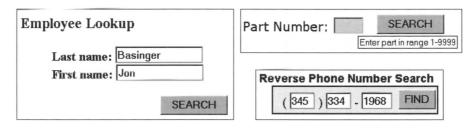

Rule: A search form should match the content being searched.

The primary element of a search form is the actual search query field. A big question is how long should the search field be? The query text field should be large enough to hold at least a few search terms without scrolling. A search field should also suggest the emphasis of search. If search is the primary emphasis of the page and users are going to form complex searches, an input size in the range 30 to 40 characters is common. A survey of the public search engines shows that most use a size of 30, 35, or 40 characters for their primary search field. This size makes the search field a fairly large element width-wise on a typical page. When search is a secondary aspect of a page, the size should be about half the size—usually from 15 to 18 characters, which should fit a few keywords for a simple query. Of course, the size of the search box should always be designed with the search terms and the page layout in mind.

Suggestion: Primary search text boxes should be about twice as big as secondary search text boxes.

The second aspect of the search form is the button to execute the search. Sometimes this is done using a form button. Other times a custom button is used. The use of a form button is probably slightly more intuitive for users. The label of the button also varies. Some favor "Search," others "Find," and some even something as simple as

"Go." A lot of this depends on the context of the search. If the word "search" is used to label the field, labeling the button "search" seems a little redundant.

| [   ] SEARCH | Search: [   ] 🔍 |

The search form should fit the types of users the site is designed for. For example, a search facility for kids might be playful and have few instructions, while a search facility for engineers might contain a variety of fields for visitors to tune their searching. Simple search forms should be separated from advanced ones.

Advanced Search-Form Design

Advanced search forms are more challenging to design, particularly if there are many ways for the user to tune the search. First, if the search is to allow Boolean searching using AND, OR, or NOT, the form must either be designed with pull-downs to separate search terms or provide explicit instructions for users on how to build Boolean queries as shown in Figure 7-8.

Creating Boolean expressions can be a serious problem for many users. Try to avoid suggesting their use in basic searches where possible.

Advanced search forms often include various fields to limit the time of search. For example, they may be able to specify a date range to search when looking for time-sensitive information. They may also be able to limit the type of data to search by format (image, PDF, sound, etc.) as well as by content type (e.g., press releases, specifications, etc.). Some search facilities allow the user to search only certain parts of a site. This may be called a *scoped* search. Unfortunately, users may not understand a site's sectioning, so it may be better to limit the site to search a topic, category, or idea rather than a section of a site. A common way to do either form of scoped search is using a pull-down as shown here.

search [products ▼] for [robot butler   ] 🔍

Suggestion: It is better to limit search to a topic, category, or idea rather than a section of a site.

Other possibilities for an advanced search facility include allowing users to limit the number of results to be returned, to set the way results should be returned, and to

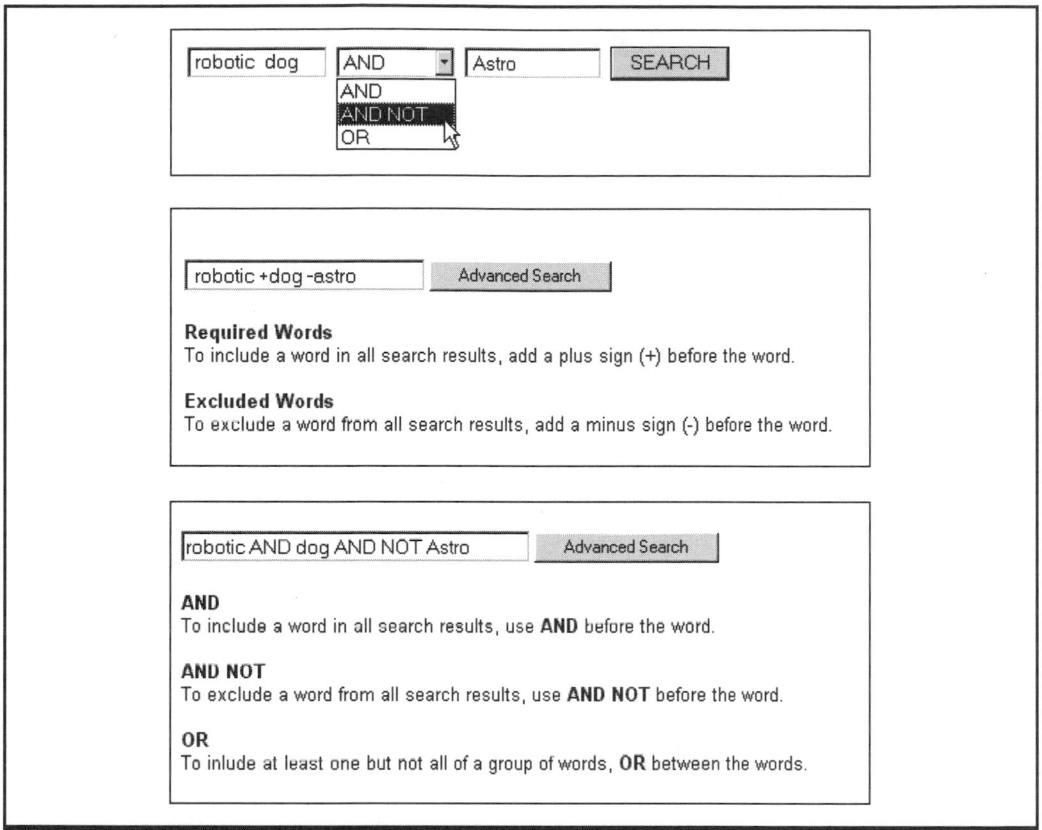

Figure 7-8.   *Boolean queries*

search in regards to meta information such as document authors. Figure 7-9 shows an example of an advanced search form.

A very important part of advanced search forms are the instructions. Not all search engines work alike, and you should provide explicit instructions for the user either directly on the search screen or using pop-up windows. Do not use a separate page for your search instructions as it forces the user to either print out the instructions or quickly memorize the information. Besides instructions, example queries and field usage should also be provided in an advanced search page.

Rule: Advanced search facilities must provide instructions and examples.

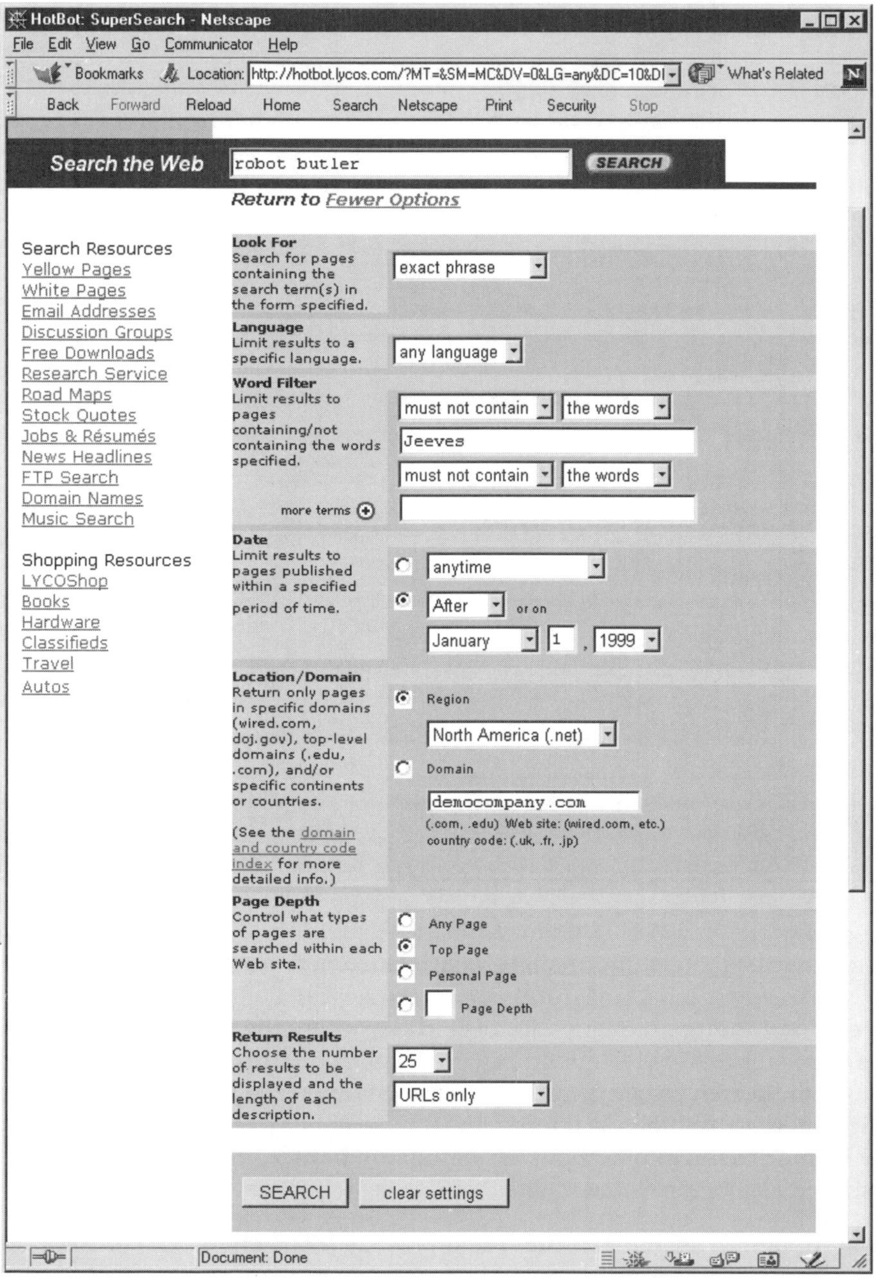

Figure 7-9. Advanced search forms should be carefully designed

Result-Page Design

Designing result pages must take into account two extreme possibilities: no results and way too much information. Even when just about the right information is returned, a well-designed result page should help the user discern what is relevant. The rule of thumb for a result page is the more information the better, as oftentimes people can't determine the value of one result over another. A well-designed result page should include the items shown in Table 7-1.

Result-Page Element	Description
Original query	The original query string used should be prominently displayed on all result pages so the users don't have to recall what search string they used.
The scope of the search and the results found	The total number of documents searched and returned should be indicated (e.g., 10,000 documents searched, 20 matches).
Context of current results	There should be some indication as to what part of the result list the user is looking at (e.g., page 2 out of 10, or items 30–40 out of 200).
Page or document titles	Each item returned should be clearly titled.
URL of returned page	The actual URL of the individual documents should be shown, as it may provide useful information to the user.
Page summaries	A brief summary of a returned page's contents should be shown. This is often picked up either from the **<META NAME="DESCRIPTION">** element or the first few lines of text in a document. A user may have the option to show or hide the page descriptions.
Date or time information of results	Minimally, the create date or date of last update of a returned document should be shown. Some search facilities also provide an indication of the time the index was last built, the time it took to search the index, and the time the query was performed.

Table 7-1.   *Common Result-Page Elements*

Result-Page Element	Description
Size of returned pages	The file size of the document returned should be indicated. This is especially important if the files being searched are large binaries.
Type of result	In some searches, other forms of data such as Adobe Acrobat, Microsoft Word, or multimedia data may be returned. Make sure to indicate the format of data with a label or icon.
Relevancy of results	A relevancy ranking should be clearly indicated. Usually, search results are ranked from highest to lowest. A percentage score or bar should be used to show the difference between items.
Keyword matches	Since users are highly annoyed when they are unable to figure out why a particular page is returned for a query, show the keywords matched and, if possible, highlight these words in context in the summary. If possible, when the user selects a document, the query terms should also be clearly highlighted.
Navigation	Navigation to move through the result set should be provided. Common buttons include "Next 10 documents" or "Previous 10 documents" where the step value changes depending on the user's preference. Navigation to see the first or last page in a result set is also sometimes used.
Refinement options	The ability to refine the query should be present. Users may be able to search against the result set or even perform a brand-new query.
Help	Help information explaining the format of the results should be available.

Table 7-1.   *Common Result-Page Elements* (continued)

Depending on the type of search engine being used, not all these items will be possible—particularly advanced relevancy and matching indication. However, designers should strive to include all elements in a result page.

> **Rule: Result pages should provide as much information as possible so users can decide what items to peruse further.**

Search result pages often miss any consideration of site navigation. When users access a result page, they are not just searching—they may also switch back to a browsing mode to investigate results. Remember, users are just looking for an answer, and they may move in and out of approaches in their hunt, so provide browsing facilities on search results when possible in case the user wants to leave the result page easily. Figure 7-10 presents a search result page that includes most of the elements listed in Table 7-1.

One aspect of search result pages, which may appear obvious but is often overlooked, is that the format of data returned should be carefully considered. For example, just listing out a page title, URL, and description may not be enough for a user to make a decision about one choice over another. For example, if a user performs a search of products, it might be possible to output small thumbnails of the products that match the user's criteria, as shown in Figure 7-11.

> **Rule: The format of the search results should fit the data that is being returned.**

The key aspect of designing a positive search result page is helping the user find and make a decision about which returned items to pursue further. However, unlike public Web search engines where very often far too much is returned, designers should also carefully consider the negative result when nothing has met a user's search criteria.

Negative Result Page

When a query results in no matches, the result page should try to help the user identify what went wrong. In some cases, it may be just that there is nothing that matches the terms. In other cases, the user may have simply used the search facility incorrectly. A good negative result page should try to help the user figure out which case it is and perform the functions shown in Table 7-2.

Figure 7-12 presents a negative result search page that provides all the features useful to help the user get back on track. Notice that the negative result page also fits with the design of the site.

> **Rule: Negative result search pages must include information on why a query failed, and potentially how to fix the query.**

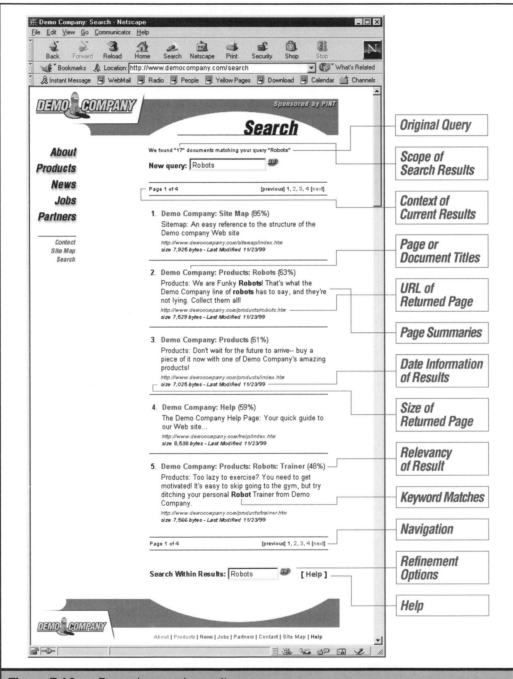

Figure 7-10.   Example search result page

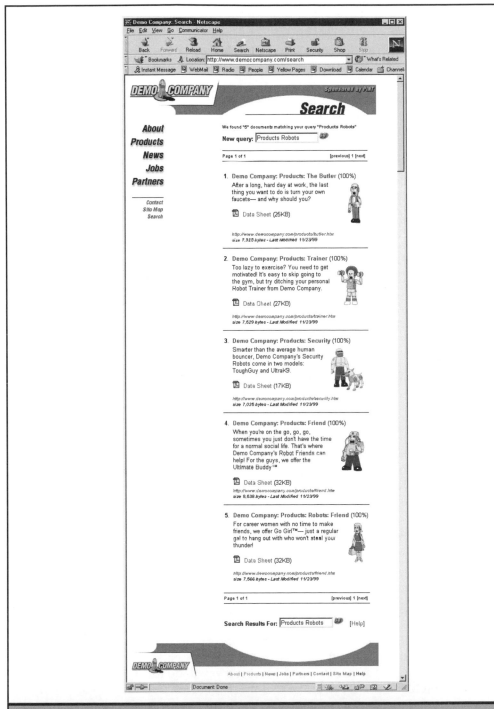

Figure 7-11.   *Search results vary based on the data searched*

Feature	Description
Clear failure message	Make sure the user knows that the query failed, and potentially why it failed. Indicate the number of documents searched and provide a clear message indicating that the search failed.
Search-again mechanism	Like a positive result page, the query used should be shown, and the option to search again should be directly available from the result page.
Help information	Probably the most important aspect of a negative result page is to provide clear and useful help. First, provide tips that might explain why the search failed. For example, often search terms are misspelled. If the search engine doesn't provide spell checking, consider adding an option to spell check the query string. If possible, show terms that are near the term searched for. Consider showing the common search terms. Lastly, make sure that help information on how to use the search facility is readily available.

Table 7-2.   *Features of a Negative Result Page*

Similar to broken-link pages, a negative result page probably comes up more than we would like. Make sure to monitor the negative queries to determine the usefulness of a search facility. Measure the percentage of negative queries, and try to discern common bad queries. If your site is missing something, the negative queries may reveal the items that users are really looking for.

Summary

While a search facility appeals primarily to power users and frequent visitors, novice users are already familiar with public search engines. Understanding how public search engines work and are used is the first step in designing a local site search facility. Designers should also understand how users move from public search sites to local sites and attempt to guide users to what they are looking for. Search facilities must be designed with the user in mind. The best way to do this is to consider what users would actually want to search for in a site. Do not fall into the trap of blindly

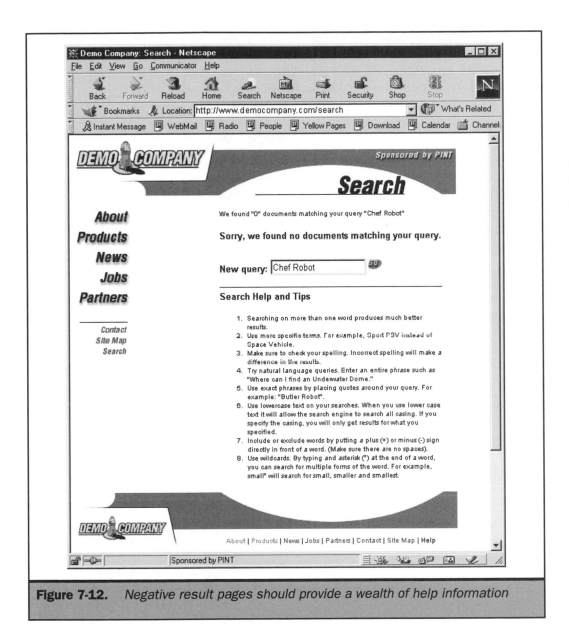

Figure 7-12.   *Negative result pages should provide a wealth of help information*

imitating the freetext search qualities of global Web search engines. When providing local search, make sure to provide both basic and advanced search forms. Format the search form carefully and provide instructions. This will help users form good queries, but in case things go wrong, make sure the negative result page provides extra help to get users back on track. Once users do receive a positive result from a search engine, make sure that enough information is provided so they can narrow down the potential choices. Having too much data is nearly as bad as having none at all. However, always consider that searching isn't everything. Do not obsess with being in the top of public search-engine results, and don't assume that all users will want to use your local search facility. Like all forms of navigation, searching is a means to an end, not the end itself. There are many ways to help a user find what they are looking for. The next chapter will present a variety of other navigational aids, such as site maps, site indexes, and help systems.

The Complete Reference

Chapter 8

Site Maps, Indexes, and Other Navigational and Use Aids

Even when a site is well structured, links are properly used, and searching is provided, users may still have difficulty finding what they are looking for. Not all users will approach site navigation in the same manner. Even when searching is available, some users may prefer to browse or navigate in a structural fashion. A few usability studies have even suggested that users find information more successfully when they avoid free text search. Regardless of navigation preference, site designers should strive to provide as many navigational choices as possible. Providing maps and other aids is not enough; we must contend with the fact that some users may need additional assistance and will turn to help systems or glossaries to further their understanding of the site. Site designers should always remember user differences. Some users will not understand navigation that seems obvious to others.

More than Searching

You may not need a search facility unless you have a very large site or very complex data. Even if you do need a search facility, it will not address every user's navigational question. Users do not always know exactly what they are looking for. There is a huge range of possibilities between a directed search for a known item and a casual browse around a site to see what is there. Sometimes a user may have a sense of what they are looking for but are interested in seeing things that are somewhat similar. Looking through a list of related items easily addresses this desire. While search engines can provide alternative search queries as suggestions, sometimes the user just needs to browse to understand the items available.

One of the biggest drawbacks to a search is that it doesn't provide a very accurate idea of scope. An unspecific or bad query might suggest there is nothing in the site, while a broad query might suggest the site contains much more than it does. Sometimes a user simply wants to understand the size and scope of a site before diving in. Just as some people rate a book by its physical size, some users may want an understanding of the number of pages in a site before they dive in. Why bother with a small site, they might reason. However, simply looking at the home page or doing a simple query of a site search engine won't reveal the depth and breadth of a site. Site designs should always strive to expose or preview what is deeper in a site. The site map is a structure that may address some of the limitations of known item searching and casual browsing. While it would seem obvious that the Web would benefit from a structural overview map, the proper use of a site overview or map is relatively uncommon on the Web. A survey of the Fortune 100 sites made at the time of this writing in mid-1999 showed that only 58 percent used site maps.

Site Maps

A map is an image that graphically represents the location of various elements within a set region or space. For example, a road map may represent the location of roads, cities, and landmarks in a bird's-eye style. A map provides both direction and distance information that a driver can use to find and reach a destination. Maps are also used to present information such as demographic data, or to visualize complex data sets. The discussion here will focus more on the use of maps for "wayfinding."

On the Web, maps are often used in the same way as road maps. A *site map* is a structural overview of a site that shows pages generally related by structural proximity. Oftentimes the physical and conceptual locations of pages are directly related, but remember, they do not have to be. Access to a site map should be from every page within a site, but generally should not be a primary navigation choice. Often, a Site Map button or link is available within a global navigation bar, but its appearance or location is less prominent than main-section navigation. Some site designs will cluster navigation aids like site map and search facilities together, as shown in Figure 8-1.

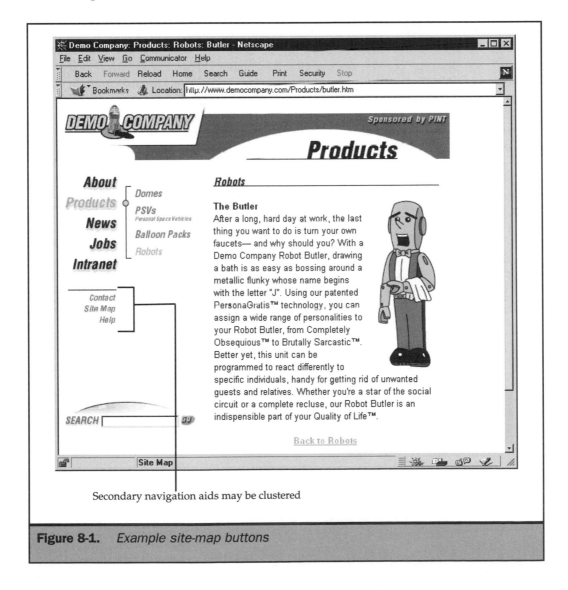

Secondary navigation aids may be clustered

Figure 8-1.   *Example site-map buttons*

The name of the Web site map link should be well considered. While simply "map" might seem appropriate, site designers must consider that if the site includes information about physical locations in the real world, the simple word "map" may be confusing. The term "site map" should be considered standard as the link name to access a structural diagram of a Web site. Do not confuse this with "site index," which will be discussed later in this chapter.

In general, activating a site-map link will load a page that provides a section-by-section overview of a site with links to many pages in the site. The user will scan the links in the map and then decide which page to access. The user could also use the site map to get a quick overview of the range of content within a site.

Textual Site Maps

The representation of a site map comes in many forms. The simplest map is a textual site map. A textual site map represents all links as basic HTML text with varying sizes, colors, or indentation to show the importance of pages within a site. An example of such a map is shown in Figure 8-2.

The arrangement of the pages can aid in a user's understanding of the site. Many sites use colored boxes or columns to section various aspects of a site, as shown in Figure 8-3.

In general, a column or downward-oriented approach to site mapping is better for larger sites given screen width constraints and the lack of rightward scrolling exhibited by users.

Textual site maps are efficient to download as well as easy to build and update. However, textual site maps may not be terribly memorable for the user. It may also be difficult to present complex organizational relationships in text form. Adding graphical icons to section heads as shown in Figure 8-4 may improve memorability and speed access by providing obvious site landmarks within a text map.

Eventually, however, a site designer may find the aesthetic and presentation options of a textual site map limiting and turn to a graphical site form.

Graphical Site Maps

While graphical site maps provide more possibility for visual design, they do so at a significant price. As discussed in Chapter 2, most sites use a flow chart or similar navigation diagram to aid in organizing a site. It is not difficult to translate such a diagram into a visual and use it as a site map by making the various page icons clickable. A simple example of a graphical site map is shown in Figure 8-5.

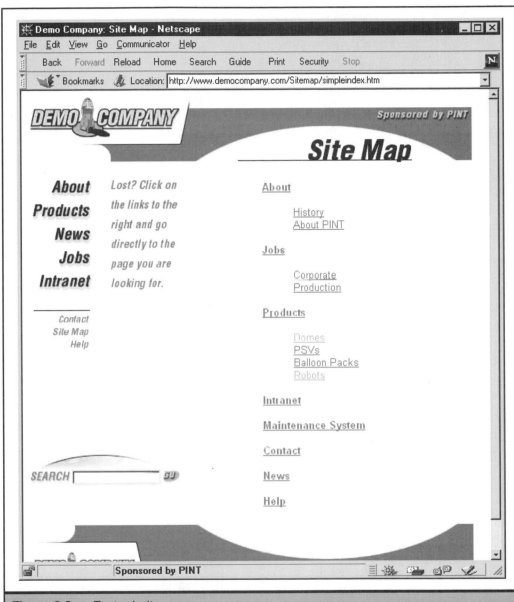

Figure 8-2.   *Textual site map*

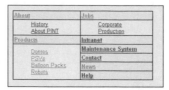

Figure 8-3. *Approaches to text-map organization*

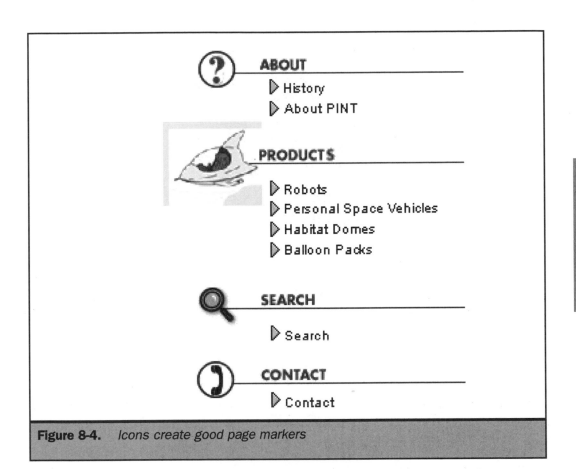

Figure 8-4.   *Icons create good page markers*

Note   *Some site-development products like Dreamweaver or FrontPage provide an easy way to save out site map images directly. Unfortunately the maps often don't work well as actual user site maps. Other flowcharting tools such as Visio may be useful to create and export site maps to a Web-friendly format.*

Like flow diagrams, many site maps are hierarchical in structure, starting with the home page graphic at the top and proceeding downward to indicate deeper pages. Such a style may only work well with a relatively deep site. A broader site would probably not fit within a typical screen size. Thus, many designers opt for a circular design or less structured site map, as shown in Figure 8-6.

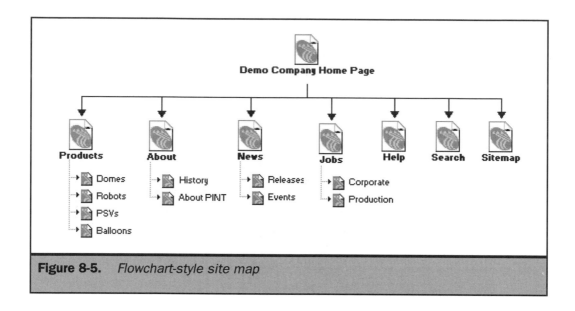

Figure 8-5. *Flowchart-style site map*

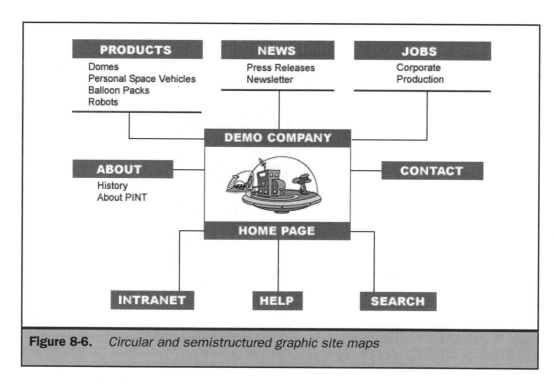

Figure 8-6. *Circular and semistructured graphic site maps*

Graphical site maps can also be used to provide more obvious clues to depth. Some have found the use of three-dimensional hybrid styles appealing, as shown in Figure 8-7. However, forms such as the one shown in Figure 8-7 can be difficult to create as well as to read, despite their sophisticated look.

One huge benefit of the graphic-site-map approach is that such site maps can be extended to fit with the theme of the site, as shown by the example site map in Figure 8-8.

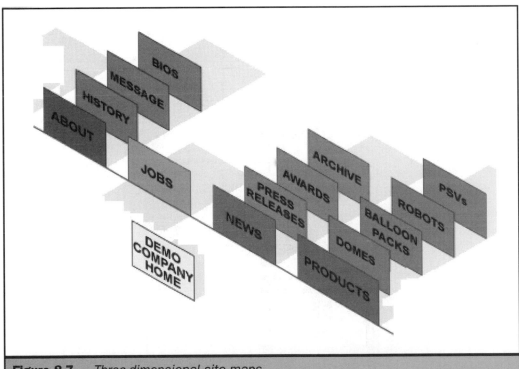

Figure 8-7.   *Three-dimensional site maps*

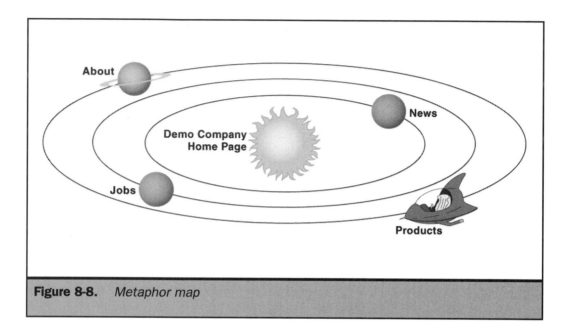

Figure 8-8.   *Metaphor map*

Another benefit of graphic site maps is that it is often easier to draw special attention to certain pages or even provide information about the content type on the page. Consider the use of icons or page-icon styles like the ones shown here:

It would be possible to provide this information in a textual site map, but it would require the user to read the content rather than quickly scan it.

While graphical site maps may provide more design possibilities, they do so at the expense of download time and updatability. Obviously, a visual site map will take more time to download than a text one. For users lost on a site, this may add insult to injury. Furthermore, it will be difficult to keep the site map up-to-date because any page changes will require a graphic change. Because of their update limitations, graphic site maps are reasonable only for relatively static sites unless their detail is limited only to the highest-level pages.

Designing Site Maps

Before considering the issues of designing site maps, consider how maps are used in the real world. Standard geographical maps help people orient themselves in three basic ways:

- They show users where they are
- They show users where they might go
- They give users an overview of their environment

Conceptually, a Web site map should serve the same purpose. In reality, most site maps do not always meet these goals.

You Are Here

Most site maps do not really show users where they are in the site. In some sense this really doesn't matter, because most site maps load over the current page. However, it might be more appropriate to show the site map in a secondary window and provide a "you are here" marker within the page. This would be similar to location directories at malls, museums, and amusement parks that provide a "you are here" indicator to help the patrons find their way. The use of a similar construct on a Web site map would certainly give the user more spatial orientation as they browsed a site. Indication of the current document could be accomplished by highlighting the page in the map with color, graphic, or size. Unfortunately, since the user could access the site map from any page on the site, adding this feature would require making the site map page dynamic. An example of this concept in action is shown in Figure 8-9.

Using a technology like DHTML, it is not terribly difficult to augment a site map to provide such a feature. By looking at the referring page for a link, the site map could highlight which page the user was on. The code below shows the basic idea how this would work:

```
<HTML>
<HEAD>
<TITLE>Demo Company: Site Map</TITLE>
<SCRIPT LANGUAGE="JavaScript" TYPE="text/javascript">
<!--
```

```
    var curDiv = "";
    var curFile = "";

    var referPath = opener.location;
    referPath = referPath.toString();
    var from = referPath.lastIndexOf("/") + 1;
    var to = referPath.length;
    var curFile = referPath.substring(from,to);

function mOvr(src,clrOver) {
    if (!src.contains(event.fromElement)) {
        src.style.cursor = 'hand'; src.style.background = clrOver;
    }
}

function mOut(src,clrIn) {
    if (!src.contains(event.toElement)) {
        src.style.cursor = 'default';
        src.style.background = clrIn;
    }
}
function pageNew (filePath,fileName) {
    var fileURL = "http://www.democompany.com/" + filePath;
    opener.location = fileURL;
    selected_page(fileName);
}

//-->
</SCRIPT>
</HEAD>
<BODY onLoad="selected_page(curFile);">

<TABLE WIDTH="300" BORDER="0" CELLSPACING="0" CELLPADDING="0">

<TR BGCOLOR="#000000">
<TD WIDTH="300"><!-- begin nested table: site map links -->
<TABLE WIDTH="300" BORDER="0" CELLSPACING="1" CELLPADDING="2">
<TR>
<TD ID="item1ID" CLASS="category" WIDTH="150" BGCOLOR="#FFFFFF"
onMouseOver="mOvr(this,'#CCCCCC');"
onMouseOut="if(curFile != 'item1.htm'){mOut(this,'#FFFFFF');}
else{mOut(this,'#CCCCCC');}"
onClick="pageNew('directory/item1.htm','item1.htm');">
<FONT FACE="arial, helvetica, sans-serif" SIZE="-2">
Item 1</FONT></TD>
<TD ID="item2ID" CLASS="category" WIDTH="150" BGCOLOR="#FFFFFF"
onMouseOver="mOvr(this,'#CCCCCC');"
onMouseOut="if(curFile != 'item2.htm')
```

```
{mOut(this,'#FFFFFF');}else{mOut(this,'#CCCCCC');}"
onClick="pageNew('directory/item2.htm','item2.htm');">
<FONT FACE="arial, helvetica, sans-serif" SIZE="-2">
Item 2</FONT></TD></TR>
<TR>
<TD ID="item3ID" CLASS="category" WIDTH="150" BGCOLOR="#FFFFFF"
onMouseOver="mOvr(this,'#CCCCCC');"
onMouseOut="if(curFile != 'item3.htm')
{mOut(this,'#FFFFFF');}else{mOut(this,'#CCCCCC');}"
onClick="pageNew('directory/item3.htm','item3.htm');">
<FONT FACE="arial, helvetica, sans-serif" SIZE="-2">
      Item 3</FONT></TD>
<TD ID="item4ID" CLASS="item" WIDTH="150" BGCOLOR="#FFFFFF"
onMouseOver="mOvr(this,'#CCCCCC');"
onMouseOut="if(curFile != 'item4.htm')
{mOut(this,'#FFFFFF');}else{mOut(this,'#CCCCCC');}"
onClick="winNew('directory/item4.htm','item4.htm','');">
<FONT FACE="arial, helvetica, sans-serif" SIZE="-2">
Item 4<BR></FONT></TD>
</TR>
</TABLE>
<!-- end nested table --></TD></TR></TABLE>

<SCRIPT LANGUAGE="JavaScript1.2" TYPE="text/javascript">
<!--
function selected_page (file) {

   switch (file) {
      case "item1.htm" :
         item1ID.style.background = "#CCCCCC";
         lastBgColor(curDiv);
         curDiv = "item1ID";
         break;
      case "item2.htm" :
         item2ID.style.background = "#CCCCCC";
         lastBgColor(curDiv);
         curDiv = "item2ID";
         break;
      case "item3.htm" :
         item3ID.style.background = "#CCCCCC";
         lastBgColor(curDiv);
         curDiv = "item3ID";
         break;
      case "item4.htm" :
         item4ID.style.background = "#CCCCCC";
         lastBgColor(curDiv);
         curDiv = "item4ID";
         break;
```

```
      default :
         break;
   }
}
function lastBgColor (divID) {
   if (divID != "") {
      var bgColor = "#FFFFFF";
    var tmpDiv = divID + ".style.background = \"" + bgColor + "\"";
      eval(tmpDiv);
   }
   return true;}
//-->
</SCRIPT>
</BODY></HTML>
```

The referring page would use this code in its links:

```
<A HREF="sitemap_nojs.htm"
onMouseOver="window.status='Site Map'; return true;"
onClick="newWindow = window.open('sitemap.htm', 'sitemap',
'toolbar=0,location=0,directories=0,status=0,menubar=0,
scrollbars=0,resizable=1,copyhistory=1,width=400,height=250');
return false;">Site Map</A>
```

Showing Scope and Destination Choices

The second and third functions of maps are generally found in most site maps. A Web site map will provide links to various pages in the site, but not all. A site map will also show the major sections and pages of a site, which should give the user an indication of the site's content. Of course, both of these map features are affected by the degree of detail provided in the map.

For all but the smallest sites, it may not be possible to show all the links in the site. Few site maps, even textual maps, show more than 100 to 200 direct links because the map quickly becomes a tangle of links or icons. If you consider using a graphical structure, you may be limited to only a few dozen pages, at most, on-screen.

In short, the site map should be created to meet the following criteria:

- Provide the appropriate level of detail
- Show important pages or site landmarks

Determining the appropriate level of detail to represent will depend on the complexity of the site. For large sites, consider using pull-down menus within a site map structure or a similar dynamic structure like an expanding tree control, as shown here:

Producing Site Maps

For small sites, site maps are easy to produce manually whether they take graphic or
textual form. For large sites, particularly those that have a great deal of dynamic

Figure 8-9.   *Provide "you are here" markers*

SITE ORGANIZATION AND NAVIGATION

content, developing a reasonably detailed map may be tedious. Automatic creation of a site navigation map is possible, but not always optimal. Numerous tools exist (www.webdesignref.com/resources) that can be used to produce textual or even graphical site maps. These maps are often more beneficial to the site maintainer looking for broken links on the site or performing similar structural maintenance.

While automatic mapping would seem a good route, particularly for larger sites, showing the complete linking relationship of a site will often produce a tangled mess of page links. Given limited screen real estate, there is little real-world evidence to suggest that a graphical site map can show more than a few dozen pages without becoming unwieldy for the user. Textual maps are better. In either case, with different levels of zooming this could be dealt with—but potentially at the expense of showing the extent of content within the site.

Automatic mapping of a site may also fail to point out which pages are important in a site and should be indicated as "site landmarks." It may be possible to use a heuristic-like number of links pointing to a page, hierarchy depth, or the amount of content in a page for a tool to determine which pages are important. However, these heuristics fail many times just as they do in search engines. The bottom line is that human guidance may be required for an automatic mapping tool to properly indicate the importance of pages.

Depending on the size of your site, you will have to choose between a graphical site map or a textual site map, as well as a hand-produced site map or a dynamically created map. No matter the form, there will always be the question of how much detail should be shown in the map. Maps for larger sites may not be able to link reasonably to every page. Site maps for larger sites may require multiple zoom levels. However, in either large or small site maps we will be concerned with how to show the importance of various points within a site. We also may be concerned with showing the amount of information at a particular location within a site. The basic site map design issues are summarized in Table 8-1.

The Benefit of "Geographical" Navigation

While some real-world mapping concepts make sense for site maps, don't take things too far. Wayfinding within a Web site isn't necessarily linear or geographical. Proximity may not matter on a Web site. Users on page A are not always required to go through page B to get to page C. The site map, as well as search engine or direct URL access, will allow them to literally teleport to any point in the site at any time. Distance measurements on maps don't make sense on the Web since there is little cost in travel time on the Web. Always remember that cyberspace isn't the same as real space; users don't necessarily form structural diagrams in their heads as they browse a site. Concepts like "up" and "down" or proximity of pages within a hierarchy may mean very little to the user. Consider this point carefully before you transform the site's architecture diagram into a site map.

Map Form	Graphical maps are useful for small sites, particularly if they are static. Graphical maps also provide opportunity for visual design. Textual maps are useful for larger sites or those that require frequent changes. Textual maps are favored because of download speed and adaptability.
Map Production Method	Small maps and most graphical maps should be produced by hand. Large maps or maps for sites with frequent structure changes should be produced dynamically.
Map Detail	Site maps for small sites should link to all pages. Large site maps should provide primary page links at minimum and may provide zoom capability to get to deeper pages. Page size or content type may also be important to site maps.
"Landmark" Indication	Site maps should indicate important pages with graphic, text, color, size, or position cues.
Location Indication	Site maps should include a "you are here" feature when possible and spawn a separate window.

Table 8-1.   *Site Map Design Considerations*

Site Indexes

A site map may fail some users, particularly if they are scanning for a known item but are forced to find the appropriate category. Even textual site maps that often resemble the table of contents of a book can be slow to scan if the user isn't familiar with the organization of the site. In the world of books, an index might be a more efficient way to find the page that a known item is referenced on. Similarly, a *site index* is an alphabetical or conceptually organized list of a site's contents. Not unlike an index of a book, a site index may provide a word or category and link to the page or pages that relate to the particular content. Be careful to organize the index in a standard alphabetical style; otherwise, the user will not be able to quickly understand the difference between an index and a map. Making a prominent letter index is an important key to making a site index easily distinguishable from a map. Unlike a map, an entry within a site index may have multiple associated pages. A basic site index is shown in Figure 8-10.

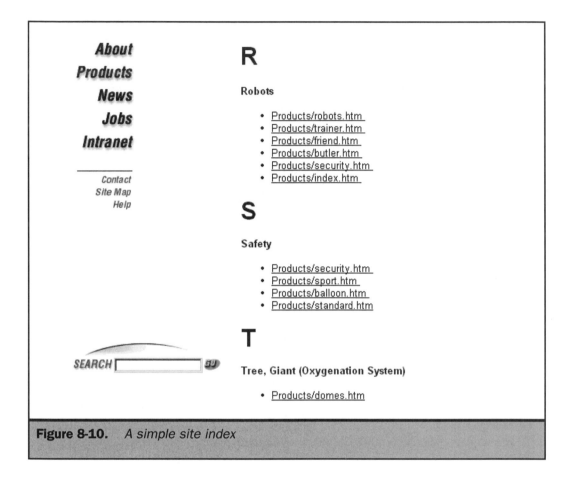

Figure 8-10.   *A simple site index*

Like a site map, access to a site index should be from every page within a site. Similarly, the site index should not be made a primary navigation choice. Like the site map, the Site Index button or link is available within a global navigation bar, but its appearance or location is less prominent than main section navigation and will often be clustered with other navigational aids.

The name of the Web site index is troublesome. While "index" might seem appropriate, site designers must take into account that the word "index" on the Web has multiple meanings and is often considered to be the primary page of a section. Site index may be a better link name, but there are still many sites that confuse the expression "site index" with that of "site map." Designers are encouraged to use the appropriate name and provide cross-linking between the two navigational aids.

Unlike site maps, the form of a site index is fairly regular and is nearly always text. It is possible to provide some graphical elements, such as icons, within a site index to indicate important index words or provide supplementary information such as content or page type. A fully graphical site index is not practical for any but the simplest sites; the only benefit would be stylizing the page to fit in aesthetically with the site. Other visual cues like color, font size, or font weight might be useful to distinguish more important concepts or pages within the index.

Generation of a site index is just as problematic as a site map. With small sites, it may be possible to come up with the words and their associated pages by hand, but tools will aid producing indexes for larger sites. Like search-engine robots, indexing tools will analyze page content to discern word relevance on a per-page basis. Site designers should use tool-based results as a guide and produce the final index by hand. Tool-created indexes will contain words of little or no relevance and could falsely associate words and pages. The reason for this is obvious. Like search engine spiders, an index tool determines word/page relationships based upon word frequency and a variety of other heuristics. This may not necessarily produce optimal results. If possible, site designers are encouraged to determine keywords within the site and create an index using only this controlled vocabulary.

A site index, while not a common structure on the Web, is in many ways preferable to a site map. A site index does not rely on a particular physical site organization so maintenance is not difficult even for a dynamically generated site. Also, because of the relatively standard form of site indexes, users will not have any difficulty figuring out how to use a site index. Lastly, a site index encourages content-based navigation rather than structural navigation, which should fit user Web habits well.

Tours

First-time visitors to complex sites as well as novice Web users may have a difficult time navigating a site regardless of the site's structure or navigation aids like site maps. One concept to help orient new users is the tour. A simple automatic or self-guiding linear path of pages can be implemented in a site, which shows the most important pages along with explanations of how to navigate the site. A theoretical concept of a guided tour is shown in Figure 8-11.

As discussed in Chapter 4, a linear structure is very easy for new users to deal with. They may welcome the loss of control in exchange for introductory site-use lessons. Theoretical support for tours as a navigation aid goes back to the earliest hypertext ideas presented by Vannevar Bush, who described "trails" through document sets that other users could follow. While many have thought tours useful in navigating cyberspace, their use is limited. Guided tours are primarily useful for novice or first-time users. Advanced users will find them limiting or even annoying.

Beyond preplanned guided tours of a particular site, some experts have promoted the use of community-built tours or paths through the Web. These community-style tours and related link systems can provide great assistance to users looking for similar content or to be oriented to a class of sites. At the same time, they may also be significantly manipulated

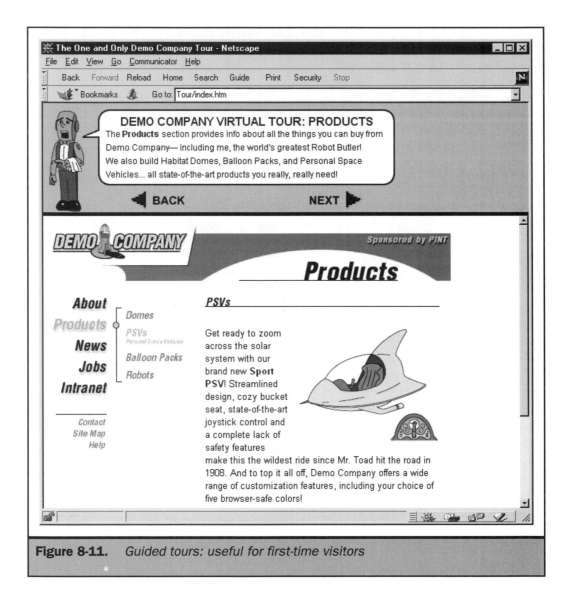

Figure 8-11. *Guided tours: useful for first-time visitors*

by the unscrupulous. Further discussion of community-based navigation systems as they relate to tours can be found in Chapter 15.

Help Systems

Regardless of the quality of implementation, some users will invariably be confused by a site's navigation or use. Unlike software, sites generally cannot rely on print documentation to answer site use questions. Online documentation is really the only approach to providing extra assistance for the user. Few sites actually have any help systems at all. A survey of the Fortune 100 sites during the summer of 1999 shows that only 11 percent had any form of help system.

When to Use Help

While few sites currently employ help, all sites should have at least a basic help system explaining site labels and navigation facilities. Figure 8-12 shows an example of a very simple help page.

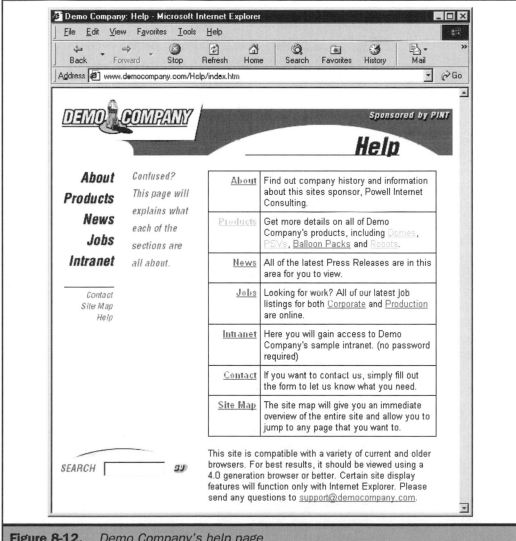

Figure 8-12.   *Demo Company's help page*

If a site requires any special technology, such as a particular browser version or plug-in, it should provide a help system indicating the site requirements. This would eliminate the need for a splash or home page covered with browser, plug-in, and technology requirement statements and buttons as shown here:

The goal of the help system should be to help users figure out any site requirements, orient themselves to the site, and determine how to accomplish their desired goal. Be careful not to hide information in a help system. If a particular page needs help, put the help information within the page rather than burying it behind a Help button. However, if this gets too overwhelming, it is possible to resort to less obvious forms of help.

The most basic way to add a help item to an object is using HTML 4.0's core TITLE attribute. Consider the following markup:

```
<FORM>
<LABEL STYLE="font-weight: bold">Phone Number:
<INPUT TYPE="TEXT"
NAME="PHONE"
SIZE="15"
TITLE="Enter phone number of form (XXX) XXX-XXXX">
</LABEL>
</FORM>
```

When the user positions their pointer over the text field, a small ToolTip window similar to a help balloon appears indicating what to do with the field, as shown here:

Phone Number: |‍

Fill this field in with a phone number of form (XXX) XXX-XXXX

Older browsers may not support the use of the TITLE attribute; however, degradation is graceful as nothing appears. While it is possible to simulate this type of help with JavaScript, it is not suggested.

Rather than using a mouse over, you could create a simple link such as the word "Help" or a simple Question Mark icon and have it create a small Help window explaining what to do with the field. The markup shown here,

```
<FORM>
<LABEL STYLE="font-weight: bold">Phone Number:
<INPUT TYPE="TEXT"
NAME="PHONE"
SIZE="15"
TITLE="Enter phone number of form (XXX) XXX-XXXX">
<FONT SIZE="-3">
<A HREF="javascript:alert('Enter phone number of form
(XXX) XXX-XXXX')">Need help?</A>
</FONT>
</LABEL>
</FORM>
```

can be used to create a simple JavaScript style help system utilizing an alert box.

Complex Help Systems

Most Web sites should rely on help systems that are immediately apparent. Instructions should be in place, ToolTips should always be on, and a Help button should be prominent on every page. However, power users may find such a heavy degree of help annoying. Within intranets and some extranets, it may be desirable to follow more conventional Windows style Help forms. In most software environments, the help system is invoked by the F1 key, which brings a Help window like the one shown here:

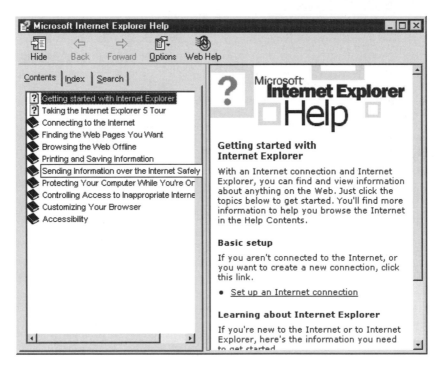

The typical Help window provides a Contents tab that shows a collapsible/ expandable outline form of the various help subjects available, an index that provides a quick lookup by a fixed vocabulary, and a free text-search query system. Setting up a similar help system for a Web site is possible. Microsoft's HTML Help (http://msdn.microsoft.com/workshop/author/htmlhelp/default.asp) provides the ability to add sophisticated help systems to Web sites. Unfortunately, the strict Microsoft approach doesn't work in all browsers because it relies on an ActiveX control only available to Internet Explorer 4.x and greater browsers. If you need cross-browser and cross-platform help, you will have to also provide Java or DHTML style help. Some software vendors—notably, Blue Sky Software (www.blue-sky.com)—offer systems to create cross-browser help. Blue Sky's aptly named WebHelp technology creates a help system that works under a variety of platforms and browsers. An example of this type of a complex help system is shown in Figure 8-13.

Note   *Netscape NetHelp technology is another possibility for online help, but at the time of this writing the technology had gained little support in the Web community and did not appear to have continued support.*

Figure 8-13.   *Typical software help for Web sites*

While complex online help systems provide a great deal of power, they can be relatively time-consuming to create. However, if users, particularly intranet users, are familiar with using standard help conventions like the F1 key, it is important to accommodate them. Microsoft has defined a special JavaScript event, **onHelp**, that can be used with most HTML elements (particularly form fields) to associate actions with the press of the F1 key. The simple example below shows how it might be used with a text field:

```
<FORM>
<LABEL STYLE="font-weight: bold">Phone Number:
<INPUT TYPE="TEXT"
```

```
NAME="PHONE"
SIZE="15"
onHelp="alert('Enter phone number of form (XXX) XXX-XXXX');
return false">
</LABEL>
</FORM>
```

Notice that the code requires a false return value since without this value the browser's help system will be invoked after the help information is presented. More complex Help windows could be displayed, but the concept is the same.

No matter how you do it, always remember that even if your help system is crafted properly you still will not remove all confusion from your site. If users still don't understand, make sure to provide an e-mail form (or at least an address) for users to ask questions. Few Web sites seem to provide any major degree of technical support, but this will certainly change as sites become more complex and the masses increasingly rely on the Web.

Glossary

Many Web sites, particularly those filled with industry-specific jargon, would benefit from a little-used site aid—the glossary. A few sites, such as online trading, that have complex jargon but appeal to people who may not be familiar with all the terms have employed glossaries successfully. However, there are relatively few glossaries used on the Web. Out of the Fortune 100 companies less than 2 percent had a glossary during the summer of 1999.

A glossary link may not necessarily be required on all pages, but should at least be readily accessible from a help system. The link name should be Glossary, Site Glossary, or Common Word Glossary. Rather than have a general link to the glossary, it is possible to provide links close to words that are often misunderstood.

```
DEMO COMPANY PRODUCTS

Robots
Habitat Domes
Balloon Packs
PSVs (glossary entry)
```

It is also possible to provide ToolTip information rather than a glossary link via the TITLE attribute, which is a core attribute for nearly all HTML 4.0 elements. Acronyms and first-word occurrences of complex ideas make perfect candidates for this approach:

```
<SPAN CLASS"word-with-glossary-entry"
TITLE="Personal Space Vehicle-- a plutonium
powered space car for personal use">
PSV</SPAN>
```

If you use the ToolTip approach for word definition, make it obvious to the user that the item is selectable. The previous example related a style sheet rule by setting the **CLASS** attribute to "word-with-glossary-entry." This **CLASS** value should relate to a style entry to make the word look different from the common text.

When implementing a full-site glossary, it should be spawned as a separate smaller pop-up window. Otherwise, it will be difficult for users to utilize it properly as they will have to consult word definitions without seeing the word in use. If the glossary is more than two dozen entries long, a letter-style link list should be provided. Very long word lists should include a search feature. Like a site index, a glossary should be implemented in text and should be easily updatable. Site designers should consider creating a print-friendly version of a site glossary for users to print out and reference as they browse the site. A visual example of a site glossary is shown in Figure 8-14.

"What's New" Sections

Sites that are consistently updated should include some form of "What's New" section in the site to aid return visitors. The use of "last updated" text along with a date on a site home page or at the bottom of a page is not appropriate because it does not indicate exactly what has changed on a site. Furthermore, because many of these indications are script generated, simply opening and saving a page may change the date of update even if no actual changes are made to the site. Rather than force the user to guess what has changed on the site, a "What's New" section will alert the return user to changes in site content. It's important to remember, however, that a "What's New" section should contain only site update information.

Unfortunately, in many cases the section is loaded with press releases, and information may not cover all forms of site updates. In the past, Web managers used to create pages that listed all changes made, similar to a revision or update list for the site. A survey of Fortune 500 sites at the time of this writing shows that the every-update-in-the-site style has fallen out of favor and has been superseded by the press-release style. This change may be due to either the difficulty of keeping such a list up-to-date or the heavy marketing focus of many sites. Over time, it is likely that some form of a recently-changed-files section will become popular as WYSIWYW- (what you see is what you want) oriented sites with heavy personalization become more commonplace.

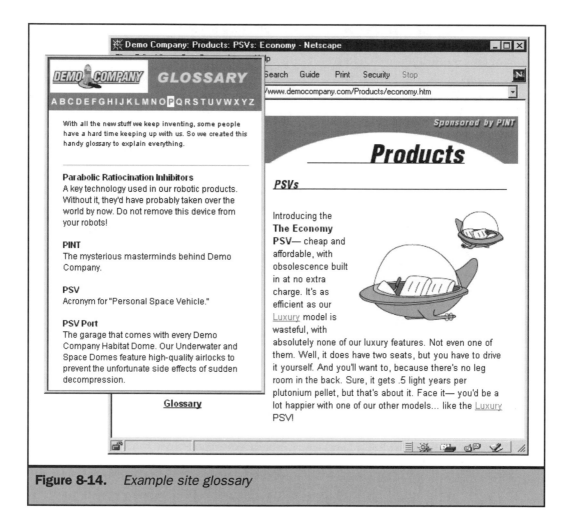

Figure 8-14.   *Example site glossary*

Summary

Site maps provide a familiar construct for Web site visitors. Just as people use a map in the real world to find their way, a site map provides a guide for users to find their way to particular pieces of information on a site. Site maps may be graphical, textual, or some combination, and are organized in a variety of ways. Site maps often provide proximity and relationship information that may not be as beneficial as it is in real-world navigation. Users may not actually form mental models of site structures like designers do. A site index often provides greater benefit to users than a site map. For new users, a site tour may help orient them to site navigation conventions. Further assistance can be provided by help systems or glossaries that help users navigate jargon-filled Web sites. For sites with frequent changes to content, a dedicated "What's New" section or a section dealing with site updates would be useful to inform repeat visitors about modified pages. Understand, however, that no single site aid meets all users' needs. The differences between users suggest that designers should strive to employ as many navigational aids as possible on a site.

The Complete Reference

Web Design

Part III

Elements of Page Design

The Complete Reference

Web Design

Chapter 9

Page Types and Layouts

The fundamental unit of a Web site is a page. Unlike those of the print world, the characteristics of a Web page can vary dramatically between sites as well as within a single site. Inspection of numerous pages shows that there are common general page types—such as home pages, search pages, or content pages—that tend to have similar characteristics. However, the similarities between page types across sites can be fragile. Even issues as basic as the suggested width and height of pages evoke contentious debate among designers. Despite this debate, Web design conventions suggest that some page layouts tend to work better than others. Designers should start exploring page layouts with these basic layouts in mind, and modify them to fit the content being presented. Extremely creative layout, while often visually inspiring, should be considered somewhat dangerous, as the purpose of page layout is always to assist the user in page use. The consistency of page layouts could go a long way to improving page usability.

What Is a Page?

This idea of a page is at the very heart of a Web site. In the simplest sense, a page is what appears in a browser window. One page equals one URL. A user types in a URL and a document appears in the window. These days, things aren't so simple. A URL might load multiple documents in the browser window, and the so-called Web page might be broken up into many smaller windows or frames. Today a "screen" may be a better analogy, but "page" is what we have and it is unlikely to change.

In the print world, a page is thought of as a component of a document like a book or a press release. A page is a "chunk" of the larger structure. Of course, the page itself is broken down into smaller chunks such as paragraphs, sentences, headers, footers, illustrations, and the like. The Web world is no different. A Web site may contain a large amount of content on a particular subject, but it is divided up or "chunked" into different pages. Each of the chunks should be a self-contained idea that contributes to the whole. When done properly, ideas can span multiple pages in a coherent flow of steps, stages, or parts. The goal in setting up Web sites is to take a body of content and spread it across a series of interrelated pages for easy digestion by the user, as shown in Figure 9-1.

Chunking content is often more of an art than a science. A designer has to make some chunks bigger and some chunks smaller than others. Unlike those in print, the dimensions of a Web page are not always fixed.

Page Sizes

The potential size of a Web page, in a theoretical sense, is both infinitely long and infinitely wide. However, given that overly long or wide pages would be difficult for a user to comprehend, use, or even print, there should be some consideration of appropriate page size. The most obvious question is what page size is appropriate? Even in paper there are numerous sizes, and the Web certainly lacks an equivalent for 8.5 × 11-inch letter size. This is both good and bad. Is it really a problem that the

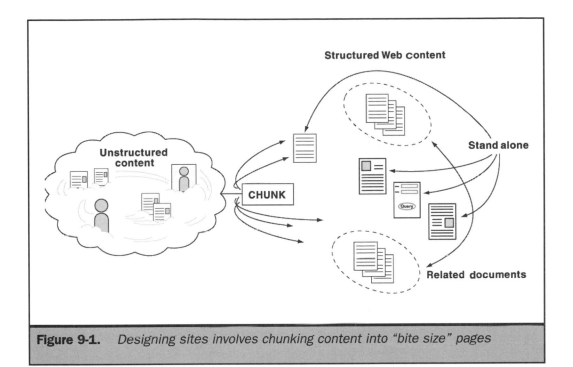

Figure 9-1.   *Designing sites involves chunking content into "bite size" pages*

Web lacks a standard page size? In the world of print, there really isn't a standard size; printed materials might range from something as small as a fortune cookie message to something as large as a poster. Brochures, CD case liners, letters, business cards, paperback books, and so on all have different sizes. The Web is the same. Just as with print, the key to a successful Web page is whether the "size" is suited to the content. If the content is too little for the dimensions selected, you may find that the page has excessive white space that may seem unusual to the reader, particularly if they are accustomed to variable page sizes. Conversely, if there is too much content, it may not fit within the user's screen, forcing the content to be split across multiple screens.

Rule: Set the size of the page to fit the purpose and the content at hand.

Despite the variation in size based upon content, there are many reasons that standard sizes are a good idea. In the print world, if we didn't settle on a particular size of paper, such as letter size, it would be very difficult to buy paper, create laser printers, and so on. On the Web, some designers struggle with a lack of standardization. Numerous designers have attempted to price their services per page, but what exactly constitutes the size of a page? Aren't bigger pages, regardless of complexity, at least slightly more costly to do than smaller ones?

This way of thinking also may be harmful to readability. If Web sites are priced on a per-page basis, this encourages customers to cram as much data as possible into a single page. It doesn't really reduce production costs, but it may result in a long, dense, cluttered page that will lack both aesthetic appeal and onscreen readability.

Fixed page sizes, which actually means a limitation on the amount of textual and visual materials appearing within one HTML file, have definite advantages when trying to decide how to "chunk" information. Like a physical sheet of paper, there is a finite number of characters that will fit on the page. Further, a fixed size gives constructive boundaries for what may appear on a given page. Finally, fixed page sizes increase readability, as the user knows what to expect when viewing a page. They know it will be a certain size, with reliable elements, and that it will print or can be emailed in a predictable manner.

Given all the potential benefits of fixed page sizes, what size makes sense? Consider first letter size paper. This is a standard 8.5 × 11-inch paper size; on a system with a typical 72dpi, this works out to be 612 pixels by 792 pixels. Consider browser chrome in a browser like Internet Explorer and you'll see that this works out to be around three screens filled with content at 640 × 480, two screens or so at 800 × 600, a screen and a half at 1,024 × 768. All the page fits, finally, at 1,280 × 1024, as shown in Figure 9-2.

What does this tell us? It lets us know that the user's screen is really the problem. The big question, then, is—what is the user's screen size? Considering computer systems first, common screen sizes include 640 × 480, 800 × 600, 1,024 × 768, 1,280 × 1,024, and

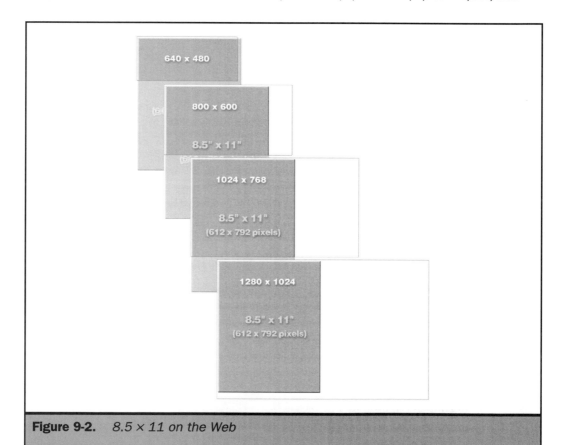

Figure 9-2. *8.5 × 11 on the Web*

1,600 × 1,200. Numerous others sizes are important as well, such as WebTV and Palm screen sizes. Table 9-1 details the common screen resolutions found.

Of course, the screen size really doesn't matter as much as designers might think. Even if a user has a particular resolution, they may not size their browser to fit the entire screen, nor may they want to. The browser "chrome" of common browsers will take up screen space. Various operating system features, such as the Windows system tray, always will take up some room anyway. Even if you assume users to use a 640 × 480 resolution, you may find as little as 570–580 usable pixels of screen width before scrolling, and 280–300 pixels of usable screen height, depending on the browser version. Figure 9-3 illustrates the screen region issues.

Resolution	Device	Comments
Varies dramatically from 3 lines by 12 characters to 310 × 100 pixels	Cell phone	Resolution often measured in characters across and lines up and down rather than pixels.
320 × 240	Palm-sized PDA	Scrolling is difficult in this environment. Single-screen full approach is common.
544 × 372	WebTV	Rightward scrolling not possible. See http://developer.webtv.net/design/ for useful information.
640 × 240	Windows CE	Half-height VGA.
640 × 480	Computer (low resolution)	Typical worst-case PC resolution.
800 × 600	Computer (standard resolution)	Probably the most common resolution circa late 1999.
1,024 × 768	Computer (high resolution)	About the limit of content expansion before significant usability problems might ensue.
1,152 × 864	Computer (high resolution)	
1,200 × 1024	Computer (high resolution)	
1,600 × 1,200	Computer (high resolution)	

Table 9-1. *Common Screen Resolutions*

ELEMENTS OF PAGE DESIGN

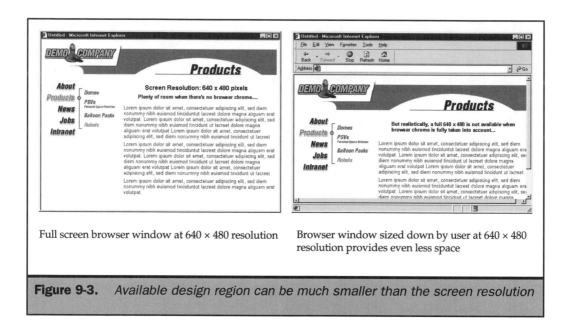

Figure 9-3. *Available design region can be much smaller than the screen resolution*

Designers often want a hard-and-fast screen height and width, but, unfortunately, the amount of room consumed by browser chrome varies dramatically. Consider Netscape 3 under Windows with all options on. The browser chrome shown here takes up a whopping 150 pixels of vertical space.

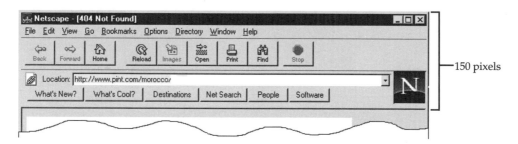

Browser chrome will vary not just by browser, but by user preference. Compare standard Netscape and Internet Explorer browser chrome to their potentially minimized sizes, as shown in Figure 9-4.

The reason that designers need to be concerned about screen size is that Web pages need to fit. It is well known that users will resist scrolling to the right, so pages need to fit the width of the screen if possible. Also, consider that very wide pages rarely print well, especially since print facilities in browsers tend not to support landscape mode.

Rule: Avoid wide pages, particularly those that cause rightward scrolling.

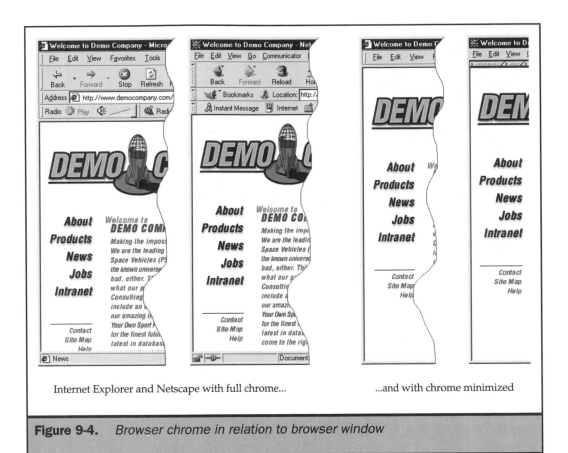

Internet Explorer and Netscape with full chrome...   ...and with chrome minimized

Figure 9-4.   *Browser chrome in relation to browser window*

When it comes to page height, it is pretty obvious that users evaluate the first screen and then decide if they want to scroll or choose something on the first screen. Statistically, users will tend to pick items within the first screen over other items that they can't see yet. It is particularly important to make sure that important items like primary navigation elements appear on the first screen. This requires that we understand the height of the screen.

Rule: Try to keep important items such as primary navigation in the first screen.

Screen height isn't as troublesome as screen width. For example, pages can be printed no matter how long they are, assuming the user wants to print a long page. There are special considerations about printing pages that are addressed in the section "Print-specific Pages" later in the chapter. Limiting content to fit screen height isn't a huge concern—while it is true that users will tend to favor content in the first screen, it is also true that they will scroll down. However, users will only scroll if they know they can. Occasionally, the way a page is laid out may not indicate that the page contains downward content, other than the scroll bar on the side of the screen. This is particularly problematic if a large amount of white space is exactly at the bottom of the page and there is no background tile or content that would suggest to the user that there is anything more. This idea is illustrated in Figure 9-5.

Some designers call the bottom of the browser screen the "fold," and it is wise to make sure that a design does not end right before or after the fold.

Suggestion: Be aware of the screen "fold," and try to hint at content beyond the first screen.

Dealing with Screen Size

Designers have a variety of ways of dealing with screen size. Some designers have taken a very inflexible stance, suggesting that users ought to have a certain size such as 800 × 600—and therefore their sites will be designed to that resolution. Period. Often, sites practicing this philosophy contain a message like the following.

This site best viewed under 800x600

While it may be written in a nice tone, messages like this basically say "go away" to users who don't have such a resolution. If you try to use some sites like this under 640 × 480 or less, they are very difficult to use. Some sites with frames are completely unusable at lower resolutions because the frames can't even be resized! Such exclusionary design based on resolution is a poor idea and does not have a place in user-centered design.

Rule: Avoid resolution entry restrictions for sites if at all possible.

About the only environment to consider resolution in a very strict manner is WebTV. WebTV sets size exactly at 544 × 372. Particularly troublesome is that if a design goes beyond 544 pixels wide, it will not fit on a WebTV screen. Rightward scrolling is not an option here. This is a pretty serious example of how a restrictive design for 800 × 600 would completely lock out users.

Rule: When designing for WebTV, consider a hard-and-fast page width of 544 pixels.

Assuming Page Size

WebTV's resolution restrictions play well to another crowd of designers—those who always assume the worst display will be the one used. Some go so far as to limit pages to be purely text-based and rely on percentage values to scale everything, while others aim to please most everybody by trying to aim for some reasonable lowest common

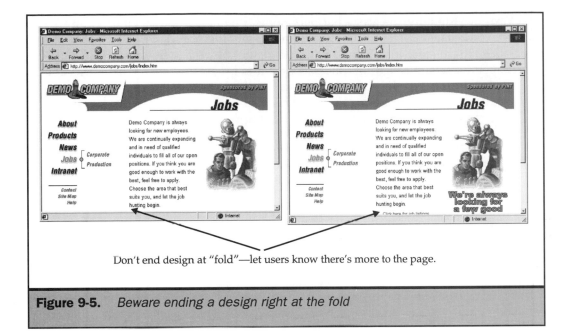

Don't end design at "fold"—let users know there's more to the page.

Figure 9-5. *Beware ending a design right at the fold*

denominator, such as 640 × 480 resolution on a Windows system with a popular browser like Netscape or Internet Explorer. If you make assumptions like a lowest base user, it may seem possible to figure out a typical screen size for the user. Consider this carefully, though. Given that the user has 640 × 480 resolution, what is the largest amount of screen area they have? This depends. Did the user full-screen the browser, or are there other items taking up screen real estate? How much browser chrome do they have? If a user full-screens and leaves the settings alone in the browser, this could be your best-case possibility. On 640 × 480, this might equate to around 580 × 300. This could be considered your potential available screen region. Table 9-2 shows how this potential area varies greatly under browsers.

Browser	640 × 480	800 × 600	1,024 ×768
Netscape 3.x	610 × 300	794 × 404	1,020 × 572
Netscape 4.x	622 × 290	780 × 410	1,006 × 570
Mozilla Prerelease	624 × 300	800 × 425	1,020 × 570
Internet Explorer 4.x /5.x	620 × 310	782 × 440	1,006 × 605
Opera 3.62	624 × 304	784 × 450	1,010 × 618

Table 9-2. *Potential Available Screen Region at Full Size with Standard Settings Under Windows*

Of course, these figures are very troublesome. Potential screen region? What happens if the user doesn't size their window up and just leaves it as the system presents it? In this case, they would have to size the browser to fit the screen. The actual opening size of a browser varies as well, and is even less than what is presented in Table 9-2. Because of the uncertainty of screen size, you might want to consider a slop factor in layouts. For example, if the probable available width is 600 pixels, you might want to provide 5 percent or more space for slop, leaving 570 pixels or less of actual width to use.

Suggestion: If designing with assumed screen sizes, be conservative and give yourself a slop factor of as much as 10 percent of the available region.

Detecting Page Size

What's interesting is that today it is actually possible to avoid making guesses about the available resolution. Using JavaScript, it is possible to sense for the screen size fairly easily, as well as for available window region, as shown by the script presented here:

```
<!DOCTYPE HTML PUBLIC "-//W3C//DTD HTML 4.0 Transitional//EN">
<HTML>
<HEAD>
<TITLE>Available Region Checker</TITLE>
</HEAD>
<BODY>
<H2>Set to the size you want to check and reload.</H2>
<HR>
<SCRIPT LANGUAGE="JavaScript1.2">
<!--
  NS4 = (document.layers) ? 1 : 0;
  IE4 = (document.all) ? 1 : 0;
  if (NS4 || IE4)
    {
     document.write("Screen height = "+screen.height+"<BR>");
     document.write("Screen width = "+screen.width+"<BR><BR>");

winWidth = (NS4) ? window.innerWidth : document.body.clientWidth;
winHeight = (NS4) ? window.innerHeight : document.body.clientHeight;

     document.write("Available height = "+winHeight+"<BR>");
     document.write("Available width = "+winWidth+"<BR>");
    }
  else
```

```
      document.write("<B>Requires 4.x generation browser</B>");
//-->
</SCRIPT>
<NOSCRIPT>
  JavaScript must be on and you must use 4.x generation or
  better browser.
</NOSCRIPT>
</BODY>
</HTML>
```

While this script does generate, it would be possible to sense for available screen region and set content appropriately. For example, consider writing out background tiles to deal with all the various screen sizes. This next script example uses JavaScript available in the 4.*x*-generation browsers to sense for screen resolution and outputs a background tile to fit. If an older browser views the page, or the scripting support is off, the browser will resort to a worst-case scenario of using the largest tile.

```
<!DOCTYPE HTML PUBLIC "-//W3C//DTD HTML 4.0 Transitional//EN">
<HTML>
<HEAD>
<TITLE>Dynamic Background</TITLE>
</HEAD>
<SCRIPT>
<!--
if (screen)
   {
    if (screen.width < 641)
     document.write('<BODY BACKGROUND-"640tile.gif">\n');
   else if (screen.width < 801)
     document.write('<BODY BACKGROUND="800tile.gif">\n');
   else if (screen.width < 1025)
     document.write('<BODY BACKGROUND="1024tile.gif">\n');
   else
     document.write('<BODY BACKGROUND="1600tile.gif">\n');
   }
  else
    document.write('<BODY BACKGROUND="1600tile.gif">\n');
//-->
</SCRIPT>
<NOSCRIPT>
<BODY BACKGROUND="1600tile.gif">
```

```
</NOSCRIPT>
   Add your page content here
</BODY>
</HTML>
```

You might consider using a script similar to this to create tables and set content to fit screen regions. However, this brings up the question of control again. Just because a user has a 2,000 × 2,000 screen, do they necessarily want the content of a page to expand to fit the available screen? Consider that a 2,000 × 2,000 image will certainly take much longer to download!

Relative Page Sizes

Another approach to dealing with page sizes relative to screen resolution is to not deal with it exactly. Why not use a relative size? For example, imagine a table layout like the following:

```
<!DOCTYPE HTML PUBLIC "-//W3C//DTD HTML 4.0 Transitional//EN">
<HTML>
<HEAD>
<TITLE>Stretch Me</TITLE>
</HEAD>
<BODY>
<TABLE WIDTH="100%" BGCOLOR="yellow">
<TR>
<TD>
<P>This table is 100% the width of the screen.  If you
stretch the browser window, the content will expand to
fit the available space.</P>
</TD>
</TR>
</TABLE>
</BODY>
</HTML>
```

The page will stretch and shrink to the available window space, as shown in Figure 9-6. Notice that the content does not reach the top and left of the screen. A Web page will have default margins on. To adjust margins, see the section on page margins that follows this discussion.

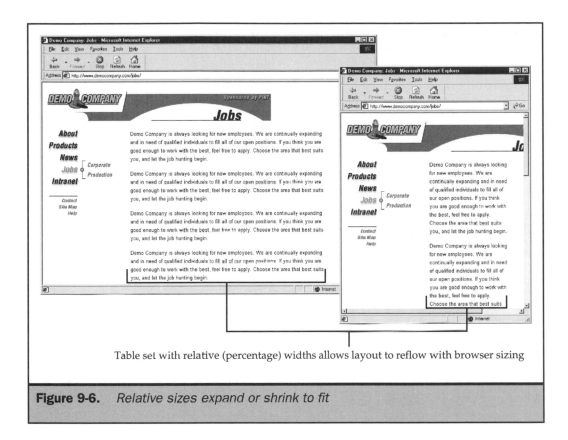

Table set with relative (percentage) widths allows layout to reflow with browser sizing

Figure 9-6.   *Relative sizes expand or shrink to fit*

Now it would seem that relative sizing would meet the needs of any resolution, but be careful as relative sizing can distort a page layout greatly—and some things, like images, just aren't meant to scale. For example, if you set an image in HTML to have a percentage height or width like so:

```
<IMG SRC="logo.gif" HEIGHT="20%" WIDTH="40%">
```

it will often look distorted, and users will see this as an error. Also consider that, even when you fix the size of some objects, layouts may become basically unreadable as the screen increases. Allowing a paragraph of text to expand to fit a 1,600 × 1,200 pixel resolution monitor will produce very long lines. Considering that optimal line length is around 12–15 words, allowing pages to stretch could actually result in significant usability problems. Of course, these problems would be of the user's own doing rather than the designer's. However, there is no guarantee that the user would see the problem from that perspective—the designer may still get blamed for creating a "bad" page. Figure 9-7 shows many of the downsides of relative layouts in action.

As one can see, the message of the page could be ruined by such distortion, and designers may be unwilling to give up control of layout.

Suggestion: Allow the user to stretch or shrink pages at will. Do not force pages to fill to an available resolution unless layout will be lost without the size increase.

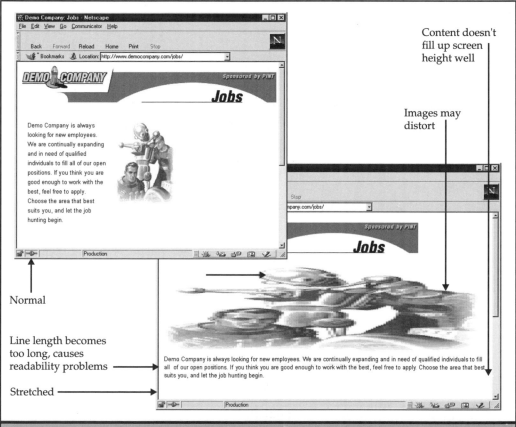

Figure 9-7. *Relative sizing can allow users to create layout and usability problems*

The section about common layouts found at the end of this chapter will present an example of using a stretchable layout that can shrink and grow reasonably without inducing serious usability problems.

Page-Size Reality Check

Before racing off to make stretchable pages or ones that fit a user's resolution, carefully consider that the point of setting the page to a particular size is to make the content more presentable. Recall the discussion about paper sizes presented earlier. A fortune cookie message doesn't belong on a letter-size sheet of paper any more than every page in your site has to stretch to fill some monster screen. Some pages ought to stretch and take advantage of every available pixel, particularly those overflowing with content. Notice that many portal sites or home pages for large e-commerce sites will stretch content to fit the screen resolution. However, do these sites necessarily allow all pages deeper in the site to stretch? No. The reality is that there is little benefit to letting a simple text document fill up a screen.

Ask a simple question: why *should* something fill the screen? One reason might be that a page doesn't look right if it doesn't fill up the screen. Users may complain that a site design looks "too small" on their big monitor. But does it need to be expanded to fit? Consider the pages shown in Figure 9-8. Both are fixed sized, but one is allowed to float to the center while the other is fixed.

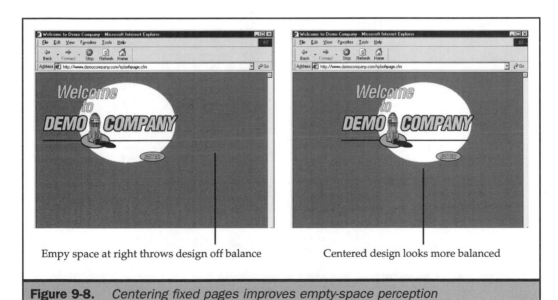

Empy space at right throws design off balance   Centered design looks more balanced

Figure 9-8. *Centering fixed pages improves empty-space perception*

Suggestion: When using fixed page sizes, make sure to center your page to reduce the perception of empty space on larger displays.

Another good trick to avoid the perception of empty space in fixed-width designs is to utilize background tiles that set up boundaries for pages or fill up any extra space with a nice pattern, as shown in Figure 9-9.

Dealing with this last idea brings up an interesting question. Why do people full-screen sites? Considering that many if not most pages do not actually stretch, what's the point? One possible reason is that it allows the user to focus on the window. Beyond making the page look better, there are good reasons to allow layouts to grow. Sites that have a great deal of content can take advantage of the extra screen real estate. However, this will backfire if too little content is presented—particularly, if a single column is used.

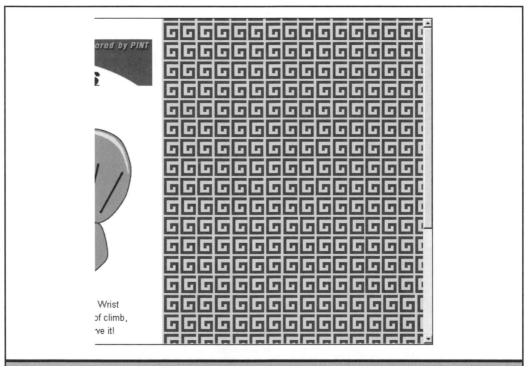

Figure 9-9. *Creative use of background tiles to fill up empty space*

Suggestion: Avoid using stretchable designs on pages with little content.

Most of the discussion has focused on page width, but what about height? Recall that unless you want to limit the content so that it doesn't scroll up and down, this isn't as critical as width. While in some viewing environments—such as Palm Pilots, Kiosks, and WebTV—scrolling is frowned on, most Web sites do scroll up and down. The question, then, is how much scrolling should be allowed. Consider that if a page is too long, it will be difficult to use, and probably will take a long time to load. If a page must scroll up and down, about 3–5 screens full is a good limit. Of course, what constitutes a full screen will vary greatly, so this is just a rule of thumb.

Suggestion: Try to fit content vertically within 3–5 screens, if possible.

If pages are longer and the content can easily be split, then do so; otherwise, let it scroll. You do not want to break up a logical unit because of an arbitrary limit unless the page has become unwieldy. Another argument against splitting is that today's users are getting used to scrolling; much effort, including improving mouse design, is being made to ease the scrolling burden on the user.

In the final analysis, no matter if you fix content, whether your page size is 640 × 480 or 2,000 × 2,000, there will always be someone who finds the content too big or too small. Pages should be set not for monitors, but for the needs of the content presented and the people viewing it. Making sure content fits viewing environment is very important. An easy way to do this is to resize your browser window to simulate other resolutions. A variety of tools exist to do this (see http://www.webdesign.com/resources/ for pointers to tools). Most Web editors, such as HomeSite and Dreamweaver, also provide utilities for browser sizes. However, a simple way to simulate resolutions is just to resize your browser to fit the test pattern tiles found at http://www.webdesignref.com/chapter9/screensizer.htm.

Page Margins

Besides considering the overall size of a page, designers should be very aware of the margins. Browsers do have margins, and they vary from version to version. Background images do not respect the margins, but foreground images do. If a page is not designed to take into account margins or control them, it is very possible the layout may be ruined in some browsers, as shown in Figure 9-10.

Under older browsers, margins varied and could not be controlled using HTML. Today, HTML and CSS provide facilities to turn off margins. If not controlled, margins will be set at the pixel values shown in Table 9-3.

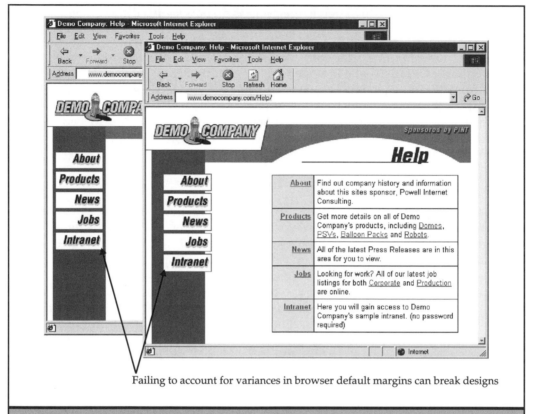

Failing to account for variances in browser default margins can break designs

Figure 9-10. *Margin problems can ruin layouts*

PC			MAC		
BROWSER	**LEFT**	**TOP**	**BROWSER**	**LEFT**	**TOP**
Netscape 3.*x*	10	16	Netscape 3.*x*	8	8
Netscape 4.*x*	8	8	Netscape 4.*x*	8	8
I.E. 3.*x*	10	16	I.E 3.*x*	8	8
I.E. 4.*x*	10	16	I.E. 4.*x*	8	8
I.E. 5.*x*	10	16			

Table 9-3. *Common Margin Offsets*

Note   *Versions of Netscape 3 on UNIX systems have reported margin offsets as high
as 22 pixels!*

Providing a slop factor of upwards of 8–10 pixels is about all that could be done
initially, but now there are a variety of ways to remove margins.

**Suggestion: Either control page margins or account for their variation with some
layout slop factor.**

Turning off the margins in HTML is not part of the specification, but both
leading browser vendors have added proprietary attributes to set page margins
from the **<BODY>** element. In Internet Explorer 4.*x* or later, set **LEFTMARGIN** and
TOPMARGIN attributes for the **<BODY>** element to 0 or any desired pixel value.
For Netscape 4.*x* or later use **MARGINWIDTH** and **MARGINHEIGHT** respectively.
A statement like

```
<BODY TOPMARGIN="0" LEFTMARGIN="0" MARGINWIDTH="0" MARGINHEIGHT="0">
```

should turn off the margins in a page completely.

 Note   *Unfortunately, some Netscape browsers may still render a 1-pixel margin, both top
and bottom, despite any manipulation.*

The HTML approach is the only reasonable approach until CSS is supported.
However, a CSS rule like

```
BODY    {margin: 0;}
```

should do the same thing as the previous HTML. CSS provides greater control for
page margins, which can be set individually for the left, top, right, and bottom.

One interesting margin workaround still employed on some sites attempting to
preserve layout on older browsers is using frames. Frames have always had margin
control, so it would be possible to use the markup shown below to kill margins on
older browsers:

```
<HTML>
<HEAD>
<TITLE>Frame Margin Trick</TITLE>
</HEAD>
<FRAMESET ROWS="99%,*" BORDER="0">
<FRAME NAME="main" SRC="mainpage.htm" MARGINHEIGHT="0"
       MARGINWIDTH="0">
```

```
<FRAME SRC="overflow.htm" MARGINHEIGHT="0" MARGINWIDTH="0">
</FRAMESET>
</HTML>
```

In this case, mainpage.htm would be set to the site's main page and overflow.htm would be a simple HTML file that matches the background color or tile of the main page. You may wonder why there are two frames used. Unfortunately, Netscape doesn't allow a 100-percent value in some versions. Regardless, this is not a good trick to employ for layout since it introduces numerous potential usability drawbacks associated with frames, as discussed in Chapter 5.

Now that the size of Web pages has been fully discussed, we should turn our attention to the various types of pages that are found in Web sites.

Page Types

There are many ways to classify Web pages. One simple way would be to consider the focus of the page. Is the page primarily a content page, a navigation page, or a task page, or is it a mixture of types? Most pages tend to be some mixture—but certain pages, like site maps, are purely navigational, and some deep content pages in a site may be nearly purely content based. Most pages—even home pages—will vary in their focus on content, navigation, or task.

Within the broad category of navigation-oriented pages, you might further classify pages. As discussed in Chapter 5 on site navigation, users tend to view entrance and exit from a site as important steps. Because of the focus on entering and leaving a site, it is important to consider whether a page is an entrance page or an exit page. A page that a user can enter on should try to orient the user by letting them know what site they are on and what things can be performed on a site. A site's home page is often the primary entrance page, but depending on how the site is used, many pages could serve as entry pages. Exit pages are less clear than entrance pages, but an exit page should provide some closure to a user's site visit. A sense of completion is an important aspect in creating a positive take-away value for the user. Often, content pages serve as exit pages because a user has found what they want. However, in task-oriented sites like a shopping site, a special exit or order-confirmation page may serve as a more explicit form of exit. In between would be pages that serve as steps during a user's visit. These intermediary pages range between providing content and acting as navigation points on the user's journey through the site. A successful journey will have a definite start (entry page), an experience of information and guidance (content and navigation pages), and finally a conclusion to the journey (exit page). Key to good Web design is making certain the user does not lose their way between the start and the finish of the journey. Thus, the importance of content and navigation.

Content-oriented pages can be categorized by type. Content pages might include things like press releases, product specifications, biographies, stories, white papers, poems, frequently asked questions, tutorials, release notes, and any other category of content imaginable. Some of the pages are somewhat unique to the Web such as FAQs, privacy pages, and so on, and will be discussed in more detail later in the chapter, but the particular form or meaning of content pages will probably depend on the organization running the sites. Navigation pages can also be categorized by type. Home pages tend to have distinct functions and looks as compared to subsection navigation pages. Special navigation pages, such as site maps, search pages, and site indices, are also found in many sites. Each of these navigation pages has already been discussed in previous chapters.

There are a variety of other ways to categorize pages, such as how they are used, printed, or viewed online, and how often they are updated. They can also be categorized by whether they are generated or are static—and if they are generated, whether they are unique by viewer (in other words, "personalized"). However, the purpose for a taxonomy of page types is simply to allow designers to discuss things in a regular organized way. Our simple taxonomy of entrance, navigation, content, and exit pages will serve this purpose well enough.

Entrance Pages

Theoretically, any page in a site can serve as an entrance page if the user knows the page's URL. In Chapter 4, sites that did not limit entry to a particular set of pages were considered porous, while sites that limited entry could be dubbed semiporous or solid depending on how limited entrance was. Yet regardless of any formal attempt to limit users, most sites tend to have only a few entry points. The home page is the main entry to a site, but certain important sectional pages or "subhome" pages might also be entry points into a site—particularly if they have special URLs or unique domains. While most sites will focus traffic through a home page, some sites may have a special entry page called a splash page.

Splash Pages

A *splash page* is a page that is used to introduce a site, to "make a splash" and leave a strong impression. A splash page is often used to set the tone of a site through the use of graphic layout, animation, or even sound. Figure 9-11 shows an example splash page. For some users, the often overly animated logos of a splash page serve as an unwanted download and may encourage them to leave. However, for some sites, a splash page is very important to set the stage for the rest of the site experience. On such sites, not having a splash page could be similar to not having an opening title sequence for a movie, leaving the user confused or disoriented. Given that a splash page could

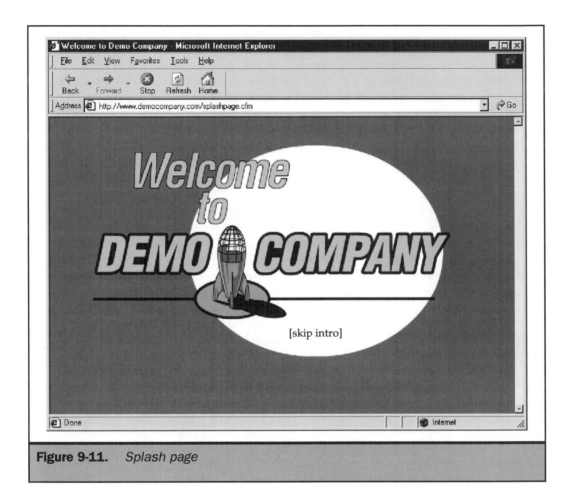

Figure 9-11. *Splash page*

be annoying to the user, there should be an easy way to skip the page. Usually, a small text link is used towards the bottom of the page for bypassing the splash page.

Suggestion: Provide an obvious link to quickly skip a splash page.

When a splash page just orients users with spinning logos and other introductory material, frequent visitors to a site may become highly annoyed even if they can skip the page. It is possible instead to issue a cookie to the user and only show a splash page to a first-time visitor.

 Consider showing splash pages only for initial visitors.

A splash page can be used for much more than just spinning a corporate logo. A splash page can be used to provide setup or installation for the site, such as figuring out if the user has the appropriate plug-ins installed. A splash page can also be used to engage the user while items used elsewhere in the site are predownloaded. For many multimedia sites heavily using Flash, a splash page is used in the same manner as an installer for traditional software.

> **Tip**   *Use splash pages for installation or preloading of site content.*

Be careful with the use of a splash page for providing important information, installing software, or prefetching site information. If a site is porous, as discussed in Chapter 4, providing many ways for the user to enter the site, a splash page may never be accessed, and thus the installation benefit may be lost.

Because of the perceived lack of value provided and the download delays caused by splash pages in the eyes of some users, they should be used with caution. However, when well executed and used infrequently (and for the appropriate type of site), a splash page is a useful way to grab a user's attention and orient them to a site.

Home Pages

A home page is generally the first page a user sees when they visit a site. The home page acts as the main entry point of a site and should be a prominent landmark in a site. As a landmark page, a home page should be unique from all other pages in a site in its appearance. Understand that the home page is often the way people visually remember a site. If it is not different, users may feel lost in a site, needing an obvious starting point.

Rule: A home page should look significantly different than other pages in a site.

In order to be distinct, home pages often are more visual than deeper pages in a site and may more prominently display organizational identity, such as a logo, than other pages. Consider the abstract page layouts shown in Figure 9-12. Can you identify the home pages?

A home page needs to set the tone for the site. The home page sets the basic design elements of a site, such as color, graphic style, font style, and so on that are used on subpages. If a home page uses a particular font for buttons, users will probably expect the rest of the site to continue using the same font. Also, the type of navigation presented will be assumed to be consistent from the home page. If the home page uses blue graphical push buttons and pull-down menus for navigation, this should be used elsewhere in the site as well.

Rule: A home page should set the visual and navigational tone of a site.

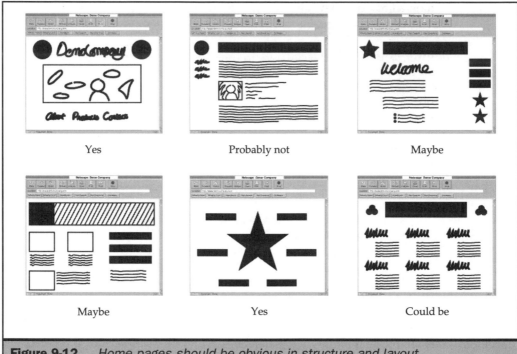

Figure 9-12.   *Home pages should be obvious in structure and layout*

Another aspect of a good home page is that it encourages people to look deeper in a site. Oftentimes a user may come to a site not knowing for sure what is provided. If the home page doesn't interest them, they may just leave. Inspection of a site's statistics logs will probably reveal that the home page is not only the primary entry page, but it is also one of the primary exit pages. Why is this? People may leave directly from the home page for a variety of reasons. Maybe they just landed at the page by accident. However, it is possible that the home page isn't doing its job. Consider that, as the entry point for a site, the home page sets the user's first impression of the site. If the page loads slowly or doesn't look interesting, there may be no reason for the user to look further.

Rule: A home page should load fast, but be dramatic enough to encourage interest.

However, there are other reasons that a user might bail out from a home page. Consider that the home page might not indicate clearly what is at the site. Many home pages don't clearly present the site's purpose and the contents of the site. Consider your home page like a magazine cover. Magazine covers have to be flashy enough to attract attention on a crowded newsstand. They have to have a variety of cover blurbs indicating what's inside the magazine.

Rule: A home page should clearly indicate what's inside a site.

Like a magazine cover, the home page of a site must be "consistently different." What that means is that the page must be recognizable but obviously changing and "fresh". Over time, the design of the site may have to change to keep the site fresh, but a complete redesign should not occur too often. Consider how often a major magazine changes its look. While it may not be a good idea to wait five years, it probably isn't a good idea to redesign your home page's look every six months. How often do the major Web sites like Yahoo! or Amazon significantly change their looks? The reality is that these sites are actually changing subtly all the time.

If return visitation is a key component of your site strategy, the home page is where to convince users to come back. You can try to encourage users to return in a variety of ways, but the most important way is to provide informational value on the home page and show them things are changing. Don't expect users to come back day after day to a page that it is just a big graphic with a few buttons near it. Isn't this just a splash page with more buttons? Try to provide some value with your home page. Indicate the key changes made to the site directly on the home page. Remember, if the home page doesn't change over time, people may assume the site's content doesn't change either. The main elements may stay the same, but secondary elements may change, and other clues may be used to let people know the site has changed. A few ways to show change include:

- Putting the date somewhere on the page
- Rotating a primary image either randomly or at a set interval (daily, weekly, or monthly)
- Putting small amounts of important changing information (press releases, etc.) on the home page
- A direct statement of the last time the page was updated
- A link to a "What's New" area

Suggestion: A home page should provide informational value and an obvious indication of site change if change is occurring.

Some sites, however, will not change terribly often, so their home page will not look dynamic. Remember, if you aren't going to update the site, don't let people know. Don't put press releases on the home page that are old, and don't put a date on the home page that changes if nothing changes in a site.

From this discussion, it is obvious that a home page has many roles to fill, as shown in Figure 9-13. It is the entry point, the update indicator, the tone setter,

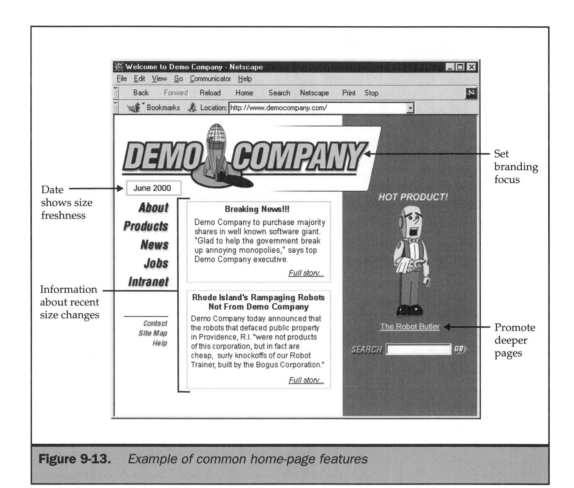

Figure 9-13.   *Example of common home-page features*

and the primary navigational landmark. Users will bookmark it or type in the URL directly. They might visit it frequently, but they probably won't do one thing common to other pages—print it. Usually a home page only provides basic or teaser information for a user about what's in a site, not detailed information that would be useful to print. Printing should therefore be considered a secondary requirement for home pages. This gives the designer more flexibility in color and background usage, multimedia, and screen width than pages deeper in a site.

Tip   *Consider printing a secondary design consideration for home pages.*

Subpages: Navigation vs. Content

From the home page, the user will select a link to explore. At this point, the user begins the middle of their visit. They have set off to do something. Because the user tends to be more focused at this point, subpages don't have to be quite as visual or unique as home pages. However, subpages generally must follow the lead of the home page, unless they are attempting to act as a "subpage" landmark. Consider, for example, that a subpage for a large section of a company such as Technical Support may be the entry page for many users. People who don't come through the "front door" of the site, so to speak, will need to orient themselves from this page. In this sense, the subpage is a landmark for a particular section. It is important, if a particular subpage is used this way, that it be distinctly different from other pages in the site. However, avoid the temptation of making it look like a home page. If the user did enter through the home page and then clicked to get to the technical support page, they would see basically something that looks like another home page. That would be quite confusing, and would potentially ruin the landmark value of each page.

> **Suggestion: If a particular subpage is a landmark or common entry page such as a "section home page" make it visually distinctive.**

Most subpages, however, will probably not be visually distinctive. In fact, most should take their design and navigation cues directly from the home page. While the purpose of the home page is to make the user keenly aware of being on a particular site, when a user journeys deeper into the site, the user's awareness needs to shift to the content. If subpages are presenting the user with new navigation, new logs, and new color schemes along the way, the user's attention will be drawn way from the content.

Consider the home page and subpage shown in Figure 9-14 and notice how it is obvious they are related, but that the subpage is more content oriented.

> **Rule: Subpages should follow the style and navigation of the home page, at least in spirit.**

Subpages will often be more focused than home pages. A subpage is generally either focused on navigation or on content. A few pages, such as site maps, might be considered purely navigation. However, it is unlikely that a page is a pure content page, since if it lacked navigation or links, it would be a so-called "orphan" page that had no way for a user to get back from other than the browser Back button. Generally, there is a balance between content and navigation in a subpage.

Navigation-Specific Pages

A variety of special navigation-focused pages, beyond home pages or main sectional pages, can be found in sites. These have been discussed in previous chapters, so they

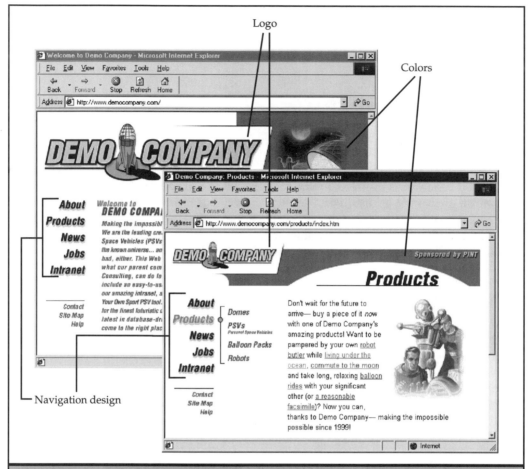

Figure 9-14.   *Logos, navigation design, colors, and other design elements are consistent between home page and subpages*

will only be mentioned here for readers to remember them as special types of pages within a site. Two of the most common special navigation pages are site maps and site indices. A site map is used to provide a structural overview of a Web site, while a site index provides a list of a site's content organized alphabetically rather than structurally. The design of these navigational pages was discussed in depth in Chapter 8. A search page is the other common navigation-specific page. Search facilities generally include a query page, result pages (both positive and negative), and, hopefully, a help page. These pages are very important for site navigation, particularly to power users. Special care should be paid to their design. Chapter 7 discusses search facilities in great depth.

Given that the focus of site maps, search, and other navigation pages is almost purely navigational, there should be, conversely, some pages that are completely content focused.

Content Pages

Content pages are those subpages that are very focused on content presentation. In some sense, a content page is a destination page. Oftentimes they are the leaf pages in a site tree and represent the "bottom" of a site. Like other subpages in a site, a content page will probably have some navigational elements, lest it be considered an orphan page. The layout of a content-focused page will vary on the content presented, but it tends to take cues from ancestor pages such as main section or home pages. Often sites tend to get less visual the deeper in, but this is not necessarily a hard-and-fast rule. Very little else can be said about content pages, as how they are structured and presented will vary based on the content. Common content pages found in commercial sites include things like press releases, product specifications, biographies, customer testimonials, technical support documentation, news articles, financial reports, legal information, and on and on. Personal Web sites might have stories, resumes, poems, and family trees, while educational sites might have syllabi, homework assignments, and presentations. Other forms of sites might have document types completely unique unto themselves. The reality is that are as many types of content pages as there are people in the world. However, there are a few types of content pages that are common on Web sites or so specific to the Web that they warrant further discussion: FAQs, legal terms, and privacy pages.

FAQ Pages

Frequently asked question, or FAQ, pages are common types of documents on the Internet. The basic idea of a FAQ page is to provide concise answers to common questions in one single document so that a user doesn't have to hunt all over a site for information. FAQs are often formatted as a single long scrolling document with an index of questions at the top, with links to each question that jump the user down the page to the appropriate question and answer. An example of a typical FAQ is shown in Figure 9-15.

There may be some question why FAQ files jump up and down a page rather than link to individual files. The main reason FAQs are often formatted as a single document is because users will want to print the entire range of questions for future reference. However, if there are too many questions, the document can become unwieldy. If a FAQ is more than a dozen or so printed pages, it is probably a wise idea to break it up into pieces that are linked to and provide a separate printable version for users who want the whole document.

Suggestion: Make FAQ pages a single document so they are easily printable, if they are of a reasonable length.

ELEMENTS OF PAGE DESIGN

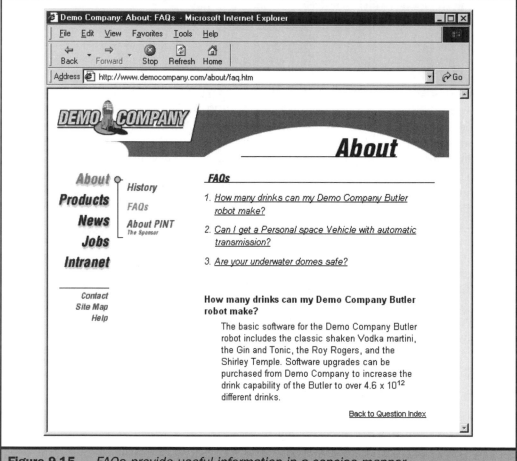

Figure 9-15.   *FAQs provide useful information in a concise manner*

When a user reads a FAQ, they will often look for the question they are interested in, read the answer, and then want to return to the list of questions. To avoid users having to scroll around, make sure to provide a link at the end of each question to link users back to the question index, which is usually at the top of the document.

Suggestion: Provide a link back to the top of the document or the list of the questions at the end of every answer.

FAQs are only useful if the answers provided actually answer the user's questions. It is a very good idea to provide a link or mechanism for a user to indicate if their question was answered. Often links like this one are included with each question.

Does this answer your question?

Other questions, such as rating of usefulness, can be asked as well. Collected information can be used to indicate which questions users mostly commonly read and if they are satisfied with the answers. This information could be useful to other users. Some sites actually provide a listing of the most popular questions accessed.

Tip   *Provide a feedback mechanism for users to rate the value of the FAQ answers provided.*

Some sites have extended the idea of rating the usefulness of a FAQ to the page itself. This does give great feedback to site designers about page use and user satisfaction. However, don't go overboard with automatic user feedback and other popularity measurements since some very useful pages may be infrequently accessed or misunderstood by some very vocal users but well understood by most others.

Legal Pages

Legal-terms pages have become commonplace within many commercial sites. Often, the bottom of a Web page on a public site includes a corporate statement. There may also be a short statement about site usage. Either of these short statements will generally include a link to another page describing the legal aspects of the site. The way legal information is linked to from pages varies. Some examples are shown here.

Read our <u>Terms and Conditions of Use</u>.

Copyright and Trademark Notice

Please click here for Terms and Conditions of use regarding this site.

The actual legal page itself tends to be an orphan page, often lacking much of the navigation or layout facilities of other site pages. However, it should still at least minimally include a way to return to the home page of the site as well as a minimal amount of branding to associate it with the site. An example legal page is shown in Figure 9-16. You'll notice that the example does not provide much in the way of legal verbiage other than some basic headings. Given that Web sites are software—and in the case of e-commerce or task-based sites, some damage could arrive from their usage—site designers should not try to use "boilerplate" legal pages modified from other sites. Just like using software, the implications of damage arising from proper or even misuse of Web sites are huge. Designers should not attempt to practice armchair

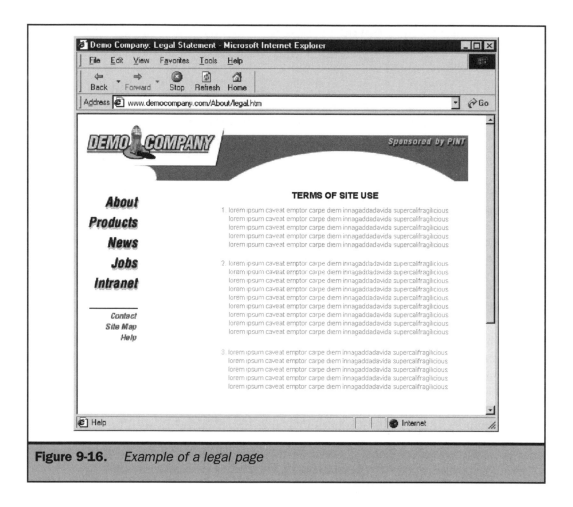

Figure 9-16.   *Example of a legal page*

law. There is already enough room for mistakes in site building without adding in the potential for legal trouble.

> **Suggestion: Consult a legal professional for drafting or inspection of any legal-terms page used to cover Web site usage.**

Copyright pages can be particularly troublesome. Designers are quick to add copyrights to pages. While the value of these statements is somewhat suspect, given the intention to apply for a copyright, they are important. Users often seem to look to copyright statements as an indication of content freshness. This then begs a question of should a copyright statement be changed every year to keep users thinking the site is up-to-date. In theory, if a change is made to a page, even a minor one, this is okay to do.

Tip   *Be careful with copyright statements; users may judge site freshness by them.*

However, utilizing the copyright statement as the only indication of a page's freshness isn't a great idea. Consider instead putting some sort of last-modified indicator on the page, like so.

Document last modified: February 19, 2000

Keeping freshness indicators up-to-date can be troublesome, but it is possible to automatically insert them with a program or even to use a simple JavaScript script, like the one shown here, at the bottom of every page:

```
<SCRIPT LANGUAGE="JavaScript">
<!--
document.write('<FONT SIZE="-1" CLASS="lastmodified">
<I>Last Modified: ');
document.write(document.lastModified);
document.write('</I></FONT>');
//-->
</SCRIPT>
```

Suggestion: Add a last-modification indication to pages.

Privacy Pages

A particular class of legal-term Web pages that has garnered much attention is the privacy-statement page. Many sites collect sensitive or personal data from users, and what sites do with this data is of particular concern to many users. Because of this concern, which is often well founded, sites should provide a privacy statement that indicates what collected data will be used for. Links to this statement should be available throughout the site and be prominently displayed on any data-collection pages. The design of this page should be like other legal pages, with only basic navigation and only organization-identifying graphics like the organization's logo or colors. However, the privacy page may also include icons associated with and links to various privacy organizations, particularly if the site is built to follow some industry standard. Figure 9-17 displays an example privacy-statement layout.

As with all legal documents, consulting a legal professional is always suggested, but one agency, TRUSTe (www.truste.org), has stepped in to provide assistance to site designers looking to craft a privacy statement. Site designers are encouraged to use sites like TRUSTe to build privacy statements. However, be careful not to just add in a large privacy statement without considering both whether it truly addresses a user's privacy concerns in an easy-to-understand manner and if it can be enforced. The fallout of posting privacy statements only to break them is enormous. Some legal experts

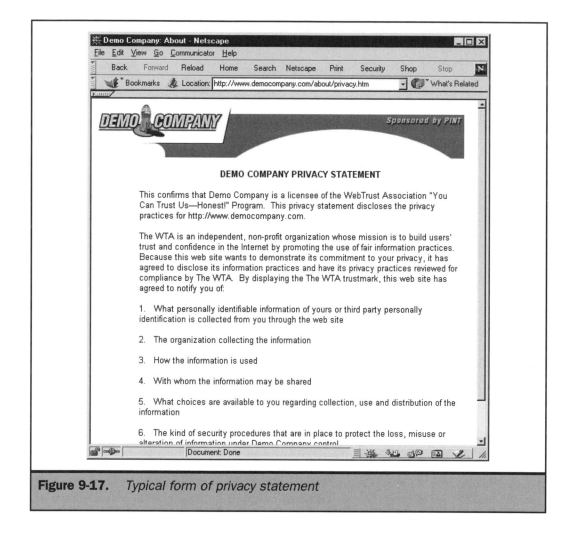

Figure 9-17. *Typical form of privacy statement*

believe a site is better off with no privacy statement than with one that is faulty or is not enforced.

> **Rule: If sensitive or personal information is collected, provide an easily accessible and understandable privacy statement.**

Task-Specific Pages

Task-specific pages are pages that allow a user to do something—particularly provide information through the interaction with various form elements. Some common task pages found in sites include shopping-cart management, database query, search pages, download pages, registration forms, guest book pages, discussion posting pages, and so on. Like content pages, there are too many possible task-specific pages that could exist within a site to provide a reasonable list of them. However, contact pages and print pages are common enough that they should be discussed further. For a general discussion of the use of form elements and other GUI widgets see Chapter 12.

Contact Pages

A contact page is a page that provides information or even a form on how to contact the owners of a site. Usually, a contact page will provide numerous methods to contact the site's owners, ranging from a simple email address or phone number to a fill-out form or even an instant chat service. An example contact page is shown in Figure 9-18.

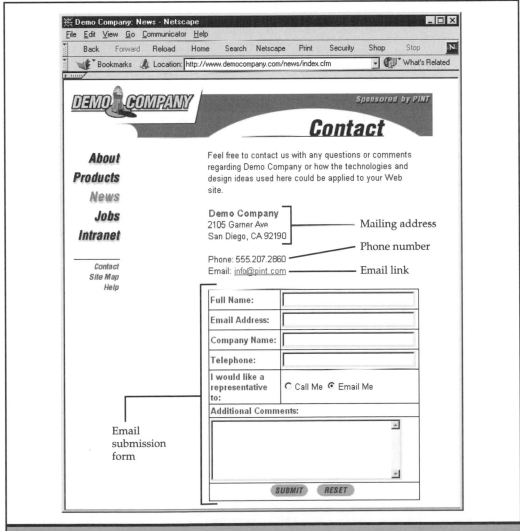

Figure 9-18.   *Contact forms should provide multiple contact methods*

Links to site-contact pages should be placed prominently on all pages within a site. Generally, the label for this link is simply "Contact." However, some sites prefer to use a more verbose link name like "How to Contact Us." A compromise might be to provide the shortened label name, but then use a scope note or the **TITLE** attribute to provide a ToolTip with more information about the forms of contact available, as shown here.

The downside of having a separate contact page reachable from content pages within a site is that it may not be associated closely enough with content, particularly if the user eventually prints the page out and consumes it offline. Because of this potential problem, some designers prefer to put full-contact information on every page just in case a user prints a page and later wants to contact the organization by phone, fax, postal mail, or email without revisiting the site. This might be a little overboard, but some form of minimal contact information such as organization name, site URL, main phone number, or email address probably should be on every page within a site. Companies with toll-free numbers increasingly make that number part of the page's visual design itself.

> **Rule: Full contact information should be available within one click of any page on a site; minimal contact information such as an email address should be included on every page.**

Print-Specific Pages

Some pages are likely to be consumed offline and thus are geared for printing. Occasionally a site may be consumed both offline and online, and two forms of the same page will exist. Notice the rise of "print version" buttons on many Web sites. In fact, many sites are now including not only links to printable pages, but special saving and email facilities to make it easier for users to use content they find. An example of this is shown here.

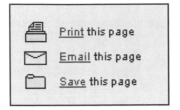

At this point, let's focus on printing pages. Many Web pages don't print well because the page is optimized for online consumption, with larger text and narrow columns. A direct print of such a page tends to waste a great deal of paper. Printed pages should be generally set in smaller type and the layout modified to utilize standard letter-size paper effectively. Colored text may not be important on a printed page, and backgrounds will burn more toner or ink than provide benefit in most cases. Furthermore, users probably do not need to see site navigation other than some indication of the site the page came from. This information may be as little as putting the organizational logo and an indication of a page's location in the site (such as what section it is in and its URL) on the print page. Advertisements may or may not be a good idea to include in the print output.

There are a variety of ways to provide print versions of pages. One possibility is to create a special print version in HTML. This could be as simple as stripping most of the HTML out or as involved as creating a special new HTML layout optimized for print.

Another approach might be to utilize a secondary print-oriented layout using a style sheet. The CSS specification indicates that it is possible to provide multiple style sheets to apply to a page, depending on the media used. To do this, two **<LINK>** elements would be included in the **<HEAD>** of a Web page like so:

```
<LINK REL="stylesheet" HREF="normal.css">
<LINK REL="stylesheet" HREF="print.css" MEDIA="print">
```

The second style sheet could be used to change text size, reduce line height, change color, remove navigation elements by setting their display property to none, and so on. Using CSS2, it is even possible to indicate where printer page breaks would occur. For example, a CSS rule like

```
.newpage    {page-break-after: always}
```

sets all elements in the class "newpage" to cause a printer page break when the page is printed in a browser such as Internet Explorer that supports this CSS2 property. Figure 9-19 shows an example of how these ideas could be applied and shows a Web page onscreen as well as the resulting printed page. To see this idea in action, see http://www.webdesignref.com/chapter9/printpage.htm.

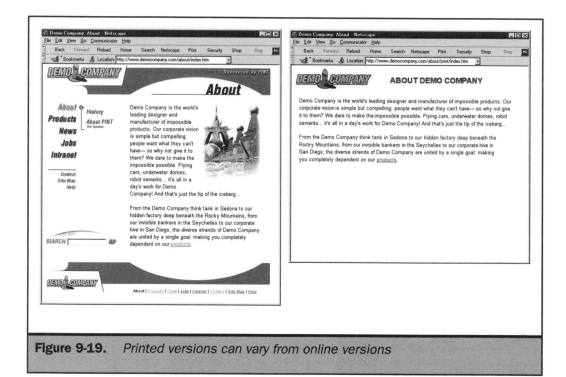

Figure 9-19.   *Printed versions can vary from online versions*

Unfortunately, not all browsers support printer style sheets. A more degradable approach would be to simply link to a page that was formatted for the printer, either using CSS or traditional HTML layout. Besides being downwardly compatible, this approach doesn't surprise the user. The user sees the page as it will print and is not surprised with something different than what is seen onscreen. Consider that just using a linked printer style could cause frustration for the user. What happens if they want to see the page exactly as it looks onscreen? Maybe they actually want to print the advertisements.

> **Suggestion: Inform users that printed pages will be different than what is seen onscreen or show the print version directly.**

Another approach to the printing issue is to utilize Adobe's Acrobat technology (www.adobe.com/acrobat) and provide a PDF (portable document format) version of the page. Using PDF, it is possible to create a high-resolution printer-oriented version of the information in a page just as it might appear in a brochure. A common use of this format is for displaying highly complex information such as technical specifications or mathematical formulas. An example of a PDF file associated with a Web page is shown in Figure 9-20.

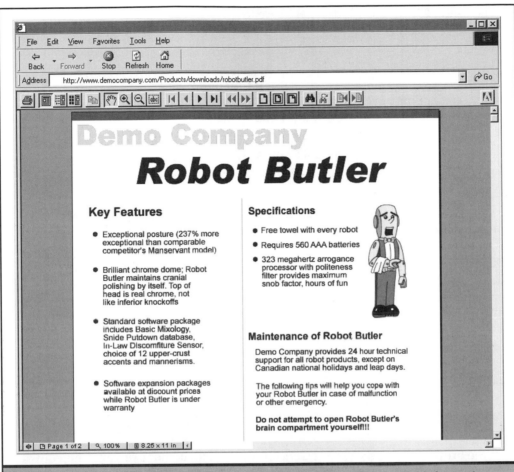

Figure 9-20. *Acrobat files make useful supplements to HTML-based information*

Suggestion: Use Acrobat PDF files for highly complex information that needs to print perfectly such as data sheets, technical drawings, and complex financial or mathematical information.

If a PDF is used, make sure to let users know what it is with an appropriately named link or PDF icon. Given the larger size of PDF files, it is also probably a good idea to indicate the file size of a linked PDF. The last time the document was modified may be useful to the user. Lastly, make sure to provide information on where to obtain the Acrobat reader for users who may not have it. All these ideas are illustrated here.

 The 2001 Annual Report is also available as a PDF (Portable Document Format) file which requires the free Acrobat Reader available from Adobe.

Suggestion: Clearly indicate Acrobat files with text and an icon, and provide information on using these files.

Restricted Printing Pages

Some designers may actually consider that some pages are not made for printing at all. An interesting possibility is limiting printing of a page with a small CSS trick. Consider a link-printer style sheet named noprint.css:

```
<LINK REL="stylesheet" HREF="noprint.css" MEDIA="print">
```

The linked file is composed of a single rule:

```
BODY    {display: none}
```

If the browser supports a linked style, it would actually not print anything out at all. Of course, while this will limit most people, the page can still be printed. A user could easily screen capture a page, save its contents and modify it, modify the browser preferences to ignore style sheets, or simply use a browser that doesn't understand printer style sheets to avoid this restriction. Generally, a designer would never want to limit the printing of a page since it takes a great deal of control from the user. However, there may be some instance (like the information changes too quickly) so it should not be saved, that the page is a sample of something purchased for viewing online only, or some bug with printing exists that may suggest that limiting printing is a good idea.

Exit Pages

While the home page serves as the main entry point to a Web site, is there a defined exit point? For content-oriented sites, there may not be one, and every page could be considered an obvious exit point. Hopefully, the user found some interesting content to satisfy their goal and left from a content page.

Not all sites can afford to lack a point of closure. Sites that have definable tasks, such as downloading software, buying a product, making a stock trade, and so on should have an obvious exit page. The exit page provides a sense of completion or closure to a visit. Closure is very important to site usability as it won't leave the user wondering if they completed the task properly.

Rule: Provide an obvious conclusion page for a task.

Probably the most common exit page seen on the Web is what might be termed the "thank you" page, as shown in Figure 9-21. A "thank you" page comes after a user has filled in a form for further information or completed some transaction such as buying

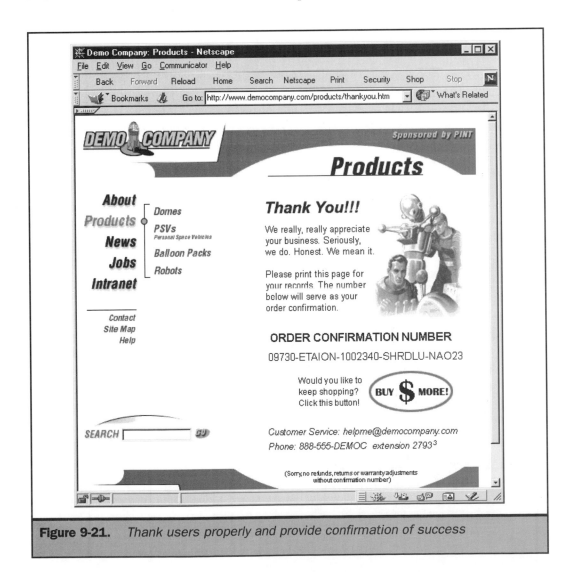

Figure 9-21.   *Thank users properly and provide confirmation of success*

a product. A "thank you" page should not only thank a user for their usage, but also provide some information such as confirmation of success, what to expect next, a tracking number, or other follow-up information. A very important aspect of an exit page is that it should provide a way back in to the site. E-commerce sites have found that just adding a link that states "Continue shopping," as well as providing a link back to the main home page, is a good way to get a few more sales.

Suggestion: Provide a way back to the site from an exit page.

Be careful with the idea of trying to get the user back into the site when they are about to leave. Some designers have abused this idea using a form of "last chance" window to hit the user up one more time. Using JavaScript, it is fairly easy to perform a task on a page as it is unloaded. Consider this modification to the **<BODY>** element of an HTML page:

```
<BODY onunload="alert('Please visit again soon!')">
```

Some sites use this idea to spawn a variety of advertisement windows, and a few even use it to trap users within the site, by endlessly redirecting them to related sites. Figure 9-22 shows a few examples of last-chance pop-ups in action.

Hitting the user with numerous pop-up windows on exit is not a good way to leave a positive feeling in a user's mind. Consider that each window has to be dismissed, and you have just created work for the user.

Rule: Let users leave in peace. Avoid "please don't go" or "last chance" pop-up windows.

Note *If for some reason, such as extreme marketing pressures, you decide not to pay attention to this previous rule, the least you could do is make the windows automatically dismiss themselves after a few seconds of viewing.*

The three major categories of pages—entrance, midvisit, and exit pages—have all been covered, along with the difference between content pages and navigation pages. A few important page types like legal pages also have been discussed in depth. However, little has been said about how these pages look. Briefly, let's explore the general ways people tend to design pages by considering the various Web design schools of thought.

Web Design Schools

As in other fields of design, there are different schools of thought about Web design. At this point in the history of Web design, these "schools" aren't well established or even clearly defined, but a few seem common on the Web.

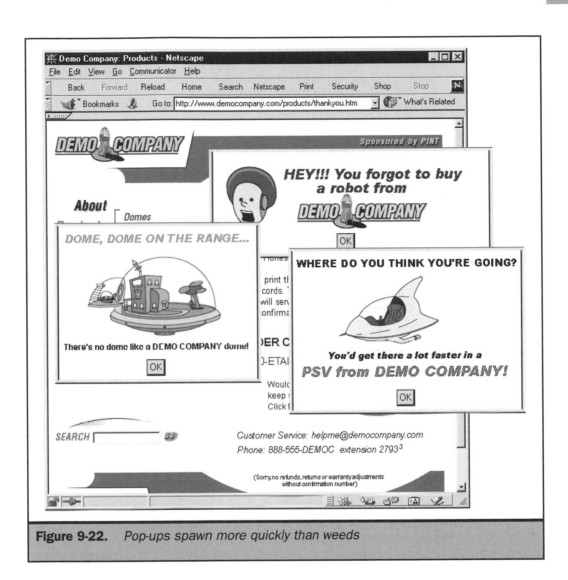

Figure 9-22. *Pop-ups spawn more quickly than weeds*

Text Design

The simplest school of thought about Web pages suggests that text is the most important design element in a page. Designers who follow the "text-first" approach favor the content over presentation and generally use minimal graphics, instead focusing on color or type choice. In the past, because of the limitations of HTML and poor support of CSS, people who took a text-first approach to Web design tended to have somewhat dismal-looking pages such as the one shown in Figure 9-23.

Figure 9-23. *Initial Web technology limited text-oriented design*

Many designers instead turned to putting text in a graphic form to achieve formatting, but did so at the expense of download time and scalability. Today, however, things are much better for text-oriented designers. Using CSS and downloadable fonts, it is possible to create nice pages with no imagery, as shown by the example in Figure 9-24.

One big downside of text design is that it relies on a technology that, so far, has been less than well supported by browsers. Secondly, text design—particularly when implemented in a traditional hypertext fashion—tends to favor somewhat unstructured or contextual links, interspersed within content, over regular navigation bars. As discussed in Chapter 6, this type of link is a very powerful way to create jumps to link related ideas, but its lack of regularity can confuse novice users that expect to see consistent navigation in a site.

Suggestion: When using text-oriented design, consider providing navigation bars as well as contextual links.

Lastly, text design can be difficult to do well. Many designers, particularly those with limited typographic backgrounds, find that it is difficult to design a compelling Web page without fancy graphic effects. However, the major benefit of text design is

Figure 9-24.   *CSS provides text designers useful tools*

significant—the pages are very fast and it is well known that responsiveness is a key aspect of site usability. Furthermore, text-oriented pages can be converted relatively easily to different environments such as much larger screens, very small screens like PDAs or cell phones, and even speech-based browsers.

> **Suggestion: Consider using a text-design philosophy on sites where download speed or display flexibility is paramount.**

Metaphor and Thematic Design

The metaphor and thematic-oriented design philosophy is interested in making Web pages look similar to what they are in real life. If a site is about cars, then structuring the site's interface as a steering wheel is a good example of this design approach. Metaphor approaches tend to be highly visual, as shown by the example in Figure 9-25.

The metaphor design has two major benefits. First, given the heavy visuals and tie-in with "real-world" ideas, the site is often highly memorable. Second, by relying on metaphors of real-world objects, users may find it familiar and easy to use. However, these benefits do come with some serious downsides. First, some users might not "get" the metaphor. For example, if you built your site interface to act like a Hewlett Packard

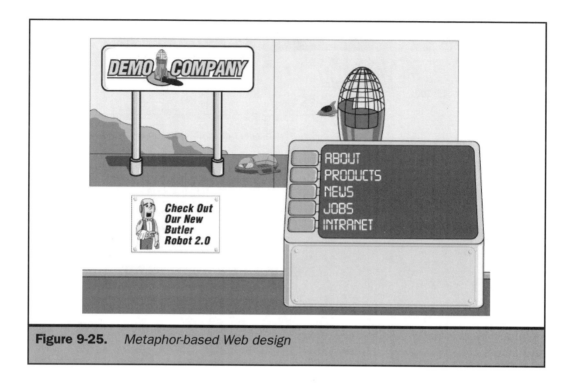

Figure 9-25.   *Metaphor-based Web design*

reverse-Polish notation (RPN) calculator, some users might find it amusing and very intuitive, particularly if they are engineers. However, for others who blocked math class out of their brain long ago and have no clue how to use a RPN calculator, the metaphor-oriented interface may provide no benefit and even be a hindrance to the user who has no previous knowledge of the metaphor. Even when a user understands the metaphor, they might not find it useful after a while. Expert users may find metaphor-oriented interfaces limiting, and frequent visitors to the site might find the interface tired after a while.

> **Suggestion: Avoid using metaphor design on sites geared towards expert users or heavy repeat use.**

Lastly, because metaphor design tends to be so visually heavy, such sites often are slower than other types of sites.

However, despite its downsides, on occasion metaphor design can be the best choice of all. Simulators are the best of example of this. For example, when you are trying to show how a car works, it is best to have a user click on the actual objects in the car such as a steering wheel, brake, and so on. Figure 9-26 shows an example of this in the context of Demo Company. Here, clicking and rolling on objects demonstrates product with movement as well as showing text describing key features.

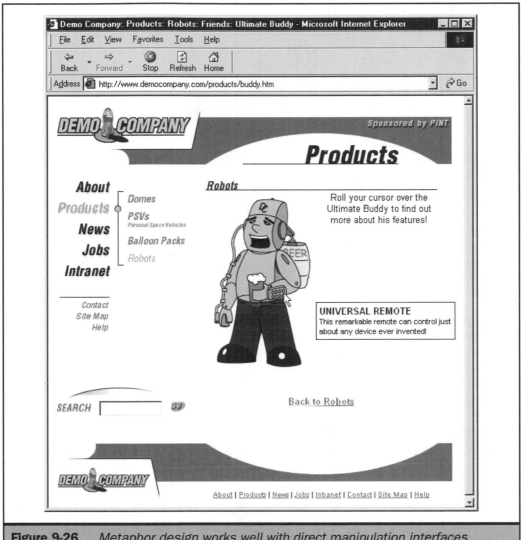

Figure 9-26.   *Metaphor design works well with direct manipulation interfaces*

GUI-Oriented Design

A very popular school of Web design could be termed "sites that act like traditional software applications." Granted, few sites following this design pattern will forsake color or graphics in favor of battleship gray menus and small icon-laden navigation bars, but the overarching sense of acting as software is at the heart of software-oriented or GUI-oriented design. Sites that use a lot of text buttons organized in palettes across the top or left of the screen basically are imitating what software applications look like. The upside of GUI design is hard to ignore. Users know how to use software. They've come to understand what to expect from menus, text fields, buttons, and so on. This knowledge the designer gets for free. GUI-oriented Web design is consistent with what people already know, so in that sense GUI design is the safest design style to practice. Rarely will a GUI-style site inspire, but at the same time it rarely upsets users. Figure 9-27 illustrates the GUI design style that is so frequently shown throughout this book.

GUI-style site design is a safe bet, particularly when there is a range of user sophistication.

Certainly the push buttons in Web-oriented GUI designs might be more colorful, but the general sense of consistency provided by software is there. This could be the

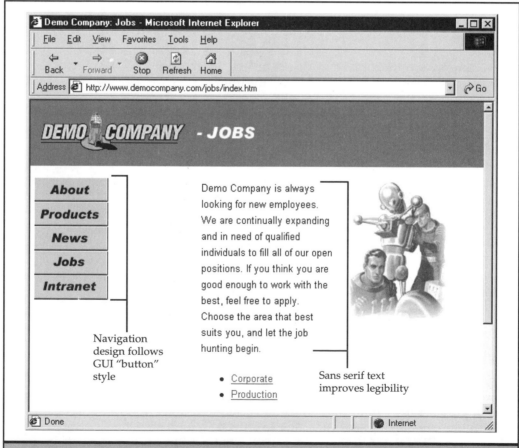

Figure 9-27.   *Software-oriented site design focuses on GUI conventions and usability*

major downside of GUI design. It doesn't leave as much room for the designer, and limits their design possibilities to the use of color or simple thematic buttons. Even font choice on navigation might be limited to common sans-serif fonts like Arial and Helvetica when GUI principles are subscribed to religiously. GUI design can be limiting to designers trying to stretch their creative wings.

Unconventional Design

The unconventional school of design favors creativity, unpredictability, and even randomness in design. Unconventional pages often damn the conventions and invent their own. The interface is an artistic opportunity for the designers to express their feelings. While these forms of designs can be the most powerful, they also can be the most dangerous to use. Unconventional interface design directly counters the usability idea of consistency. Why rely on what people already know? That's boring. Give them something new! Of course, a site following such a practice forces the user to learn new interfaces, and could send many users packing. On the other hand, when the experience is fun or provides a motivating payoff, users may stick around nonetheless. Remember—users can also be quite curious, and when their curiosity is piqued, what is considered usable may be not as important as what is consider new or unusual. While the unconventional school of Web design is probably the most fun and certainly tends to attract great interest in the design community, it is practical for only a relatively small class of sites. Few corporate sites would be willing to risk their site to an unconventional design. Heavy-use sites or task sites may find the use of an unconventional design highly damaging. Imagine a user struggling with new bizarre interface concepts when trying to find information about a business or pay their bills. Figure 9-28 suggests what a self-interested designer might have done with the Demo Company site.

> **Suggestion: Avoid unconventional or very artistically oriented interface designs on task-driven or frequent-use sites.**

Of course, sites meant to entertain users may find unconventional design the best approach. Sites designed as art are an obvious place for unconventional design. Designer portfolios, personal homes, and any site whose primary purpose is to provide a creative outlet for the designer rather than serve the users will find unconventional design appropriate. In short, any site where the main goal is to interact with a user on a more emotional level, with no worry about leaving some people behind, may find unconventional or art-first designs appropriate. Designers are highly encouraged to explore these boundaries of the Web and push the limits. It makes them better designers. A pet project is a great way to safely do this and lets the designer not worry about what other people think—or even if people understand the site. Of course, don't try this kind of design on a paying client unless they asked for it or you are willing to lose them!

| Tip | *Sites designed purposely to be unconventional are a great way to explore new ideas.* |

ELEMENTS OF PAGE DESIGN

Figure 9-28.   *An interesting design, but Demo Company management might not appreciate an unconventional design*

Layout Examples

The next section provides some examples of the most common layouts used in Web sites. While there are countless variations of layouts, most tend to be somewhat related to the ones presented here. Of course, freestyle designs that seem to follow no pattern at all may be the most common of all, and are particularly popular among personal home-page builders. The examples presented speak only about general layout and say nothing about the particular stylistic aspects of a particular layout. The use of color, text, and imagery is highly related to personal taste and current social and visuals trends. Some classical trends, such as the use of symmetry and white space, tend to weather short-lived fads, but little else can be said, so focus will be placed on general layout and leave the designer free to be as creative as they like within the defined regions.

TLB Pages

TLB, or top-left-bottom, is one of the most common design styles used on the Web today. The basic idea of this design is that the top of the page is reserved for page labeling, branding information, and, potentially, primary navigation. The left side of the screen contains navigation elements. If the site is small, the left contains the site's primary navigation and the top contains solely labeling information, but more often the left is reserved for secondary navigation information. As the user clicks through the main sections, the choices on the left change. Consider that this is really no different than a traditional GUI application. In a GUI, the user selects menus that drop down to present more specific choices. The only difference here is that the position of the menu is fixed to the left of the screen. Of course, as discussed in Chapter 12, it is possible to actually directly imitate GUI styles with modern Web technology. The last location in a TLB design is the bottom of the screen, which is generally reserved for text links to supplement the other navigation and supplementary information such as copyright information, legal terms, or contact info.

TLB designs are so common that users should already be very familiar with how to use sites using this layout. From a usability perspective, the major complaint about TLB designs is that the left-hand navigation often takes up a great deal of screen real estate that could be used for content, and the user in some sense has to "jump" over the navigation to reach the content. When using fixed page widths restricted to account for small monitors, the column for content can be somewhat restrictive so that some content, such as tables, has to be reformatted, or the page scrolls a great deal. However, letting the content expand infinitely to the right is not always a good solution as it may make the page difficult to read. In fact, often TLB designs are restricted eventually on the right by a third column of information or a background color. This creates a familiar page approach to design. Figure 9-29 illustrates a TLB design.

Tip *Consider limiting the right-hand margin in TLB designs to create a consistent page look.*

The major downside of TLB layouts, besides their potentially limiting content region, is that they generally look more navigationally focused than content focused, and may not provide as much design opportunity as some other forms of layout.

Header-Footer Pages

A header-footer design provides navigation on both the top and bottom of the page, with the entire width of the page used for content. This type of design is good for content-oriented sites, though it does limit the amount of area used for navigation. Generally, the top of the screen is used for branding, graphical navigation, and page headings, while the bottom of the screen is used to repeat text links and to provide supplementary information such as text links—particularly if the top navigation can scroll off the page. Using frames, it is possible to fix the position of the top and bottom navigation regions so they don't scroll offscreen. If this is the case, a redundant set of navigation is not as necessary, and the bottom may be reserved instead solely for useful information like legal terms, copyrights, or contact information. Figure 9-30 shows an example of header-footer design.

> **Suggestion: Use header-footer design for content-focused sites, particularly when wide content is common.**

Floating Window Pages

An increasingly popular page-layout style could be termed the floating card, or window, style. The basic idea is to create a region in the middle of the screen for

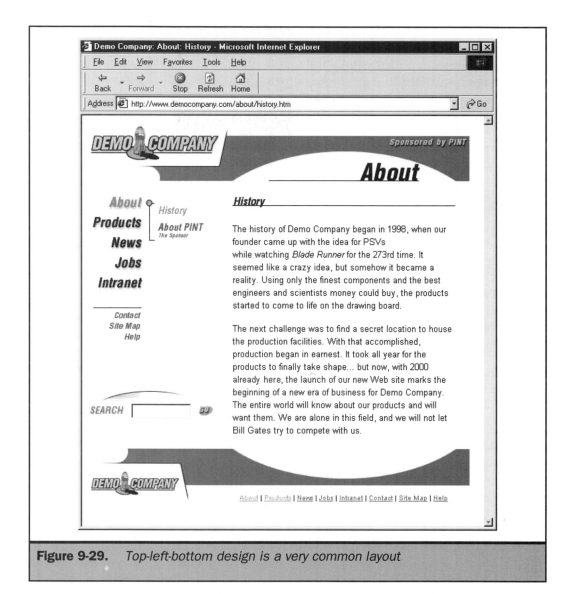

Figure 9-29.   *Top-left-bottom design is a very common layout*

content. The region can either be fixed in size from page to page or be a scrolling window. Generally, fixed card–style design won't work unless a very limited amount of content is presented. However, utilizing frames, it is possible to create a central region of content that scrolls. The benefit of this style of design is that it provides a fixed region to design for but doesn't look as unusual on varying screens since it is usually positioned within a lush background and floats in the center of a screen. Of course, executing this design tends to require the use of frames, which often results in the navigation problems discussed in Chapter 5. A particularly troublesome part of

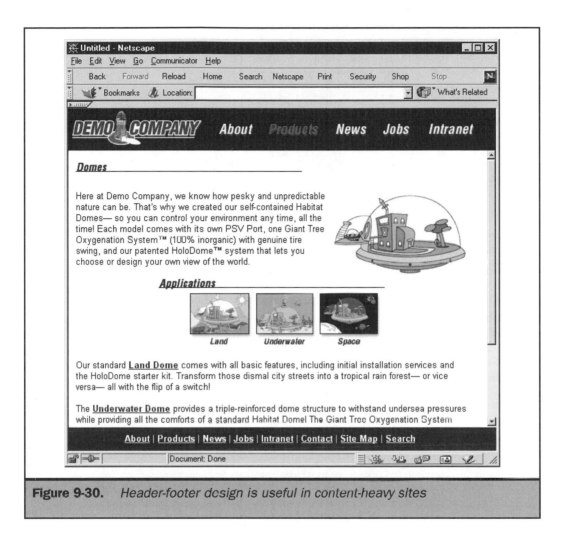

Figure 9-30. *Header-footer design is useful in content-heavy sites*

executing this type of design is that, because of frame implementations in browsers, it is not possible to do things the easy way.

The simplest way to execute a scrolled window–style design might be to do something like this:

```
<!DOCTYPE HTML PUBLIC "-//W3C//DTD HTML 4.0 Transitional//EN">
<HTML>
<HEAD>
<TITLE>The Easy Way</TITLE>
</HEAD>
<BODY BGCOLOR="blue">
```

```
<DIV ALIGN="CENTER">
<IFRAME SRC="http://www.Demo Company.com" HEIGHT="90%"
        WIDTH="600" BORDER="0">
</DIV>
</BODY>
</HTML>
```

Of course, this relies on the **<IFRAME>** element that is not currently well supported in browsers beyond Internet Explorer, though it is part of the HTML specification and should eventually be supported. In reality, a much more complicated approaching using a variety of frames may be required, as shown by the markup here:

```
<!DOCTYPE HTML PUBLIC "-//W3C//DTD HTML 4.0 Transitional//EN">
<HTML>
<HEAD>
<TITLE>Floating Window in Frames</TITLE>
</HEAD>
<FRAMESET ROWS="71,*,34" BORDER="0" FRAMEBORDER="0"
     FRAMESPACING="0">

<FRAME NAME="top" SRC="top.htm"
     SCROLLING="NO" FRAMEBORDER="No"
     FRAMESPACING="0" NORESIZE MARGINWIDTH="0" MARGINHEIGHT="0">

<FRAMESET COLS="170,423,*" FRAMEBORDER="0" FRAMESPACING="0">
   <FRAME NAME="left" SRC="left.htm" SCROLLING="No"
      FRAMEBORDER="No" NORESIZE FRAMESPACING="0"
      BORDERCOLOR="#FFFF00" MARGINWIDTH="0" MARGINHEIGHT="0">
   <FRAME NAME="center" SRC="contentpage.htm" SCROLLING="AUTO"
      FRAMEBORDER="No" NORESIZE FRAMESPACING="0"
      MARGINWIDTH="0" MARGINHEIGHT="0">
   <FRAME NAME="right" SRC="right.htm" SCROLLING="No"
      FRAMEBORDER="No" NORESIZE FRAMESPACING="0"
      MARGINWIDTH="0" MARGINHEIGHT="0">
</FRAMESET>

<FRAME NAME="bottom" SRC="bottom.htm" SCROLLING="NO"
     FRAMEBORDER="No" FRAMESPACING="0" NORESIZE
     MARGINWIDTH="0" MARGINHEIGHT="0">

<NOFRAMES>
<BODY>
This site heavily uses frames. If you do not have a
```

```
frames-compatible browser it is not possible to proceed
beyond this point. Please e-mail
<A HREF="mailto:gripes@democompany.com">gripes@democompany.com</A>
to register a complaint.
</BODY>
</NOFRAMES>
</FRAMESET>
</HTML>
```

This markup sets up a set of frames that define the top, bottom, and sides of the window and leaves the middle for content. An example of this design in action is shown in Figure 9-31.

The challenge of using the fixed window approach is dealing with the frame-rendering problems in browsers. Testing is very important with this type of layout.

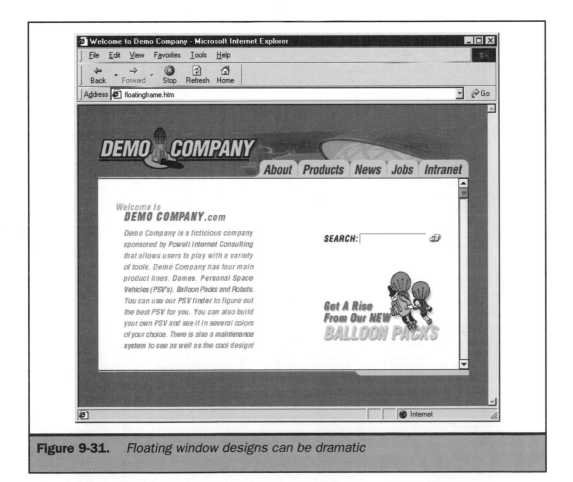

Figure 9-31.   *Floating window designs can be dramatic*

When building scrolling card-style pages, be careful to make sure that frame lineup is precise under all browsers.

As discussed earlier in the chapter when talking about page sizes, fixed pages may look rather small on large monitors. Unlike TLB layout, header-footer and scrolling windows can be centered to reduce the perception of empty space. Of course, the only way to truly deal with space issues is to create a stretchable page with relative sizing.

Stretchable Pages

Stretchable pages are rising in popularity, particularly as more users access the Web with high-resolution monitors. However, as discussed earlier, letting a page stretch is dangerous since things can distort. Some items should be fixed and others allowed to stretch. Consider, for example, the situation where the navigation column and margins are fixed while the center column is free to stretch however the user wants:

```
<!DOCTYPE HTML PUBLIC "-//W3C//DTD HTML 4.0 Transitional//EN">
<HTML>
<HEAD>
<TITLE>Stretch Me</TITLE>
<BASEFONT FACE="Arial">
</HEAD>
<BODY BGCOLOR="#006699"  LEFTMARGIN="0" TOPMARGIN="15">
<TABLE BORDER="0" WIDTH="100%" CELLSPACING="0" CELLPADDING="0">
<TR>
   <!-- just a gap -->
   <TD WIDTH="20" BGCOLOR="#006699">   </TD>
   <!-- navigation column fixed size -->
   <TD WIDTH="100" BGCOLOR="#FFCC00" VALIGN="top" >Navigation
         <BR><BR>
      <A HREF="#">Link</A><BR>
      <A HREF="#">Link</A><BR>
      <A HREF="#">Link</A><BR>
      <A HREF="#">Link</A><BR>
   </TD>
   <!-- just a gap -->
   <TD WIDTH="20" BGCOLOR="#FFFFFF">   </TD>
   <!-- content region variable size -->
   <TD WIDTH="100%" BGCOLOR="#FFFFFF" VALIGN="top">
   <H2 ALIGN="center">Stretch Demo</H2>
Content goes here. Content goes here. Content goes
```

```
here. Content goes here. Content goes here. Content
goes here. Content goes here. Content goes here.
Content goes here.
</TD>
<!--right margin gap-->
<TD WIDTH="20" BGCOLOR="#006699">   </TD>
</TR>
</TABLE>

</BODY>
</HTML>
```

While this design does fit to whatever screen the user wants, it can be rather limiting. Consider that creating stretch points limits the design to simple colors or patterns since the relative areas are elastic and would distort an image placed there.

| Tip | *Avoid stretchable pages when content is minimal, or they may distort when stretched.* |

The Road to Common Site Looks

Designers may feel that the previous discussion will stifle creativity, yet consistency is common even with the world of print. Consistency can be good. Users know what to expect. They are faster and more efficient when they understand a site. Consider the frame grabs of two popular e-commerce sites shown in Figure 9-32. They really are the same design, and for good reason. Users will know how to shop right away.

Common layouts benefit not only the user, but the designer as well. Common layouts can be implemented as templates that allow for the cost-effective construction of large sites. Even novices can easily apply common layouts with decent success. Remember, not everyone who is building sites will need or want to go to art school. Already the W3 has issued core styles (http://www.w3.org/StyleSheets/Core/) that they are encouraging people to use. Hopefully, this will improve the look of many sites.

Consistency between sites does, however, limit creativity to some degree. Rather than be pessimistic about the design options open to you, it would be smarter to say that consistent site designs allow creativity to operate within certain parameters. Within a similar site, there may be many ways to do the same general design. Type choice, color, and artistic style such as the use and treatment of illustration or photo can make sites with the same basic structure appear very different.

Rule: Strive always in Web design to be the same, but different.

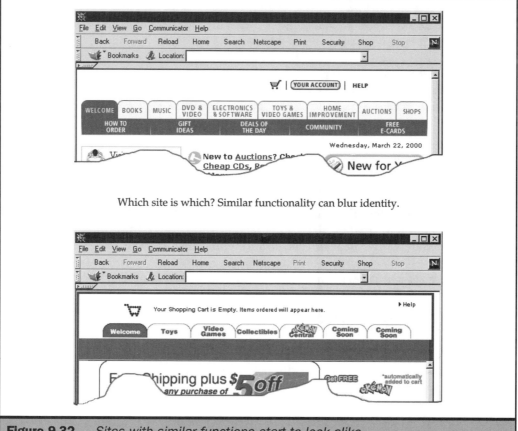

Which site is which? Similar functionality can blur identity.

Figure 9-32.   *Sites with similar functions start to look alike*

Summary

Web pages are not print pages. While certain characteristics like size and layout are often similar, the dynamic nature of the Web environment can make design difficult. Users can view pages under a variety of resolutions, and designs will literally break if designers aren't careful. Even something as simple as the user adjusting their font size can ruin a nice layout. The design considerations of pages vary on the type of the page as well as its content. Always remember that the beauty of the Web is that pages can easily be changed to fit presented content. While it would be very difficult to say what is a proper page design style, a few common schools of Web design exist, as do common layouts. Designers should consider these designs, but also think about experimenting as well. So far, little has been said about the actual components of a page such as text, color, images, and form elements. The next few chapters will investigate the proper use of these page elements.

The Complete Reference

Web Design

Chapter 10

Text

The heart and soul of a Web page is text. Whatever anyone says about the future of multimedia online, most Web pages are dominated by textual information. Assuming that your site relies heavily on text, the way that you use text may significantly influence the user's experience. The simple choice of a typeface could hurt site usability just as much as it could improve site memorability by building brand. Formatting text could also make the text easier or harder to deal with. The art or process of using type is traditionally termed *typography*. In short, typography is concerned with the aspects of text use that make it readable—or if you prefer, simply usable, as well as expressive. The use of words themselves and the style of writing employed might affect the user's experience just as much as how it is presented.

Medium Matters

As mentioned throughout this book, the medium of the Web greatly affects what we can do with it. While there is a great deal of knowledge concerning how type is used on paper, not all of it maps well to the Web. Technologies like HTML and CSS are not always powerful enough to do things that are feasible on paper, at least not easily. Even if we were provided with simple absolute control over page layout, we still would have trouble. As discussed in Chapter 11, the Web does not support any particular fixed page width or length. Even if there were such conventions and they were followed, page designers do not have as much control over the final presentation as they think. Users are always free to change their screen size, increase or decrease their font size, change the font used, or even change their screen colors. Designers have to get used to the fact that the Web is not static—it's a fluid medium where presentation varies greatly from user to user and moment to moment. Nowhere is this lack of control more obvious than the use of text within Web pages. Text flow is very dynamic: a user simply has to increase their font size, shrink their window, or expand their window to ruin a nicely formatted page, as shown in Figure 10-1.

Many designers cannot accept the fact that Web technologies like HTML don't allow them common typographic facilities like adjustable line spacing. They become very frustrated when they find that even simple things like relative text size are not predictable online. Notice the dramatic difference between font sizes on a Macintosh and PC screen as shown in Figure 10-2.

Taking Control of Text Using Graphics

What's a designer to do? Some will invariably fight with the medium and attempt to wrestle control back. Typically, these designers put all their text into image format. Making their text graphic allows designers a degree of control over letter spacing, font choice, and a variety of other facilities they have come to expect from print. This approach is flawed to the core. Putting textual content into an image form makes a Web page load more slowly.

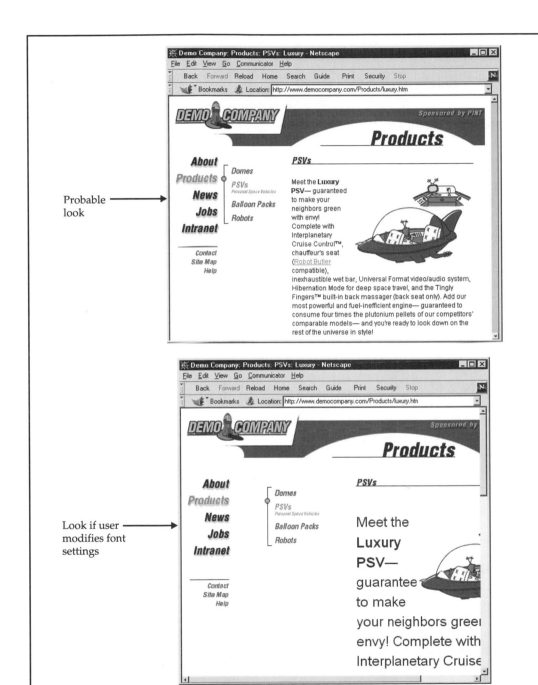

Probable look

Look if user modifies font settings

Figure 10-1. *Examples of text-layout challenges on the Web*

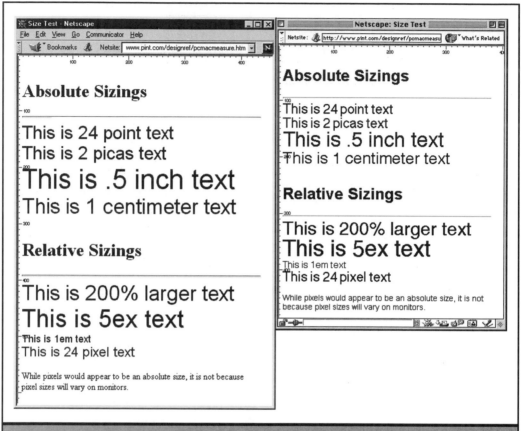

Figure 10-2.   *Screen font sizes aren't the same on Mac and PC*

No amount of graphic optimization is going to make the phrase "Web pages need to be fast" in a graphic form quicker than ASCII text saying the same thing, as shown in Figure 10-3.

Besides the problem of file size, graphic text must be formatted for a particular screen size. A graphic text label using a 24-point font size may look quite nice at 640 × 480 resolution. Consider what it looks like at 1,024 × 768. The pixels don't get any bigger, so it is either small or distorted, as shown in Figure 10-4.

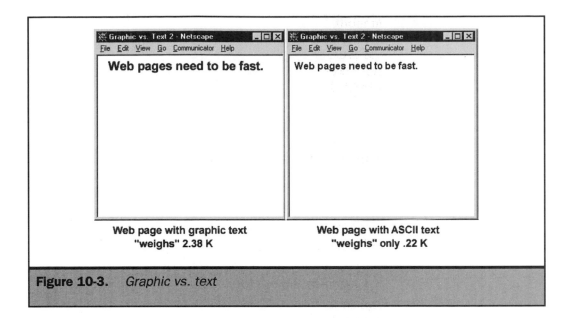

Figure 10-3.   *Graphic vs. text*

Users have no way of fixing the sizing issue. If, however, text is presented as regular HTML text, it is possible for the browser to override any sizing. This enables the user to improve the page's readability. Other problems with using graphic text include:

- **Difficulty updating**   You need to use an image-manipulation tool to make a simple text change. If you use ALT text, you actually have to update both the image and the text—in short, doubling the work.

- **Accessibility is limited**   Users using nonvisual browsers will have problems with graphic text unless the ALT attribute is used. As previously mentioned, accessibility may be limited regardless of ALT attributes if the images do not size based on screen resolution.

- **Search engines ignore it**   Search engines will not index graphical content, though they may be able to index ALT text if it is provided.

Despite its problems, graphical text does have its place. Until downloadable font technology is straightened out, graphic headings and buttons that must be rendered with a particular effect will still have to be created as graphics. For most text, though, it is better to use text itself rather than images.

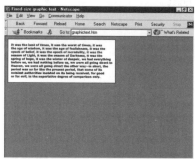

Graphic text at 640 x 480 screen resolution

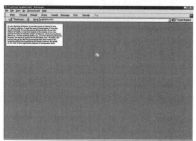

Graphic text at 1024 x 768 screen resolution

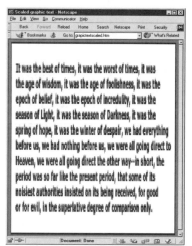

The <IMG> tag allows the use of percentage values to define image height and width (100% for each dimension in this example). This makes image display completely dependent on how the user's browser is sized, as show here.

Figure 10-4. *Absolute sizing of text backfires as graphic changes size*

Throwing Up Your Arms

On the other end of the spectrum are those who literally throw up their arms and don't even try to control text layout to any major degree. This is nearly as bad as the previous situation. The reason we want to control layout is to improve the readability of text. If our text is easier to read, it is more likely the user will actually bother to read it, and even act upon any message we are attempting to convey. The use of a particular typeface, size, and style, and the overall layout of text all affect how well or how poorly text conveys information to the user. Traditional typographic conventions have striven to improve the legibility or readability of text. The word "usability" could easily be used instead, but the meaning is basically the same. Take a look at the Web pages shown in Figure 10-5. The page on the top shows a typical page lacking any major typographic improvements. The one on the bottom has applied some basic techniques to improve readability.

Modern-Day Baskerville

Should we strive to apply any and all typographic conventions from print to the Web directly? No, because some ideas just don't make sense or need modification. For example, the concept of copy fitting is well known in print publishing. Copy fitting is the process of taking text and trying to fit it within a predefined space such as a piece of paper. Copy fitting requires the designer to literally count the characters and determine how to fit them in the page by changing the type size, type family, line spacing, layout, or even by editing the text. On the Web, we could limit our pages to a particular size, as discussed in the previous chapter, but we could also let things scroll. We are not confined by the same limitations as paper, and this can be a blessing. We really can't worry about things like widows in Web text. Because text can reflow simply by the user resizing their screen or changing their font size, a paragraph may have a widow (a short line of text that is less than half the size of a normal line) no matter what we do. The concept of a page doesn't hold up on screen. The user creates and destroys widows simply by using the scroll bar. Not all the ideas of print type layout make sense for the Web. As a designer, you should strive to work with the medium, not against it. Consider the history of print design. John Baskerville was an English type designer in the mid-1700s who designed typefaces that took into account how the print process worked, starting from the properties of the metal used to manufacture type. Baskerville considered the whole process and the state of printing technology when he designed his typefaces. We should always remember that the Web, and its support for text layout, is still very primitive. Be a modern-day Baskerville.

The rest of this chapter will provide a brief overview of typography and its terms. We'll follow with a discussion of many traditional uses of type and how they may be accomplished using standard Web technologies like HTML or CSS. The chapter will conclude with a discussion of how to format text for usability.

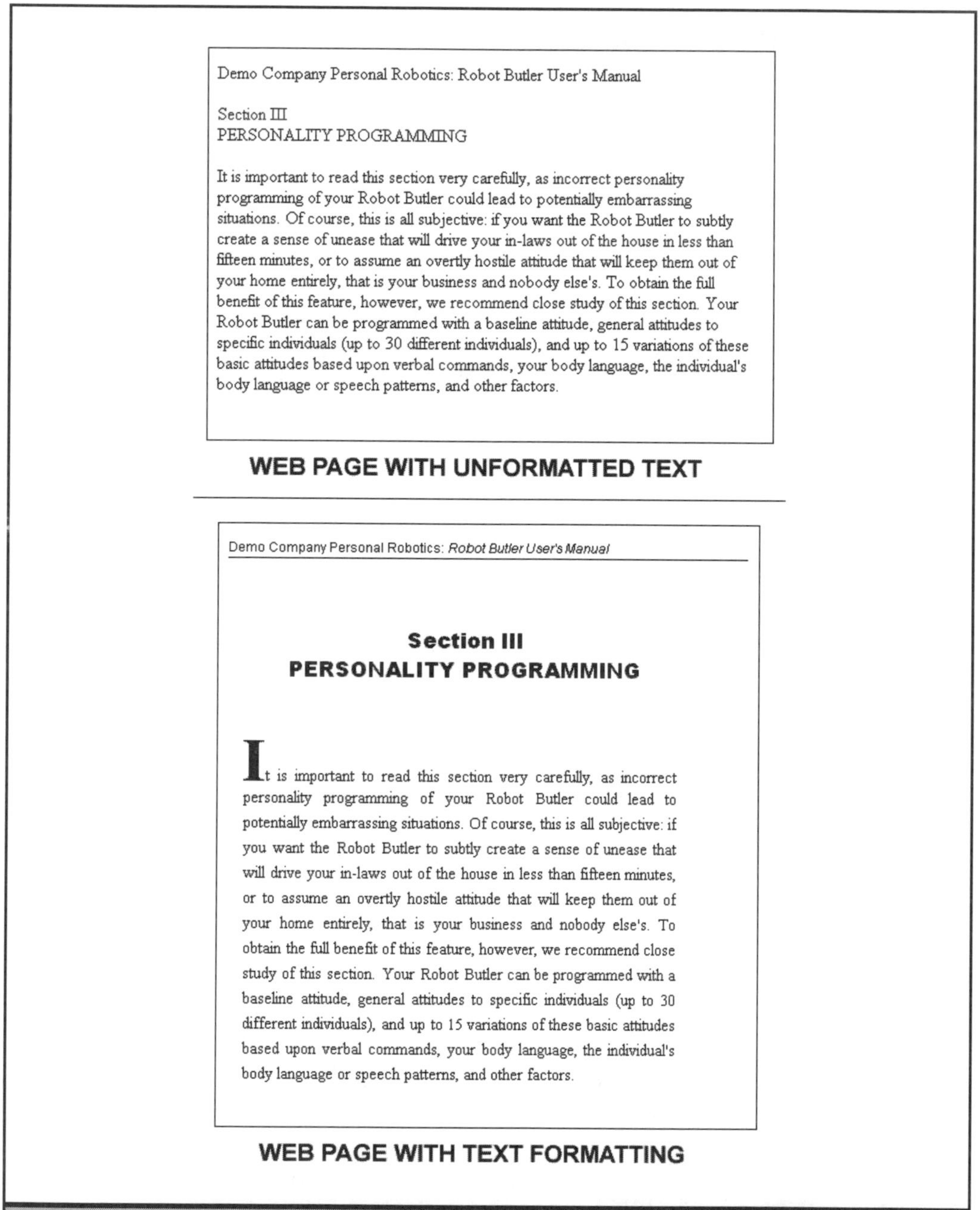

Demo Company Personal Robotics: Robot Butler User's Manual

Section III
PERSONALITY PROGRAMMING

It is important to read this section very carefully, as incorrect personality programming of your Robot Butler could lead to potentially embarrassing situations. Of course, this is all subjective: if you want the Robot Butler to subtly create a sense of unease that will drive your in-laws out of the house in less than fifteen minutes, or to assume an overtly hostile attitude that will keep them out of your home entirely, that is your business and nobody else's. To obtain the full benefit of this feature, however, we recommend close study of this section. Your Robot Butler can be programmed with a baseline attitude, general attitudes to specific individuals (up to 30 different individuals), and up to 15 variations of these basic attitudes based upon verbal commands, your body language, the individual's body language or speech patterns, and other factors.

WEB PAGE WITH UNFORMATTED TEXT

Demo Company Personal Robotics: *Robot Butler User's Manual*

Section III
PERSONALITY PROGRAMMING

It is important to read this section very carefully, as incorrect personality programming of your Robot Butler could lead to potentially embarrassing situations. Of course, this is all subjective: if you want the Robot Butler to subtly create a sense of unease that will drive your in-laws out of the house in less than fifteen minutes, or to assume an overtly hostile attitude that will keep them out of your home entirely, that is your business and nobody else's. To obtain the full benefit of this feature, however, we recommend close study of this section. Your Robot Butler can be programmed with a baseline attitude, general attitudes to specific individuals (up to 30 different individuals), and up to 15 variations of these basic attitudes based upon verbal commands, your body language, the individual's body language or speech patterns, and other factors.

WEB PAGE WITH TEXT FORMATTING

Figure 10-5.   *Type on the Web: "Do nothing" vs. "do something"*

Typography Terminology 101

Typography has a rich history as well as many rules and terms. Web designers should be familiar with the vocabulary and some of the basic tenets of text usage that have been established in the print world. Don't fall asleep as you read on. Remember, the more we focus on the various aspects of letters and the use of type, the better we will be able to fix subtle problems that the reader may not be consciously aware of.

Text is made up of characters. Characters can be letters, numbers, punctuation, and a variety of special characters. With letters, we have both uppercase and lowercase letters. We can also describe various parts of the individual letters. For example, *ascenders* are the parts of lowercase letters that protrude upwards away from the main part of the letter. *Descenders* are the parts of letters that protrude downward and hang below the baseline, which all characters sit on. The letters b, d, f, h, k, l and t have ascenders while the letters g, j, p, q, and y have descenders. Ascenders and descenders are important because they help readers to recognize words more easily by providing variation in letter forms when combined in a word. The *baseline* is an imaginary line that text appears to sit on; descenders go below this line. The imaginary line that marks the top of lowercase letters that lack ascenders is called the *meanline*. Between these two lines, characters may be measured by their *x-height*, which is the height of the body or main part of a lowercase letter not including any descender or ascender. Basically, it is the distance from the meanline to the baseline. It is simplest to think of x-height simply as the height of a lowercase x character. Figure 10-6 provides a graphical overview of all these type terms.

There are many more terms that help classify letter shapes. Some of these are shown in Figure 10-7. The purpose of knowing all these terms is simply to be able to understand the differences between different character styles. Readers interested in a complete discussion of typography terms should see the links at the support site www.webdesignref.com.

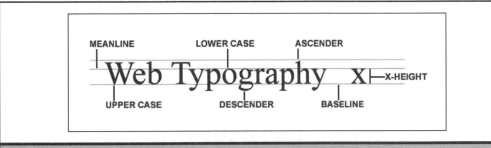

Figure 10-6.   *Some common type terms*

ELEMENTS OF PAGE DESIGN

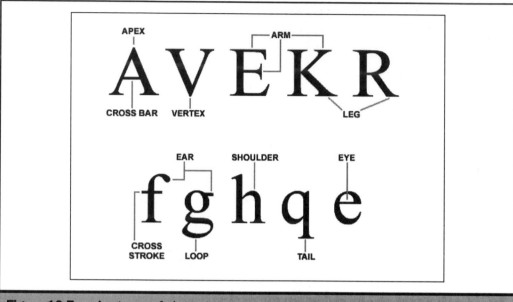

Figure 10-7. *Anatomy of characters*

Fonts

A *font* refers to the style of the type used on a computer. The term comes from the print publishing industry where it referred to a particular size of a particular typeface. On the computer, this term is often interchangeable with the word "typeface." On the Web, typefaces are generally classified in only a few basic ways. First, by distinguishing if the typeface is *serif* or *sans serif*. A serif font is one that has short starting or finish strokes protruding from certain parts of letters, like T or h. In contrast, a sans serif font lacks these extra strokes. Notice the difference between Arial, a common sans serif font, and Times, the most common serif font on the Web.

Arial is a sans serif font

Times is a serif font

Beyond this form, there are varieties of other ways to categorize type...but there is little agreement as to what degree we should distinguish typefaces. Beyond sans serif and serif, some other common typefaces categories include script and decorative. Some may refer to the decorative typefaces as novelty or display typefaces. Other categories of type are possible, and many subcategories may also exist. Exactly what categories exist and which font is in which category is an area for heated debate among typographers. Table 10-1 should serve as a basic guide for Web designers to the common categories of typefaces that exist.

Typeface Variety	Category Within Each Typeface	Example
Serif Typeface	**Old Style** This type appeared between the 15th and 17th centuries. They have little contrast between thick and thin strokes, bracketed serifs, and small x-height.	Bembo
	Transitional This is a group that combines elements from both the Old Style and Modern groups and appeared in the 17th and 18th centuries. The typical characteristics include a large x-height, more contrast between thick and thin strokes than is seen in Old Style faces, and thin bracketed serifs.	Times Roman
	Modern This typeface originated in the 18th century and was used in the 19th century as well. Fonts in this category usually display a contrast between thick and thin strokes, small x-height like Old Style, and usually unbracketed serifs.	Bodoni
	Slab Serif This typeface features heavy lines and curves of equal width, with rectangular serifs the same width as the strokes themselves. The x-height is generally large. Some slab serifs have an "Egyptian" feel to them.	Clarendon

Table 10-1.   *Common Typefaces*

ELEMENTS OF PAGE DESIGN

Typeface Variety	Category Within Each Typeface	Example
Sans Serif Typeface	**Geometric** The x-height of these tends to be small, and the strokes of the characters tend to be the same width. Like their name, they tend to be mathematical in their proportions.	Futura
	Grotesque These tend to have more stroke variation than other sans serif fonts, and have a large x-height. They are not as geometric in feeling.	
	Humanist These have a small x-height similar in proportion to Old Style.	Gill Sans
Script Typeface	**Brush script** This type looks as if it were lettered with a brush.	Cursive
	Calligraphic In this type of typeface, the designs appear to have been drawn with a broad-edged pen.	
Decorative Typeface	Also called display or novelty typefaces, many of these fonts are too intricate or irregular to be useful for text unless at very large size or for a few words.	Ransom Note

Table 10-1. *Common Typefaces* (continued)

Proportional vs. Monospaced Fonts

While there are literally thousands of fonts that can be used, the use of different font families within standard Web text is actually very limited. By default, Web browsers only support two basic font types: proportional and monospace fonts. A *proportional font* consists of characters that take up only as much space as they need within a word or a line of type. By default, text in HTML is rendered in a proportional font when not specified—typically, Times. With *monospaced fonts* (also called fixed-width or nonproportional), each character occupies exactly the same amount of space regardless of its actual width. Web browsers also support a single monospaced font—typically, Courier. Setting Web text into a monospaced font is easy with HTML using the **<TT>** element, as shown here:

```
<TT>This is now monospaced</TT>
```

A specific monospaced typeface such as Courier can be specified using the **<FONT>** element, which will be discussed in the next section. Proportional fonts should be used for most text, as they have the following two advantages:

- You can include more characters in a given amount of space if they can vary in width.
- Text is easier to read because the words appear as a cohesive unit within a sentence.

Note the readability and the amount of room taken up by the sample text shown in Figure 10-8.

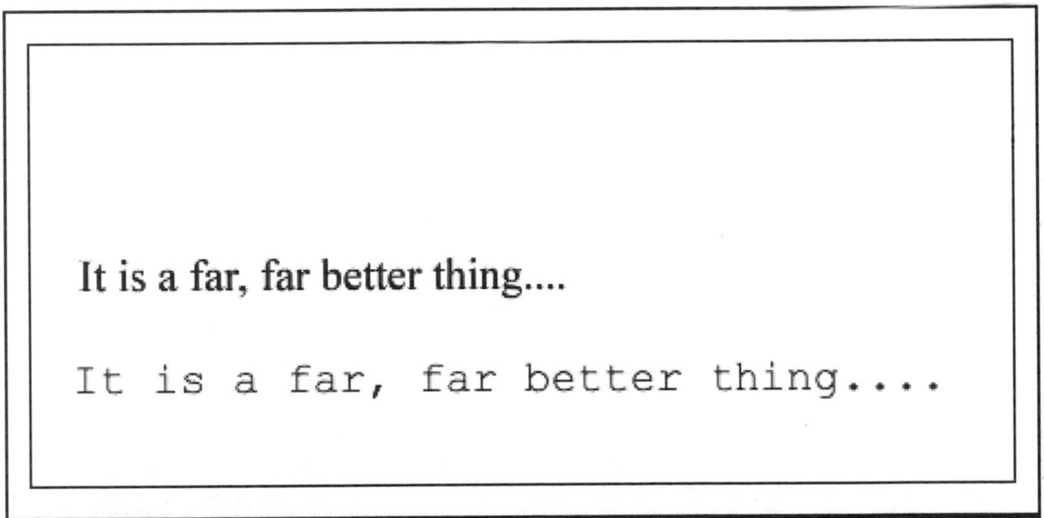

It is a far, far better thing....

It is a far, far better thing....

Figure 10-8.   *Proportional vs. monospace text*

ELEMENTS OF PAGE
DESIGN

In general, you should consider using monospaced type within Web pages for computer code, certain technical data, or to bring special emphasis to words or phrases.

Setting Fonts in Web Pages

While Web pages support two primary generic font types, proportional and monospaced, it is possible to set the font itself. Use the **FACE** attribute for the **<FONT>** tag to set the name of the font used to render text in a Web page:

```
<FONT FACE="Courier">This is now monospaced</FONT>
```

A Web browser will read this HTML fragment and render the text in the font named in the **FACE** attribute—but only for users who have the font installed on their systems. Multiple fonts can be listed using the **FACE** attribute:

```
<FONT FACE="Arial, Helvetica, Sans-serif">This should be in a
different font</FONT>
```

Here, the browser will read the comma-delimited list of fonts until it finds a font it supports. Given the fragment shown above, the browser would try first Arial, then Helvetica, and finally a sans serif font before giving up and using whatever the current browser font is.

When using CSS, specify the **font-family** property to set the font, either by specifying a specific font such as Arial or a generic family such as sans serif, which should be built in to the browser. Quote any font names that contain white space, and be careful to note that font names may have to be capitalized. Like the **<FONT>** tag, CSS supports a comma-separated list to select text from. So, to set the font for all paragraph tags, you would use a simple CSS rule like this:

```
P    {font-family: Arial, Helvetica, Sans-serif}
```

A little guesswork can be applied when setting Web fonts so that the page renders correctly. Most Macintosh, Windows, and UNIX users have a standard set of fonts, as shown in Appendix C. Furthermore, CSS specifies one font face for every category that should be built into the browser. If equivalent fonts are specified, it may be possible to provide similar page renderings across platforms. Recommended faces to use within Web pages are shown in Figure 10-9.

Because many of these fonts are specific to a particular operating system, you may have to specify fallback equivalents unless you decide to use downloadable fonts, which will be discussed in the next section. Traditionally, without relying on downloadable fonts, the combinations listed below have been considered useful

Figure 10-9.   *Common Web fonts*

to specify within Web sites because the fallback fonts are fairly similar and users generally have them installed:

```
Arial, Helvetica, sans-serif
Times New Roman, Times, serif
Courier New, Courier, mono
Georgia, Times New Roman, Times, serif
Verdana, Arial, Helvetica, sans-serif
```

Using Downloadable Fonts

With traditional HTML and even basic CSS, font choice is very limited on the Web. Designers often resort to putting text into an image form in order to use a nonstandard font in a page. However, this solution is not optimal. Fortunately, the major browser vendors have developed their own versions of downloadable fonts. Microsoft's solution is called OpenType (www.microsoft.com/typography). Netscape's solution, called Dynamic Fonts, is based on TrueDoc (www.truedoc.com). Currently, only Netscape 4.0 and Internet Explorer 4.0 and above support downloadable fonts. Unfortunately, neither solution is perfectly implemented.

Netscape's Dynamic Fonts

To use a dynamic font under Netscape, page authors should use the **FACE** attribute of the **<FONT>** element or a style sheet attribute to set the font face. If the user does not have the font installed on the system, a downloadable font linked to the page can be fetched and used to render the page. To include a link to a Netscape font definition

file in Portable Font Resource (PFR) format, use the **<LINK>** element by setting
the **REL** attribute to **fontdef** and the **SRC** attribute equal to the URL where the font
definition file resides. The **<LINK>** element must be found within the **<HEAD>** of the
document. You will have to create a PFR file using a tool such as HexMac's Typograph
(www.hexmac.com). A more complete list of tools can be found at www.truedoc.com.
An example of how this element would be used is shown here:

```
<!DOCTYPE HTML PUBLIC "-//W3C//DTD HTML 4.0 Transitional//EN">
<HTML>
<HEAD>
<TITLE>Netscape Font Demo</TITLE>
<LINK REL="fontdef"
     SRC="http://www.bigcompany.com/fonts/ransom.pfr">
<STYLE>
<!--
  .special   {font-family: ransom; color: green; font-size: 28pt;}
-->
</STYLE>
</HEAD>
<BODY>
<FONT FACE="ransom">
  Content rendered in the font "newfont" which is part of
  the pfr file.
</FONT><BR>
<SPAN CLASS="ransom">You can use CSS rules to access the
new font as well</SPAN>
</BODY>
</HTML>
```

Note that there may be many fonts in the same font definition file. There is no limit
to how many fonts can be used on a page. Once the font is accessed, it is used just as if
it were installed on a user's system. You can use either CSS or normal HTML **<FONT>**
syntax to access the downloadable font.

   *One drawback to the Netscape approach to dynamic fonts is that it may cause screen
flashing in many versions of Netscape. This can be disorienting for the user and has
somewhat limited the use of this technology.*

Microsoft's Dynamic Fonts

Microsoft also provides a way to embed fonts in a Web page. To include a font, you
must first build the page using the **<FONT>** element or style-sheet rules that set fonts.
When creating your page, don't worry about whether or not the end user has the font

installed; it will be downloaded. Next, use Microsoft's Web Embedding Fonts tool or a similar facility to analyze the font usage on the page. The program should create an .eot file that contains the embedded fonts. Then, add the font-use information to the page in the form of cascading style sheets (CSS) style rules, which are basically those defined in CSS2, as shown here:

```
<!DOCTYPE HTML PUBLIC "-//W3C//DTD HTML 4.0 Transitional//EN">
<HTML>
<HEAD>
<TITLE>Microsoft Font Test</TITLE>
<STYLE TYPE="text/css">
<!--

  @font-face {
    font-family: Ransom;
    font-style:  normal;
    font-weight: normal;
    src: url(fonts/ransom.eot);
  }

  .special {font-family: Ransom; color: green;
            font-size: 28pt;}
-->
</STYLE>
</HEAD>
<BODY>
<FONT FACE="Ransom" SIZE="6">
Example Ransom Note Font</FONT><BR>
<SPAN CLASS="special">
This is also in Ransom</SPAN>
</BODY>
</HTML>
```

Notice how it is possible to use both typical style-sheet rules like a **CLASS** binding as well as the normal **<FONT>** tag. A possible rendering of font embedding is shown in Figure 10-10.

As in the Netscape approach, you must first create a font file and reference it from the file that uses the font. It may be useful to define a fonts directory within your Web site to store font files, similar to storing image files for site use.

The use of **@font-face** acts as a pseudoelement that allows you to bring any number of fonts into a page. For more information on embedded fonts under Internet Explorer, and links to font-file creation tools like WEFT (Web Embedding Font tool), see the Microsoft Typography site (www.microsoft.com/typography).

Figure 10-10.   *Embedded fonts increase design choices*

While downloadable font technology is improving, you must still include both technologies within pages built for public consumption—despite the fact that CSS2 defines the Microsoft syntax. Even when downloading fonts is done correctly, the user still may experience annoying flashing, or the text may not work properly with background colors and images. Once perfected, downloadable font technology will drastically change type use on the Web, enabling users to create beautiful pages as well as ones overloaded with font families. Experienced designers should consider that a limited selection of fonts may be best for inexperienced page builders who might pick illegible fonts to use online.

Setting Font Styles

The style of a font, regardless of its family, may vary. The most common style is when the characters are upright. This is called "Roman," or simply "normal" (as is done in CSS). By default, HTML uses Roman style, as does CSS, if you don't specify a particular style. To explicitly set font style to Roman, use a style rule like the following:

```
<SPAN STYLE="font-style: normal">This text is Roman.</SPAN>
```

The other font style possibility is italic, where the letters slant to the right. Setting text in italic in HTML is simple using the **<I>** element:

```
<I>This is italic text</I>
```

It is also possible to use the **font-style** rule in CSS to set the style rule, as shown here:

```
<SPAN STYLE="font-style: italic">This is italic</SPAN>
```

Lastly, you can specify to set text in a style called oblique. Traditionally, oblique text would be a slanted sans serif face. In many situations, oblique text looks identical to italic text and is more in reference to an oblique family name if one exists. Text style can be set to oblique only using CSS:

```
<SPAN STYLE="font-style: oblique">This is oblique</SPAN>
```

An italicized font isn't necessarily one that is just tilted. If the family supports an italic or oblique style, the actual characters may be different, particularly the lowercase characters f, g, a, and k. Other characters may change as well; it simply depends on the font used.

Setting Font Weight

The weight of a font refers to the thickness of its stroke. Changing the weight brings emphasis to text. Many designers prefer to bring emphasis to text using italics rather than bold, but the choice is up to you. Setting text bold in HTML is easy using the **<B>** tag:

```
<B>This is bold text</B>
```

HTML does not afford any great control over the weight of text. Under CSS, you can specify the weight using the **font-weight** property. Values for the property range from 100 to 900, in increments of 100, with 900 being very bold and 100 light. Normal text is set at 400 weight, and 700 corresponds to the use of the **<B>** tag. Keywords are also supported, including **bold**, **bolder**, and **lighter**, which are used to set relative weights. Some browsers may also provide keywords such as **extra-light**, **light**, **demi-light**, **medium**, **demi-bold**, **bold**, and **extra-bold**, which correspond to the 100 to 900 values.

Because font families also include bold values, and the meaning within them varies, the numeric scheme is preferred. A few examples are shown here:

```
STRONG              {font-weight:   bolder}
.special-emphasis   {font-weight:   900}
H2                  {font-weight:   demi-bold}
```

Unfortunately, many supposed CSS-compliant browsers do not support the various weights well and default to just bold or nonbold text.

Specifying Font Variants

Yet another variation of a font that can add emphasis to text is the use of small capitals, or small caps. This style is often used in legal documents. In HTML you will have to manually size text down and type in all capital letters:

```
<SMALL>THIS IS MANUAL SMALL CAPS</SMALL>
```

CSS provides the **font-variant** property, which can be set to **small-caps** to display the current font as small uppercase letters:

```
EM      {font-variant: small-caps}
```

Reversing Text

Using white letters on a black or another color background can create a striking effect, but it may also be much harder to read. Reverse type appears smaller, and the color may overpower the text. On the Web, we don't have to worry about ink-bleeding issues with reversed type, but because of readability issues you will probably still have to up your font size 1 or 2 points when using reversed text. You should also avoid using very thin typefaces in a reversed fashion. Setting text in reversed style is fairly easy with a style-sheet rule:

```
.reverse   {background-color: black;  color: white;}
```

and then accessing it whenever you want to reverse text, like so:

```
<SPAN CLASS="reverse">Reverse It!</SPAN>
```

In vanilla HTML, it is much harder to reverse text. You will have to rely on tables and background colors to achieve the effect unless you want to resort to making an image. The markup below achieves the same effect as the style rule:

```
<TABLE CELLPADDING="0" CELLSPACING="0">
<TR>
 <TD BGCOLOR="black">
  <FONT COLOR="white">Reverse It!</FONT>
 </TD>
</TR>
</TABLE>
```

Not only is the HTML approach messy, it doesn't necessarily work well in all situations. Consider the following markup to reverse a single letter. It works, sort of, but it's awkward.

```
<TABLE CELLPADDING="1" CELLSPACING="0" BORDER="0">
<TR>
 <TD ALIGN="center" BGCOLOR="black"><FONT
```

```
COLOR="white">R</FONT></TD>
 <TD>everse only the R</TD>
</TR>
</TABLE>
```

To effectively reverse a single character in a Web page without using style sheets, you will probably have to resort to an image.

Text Casing

One last way to change the general appearance of text is to case it differently. As you already know, text has both uppercase and lowercase. You should be cautious with the use of uppercase in Web pages as TYPING IN ALL UPPERCASE IS CONSIDERED THE EQUIVALENT OF SHOUTING. Also consider that when you TYPE IN ALL UPPERCASE IT IS MUCH MORE DIFFICULT TO READ than when you type in mixed case because the letter forms are much less distinguishable. Last but not least, when type is set in all caps it can be much longer than the same type set in lower or mixed case. This can be very important if you are making buttons or have a fixed region like a table or column to put text into. You may have to make the size of the text smaller to fit the text into the defined area. This could make the text illegible. Setting the case of text is generally a manual process, though CSS does define the **text-transform** property that can be used to uppercase text automatically. The example here shows how a class called upper is changed to uppercase automatically:

```
.upper   {text-transform: uppercase}
```

It is also possible to specify values of **lowercase**, **capitalize**, or **none** for the **text-transform** property. Uppercase text should be used sparingly, but it may be useful within navigation or within section labels or headings.

Sizing Font

Traditional text measurement specifies font size in points. A point is 1/72 of an inch. The point size of text is measured from the top of the ascender to the bottom of a descender. Even though text is set to a particular point size, it may not look the same size on screen or paper. The size of the characters optically is determined greatly by their x-height measurement. The x-height is the height of the body or main part of a lowercase letter not including any descender or ascender, or simply the height of the font's lowercase x character. Since most text will be composed of lowercase letters, a font with a small x-height will look smaller than one with a larger x height, even though both may be set to the same point size. Figure 10-11 illustrates the point measurement system and shows the size variation between fonts.

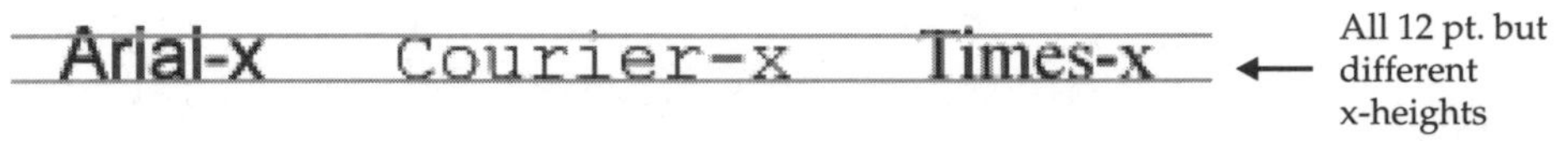

All 12 pt. but
different
x-heights

Figure 10-11. *Font Measurement in points and x-height*

Font Sizes in HTML

HTML does not provide a fine-grain measurement system for fonts. The **<FONT>** tag does provide a **SIZE** attribute that sets the size of type. In a Web page, there are seven sizes for text, numbered from 1 to 7, where 1 is the smallest text in a document and 7 is the largest. To set some text into the largest size, use **<FONT SIZE="7">**This is big**</FONT>**. By default, the typical size of text is 3; this can be overridden with the **<BASEFONT>** element discussed in Appendix C. Sizing is not exact in HTML; however, if the user has not modified their browser settings, the size corresponds to the point sizes in Table 10-2. Designers are warned that these are only guidelines. If exact point sizes are required, CSS should be used or the text made into an image.

Relative sizing with HTML is possible. If the text should just be made one size bigger, use a relative sizing value such as **<FONT SIZE="+1">** instead of specifying the size directly. The **+** and **-** nomenclature makes it possible to bring the font size up or down a specified number of settings. The values for this form of the **SIZE** attribute should range

<FONT SIZE="n">	**Typical Point Size**
1	8
2	10
3	12
4	14
5	18
6	24
7	36

Table 10-2. *Typical <FONT SIZE> and Point Size Equivalents*

from +1 to +6 and -1 to -6. It is not possible to specify **<FONT SIZE="+10">** because there are only seven sizes. If the increase or decrease goes beyond acceptable sizes, the font generally defaults at the largest or smallest size, respectively. It is also possible to use the **<BIG>** and **<SMALL>** elements, which correspond to **<FONT SIZE="+1">** and **<FONT SIZE="-1">,** respectively. Under strict HTML 4.0, this is the preferred method as the **<FONT>** tag is depreciated.

Font Sizing Under CSS

CSS provides more control over font sizes than HTML. The **font-size** property sets the relative or physical size of the font. Values may be mapped to a physical point size or to a relative word describing the size. Physical point size can be set in points (**pt**), picas (**pc**), centimeters (**cm**), millimeters (**mm**), inches (**in**), pixels (**px**), x-height values (**ex**), and em values, which are equivalent to the current font size in use (**em**). It is also possible to use keywords like **xx-small**, **x-small**, **small**, **medium**, **large**, **x-large**, and **xx-large** that map to browser-defined sizes that are probably very similar to the HTML font sizes from 1 to 7. Relative sizing can be accomplished using the keywords **larger** or **smaller** as well as positive percentage values like **50%** or **200%**. A few example rules are shown here:

```
P          {font-size: 18pt}
STRONG     {font-size: larger}
H1         {font-size: 200%}
```

This is a clear case where CSS provides more control options than HTML. While point size may appear to provide the most control, unfortunately point size is not perfectly equivalent across PC and Macintosh displays. The PC tends to display text about 33 percent larger for the same point size as a Mac. Designers looking for precise control may have to resort to measurements like pixels or give up and use relative sizing, particularly the **x-height** measure. A more complete discussion of these cross-platform text-size issues can be found in Appendix C.

Text Layout

Once you have selected your font to use and begun to set basic features such as size and style, you may begin to experiment with formatting text in various ways. Traditionally, Web page designers have relied heavily on tables to lay out text on a page. We will provide only basic reminders of how this can be accomplished, as there is no doubt that over time this approach to text layout will be replaced with CSS. HTML tables are far too complex and bind layout very closely to content. Readers looking to find more information about table layout are encouraged to see the companion book *HTML: The Complete Reference* (Osborne/McGraw-Hill, 1999) for more information.

Text Alignment

The first question about text layout usually has to do with aligning text. The default on the Web is to leave the text flush left with a ragged right side. In HTML you do not have to do anything to force this alignment, but you can explicitly set it with the **ALIGN** attribute on common block elements like **<P>**.

```
<P ALIGN="left">This paragraph is aligned to the left</P>
```

This can also be done in CSS using the **text-align** property.

```
P   {text-align: left;}
```

Setting the alignment in the opposite style, flush right with a ragged left side, is possible simply by changing the value to **RIGHT** in the two examples. Making the text flush both left and right, or justified, is possible by setting the value to **JUSTIFY**. To center text, you can use the **<CENTER>** element or the **ALIGN** attribute set to **center** on most major block elements. This may not produce the desired effect unless you manually add line breaks at the appropriate points, because the text won't really seemed centered except as a block relative to the whole page. CSS also supports a center value for the **text-align** property. Lastly, it is possible to format text in more of a random or asymmetrical style. The easiest way to accomplish this is using the **<PRE>** element in HTML. Unfortunately, the **<PRE>** element will also convert the text to a monospace font like Courier. The following example illustrates the use of all the formatting in both HTML and CSS. Notice that this overrides the various **ALIGN** attributes and forces the **<PRE>** tag to render in the default style. This example would work equally well in a CSS and non-CSS supporting browser.

```
<!DOCTYPE HTML PUBLIC "-//W3C//DTD HTML 4.0 Transitional//EN">
<HTML>
<HEAD>
<TITLE>Text Alignment in HTML and CSS</TITLE>
<STYLE TYPE="text/css">
<!--
  .flushleft  {text-align: left;}
  .flushright  {text-align: right;}
  .centered  {text-align: center;}
  .justified  {text-align: justify;}
  .random   {font-family: Serif;
             font-size: 1em;}
-->
</STYLE>
</HEAD>
```

```
<BODY>
<P ALIGN="LEFT" CLASS="flushleft">
On the Web text is normally aligned to the left with a
ragged right side.  This is the most common layout of
text and while it is highly readable with good variation
between lines, it can get somewhat boring.<BR>
Consider spicing up your layouts with other text layout
styles.</P>
<BR><BR>
<P ALIGN="RIGHT" CLASS="flushright">
Aligning your text to the right is not always considered
the best thing to do because it may make it difficult to
read.<BR>
Readers may not be able to easily track the text because
of the uncommon layout style.<BR>
However, for effect you may find that flush right text
can be bring attention to the content.</P>
<BR><BR>
<P ALIGN="CENTER" CLASS="centered">
Centered text can be a real problem for large amounts of
copy. <BR>
The reader's eye will bounce back and forth across lines
of varying length. <BR>
In reality you are going to have to set all the lines of
centered text <BR>one <BR>by <BR>one.<BR>
If you just center whole paragraphs at a time you aren't
going to get the effect you are looking for.</P>
<BR><BR>
<P ALIGN="JUSTIFY" CLASS="justified">
While justification seems like a good idea it really isn't.
Depending on how it is implemented in the browser and what
the text says, justification may result in rivers of
white space within your text.  These rivers may break up
the layout of your text drawing undue attention to the
whitespace. Depending on your screen size the rivers may
grow or shrink. If you really want to justify
your text on the Web you are going to have to put up with
them.</P>
<BR><BR>
<PRE CLASS="random">
  Asymmetrical or
    random
formatting
```

```
      seems like a lot of fun.
   It can be.
        However,
      this style of formatting
 isn't appropriate for everything and should be
      used sparingly for things like poetry.
Remember, it will be very
     difficult for a browser to reflow
 such random text and generally this
   will force
           RIGHT SCROLLING
for users
with smaller screens.
</PRE>
</BODY>
</HTML>
```

The rendering for this example is shown in Figure 10-12. Notice that the flush right and centered text is difficult to read. The asymmetrical text is also very difficult to follow, but when used properly it can bring emphasis to text.

While justified text seems a good approach over the tried and true flush left, ragged-right style, "rivers" of white space can be created in the document, depending on the content and how the user resizes their browser; this may ruin its readability. Remember, justification works by inserting spaces between words to even the lines up. The more words in the line, the less noticeable will be the inserted spaces. If the text is in a small column or the browser window is resized dramatically, the gaps between words will become more noticeable, as shown in Figure 10-13.

Suggestion: Avoid using justified text in Web pages.

Line Length

When laying out our text, we should strive to make the length of a line of text somewhere between 50 and 70 characters, or roughly anywhere from 7 to 15 words. This idea corresponds with cognitive science and usability concepts discussed in previous chapters. Studies suggest that that the human eye can focus on an area about four inches wide without having to turn one's head. This space corresponds to around 24 picas for standard 12pt Times. If we are playing with type size, we may consider that our optimal line length is often calculated as twice the point size in picas. So, when using 24pt font we want to use line lengths of 48pc. If we set line lengths too short, the reader may have trouble reading the text, as phrases are often broken across lines. Lines that are very long will cause problems for the reader because it will be difficult for them to track text. You have probably experienced such problems.

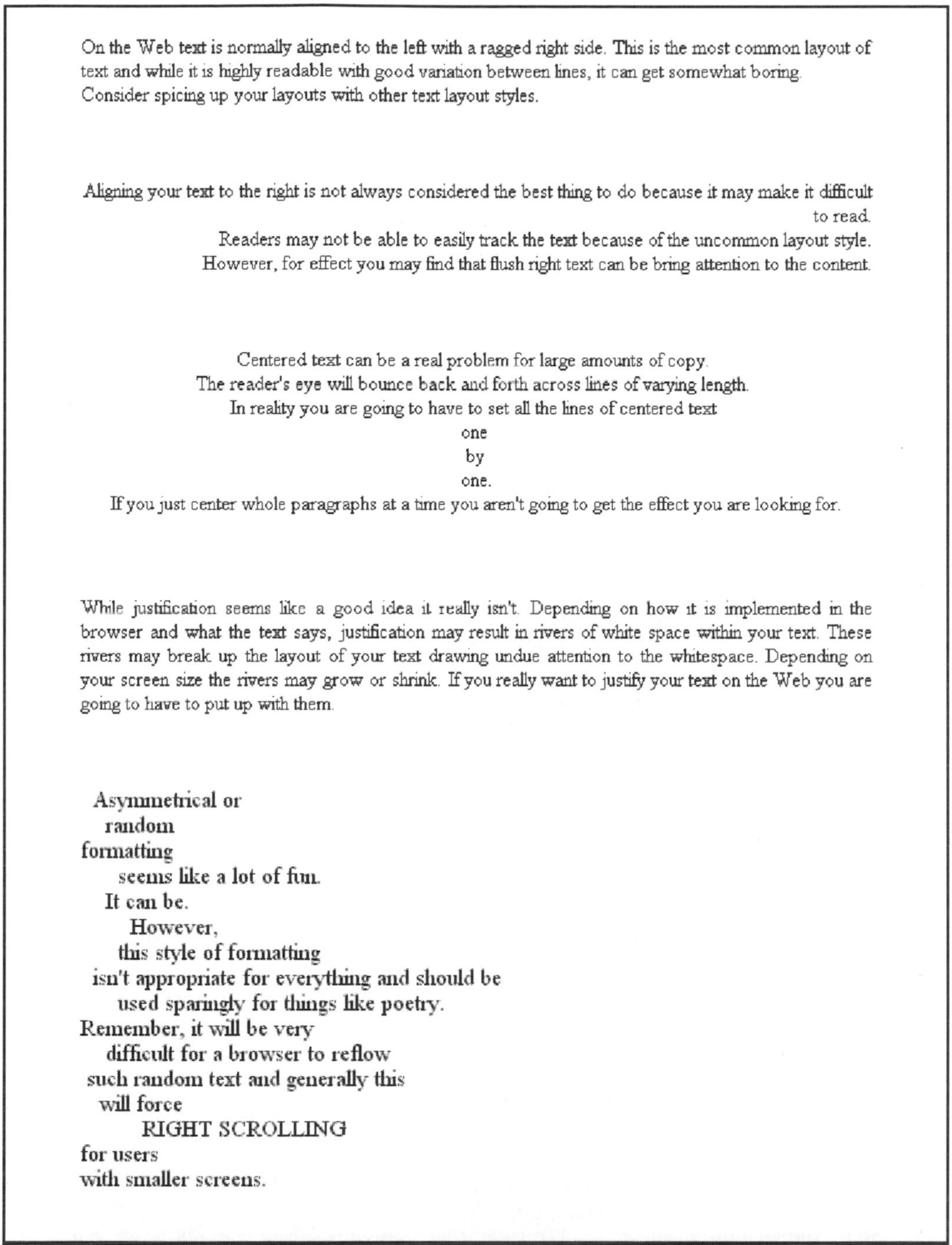

On the Web text is normally aligned to the left with a ragged right side. This is the most common layout of text and while it is highly readable with good variation between lines, it can get somewhat boring. Consider spicing up your layouts with other text layout styles.

Aligning your text to the right is not always considered the best thing to do because it may make it difficult
to read.
Readers may not be able to easily track the text because of the uncommon layout style.
However, for effect you may find that flush right text can be bring attention to the content.

Centered text can be a real problem for large amounts of copy.
The reader's eye will bounce back and forth across lines of varying length.
In reality you are going to have to set all the lines of centered text
one
by
one.
If you just center whole paragraphs at a time you aren't going to get the effect you are looking for.

While justification seems like a good idea it really isn't. Depending on how it is implemented in the browser and what the text says, justification may result in rivers of white space within your text. These rivers may break up the layout of your text drawing undue attention to the whitespace. Depending on your screen size the rivers may grow or shrink. If you really want to justify your text on the Web you are going to have to put up with them.

   Asymmetrical or
   random
formatting
      seems like a lot of fun.
   It can be.
      However,
      this style of formatting
isn't appropriate for everything and should be
      used sparingly for things like poetry.
Remember, it will be very
   difficult for a browser to reflow
such random text and generally this
   will force
         RIGHT SCROLLING
for users
with smaller screens.

Figure 10-12.   *Rendering of text-formatting example*

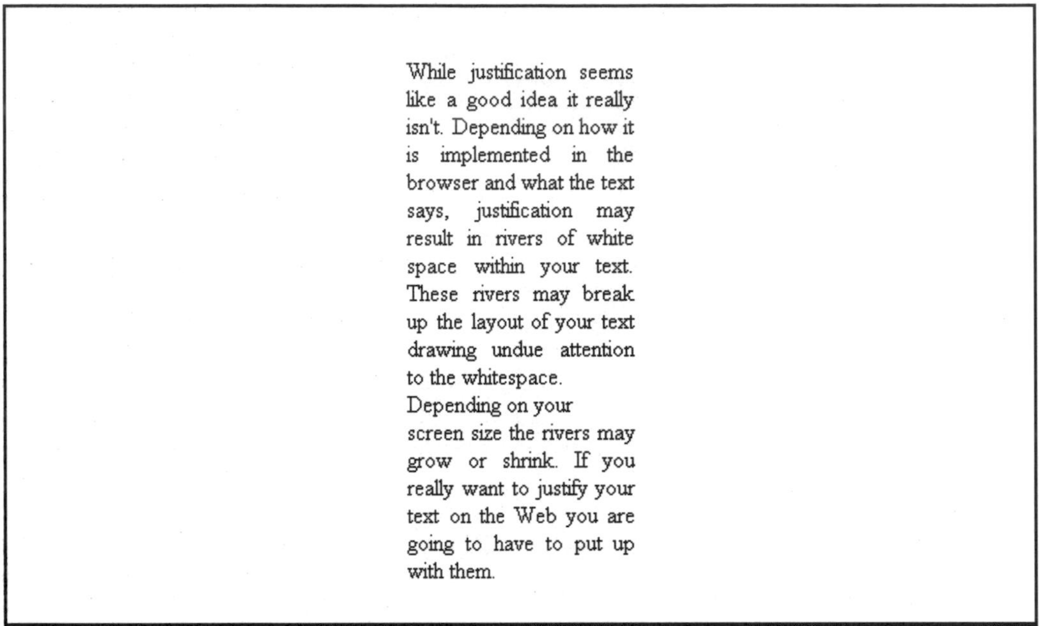

While justification seems
like a good idea it really
isn't. Depending on how it
is implemented in the
browser and what the text
says, justification may
result in rivers of white
space within your text.
These rivers may break
up the layout of your text
drawing undue attention
to the whitespace.
Depending on your
screen size the rivers may
grow or shrink. If you
really want to justify your
text on the Web you are
going to have to put up
with them.

Figure 10-13.   *Narrow columns or browser windows cause rivers*

To set line length, we may consider setting regions off by using **<DIV>** tags to create various line lengths as shown here:

```
<DIV STYLE="font-size: 12pt; width: 24pc">
  Insert your text here
</DIV>
```

However, if we are using tables in HTML with a 12pt Times font standard, we should be using columns of text somewhere between 350 and 400 pixels wide for optimum online reading. You can certainly use longer lengths if you like, but you should increase your font size and the space between lines as you increase line length. Otherwise, the text will become unreadable.

Note   *The line-length rules of thumb suggested will result in wasted paper when printing. To combat this problem, many sites using the suggested sizing provide a special button to a "printer friendly" version of the text or even link to an Adobe Acrobat equivalent of the text. As CSS matures and browsers begin to support media-based style sheets, this may change, but for now always consider that sizing for screen may not be optimal for printer.*

Line Spacing

Line spacing or *leading* is the term for the space between lines of text. The idea of line spacing is generally to add a little extra space between the lines of type so that it is easy for a reader to track which line they are on. Normal HTML text will render generally in whatever style the browser decides, typically close to single spacing. If you want to increase line spacing, you will have to manually insert **
** elements at the end of every line. Not only is this approach tedious, but text reflow when the user sizes their screen smaller than the longest line will ruin the layout unless the text is constrained by a fixed-width table cell. Even then, if the user overrides the default font size, all the spacing will be ruined.

CSS provides support for setting line spacing using the **line-height** property. The value of the line height can be specified in a variety of forms, but it would most often be written in points (**pt**), pixels (**px**), or percentage values (**%**). We can set **line-height** for the entire body of a document or for selected areas of text as shown here:

```
BODY          {line-height: 1.5em}
P.double      {line-height: 200%}
```

The print rule of thumb is to set line spacing to around one-third to one-half above the type size. So if you are using 12pt font, set **line-height** to 18pt or greater. If we don't know the current font size, it is easy to specify this as 1.5em. Some typefaces, particularly sans serif fonts like Arial or Helvetica, have very large x-heights, so they will need to have more line spacing to make it easier to read. Given how hard it is to read online text, you might consider using a **line-height** of 2em or 200%. If you plan on making very long lines, you should increase the **line-height** accordingly to improve readability.

Rule: Increase line height to improve online text readability.

Figure 10-14 shows the effect of **line-height** on various forms of text.

 The origin of the word "leading" has to do with the fact that in the days of mechanical type setting the operator would actually place small strips of lead between the lines to give them space.

Letter Spacing and Word Spacing

Besides opening up the space between lines, we can modify the space between words or even characters. The concept of adjusting spacing between characters to improve readability is called *kerning*. Adjustment of letter spacing in HTML is not accurate. While it is possible to insert a single full space between letters just by hitting the SPACEBAR between characters, HTML collapses multiple spaces, so any real formatting has to be done with the nonbreaking space entity specified by ** **. Page designers who have used WYSIWYG editors may already be familiar with this entity, which is littered throughout many poorly designed pages.

No Spacing Set

Just because the Web may not afford as many facilities for type control as print does not mean that we should abandon all hope of control over our text. The reality is that type control is improving and with some effort we can improve the presentation of our text dramatically. Choosing the appropriate typeface, size, style, spacing, and line weight can go a long way to improving the readability of a Web page.	Just because the Web may not afford as many facilities for type control as print does not mean that we should abandon all hope of control over our text. The reality is that type control is improving and with some effort we can improve the presentation of our text dramatically. Choosing the appropriate typeface, size, style, spacing, and line weight can go a long way to improving the readability of a Web page.

1.5 em Spacing

Just because the Web may not afford as many facilities for type control as print does not mean that we should abandon all hope of control over our text. The reality is that type control is improving and with some effort we can improve the presentation of our text dramatically. Choosing the appropriate typeface, size, style, spacing, and line weight can go a long way to improving the readability of a Web page.	Just because the Web may not afford as many facilities for type control as print does not mean that we should abandon all hope of control over our text. The reality is that type control is improving and with some effort we can improve the presentation of our text dramatically. Choosing the appropriate typeface, size, style, spacing, and line weight can go a long way to improving the readability of a Web page.

Figure 10-14.   *Line spacing should be adjusted to improve readability*

CSS provides letter-spacing control using the **letter-spacing** property. You can set the value of this property to a positive value like 3pt or a negative value like -4pt to tighten up spacing between letters. Normally, we aren't terribly concerned with kerning HTML text unless the text is very large, such as in a headline. In fact, you should avoid letter spacing in lowercased body text. It is considered bad practice. However, in headlines we may notice large gaps between certain letter combinations like Yo, Ya, Wa, We, Te, To, and numerous others. Reducing the space between the characters is possible, but it can be tedious. However, in headlines, reducing the spacing between lines, words, and letters can make the text more pleasing to look at and easier to read.

CSS also provides control over intraword spacing using the **word-spacing** property. You can set this to a positive value like 2em to open spaces between words or a negative value like –5pt. In general, you should try to keep word spacing in your headlines and body text fairly close. The general rule of thumb from the print world for word spacing is to be able to imagine the width of a lowercase l between words. Note that because the l character changes size with font choice and size, the word spacing would also change according to this rule. The code below illustrates adjusting a headline in various ways. The colored text is solely used to show which characters are being kerned.

```
<!DOCTYPE HTML PUBLIC "-//W3C//DTD HTML 4.0 Transitional//EN">
<HTML>
<HEAD>
<TITLE>Kerning Is Here?</TITLE>
<STYLE TYPE="text/css">
<!--
.style1   {font-size: 36pt;
          color: red;
          line-height: .9em;
          letter-spacing: -2pt;
          word-spacing: .5em;}
.style2   {font-size: 36pt;
          color: green;
          line-height: .9em;
          letter-spacing: -1pt;}
  .style3   {font-size: 36pt; color: green;}
  /* kerning classes */
  .tight   {letter-spacing: -5pt; color: yellow;}
  .tighter   {letter-spacing: -6pt; color: purple;}
  .tightest   {letter-spacing: -8pt; color: orange;}
  -->
</STYLE>
</HEAD>
<BODY>

Full Kerning
<H1 CLASS="style1">Demo Company Incorporated
<SPAN CLASS="tight">Wa</SPAN>rmly
<SPAN CLASS="tight">We</SPAN>lcomes
<SPAN CLASS="tightest">Yo</SPAN>
<SPAN CLASS="tighter">u  
To</SPAN> Our Homepage</H1>

Simple Letter Spacing and Line-height Reduction
<H1 CLASS="style2">Demo Company Incorporated Warmly
Welcomes You To Our Homepage</H1>

Regular Style
<H1 CLASS="style3">Demo Company Incorporated
Warmly Welcomes You To Our Homepage</H1>
</BODY>
</HTML>
```

The improvement when adjusting spacing in a headline can be dramatic. You often find that you can fit much more type in the same area as well as create a more pleasing looking headline if you take the time to adjust the layout, as shown by the rendering in Figure 10-15. However, you will notice that certain characters, such as the lowercase p and the uppercase Y on the line below it tend to run a bit too close to each other for comfort.

While the support for character and word spacing is pretty buggy in 4.x and early 5.x generation browsers, over time it will certainly improve. However, any graphic text that you produce such as buttons and labels, particularly if it is in larger text, should be kerned. If you are going to avoid using HTML and CSS text and incur all the downside of graphic text, you might as well enjoy the upside. Be aware that text manipulated in many programs may be autokerned in such a way as to look odd to some designers. If you want to examine your text, you should try to focus on the spaces between letters and look at the actual letters themselves. A trick that designers often use is to squint while they look at text, look at the text upside down, reversed, backwards, or anything else you can think of so that they don't concentrate on the word but the actual characters and the spaces between them.

Full Kerning

Demo Company Incorporated Warmly Welcomes You To Our Homepage

Simple Letter Spacing and Line-height Reduction

Demo Company Incorporated Warmly Welcomes You To Our Homepage

Regular Style

Demo Company Incorporated Warmly Welcomes You To Our Homepage

Figure 10-15. *Headline text often needs adjustment*

Setting Type Hierarchy

Type can be used to improve the organization of a page greatly. Consider creating a type hierarchy for your Web pages. The concept here is to create a size and emphasis of text pattern that matches the importance of the page. Imagine setting your headlines in large font and your footer information in small font. This is the crudest type of example, but with simple sizing and style adjustments we can give an importance to the elements on the page that should help back up any page structure we may have come up with. In order of importance, you should run your text objects from large to small, dark to light, dense to spread out, and so on. Each font and style you use should have a unique voice so your hierarchy is obvious. The concept of type voice is easy if you consider the page being read aloud by a talking browser. You would probably want the device to read the important things loudly and the less important things softly. You might even consider that some things would be said with a different tone if they were a form of aside. HTML implicitly provides a very simple type hierarchy through headlines, body text, and links, but you could consider improving or extending this hierarchy.

> **Suggestion: Create a type hierarchy by varying text color, size, style, and position to improve page usability.**

Headings and Subheadings

Headings and subheadings or simply subheads can be used to draw a user into a page. Headings also provide a structure for your page. The main heading is often used to indicate what the page is about while the subheads are used to indicate various sections of text. You should be careful not to have just a simple heading followed by huge amounts of body text broken into paragraphs and the occasional figure. Such text will look daunting for the reader and provide no easy entry points other than starting at the first line and reading. In HTML, we generally indicate a heading with a heading tag like **<H1>**, **<H2>**, **<H3>**, **<H4>**, **<H5>**, or **<H6>**. The formatting provided by these tags is relatively simple. The more important the heading, the larger or more distinctive the heading is rendered. Headings in HTML are arranged from most important and largest (**<H1>**) to least important and smallest (**<H6>**). It has been noted that designers rarely use headings beyond **<H3>**. Mostly this has to do with the lack of visual distinction in standard HTML of the smaller headings.

Using style sheets, we can provide a greater distinction between our subheads. The first thing to do to improve headings in Web pages is to remove the implicit returns from headings by setting their display property to **inline**. This improves headings by more closely relating subheads to their content. In normal HTML, there is often quite a gap between headings and their related content. Next, we might consider making the headlines much more visually distinctive using color, size, spacing, or even bars. The markup below illustrates a few possibilities:

```
<H2 STYLE="display: inline; color: green;">Important Headline</H2><BR>
<DIV ID="section1" STYLE="width: 24pc">
Text here for section.</DIV><BR><BR>

<H2 STYLE="display: inline; color: red;">
Important Headline</H2><BR>

<DIV ID="section1" STYLE="margin-left: 2em; width: 24pc">
Text here for section.</DIV><BR><BR>

<H2 STYLE="border-bottom-style: double; border-color: black;
          color:orange; font-size: 24pt; width: 9em;
       display: inline">Important Headline</H2><BR>
<DIV ID="section1" STYLE="width: 24pc">Text here for section.</DIV>
```

The rendering of the previous example is shown in Figure 10-16. Be aware that using the **display** property may cause erratic behavior at times.

The basic technique of bringing the headings out could also be applied to text like frequently-asked-question (FAQ) pages. Consider making the questions visually distinctive from the answers. This will improve the user's ability to quickly scan the page for the content they are looking for.

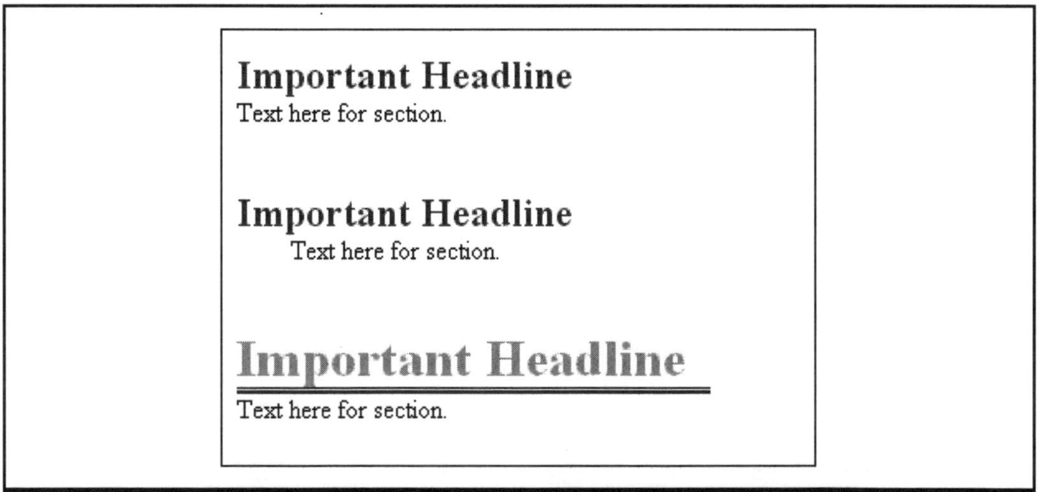

Figure 10-16. *Vary headings to improve page hierarchy*

Heading Layout Problems

Because headings are often set in larger text, we may have to kern the characters of the heading and reduce the line spacing to make them look nice. If our headings are done in CSS rather than as an image, we may run into a problem. Negative line spacing can cause problems when the descenders on the line above smash into the ascenders on the line below. Figure 10-17 shows the demo of kerned headlines from earlier in the chapter where the ascenders and descenders begin to collide because the browser has been resized. You may consider manually setting your line breaks as well as setting hard widths to avoid this type of resizing problem.

Indicating Paragraphs and Sections

When presenting large bodies of text, it is useful to break them up into smaller units such as paragraphs and sections (which may include multiple paragraphs). The most basic way to format paragraphs in HTML is with the **<P>** element.

```
<P>Too lazy to exercise? You need to get motivated!</P>
<P>It's easy to skip going to the gym, but try ditching your
personal Robot Trainer from Demo Company. He's pushy, he's
persistent, and it's all for your own good. Complete with hand
weights, leg warmers and an audio database of every disco song
ever recorded, this model will have you sweating to the beat
in no time.</P>
<P>If you miss a workout session, the Robot Trainer will make
sure you get back on schedule. How? Simple-- he'll follow you
everywhere you go until you get back into the swing of things!</P>
```

<P> is a block-level element; block-level elements such as **<P>**, **<DIV>**, and **<TABLE>** always receive the equivalent of two line breaks after the element, as shown in Figure 10-18.

Demo Company Incorporated Warmly Welcomes You To Our Homepage ↑

Careful as ascenders and desenders may collide

Figure 10-17. *Tight-leading problems*

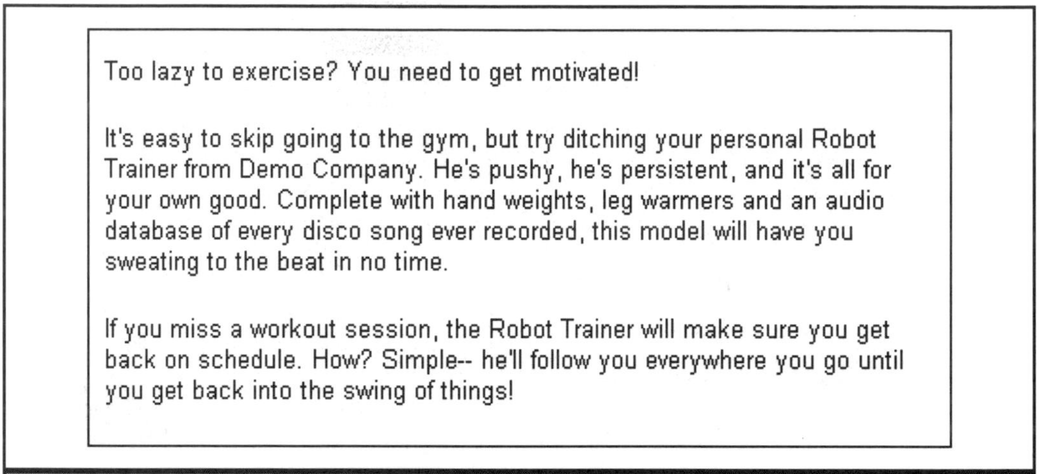

Too lazy to exercise? You need to get motivated!

It's easy to skip going to the gym, but try ditching your personal Robot Trainer from Demo Company. He's pushy, he's persistent, and it's all for your own good. Complete with hand weights, leg warmers and an audio database of every disco song ever recorded, this model will have you sweating to the beat in no time.

If you miss a workout session, the Robot Trainer will make sure you get back on schedule. How? Simple-- he'll follow you everywhere you go until you get back into the swing of things!

Figure 10-18.   *Basic paragraph rendering*

In print, this style of paragraph is not indented. When paragraphs are indented, they generally do not receive two line breaks; rather, they receive only one. A simple way to create this form of paragraph layout is to separate the paragraphs with the **
** tag, and to use multiple nonbreaking spaces **( )** or invisible images to indent the first line of each paragraph. A rendering of the last example with indents created with nonbreaking spaces is shown in Figure 10-19.

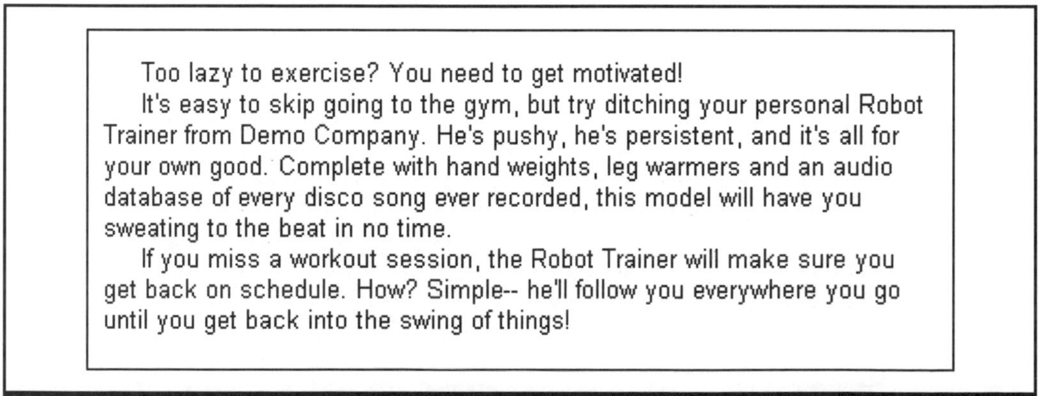

    Too lazy to exercise? You need to get motivated!
    It's easy to skip going to the gym, but try ditching your personal Robot Trainer from Demo Company. He's pushy, he's persistent, and it's all for your own good. Complete with hand weights, leg warmers and an audio database of every disco song ever recorded, this model will have you sweating to the beat in no time.
    If you miss a workout session, the Robot Trainer will make sure you get back on schedule. How? Simple-- he'll follow you everywhere you go until you get back into the swing of things!

Figure 10-19.   *Indented paragraphs using HTML*

The two approaches discussed so far work well under most browsers. There are, however, more advanced techniques using CSS that will work under the 4.0 versions of Netscape and Internet Explorer. Here, the style property **text-indent: 2em** indents the first line by 2ems, while **margin-top: 0** removes the extra break between paragraphs. To set this document wide, consider using a CSS rule like the following:

```
P       {text-indent: 2em; margin-top: 0}
```

A rendering of this rule applied to the example paragraphs is shown in Figure 10-20.

Initial Caps

Another way to mark the beginning of a paragraph or section is to set off the first letter, or "initial cap." This is generally used more for sections than for paragraphs.

Raised Initials   One style of initial cap is the raised initial. In this case, the first letter of the section lies on the same baseline as the rest of the first line, but is much larger than the other text. This effect can be achieved using basic HTML, although as Figure 10-21 shows, it tends to create extra space between the first line and the rest of the text.

```
<FONT SIZE="+5"><B>D</B></FONT>emo Company Robots are your best
investment in artificial intelligence...
```

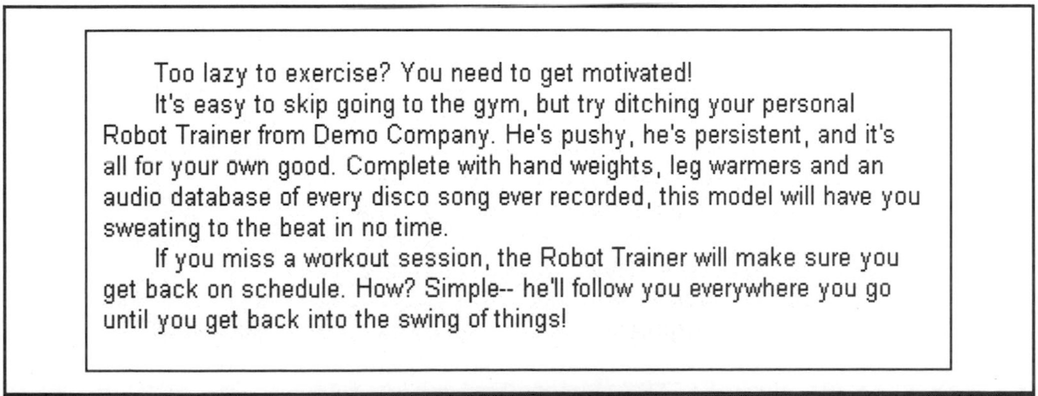

> Too lazy to exercise? You need to get motivated!
> It's easy to skip going to the gym, but try ditching your personal Robot Trainer from Demo Company. He's pushy, he's persistent, and it's all for your own good. Complete with hand weights, leg warmers and an audio database of every disco song ever recorded, this model will have you sweating to the beat in no time.
> If you miss a workout session, the Robot Trainer will make sure you get back on schedule. How? Simple-- he'll follow you everywhere you go until you get back into the swing of things!

Figure 10-20.   *Indented paragraphs using CSS*

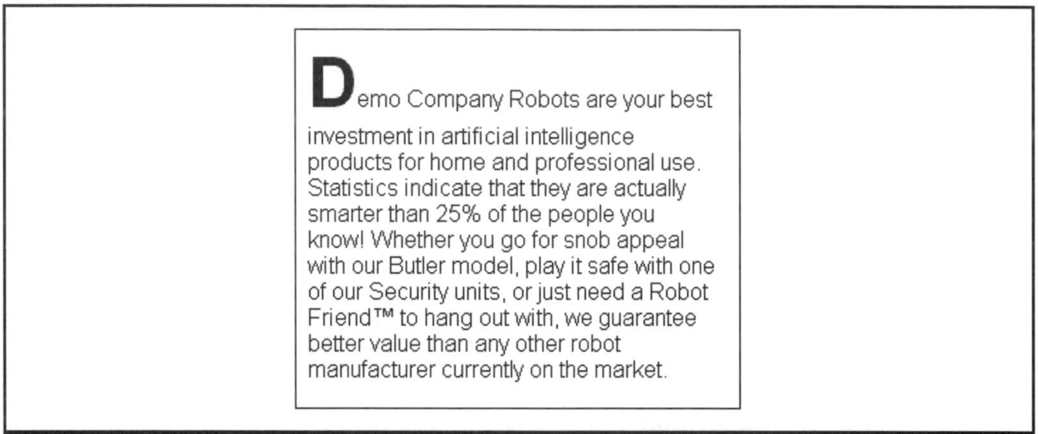

Figure 10-21.   *Raised initial using HTML*

A better effect can be achieved using graphics. A simple GIF of the letter M can be added to the first line with the **<IMG>** element.

```
<P><IMG SRC="bigD.gif" WIDTH="30" HEIGHT="37" ALT="" BORDER="0"
ALIGN="ABSBOTTOM">emo Company Robots are your best investment in
artificial intelligence...
```

By using the **ABSBOTTOM** attribute, it is possible to achieve the effect shown in Figure 10-22 (in browsers that support the **ABSBOTTOM** attribute).

Style sheets offer another means to do this: the **first-letter** pseudoelement. Including the rule **P:first-letter {font-size: 48pt; font-weight: bold}** in a style sheet should make the first letter work as a raised initial, provided that the rest of the text is set to a smaller font size, such as 12 points. At the time of this writing, however, few browsers support this, and it creates a line-spacing problem similar to the one shown in Figure 10-21.

Drop Initials   Drop initials set the initial cap into the text, usually taking up the first part of several lines of text. Graphics provide the most efficient means to do this in Web pages, as shown here:

```
<IMG SRC="bigM.gif" WIDTH="35" HEIGHT="35" ALT="" BORDER="0"
ALIGN="left">ixing drinks is just one of the many skills
available with our line of Robot Butlers....
```

> **D**emo Company Robots are your best investment in artificial intelligence products for home and professional use. Statistics indicate that they are actually smarter than 25% of the people you know! Whether you go for snob appeal with our Butler model, play it safe with one of our Security units, or just need a Robot Friend™ to hang out with, we guarantee better value than any other robot manufacturer currently on the market.

Figure 10-22. *Raised initial using graphics*

In this case, the image is aligned to the left of the text, which flows around it as shown in Figure 10-23.

This is all very well and good using a letter like M with straight ascenders, but what if the first letter has a different shape? Figure 10-24 shows how this might look using the letter A (in this case, a GIF employed as in the previous drop initial example). The slope of the A creates a significant gap between the uppercase A and the lowercase l in the word All, which makes this difficult to read.

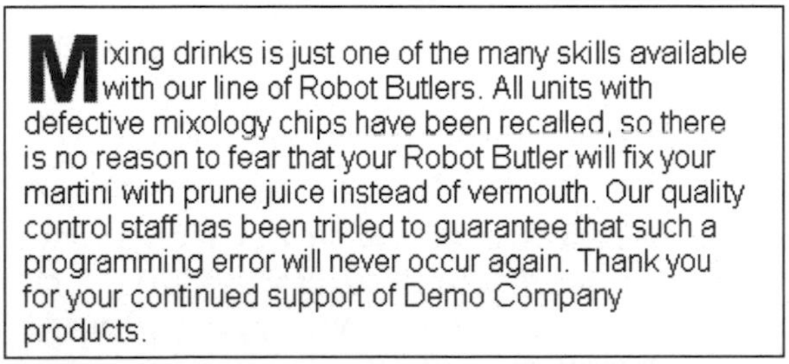

> **M**ixing drinks is just one of the many skills available with our line of Robot Butlers. All units with defective mixology chips have been recalled, so there is no reason to fear that your Robot Butler will fix your martini with prune juice instead of vermouth. Our quality control staff has been tripled to guarantee that such a programming error will never occur again. Thank you for your continued support of Demo Company products.

Figure 10-23. *Drop initials using graphics*

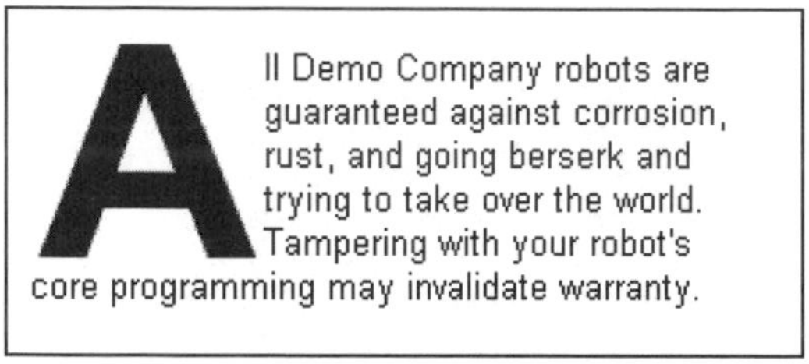

Figure 10-24.　*Drop-initial problem with irregular letter shapes*

In modern browsers (4.x and beyond), positioning using CSS, as in the following listing, allows a greater degree of control:

```
<DIV ID="Layer1" STYLE="position:absolute; width:80px;
height:130px; top: 15px; z-index:1; font-family: Arial;
font-size: 100px; font-weight: bold">A</DIV><BR>

<DIV ID="Layer2" STYLE="position:absolute; width:350px;
height:115px; z-index:2; left:12px; top: 32px;
font-family: Arial; font-size: 13px;">
<IMG SRC="space.gif" WIDTH="50" HEIGHT="1" BORDER="0">
ll Demo Company robots are<BR>
<IMG SRC="space.gif" WIDTH="55" HEIGHT="1" BORDER="0">
guaranteed against corrosion,<BR>
<IMG SRC="space.gif" WIDTH="62" HEIGHT="1" BORDER="0">
rust, and going berserk and<BR>
<IMG SRC="space.gif" WIDTH="67" HEIGHT="1" BORDER="0">
trying to take over the world.<BR>
<IMG SRC="space.gif" WIDTH="72" HEIGHT="1" BORDER="0">
Tampering with your robot's<BR>
core programming may invalidate warranty.</DIV>
```

In this example, a layer is created for the letter A, which is set to a precise size of 100 pixels; using measurements that can vary between browsers and systems would make this a very unstable approach. Another overlapping layer is created for the rest of the text, which is set to a size of 13 pixels. Breaks were entered where needed with the **
** tag, and an invisible pixel was used to adjust the indentation of each line. The actual image is only 1 pixel by 1 pixel; its width is adjusted using the **WIDTH** attribute. (Nonbreaking spaces could be used instead, but this approach offers more control.) The result is shown in Figure 10-25.

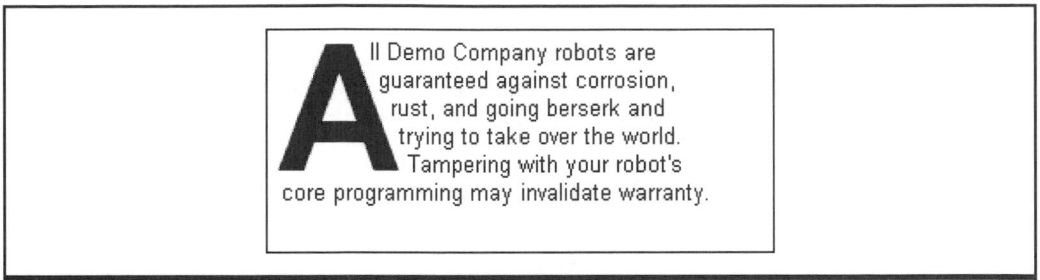

Figure 10-25. *Drop initial A created with layered CSS positioning*

The use of images can be dispensed with completely by creating a separate positioned layer for each line of text. This is not as complicated as it might seem if a tool like Macromedia's DreamWeaver is used. This approach also will provide the greatest level of layout control—in browsers that support CSS to this degree.

Hung Initials The third variety of initial cap, the hung initial, places the initial in the margin to the left of the text. In HTML, this can be done simply by using a graphic letter and a table, as shown here:

```
<TABLE WIDTH="400" CELLSPACING="0" CELLPADDING="0" BORDER="1">
<TR>
<TD VALIGN="top" WIDTH="39"><IMG SRC="bigM.gif" WIDTH="35"
HEIGHT="35" BORDER="0" HSPACE="2" VSPACE="2"></TD>

<TD VALIGN="top" WIDTH="361">ixing drinks is just one of the many
skills available with our line of Robot Butlers...</TD>
</TR>
</TABLE>
```

The graphic letter goes into one table cell, while the text goes into another; Figure 10-26 shows a rendering of this with the table border turned on.

Rules

Another means of separating sections of text is the rule: a straight line across a portion of the page. HTML provides for this with the **<HR>** element. Used without any additional attributes, **<HR>** produces a shaded gray line that extends all the way across whatever element contains it (document body, table cell, etc.). Width, size (thickness), alignment, and shading can all be set in HTML, as shown here:

```
<HR WIDTH="50%" SIZE="1" ALIGN="left" NOSHADE>
```

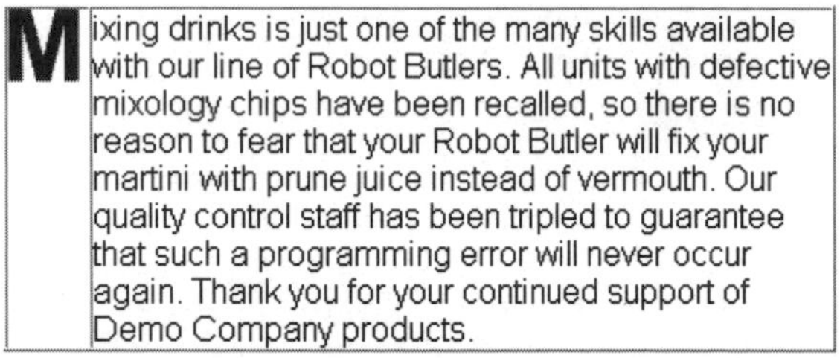

Figure 10-26.   *Hung initial created with graphic and table*

This code will produce a horizontal line half the width of the element it is contained in, 1 pixel thick, aligned to the left, with no shading. Horizontal rules have a default width of 100 percent; values can be set with percentages or pixel values. Alignment can be set to **left**, **center** or **right**; **center** is the default. Size must be set in pixels. Horizontal rules display as a shaded line unless the **NOSHADE** attribute is set. Internet Explorer 4.0 and later supports a **COLOR** attribute as well:

```
<HR WIDTH="300" SIZE="3" NOSHADE COLOR="red">
```

This code will produce a red rule in Internet Explorer, but it will appear gray in other browsers. A simple way around this would be to use a graphic to create a colored rule:

```
<IMG SRC="redline.gif" HEIGHT="1" WIDTH="300">
```

CSS can also be used to apply color to the **<HR>** element, but this may not be supported by all browsers.

Pull Quotes

In print, it is sometimes useful to enhance a page of text with one or two pull quotes. In addition to varying the text flow, pull quotes are used to draw the reader's attention by highlighting a statement from the text. In Figure 10-27, most of the paragraphs are set to a default font size and face with no further embellishment beyond a left margin of 10 pixels.

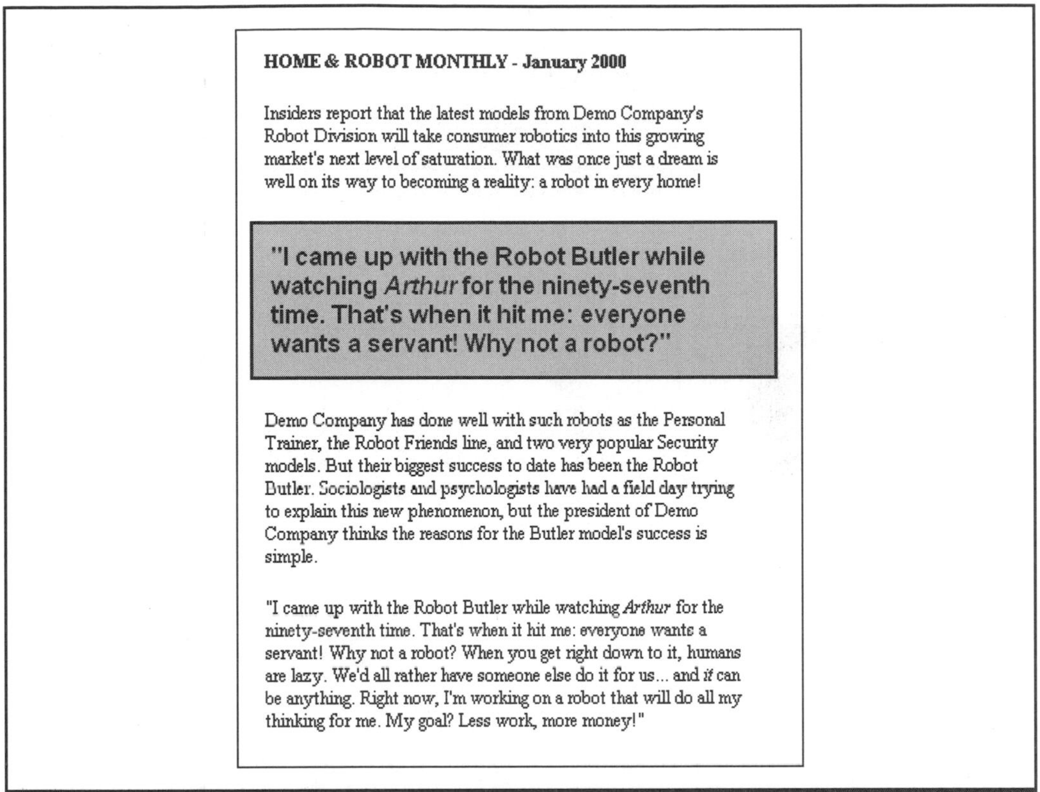

HOME & ROBOT MONTHLY - January 2000

Insiders report that the latest models from Demo Company's Robot Division will take consumer robotics into this growing market's next level of saturation. What was once just a dream is well on its way to becoming a reality: a robot in every home!

"I came up with the Robot Butler while watching *Arthur* for the ninety-seventh time. That's when it hit me: everyone wants a servant! Why not a robot?"

Demo Company has done well with such robots as the Personal Trainer, the Robot Friends line, and two very popular Security models. But their biggest success to date has been the Robot Butler. Sociologists and psychologists have had a field day trying to explain this new phenomenon, but the president of Demo Company thinks the reasons for the Butler model's success is simple.

"I came up with the Robot Butler while watching *Arthur* for the ninety-seventh time. That's when it hit me: everyone wants a servant! Why not a robot? When you get right down to it, humans are lazy. We'd all rather have someone else do it for us... and *it* can be anything. Right now, I'm working on a robot that will do all my thinking for me. My goal? Less work, more money!"

Figure 10-27. *Pull quote created with CSS*

The pull quote, which is drawn from later in the text, uses CSS rules to distinguish the pull quote from the rest of the text:

```
<P STYLE="background: #99FFFF; width: 22pc; margin-left: 0;
padding: 12px; font-family: Arial; font-size: 12pt;
font-weight: bold; border-style: solid; border-width: thin;
border-color: #000000">"I came up with the Robot Butler while
watching <I>Arthur</I> for the ninety-seventh time. That's when
it hit me: everyone wants a servant! Why not a robot?"...
```

The result is a box with a blue background, a black border, extra padding between the border and its content, and a larger sans serif font.

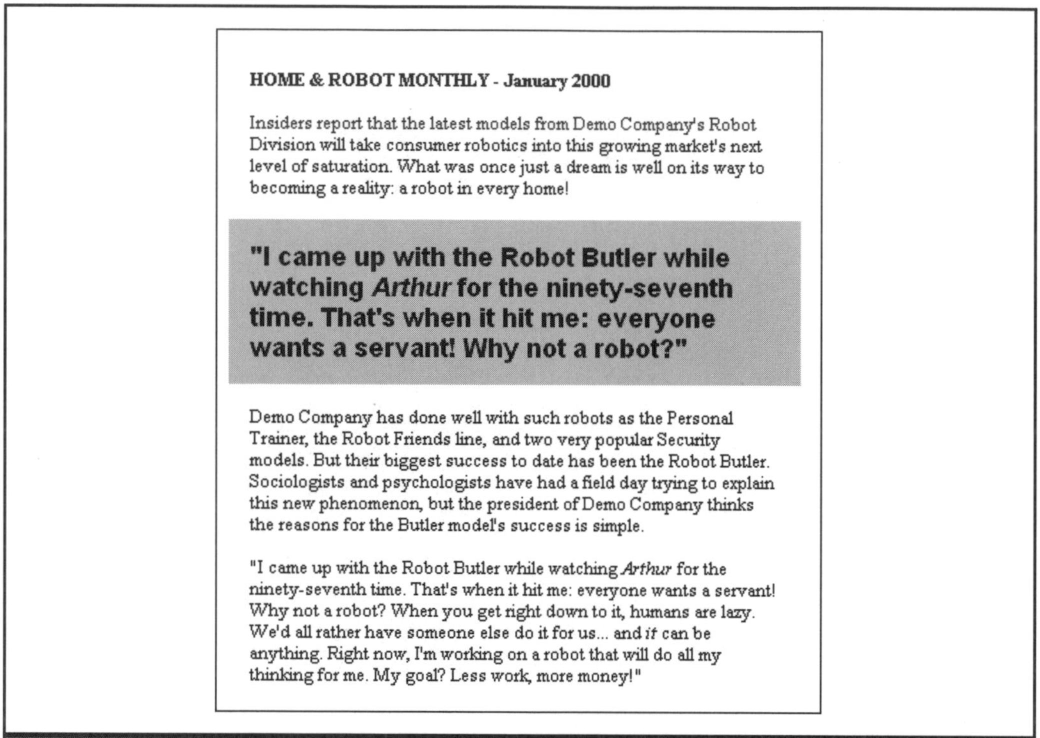

Figure 10-28. *Pull quote created with HTML table*

Figure 10-28 uses a table to create a similar effect:

```
<TABLE WIDTH="400" BORDER="0" CELLSPACING="0" CELLPADDING="15">
<TR>
<TD><FONT FACE="Times New Roman" SIZE="-1">
<B>HOME &amp; ROBOT MONTHLY - January 2000</B><BR><BR>

Insiders report that the latest models...</FONT></TD>
</TR>

<TR>
<TD BGCOLOR="#99FFFF">
```

```
<FONT FACE="Arial, Helvetica, Sans-serif" SIZE="+1"><B>"I came up
with the Robot Butler...</B></FONT></TD>
</TR>

<TR>
<TD><FONT FACE="Times New Roman" SIZE="-1">Demo Company has done
well... FONT></TD>
</TR>
</TABLE>
```

In this instance, cell padding is used to set off the text, the **<FONT>** tag is used to set font face and size, and the **BGCOLOR** attribute of the table data element **<TD>** is used to apply a light-blue color to the background of the pull quote. This approach is more likely to work on a greater variety of browsers.

Sidebars

Like pull quotes, sidebars stand apart from the rest of the text on a page. Instead of drawing attention to the main text, however, they serve to provide additional information related to the subject at hand. This can also be done with tables:

```
<TABLE WIDTH="400" CELLSPACING="0" CELLPADDING="12" BORDER="0">

<TR><TD ALIGN="center" COLSPAN="3"><B>HOME &amp; ROBOT MONTHLY -
January 2000</B></TD></TR>

<TR>
<TD WIDTH="200" VALIGN="top">Insiders report...</TD>

<TD WIDTH="200" VALIGN="top" BGCOLOR="#CCFFFF">
<FONT FACE="Arial, Helvetica, Sans-serif" SIZE="-1">
The history of Demo Company began in 1998...
</FONT></TD>
</TR>
</TABLE>
```

The result, shown in Figure 10-29, uses two side-by-side table cells, two different fonts, and a background color in the right-hand cell to create two columns. The **CELLPADDING** attribute of the **<TABLE>** element is used to create padding and prevent the two text areas from butting up against each other.

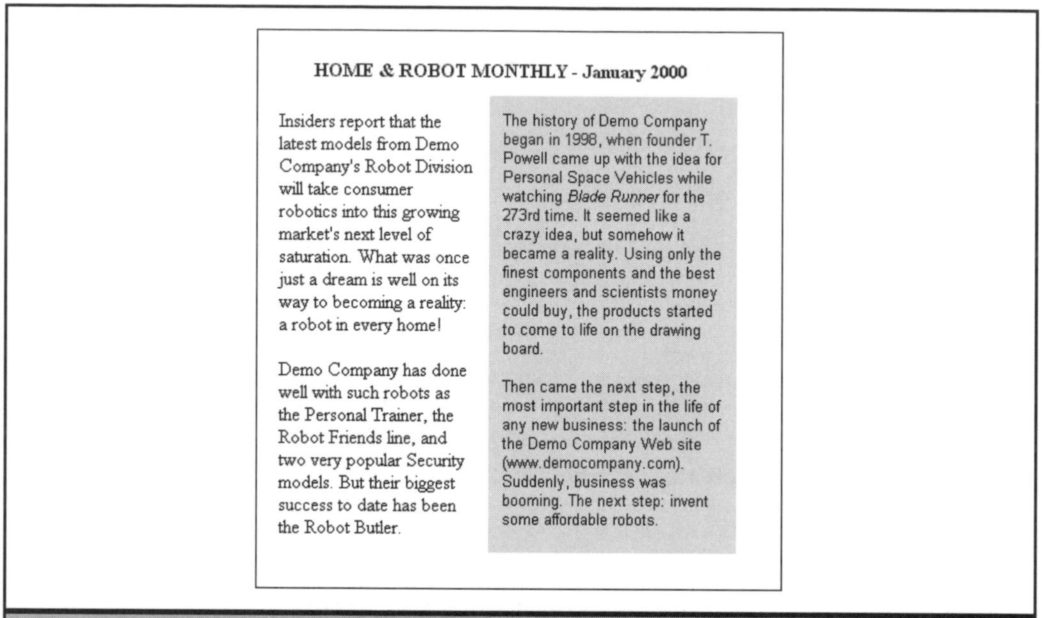

HOME & ROBOT MONTHLY - January 2000

Insiders report that the latest models from Demo Company's Robot Division will take consumer robotics into this growing market's next level of saturation. What was once just a dream is well on its way to becoming a reality: a robot in every home!

Demo Company has done well with such robots as the Personal Trainer, the Robot Friends line, and two very popular Security models. But their biggest success to date has been the Robot Butler.

The history of Demo Company began in 1998, when founder T. Powell came up with the idea for Personal Space Vehicles while watching *Blade Runner* for the 273rd time. It seemed like a crazy idea, but somehow it became a reality. Using only the finest components and the best engineers and scientists money could buy, the products started to come to life on the drawing board.

Then came the next step, the most important step in the life of any new business: the launch of the Demo Company Web site (www.democompany.com). Suddenly, business was booming. The next step: invent some affordable robots.

Figure 10-29.   *Sidebar created with HTML table*

Formatting Tables

As already discussed in this chapter, **<TABLE>** and its associated elements can be used as a means to lay out text and graphics in a Web page. Tables were actually meant to be used as *tables*...a means of presenting information in an organized fashion. Financial data, statistics, and concise summaries of information already covered in detail somewhere else are all prime candidates for this sort of presentation. Consider this simple table summarizing the selling points of a line of robots:

```
<TABLE WIDTH="500" CELLSPACING="0" CELLPADDING="3" BORDER="1">
<TR>
    <TH WIDTH="170">Robot Model</TH>
    <TH WIDTH="180">Standard Features</TH>
    <TH WIDTH="150">Price</TH>
</TR>
<TR>
    <TD>Butler</TD>
```

```
    <TD>Sarcasm, Drink Mixing</TD>
    <TD>30,000 credits</TD>
</TR>
<TR>
    <TD>Trainer</TD>
    <TD>Enthusiasm, Gym Shorts</TD>
    <TD>32,000 credits</TD>
</TR>
<TR>
    <TD>Security (ToughGuy)</TD>
    <TD>Limited vocabulary</TD>
    <TD>40,000 credits</TD>
</TR>
</TABLE>
```

As shown in Figure 10-30, this isn't formatted very well. The table header element **<TH>** has a default alignment of **center**, while the table data element **<TD>** has a default alignment of **left**. (Note that the content of **<TH>** is automatically rendered as bold text.)

It is possible to use a style sheet in the head of the document to format the table like this:

```
<STYLE TYPE="text/css">
<!--
TH {font-family: Arial; font-size: 11pt; text-align: left}
TD {font-family: Arial; font-size: 9pt}
-->
</STYLE>
```

Robot Model	Standard Features	Price
Butler	Sarcasm, Drink Mixing	30,000 credits
Trainer	Enthusiasm, Gym Shorts	32,000 credits
Security (ToughGuy)	Limited vocabulary	40,000 credits

Figure 10-30.   *Table with no text formatting*

Robot Model	Standard Features	Price
Butler	Sarcasm, Drink Mixing	30,000 credits
Trainer	Enthusiasm, Gym Shorts	32,000 credits
Security (ToughGuy)	Limited vocabulary	40,000 credits

Figure 10-31.   *Basic text formatting enhances tables*

Here, font formatting has been applied to the **<TH>** and **<TD>** cells using CSS information in the head of the document. The alignment of the **<TH>** cells has been set to **left**. As Figure 10-31 shows, even with the border set to zero in the HTML, this table is easier to follow. The larger text in the **<TH>** cells clearly establishes the relationship of the columns, which is further enhanced by consistent alignment of the text in each column.

This table is clearly oriented along the horizontal axis; while a more vertical organization is possible, horizontal orientation is more suitable for Web pages. Even so, a larger table with more rows may tend to be harder to read. Figure 10-32 applies a background color to every other table row in order to improve readability and maintain the proper relationship between information.

Robot Model	Standard Features	Price
Butler	Sarcasm, Drink Mixing	30,000 simoleons
Trainer	Enthusiasm, Gym Shorts	32,000 simoleons
Security (ToughGuy)	Limited vocabulary	40,000 simoleons
Security (UltraK9)	Bark worse than bite	45,000 simoleons
Robot Friend (Male)	Bottomless Beer Keg	48,000 simoleons
Robot Friend (Female)	Multidimensional Handbag	48,000 simoleons

Figure 10-32.   *Alternating colors in table rows*

In Figure 10-32, the CSS information in the document head includes a class rule:

```
.shaded {background: #CCFFFF}
```

In this case, the rule is applied to alternating table rows.

```
<TR CLASS="shaded">
```

This will work in CSS-compliant browsers. For backwards compatibility, background color could be added to the table cells in alternating rows using the **BGCOLOR** attribute:

```
<TR BGCOLOR="#CCFFFF">
    <TD>Butler</TD>
    <TD>Sarcasm, Drink Mixing</TD>
    <TD>30,000 simoleons</TD>
</TR>
```

Various design embellishments can also be added. Horizontal lines can be added to separate all the rows, or to separate the header row from the other rows, and to delineate the end of the table. In a three-column table like this one, the **COLSPAN** attribute can be used to make a cell that spans three columns:

```
<TR>
<TD COLSPAN="3"><IMG SRC="line.gif" HEIGHT="3" WIDTH="480"></TD>
</TR>
```

As shown in Figure 10-33, graphic lines are used in this example. The same image source was used for all the lines in this table; the thinner lines were created simply by setting the **HEIGHT** attribute to **1** instead of **3**. (When working with solid colors, it is feasible to resize images in this fashion, but it is not advisable when working with more complicated images.)

There are many ways to present tables. In some cases, it is desirable to have the table borders turned on. The essential thing to remember is that the information in the table is more important than the look and feel of the table itself. Thick borders, excessive and inconsistent coloring of table cells, and extraneous graphics will not enhance a table's usefulness. When presenting information in table form, keeping it simple is your best bet.

ELEMENTS OF PAGE DESIGN

Robot Model	Standard Features	Price
Butler	Sarcasm, Drink Mixing	30,000 credits
Trainer	Enthusiasm, Gym Shorts	32,000 credits
Security (ToughGuy)	Limited vocabulary	40,000 credits

Figure 10-33. *Table with horizontal lines for organization*

Details

In Web page design, the devil is truly in the details. Remember the following Web design rule:

Rule: The details of a site may heavily influence the take-away value.

Users will often notice a bad copyright symbol or improper use of quotes before they notice that the navigation for the site is illogical. Formatting text is all about the details. Especially careful consideration should be paid to special characters and punctuation layout.

Special-Character Consideration

Adding special characters to Web pages is easy if you understand character entities. It is possible to insert special symbols such as the copyright character by specifying a character entity like **©** or **©**. Unfortunately, we may not always be happy with the text layout of these characters because in many fonts they are oversized. Consider reducing the point size on these characters either using the **<SMALL>** element in HTML or using a style rule like **<SPAN STYLE="font-size: 0.8em">** around the character entity. You need to be particularly careful to check if the font you are using supports the particular symbol you have selected. Be very cautious with some characters like **™**, which sets the trademark symbol. You may find that the character is not supported on all systems. However, it is simple enough to get around this problem using style sheets. Just create a very small TM in small caps and then set a vertical alignment in a superscript style. If necessary, you might even make your own small GIF images to replace troublesome special characters.

Dashes can be particularly troublesome for layout. First, make sure you are using the correct dash. A short dash or en dash is specified in HTML with **–** while a long dash or em dash is specified with **—**. The purpose of the em dash is to shift to a new point in a sentence. A short dash is generally employed when specifying ranges like 4–7 or simply to indicate the word "to." A particular troublesome problem with dashes is that when used with capital letters, they may not appear to line up vertically. The reason for this is that the dash is aligned to the middle of the lowercase x. The dash may look low next to some capital characters, particularly those in a font with a small x-height. This subtle problem is shown in Figure 10-34.

You should shift the text up using the **vertical-align** attribute as shown here:

```
<SPAN STYLE="font-size: 36pt">
LOOK AT THE DASH&#151;DOES IT SEEM LOW?</SPAN><BR>
<SPAN STYLE="font-size: 36pt">
LOOK AT THE DASH NOW<SPAN STYLE="vertical-align: 10%;">&#151;
</SPAN>BETTER?</SPAN>
```

As with the problem with dashes, you should consider reducing the size of any bullets that you use, even in lists. You may even consider setting their position relative to text differently.

Quotes can also be troublesome. Understand the difference between prime marks like " and ', and so-called smart or curly quotes like "" and ''. The prime marks are used for measurements like feet and inches and for basic quotes within code. If we want to use smart quotes, we should resort to the entities “ and ” for opening and closing smart quotes. Unfortunately, this isn't always dealt with carefully—particularly when importing text from word-processing programs. In this situation, the smart quotes are often ruined and may render on some systems as empty boxes or other strange characters.

Other details that may be important include the use of the ellipsis … rather than three periods . . .. HTML does support a special entity …, which can be used to insert real ellipses. Some designers may not find this entity adequate as it often looks as bad as three periods. If you want such fine control, consider adjusting letter spacing between the three periods to create your own style of ellipsis.

Lastly, you may consider hanging your punctuation outside the current paragraph, particularly when using headlines or large type that is justified. If you do not, any punctuation characters starting or ending a line will cause small gaps in your nicely laid-out text. An example of hung punctuation vs. regular punctuation is shown in Figure 10-35.

ELEMENTS OF PAGE DESIGN

LOOK AT THE DASH—DOES IT SEEM LOW?
LOOK AT THE DASH NOW—BETTER?

Figure 10-34.   *Subtle dash line problem*

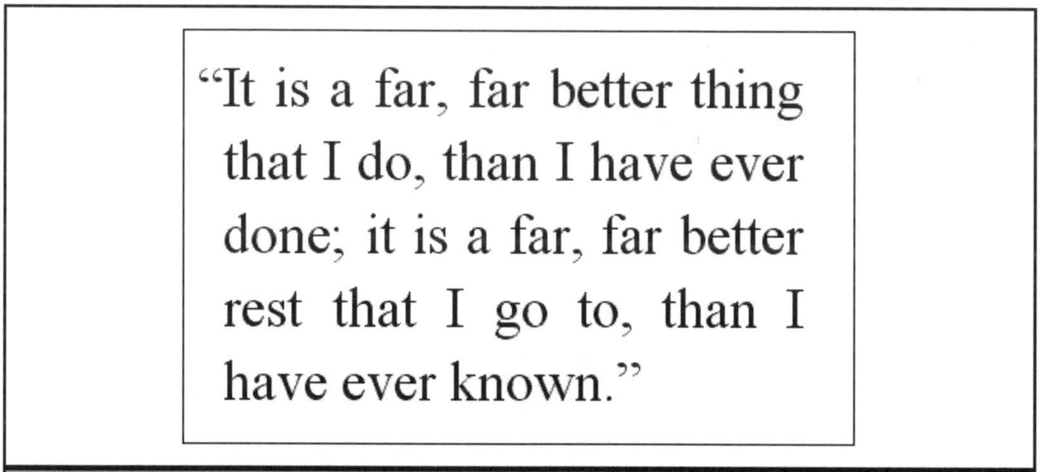

> "It is a far, far better thing that I do, than I have ever done; it is a far, far better rest that I go to, than I have ever known."

Figure 10-35. *Hanging punctuation in large justified text*

Fancy Text Layouts

We can have great control over page layout if we want it. Sophisticated text layout is possible using style sheets, particularly when you use positioning. This has already been mentioned earlier in this chapter (see "Drop Initials" above); Figure 10-36 shows a few more examples.

Laying a page out with such sophisticated runarounds can be a real chore. Consider the code just to create the simple pyramid of text shown in Figure 10-36:

```
<!DOCTYPE HTML PUBLIC "-//W3C//DTD HTML 4.0 Transitional//EN">
<HTML>
<HEAD>
<TITLE>Secrets of Ancient Egypt</TITLE>
</HEAD>

<BODY BGCOLOR="#0035FF" TOPMARGIN="10" LEFTMARGIN="10"
MARGINHEIGHT="10" MARGINWIDTH="10">

<DIV ID="Layer1" STYLE="position:absolute; width:440px;
height:345px; z-index:1; top: 20px; left: 20px">
<IMG SRC="bluepyramid.gif" WIDTH="440" HEIGHT="345" BORDER="0">
</DIV>
```

```
<DIV ID="Layer2" STYLE="position:absolute; width:320px;
height:250px; z-index:2; top: 75px; left: 80px;
font-family: Verdana; font-size: 13px; line-height: 160%;
text-align: center">
In<BR>
ancient<BR>
Egypt, all<BR>
they wanted<BR>
was to live forever.<BR>
Their odds of success<BR>
were much better than a<BR>
Web designer's chances of creating<BR>
a truly creative layout guaranteed to<BR>
work correctly on all browsers, all the time.</DIV>
</BODY></HTML>
```

Given the lack of tools that create style-sheet–based layouts, it is no wonder we don't rush quickly back to image-based layouts. Not so fast—the hard work pays off. These designs scale, and are searchable, printable, and much faster than image layouts on download.

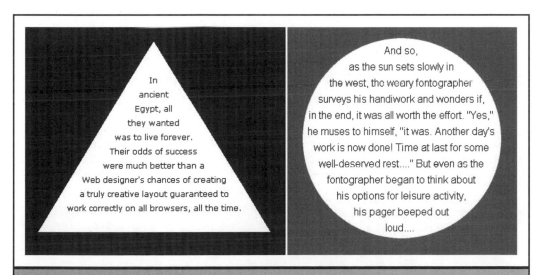

Figure 10-36. *Sophisticated text layout is possible with CSS*

Special Text Effects

While the previous section suggests that it is possible to create sophisticated layouts using style sheets, what about buttons and fancy text effects? Actually, basic 3-D text, drop shadows, raised buttons, and just about anything you can come up with is possible in CSS.

Making drop-shadowed text, particularly if you can download a font, doesn't require you to go to PhotoShop. Making a button is just as easy. The button shown here (as rendered by Internet Explorer 5.0)

was produced with the following markup:

```
<DIV NAME="Layer1" STYLE="position: absolute; z-index: 1; width: 125;
    height: 50; top: 52; left: 52; background: #0000CC"></DIV>

<DIV NAME="Layer2" STYLE="position: absolute; z-index: 2; width: 125;
    height: 50; top: 50; left: 50; background: #99FFFF"></DIV>

<DIV NAME="Layer3" STYLE="position: absolute; z-index: 3; top: 66;
    left: 57; background: none; font-family: Arial; font-size: 18px;
    font-weight: bold; color: #FFFFFF">HOME PAGE</DIV>

<DIV NAME="Layer4" STYLE="position: absolute; z-index: 4; top: 65;
left: 56; background: none; font-family: Arial; font-size: 18px;
font-weight: bold; color: #0000CC">HOME PAGE</DIV>
```

Note *Complex CSS rules such as the ones used in these examples are not always well supported even in browsers that claim compliance. This is yet another reason to fully test your Web pages.*

Creating dramatic text effects like this

no longer requires any fancy filter or illustration work. Of course, now you have to know CSS pretty well. The code that produces this effect, rendered in IE 5.0 above, is shown here.

```
<DIV NAME="Layer1" STYLE="position: absolute; z-index: 1; width: 300;
height: 215; top: 10; left: 10; background: red"></DIV>

<DIV NAME="Layer2" STYLE="position: absolute; z-index: 2; width: 295;
height: 380; top: 25; left: 11; background: none; font-family: Arial
Black; font-size: 18pt; text-align: center; line-height: 90%;
border: none">THE TIME HAS COME<BR>FOR ALL BROWSERS<BR>
TO GET REAL WITH</DIV>

<DIV NAME="Layer4" STYLE="position: absolute; z-index: 4; top: 80;
left: 10; background: none; font-family: Arial; font-size: 50pt;
color: white; text-align: center; letter-spacing: -15px">CSS</DIV>

<DIV NAME="Layer5" STYLE="position: absolute; z-index: 5; top: 80;
left: 30; background: none; font-family: Verdana; font-size: 70pt;
font-style: italic; text-align: center; letter-spacing: -15px;
color: yellow;">CSS</DIV>

<DIV NAME="Layer6" STYLE="position: absolute; z-index: 6; top: 80;
left: 70; background: none; font-family: Arial Black; font-size: 90pt;
text-align: center; letter-spacing: -15px">CSS</DIV>
```

The code above used positioned layers to overlap text. This example uses the Wingdings font to create a teardrop shape, then layers more text over it to create an initial cap effect:

```
<DIV NAME="Layer1" STYLE="position: absolute; z-index:1;
width: 100; height: 100; left: 10px; top: 0px;
font-family: Wingdings; font-size: 202px;
color: black">S</DIV>

<DIV NAME="Layer2" STYLE="position: absolute; z-index:2;
width: 60; height: 100; left: 41px; top: 70px;
font-family: Verdana; font-size: 100px;
font-weight: bold; color: white">S</DIV>

<DIV NAME="Layer3" STYLE="position: absolute; z-index:3;
left: 116px; top: 148px; font-family: Verdana;
font-size: 20px; font-weight: bold; color:
black; letter-spacing: -2">omewhere on the Web...</DIV>
```

This last example uses Microsoft's proprietary filter extensions to CSS to create a glow around a section of text:

GLOW FILTER

```
<!DOCTYPE HTML PUBLIC "-//W3C//DTD HTML 4.0 Transitional//EN">
<HTML>
<HEAD>
<TITLE>Fuzzy Fonts Attack</TITLE>
<STYLE TYPE="text/css">
<!--
.blur    {height: 10; width: 400;
         font-family: Arial Black;
```

```
                font-size: 35pt; font-style:
                bold; color: black;
                filter: Glow(Color = lightblue, Strength = 15); }
-->
</STYLE>
</HEAD>
<BODY BGCOLOR="#FFFFFF">

<DIV NAME="Layer1" CLASS="blur">GLOW FILTER</DIV>

</BODY>
</HTML>
```

Microsoft has introduced some text filters that can greatly simplify the application of such styles, but cross-browser support is so limited that they should be avoided.

Text-Design Issues for the Web

Bottom line—the Web isn't paper. The actual resolution of screens is usually very low: around 72 pixels per inch. Compared to even a typical laser printer, this is very low. Furthermore, glare and refresh rate make reading online difficult. Eyestrain is frequent, and many usability experts as discussed in Chapter 3, have suggested that people just don't read online—and when they do, it is much slower. Designers should always strive to make their Web pages more readable. Standard rules like keeping your line lengths short and increasing your leading apply to the Web as well as paper. However, print rules of thumb about font sizing often have to be adjusted upwards to deal with the lack of screen resolution. Some print suggestions don't
work as expected, some are open to debate, and some just don't make sense at all.

Serif vs. Sans Serif

Some design experts consider serif typefaces more readable than sans serif typefaces because the serifs help define the characters, making them easier to recognize, and could even provide a direction for the eye to easily move from letter to letter. Traditional print design rules suggest that a legible serif font be used for body text while a contrasting sans serif font be used for large titles and headings. The Web, not breaking with tradition, generally uses Times as the default body copy for text; however, it does not change heading styles to a sans serif font. There is some debate whether or not serif text should be used onscreen, particularly when small. If you combine this with antialiasing, discussed in the next section, serif text can become very hard to read. The jury is still out on the serif vs. sans serif debate. All that can be said for sure is to be careful with small serif text and consider increasing your font size no matter what you use.

Aliased vs. Antialiased Text

While not a consideration for normal HTML text, it is possible when using text in graphics or using a downloadable font to antialias text. Aliased images are those that have jagged edges, while antialiased images are those that have their edges smoothed out. The problem with antialiased text is that when the text is small it tends to look fuzzy, not smooth—particularly when antialiasing crisp sans serif fonts like Arial. A demonstration of the readability problem with antialiasing is shown in Figure 10-37.

In image form, antialiased images will be slightly larger because of the extra details required in the image—yet another strike against doing this.

Suggestion: Avoid antialiasing small text.

However, when it comes down to it, some people prefer antialiasing. Just make sure you actually try your small text both antialiased and aliased before jumping on a particular bandwagon.

Number of Fonts to Use

Traditionally, designers have held that you should use only two types of fonts in a document, usually a sans serif for headlines and a serif for body copy. Of course, the styles and size of these may change, but using multiple fonts—particularly of the same font type like sans serif—is considered to be poor style. Some designers think you can go higher, particularly if the contrast between the fonts is obvious enough. Remember that a user might not be able to tell the difference between an Arial and a Helvetica font like you can. If you establish your type hierarchy on such subtle differences, it is bound to fail. Worse, even if they do notice they may consider such variations erroneous rather than intentional. Using radically different fonts next to each other brings attention to content and may aid greatly in setting up a type hierarchy.

However, while the two-fonts-per-document rule works well in print, it might need to be modified for the Web. Instead, you may consider three fonts: one for your headlines, one for your body text, and one for your navigation.

Suggestion: Consider three fonts per page: one for page labels and headlines, one for body text, and one for navigation.

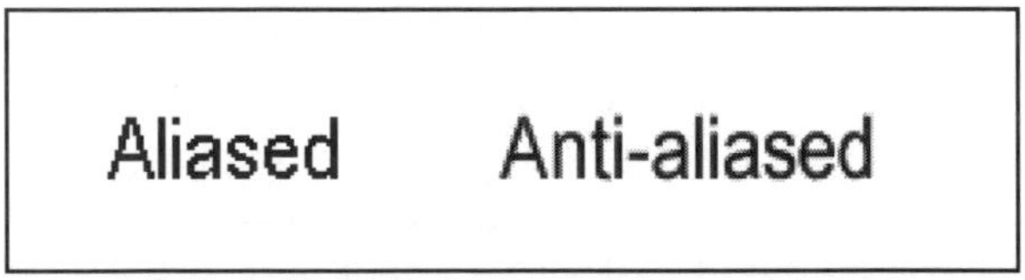

Figure 10-37. *Comparison of aliased and antialiased Arial font at 12pt*

You'll probably end up making your headlines and navigation in a sans serif font. Just make sure that you vary the headlines and navigation enough either in size, color, or family.

Columns on the Web

Traditional print design has relied extensively on columns when laying out text. Columns on the Web are very different. Unless you have very sophisticated sensing, it is not guaranteed that the user will be able to see your complete page at once. Columns that wrap up and down make little sense on the Web. Netscape's proprietary **<MULTICOL>** tag showed just how useless this design is. Remember, the text read direction is not a top-left to bottom-right style, but more a top-left down the page to its bottom. Imagine having the user scroll up and down the page just to follow text. When using columns, they should continue to run down the page until the content is finished, as shown in Figure 10-38.

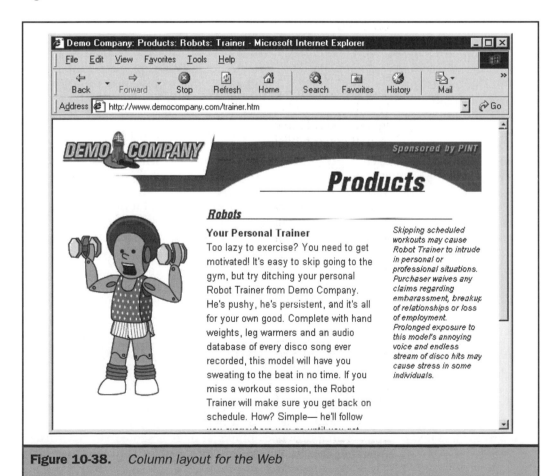

Figure 10-38. *Column layout for the Web*

Rule: Columns of text in Web pages should never wrap up and down.

The size of the columns should not be much more than around 300 pixels or so (around 24pc for 12pt font) if it is heavy on body text. You may find that a design with a main center column of around 300 to 400 pixels with a left navigation column and a right pull quote or supplementary column works well. Many heavily used sites have employed such a design successfully.

Is White Space Good or Bad?

Traditional type design suggests that judicious use of white space makes a page much more readable. The white space can give readers a place to rest their eyes, or it may direct a user's focus, emphasize certain bits of text, and just provide an open, airy look to a page. Unfortunately, many designers tend to cram as much content as possible into a page. Some experts suggest that this is very much a bad idea and that online is no different than print. White space is very good. In fact, Web pages may need even more white space—as much as 40–60 percent white space on a page. However, some usability experts, notably Jared Spool (Spool 1999), suggest that white space actually may not improve page usability—and may even hinder it. This goes so far against conventional wisdom that it is very hard to believe. The probable answer is that the user can "cover more ground" quickly when looking through relatively dense text pages formatted for skimming. However, this answer suggests that people are navigating content but not consuming it. Maybe they are simply printing the content out for later use. Yet once they do, it is certain they want it easy to read!

Rule: Navigation-focused pages generally require less text white space than consumption pages.

The white-space issue is certainly troublesome; the concept that it may be bad makes sense if users are skimming. As discussed in Chapters 6 and 7, you need to balance clicking and scrolling. If you have a lot of white space, you may not be giving people the amount of content they need at an adequate pace. Always consider what the user is doing with data and where it will ultimately be consumed.

Rule: Always use white space to complement the use of information.

Always Consider the Medium of Consumption

Probably the most important thing to consider when discussing text layout on the Web is where the information is actually consumed. Many designers put so much text within pages that users invariably print the pages. Much of the time, these pages don't print terribly well. Other times people create text for online consumption. Often, this means much less text per page with lots of use of links. If there is some reason the user would want to print the content, it isn't easy to collect the content together for printing.

When users read online, they generally want less text, large size, narrow columns, and large line height. However, when printing, users may want a lot of content per page, possibly expanding to fit the paper or even using a smaller font size and line height. If printing becomes an issue, you may find it useful to provide a link to an Acrobat version of your content (www.adobe.com/acrobat) or provide a link to a page that is formatted for print output. Many sites now provide printable versions of text. An article at an online magazine may be broken up into several pages for online reading, complete with graphics, advertisements, and site navigation. While these pages may be printable, the resulting printout may be too cluttered to be useful. And if the pages use advanced layouts such as the pyramid text shown earlier in this chapter, it may not be printable at all. This has led to the increased use of the already ubiquitous "Click here for a printer-friendly version" and similar links.

Writing for the Web

As discussed in previous chapters, users tend to be involved in some balance of navigating content, consuming content, or performing a task such as form fill-out. Up to now we have focused a great deal on users navigating content—but what about when they are ready to actually read a page?

Reading *vs.* Scanning

If you're coming to the Web with a print-oriented mindset, you're in for a rude shock: studies have shown that reading on the Web generally takes more time than reading the same text on paper. If that wasn't bad enough, many users won't even read the page online. Web experts have determined that users tend to scan quickly over the content of Web pages, looking for something that will catch their attention and lead them to click on a link, or back up and read the page more closely. If something doesn't grab them right away, they are highly likely to move on to another page or site. Page length can be daunting, too; a person skimming over a Web page hoping to be engaged probably won't feel like scrolling down to read more if the text in the initial screen hasn't already done its job. A few key concepts will help counter this trend:

- **Keep your text short and concise.** Experts suggest that you should write only half as much text as you would when writing for print. This makes the online reading process smoother by overcompensating for the slow online reading-time rule mentioned above. Keep paragraphs short as well; nothing scares users away faster than long, unbroken columns of text that extend far below the bottom of their browser window.

- **Get to the point right away.** Don't preface your page with a long, rambling, and circuitous opening. If your English professor taught you to start with the general and work up to the specific, forget it. Cut to the chase and tell users your conclusion in the very first sentence. Use the journalistic technique known as the "inverted pyramid"—tell them what you're going to tell them immediately, *then* fill in the details, followed by whatever background material seems appropriate.

- ■ **Use headings to provide meaning.** Headlines aren't much use if they're clever but don't tell the user what the main content is about. Headers should let users know why they should stop and read a Web page. Meaningful use of subheadings adds structure, and additional meaning, to a page.

- ■ **Highlight the ideas expressed in the page.** Pull quotes and highlighted text, if selected well, will emphasize what the page is about and help users decide if the page interests them. It's better to have someone leave a page because the topic leaves them cold than to have them leave simply because they can't figure out what the page is about. Don't emphasize text with underlining, as this may be confused with hyperlinks. If your hyperlinks are chosen well, the clickable text should provide additional hints to your page's meaning.

- ■ **Use lists to summarize information.** When dealing with important information, don't embed it in a paragraph if it can be broken out into bulleted or numbered lists instead. This places the information out in plain view of the skimming reader, instead of forcing the reader to dig for it in a large block of text.

The inverted-pyramid structure is just one of the tools that can make online writing more user friendly. Applied to the Web, it can be used to get a basic point across and motivate users to scroll down to the more general information lower in the page. Hypertext adds even more variations to writing on the Web. On the simplest level, it can be used to break a piece of writing up into smaller pages, to be connected by linear linking and read in sequence. This can keep page scrolling to a minimum and make page content easier for readers to process quickly. Ending each page in a fashion that will encourage readers to move on, and starting each page with writing that reinforces the reader's desire to continue, can work wonders and keep users from defecting to another site.

Nonlinear Writing

Of course, the Web offers more choices than a simple linear progression. The options are many, but it is important not to go overboard. While it is possible to create an incredibly complex hypertext document that branches off in multiple directions, it would be wiser to provide short blocks of information to create a much larger whole. Optimally, the basic information you are trying to convey could be organized in a fairly linear fashion, while more detailed examinations of its implications could branch out in many directions. If you were an expert in canine health concerns, you might be tempted to create a huge Web page that imparts all your years of accumulated knowledge in one huge lump. But dog owners would be more likely to read a simple site about canine health; the main focus could be about nutrition and the basic care of dogs, with additional pages that go into more detail on those topics, well-placed hyperlinks to pages discussing how to recognize the symptoms of canine diseases, and even deeper pages that might be of more interest to veterinarians than to laypeople. This site could be a great resource for a wide variety of people as long as it is written and structured to draw them in and guide them to the level of information they require.

Danger Words

It is important to remember that certain ordinary words have taken on extra meaning on the Web. The word "links" could easily refer to sausages or to golf, but on the Web those meanings may be secondary. Choice of vocabulary is an issue.

Suggestion: Be careful of using words that have alternate Web meanings.

For example, at a Web site about golf courses, it might be impossible to avoid using "links" as it relates to the game, so it would be imperative to use the word "hyperlinks" when referring to clickable text in the site in order to reduce any potential confusion. The following table lists a few words to use carefully due to their online significance:

home	page	browse/browser
explore/explorer	navigate/navigator	robot
stop	back	forward
source	script	spider
map	index	site

◼ Summary

While HTML may not afford the designer much possibility to lay out text on a page, CSS provides everything from leading to kerning. Perfect positioning is possible if you want to spend the time. While font control isn't perfect yet, downloadable fonts are on the way. Spending the time to lay out pages well by increasing line height, reducing line length, changing font size, and generally dealing with small details pays off in highly readable pages more likely to invite the user to stay and read a while. However, now that we have better text control we are literally armed and dangerous. If we're not careful, we can just as easily mess up our organized site and page with poor type layout. More damage can result if we blindly utilize technologies that are not consistently supported in browsers, which can end up in ruined layouts or difficult-to-read pages. With the power of CSS, we can take display control back away from the user. Just remember the lessons from previous chapters before you yank control from them—the user's experience should always be our number-one concern.

Chapter 11

Colors, Images, and Backgrounds

For most people, the Web is a visual medium. While the disabled or those accessing the Web from a nongraphical environment can still interact with Web pages, they often miss a great deal of information that only images can provide. The lure of a graphical environment is precisely the way in which imagery enhances the users' comprehension and experience of the material. Colors, images, and backgrounds are used on the Web to make sites more interesting to look at, but to also inform, entertain, or even evoke subliminal feelings in the user. However, each addition comes with both benefits and problems. When a designer reviews all of the details, conflicts, potential for missteps, and pitfalls of image use in the Web environment, the "text-only" school of design begins to look rather reasonable.

If color is used incorrectly or with no attention to cultural meanings, it may evoke a negative feeling or perhaps simply confuse a user who is used to seeing only blue hyperlinks. Most designers are well aware of the fact that too many images may result in a "slow" page, but they can forget other usability issues such as insufficient contrast between background images and foreground text, or that many small images may actually result in a slower page than a few large images due to demands upon the server. The demand for "small" images ignores whether an image is in an appropriate file format—the choice between a GIF and a JPEG can make or break some images. While personal taste may dictate much image use, there are some general guidelines for image preparation and use that will keep even image-heavy pages usable. And, yes, in some cases, not using images at all may be the most appropriate design choice.

In this chapter, color, images, and the use of backgrounds will be covered. Colors are the building blocks of imagery, and attention to color will increase awareness of how images both affect us as Web page users and are affected by us as Web page designers. The use of background imagery in either a thoughtful or careless manner can make the difference between an outstanding site and an unusable one. While it is not possible in the space of one chapter to cover all of the intricacies of imagery on the Web, this chapter should provide constructive guidelines for experimentation and development of a sense for effective imagery use.

Color Basics

What exactly is color? This is not a simple question, as the discussion in Chapter 3 suggested. Color is generally described as having three components: hue, saturation and value. These and other color terms are defined in Table 11-1.

Hue describes the quality of the color itself, as related to the basic chromatic colors red, yellow, and blue. *Saturation* can be described as the purity of the color in relation to achromatic (colorless) values such as gray. A fully saturated blue, for instance, would be "pure" blue, while the darker blue in an artist's palette may actually be "diluted" by other pigments such as gray or black. Finally, *value* (also referred to as *brightness*, or *lightness*) describes how much a color appears lighter or darker than another under the same viewing conditions. Manipulating these qualities gives the designer control over what the user perceives as "color."

Term	Description
Hue	The color attribute identified by color names, such as "red" or "yellow."
Value	The degree of lightness or darkness of a color.
Saturation	The relative purity of a color—also referred to as intensity. The "brighter" the intensity of a color, the more saturated it is. New jeans are saturated with blue; faded ones are less saturated with blue.
Chromatic hues	All colors other than black, white, and gray.
Neutral colors	A black, white, or gray—otherwise known as "nonchromatic hues."
Monochromatic	A color combination based on variations of value and saturation of a single hue.

Table 11-1.   *Basic Color Terminology*

The human eye processes visual information when light passes through the cornea, or lens, of the eye and is focused in the sensitive area at the back of the eye known as the retina. The retina is comprised of two kinds of photosensitive cells: cones and rods. The six million or more cones in each eye process both chromatic information (red, blue, green) and achromatic information (white, black, and grays). Color vision is enhanced by higher levels of light; at lower light levels, the cones can also process achromatic hues. At even lower light levels, the ten million rods in the eye take precedence, as they process values of black, white, and gray. At noon on a bright day, your vision would be produced primarily by the action of the cones; at dusk, when everything looks gray, the rods are doing most of the work. Interestingly, the central area of the retina, called the fovea, is made up entirely of cones. The fovea is also linked directly to the optic nerve, which means that the color information it processes gets to the brain much faster than the information processed by cells located elsewhere in the retina. Physically, color information would appear to have greater significance than achromatic information.

Human color perception does not adhere to some exact standard. The point of this discussion is not that a designer needs to understand ocular physiology—the key concept to take away is that there is significant variation in how different users are able to see visual information, and that the viewing environment will play an important role in how well particular images and combinations of images can be seen. Limitations built into the Web viewing environment add yet another level of complexity to this situation. The main points to take away from a discussion of how the eye works is not terminology about how eyes work, but simply that everyone's eye will work slightly differently, and the viewing environment will play an important role in how well something can be seen. We will start by examining color on the Web.

Colors on the Web

There are several significant factors relating to how color can and cannot be used on the Web. Most important is bit depth, the most basic component for generating colors for display on computer monitors. However, not all browsers and computer systems are able to support the same range and degree of colors, leading to identification of browser-safe colors—colors that can be relied upon to display more or less the same regardless of the user's Web viewing environment. In conjunction with this "safe" color palette, there are a variety of ways to specify colors in HTML and CSS, particularly using hexadecimal values and reserved color names. Difficulties arise due to the fact that, while CSS color can be applied to nearly any element within an HTML page, HTML itself limits use of foreground and background color to a select few elements. Complicating the mix a bit more is the issue of contrast. High contrast is almost indispensable for creating usable Web pages. As you can see, color reproduction on the Web is no simple task. Throw in yet more esoteric display issues, such as gamma control and hardware support, and the lovely shade of brown you slaved to create devolves into onscreen mud. Color manipulation in the Web environment is not for the faint of heart!

Bit Depth

Bit depth, sometimes referred to as color depth, is the term given to the number of bits used to describe color in an image or on a monitor. The basic idea is simple: the more bits used to specify a color, the more possible colors can be described. In short, the more bits, the more colors you can specify. One bit can be used to specify two colors, typically black and white. When using two bits to describe color, we can reference four colors; three bits allow for eight colors, and so on. Notice that the number of colors specified by the bit depth is simply 2 raised to the nth power where n is the number of bits, as shown in Table 11-2.

A firm understanding of bit depth is important for a Web designer. Not all users will have video cards capable of displaying colors beyond even 8-bit. More important for the designer, bit depth is directly related to file size. The higher the bit depth, the greater the number of colors. The greater the number of colors, the larger the file size. Therefore, reducing the number of colors will aid in lowering the file size of your images and improve the download time of your Web pages. Further consideration of this limitation will be discussed later on in the chapter.

Bits	Number of Possible Colors
32	16,777,216 (24 bits) plus 8 bits used for control information
24	16,777,216
16	65,536
8	256
7	128
6	64
5	32
4	16
3	8
2	4
1	2

Table 11-2. *Bit Depth and Colors Specified*

Defining Color on the Web

Computer monitors display colors using varying amounts of red, green, and blue. This is called RGB color; this is considered an additive form of color, because red, green, and blue light in equal amounts "adds" up to white light. This is completely different from the way colors are set in print. In print, CMYK (cyan, magenta, yellow, black) is the more common color scheme. The colors you see on a printed piece are the parts of the spectrum reflected back to your eyes as white light hits the ink. CMYK is considered subtractive color since, in theory, if you were to mix pure cyan, magenta, and yellow, they should absorb all color to produce black [due to impurities in all printing inks, however, these three don't actually produce black, which is why black (K) ink must be added]. Anyone familiar with Photoshop or similar programs will probably know both these formats. In RGB formatting within a program like Photoshop, each of the three elements—red, green, and blue—can have values from 0 to 255, generally expressed as three numbers separated by commas. So, in the RGB triplet 102,153,204, the number 102 is the red value, 153 is the green value, and 204 is the blue value. All this is very well and good when you're working in a graphics program, but the Web does not normally measure color with decimal values. Rather, the Web relies on hexadecimal values.

Undoubtedly in HTML you may have seen markup like:

```
<FONT COLOR="#FF12AC">Hot Pink!</FONT>
```

In HTML, color is specified by a hexadecimal RGB triplet preceded by the pound sign "#." The color is six digits long—two hex digits for each byte. So, in the RGB triplet #FF12AC:

- The first two digits (FF) represent the intensity of the red component of the pixel, which is at full strength because a byte cannot be greater than FF.

- The next two digits (12) represent the intensity of the green component of the pixel, which is fairly low.

- The last two digits (AC) represent the intensity of the blue part of the pixel, and it's fairly high.

The end result is a bright-pink pixel.

In HTML and CSS, we measure color in a hexadecimal range from 0–FF which is equivalent to 0–255 in decimal. It's relatively easy to translate RGB values to hexadecimal values by referring to a translation chart. A hex code for a midrange blue like 102,153,204 would read #6699CC. It also is possible to reference the color by name in the code (i.e., "black"). The 16 basic names originally defined by Microsoft are now part of the HTML specification; these appear alongside their hexadecimal values in Table 11-3.

These are just a few of the colors available. By using RGB triplets translated to a hex value, it is possible to use 256 shades of red, green, and blue to create colors—

Color Name	Hex Value
Black	#000000
White	#FFFFFF
Gray	#808080
Silver	#C0C0C0
Green	#008000
Lime	#00FF00
Olive	#808000
Yellow	#FFFF00

Table 11-3.   *HTML Specification Colors*

Color Name	Hex Value
Aqua	#00FFFF
Teal	#008080
Blue	#0000FF
Navy	#000080
Fuchsia	#FF00FF
Purple	#800080
Red	#FF0000
Maroon	#800000

Table 11-3.   *HTML Specification Colors* (continued)

somewhere around 16.4 million colors! There are over one hundred more color names defined by Netscape, which are largely supported by the newer versions of Explorer and other browsers. Believe it or not, they include such varied color names as tomato, thistle, and lightcoral.

> **Online: The full list of color names and their hexadecimal and RGB equivalents can be seen online at www.htmlref.com/Reference/AppE/colorchart.htm.**

One could, of course, use any word, such as pineapplesherbet (not a real value), as a color value; browsers will attempt to render them, but if they are not recognized color names, the rendering will have no relation to the meaning of the word. Our imaginary value pineapplesherbet renders as a shade of blue in Internet Explorer, but as a completely different—much darker blue—color in Netscape. Either way, it doesn't look like pineapple sherbet. Because of this fact, it is important to specify the exact color you wish to reproduce with its correct hexadecimal value in order to avoid different browser interpretations. For example, the defined color name aquamarine is equivalent to an RGB value of 127,255,212, which translates to a hexadecimal value of 7FFFD4. Unfortunately, as with many of the other named colors, this is not a browser-safe color. In general, it is preferable to use a hexadecimal code to indicate color. Doing so greatly reduces the chance that the color will be rendered incorrectly.

> **Rule: To ensure the appropriate color is produced, always use a hexadecimal value over a named color except in the case of basic colors like white, black, red, and so on.**

Browser-Safe Color

What are the browser-safe colors, and why is it important to use them? The first step in answering this question is to ask another question: what controls the colors that can be displayed on a computer? These colors are controlled by the computer's video card and limited by the capacities of the monitor being used. The range of colors can vary anywhere from 256 colors and below on the low end, all the way up to millions and "true color" on the high end. Some older systems may even only support 16 colors. In order to be completely safe for all systems, Web design must concentrate on the lowest common denominator. But how can we predict what that is going to be? We can't, really. Many of the newer systems available today are more likely to have all the colors needed to display all of your images, but we must play it safe and assure that those who only have 256-color capability will not have a terrible experience.

So how do we figure what those 256 color are? The 256 colors supported by a PC are not the same as those supported by a Macintosh; most of them are the same, but 40 are actually different. That leaves 216 colors that will be guaranteed to be "safe" and display correctly regardless of the platform or video card. What happens if you use a color that is not one of the 216 Web-safe colors? Quite often, nothing. If a user's computer can display more colors, then it probably will not have any problems with rendering the color you chose, as long as the color is in that computer's palette. But what happens if they do have only 256? In these cases, their computer will try to re-create the color by using a technique called *dithering*.

Dithering is a process through which the computer attempts to re-create the desired color by using those it has available. It will do this by using two or more colors in a dithered (speckled or dotted) pattern to try to visually re-create the color it doesn't have, as shown in Figure 11-1. You can see a better example of this in our dithering demo at www.webdesignref.com/chapter11/designdemos/dither.htm. Dithered images can look terrible, and reflect poorly on the designer. Paying attention to the Web-safe palette, it is possible to avoid most instances of dithering.

So how do we use the browser-safe colors? When creating your graphics, it is important to make sure that you are using the correct color palette within your graphics software. Programs like Adobe Photoshop and Illustrator all come with a set of Web-safe swatches that you can load. In HTML, you will need to convert these colors to their hexadecimal value.

Whether setting colors in an HTML document or in a graphics program, the hexadecimal coding convention for browser-safe colors can easily be memorized. It is also fairly simple to move between hexadecimal, RGB, and percentage color standards. In RGB, the values are all multiples of 51, from 0 to 255; in terms of percentages, which may be used with CSS (see "CSS and Colors," below), it's a standard 20 percent difference, from 0 percent to 100 percent; the safe hexadecimal

Non–Web-Safe Colors

Non-safe - True color

Non-safe - 256 color

Figure 11-1.   *Dithering example*

values assigned to these values are fixed. This simple rule of thumb is shown in Table 11-4.

Given how quickly computer technology is advancing, does any of this matter? As we discussed earlier, the majority of newer systems today will have a much greater color capacity than 256. So what do you design for? Or, to put it differently,

RGB Value	Multiplier	Percentage Value	Hexadecimal Value
255	x5	100	FF
204	x4	80	CC
153	x3	60	99
102	x2	40	66
51	x1	20	33
0	x0	0	00

Table 11-4. *RGB/Hexadecimal Equivalents*

why should you limit your designs to the lowest common denominator? It's very hard to say. If you have a specific target audience and you know what they have, such as an internal company intranet, then you can definitely design around these parameters. Since the majority of the time you don't know what your users are going to have, you are going to have to make your own decisions on what you want to do. Someone might get left out in the cold, but that's the risk you have to take. However, since it is possible to do exciting, quality design within the boundaries of Web-safe color palettes, why take the risk at all? Before using a non–Web-safe color, ask yourself if you can use a Web-safe color and achieve comparable results.

Hybrid Colors

In their quest to beat the 216-color limitations of the Web-safe palette, designers have come up with a simple workaround generally referred to as hybrid colors. Taking advantage of the smallness of pixels and the human mind's tendency to fill in the blanks in visual information, hybrid colors simply take two or more Web-safe colors and combine them in some pattern—usually a checkerboard, but sometimes stripes— to trick the eye into seeing a different color. In a sense, this is a form of intentional, controlled dithering that, if done properly, the end user will not notice.

> **Suggestion: To safely break the 216-color barrier, use predithered patterns or so-called hybrid colors.**

In the following illustration, the area on the left that appears to be gray is actually a checkerboard made up of single-pixel black and white squares, as shown on the right.

Online: color demos of this concept in practice can be viewed at
www.webdesignref.com/Chapter11/designdemos/hybrid.htm.

Various tools, such as BoxTop's ColorSafe plug-in for Photoshop (http://
www.boxtopsoft.com), can aid designers in creating hybrid colors quite easily. In
the end, however, the real decision is whether you can design within the constraints
of the Web-safe palette. By remaining within that range as much as possible, you
maximize the usability of your Web site.

HTML and Colors

There are numerous ways to set colors in HTML. The elements (tags) where setting the
color is an option include the background color of the document body, the default color
of text in the document, the colors of links, the color of fonts used in the document, and
background colors in tables. The next few pages provide an overview on how to use
color attributes within these HTML elements.

Document-Wide Color Settings

Two basic document-wide color settings can be defined using the **BODY** element:

```
<BODY BGCOLOR="#FFFFFF" TEXT="#000000">
```

This will provide the document with a white background, and the default color for
text in the document will be black. In addition, the **BODY** element has three attributes
that define the colors for three different text-link states:

```
<BODY LINK="blue" ALINK="red" VLINK="purple">
```

The **LINK** attribute defines the color of unvisited links in a document. For example,
if you've set your background color to black, it might be more useful to use a light link
color instead of the standard blue. The **ALINK** attribute defines the color of the link
as it is being clicked. This is often too quick to be noticed, but can create a flash effect
if desired. For a more subdued Web experience, it might be better to set the **ALINK**

attribute to match either the **LINK** attribute or the next one, **VLINK**. The **VLINK** attribute defines the color of a link after it has been visited, which under many user agents is purple. Many authors wish to set the value of the **VLINK** attribute to red, which makes sense given standard color interpretation. So, using the last attributes, creating a white page with green text, red links, and fuchsia-colored visited links could be accomplished using the code presented here:

```
<BODY BGCOLOR="#FFFFFF" TEXT="#008000" LINK="#FF0000"
      VLINK="#FF00FF" ALINK="#FF0000">
```

Link-Color Issues

Try not to choose link colors that might confuse your viewers. For example, reversing link colors so that visited links are blue and nonvisited links are red could confuse a user. While it is unlikely that a page author would do such a thing, it has been seen more than once—particularly in situations where the look and feel is the driving force of the site. Other common problems with link color changes include the idea of setting all link values to blue with the belief that users will revisit sections, thinking they haven't been there before! While this may make sense from a marketing standpoint, the frustration factor due to the lost navigation cues may override any potential benefit from extra visits. As the last example showed, setting the link colors all to red could have a similar effect of encouraging the user to think they have seen the site already. It is also important to make sure that you do not set your links to the same color as the regular text on the page. Relying on underlining to be the definition of the link is extremely dangerous, since most browsers have the option to turn off underlining. Make sure that your link color is going to contrast enough with the paragraph containing it in order to avoid forcing your user have to figure out if there are any links on the page.

<BASEFONT>: Not Recommended

Finally, the **<BASEFONT>** element supports color values in Internet Explorer 4 and higher. The code

```
<HTML>
<HEAD>
<TITLE>Untitled</TITLE>
</HEAD>
<BODY BGCOLOR="#FFFFFF" TEXT="#000000">
<BASEFONT FACE="Arial" SIZE="4" COLOR="maroon">
<B>Color me maroon!</B>
</BODY>
</HTML>
```

will display a size 4 Arial font in a maroon color under those browsers. Note that the only value supported by Netscape for this element is the **SIZE** attribute. **BASEFONT** is not a particularly good way to set font values of any sort for a document unless you're absolutely certain your site will only be viewed under Internet Explorer.

> **Suggestion: Due to poor cross-browser support, avoid using the <BASEFONT> element to set font values in a document—especially where colors are concerned.**

Colors and Fonts

Font colors, as well as all other font values, are better controlled through the **<FONT>** element. Focusing on colors exclusively, using **<FONT>** is pretty simple. This code

```
<FONT COLOR="red">Red text!</FONT>
```

will produce red text, as will this:

```
<FONT COLOR="#FF0000">Red text!</FONT>
```

For a more detailed discussion of fonts, see Chapter 10.

Color and Tables

Tables also can be assigned background colors in several ways. The **BGCOLOR** attribute is valid for **<TABLE>**, **<TR>**, **<TH>**, and **<TD>**:

```
TABLE BORDER="1" CELLSPACING="0" CELLPADDING="8" BGCOLOR="green">
<TR>
<TH BGCOLOR="lightblue">A</TH>
<TH BGCOLOR="lightblue">A</TH>
<TH BGCOLOR="lightblue">A</TH>
</TR>

<TR BGCOLOR="orange">
<TD>B</TD>
<TD>B</TD>
<TD>B</TD>
</TR>

<TR>
<TD BGCOLOR="red">C</TD>
<TD BGCOLOR="white">C</TD>
```

```
<TD BGCOLOR="blue">C</TD>
</TR>

<TR>
<TD> </TD>
<TD> </TD>
<TD> </TD>
</TR>
</TABLE>
```

In this code, the header cells (**TH**) in the first row will have a light-blue background; all three cells (**TD**) in the second row will have an orange background as defined for the entire row (**TR**); the three cells in the third row will have different background colors as defined by the **BGCOLOR** attribute for each **<TD>** tag; and the cells in the last row, which have no background color defined for themselves or their row, will default to the green background color defined in the **<TABLE>** tag, as shown in Figure 11-2.

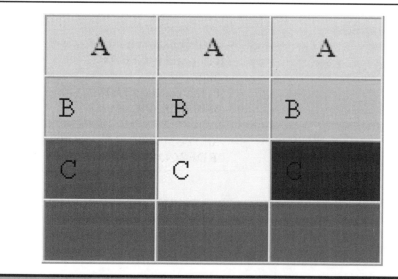

Figure 11-2.   *BGCOLOR applied to different table elements*

Note that the **CELLSPACING** attribute for **<TABLE>** is set to zero; if it is set to a higher value, the background color will display in the areas between cells in Internet Explorer.

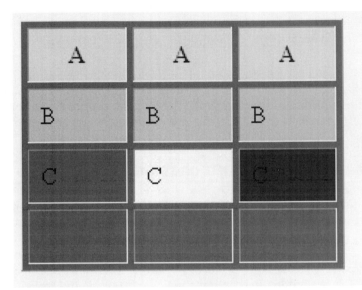

Don't forget that if the **CELLSPACING** attribute is not included, most browsers will render the table with several pixels of cell spacing by default. Be sure to set it to zero to prevent inadvertent display of spacing.

Some grouping elements associated with tables, like **<THEAD>** and **<TFOOT>**, as defined in the HTML 4.0 spec, also accept **BGCOLOR**, but so far only IE 4 and higher support the use of this attribute.

Additional proprietary attributes have also been defined for table elements. Internet Explorer 4 and higher define a **BORDERCOLOR** attribute for **TABLE**. Under IE 4 and higher, the code

```
<TABLE BORDERCOLOR="#FF0000" BORDER="1">
<TR><TD>. . . content . . .</TD></TR>
</TABLE>
```

will render a table with a red border around the entire table and its cells. Netscape 4 and higher may render a red outline only around the four sides of the table, but the effect is completely different from the IE rendering. Under IE 4 and up, **BORDERCOLOR** can also be applied to rows (**TR**), headers (**TH**), and cells (**TD**).

ELEMENTS OF PAGE
DESIGN

IE 4 and up also provide two more border-color attributes: **BORDERCOLORDARK** and **BORDERCOLORLIGHT**:

```
<TABLE BORDERCOLORDARK="#FF0000" BORDERCOLORDARK="#0000FF"
       BORDER="4">
<TR><TD>...content...</TD></TR>
</TABLE>
```

Under IE 4 and up, this will render a two-tone outer border for the table in which the top and left outer borders are blue, while the lower and right outer borders are red. It will have no effect in Netscape. Experiment with the elements and attributes under different browsers to understand and control display variations between browsers.

Contrast Issues with Backgrounds and Foregrounds

Page authors must also be extremely careful when setting text and background colors. Readability must be preserved. Page designers are often tempted to use light colors on light backgrounds or dark colors on dark backgrounds. For example, a gray text on a black background might look great on your monitor—but if the gamma value of another person's monitor is much different than your monitor, it will be unreadable. White and black always make a good pairing, and red is certainly useful. The best combination, in terms of contrast, is actually yellow and black, but imagine the headache from reading a page that looks like a road sign. Despite the high contrast, designers should be careful of white text on a black background when font sizes are very small, particularly on poor-resolution monitors.

Color and Other HTML Elements

The only other HTML element that supports color is the horizontal rule **<HR>**; this is a proprietary use of the **COLOR** attribute defined by Microsoft, so while this code

```
<HR NOSHADE SIZE="1" COLOR="black">
```

will render a solid black rule under IE 4 and higher, other browsers will ignore the **COLOR** attribute and render the rule in default gray.

 *Limited browser support makes it a poor choice to set colors for the **<HR>** element; for colored rules, a simple graphic might make a better option.*

CSS and Colors

So far, we have discussed applying color values to various HTML elements using named values like red or hexadecimal values like #FF0000. The number of HTML elements that support such attributes as **COLOR** and **BGCOLOR** is rather limited. Using CSS (cascading style sheets) opens up a whole new world of color possibilities, both in terms of expressing color values, and in the number of HTML elements to which you can apply color. Chapter 10 has already covered some CSS basics (see "Setting Fonts in Web Pages") such as applying inline and document-wide style, so this discussion will jump directly to color issues.

Extended Ways of Expressing Color Values

Applying a color to a font with CSS is as easy as setting a font family or font size. To make all text in a document black, simply place the following style-sheet info in the head of the document:

```
<STYLE TYPE="text/css">
<!--
BODY {color: black}
-->
</STYLE>
```

Using hexadecimal values, setting

```
BODY {color: #000000}
```

will produce the same effect in CSS-compliant browsers. However, you could also use this approach, in this case for a red font:

```
BODY {color: #F00}
```

This is thanks to CSS's increased support of color values.

THREE-DIGIT HEXADECIMAL COLORS   CSS also supports a sort of condensed hexadecimal code, where black would be #000, blue would be #00F, and so on. Browser support is variable, however; IE 4 and higher will support the document-wide style rule shown above, but Netscape browsers will not. Apply this to an inline style like **<FONT STYLE="color: #F00">**Red text!**</FONT>,** however, and it will work in Netscape 4 and better. Set a document-wide style like

```
<STYLE TYPE="text/css">
<!--
P {color: #00C}
-->
</STYLE>
```

and CSS-compliant Netscape browsers will render paragraph text in blue.

RGB COLOR VALUES   Photoshop users will appreciate another CSS color-value approach: RGB values. No need to convert RGB values to hex with this technique:

```
<STYLE TYPE="text/css">
<!--
SPAN {color: rgb(0,0,255)}
-->
</STYLE>
```

Netscape 4 and higher, and IE 4 and higher, all support this approach, in which the color value is defined by the letters rgb (lowercase) followed by three RGB values in parentheses: rgb(0,0,255). Again, Netscape does not apply this to all elements; if you try using it with the **BODY** tag, it will only work in Internet Explorer.

RGB COLOR VALUES USING PERCENTAGES   CSS offers a final new approach, pretty much like the last one except it uses percentage values. To create paragraph text in red, for instance, use the following code:

```
<STYLE TYPE="text/css">
<!--
SPAN {color: rgb(100%,0%,0%)}
-->
</STYLE>
```

As with the 51 rule for working on browser-safe colors in Photoshop and similar graphics programs, it is easy to create browser-safe colors easily by remembering the 20 percent rule as shown in Table 11-3, above, or online at www.webdesignref.com/chapter11/designdemos/bschart.htm.

Of course, using these techniques limits your user base to those with 4.0 browsers and higher. Therefore, the best idea is to let designs degrade gracefully. Using inline style, you can easily set a paragraph to have a light-blue background with this code:

```
<P STYLE="background-color: rgb(60%,60%,100%)">. . . text . . . </P>
```

The paragraph will display in all browsers, but the background color will only appear in CSS-compliant browsers. The key here is to avoid making partially supported CSS capabilities a key part of your design. In the long run, when implementation becomes more commonplace, extended color values like this will primarily serve to make it easier to translate values from the design environment, like Photoshop, into the Web environment.

Color-Reproduction Issues

Beyond the basics of color display, there are various aspects of monitors that can affect the display of colors. This section will discuss several of them, including color shifting, gamma correction, and types of monitors. While you may develop your designs on a 21-inch top-of-the-line monitor, your users will probably be viewing your creation using much lower-end displays.

Color Shifting

Here's the bad news: even the Web-safe palette isn't Web safe under some conditions.

Computers may support a range of color settings, which generally include the following:

- True color
- Millions of colors
- 65,536 colors (high, or thousands, of colors)
- 32,768 colors
- 256 colors

The monitor does not really determine the number of colors that can be displayed, except in terms of its inherent limitations due to cost, model, manufacturer, and intended use. The number of available colors is actually defined by the computer's video card. In our lowest-common-denominator scenario (256 colors), 8 bits are employed to display colors. (Remember—2 to the 8th power is 256.) For more colors, the computer must allocate more memory to process colors. High (16-bit) color produces over 65,000 colors, while 24-bit provides literally millions of colors. This may really be overkill, as studies have shown that the average person cannot tell 16-bit and 24-bit color apart. On the other hand, 8-bit and 16-bit are fairly easy to distinguish.

Due to simple mathematics, 16-bit displays have some problems with the accurate display of the 216 Web- or browser-safe colors discussed earlier in this chapter. High-color monitors were originally intended for print designers, who work with CMYK—a four-value system—rather than RGB—a three-value system. Sixteen divided by 4 yields a handy 4 bits per color channel if you're working in CMYK. But if you're working in RGB, you run up against a troublesome issue. You can't split a bit, so in 16-bit RGB you wind up with 5 bits per color channel; the 16th bit either vanishes into some electronic limbo or is assigned arbitrarily to one of the three channels, depending on the system. A color channel with 5 bits can produce 32 different colors; multiply that by 3 and you get 32,768 colors—not quite the 65,000+ you'd get in CMYK.

The Web-safe palette, on the other hand, divides each color channel into six values. Since 32 can't be divided exactly by 6, the colors defined by the Web-safe palette won't necessarily match the colors defined by a 16-bit color setting. Thus, on some systems, some of the Web-safe colors may shift their values slightly. To make matters worse, different components of a Web page may be affected differently. Remember, a Web browser is a program; the part of that program that processes GIF images may process a certain color one way, while the part of that program that processes HTML may shift the same value somewhat differently when rendering a background color. This can result in an image not matching a background, even though you've taken great pains to keep that shade of red to the correct value. More information on this issue can be found at http://www.macromedia.com/go/13901/. The unpredictable nature of interactions between video cards and monitors is further compounded by the rendering inconsistencies of the browsers themselves.

Gamma Correction

Gamma correction changes the overall brightness and color saturation of an image as it is displayed on a monitor. If a display is gamma corrected, the nonlinear relationship between pixel value (the number assigned to a particular color tone) and displayed intensity (the way it actually looks) has been adjusted for. To get an idea of what this means visually, take a look at www.webdesignref.com/Chapter11/designdemos/gamma.htm.

To understand gamma, we need to delve a little deeper into the inner workings of monitors. The concept of gamma correction is to adjust a monitor so that it boosts the voltage in a manner consistent with other monitors. Computers send a certain voltage to monitors, which controls the electron emissions that tell the pixels on the screen which colors they should display. The monitor, in turn, boosts the signal by increasing that voltage a certain amount, which may be as high as 2.5 times the original voltage. But since the original voltage, which varies for different colors, is usually less than 1 volt, this may not account for much. Variations in the amount a monitor boosts this voltage will cause different monitors to display the same color differently. Brightness and contrast are both affected. Browsers with incorrect gamma correction will look darker and have less contrast. This is not just a matter of brightness, as gamma settings also affect the ratios between the levels of red, blue, and green.

Macintosh computers are generally regarded as better in this department, and with good reason: they were meant to be used in the creation of graphics (originally for print), while this has only become a recent concern for PCs. As it stands, Macs are set to a gamma setting of 1.8 and PCs are set to 2.5. Macs default to "corrected" gamma, which means the video signal is absolutely true to the source data—which is what a print designer needs. Most Windows PCs display "uncorrected" gamma, just like television, which skews midtones to be 10–15 percent darker and more saturated. For this reason, many experts suggest that once Web designers get their gamma set up correctly, they should work with an average gamma of 2.2 in mind. Gamma-correction software can be implemented by technicians, or you can do it yourself. Photoshop 5.5 actually allows designers to preview an image's appearance under various gamma settings. Most recent Web-specialized graphics programs (Photoshop, Fireworks, ImageReady) now have this ability to gamma preview images, as well as to batch process images to use a selected gamma value. If you are working on low-contrast designs, understanding the lack of gamma correction on the average PC monitor will help you avoid creating muddy, indistinct imagery.

Monitor Types: CRT vs. LCD

Most desktop computer monitors are cathode ray tube (CRT) display devices, just like a television monitor. The inside of a CRT monitor screen is covered with thousands of phosphor dots. Three of these dots—one red, one green, one blue—make up a pixel. The phosphor dots glow in response to charges emitted by an electron gun at the back of the monitor. As noted above, however, color processing begins in a computer's video card, not in the monitor. Using a digital-to-analog circuit (DAC), a computer monitor translates the digital information from the video card into an analog signal that controls the monitor's electron gun. Sudden and erratic variations in a monitor's color display may be caused by problems with the DAC. When encountering serious color distortion, always test the monitor on a different computer before blaming the wrong piece of hardware for the problem.

Another issue with CRT monitors is flicker. This occurs when the phosphor dots inside the screen, which have been stimulated by electron streams, begin to lose their charge before it is refreshed. Setting your monitor to a refresh rate above 70Hz should take care of this; although the Video Electronics Standards Association (VESA) defines 85Hz as the standard, this may be more than is required. Setting the refresh rate too high can cause damage to a monitor. There are several types of CRT monitors, such as aperture grille and shadow mask, but this is beyond the scope of this discussion.

Liquid crystal display (LCD) monitors, long used for laptop computers, are becoming more commonly used as desktop monitors, as the technology has improved sufficiently to make larger screens feasible and affordable. Since LCD monitors don't need room for an electron gun, they are "flat" and take up, on average, only a third of the space needed for bulkier CRT monitors. Other factors in their favor include a complete lack of cathode-ray emissions—making them easier on the eyes—and significantly lower power requirements. The upswing in LCD monitor use has several ramifications in terms of color use.

First, many LCD screens, particularly smaller ones, may only handle thousands, or even hundreds, of colors, and also tend to support a narrower range of screen resolutions. Larger (and/or more expensive) ones are more likely to handle millions of colors, or true color. Brightness may also be a concern, as LCD monitors are backlit, and their brightness levels may vary more than that of CRTs. The most important color issue for LCD monitors has to do with the angle of view. They need to be viewed head-on for best results, but even so, light variations caused by the orientation of the screen surface may cause the same color to look somewhat darker at the top of the screen and lighter at the bottom, or vice versa. Given this, LCD screens are probably a poor choice for doing graphic design for Web sites (or any other medium) unless your lighting conditions are very well controlled. From a designer's viewpoint, this reinforces the importance of choosing well-contrasted and coordinated colors for Web pages.

ELEMENTS OF PAGE DESIGN

Color and Usability

When using color, it is wise to take two key factors into account. The first, the meaning of colors, is highly subjective, but there are common color associations that can be kept in mind while designing pages. The second concerns the use of contrast; without proper contrast, even the most colorful layouts may be difficult for the end user to interpret. Once we've covered these questions, we'll move on to consider images.

The Meaning of Color

Beyond the physical aspects of color perception (see "Color Basics" earlier in this chapter), it's easy to get hung up on a much trickier issue: the meaning of color. Artists, philosophers, scientists, religious thinkers, and countless others have pondered this question for centuries, but none have reached the same conclusions. The poet Goethe spent a large portion of his life developing a theory of colors—most of which has been consigned to the dustbin of philosophy by modern thinkers. Even setting aside highly codified color/concept schemas such as those used in Tibetan religious art—or the changing colors of the liturgical seasons in Western churches—it is difficult to apply specific meanings to specific colors. In the West, black is largely associated with death and somber thoughts—while in Japan, the color associated with death is white, a complete reversal of the Western viewpoint. Considering that the Web is an international medium of communication, it may not be practical to take culturally accepted color meanings for granted. Bearing in mind the Western cultural background of this book's production, Table 11-5 lists some common meanings people may associate with certain colors.

Even without the complications of cultural associations, Web conventions also use color to convey meanings. Earlier in this chapter, the significance of hyperlink colors was brought up—people are used to clicking on blue text to go somewhere else, and know purple text means they've already been there. Changing the color of hyperlinks is always a questionable proposition, especially if the audience for the site is not made up of experienced users—they may see light-blue text and never think to click because they know that regular links are blue. But the messages may be subtler and more difficult to pin down. Reflect on what you think when you see a Web page with red text on a black background. How often does this make you think "Amateur!" in terms of the site's designer? How do you respond to sites that do not have a white background on text-heavy pages? Every Web user brings a host of unacknowledged expectations about what colors, or combinations of colors, mean in the browser window.

Issues like color-blindness and contrast problems have been touched on briefly. What does it do for the usability of a site if a certain percentage of users might not be able to distinguish a foreground image from a background color, or if text buttons disappear into a dim sidebar? It means frustrated users, a bad Web experience, and a strong likelihood that your site will lose visitors. Color issues are not simply aesthetic concerns, but go right to the core of a site's very *raison d'être*: Can an ordinary user under "real-world" conditions easily and effortlessly navigate through that site, and wish to make a return visit?

Color	Association
Red	Hot, error, stop, warning, aggression, fire, lushness, daring
Pink	Female, cute, cotton candy
Orange	Warm, autumnal, Halloween
Yellow	Happy, caution, sunny, cheerful, slow down
Brown	Warm, fall, dirty
Green	Envy, pastoral, jealousy, inexperience, fertility, newness
Blue	Peaceful, sadness, water, male
Purple	Royalty, luxury
Black	Evil, death, mourning, ghostly, night, fear
Gray	Overcast, gloom, old age
White	Virginal, clean, innocent, winter, cold

Table 11-5.   *Common Concepts Associated with Colors (Subject to Cultural Bias)*

The proliferation of PDAs, phones, and Palm devices raises another interesting aspect of Web site design. What do you do when you do not have color to work with? Can you design a site that works well in all conditions? Two-tone devices, usually displaying with a greenish-gray background and grayish-black text, challenge design ingenuity in a number of ways. The safest approach is probably to design a separate site for each browsing platform so that you can design completely within a particular visual environment. Browser sensing then directs the incoming user to the version of the site appropriate to their display device.

Contrast Problems

One common design problem is when the elements of a design do not contrast enough. The general problem arises when the designer, who is statistically more likely to be designing on a Mac, doesn't realize that, in general, PC monitors display darker than their Mac does (see "Gamma Correction," above). This becomes a problem when you try to create some sort of subtle color differences between two elements on top of, or next to, each other. Then you move to another system, the PC for example, and discover that you can't see the difference between the two, or that the foreground image did not contrast enough from the background color and now seems to disappear completely. An online demonstration of this problem can be found at www.webdesignref.com/chapter11/

designdemos/usability.htm. The solution: make sure to never have elements that require a precise rendering in order for the difference to be apparent. If it is used as a nonmain element—one whose disappearance wouldn't affect the overall look of the page—this might be acceptable. But if your design requires that everything appear in order to not fall apart, then you will need to modify your design.

The flip side of low contrast is exaggerated high contrast. Bright neon colors on a black background offer a great deal of contrast, but is it an effective or usable design? Using color and contrast to bring attention to particular parts of a site is a balancing act—how do I make the navigation obvious without making it obtrusive? How do I highlight a special site feature without overwhelming the page? What can I do with text color that will emphasize key items but not create a billboard effect? Using dramatic colors (often in combination with animation) against a relatively neutral background of black or white is a fast way to grab the user's attention—but it can be an equally fast way to generate a negative response to the site. In general, large blocks of very bright colors are not easy to use in a Web page. They risk overwhelming the user, which causes a negative reaction and may result in loss of return visitation, increase in complaints, and less effective communication of site information. In either case—low contrast or high contrast—the fundamental demand upon the designer is to exercise judgment on how to present content in a visual manner.

At the heart of all of these issues is the simple fact that people want to see pictures, and not just pages of text, when they browse the Web. Blocks of color can only go so far to communicate certain messages, no matter how many colors have been applied to them. At some point, images must become part of the design.

Images

The Web revolution could perhaps be said to have started in 1993 when Mosaic first made it possible to display images in Web pages. Since those early days of clunky, dithered GIFs slapped unceremoniously beside barely formatted text, the use of images has evolved along with the possible uses of the Web, and the increasing desires and expectations of designers and users alike. While Web page design may have becomes subtler and wider ranging as the underlying assumptions of Web use have developed and spread, many of the fundamental issues governing proper image use remain the same. This section will examine the HTML underpinnings of image use, the types of images best suited to Web use, emerging image formats, and related usability concerns.

Using Images

Why do we use images? They are a fast way to represent things in a visual communication medium. An image can represent, not just explain, and serves to communicate thoughts, concepts, ideas, and directions—either in conjunction with textual data or as a more comprehensible replacement for that data. Think of a map with driving directions. Just the map or just the text could each probably get you to your destination. The combination of the two provides a more complete method of communication than either by itself.

Text rendered as an image, such as a button, a headline, or a caption, allows the designer to convey other things besides the straightforward meaning of the text. Color, font style, size, graphic effects, and placement on the page all work together to emphasize that particular information—here is the navigation, look at this important break in the paragraph, this is a particular type of staff picture—perceptibly enhancing (or sometimes detracting from) the experience of the site were it only text and blocks of color. And, of course, images can be used simply for the joy or whimsy of including a particular picture in a specific place in the site. As with any other visual element on the page, the key to effective use of Web imagery is good judgment. Knowing what images to use, how to prepare them, why to use one format over another, and when to refrain from using them are all necessary parts of being a good visual designer.

When preparing images for use on your Web site, there are several things to keep in mind beyond file size and compression. First, where do you store the images? It is a good idea to keep your images in their own directory. For most sites, you are going to end up with a lot of images, and it is much better, for organizational reasons, if you have them separated from everything else. Create a directory named "images" and keep all of the site images in it. It will dramatically improve maintenance operations on the site if all images are in one location.

Rule: Always store your images in a separate directory.

It's also important how you name your images. It is extremely important to name your images in a manner that makes sense. When the directory is viewed, they will be in alphabetical order, so you want to make related images show up next to one another. For example, you could name your navigational images HNabout.gif, HNproducts.gif, and HNcontact.gif (HN standing for Home Navigation). That way, alphabetically, all the HNs will show up together in the directory. If the images were to have rollovers, you could name those HNOabout.gif, HNOproducts.gif, and HNOcontact.gif (HNO standing for Home Navigation On). Again, they will always show up next to one another in the images directory. You could continue this throughout the entire site by using names such SN for Sub Navigation or PI for Product Images. Create your own standards, but keep the names as short and to the point as you can, while still making sure that you can figure out what they are.

Rule: Name your images in a logical fashion that groups them by purpose or usage.

HTML and Images: The <IMG> Tag

To insert an image into a Web page, simply use the **<IMG>** element and set the **SRC** attribute of the element equal to the URL of the image. The form of the URL may be either an absolute URL or a relative URL. The best approach is to use a relative URL to an image found in your images directory. To insert a GIF image called logo.gif residing in that directory, use

```
<IMG SRC="images/logo.gif">
```

Of course, an absolute URL could also be used to reference an image on another server, for example:

```
<IMG SRC="http://www.democompany.com/images/logo.gif">
```

Although using absolute URLs for linking in your images works, it is going to limit the mobility of your Web site. Imagine trying to make a copy onto a CD-ROM. Therefore, using relative links will be a better long-term solution. Using an external URL is not advised since images may move and cause the page to load at an uneven pace.

Rule: You can't use the <IMG> tag without the SRC attribute.

To set up a simple example, first create a directory to hold your images. Now place a GIF format image named photo.gif in that directory. To retrieve an image off the Internet, you can simply right-click with your mouse on an image and save the file to your directory. Macintosh users will have to hold the mouse button down on an image to access the menu for saving the image. Once you have a GIF image, you should be able to use a short piece of HTML markup to experiment with the use of **<IMG>,** as shown below:

```
<!DOCTYPE HTML PUBLIC "-//W3C//DTD HTML 4.0 Transitional//EN">
<HTML>
<HEAD>
<TITLE>Image Example</TITLE>
</HEAD>
<BODY>
<H2 ALIGN="CENTER">Image Example</H2>
<IMG SRC="images/photo.gif" WIDTH="234" HEIGHT="150" BORDER="0">
</BODY>
</HTML>
```

A possible rendering of the image example is shown in Figure 11-3.

This is the simplest way to use an image. Of course, you will immediately want to expand your image-handling abilities, as this is also a relatively dull way to use an

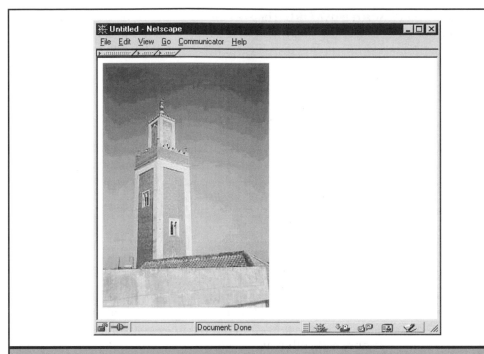

Figure 11-3.   *Possible rendering of a simple <IMG> example*

image. To expand these abilities, you will need to understand the **<IMG>** element's attributes.

<IMG> Attributes

Besides **SRC**, there are numerous other attributes to the **<IMG>** element. Two of them, **ISMAP** and **USEMAP**, have been discussed at length earlier in this book (see Chapter 6, "Image Maps"). Some commonly used attributes are discussed here briefly; for a more detailed examination of **<IMG>** and its attributes, see Chapter 5 of the companion volume *HTML: The Complete Reference*.

ALT   The **ALT** attribute provides alternative text for user agents that do not display images, or for graphical browsers where the user has turned off image rendering:

```
<IMG SRC="images/logo.gif" ALT="Demo Company Logo">
```

The **ALT** attribute's value may display in place of the image or be used as a ToolTip or placeholder information in image-based browsers. Any HTML markup found in the **ALT** element will be rendered as plain text. If the option to display images is turned off, the browser will display the alternative text, as shown here.

Many modern graphical browsers will also display the **ALT** text as the ToolTip for the image once the pointer is positioned over the image for a period of time, as shown in Figure 11-4. A browser may also show the **ALT** text as images load, giving the user something to read as the page renders.

While theoretically there is no limit to the **ALT** text that may be used, anything more than a few hundred characters may become unwieldy. Some browsers, including some versions of Netscape 4, do not handle long ToolTips properly and may not wrap the descriptive text.

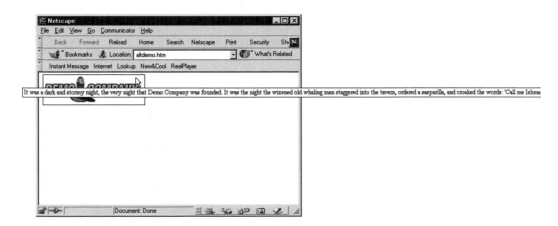

Another reason to keep the **ALT** text short is that the ToolTip only stays visible for a matter of seconds. If there is too much to read, it will disappear before the user is able to finish reading.

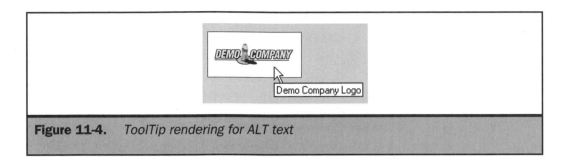

Figure 11-4.   *ToolTip rendering for ALT text*

The **ALT** attribute's importance becomes clear when you reflect on how many people access the Web from a text-only environment. Unfortunately, setting alternative text does not always provide a substantial benefit. Do the recent examples above really help by backing up the Demo Company logo graphic with the actual words "Demo Company logo"? Would simply "Demo Company logo" be sufficient, or insufficient? Try to make **ALT** text reflect the meaning of an image; if an image is merely decorative, like a graphic bullet for a list item, setting it to no value (**ALT=""**) is perfectly acceptable.

> **Suggestion: ALT text should reinforce the meaning of significant images; if an image does not convey essential meaning, leaving the ALT value blank is better than cluttering the page with unnecessary ToolTips.**

Height and Width

One all-too-common sight on the Web is text that loads in quickly, only to suddenly reflow all over the place when the images pop in a few seconds later. This is caused by designers neglecting to use the **HEIGHT** and **WIDTH** attributes of the **<IMG>** tag:

```
<IMG SRC="images/sequoia.jpg" HEIGHT="150" WIDTH="40">
```

Using these attributes resolves this problem because when visual browsers read these attribute values, they reserve the space defined by those dimensions.

> **Rule: Always use the HEIGHT and WIDTH attributes with the <IMG> tag.**

When these attributes are used in an HTML document, text will flow around where the images are supposed to go even if the images finish loading long after the text. For more complicated layouts, where cut-up images may be assembled jigsaw-puzzle style in a table, it is very important to use these attributes accurately and in a way that matches the dimensions of the table cells holding the images. Using these attributes has the additional benefit of improving the perceived download time, as users can begin reading the page before the all of the images have finished loading.

Some designers misuse the **HEIGHT** and **WIDTH** attributes to resize images with HTML. It is usually easy to spot this mistake: whether they are shrunken or expanded by decreasing or increasing the attribute values, images resized in HTML tend to look distorted.

Rule: Never use the HEIGHT and WIDTH attributes to resize images with HTML. If a smaller version of an image is needed, create a smaller version of the image and use HEIGHT and WIDTH correctly.

Images and Borders

Browsers tend to render images whose **BORDER** attribute remains undefined with no border, with one notable exception. While the image

```
<IMG SRC="images/sequoia.jpg" HEIGHT="150" WIDTH="40">
```

will render without a border, making it a link

```
<A HREF="sequoiafaq.htm"><IMG SRC="images/sequoia.jpg"
    HEIGHT="150" WIDTH="40"></A>
```

will render with a colored border, usually blue. This is the Web's graphic equivalent of underlining text links. In the early days, this was a good way to let users know that an image was a link. Nowadays, with graphic navigation conventions fairly well established, this is more of a nuisance than a boon. Setting all images to have a border of zero is a good idea most of the time.

Rule: Always set an image's BORDER attribute to zero unless you have a specific design reason to do otherwise—and remember that linked images with no BORDER attribute will render with colored borders by default.

Other <IMG> Attributes

A few other useful attributes are shown here:

Attribute and Value(s)	Usage Example	Function
ALIGN="BOTTOM I LEFT I MIDDLE I RIGHT I TOP"	**<IMG SRC="photo.jpg" ALIGN="RIGHT">Text....**	Aligns an image relative to text or other inline elements
HSPACE="*number***"**	**<IMG SRC="photo.jpg" HSPACE="***x***">**	Creates a horizontal margin of *x* pixels on the left and right sides of the image

Attribute and Value(s)	Usage Example	Function
VSPACE="*number*"	<IMG SRC="photo.jpg" VSPACE="*x*">	Creates a vertical margin of *x* pixels on the top and bottom sides of the image

Image Types

Computer-based images come in two basic varieties: *vector images* and *bitmapped images*. The Web only supports bitmapped images, unless plug-ins are employed; this will be discussed later in the section "Vector-Based Art on the Web: Flash." A bitmap image is basically a collection of pixels of different color values. Because of the large number of pixels and color information in an image, bitmaps can be very large. An uncompressed bitmap image at 640 × 480 pixels with 24 bits of color information would take up nearly 1MB. This makes it impractical to transmit raw bitmaps across the Internet.

One approach to dealing with the size problem is to compress the images. In general, there are two forms of image compression: *lossless* and *lossy*. Lossless image compression means that the compressed image is identical to the uncompressed image. Because all the data in the image must be preserved, the degree of compression, and the corresponding savings, is relatively minor. Lossy compression, on the other hand, does not preserve the image exactly, but can provide much higher degrees of compression. With lossy compression, the image quality is compromised for a smaller byte count. Because the human eye may barely notices the loss, the trade-off may be acceptable.

While the HTML standard says nothing about what image formats can be used on the Web, browsers tend to support the same image types. On the Web, the primary image formats are GIF (Graphics Interchange Format) and JPEG (Joint Photographic Experts Group). Given the historical association between UNIX and the Internet, the X image formats—XBM (X Bitmaps) and XPM (X Pixelmaps)—are often supported natively by browsers. Page designers are warned to use only GIF and JPEG images, as these are the most commonly supported.

GIF

GIF images are probably the most widely supported image format on the Web. There are two basic types of GIF: *GIF 87* and *GIF 89a*. Both forms of GIF support 8-bit color (256 colors), use the LZW (Lempel-Ziv-Welch) lossless compression scheme, and generally have the file extension .gif. GIF 89a also supports transparency and animation, both of which will be discussed later in this section.

The run-length encoding compression scheme used by the GIFs works well with large areas of continuous color, so GIF is very efficient in compression of flat-style illustration. Figure 11-5 shows the GIF compression scheme in practice. (To see an extended online version of this, go to www.webdesignref.com/Chapter11/

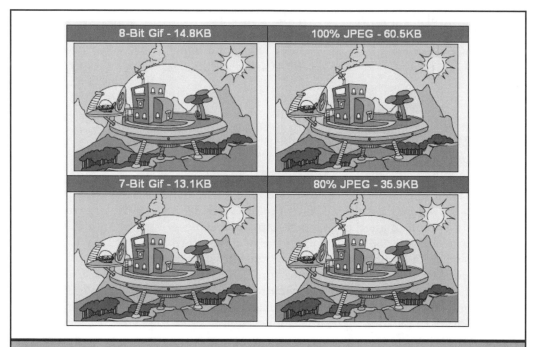

Figure 11-5.   *GIF compression scheme comparison*

designdemos/gifsize.htm.) The images with large, horizontal, continuous areas of color compress a great deal, while those with variation do not. Simply taking a box filled with lines and rotating it 90 degrees shows how dramatic the compression effect can be.

As mentioned earlier, GIF images only support 8-bit color for a maximum of 256 colors within the image. Consequently, some degree of loss is inevitable when representing true-color images, such as photographs. Typically, when an image is remapped from a large number of colors to a smaller color palette, dithering occurs. As discussed earlier, dithering attempts to create the desired color that is outside of the palette by taking two or more colors from the palette and placing them in some sort of checkered or speckled pattern to attempt to visually create the illusion of the original color. Making sure to use the appropriate file format for the right types of images and making sure that flat or illustrative type images use Web-safe colors will help reduce any dithering that may take place.

The bit depth of a GIF will also affect its file size. The higher the bit depth, the more colors and the greater amount of information required. All of these factors will make the file size of the image larger. It would make sense then that, if you can limit the number of colors as much as possible without reducing the quality of the image, you could create some extremely small files.

GIF images also support a concept called *transparency*. One bit of transparency is allowed, which means that one color can be set to be transparent. Transparency allows the background that an image is placed upon to show through, making a variety of complex effects possible. Transparency is illustrated in Figure 11-6.

Online: A transparency example can be seen at www.webdesignref.com/ Chapter11/designdemos/transparent.htm.

GIF transparency is far from ideal. There are a variety of issues, which are displayed at the online demo. To have a better understanding of these, it is first important to understand what *anti-aliasing* is.

Everything that is displayed onscreen is made up of pixels. Pixels are square. It should therefore be obvious that creating an image that has rounded edges may pose some problems. Anti-aliasing allows us create the illusion of rounded or smooth edges by partially filling the edge pixels in an attempt to blend the image into the background. An example of this can be seen in Figure 11-7 and online at www.webdesignref.com/Chapter11/designdemos/antialias.htm.

Anti-aliasing complicates attempts to use transparency to create more pleasing GIFs. When creating a transparent GIF, you are able to make one color transparent, or drop, in order to allow the background color or image to show through the transparent areas of the foreground image. Since anti-aliased images have partially filled pixels around the edges to give them their smooth appearance, these colors are not the same as the background color. Therefore, they do not drop out. The result can be a halo effect around the image when placed on a background color that was not similar to the one in the original image. There are ways to try and get around this by making the images color-keyed, in which you match the background of your image to the background of your page and don't use a transparency. You can also make the image aliased, which lacks the blended look of an anti-aliased image and will appear jagged around the edges, but will allow for perfect transparency. Another option is to

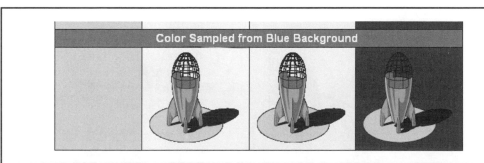

Figure 11-6.   *Transparency with GIF images*

Figure 11-7.   *Anti-aliasing*

use an alpha transparency. This is created by using an alpha channel to try to create a better transparency. This works quite well, but can have some adverse affects. It may tend to make the image appear a little jagged around the edges, but can be quite useful when trying to place an image on top of a complex background. A comparison between an anti-aliased image and an aliased image can be seen in Figure 11-8.

> **Online: Examples can be seen at www.webdesignref.com/Chapter11/ designdemos/antialias.htm.**

 When using small text in a graphic, it may be a good idea to leave it aliased; anti-aliasing introduces an element of fuzziness that will make smaller font sizes very difficult to read.

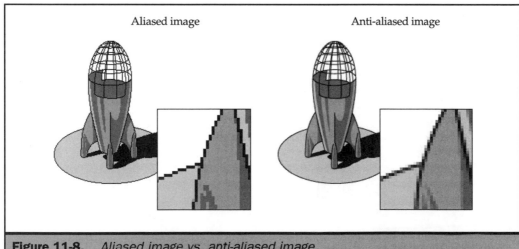

Figure 11-8.   *Aliased image vs. anti-aliased image*

GIF images also support a feature called *interlacing*. Interlacing allows an image to load in a venetian-blind fashion rather than from top to bottom a line at a time. The interlacing effect allows a user to get an idea of what an image looks like before the entire image has downloaded. The idea of interlacing is shown in Figure 11-9. The previsualization benefit of interlacing is very useful on the Web, where download speed is often an issue. While interlacing a GIF image is generally a good idea, occasionally it comes with a downside; interlaced images may be larger than noninterlaced images. It would also be a bad idea to use interlacing for images that have text on them, since it would be impossible for the text to be read easily until the download was complete.

Online: For more on this topic, visit www.webdesignref.com/Chapter11/ designdemos/intgif.htm.

The GIF89a format also supports animation. This works by stacking GIF after GIF in a manner similar to a flip book to create the animation. The animation extension also allows timing and looping information to be added to the image. Animated GIFs are one of the most popular ways to add simple animation to a Web page because nearly every browser supports them. Browsers that do not support the animated GIF format generally display the first frame of the animation in its place. Even though plug-ins or

Figure 11-9.   *Example of interlacing*

other browser facilities are not required, authors should not rush out to use animation on their pages. Excessive animations can be distracting for the user, and are often inefficient to download. Since the animation is basically image after image, the file size is the total of all the images within the animation combined, and can result in a much larger image than the user is willing to wait for. Thus, it is very important to make sure that every frame of the animation is compressed as much as possible. One approach to combat file bloat is to optimize the image by replacing only the moving parts of an individual animation frame. By replacing only the portion of the frame that is changing, you can use smaller images in some frames to help cut the file size down. Many of the GIF animating applications have a feature built in that will go through and optimize the images for you. This may result in a dramatic saving of file size, as shown in Figure 11-10.

> **Online: A more extended look at animated GIFs can be viewed online at www.webdesignref.com/Chapter11/designdemos/animate.htm.**

JPEG

The other common Web image format is JPEG, which usually is indicated by a filename ending with .jpg or .jpeg. JPEG, which stands for the Joint Photographic Experts Group—the name of the committee that wrote the standard—is a lossy image format designed for compressing photographic images that may contain thousands, or even millions, of colors or shades of gray. Because JPEG is a lossy image format, there is some trade-off between image quality and file size. However, the JPEG format stores high-quality 24-bit color images in a significantly smaller amount of space than GIF, thus saving precious disk space or download time on the Web.

Note that JPEGs can be saved in both RGB and CMYK formats; don't use a CMYK JPEG by mistake, or you may wind up with something like this when it renders in a browser.

RGB JPEG displayed by Netscape   CMYK JPEG displayed by Netscape

While the JPEG format may compress photographic images well, it is not well suited to line drawings or text. The degree of compression in JPEG images, which shows how the format favors photographs, is shown in Figure 11-11.

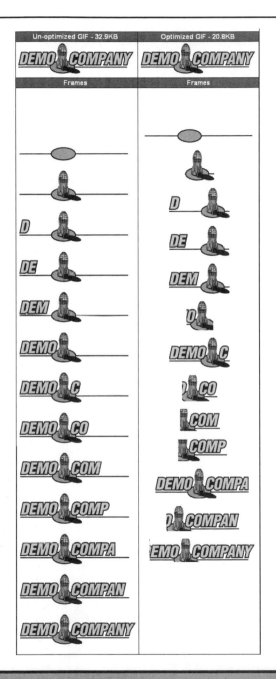

Figure 11-10.   *Example of animated GIF frames and optimization*

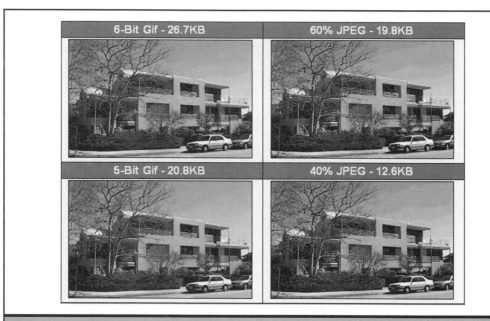

Figure 11-11.   *Comparison between GIF and JPEG formats*

Online: You can see more of this at www.webdesignref.com/Chapter11/designdemos/gifjpeg.htm.

Note that when illustrations are saved in JPEG format, they may acquire extraneous information, often in the form of unwanted dots or other residue. JPEG images do not support animation, nor do they support any form of transparency. Web designers needing such effects must turn to another image format, such as GIF. JPEG images do support a form of interlacing in a format called *progressive JPEG.* Progressive JPEGs fade in from a low resolution to a high resolution, going from fuzzy to clear. Like interlaced GIFs, progressive JPEG images are slightly larger than their nonprogressive counterparts. Because JPEG is so well suited to photographs and GIF to illustrations, it is possible to obtain better-quality images in a smaller file size simply by selecting the best file format.

Online: For more about progressive JPEGs, visit www.webdesignref.com/Chapter11/designdemos/jpegsize.htm.

Wavelet Compression: JPEG 2000

Still in the works is a new, improved JPEG standard that will vastly improve the display of photographic images on the Web. Regular JPEGs use a compression system called DCT that compresses visual information into blocks of 8 pixels by 8 pixels; the blocks load in sequence as the image is rendered. The JPEG 2000 standard, in turn, uses something called wavelet compression. Images will be converted into a series of wavelets, rather than square blocks of pixels, and will not need to discard as much information as the current JPEG approach. In addition to improved compression, designers will be able to choose from a range of resolution levels for each JPEG 2000 image—and users will be able to select how much of that resolution they want to display. JPEG 2000 will also allow for possible CMYK display on the Web and contain additional information, including some that will correct color display for a variety of systems and platforms.

AOL Compression Issues

America Online users often encounter blurry images when viewing Web pages, particularly non-AOL pages. The reason for this is AOL employs its own compression format, created by the Johnson-Grace company (now owned by AOL), which converts GIF, JPEG, and even BMP files into their own .ART format.

On the consumer end, AOL users can deselect User Compressed Graphics from their Web preferences menu. On the designer end, you can at least *try* to minimize display issues under AOL. Photoshop 4 and higher, and other graphics programs, allows you to save thumbnail previews of an image so that you or someone else can see a preview of the image before opening it. This thumbnail information is, of course, included in the file; when AOL compresses such an image, it reads the preview— itself a scaled-down JPEG image—first, assumes that this is the image itself, and tries to display it at the size defined for the "real" JPEG. Adobe claims that images created on PCs will have this problem, but not those created on a Mac, which does not actually answer the problem. Your best bet is to make certain that all images you create for Web use are not saved with thumbnails.

FlashPix

Another emerging graphics format, FlashPix, allows the creation of zoomable, scrollable, pixel-based images. This is possible by using proprietary software to create images that the computer can use to display the requested portion on the fly. It is not as fast as zooming in on a flash file, but is rather interesting—particularly because it allows one file to contain a wide variety of information about an image. With the appropriate plug-in, you can view demos at www.flashpix.com that allow the user to choose zoom factor, image resolution, brightness, contrast, sharpness, and red/blue/green levels, and then download a version of the image that fits those requirements! Unfortunately, this format is not widely known or supported. Only time will tell if it will catch on with the Web public.

PNG

The Portable Network Graphics (PNG) format has all of the features of GIF89a in addition to several other features. Notable features include greater color-depth support, color and gamma correction, and 8-bit transparency. In addition, the compression algorithm for PNG is nonproprietary, making PNG a likely successor of GIF. Internet Explorer 4 supports inline PNG images in a limited way. Some versions of Netscape Communicator require a plug-in, while later versions provide limited support. No 4.*x*-generation browser supports PNG well enough to rely on the format, so Web designers are warned to avoid using the format unless browser sensing is utilized so as to guarantee images will render properly. For more information, see the online demo www.webdesignref.com/chapter11/png.htm.

> **Suggestion: Limit graphics formats in Web pages to JPEG and GIF until other formats become generally supported.**

Image-Related Issues

There are a number of issues associated with the use of images on the Web. Contrast concerns, already discussed above in "Contrast Problems" and "Contrast Issues with Backgrounds and Foregrounds," are worth considering again before proceeding. Usability questions, such as those raised by the fact that there are visually impaired users on the Web, are also quite important. Download and compression issues are practically two sides of the same coin. Finally, what about the legal ramifications of using images created by someone else? We'll take a look at each of these before concluding the section on images.

Matching Image and Background Colors

When creating images for use against backgrounds (see below, "Document-Wide Backgrounds"), it is important to make sure they match properly. Macromedia's Dreamweaver program, probably the best WYSIWYG tool for editing HTML pages, has a convenient Eyedropper tool that will allow you to sample colors from anywhere—text, images, backgrounds, even the color from the top bar of the program window. While not used to create images directly, this tool is useful in determining the exact hexadecimal color value of any colored element in a Web page.

Usability and Images

Images definitely improve the Web, but there are downsides to their use. When building a site that relies heavily on color, it is important to consider those who, for physical reasons, will perceive color in a dramatically different way than the average user. Many people suffer from some form of color-vision deficiency, often called color blindness.

The most common color-vision problem is red-green color blindness. Other forms of color blindness, such as blue-yellow color blindness—or even true color blindness, where the person can only see in shades of gray—are less common than red-green color-vision deficiency. Dealing with color-vision problems on the Web boils down to a few commonsense considerations.

> **Suggestion: Don't rely solely on color as a cue in links and informational graphics.**

TEXT-LINK COLOR   Within Web pages, red and green are occasionally used as link colors, green usually being the unvisited link color and red the visited color. If this is the case, consider using a dark shade of green and a light shade of red. This way, the color-blind user will see the link change intensity from dark to light as links are selected, and will be able to tell the difference between visited and unvisited links even if they appear to be the same color. A good combination for green/red links that deal with color blindness on a Web page is shown here:

```
<BODY TEXT="#000000" LINK="#006600" ALINK="#FF0000"
VLINK="#FF9999">
```

The most important consideration is link color. Users need to be able to easily distinguish the difference between normal text and link text. Normal link feedback includes colors, underlining, and cursor change. If underlining is removed, consider how difficult it would be for color-vision–deficient users to make out links. If underlining is removed, you must make sure to vary the intensity of link colors significantly from each other as well as from the surrounding text.

GRAPHIC-LINK COLOR   Color should also be used carefully in graphical text buttons. Though graphic text will often look different than normal text or graphic labels in a page, make sure that color isn't the main difference. Try to vary the size, style, or font of clickable graphics to indicate what graphical text is a link. Figure 11-12 shows two

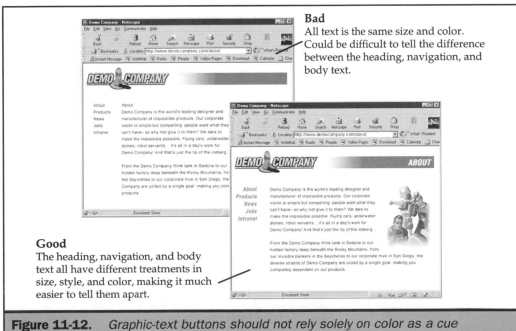

Bad
All text is the same size and color. Could be difficult to tell the difference between the heading, navigation, and body text.

Good
The heading, navigation, and body text all have different treatments in size, style, and color, making it much easier to tell them apart.

Figure 11-12.   *Graphic-text buttons should not rely solely on color as a cue*

screens with graphical text and labels. The first screen relies solely on color as the differentiating factor for clickable graphic text while the second screen uses size and style to further indicate what is a graphic link.

COLOR IN INFORMATIONAL GRAPHICS   When using color as a key in an informational graphic such as a pie chart, consider using labels as well, or patterns, in case color cannot be seen, as shown in Figure 11-13.

Avoid red-green combinations when possible.

Finally, use colors with different lightness values. While color perception is a problem for some, intensity is usually not. Even if a user won't be able to distinguish color, they will be able to distinguish intensity.

MINIMIZING USE OF GRAPHICS   Then there is always the option to simply not use images. This is obviously not the most visually pleasing solution. Using strictly text is going to be far less interesting, and there may be information that requires the use of images to make sense. It is possible to have two versions of a site—one with text and images, and one that is text-only. It is a possible solution, but depending on how you are maintaining your data (for example, not using a database to populate content), you could be creating an enormous amount of maintenance work to serve the needs of a small audience. How about **ALT** text? Writing really good **ALT** text could be extremely useful. If the user can't see the images, then the **ALT** text will take their place. Speech-based browsers, once developed, might "speak" the **ALT** text for the visually impaired. Overall, judicious use of carefully selected and optimized imagery in conjunction with thoughtful use of color will allow you to create powerful Web pages that are usable for the large majority of users.

Download/File Size Issues

Another concern related to images is the matter of images slowing page-download speeds.

In fighting this problem, choosing the correct file format can make a huge difference. By choosing the correct format, you will be able to compress the images in the most effective way, thereby reducing the file size and allowing the page to download faster. It is important to be careful not to overoptimize through cutting the image into too many small pieces. While this does work to a certain extent, every image is a request to the server. Too many server requests can also start to slow the page down. The key is to find a good balance between number of files and file size. Experience and experimentation will teach where that balance lies.

You can also attempt to fool the user. One way to speed up pages is to reuse imagery across pages. For example, if you use the same navigational area across the top of all of your subpages, calling the same images on multiple pages, you take advantage of the browser's own image caches. This means that your user downloads an image once and then reuses it, speeding up their experience of the site. It has the added benefit of reducing the number of calls to the server, reducing traffic, and improving overall performance, which further speeds up the site for the end user. By cutting things up appropriately so that images that appear on multiple pages can be cached, it will save the browser from having to redownload the images on every page.

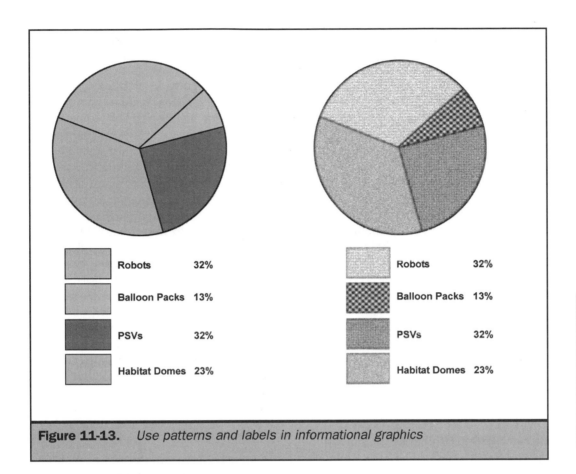

Figure 11-13.   *Use patterns and labels in informational graphics*

While not exactly an "image" issue, the importance of good underlying code cannot be emphasized enough. The number of visually exciting sites brought to grief by poorly executed code is a shame, especially when good code is more a matter of attention to detail and good testing than anything else. The bottom line is your images will perform better when your HTML is at its best.

Compression Issues

Another approach to reducing the byte count in an image is through compression. As discussed previously, image compression is handled by the image-file format, so choosing the correct format for a particular image is integral to reducing byte count. A basic rule of thumb is to use GIF images for illustrations and JPEGs for photographs. Also, by setting the degree of compression when using a JPEG image, you can reduce file size with a small sacrifice in image quality. Because the human eye can't often perceive the difference between an image of high quality and one of medium quality, tuning the image can often result in significant file-size savings without visual penalty.

While image size is certainly important to improving the loading time of Web pages, designers shouldn't get carried away with optimizing images without consideration for the rest of the Web process. There are many more factors than image size that affect Web page performance. Some of the factors affecting page performance include the type and configuration of the Web server, the distance "traveled" on the Internet between the server and the end user, the traffic levels on the Internet at the time of site access, the software being used on the server to deliver the site and on the user's system to view the site, and even the processing speed of the user's computer. All of these factors affect the user's experience. Good HTML is one the best and easiest ways to improve site performance. As mentioned earlier in this chapter and also discussed below, a proven way improve page performance is to specify the table widths, and the width and height of images, so that the browser is able to "block out" the page before the actual data arrives at the user's system. Then, all the browser has to do is toss each bit of data or each image into its proper holding cell as that information finally arrives. This lets the user read ahead and view the faster-loading images rather than having to wait for everything to arrive before the browser can render the page.

Be aware of your site's hosting environment. There is little reason to optimize images or code for a Web site that will be hosted on a slow, poorly connected, or improperly configured server. In the end, the only true measure of the site is the quality of the end-user experience. What the user experiences is what counts, not the bytes transferred or the number of connections made. Top-quality Web design will include evaluation and optimization of all factors that go into page delivery, not just images.

Preloading Images

Preloading images is a possible method for improving Web page performance. You could selectively place an image or two for the next page at the bottom of a previous page, scaled to a 1 × 1 pixel size in the code, which renders it invisible on the page where it preloads. Once it has been placed in the user's browser cache, it will render very quickly once the user requests the page where it is normally sized and is supposed to display. There are limited uses for this trick. It works best when you have a series of pages where the user will spend some time reviewing the visual materials before moving in a linear fashion to the next page in the series. This way, each image has been prepared for a guaranteed viewing session. This works well to a certain extent, but don't forget that it still has to download on whatever page you hide it on. The first page of the series will always have a significantly longer download time than the other pages, and this may cause users to exit before they get into the progression of images. Make sure that you don't try to preload too many images in this manner, and make sure that it isn't going to hurt the preloading page too much. A photo journal or photo essay would be a good candidate for this type of image work.

You can also use JavaScript to run a status bar to let the user know that something is downloading if you just can't avoid having a large download.

Obtaining Images

So, you see all the really cool sites out there, but where do you get the cool images? There are a variety of ways in which to obtain great images. The first way would be to buy them. You can go about this a couple of ways. You could commission a photographer to take some pictures for you— in other words, pay for the photo shoot. You could also buy images from a vendor. There are many vendors that do nothing but sell images. As you might expect, good images cost significant amounts. There are also usability rights that must get cleared. You may get charged, depending on how you plan to use them—don't assume that paying one price will always get you limitless use rights. You may only have purchased the right to use it on one page of your site, or only on the Web, not on related print materials, and so on. These issues will vary from vendor to vendor. Obtaining images is actually relatively easy, but obtaining good images on a relatively tight budget with unlimited usage rights can be challenging. Finally, there are few images that can be used "as is," even if they are of good quality.

The expense of licensing images and the ease with which images can be copied have convinced many people that they can simply appropriate whatever images they need. Unfortunately, this is stealing the work of others. While there are stiff penalties for copyright infringement, it can be difficult to enforce these laws. Also, some page designers tend to bend the rules thanks to the legal concept called *fair use,* which allows the use of someone else's copyrighted work under certain circumstances.

There are four basic questions used to define the fair-use concept.

First, is the work in question being appropriated for a nonprofit or profit use? The fair-use defense is less likely to stand up if the "borrowed" work has been used to make money for someone other than its copyright holder.

Second, is the work creative (for example, a speculative essay on the impact of a recent congressional debate) or factual (a straightforward description of the debate without commentary)? "Fair use" would cover use of the factual work more than use of the creative one.

Third, how much of the copyrighted work has been used? It is possible to use someone else's image if it is changed substantially from the original. The problem is determining what constitutes enough change in the image to make it a new work. Simply using a photo-editing tool to flip an image or change its colors is not enough. There is a fine line between using portions of another person's work and outright stealing. Even if you don't plan on using uncleared images, be careful of using images from free Internet clip-art libraries. These so-called free images may have been submitted with the belief that they are free, but some of them may have been appropriated from a commercial clip-art library somewhere down the line. Be particularly careful with high-quality images of famous individuals and commercial products. While such groups may often appreciate people using their images, the usage is generally limited to noncommercial purposes.

The third fair use question leads to the fourth. What impact does the image have on the economic value of the work?

This whole discussion begs many legal questions that are far beyond the scope of this book. Suffice it to say that in the long run, it's always safer to create original work, license images, or use material in the public domain. Just because many Web designers skirt the law doesn't mean you should.

If you are artistically gifted, you can try creating the images yourself. You can use programs such as Adobe Photoshop to create entirely new and unique images. If you are not an artist, you can hire a graphic designer or a design firm to create original images for you. This can be an expensive proposition, and usually means that you will still have to purchase some stock imagery to use as the building blocks for your new designs. At base, unless you wish to limit your visual expression to unaltered clip art, you will need to invest part of your Web site budget into development of imagery.

Now that you are an image creator, you have to worry about controlling your visual property. How do you prevent someone from stealing your images off of your Web site? You could try to use some advanced scripting or programming to prevent it. You could create images that are multipart and difficult to collect. You could embed a watermark within Photoshop using Digimarc technology (www.digimarc.com), and so on. The issue, however, comes down to two points: how will you know if someone took images from your site, and what are your legal options if they do? You could have a legal team to constantly check for illegal use and then decide if you wanted to prosecute image thieves to stop them from using your images. Or, you could limit the images you use on your site to those you are willing to lose control over. However, you will always want to protect your logo, your brand name, and images of your products.

Cutting Up Images

One common, and highly useful, approach to building graphically appealing layouts involves cutting up images and using tables as a "framework" to hold them in place. This is discussed in considerable detail in Chapter 7 of the companion volume, *HTML: The Complete Reference*. The first thing to watch out for is to make sure the images inserted in a table have their **WIDTH** and **HEIGHT** values defined, and that those values match those of the table cells. The **HEIGHT** attribute for table cells is not generally supported, but it won't hurt to include it. If things don't add up, the layout won't either.

Another concern is the complexity of the table involved. In its years of building Web sites, the author's company has encountered code left over from clients' previous Web designers—code that tried using the cutup approach but made it too complicated, often resulting in pages that only worked in one browser, if that. Some used multiple nested tables to create truly unwieldy code that made little sense from a design standpoint, much less from the HTML side of the equation.

A highly simplified version of table/image layout is shown in Figure 11-14.

The layout on the left of the figure represents a page that was created with a single table. Cells with a gray background contain images. As you can see, this layout will require a lot of **ROWSPAN** and **COLSPAN** attributes in the table cells. While this may

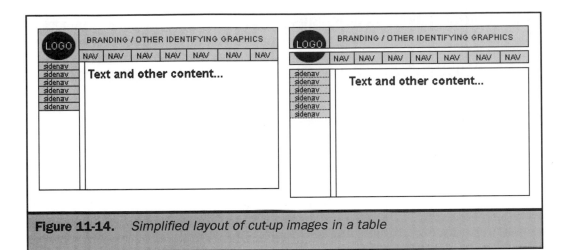

Figure 11-14.   *Simplified layout of cut-up images in a table*

work reasonably well with such a grid-based layout, designers sometimes take this approach even farther to create unusual image alignments. What this approach overlooks is the simple fact that you can stack tables, much like a layer cake, and achieve the same effect. The layout on the right simulates what this page would look like if you made three tables and cut the logo image in half. Now there's no need to mess around with **ROWSPAN**. Just make sure the two halves are the same width, and apply the appropriate **WIDTH** value to both the images and the table cells. For the second table from the top, be certain that the width of the seven navigation buttons adds up to the width of the longer branding image in the top table, and again make sure that width values all add up within the second table as well, as shown here.

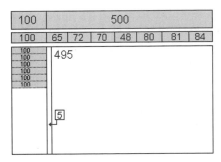

Rule: when creating layouts with cut-up images and tables, make sure that WIDTH and HEIGHT values for images and table cells always add up appropriately.

The dotted lines around the sidenav images in table 3 of the right-hand layout indicate that they are all in one table cell now. With that table cell's vertical alignment set to **VALIGN="TOP"** and a single **
** tag placed after each image, these buttons will "stick" to the top of the cell. The rest of that cell can be filled in with another image, or, even more simply, an appropriate background color set with the table cell's **BGCOLOR** attribute. Make sure to set **VALIGN="TOP"** for the text/content table cell as well.

*Always make sure that the closing **</TD>** tags in graphics/table layouts are closed up against the final HTML element in each cell; otherwise, some browsers may throw in an extra return and destroy the layout.*

After double-checking that everything adds up correctly, make sure that the tables have their **CELLPADDING** and **CELLSPACING** attributes set to zero. This is very important. For example, if you had an image that was 100 pixels wide, and you tried to place it into a **<TD>** that was also 100 pixels wide, no problem. But, if there was cellpadding, which affects the interior space of the **<TD>**, and it was set to 5, you would have to deduct 5 from each side of the **<TD>** and realize that you could only make the image 90 pixels wide without breaking the rest of the table. With the tables' **BORDER** attributes set to zero and no **
** tags or other content between the tables themselves, this page should look like one seamless layout.

> **Rule: For cut-up images and tables to work together properly as layouts, always set the table's CELLPADDING and CELLSPACING values to zero.**

One advantage to this kind of layout is that it can enable designers to better mix graphics-style images with more photographic images. If the logo in the previous examples included a photograph of a lion, for example, that image could be saved as a JPEG, while the graphics text in the buttons could be saved as GIFs—as long as you were careful to make the logo's background match that of the surrounding GIFs, assuming that the layout required this.

Macromedia's FireWorks program is indispensable for this kind of layout, as it has extensive tools for cutting up layouts, matching colors, and optimizing images in the formats best suited to their intent. Macromedia offers online tutorials and trial downloads at http://www.macromedia.com/support/fireworks/.

Vector-Based Art on the Web: Flash

Beyond the formats already discussed—GIF, JPEG, BMP, and PNG—there are quite a few other image formats that can be used on the Web, as long as you have the appropriate plug-in installed. Many of these formats are vector-based. Anyone who has worked with Photoshop and Illustrator, or another vector-based graphics program like Freehand, knows what this means. While Photoshop produces images like GIF and JPEG that are essentially comprised of a mosaic of pixels, vector-based images use mathematically defined curves (Bézier curves, to get technical) to define images. Computers read this mathematical information and create the image on the monitor screen. A 100 × 100 pixel square with a 2-pixel red border would be defined mathematically, not by a collection of colored dots. If a Web browser could process images in this fashion, it would be feasible to scale images effectively on the Web; if you changed the part of the equation defining the height and width of the square, the browser could increase its size without impacting any other aspect of the image, removing the distortion problems you get if you resize a GIF or JPEG using HTML. Unfortunately, browsers do not support this image type, and designers are dependent upon plug-ins to display vector-based formats.

One vector-based image format is becoming relatively common on the Web: Macromedia's Flash, which is primarily used to create animations. Needless to say, this requires the Flash plug-in, but the end result is often worth it. A Flash animation (file extension .swf) is superior to an animated GIF in several ways. First, it can contain a great deal more information than a GIF, allowing more sophisticated and complex effects. The image is scalable and can expand or contract to fit a relative display region, thus becoming larger on top-of-the-line monitors, yet scale down to fit reasonably comfortably within low-end displays. The crowning advantage is that .swf files can be smaller in kilobyte size than a comparable GIF animation—particularly in larger, more detailed images. If you view the animation at http://www.democompany.com/splashpage.cfm, you can right-click on the image (on a PC) or CTRL-click (on a Mac), and then select a dialog that will let you zoom in and examine its details.

In the rush to create compact animations for the Web, most people have overlooked one obvious application of Flash: it can also be used to create scalable still images like the one at www.webdesignref.com/Chapter11/designdemos/flash.htm. With a little browser sensing, it might be possible to set a Flash image to take up a certain percentage of available screen space, as well as other effects along this line. In general, still images in Flash are usually not smaller when compared to their GIF counterparts, but imagine if you wanted to display a detailed technical diagram. With the GIF, you would have to make it large enough to see all the details, thus increasing the file size significantly as well as taking up a lot of physical space. With a Flash image, you could direct the user to zoom in and be able to see the minute details much clearer in a smaller amount of physical space, and with a smaller file size.

The great drawback is that not all users have the properly installed plug-in that will enable them to view your creation. Any time you rely on a user-installed plug-in for Web site display, you are asking for trouble. A certain portion of your audience will not have the plug-in at all, another portion will have an outdated version and not want to upgrade (perhaps due to a bad installation experience), another portion will have the latest version but will have installed it improperly or have a conflict between the plug-in and another program on their system, and so on. You should be willing to experiment with new technologies, but be aware that you may be opening yourself up for user complaints that your site is "broken," or that you may be turning away users because they do not use that technology. Never use technologies like Flash in mission-critical portions of your site, such as basic navigation.

Other, generally more specialized Web sites may also use other vector-based formats, which will require appropriate plug-ins. AutoCAD, the layered, vector-based program used to create architectural renderings, can be used on the Web—but file sizes are considerable, so this remains largely limited to serious architecture-oriented Web sites. Illustrator, Freehand, and fractal images *can* be used on the Web, but between additional software requirements on the user's end and file-size considerations, it's not very practical to consider any of these except in very specific circumstances focused on a very specific group of users—and certainly not on the Web at large.

Background Images

This chapter has already discussed how to set background colors for various HTML elements such as **<BODY>** and **<TABLE>**. It is also possible to change the background of a Web document by applying a background image to the **<BODY>** tag. Background images can also be applied, with varying measures of success, to some other elements. And, as might be expected, CSS can be used to expand these possibilities in various ways. The key to background images is to test them thoroughly and to anticipate a variety of rendering problems. Used with care and forethought, background images can greatly enhance your site.

Document-Wide Backgrounds

To set a background image for a Web page, simply use the **BACKGROUND** attribute with the **<BODY>** tag, and set the value just as you would with **<IMG SRC>**:

```
<BODY BACKGROUND="images/background.gif">
```

The image used must be a GIF or a JPEG file. Internet Explorer also supports bitmap files (.bmp), but this is not really a viable option unless users will be limited to a Microsoft-exclusive environment. Images accessed in this fashion repeat, or *tile*, in the background of a Web page. This can make or break a Web page design. Imagine someone who used the **BACKGROUND** attribute to place a 200 × 300 pixel JPEG of a favorite dog on his or her home page. The dog's image would repeat, both vertically and horizontally, in the background of the page. This would make the dog's owner very happy—and make the page very difficult to read. Figure 11-15 shows an example of a bothersome repeating background.

In general, complex background images tend to be a poor design decision. Taking the subtle approach can backfire as well. Some users attempt to create a light background like a texture or watermark thinking that, like paper, it will have a sophisticated effect. The problem with this is that under many monitors, the image may be difficult to make out at all, or the texture may even blur the text on top of it slightly. Just like setting background colors, the most important consideration is the

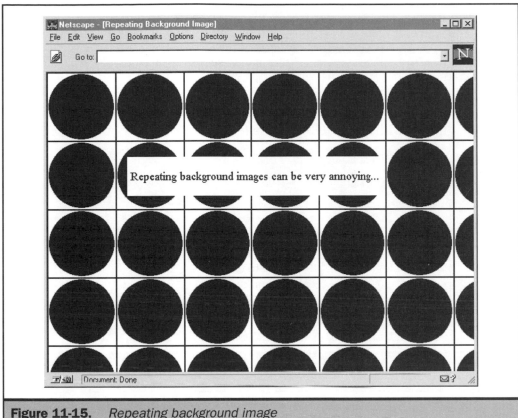

Figure 11-15.   *Repeating background image*

degree of contrast. Always attempt to keep the foreground and background at a high level of contrast so that users can read the information. Unless you are absolutely certain the background image will not interfere with text readability, don't use it.

If a background is desired, image-manipulation programs such as Photoshop can be used to create seamless background tiles that are more pleasing to the eye and show no seam. Figure 11-16 demonstrates the idea of a repeating background tile.

The best use of the background tile, however, is to enhance page layout by framing rather than filling the text and content display area. A single GIF 5 pixels high and 1,200 pixels wide could be used to create a useful page layout. The first 200 horizontal pixels of the GIF could be black, while the rest could be white. Assuming 1,200 pixels as the maximum width of a browser, this tile would only repeat vertically, thus creating the illusion of a two-tone background. This has become a very common use of a background image on the Web. Many sites use the left-hand column for navigation buttons, while the remaining area is used for text, as shown in Figure 11-17.

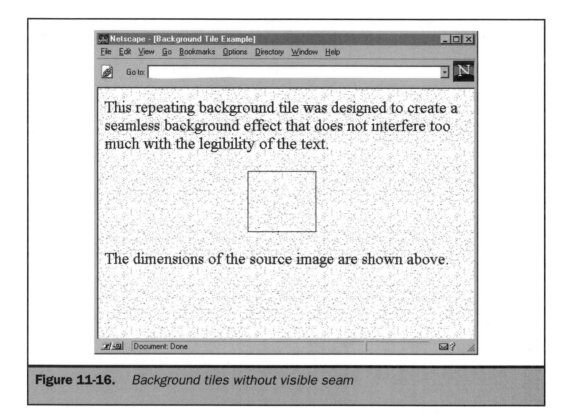

Figure 11-16.   *Background tiles without visible seam*

However, to guarantee that content appears on top of the appropriate section of the background image, you may be forced to use tables.

Intelligent use of the background image combined with creative table layouts can deliver good-looking pages with little performance cost. Depending upon navigational needs, the fundamental look and feel for an entire site can be created with a dozen images with a cumulative image weight of less than 50KB. This will not be the most elaborate site ever seen, but may be just the ticket for a simple intranet or extranet design.

Be very careful when segmenting the screen using a background tile. For example, many people are tempted to create page layout with vertical sectioning, as shown in Figure 11-18.

However, there is a problem with this layout. Won't the black bar repeat? Quite possibly, because the length of the content is hard to determine. Viewers may find the black bar repeating over and over, with content being lost wherever the black strip repeats. A solution might be to make the background tile very tall. However, this not only increases file size, but begs a question of how tall is tall enough? Because content

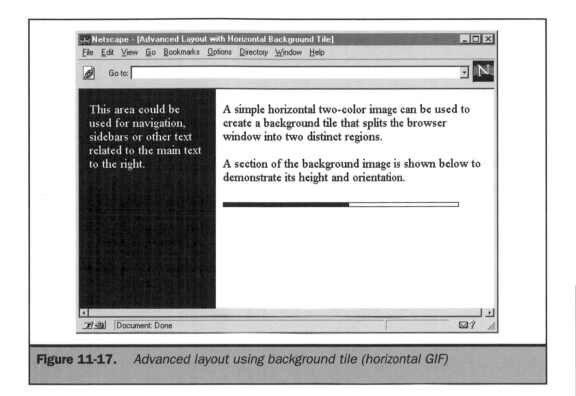

Figure 11-17. *Advanced layout using background tile (horizontal GIF)*

may vary from page to page and increase or decrease over time, determining the width is next to impossible. A left-oriented sidebar tile is not affected by the same type of constraints, given that pages generally do not scroll left to right, and monitor sizes tend to not exceed 1,200 pixels. There are options using style sheets, discussed below, that get around certain of these constraints.

You might be tempted to minimize the file size of your background tile in order to reduce download time. Sometimes you will encounter a situation where you can see a screen "paint" the background image. The cause of this is the designer made the background image a single pixel tall, causing the background to tile as many times as the screen is high in pixels. With a slow video card, this may produce an annoying sweeping effect as the image fills in, pixel by pixel, down the screen. To avoid the background-painting problem, balance physical file size and download size. If colors are kept to a minimum, there is no harm in making the image 20 or 30 pixels high. It will still be only a few kilobytes in size and will not incur any significant download penalty.

> **Suggestion: Do not make a background tile a very small height or width (e.g. 1-2 pixels) as an annoying monitor flashing effect may result.**

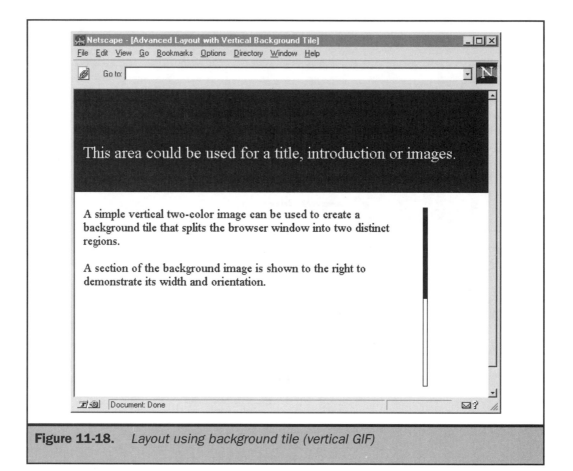

Figure 11-18.   *Layout using background tile (vertical GIF)*

CSS and Backgrounds

CSS provides additional methods to apply background to Web pages. Rather than use the **BGCOLOR** attribute to set a light-blue background to a page, you could use the following:

```
<BODY STYLE="background-color: #99CCFF">
```

You could also apply this style to **<BODY>** in the head of the document. Using CSS for background colors for other elements has been discussed earlier in this chapter; it can also be used to apply colors to table elements. Instead of

```
<TD BGCOLOR="silver">...content...</TD>
```

you could use

```
<TD STYLE="background-color: silver">...content...</TD>
```

or set this in the head of the document:

```
TD { background-color: silver;}
```

By setting a style in a style sheet, you then empower yourself to employ that style wherever you can apply CSS operations. As discussed throughout the book, CSS is a powerful tool in a Web designer's tool belt.

LIMIT TILING WITH STYLE SHEETS The real benefit of using CSS with background, however, is to limit tiling of background images. Misbehaving background tiles can ruin an otherwise excellent design. For example, what if you wished to use one large image in the background of a page? Using only regular HTML, you would have to create a maximum estimated size image, and hope that no one would view it on a larger monitor or with a larger browser-window size than you had estimated. There is no way to guarantee that no one would use a larger monitor, and you would risk ruining the viewing experience of users with smaller monitors.

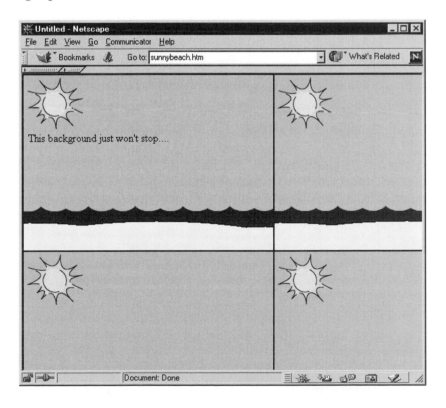

Luckily, CSS provides a way to limit background tiling in Web pages:

```
<BODY BGCOLOR="#99CCFF"
      STYLE="background: #99CCFF url(sunnybeach.gif) no-repeat">
```

The background will only appear once.

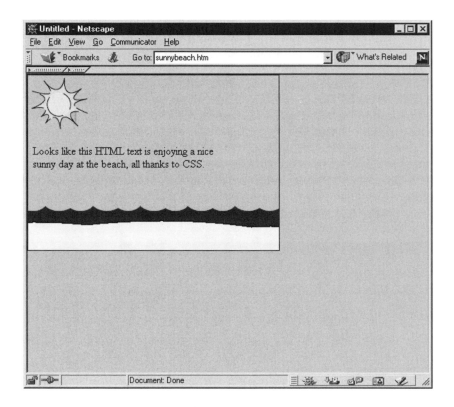

Other values you can use instead of **no-repeat** are **repeat-x** and **repeat-y**, to limit tiling to one axis only.

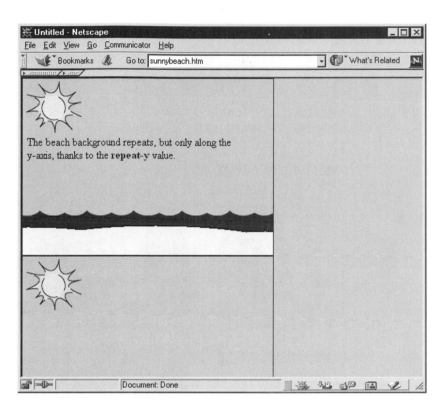

Needless to say, this will only work in CSS-compliant browsers. If you want the background image to display in older browsers, even though it will repeat, be sure to include it using the **BACKGROUND** attribute as well:

```
<BODY BGCOLOR="#99CCFF" BACKGROUND="images/sunnybeach.gif"
 STYLE="background: #99CCFF url(images/sunnybeach.gif) no-repeat">
```

One thing to note about using these types of background treatments, however, is that if the background doesn't move, it means that your content, including foreground images, will scroll over the background image. It may be necessary to make all foreground images transparent in order to maintain the effect that you are aiming for with your design.

Background Images in Tables

Using simple HTML, it is possible to apply background images to tables as well. Defining a table with the code

```
<TABLE WIDTH="220" BORDER="1" CELLPADDING="0" CELLSPACING="0"
      BACKGROUND="smalltabletile.gif">
.... other table elements...
</TABLE>
```

would place a repeating background tile behind the table, as shown here.

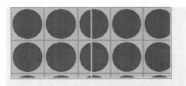

Internet Explorer   **Netscape**

The table on the left, displayed in Internet Explorer, renders the tile in a repeating background behind the entire table. The table on the right, displayed in Netscape, applies the background to each separate table cell. This is a radical cross-browser split that makes this approach impractical.

The same attribute can be applied to table rows (**<TR>**), but this will not display in Internet Explorer, and Netscape, as above, applies the tile to each cell in the row, not the row as a whole.

The only practical way to use backgrounds with tables is with table cells, as in this code:

```
<TABLE WIDTH="220" BORDER="1" CELLPADDING="0" CELLSPACING="0">
<TR>
<TD WIDTH="110" BACKGROUND="bigtabletile.gif"> <TD>
<TD WIDTH="110" BACKGROUND="smalltabletile.gif"> </TD>
</TR>
</TABLE>
```

As you can see here, this doesn't look too great.

Use the **HEIGHT** attribute in the table cell with the large title, and adjust the **WIDTH** attribute to make the cell match the dimensions of the tile, like this:

```
<TABLE WIDTH="220" BORDER="0" CELLPADDING="0" CELLSPACING="0">
<TR>
<TD BACKGROUND="bigtabletile.gif" HEIGHT="100" WIDTH="100"
ALIGN="CENTER"><B>HELLO!</B></TD>
<TD WIDTH="120" BACKGROUND="smalltabletile.gif"> </TD>
</TR>
</TABLE>
```

This will produce the following renderings in Internet Explorer 5 and Netscape 4. Older browsers like Netscape 3 will not support the background image at all.

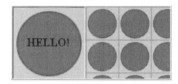

While this can be used for some nice effects, it is somewhat unwieldy, particularly if the user has their font settings set high.

Once again, this is a situation that can be better controlled through the use of CSS.

CSS and Background Images in Tables

Consider the large-font problem shown above. CSS can be used to limit the tiling of a table-cell background:

```
<TD HEIGHT="100" WIDTH="100" ALIGN="CENTER"
    STYLE="background: url(smalltabletile.gif) no-repeat">
```

Of course, that doesn't help with the font problem.

This can also be adjusted with CSS:

```
<TABLE WIDTH="220" BORDER="0" CELLPADDING="0" CELLSPACING="0">
<TR>
<TD HEIGHT="100" WIDTH="100" ALIGN="CENTER"
STYLE="background: url(bigtabletile.gif) no-repeat">
<FONT FACE="Arial" STYLE="font-size:
16px"><B>HELLO!</B></FONT></TD>
<TD WIDTH="120" BACKGROUND="smalltabletile.gif"> </TD>
</TR>
</TABLE>
```

Setting the font size with pixel values is advisable in a situation like this, since it circumvents the user increasing their browser's font size and breaking the table.

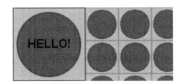

Online: For more examples of using CSS with table layout, visit www.webdesignref.com/chapter11/css/tables.htm.

CSS and Background Images for Other HTML Elements

While the basics have already been covered, bear in mind that CSS can also be used to apply background images to other HTML elements. For example,

```
<P STYLE="padding: 5px; background: url(spottedtile.gif)">
Talking over<BR>a big old tile<BR>
can sure be<BR>hard to read...</P>
```

will produce the following.

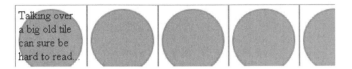

Again, using **no-repeat**, **repeat-x**, or **repeat-y** can control if and how the background repeats. For more demos, visit www.webdesignref.com/chapter11/css/backgrounds.htm.

Using CSS for Back Compatibility

Some older browsers, such as Netscape 2, support font colors but not background color attributes for table cells (**TD**) and headers (**TH**). So, if you wanted to create white text against a black background using tables, you could use a bit of code like this:

```
<TABLE BORDER="1" CELLPADDING="5">
<TR><TD BGCOLOR="#000000">
<FONT SIZE="4" STYLE="color: white">Is this text legible?</FONT>
</TD></TR>
</TABLE>
```

In more recent CSS-compliant browsers, the table cell will have a black background and the text will be white. Under Netscape 2, which does not support **BGCOLOR** for the **<TD>** tag or CSS, text and background will both display as default values. Even Netscape 2 supports this code:

```
<BODY BGCOLOR="#FFFFFF" TEXT="#000000">
```

Unfortunately, while Netscape 3 and Internet Explorer 3 support background color values for table cells, they do not support CSS—so those browsers will render a black table cell with black text, making the text illegible. Of course, you can also apply the table cell's background color with CSS:

```
<TABLE BORDER="1" CELLPADDING="5">
<TR><TD STYLE="background: black">
<FONT SIZE="4" STYLE="color: white">Is this text legible?</FONT>
</TD></TR>
</TABLE>
```

Now this will display the desired white text/black background in CSS-compliant browsers and black text/white background in Netscape 3 and earlier. The problem here is, you lose the effect in Netscape and IE 3 even though they support HTML tags that would make this effect possible in those browsers. This leads to a prickly issue: how far do you want to take backwards compatibility? All the way to Mosaic? Are there enough people out there using Netscape 2 to even make this a viable concern? Possibly not. Remember that no matter how hard you try, you can't create a Web site that 100 percent of Web users can access unless you want to present bare-bones, unformatted text with no graphics or color. Chapter 13 discusses issues of browser profiling that may be useful for dealing with sticky situations such as this.

Summary

To recap, this chapter has examined various issues surrounding the use of colors and images on the Web. Color reproduction on the Web is difficult. Given the range of color support in end-user hardware, designers often focus on the so-called Web-safe set of colors. However, the reality is that even when using only these colors, users may interpret the color differently or the hardware may not display quite the same. Designers should also be aware of the usability concerns related to color. Contrast should be kept high at all times. Images should be used on the Web as well, in spite of anything said by usability curmudgeons. Without imagery, Web sites can become quite boring. However, images should be properly optimized lest download time become a key concern. Choosing the correct file type—either GIF or JPEG—and tuning color and quality is the best way to reduce image file size. New image formats such as PNG promise improved download support and image use for the Web, but so far their use is not suggested. When using images, always be aware of the numerous usage details. For example, improper use of transparency and anti-aliasing can ruin an image, while background tiles are easily ruined when seams can be seen in the tile, or they are made too small or wide. Designers certainly have their hands full with the color and imagery on the Web, and nothing was even said about making something look pleasing. The next chapter will look at the relationship between Web page design and GUI interface design, and what Web designers can and should learn from it.

Chapter 12

Building Interactivity Using GUI Features

A Web site should be regarded as a modified form of a traditional graphical user interface (GUI) driven program. While not all conventions like double-clicking survived the translation to the environment of the Web, many conventions have. It is important for Web designers to understand the traditions of GUI design so as not to utilize GUI features like menus, fill-in fields, and so on in ways that may confuse a user already familiar with how software applications tend to use these items. This chapter will explore various GUI features used on the Web. Special focus will be paid to usability concerns as well as unusual uses of GUI elements on the Web. As the discussion proceeds, never assume that the Web is exactly the same as a GUI-driven software application. Differences do occur; some Web technologies like HTML forms do not yet provide all the interactive elements commonly found in software applications. The next chapter will continue this exploration and show how Web technology will affect design.

Web Sites and Traditional GUIs

It is tempting to simply apply the rules of interface design used to build typical GUI software applications to the Web. Considering that a Web site is at base a form of software, this makes a great deal of sense. However, Web design is not quite standard GUI design. It borrows heavily from GUI design principles, but it has its own conventions as well, as summarized in Table 12-1.

What makes Web sites different from GUI applications? First, consider the delivery and medium of the Web. Web sites generally are delivered incrementally, often a page at a time. Software applications tend to be installed, either after downloading a complete package off the Internet or using a CD-ROM or diskette. The simple fact that the software application is completely installed in most cases makes it much more responsive than a Web-delivered one. However, the benefit of the Web's incremental delivery approach is that the user does not have to actually install anything more than they need. Web sites lack what could be called the "install-uninstall barrier" of a traditional application. With most software, the user has to have the initiative to find, download, or purchase a piece of software and then install it—just to try it out. If the program isn't quite what they are looking for, they may even have to reverse the procedure with an uninstaller. Because of the hassle of installation and removal, users may be hesitant to try something new, and slow to remove a less-than-ideal package. However, Web sites do not have such an install-uninstall barrier. A simple click, and the user is off to another site.

The install-uninstall barrier has interesting ramifications for Web design. Because Web sites do not have this barrier, they often have to perform very well because the user can easily move on to a competing site. Because of this, many sites strive to become "sticky." Sticky sites keep users coming back often by providing a valuable service that is difficult to transfer to another site. Consider why sites offer free email accounts, calendars, and massive customization. It makes users less likely to want to move on, even if the site isn't quite perfect.

Suggestion: Provide a useful service that is difficult to transfer between sites to improve site "stickiness."

Another interesting aspect of software design vs. Web design is the heavy reliance on documentation. Web site designers building public sites generally cannot expect users to read a manual in order to use their site, regardless of whether the manual is provided online in the form of a help section or offline in the form of a printed manual. The function and use of sites must be obvious. Unfortunately, creating such a site can be difficult; there are bound to be aspects or operations of the site that users will not understand, no matter how well the site is designed. Documentation should still be provided. Public sites may provide help in the form of online help pages. Internal Web projects such as intranet or extranet sites may actually provide hardcopy documentation or even hold training classes. However, as with software applications, expecting users to access help documents or read the manual is difficult. Given that users have come to expect Web sites to be obvious to use, it is problematic to rely on documentation to make up for site flaws.

Suggestion: Provide online documentation (or, in some cases, printed documentation), but don't rely on the user accessing it.

The degree of marketing influence on interface design is much greater with Web sites than for most commercial software applications. Given two word-processing programs, it would be somewhat difficult to correctly identify the programs after only a brief inspection. Most software applications only subtly brand with their interface. Rarely do you see software programs with bright hot-pink, oddly shaped buttons; most tend to lay out the screen in about the same way and utilize similar icons. On the Web, however, marketing is often directly integrated into the user interface. In some sense you could say that with a Web site, the package and the application are one and the same. In the case of software, often the branding is done mostly through the box, documentation, and other collateral material: the installation screen, a splash dialog shown on startup, functionality of the program, and subtle interface details in the program. Web sites are more heavy-handed in their integration with marketing demands because they lack many of the outlets for branding beyond the interface, such as documentation or the box.

However, one of the largest differences between GUI design and Web design is that with GUI design there is a lack of recognized groups, such as operating-system vendors, to set a standard. While the World Wide Web Consortium certainly tries to influence how people approach Web design, they do not wield the power of interface standards that Apple or Microsoft has with application developers. The Web lacks recognized standards of interface design. Instead, conventions of design have arisen

GUI Principle	Commentary	Web Principle	Commentary
Metaphors from the real world	Concrete metaphors from the real world should be applied so that users have expectations to apply to the computer environment.	Metaphors from the real world, including GUI metaphors	Given the familiarity people have with GUI systems, the Web variation could be "Metaphors from the real world including existing software metaphors." The window, icon, mouse, and pointer approach is a metaphor of its own for many users. Break with it too much within a Web page and you'll go against a user's expectations of how the site should act.
Direct Manipulation	Users want to feel that they are in control of the computer's activities.	Direct manipulation	This is as true for a Web site as for a software application. The only downside is that direct manipulation may be difficult to sustain in a network delivery environment with relatively slow response times.
See-and-point (instead of remember-and-type)	User interfaces should rely on recognition rather than recall. In practice, make sure to present choices plainly onscreen so a user can simply choose from them.	See-and-point (instead of remember-and-click)	No major difference here, except that we do not have to deal with the downsides of keyboard command interfaces on the Web. Given the amount of sites a user may see, this becomes more important within a space of Web sites as users will probably not be able to memorize many specific details from all the sites they visit.

Table 12-1.   *General Principles of GUI Design Modified for the Web*

GUI Principle	Commentary	Web Principle	Commentary
Consistency	Effective applications are both consistent within themselves and with one another.	Consistency	This applies directly to the Web. Web sites should be consistent internally *and* follow conventions set by other Web sites. The only nuance to this idea on the Web is that a centralized body such as an operating-system vendor is lacking to enforce conformance to conventions.
WYSIWYG (what you see is what you get)	The user gets exactly what they see—no more, no less. Secrets are not kept from the user. A particularly important aspect of this idea early on was to make sure that what is seen onscreen is what shows up on paper when printed.	WYSIWYW *(what you see is what you want)*	For the Web, WYSIWYG should be modified to WYSIWYW (what you see is what you want). Users may like to modify sites to display information they are interested in rather than what is set out for them. In a diverse environment like the Web, with many ways to access information (including cell phone, PDA, and computing systems of all shapes and sizes), the idea of WYSIWYG doesn't work well. The printing aspect may still be somewhat important, but recall the medium-of-consumption discussion in Chapter 3 and consider that for many users, exact printing may be less important than appropriate printing. Notice all the print versions vs. Web version pages that exist in content-rich sites.

Table 12-1. *General Principles of GUI Design Modified for the Web* (continued)

ELEMENTS OF PAGE DESIGN

GUI Principle	Commentary	Web Principle	Commentary
User control	The user, not the computer, initiates and controls all actions.	Balance of control	Addressing the control issue presented in Chapter 3, control should be given to the user, but as this rule was actually applied, the appearance of control again is more the issue. Users should be guided in many situations, depending on the purpose of the site.
Feedback and dialog	Keep the user engaged and provide plenty of feedback, such as messages and status indicators, to let a user know what is going on.	Feedback and dialog	On the Web, this is more important than ever, especially considering the responsiveness problem of the Web. Sites should provide more feedback to the user.
Forgiveness	Users will make mistakes, so we have to forgive them and allow them to undo things or keep them from doing things that could be very damaging.	Forgiveness	This rule certainly applies to Web sites. Not every site provides adequate confirmation of important actions, such as order placement, that are difficult to undo. As sites becomes more software-like, this rule will become more and more important.
Perceived stability	Users will find comfort in a computer environment that remains familiar rather than changing randomly.	Perceived stability	This rule is well applied in GUI applications. Notice that menus don't jump around the screen or change their ordering. Unfortunately, Web sites more often than not do not give an appearance of stability and may change button style, position, or even choices almost arbitrarily. Sites could be improved dramatically just by strict conformance to this principle.

Table 12-1.   *General Principles of GUI Design Modified for the Web* (continued)

GUI Principle	Commentary	Web Principle	Commentary
Aesthetic integrity	An interface should be clear and pleasing. Design should be consistent, but objects that are different should be distinctly different.	Aesthetic integrity	For the Web, this is very important. Users will judge sites severely if they have poor appearances.
		Quality content	Web sites are heavily geared towards content. Web sites should provide quality content that is well written, provides the appropriate level of detail, is clear and easy to comprehend. and is, above all, accurate.
		Time sensitive	Web sites need to be sensitive to time. Time of delivery is the most important aspect of sites. Users will not stand for inefficient delivery. Timeliness of content and interface may also be important as well. Sites tend not to be as static as traditional software.

Table 12-1. *General Principles of GUI Design Modified for the Web* (continued)

online, partially influenced by the innovations of browser vendors and individual site creators, as well as from previous GUI design ideas. Understanding GUI design conventions is important for Web designers, as many of them can be quickly applied to Web sites.

GUI Design Implications

Graphical interface design has nearly 20 years of commercial experience. Many of the ideas of Web design follow directly from early findings from Xerox, Apple, and (later) Microsoft. Apple, in particular, has been very influential in the field of interface design.

In fact, the Macintosh operating system was developed with ten interface principles in mind, most of which relate directly to the usability ideas of Chapter 3. Given the extreme importance of these principles in shaping modern interface design, it is interesting to see how they apply to the Web. As it turns out, most hold up quite well. Designers should try to apply these principles to the Web.

However, some of the rules should be modified with the Web in mind, and a couple of new rules ought to be added given the different medium of the Web. Remember that network and content aspects of the Web are different than traditional software. Table 12-1 presents the original Apple interface design principles, along with commentary and possible modification for use on the Web.

While the previous discussion shows just how much GUI conventions influence Web conventions, Web conventions are still emerging, and many designers seem completely oblivious to useful GUI design ideas. The rest of the chapter will present the various interface features used in interactive design and explain how they are used on the Web. Careful attention will be paid to features that are used slightly differently than within traditional software applications.

Windows

The first interface component to consider is the window. All Web pages are displayed in a window—the browser window. The browser window serves as the frame for a page. Without this framing device, site design may often look strange, as shown in Figure 12-1.

The exact look of the browser window varies in look from browser to browser. In some situations, the browser window may not be terribly evident. WebTV provides few framing features. Many embedded browsers, such as cellular-phone browsers, also lack such obvious framing features. A textual browser like Lynx running from a UNIX prompt also does not provide much framing. Figure 12-2 shows the range of framing effects for a browser.

It is even possible now to customize the look of browsers. NeoPlanet (www.neoplanet.com) and HotBar (www.hotbar.com) both provide methods to provide custom toolbar backgrounds and designs, or *skins*, for a browser, as shown in Figure 12-3.

Creating New Windows

It is possible to customize windows in HTML and JavaScript. The simplest way to create a new window is using the **TARGET** attribute modification of the anchor element. For example,

```
<A HREF="http://www.democompany.com" TARGET="_blank">Open window</A>
```

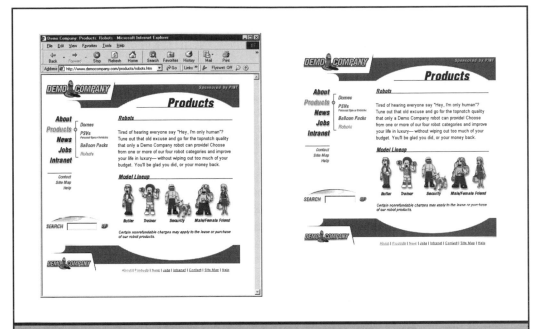

Figure 12-1. *The browser window frames a Web page*

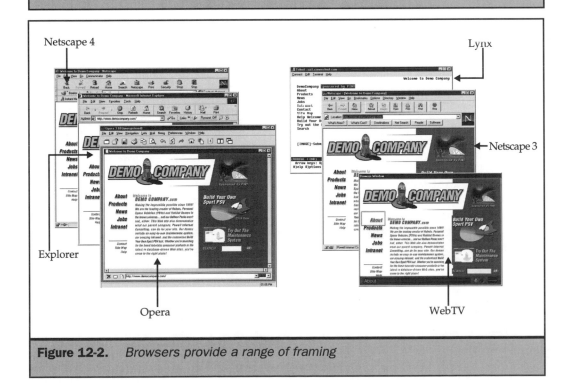

Figure 12-2. *Browsers provide a range of framing*

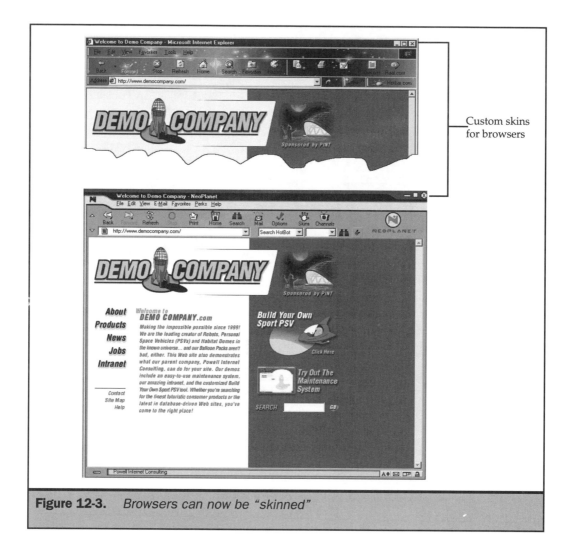

Custom skins
for browsers

Figure 12-3. *Browsers can now be "skinned"*

would open a new browser window with the DemoCompany site in it. Using
JavaScript, it is possible to modify the window that is opened. The window can be
sized, and the particular buttons shown can be limited as well. All of the buttons,
fields, scrollbars, and other functional, non-content portions of the browser are often
called *chrome*; the code shown here opens up the DemoCompany site in a chromeless
window and sizes it to 500×600 pixels.

```
<!DOCTYPE HTML PUBLIC "-//W3C//DTD HTML 4.0 Transitional//EN">
<HTML>
<HEAD>
```

```
<TITLE>Window Opener</TITLE>
</HEAD>
<BODY>

<A HREF="http://www.democompany.com"
onClick="newwindow=window.open('http://www.democompany.com',
'democompany','width=600,height=500'); return false">
Open window</A>

</BODY>
</HTML>
```

Note *It is possible, using JavaScript, to turn on some buttons, status bars, and so on. It isn't an all-or-nothing situation when creating new windows. See JavaScript documentation on the **window.open()** method for specific syntax on allowing buttons.*

Figure 12-4 shows the rendering of the chromeless window. Notice in the figure that much of the control has been taken away from the user. They aren't sure where they are since the URL is hidden, browser buttons they may have come to rely on have been hidden, and even scrolling the page seems difficult. It should be evident that browsing a site within this type of window might be frustrating for some users—particularly novices. Unfortunately, some designers use this technique to create a fixed page size so they don't have to worry about their design stretching to fit a browser window. While the framing effect of the perfectly sized chromeless window might improve the look, the usability trade-offs are significant. Designers are warned not to use this technique unless absolutely necessary. Secondary windows that present a short message such as an alert can be significantly modified, but the primary window the user will use to navigate your site should not be modified in most situations.

Suggestion: Avoid modification of the appearance of the user's primary browser window.

When opening new windows, you have to be careful that the window is visible to the user. Occasionally, it may move out of the way or be positioned behind other windows if it is automatically lowered. In order to combat these problems, you may wish to position and raise created windows. To set the position in Netscape 4 and beyond, set the **screenX** and **screenY** parameters when creating the window. For Internet Explorer 4 and beyond, set the **top** and **left** parameters. Simply focusing the created window using its **focus()** method should bring it back to the top. The following code shows how this would be accomplished using a link to trigger the new window:

```
<!DOCTYPE HTML PUBLIC "-//W3C//DTD HTML 4.0 Transitional//EN">
<HTML>
<HEAD>
```

```
<TITLE>Window Opener 2</TITLE>
</HEAD>
<BODY>

<A HREF="http://www.democompany.com"
onClick="newwindow=window.open('http://www.democompany.com',
'democompany','width=600,height=500,screenX=100,screenY=100,
top=100,left=100'); newwindow.focus(); return false">
Open window</A>

</BODY>
</HTML>
```

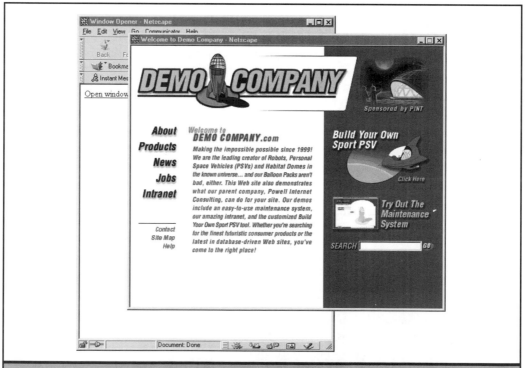

Figure 12-4. A chromeless window lacks expected surrounding browser "chrome" and buttons

Full-Screen Windows

Creating a window that fills up the screen and even removes browser chrome is possible in many browsers. It is possible under 4.*x* generation browsers and beyond to figure out the current screen size and then create a new window that fits most or all the available area. In the case of Netscape, you may have difficulty covering the entire window because of the way the height and width of the screen are calculated. However, the script presented here should work to fill up the screen in both browsers:

```
<SCRIPT LANGUAGE="JavaScript1.2">
<!--
newwindow=window.open('http://www.democompany.com','main','height='
+screen.height-2+',width='+screen.width-2+',outerHeight=' +
screen.availHeight + ',outerWidth=' + screen.availWidth+'screenX=0,
screenY=0,left-0,top=0,resizable=no');
//-->
</SCRIPT>
```

The previous "poor man's" script does keep the browser chrome and may not quite fill up the window. It is possible under 4.*x*-generation browser to go into a full-screen mode that completely fills the screen. Using Internet Explorer, it is quite easy using a JavaScript statement like the following:

```
Newindow=window.open('http://www.democompany.com', 'main',
'fullscreen=yes');
```

However, Netscape needs a much more complicated script and will even prompt the user if a security privilege should be granted to go full screen. A script that works in both browsers is shown here:

```
<SCRIPT LANGUAGE="JavaScript1.2">
<!--
if (document.layers) {
 netscape.security.PrivilegeManager.enablePrivilege('UniversalBrowserWrite');
 window.open('http://www.democompany.com','newwin','titlebar=no,width=' +
 window.screen.availWidth+',height='+window.screen.availWidth+',screenX=0,
screenY=0')
 }
 else if (document.all) {
    window.open('http://www.democompany.com', 'newwin', 'fullscreen=yes');
 }
//-->
</SCRIPT>
```

It is important to note that many users will not know how to get out of full-screen mode. The key combination ALT-F4 should do the trick on a Windows system. However, users may not know this, so you should provide a close button or instructions on how to get out of full-screen mode.

> **Rule: When using full-screen window, inform the user how to exit or provide a close button.**

While some may dislike Netscape's prompt of the user, it is probably a good idea not to force a full screen. Consider that users may want to keep another window open while they browse your site, or copy content from your site into another document. Forcing full screen takes their options away.

> **Suggestion: Do not go full screen without asking the user first.**

Modal Windows

Beyond going full screen, it also is possible to create so-called modal windows. A *modal window* is one that does not allow the user to use other windows within the browser until the window is closed. Users often encounter modal windows in the form of alert windows providing important information to the user. It is possible, with some careful scripting, to create a generic modal window; however, this is not a good idea unless you are simply creating a visual replacement for an alert, confirm, or prompt window. A brief discussion of how to create such windows will be presented later in the following sections. However, do not create modal windows that aren't prompting the user for action or data, or alerting them to important system messages, as it takes too much control away from the user.

> **Rule: Do not create general modal windows. Reserve modality for alerts, prompts, and confirmation windows.**

Subwindows

Subwindows are secondary windows that are presented to a user to allow them to perform a task on, or inform them about, what's going on in the primary browser window. From GUI parlance, these windows are generally called dialog boxes since they are used to carry on a dialog with a user. A common use of a dialog box on the Web is to alert users about errors made during form fill-out, to warn them about irreversible actions such as deleting content or making a payment, and to collect small bits of information from them such as login or password information. Dialog boxes can contain just about any amount of information and may be customized to look a particular way. However, in the case of most Web sites, dialogs are created using simple JavaScript and tend to have a standard look and feel unless the designer has gone specifically out of their way to customize their presentation.

Alerts

In a GUI application, an *alert box* is a small dialog box used to present an important message to the user. Often, alerts are used to inform users of errors made—particularly during form fill-out. Alerts can be created directly in JavaScript using the **alert()** method of the window object. For example, consider the following markup:

```
<FORM>
<INPUT TYPE="button" VALUE="Press Me"
onClick="window.alert('Red Alert!')">
</FORM>
```

Pressing the form button creates a browser modal dialog with a short message saying "Red Alert!" in a JavaScript-capable browser. The alert usually contains a special icon, a message indicating that it is the browser issuing the alert and not some other application on the user's system, and an OK button used to dismissed or close the dialog. However, the specific rendering of the alert box varies fairly significantly from browser to browser. Figure 12-5 shows a variety of renderings for the alert.

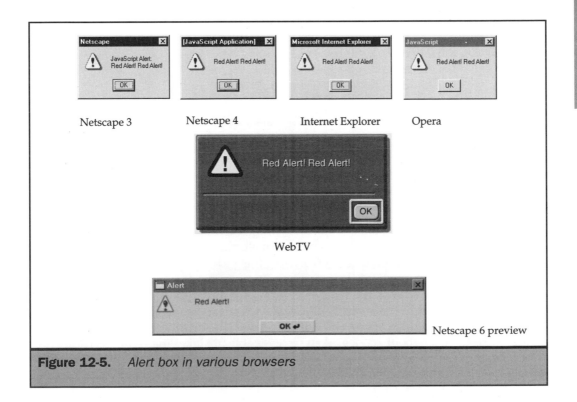

Figure 12-5.   *Alert box in various browsers*

It is important to consider the modal nature of an alert message. Recall that a modal window is one that blocks action within the application. In the case of the alert, the user must dismiss the dialog in the window before continuing on in the current browser window, though in many modern operating systems they can switch to another application before closing the alert. A system modal dialog would be one that blocks all action on the user's system until dismissed. In the 4.x and early 5.x generation browsers, it is impossible to create system modal dialogs from JavaScript. Hopefully this will continue to be the case, as system modal dialogs can be very annoying to users and should only be used for very important system-level messages. However, do not create modal windows that aren't prompting the user for action or data, or alerting them to important system messages, as it takes too much control away from the user. Avoid welcoming people to your site or providing noncritical information to the user by using an alert.

Suggestion: Use alerts to inform the user of important issues, not general information.

Custom Alerts

The look and feel of JavaScript-generated alert boxes usually leave something to be desired. The size and style of the dialogs is not easily modified using the basic **window.alert()** JavaScript method. However, it is possible to create custom alert dialogs—complete with their look and feel and buttons. For example, consider the custom alert shown here.

To create an alert of this style requires creating a custom piece of JavaScript that creates a special modal window that acts like an alert complete with an OK button to dismiss the dialog. However, before presenting this technique, consider when custom alerts should really be used. While it may be nice to create alerts that fit with the marketing aspects of a site, it may be more important not just to expand on the meaning of the alerts. In traditional GUI design, there are three forms of common alerts: informational alerts, which provide important information; warning alerts, which warn the user about actions taken or reversible mistakes made; and error alerts, which present very important information such as a serious error or failure. The typical icons for each of these dialogs are shown in Figure 12-6.

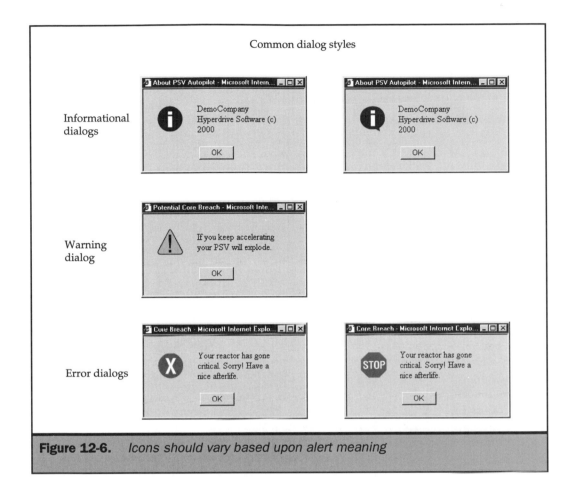

Common dialog styles

Figure 12-6. *Icons should vary based upon alert meaning*

A custom alert script to present informational, warning, and error alerts is presented here:

```
<!DOCTYPE HTML PUBLIC "-//W3C//DTD HTML 4.0 Transitional//EN">
<HTML>
<HEAD>
<TITLE>Custom Alerts</TITLE>
<SCRIPT>
<!--
function customAlert(alerttype, title, msg)
{
var icon;
```

```
if (alerttype == "error")
 icon = "icons/stop.gif";
else if (alerttype == "info")
 icon = "icons/info.gif";
 else
 icon = "icons/exclaim.gif";

newalert = window.open("", "newalert", "width=300,height=150,modal=yes");

newalert.document.write('<!DOCTYPE HTML PUBLIC "-//W3C//DTD HTML 4.0
 Transitional//EN">');
newalert.document.write('<HTML>');
newalert.document.write('<HEAD>');
newalert.document.write('<TITLE>'+title+'</title>');
newalert.document.write('</HEAD>');
newalert.document.write('<BODY BGCOLOR="#CCCCCC" onblur="self.focus()">');
newalert.document.write('<TABLE CELLPADDING="10">');
newalert.document.write('<TR>');
newalert.document.write('<TD WIDTH="50">');
newalert.document.write('<img src='+icon+' width="50" height="50"
border="0" alt="" align="left">');
newalert.document.write('</TD>');
newalert.document.write('<TD WIDTH="150">');
newalert.document.write(msg);
newalert.document.write('</TD></TR><TR>');
newalert.document.write('<TD ALIGN="CENTER" COLSPAN="2">');
newalert.document.write('<FORM><INPUT TYPE="BUTTON"
VALUE="   OK   " onClick="window.close()">');
newalert.document.write('</FORM></TD></TABLE>');
newalert.document.write('</BODY></HTML>');
newalert.focus();
}
// -->
</SCRIPT>
</HEAD>
<BODY BGCOLOR="#CCCCCC">

<FORM>
<INPUT TYPE="button" VALUE="Info Dialog"
onClick="customAlert('info','Core Breach',
'DemoCompany Hyperdrive Software (c) 2000')">
```

```
<INPUT TYPE="button" VALUE="Warning Dialog"
onClick="customAlert('warn','Potential Core Breach',
'If you keep accelerating your PSV will explode.')">

<INPUT TYPE="button" VALUE="Error Dialog"
onClick="customAlert('error','Core Breach',
'Your reactor has gone critical. Sorry! Have a nice afterlife.')">
</FORM>
</BODY>
</HTML>
```

Online: http://www.webdesignref.com/chapter12/customalerts.htm.

Note that the scripts presented here assume the user has the images locally for each type of dialogs. These icons can easily be saved from the working example online. Also note that the example does not create a modal alert dialog under Internet Explorer. Internet Explorer 5 and beyond support a method, **window.showModalDialog()**, that can be utilized to create that type of display. A cross-browser version that supports modal dialogs in browsers is somewhat long and involved, and will not be listed here. It can be found online at http://www.webdesignref.com/chapter12/modalalerts.htm.

Confirms

In a GUI application, a confirm dialog box is presented when a confirmation is required before performing some task. The confirm is often user as an "are you sure?" question for the user, and it is usually presented before the user performs some task that may not be easily reversible such as deleting a file or placing an order. Confirmation dialogs can be created directly in JavaScript using the **confirm()** method of the window object. For example, consider the following markup:

```
<FORM>
<INPUT TYPE="button" VALUE="Press Me"
onClick="window.confirm('Do you really want to blow up the ship?')">
</FORM>
```

The **confirm()** JavaScript method creates a browser modal dialog with a short message asking the user a simple question and allowing them to press an OK or cancel button in response to the question. Like the alert dialog, the specific rendering of a confirmation dialog varies from browser to browser. Figure 12-7 shows a variety of renderings of confirm dialogs generated from JavaScript.

The use of confirms should be limited to those situations where you want to warn the user of an action they are about to take or to have them answer a simple question.

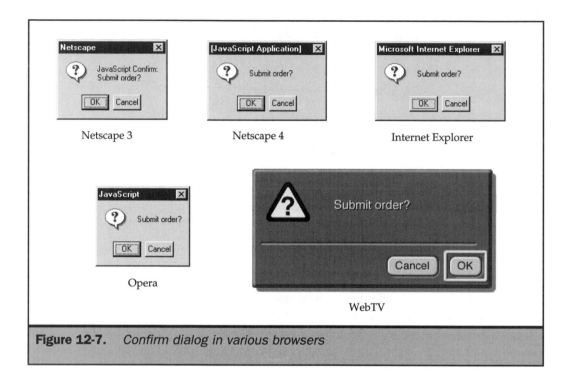

Figure 12-7.   *Confirm dialog in various browsers*

Typical uses of a confirm dialog would be to ask the user if the contents of a form should be submitted for processing or an irreversible task such as deleting an online account should be allowed to take place.

> **Suggestion: Use a confirmation dialog to verify the execution of an irreversible or important task such as form submission.**

When asking confirmation questions, consider the formation of the question carefully since the standard JavaScript confirmation dialog buttons are labeled OK and CANCEL. Consider using simple yes/no questions like "Delete the file?".

Custom Confirm Dialogs

Like alert dialogs, the look and feel of JavaScript-generated confirmation dialogs may leave something to be desired. The size, style, and buttons cannot be modified using the basic **window.confirm()** JavaScript method. As with alerts, it is, of course, possible to create custom confirm dialogs that fit with the look and feel of a site similar to the one shown here.

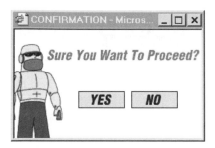

However, besides controlling the look and feel of the window, designers may be encouraged to provide different icons and button text for confirm dialogs, depending on the type of confirmation. A custom confirmation dialog script could be created similar to the one presented for alerts. An example of a custom confirm script can be found online at http://www.webdesignref.com/chapter12/customconfirm.htm.

Prompts

A prompt dialog box is presented when a small amount of information is needed from the user to perform some task. Usually, a prompt dialog is used to collect a single line of information in answer to some question. For example, the user may be prompted to enter a special offer code. Prompt dialogs can be created directly in JavaScript using the **prompt()** method of the window object. For example, consider the following markup:

```
<FORM NAME="testform">
Answer: <INPUT TYPE="text" VALUE="" NAME="favcolor" SIZE="20">
<INPUT TYPE="button" VALUE="Ask Me"
onClick="document.testform.favcolor.value=window.prompt
('What is your favorite color?',' ')">
</FORM>
```

The **prompt()** JavaScript method creates a browser modal dialog with a short message asking the user a simple question. A default answer can also be provided. When prompted, the user can press the OK button when done or the cancel button to not respond. Like the alert and confirmation dialogs, the specific rendering of a confirmation dialog varies from browser to browser. Figure 12-8 shows a variety of renderings of prompt dialogs generated from JavaScript.

The use of prompts should be limited to those situations where you want to collect a single line of text—usually a short answer to a simple question. Typically, the prompt dialog is used to ask the user for their name, or for a value to put in a form field that wasn't filled in.

Suggestion: Use prompt dialogs only to ask a user to provide a short word or numeric answer to a simple question. Do not ask questions that would result in a multiple-line answer.

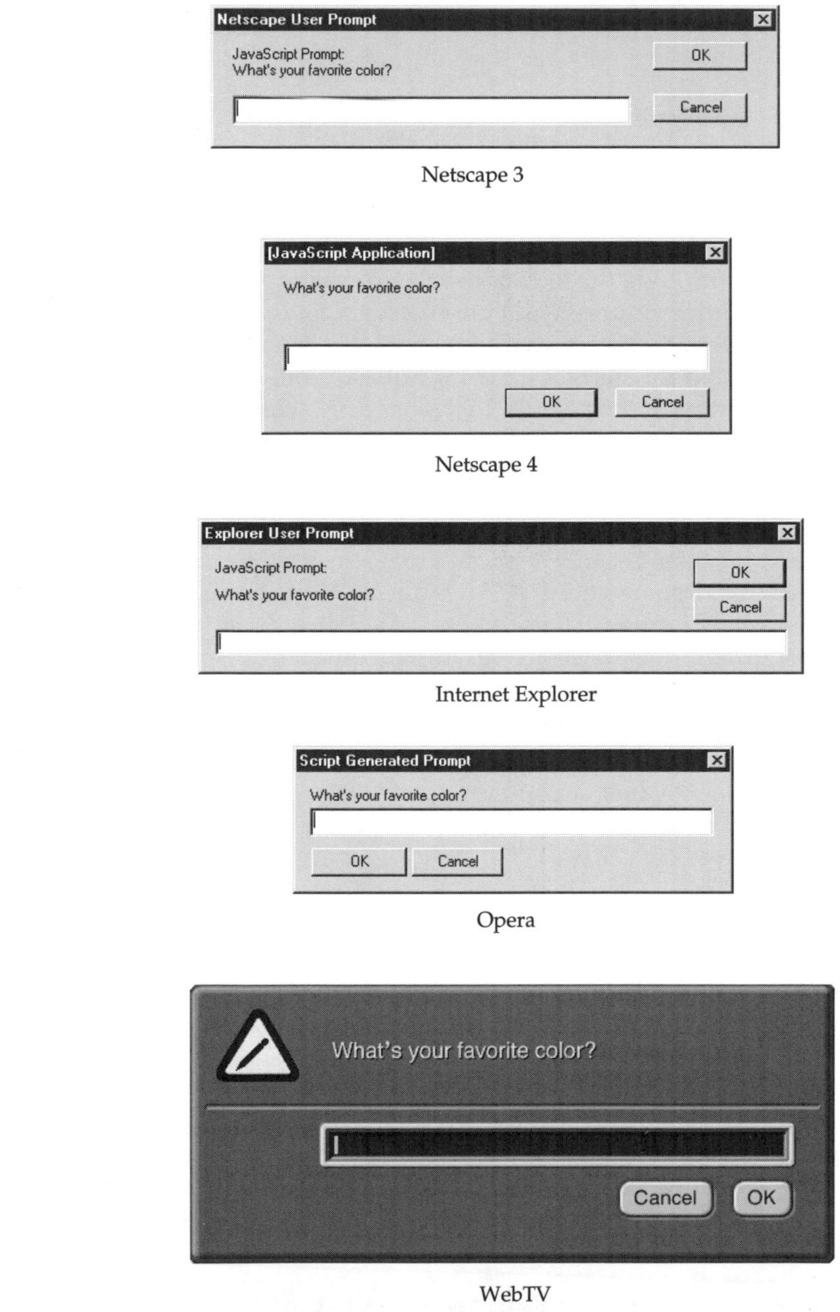

Figure 12-8.   *Prompt dialog in various browsers*

Make sure that you clearly indicate what type of information you are looking to collect such as a number or text string.

Custom Prompt Dialogs

Like the previous dialogs, the look and feel of JavaScript-generated prompt dialogs may leave something to be desired. The size, style, and buttons cannot be modified using the basic **window.prompt()** JavaScript method. As with alerts and confirms, it is obviously possible to create custom prompt dialogs that fit with the look and feel of a site similar to the one shown here.

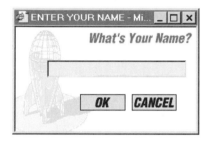

A custom prompt dialog script could be created similar to the ones presented for alerts and prompts, and can be found online at http://www.webdesignref.com/chapter12/customprompt.htm.

Forms

The primary way that a user interacts with a Web site besides selecting links is through the various form elements such as text fields, radio buttons, pull-down menus, and so forth. GUI design theory has a great deal to say about how to use these elements properly, but, unfortunately, given the limited capabilities of HTML form features, sometimes it is difficult to implement a modern GUI from within a Web page. The next few sections discuss each of the form elements and provide an overview of their proper use.

Labels

Form elements should be clearly labeled. A label should provide a description that indicates what a form element does or what kind of data should be entered in the element. Labels may include both text and graphics. Here are a few examples of labels.

The position of labels should be close to the field they are describing. Oftentimes the label is either to the left or above the field. Sometimes a table may be used to associate the label and the field together. All three ideas are shown here.

Name:

Name:

Name:

Labels and Field Selection

In some browsers, the **<LABEL>** contents can be clicked on to select the field. The idea is that when the label receives focus from the user, either by clicking on it or using an accelerator key, the focus should switch to the associated field. The reality is that in many browsers this doesn't work. This is a big reason not to use an **ACCESSKEY** attribute on a label, but rather on the field, as discussed later in the chapter. However, the click-select action of the label can easily be simulated using a little bit of JavaScript. For example, consider the markup here:

```
<FORM NAME="myform">
<LABEL onClick="document.myform.firstname.focus()">
First Name:
 <INPUT TYPE="text" NAME="firstname">
</LABEL>
</FORM>
```

In this example, a modern browser will bring the cursor to the associated field when the user clicks on the label by using the **focus()** method on the field. Fortunately, older browsers will just ignore the **<LABEL>** tag as well as the JavaScript on the associated intrinsic event-handler attribute.

Text Fields

HTML provides for single-line text fields using markup like the following:

```
<INPUT TYPE="TEXT">
```

For eventual processing by server-side programs or validation by client-side scripts, the fields should always be named with **NAME** as well as **ID** attribute:

```
<INPUT TYPE="TEXT" NAME="age" ID="age">
```

In the future, the ID attribute will be the only naming required, but the **NAME** attribute should be used for backward compatibility.

Setting the size of the text field will depend on the data being entered, but it is far better to use HTML to limit the field size to a particular range rather than allowing the user to enter more data than is allowed. For example, consider if you are asking for the user's age, two or perhaps three digits should be the maximum allowed. Two digits would allow a range of 0–99. Setting the size of a text field is easy in HTML—it requires specifying the size of the field in number of characters to show using the **SIZE** attribute like so:

```
<INPUT TYPE="text" NAME="age" SIZE="2">
```

Suggestion: Set the length of text fields to reasonably fit data being provided.

Age: 58   *not*   Age: 58

One troublesome aspect of the text input field in HTML is that the size of the field doesn't seem to always match the amount of data that can be input in the field visually. Consider the fields and data shown in Figure 12-9. Without applying style-sheet rules, there isn't necessarily any guarantee the data will not extend past the region provided or not fill up the region itself. This is an annoying quirk that varies amongst browsers and versions.

The visual size of a field doesn't necessarily limit the amount of data that can be put in the field under HTML. To limit the field, you would have to use the **MAXLENGTH** attribute like so:

```
<INPUT TYPE="TEXT" NAME="age" SIZE="2" MAXLENGTH="2">
```

Once the user hits the limit, the browser should not allow more data to be entered and will probably sound the system beep or perform some other indication the limit has been reached if the user continues to type. If you do not set the **MAXLENGTH** attribute, the data will not be limited and the field will scroll to the right as a user types in data. Consider that you should really always try to set **MAXLENGTH**. A user maliciously copy-pasting, say, 10,000 characters into a field may cause problems for server-side processing. Hackers often utilize unconstrained fields that are run on servers to try to run commands from the form. Furthermore, if passed using the **GET** attribute, there is actually a limit to the amount of data that can be passed before being truncated.

Rule: Always set your MAXLENGTH for a text field.

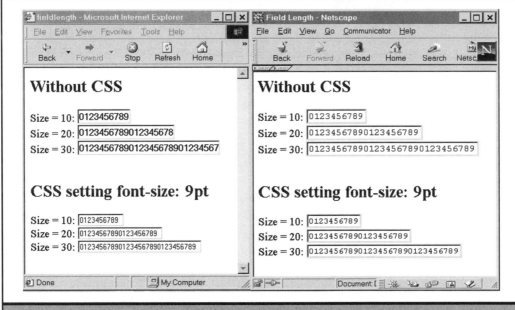

Figure 12-9.   *Example of imprecise text-field sizing in Internet Explorer and Netscape*

Always attempt to make a text field large enough to hold the data without scrolling. Users should be able to see all the text they have input lest they forget what they entered. The only time the **MAXLENGTH** value should be larger than the actual size of the text field is when the field is too big to fit the available screen real estate.

> **Rule: Only allow a text field to scroll rightwards when there is a premium on screen real estate and the data to be entered is larger than the available screen region.**

Some form designers prefer right-aligned form fields. It is possible to do this using a style sheet rule like so:

```
Username: <INPUT TYPE="TEXT" NAME="username" SIZE="20"
          STYLE="text-align: right">
```

Unfortunately, while this may be somewhat common in GUI applications, it is relatively uncommon on the Web. One large reason is probably that browsers seem to be confused on how to interpret this. Consider Internet Explorer and Netscape's interpretation of the markup shown here.

Internet Explorer aligns fields fine

Username: [Thomas]

Netscape 4.x may do something odd

Username: [Thomas   ]

Password Fields

A password field is a modified single-line text field that does not echo the characters typed to the screen, instead showing an asterisk or similar character. The main purpose of the password field is to provide limited security by making "shoulder surfing"—where a person looks over your shoulder to see your password—more difficult. The syntax for the password text-field form is similar to a single-line text field:

```
<INPUT TYPE="PASSWORD" NAME="secretpass" SIZE="10" MAXLENGTH="10">
```

The rendering of the password field is fairly similar in browsers and should look something like this.

Password: [**********]

Given that a user will not be able to see what they are typing, it is very unwise to let the field scroll. Imagine a user typing a very long password and they suddenly forget what letter they just typed as the field scrolls. Because they won't be able to judge the number of characters easily, they will probably be forced to reenter the entire password. To combat this potential problem, set the **MAXLENGTH** and **SIZE** the same to avoid scrolling.

Rule: Never allow password fields to scroll.

Another consideration with passwords is that they tend to have a maximum length. Make sure to limit the password field to match the length.

Rule: Limit the length of password fields to match password sizes.

An obvious rule that should not have to be stated is not to use default values with password fields. All the user has to do is view the source in order to see what the password is!

Rule: Do not use default values with password fields.

Multiline Text Entry

A multiline text area defined in HTML using the **<TEXTAREA>** element is used to collect larger amounts of data such as comments. Setting the **COLS** attribute to the number of characters across and the **ROWS** attribute to the number of lines to show in the box before scrolling can be used to size a text area. For example, the HTML markup

```
<TEXTAREA NAME="comments" ROWS="8" COLS="40">

</TEXTAREA>
```

creates a multiline text entry region 40 characters across with 8 lines showing at a time.

One interesting aspect to the **<TEXTAREA>** element is that there is no obvious way to set the maximum amount of content that can be entered in the field. For browsers that support all the core events such as **onkeypress**, we could easily limit the field. For example:

```
<HTML>
<HEAD>
<TITLE>Limited Text Area</TITLE>
</HEAD>
<BODY>
<FORM NAME="myform">
Comments:<BR>
<TEXTAREA NAME="comments" ROWS="4" COLS="40"
onkeypress='return (document.myform.comments.value.length < 100)'>
Will be limited to 100 characters in a compliant browser.
</TEXTAREA>
</FORM>
</BODY>
</HTML>
```

Of course in many browsers, such as the Netscape 4.*x* generation, the preceding script will not work despite the fact that this is a standard event. The only workaround to deal with the unlimited field length would be to sense the field length when its contents change or at submit time and reduce it to the proper number of characters. The following example illustrates one approach to this problem:

```
<!DOCTYPE HTML PUBLIC "-//W3C//DTD HTML 4.0 Transitional//EN">
<HTML>
<HEAD>
```

```
<TITLE>Limited Text Area</TITLE>
<SCRIPT>
<!--
function checkLimit(field, limit)
{
 if (field.value.length > limit)
 {
 alert("Field limited to "+limit+" characters");
 // Change it to the limit
  var revertfield = field.value.slice(0,limit-1);
  field.value = revertfield;
  field.focus();
 }
}
//-->
</SCRIPT>
</HEAD>
<BODY>
<FORM NAME="myform">
Comments:<BR>
<TEXTAREA NAME="comments" ROWS="8" COLS="40"
 onChange='checkLimit(this, 100)'>

Try entering 10 more characters to pass 100 characters
in this field. Then click outside.
</TEXTAREA>
</FORM>
</BODY>
</HTML>
```

Tip *Be careful with **<TEXTAREA>** fields as they have no limit to the amount of entered text without scripting.*

A default value can be set for the element by including text information within the tag. Be careful as this area takes plaintext and all returns, tabs, and spaces, and even HTML markup will be shown onscreen, though character entities should be interpreted.

```
<TEXTAREA NAME="comments" ROWS="8" COLS="40">
S P A C E S work here
so do
     TABS and
```

```
RETURNS.
Watch out for <B>HTML</B> in here.
What about character entities like &copy;
</TEXTAREA>
```

Probably the most troublesome aspect of the **<TEXTAREA>** element is that the wrapping of text is not supported in a standard way between browsers. In fact, by default many versions of Netscape will not wrap text while Internet Explorer will, as shown here.

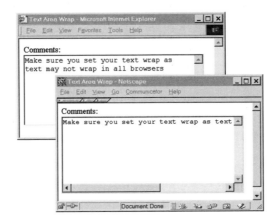

The solution to this is simply to define the **WRAP** attribute to a value of "soft" so that both browsers will exhibit the same behavior, like so:

```
<TEXTAREA NAME="comments" ROWS="8" COLS="40" WRAP="SOFT">
Everything is fine with this field now that the wrapping
has been set.
</TEXTAREA>
```

Rule: Set text wrapping in multiline text regions.

 Interestingly, the HTML 4.0 specification does not even address the wrapping problem at all.

Check Boxes

Check boxes should be used to indicate optional values. The basic idea with a group of check boxes is that the user may select as many or as few as they like of the set values. Setting check boxes in HTML is easily done using the **<INPUT>** element as shown here:

```
<FORM NAME="myform">

<B>PSV Options</B><BR><BR>
Asteroid Bumpers:
<INPUT TYPE="checkbox" NAME="bumpers">
<BR>
Blackhole Detector:
<INPUT TYPE="checkbox" NAME="detector">
<BR>
Autopilot: <INPUT TYPE="checkbox" NAME="autopilot">
<BR>

</FORM>
```

The rendering of the check box does vary under some browsers, but the major browsers render the markup nearly identically as shown in Figure 12-10.

It is possible to modify the look and feel of a check box using a set of images to represent the on and off stages. Radio buttons can be handled much the same way, and a script to customize the look of both will be presented in the section on radio buttons later on in this chapter.

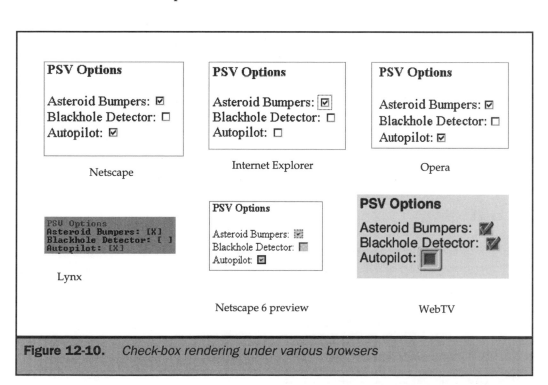

Figure 12-10.   *Check-box rendering under various browsers*

ELEMENTS OF PAGE DESIGN

When using check boxes, designers should think carefully about the amount of mouse travel between choices. Notice, for example, how the check boxes here incur more mouse travel when laid out horizontally.

PSV Options

Asteroid Bumpers: ☑
Blackhole Detector: ☐
Autopilot: ☑

PSV Options

Asteroid Bumpers: ☑   Blackhole Detector: ☐   Autopilot: ☑

Traditionally, GUI design has tended to cluster items together, but Web pages do scroll, so a vertical element might make more sense.

Suggestion: Consider vertically aligning related check boxes to decrease mouse travel.

Be careful when creating large groupings of check boxes as they may take up a great deal of screen real estate. Further, consider that while check boxes may be easy to use, with too many a user may not be able to scan them effectively. Consider the 7 +/-2 choices memory consideration presented in Chapter 3; it is probably wise to keep groups of related check boxes limited to about ten.

Setting a check box to be checked by default is very easy using HTML. Unfortunately, very often forms are designed with values that must be deselected by a user to opt out of receiving email solicitations. Some email solicitation forms are even designed in a somewhat sneaky fashion with text very small near the label. Considering that users will not necessarily read check box labels carefully, do not default check boxes for follow-up information.

Let users opt in and not out of emailings. Do not precheck such check boxes—require the users to select it themselves.

Radio Buttons

Radio buttons are used to select one item out of a group. Groups of radio buttons are defined similarly to check boxes. The main difference syntaxwise besides setting the **TYPE** attribute for the **<INPUT>** element to **RADIO** is that all the fields must have the same value for the **NAME** attribute to preserve the radio functionality between the fields. Consider the markup here that demonstrates the problem as well as the correct approach:

```
<FORM>
<H2>Different NAME Attributes</H2>
<INPUT TYPE="radio" NAME="notequal"> choice 1
```

```
<INPUT TYPE="radio" NAME="names"> choice 2
<INPUT TYPE="radio" NAME="donotwork" CHECKED> choice 3

<H2>NAME Attribute Set Properly</H2>
<INPUT TYPE="radio" NAME="samename"> choice 1
<INPUT TYPE="radio" NAME="samename"> choice 2
<INPUT TYPE="radio" NAME="samename" CHECKED> choice 3
</FORM>
```

Notice in the rendering shown here that it is possible to select all the choices in the first example, while the second one preserves the one-of-many radio selection method.

Different NAME Attributes

⦿ choice 1 ⦿ choice 2 ⦿ choice 3

NAME Attribute Set Properly

○ choice 1 ⦿ choice 2 ○ choice 3

Another small implementation problem with a radio buttons under HTML is that a value is not selected by default. This creates a mysterious state for the user that they can't return to as shown here.

Mysterious initial state with nothing set

○ choice 1 ○ choice 2 ○ choice 3

Once clicked unable to return to first state

○ choice 1 ○ choice 2 ○ choice 3

Setting the first field selected by inclusion of the **CHECKED** attribute solves this troublesome interface quirk.

Rule: Always check an initial radio button by default.

Another more potentially troublesome aspect of radios is determining when they should be used. Some designers feel that radios should be used for yes/no questions rather than pull-downs. This makes sense when you consider that they show both choices at once. The screen real estate saved by the pull-down is minimal. However, some designers further suggest that maybe a check box with a different label makes more sense since it is only one control to manipulate rather than two. It makes some sense until you consider that the wording of the label may get somewhat confusing. Consider the example shown here for asking users if they want to receive email solicitations. Radio buttons are the best way to present this information since the normal pull-down menu hides possible choices; the pull-down with all choices shown looks nonstandard, and the check box is confusing.

Send me annoying email! ☑

Do you want to receive our annoying e-mail? Yes ⊙   No ○

Do you want to receive our annoying e-mail? yes ▾

Do you want to receive our annoying e-mail?

Rule: Use radio buttons for yes/no questions rather than pull-down menus or check boxes.

The main advantage of radio buttons is that they are all exposed, allowing the user to easily choose from them. However, since all choices must be looked at in a radio group, the number of selections has to be limited enough for the user to consider all at once lest they make a mistake. This means the short-term memory rule of 7 +/-2 items should be strictly enforced.

Suggestion: Avoid more than eight items in a radio group.

Beyond memory considerations, when more than eight items are presented, screen real estate may become an issue.

Suggestion: Use pull-downs if more than eight items are in a selection of one-choice-of-many to save screen real estate, as stated by this rule.

If radio buttons are to be used, unlike check boxes, the grouping of radio buttons isn't quite as critical since the user will only make one choice, but it is wise to consider vertical alignment with radios as well—particularly when there are many choices.

 Vertical alignment is useful for larger groups of radio buttons.

Like check boxes, the rendering of radio buttons is similar amongst the major browsers, but does have differences in some viewing environments as shown in Figure 12-11.

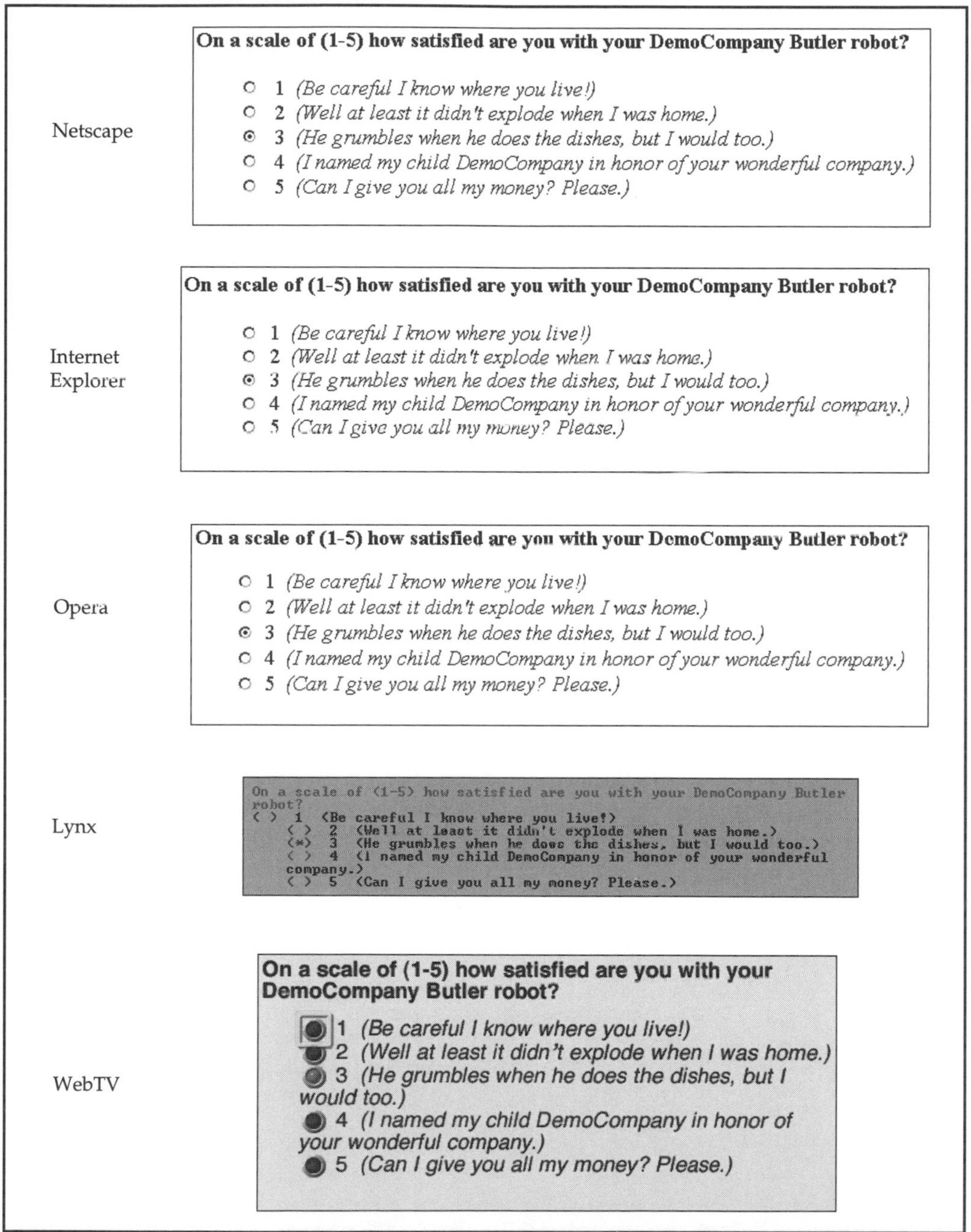

Netscape

On a scale of (1-5) how satisfied are you with your DemoCompany Butler robot?

   ○ 1 *(Be careful I know where you live!)*
   ○ 2 *(Well at least it didn't explode when I was home.)*
   ⊙ 3 *(He grumbles when he does the dishes, but I would too.)*
   ○ 4 *(I named my child DemoCompany in honor of your wonderful company.)*
   ○ 5 *(Can I give you all my money? Please.)*

Internet Explorer

On a scale of (1-5) how satisfied are you with your DemoCompany Butler robot?

   ○ 1 *(Be careful I know where you live!)*
   ○ 2 *(Well at least it didn't explode when I was home.)*
   ⊙ 3 *(He grumbles when he does the dishes, but I would too.)*
   ○ 4 *(I named my child DemoCompany in honor of your wonderful company.)*
   ○ 5 *(Can I give you all my money? Please.)*

Opera

On a scale of (1-5) how satisfied are you with your DemoCompany Butler robot?

   ○ 1 *(Be careful I know where you live!)*
   ○ 2 *(Well at least it didn't explode when I was home.)*
   ⊙ 3 *(He grumbles when he does the dishes, but I would too.)*
   ○ 4 *(I named my child DemoCompany in honor of your wonderful company.)*
   ○ 5 *(Can I give you all my money? Please.)*

Lynx

```
On a scale of (1-5) how satisfied are you with your DemoCompany Butler
robot?
( )   1   (Be careful I know where you live!)
   ( )   2   (Well at least it didn't explode when I was home.)
   (*)   3   (He grumbles when he does the dishes, but I would too.)
   ( )   4   (I named my child DemoCompany in honor of your wonderful
   company.)
   ( )   5   (Can I give you all my money? Please.)
```

WebTV

On a scale of (1-5) how satisfied are you with your DemoCompany Butler robot?

   ⦿ 1 *(Be careful I know where you live!)*
   ● 2 *(Well at least it didn't explode when I was home.)*
   ● 3 *(He grumbles when he does the dishes, but I would too.)*
   ● 4 *(I named my child DemoCompany in honor of your wonderful company.)*
   ● 5 *(Can I give you all my money? Please.)*

Figure 12-11.   *Radio buttons are relatively consistent in appearance*

As mentioned in the section on check boxes, it is possible to modify the appearance of both GUI elements using JavaScript. The markup and script code presented here shows this in action. A rendering of the example is shown in Figure 12-12.

```
<!DOCTYPE HTML PUBLIC "-//W3C//DTD HTML 4.0 Transitional//EN">
<HTML>
<HEAD>
<TITLE>Custom Checkboxes and Radios</TITLE>
<SCRIPT LANGUAGE="JavaScript">
<!--
  ns4 = (document.layers)? true:false;
  ie4 = (document.all)? true:false;

  function initialize() {
    psv = new checkBox('DomeSelector','psvImg','yes','no');
    tree = new checkBox('DomeSelector','treeImg','yes','no');
    dome = new radio('DomeSelector','domeImg',3,'Land');
  }

  function loadImage(imgObj,imgSrc) {
    eval(imgObj+' = new Image()');
    eval(imgObj+'.src = "'+imgSrc+'"');
  }

  loadImage('button0','../images/button0.gif');
  loadImage('button1','../images/button1.gif');
  loadImage('radiobutton0','../images/radiobutton0.gif');
  loadImage('radiobutton1','../images/radiobutton1.gif');
  loadImage('checkbox0','../images/checkbox0.gif');
  loadImage('checkbox1','../images/checkbox1.gif');

  function submitForm() {
    str = "You want a PSV port = " + psv.value + "\n";
    str += "You want a Tree Oxygenation System = " + tree.value + "\n";
    str += "You selected dome application is " + dome.value + "\n";
    alert(str);
  }

  function changeImage(layer,imgName,imgObj) {
    if (ns4 && layer!=null) eval('document.'+layer+'
.document.images["'+imgName+'"].src = '+imgObj+'.src');
    else document.images[imgName].src = eval(imgObj+".src");
```

```
  }

  function radio(layer,imgNames,length,defaultValue) {
    this.layer = layer;
    this.imgNames = imgNames;
    this.length = length;
    this.change = radioChange;
    this.value = (defaultValue)? defaultValue : "undefined";
  }

  function radioChange(index,value) {
    this.value = value;
    for (var i=0; i<this.length; i++)
    changeImage(this.layer,this.imgNames+i,'radiobutton0');
    changeImage(this.layer,this.imgNames+index,'radiobutton1');
  }

  function checkBox(layer,imgName,trueValue,falseValue,defaultToTrue)
{
    this.layer = layer;
    this.imgName = imgName;
    this.trueValue = trueValue;
    this.falseValue = falseValue;
    this.state = (defaultToTrue) ? 1 : 0;
    this.value = (this.state) ? this.trueValue : this.falseValue;
    this.change = checkBoxChange;
  }

  function checkBoxChange() {
    this.state = (this.state) ? 0 : 1;
    this.value = (this.state) ? this.trueValue : this.falseValue;
    changeImage(this.layer,this.imgName,'checkbox'+this.state);
  }

//-->
</SCRIPT>
<STYLE>
<!--
#DomeSelector   {position: relative;}
-->
</STYLE>
<BASEFONT SIZE="2" FACE="Arial,Helvetica,sans-serif" COLOR="Black">
```

```
</HEAD>
<BODY onLoad="initialize()" BGCOLOR="#FFFFFF">

<DIV ID="DomeSelector">
<TABLE BORDER="0" CELLSPACING="0" CELLPADDING="3">
<TR>
<TD COLSPAN="2" ALIGN="CENTER">
<FONT SIZE="+2">Dome Selector</FONT><HR>
</TD></TR>

<TR>
<TD COLSPAN="2"><FONT SIZE="+1">Applications</FONT><BR></TD>
</TR>

<TR>
<TD><A HREF="javascript:dome.change(0,'Land')">
<IMG NAME="domeImg0" SRC="../images/radiobutton1.gif" WIDTH="20"
HEIGHT="20" BORDER="0" ALT=""></A></TD>
<TD>Land</TD>
</TR>

<TR>
<TD><A HREF="javascript:dome.change(1,'Underwater')">
<IMG NAME="domeImg1" SRC="../images/radiobutton0.gif" WIDTH="20"
HEIGHT="20" BORDER="0" ALT=""></A></TD>
<TD>Underwater</TD>
</TR>

<TR>
<TD><A HREF="javascript:dome.change(2,'Space')">
<IMG NAME="domeImg2" SRC="../images/radiobutton0.gif" WIDTH="20"
HEIGHT="20" BORDER="0" ALT=""></A></TD>
<TD>Space</TD>
</TR>

<TR>
<TD COLSPAN="2"><BR><FONT SIZE="+1">Options</FONT><BR></TD>
</TR>

<TR>
<TD><A HREF="javascript:psv.change()">
```

```
<IMG NAME="psvImg" SRC="../images/checkbox0.gif" WIDTH="20"
HEIGHT="20" BORDER="0" ALT=""></A></TD>
<TD>PSV Port</TD>
</TR>

<TR>
<TD><A HREF="javascript:tree.change()">
<IMG NAME="treeImg" SRC="../images/checkbox0.gif" WIDTH="20"
HEIGHT="20" BORDER="0" ALT=""></A></TD>
<TD>Tree Oxygenation System</TD>
</TR>

<TR>
<TD COLSPAN="2" ALIGN="RIGHT">
<BR>
<A HREF="javascript:submitForm()"
onMouseDown="changeImage('DomeSelector','submitImg','button1')"
onMouseUp="changeImage('DomeSelector','submitImg','button0')"
onMouseOut="changeImage('DomeSelector','submitImg','button0')">
<IMG NAME="submitImg" SRC="../images/button0.gif" WIDTH="85"
HEIGHT="30" ALT="Submit" VSPACE="10" BORDER="0"></A>
</TD>
</TR>

</TABLE>
</DIV>
</BODY>
</HTML>
```

Online: http://www.webdesignref.com/chapter12/customradios.htm.

One disturbing use of radio buttons that bears mentioning before moving to the next GUI element is the use of radio buttons to navigate a site. This is a completely nonstandard use of this feature and is highly confusing. While pull-downs have been used successfully for navigation on the Web and offer the same one-choice-of-many that radio buttons do, users have tended to understand from software applications that a menu selection will trigger an action while a radio button will not.

Rule: Do not use radio buttons for navigation.

Figure 12-12. Custom radio buttons and check boxes can fit with a site's design style

Pull-Down Menus

Pull-down menus, as defined in HTML using the **<SELECT>** menu, provide a simple one-of-many selection capability similar to radio buttons. The main advantage of pull-downs is that they save screen real estate. However, pull-downs do hide values from the user, forcing them to expose the values—which takes effort as well as potentially having to memorize the values shown if they have second thoughts later on. Certainly pull-downs do not rely on recognition, but rather on recall, the downsides of which have been discussed numerous times—particularly in Chapter 3. However, the screen-real-estate issue alone makes pull-downs worthy of consideration. Setting up a simple pull-down menu can be done like so:

```
<SELECT NAME="robotchooser">
    <OPTION>Butler
    <OPTION>Security
    <OPTION>Trainer
    <OPTION>Friend
</SELECT>
```

Indicating a default choice isn't as great problem as it is with radio buttons. A pull-down menu will always start on the first choice presented. It might be a good idea to utilize the **SELECTED** attribute to preselect a choice, similar to setting the first radio button rather than relying on the default action of the browser.

Tip *Do not rely on the browser's default action with pull-downs. Always set a SELECTED value as an initial state.*

Designers occasionally create nonchoice items like so, which may in some sense ruin the logic of the feature—which is "now choose one of the items but not the first one," as shown here:

```
<SELECT NAME="robotchooser">
    <OPTION>Choose your robot
    <OPTION>Butler
    <OPTION>Security
    <OPTION>Trainer
    <OPTION>Friend
</SELECT>
```

The assumption would be that we would validate the form in this previous situation and alert the user that they have to choose something. Another potential downside of **<SELECT>** menus is that they lack any form of separator or grouping facility. Occasionally, designers will use an entry filled with dashes or a blank entry to simulate a separator, like this:

```
<SELECT NAME="robotchooser">
        <OPTION>Choose your robot
        <OPTION>------------------------
        <OPTION>Butler
        <OPTION>Security
        <OPTION>Trainer
        <OPTION>Friend
        <OPTION>    Male
        <OPTION>    Female
</SELECT>
```

Tip *Be wary of using special characters in pull-downs—particularly nonbreaking spaces—as they often do not render properly.*

HTML 4 introduces the **<OPTGROUP>** element, which should be used to segment choices into groups, or even to create submenus. For example, consider the markup shown here:

```
<SELECT NAME="robotchooser">
   <OPTION>Choose your robot
   <OPTION>------------------------
   <OPTION>Butler
   <OPTGROUP LABEL="Security Models">
      <OPTION>Man
      <OPTION>K-9
   </OPTGROUP>
   <OPTGROUP LABEL="Friend Models">
      <OPTION>Female
      <OPTION>Male
   </OPTGROUP>
   <OPTION>Trainer
</SELECT>
```

In a prerelease version of the new version of Netscape, **<OPTGROUP>** renders as a section name that cannot be selected, as shown here.

Until **<OPTGROUP>** is more commonly supported in browsers, it should be avoided.

The renderings of traditional pull-downs are fairly similar in the major browsers, but, of course, they have rendering differences in the appliance or text-only environments as shown in Figure 12-13. These environments may find radio buttons a much better choice.

Consider radio buttons over pull-downs if you are dealing with alternative access users.

One interesting aspect of the use of a pull-down menu is that when the **SIZE** attribute is added, it generally results in a window that acts like a pull-down, allowing

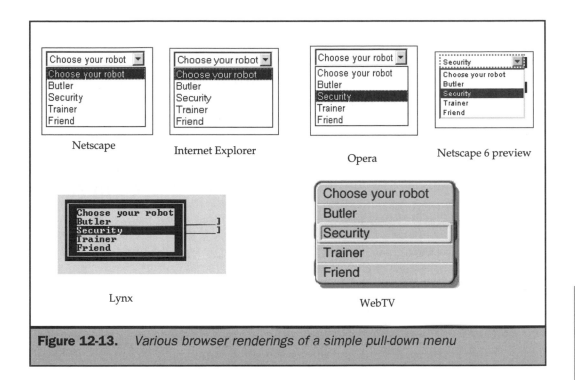

Figure 12-13. *Various browser renderings of a simple pull-down menu*

only one choice out of many, but looking like a scrolled list. Many users won't understand that the following features shown here do the same thing.

The same?   or   Different?

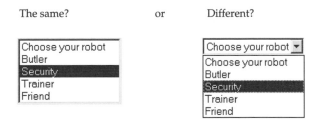

> **Suggestion: Avoid changing the display of single-choice pull-down menus with the SIZE attribute.**

It is possible, of course, through the use of style sheets, to significantly change the look and feel of pull-downs, and in fact to create your own pull-downs. Many designers have experimented with a variety of cascading menu scripts to create navigation systems for sites. An example of this is presented in the section later in this chapter entitled "Advanced Web GUI Features." For now, let's take a look at the use of pull-downs for navigation in Web pages.

Using Pull-Downs for Navigation

A common use of pull-down menus in Web sites is for navigation. The basic idea is that a selection of sites or pages is shown in a pull-down and when selected, the user is instantly whisked to the page. The pull-down, like a typical application menu, tends to be on the top of pages and saves a great deal of screen real estate over conventional navigation bars—of course, it does so by hiding the links. While this use for the pull-down seems perfectly acceptable, it now means there are two uses for a pull-down: one will cause the user to navigate the page, while the other is just used within form elements. Some users may be confused with the dual use if the context of use is not kept clear. A pull-down used for navigation should not be within a form. It should be clearly labeled, and probably should use some type of trigger button labeled "go" or something similar to indicate the purpose of the pull-down.

> **Rule: Make the result of navigation pull-down clear by context, labels, and possibly a trigger button.**

Assuming that users understand the use of pull-downs for navigation, there are numerous implementation issues to avoid. The first is the issue of a go button to trigger the page load. Many sites prefer to use pull-downs that trigger a page load immediately. While this is very fast, it can be somewhat of a hair-trigger form of navigation. It is very easy for a user to slip up on the mouse—particularly on a long pull-down—and accidentally trigger a page load. To combat this, a special form button often with a label of go is used next to the menu to actually trigger the page load. The two approaches are illustrated here.

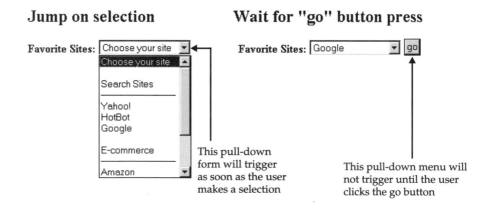

A big problem of considering the no go button approach is what to do when the user has turned their JavaScript off. In many sites, without JavaScript the navigation completely breaks and the user is left pulling menus that don't do anything. The use of the go can trigger a backup call to a server-side program to redirect the page.

Rule: Make sure pull-down navigation degrades gracefully when JavaScript is off.

It is possible to have the go button show up only when script is off, or it can be left on the screen all the time. However, leaving it onscreen does result in a troublesome usability problem since the user is never able to click the button before a new page loads, which could annoy the user greatly.

Rule: If a go button is shown onscreen with pull-down navigation, make sure the user can actually click it.

Having the go button trigger the page load is probably a good way to go rather than automatic selection, since it does give a sense of closure to the user's action and avoids the hair-trigger effect this form of navigation often exhibits.

The last problem with pull-downs for navigation has to be with the state the menu is left in. First consider, for example, the user pulling the menu down and resting it on a separator. Shouldn't the menu reset to the top like a traditional menu in an application? Most, for some reason, do not. Second, consider that a user does select a legitimate choice and is sent to a new page. Once at that page, they back up—only to find the pull-down selecting the choice they just made. Suddenly deciding that the page they had selected was correct, they have to either reload the page to reset the pull-down or choose some false choice and try again. The basic problem is that most of the time the menu is not reset when the user reloads the page or selects a nonactive item like a separator.

Rule: Reset a pull-down when users back out of a page as well as when they select separator items.

The best way to really understand these problems is by accessing the examples located at http://www.webdesignref.com/chapter12/pulldownproblems.htm. A complete script is presented here that deals with all the problems and provides cosmetic improvements to the pull-down navigation style:

```
<!DOCTYPE HTML PUBLIC "-//W3C//DTD HTML 4.0 Transitional//EN">
<HTML>
<HEAD>
<TITLE>Select Navigation</TITLE>
<STYLE>
```

```
<!--
   .nochoice    {color: black;}
   .choice      {color: blue; }
-->
</STYLE>
<SCRIPT>
<!--
function redirect(pulldown) {
  newlocation = pulldown[pulldown.selectedIndex].value;
  if (newlocation != "")
   self.location = newlocation;
 }

function resetIfBlank(pulldown){
   possiblenewlocation = pulldown[pulldown.selectedIndex].value;
   if (possiblenewlocation == "")
pulldown.selectedIndex = 0; /* reset to start since no movement */
 }
//-->
</SCRIPT>
</HEAD>
<BODY>
<FORM NAME="navForm">
<B>Favorite Sites:</B>
<SELECT NAME="menu" onChange="resetIfBlank(this)">
<OPTION VALUE="" CLASS="nochoice" SELECTED> Choose your site
<OPTION VALUE="" CLASS="nochoice">
<OPTION VALUE="" CLASS="nochoice">Search Sites
<OPTION VALUE="" CLASS="nochoice">--------------------------
<OPTION VALUE="http://www.yahoo.com" CLASS="choice">Yahoo!
<OPTION VALUE="http://www.hotbot.com" CLASS="choice">HotBot
<OPTION VALUE="http://www.google.com" CLASS="choice">Google
<OPTION VALUE="" CLASS="nochoice">
<OPTION VALUE="" CLASS="nochoice">E-commerce
<OPTION VALUE="" CLASS="nochoice">--------------------------
<OPTION VALUE="http://www.amazon.com" CLASS="choice">Amazon
<OPTION VALUE="http://www.buy.com" CLASS="choice">Buy.com
<OPTION VALUE="" CLASS="nochoice" CLASS="choice">
<OPTION VALUE="" CLASS="nochoice">Demos
<OPTION VALUE="" CLASS="nochoice">--------------------------
<OPTION VALUE="http://www.democompany.com"
```

```
CLASS="choice">DemoCompany
</SELECT>
<INPUT TYPE="button" VALUE="go"
onClick="redirect(document.navForm.menu)">
</FORM>
<SCRIPT>
<!--
document.navForm.menu.selectedIndex = 0;
//-->
</SCRIPT>
</BODY>
</HTML>
```

**Online: The complete script can be found at
http://www.webdesignref.com/chapter12/pulldownnav.htm.**

Certainly, using pull-downs as a navigation device is a break from traditional GUI conventions. Another interesting difference is that GUI conventions suggest that when there are over 15 items, a pull-down should not be used; rather, a scrolled list of some sort should be used. Yet these form elements, which are discussed next, are relatively rare in Web sites.

Scrolled Lists

A scrolled list is one where the user can choose multiple items out of the choices presented. Functionally they are equivalent to the check box, though they take up less screen real estate. To create a scrolled list, simply change a **<SELECT>** element by adding the attribute **MULTIPLE** and setting a **SIZE** attribute equal to the number of choices that should be shown at a given moment. An example is shown here:

```
<B>Security Robot Extras:</B><BR>
<SELECT NAME="extras" SIZE="3" MULTIPLE>
   <OPTION>Austrian accent
   <OPTION>Fame thrower
   <OPTION>One-liner catch phrase software upgrade
   <OPTION>Permanent facial sneer
   <OPTION>Rocket fists
</SELECT>
```

Browsers rendering examples of a scrolled list are shown in Figure 12-14.

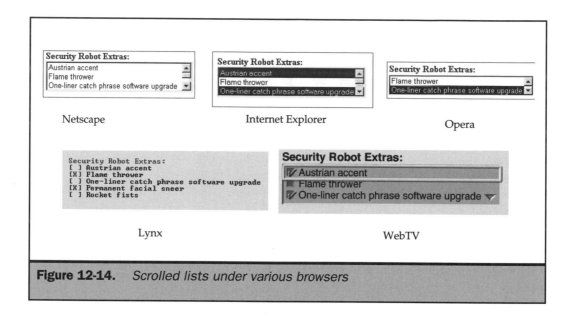

Figure 12-14. *Scrolled lists under various browsers*

Notice that in the alternative browsers, like WebTV or text-only environments, scrolled lists are significantly modified or even changed into check boxes.

Suggestion: Avoid scrolled lists if you expect alternative browsing environments; use check boxes instead.

What's interesting is that scrolled lists are actually relatively unused in large public Web sites. Probably the main reason is that, for some users, they are confusing compared to check boxes. Consider, how do you select multiple non-contiguous items in the list? Which key is held down? CTRL? SHIFT? Now consider other operating systems and browsers—is it the same? What you'll find if you actually watch novice users is that they often approach these form elements in a trial-and-error fashion. Because of this, if they must be employed, always provide a statement about what keys should be held for multiple selections.

Rule: When using scrolled lists, make sure to provide some form of instructions for novice users on how to select multiple items.

Push Buttons

HTML forms support simple push buttons using the following syntax:

```
<INPUT TYPE="BUTTON" VALUE="Push Me">
```

The rendering of such buttons is very plain and tends to look something like this.

However, without the use of scripting language, a push button will do nothing. It is possible to cause anything to happen—for example, triggering an alert to fire or a page to load, as shown here:

```
<FORM>
<INPUT TYPE="BUTTON" VALUE="Say Hello" onClick="alert('Hello')">
<BR><INPUT TYPE="BUTTON" VALUE="Load a page"
onClick="window.location='http://www.democompany.com'">
</FORM>
```

From experience with software applications, a user would expect a significant action to happen when a form button is pushed—such as a document to print, an alert to be dismissed, and so on. Users would not expect this to be used for page loading; rather, normal links or graphical buttons tend to be used for that action.

Suggestion: Do not use default form-style push buttons for navigation; instead, reserve them to cause actions.

It is possible to change the rendering of a push button using images. This will be demonstrated using a submit button later on in the chapter.

Reset Buttons

A reset button may be useful to include on complex forms to reset values back to their default state. The syntax for the reset button is one of the simpler forms of the **<INPUT>** element:

```
<INPUT TYPE="RESET" VALUE="Reset Fields">
```

Web conventions seem to suggest that the reset button be placed near the form submission and be labeled something like "Reset," "Reset Fields," or "Reset Form." If there are no default values used in the form, a more appropriate label might be "Clear Form" or "Clear Fields."

The main problem with the reset button is that it is often so close to the submit button that the user might literally slip and press it accidentally, thus possibly losing a great deal of entered information. To avoid a hair-trigger reset button, attach a JavaScript to get confirmation from the user, as shown here:

```
<FORM onReset="return confirm('Clear the form?')">
...other fields in the form...
<INPUT TYPE="RESET" VALUE="Clear Fields">
</FORM>
```

Rule: Provide a confirmation on a form reset button to avoid accidents.

One might also wonder why the reset button is so close to a form-submission button. While this is somewhat a mystery, convention has put it there. You may consider putting it someplace else more out of the way.

Suggestion: Consider moving your reset button away from the submit button.

Submit Buttons

A submit button is a special class of push button that triggers the contents of a form to be sent to a server-side program as specified by the value of the **ACTION** attribute in the <FORM> tag. For example,

```
<FORM ACTION="saveit.pl" METHOD="POST" NAME="testform">
...form elements here...
<INPUT TYPE="SUBMIT" VALUE="SUBMIT">
</FORM>
```

would trigger the execution of the program saveit.pl, which would receive the contents of the form. Because a submit button may cause an action that could be irreversible, it is always a good idea to use a confirmation dialog to warn a user before they submit something, as discussed previously in the chapter and as shown here:

```
<FORM ACTION="saveit.pl" METHOD="POST" NAME="testform"
onSubmit="return confirm('Are you sure?')">
...form elements here...
<INPUT TYPE="SUBMIT" VALUE="SUBMIT">
</FORM>
```

Rule: Provide a final chance before submitting important information or starting a difficult-to-reverse action.

The location of a submit button is generally at the bottom of a form. However, unlike many GUI-based form applications on the Web, it is not necessarily at the far right or the center of the screen. On the contrary, it generally appears on the left or the center of the bottom of the screen—generally near the reset button.

Suggestion: Keep the submit button at the bottom of the form, either in the center or on the left side.

The look and feel of the submit button is usually the same as any normal push button, though designers may wish to change the style of the button using an image, as discussed in the next section.

Image Buttons

Using script, it is possible to utilize an image instead of a typical HTML form field as a push button. Unlike HTML, multiple states (including animated states) are possible. An example of an image button is shown here.

Using the **<INPUT TYPE="IMAGE">** element or a script to make more visually appealing image buttons is relatively straightforward. An example of this is presented here:

```
<HTML>
<HEAD>
<TITLE>Image Submit Button</TITLE>
</HEAD>
<BODY BGCOLOR="#FFFFFF">

<FORM NAME="Form" ACTION="submit_img.htm"
onSubmit="javascript:alert('The form is being submitted.');">
    <INPUT TYPE="text"><BR>
    <INPUT TYPE="image" SRC="../images/button0.gif" WIDTH="85"
     HEIGHT="30" BORDER="0">
</FORM>

</BODY>
</HTML>
```

Before you quickly run out to change all form buttons, consider first the download expense as well as the degradability of these buttons. Designers should consider if the visual improvement of the button is that important to the user experience and if the buttons will even be viewable under all browsing conditions. A simpler idea might be just to apply some simple style-sheet rules to color buttons to match a site design.

Suggestion: Provide a degradable state for image buttons with scripting or images off.

 *HTML 4 defines the **<BUTTON>** element, which is a much easier approach to adding image buttons. However, this element is not well supported at the time of this writing and should be avoided.*

File Upload Controls

A special type of form control supported in HTML is the file upload control. This control can be used to browse the user's local system and attach a file for uploading. The syntax of the field is relatively simple, as shown here:

```
<INPUT TYPE="file" SIZE=30 NAME="upfile">
```

File upload does not work on every browser, but on the ones that are supported, it looks fairly similar on all browsers, as shown in Figure 12-15. Notice that, as expected, this form element does not work in alternative or restricted browsing environments.

Rule: Make sure to consider the environment of use before using a file upload facility. This may not make sense for users that do not have file storage.

The file upload facility as implemented under HTML provides little room for customization. The only possibility is that the size of the path field may be set. However, designers should not modify or limit the size of the file field given that you will have no idea of the length of the directory path that may be required to attach a file on a user's system. Also, there is really no option to change the layout of the field or the associated browse button.

It is possible to implement a file upload system using Java or JavaScript and to produce an interface similar to the one shown in Figure 12-16.

Examples of file upload use as well as associated Perl code to save a file to a server can be found online at http://www.webdesignref.com/chapter12/fileupload.htm.

Usable Forms

Creating a usable form need not be hard. The most common mistake is that forms are simply not well laid out. Consider the forms shown in Figure 12-17. The form with well-aligned fields at least appears to be easier to fill out.

Primarily, forms will be laid out in an up-and-down fashion on a Web page, rather than a left-to-right fashion, to fill up a fixed-sized dialog. However, the exact layout of the form will depend greatly on the data presented. For example, consider the two possible layouts for collecting a user's name shown here:

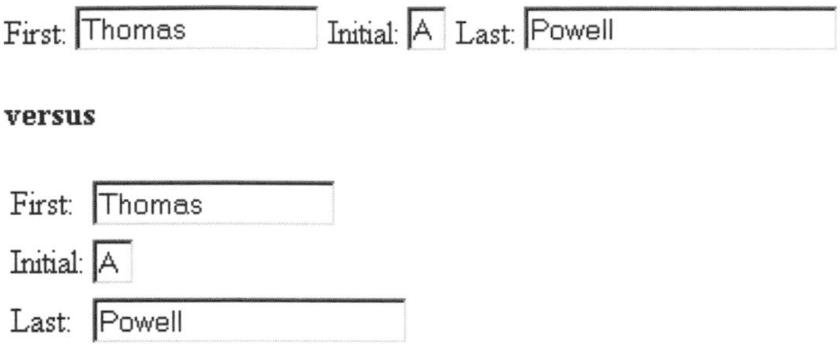

First: Thomas   Initial: A Last: Powell

versus

First: Thomas

Initial: A

Last: Powell

Which field layout is easier to understand? Which is the more efficient use of screen real estate? On the Web, fields tend to be filled out generally up to down, though it might make sense to arrange fields left to right because of context.

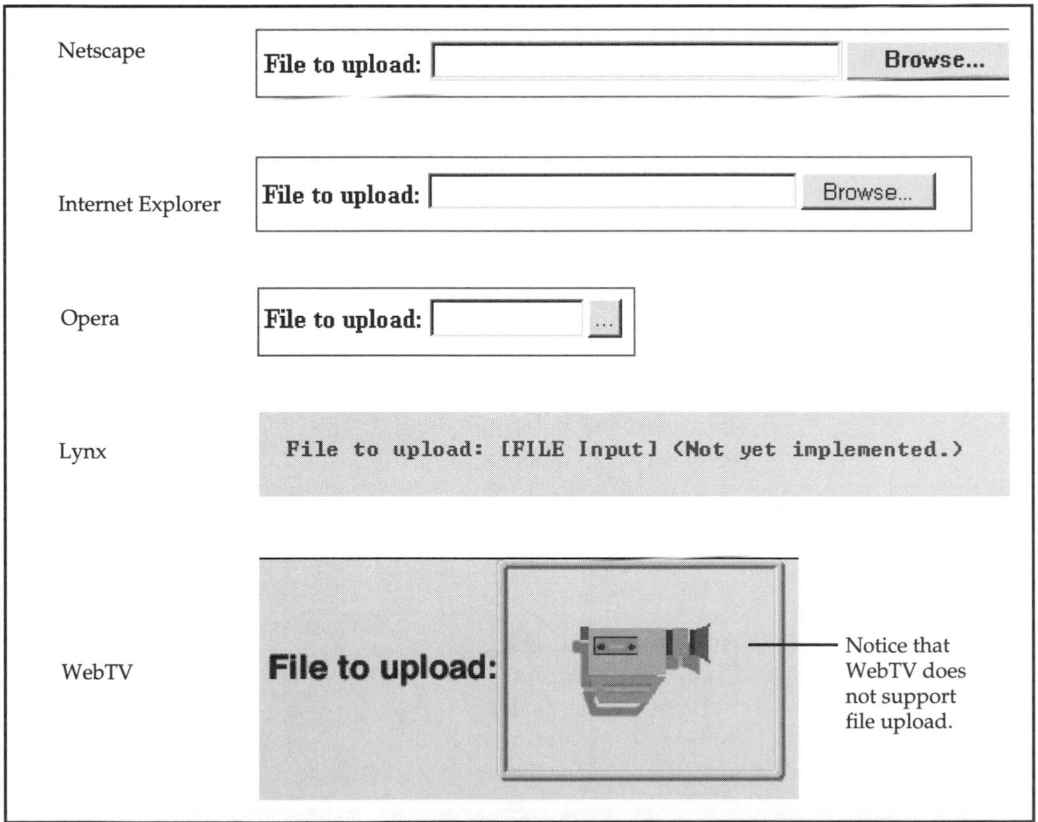

Figure 12-15. *Rendering of the file upload control*

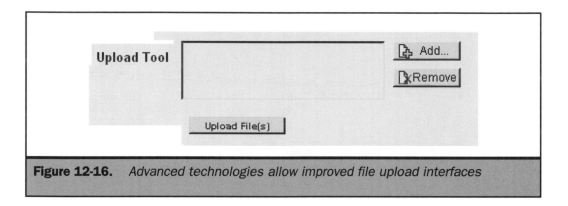

Figure 12-16. *Advanced technologies allow improved file upload interfaces*

Suggestion: Generally, lay out form elements up to down, but consider left to right based on the context of the information being asked for.

Regardless of how forms are laid out, in most cases HTML tables will be used. So far in the 4.*x* and earlier 5.*x* generation of browsers, the use of style sheets and form elements for layout of the fields is a dangerous mix. For the near term, consider using tables over CSS for form pages.

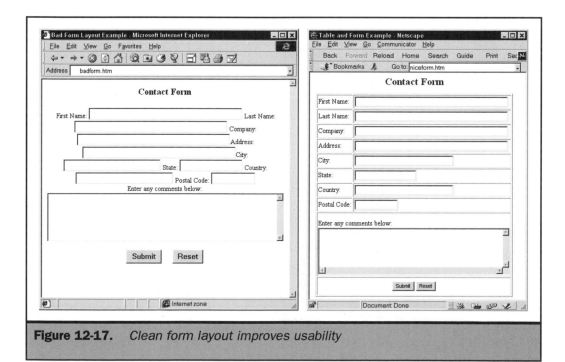

Figure 12-17. *Clean form layout improves usability*

Suggestion: Consider keeping table borders on when formatting table elements as they help associate labels and fields.

To format text fields, you might try to use HTML markup like **<FONT>**, **<TT>**, **<B>**, and so on around form elements. However, browsers will not necessarily interpret the markup properly. Consider the example here:

```
<FORM>
    <FONT COLOR="red"><I>
    Username: <INPUT TYPE="TEXT" NAME="Username" SIZE="20">
    </I></FONT>
</FORM>
```

The label of the field will be rendered in red and italic in every browser; however, what happens to the content in the text field varies. Under some browsers, it will render in italic, but not red; in others, the text field is unaffected. Using style sheets, this situation improves somewhat, but designers should be very careful to limit the type of formatting performed. Probably the easiest addition would be to provide a subtle color to fields, like so:

```
<INPUT TYPE="TEXT" NAME="USERNAME" SIZE="20"
    STYLE="background-color: yellow">
```

Tip   *Avoid trying to apply anything more than simple HTML or CSS formatting to form fields.*

Style can be applied to a field to indicate what state it is in. For example, as the user tabs through a set of fields, consider having the background color of each field change slightly. Also, a field could change color when it is in error. This can be done using JavaScript and CSS.

One of the biggest mistakes designers tend to make when working with forms online is directly copying the look and feel of an existing paper form. When users are highly familiar with a particular type of form that they fill in every day, it may be useful to do this since it would be improve the user's comfort level with the form and not require retraining for people to use the online version. However, in most cases, written forms have different usability issues than online ones. Remember the environment-of-consumption discussion presented in Chapter 3. It is important to gear the form to how the user is going to be filling it out—in this case, probably using a keyboard and a mouse. To improve usability, always try to make the form simpler to read and use online.

Suggestion: Imitate real-world forms directly if users are very used to filling them out; otherwise, focus on reducing the amount of data entry.

One way to improve usability of forms is to consider that users will have to use keyboards to enter in text data. There may be a great deal of keyboard-to-mouse, back-and-forth movement in a form. Try to minimize this in two ways. First, make the form keyboard friendly by encouraging tabbing, using accelerator keys, and providing default data values. How to implement each of these ideas is discussed later in the chapter.

Rule: Make forms keyboard friendly.

Second, make sure to limit the mouse travel between form elements. If users are going to be moving from field to field with their mouse, try to limit the distance between fields.

Rule: Limit mouse travel between form elements.

In order to limit mouse travel, you often end up grouping associated items together.

Fields that are associated with each other should be grouped together. The easiest way to do this is to put the fields within a table. The table may have a background color to make the grouping more obvious. It is also possible using the HTML elements **<FIELDSET>** and **<LEGEND>** to quickly create form grouping. The two approaches are illustrated here.

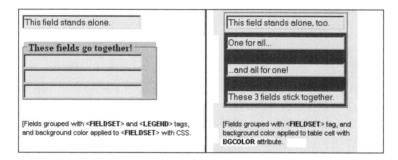

When grouping items, it is important, of course, to group items that make sense together—not just to limit mouse travel or to create colored sections. However, one of the most important form improvements that can be made is making sure that fields that are required are clearly noted to the user.

Required Fields

When a user is trying to fill in a form, it is very important to indicate which fields in the form are required. Nothing can annoy a user more than trying to guess what fields are required and being forced to keep resubmitting until all the mandatory fields are filled in. The most common way that required fields are indicated on the Web is using an asterisk next to the field. Despite the common use of the asterisk for required fields, it is a good idea to indicate somewhere on the form that the asterisk indicates a required field. Color is also used by itself, or with the asterisk. However, avoid just coloring a field name to indicate a required field since a user may be unable to see the color. Last but not least, it might just be best to indicate the required field by explicitly putting the word *"required"* next to it. All these techniques showing required fields are illustrated here.

* Indicates required fields

(*) Name:

Name: *

Name: *required*

Rule: Label all required fields carefully using an asterisk or the word *"required."*

Tabbing Forms

One good way to improve form fill-out is to improve the movement between fields using the TAB key. Normally, a browser will tend to tab through fields left to right, top to bottom. However, the basic tab movement is more an artifact of the order in which fields are defined. If you want to explicitly set a tabbing order, HTML 4.0 has included the **TABINDEX** attribute for many elements.

Set the **TABINDEX** to a value between 0 and 32767. Hopefully you don't have 32,000 fields in your form, but the specification says you can set tab values that high! Tabbing will proceed from the lowest positive value to the highest value. Fields with a **TABINDEX** set to 0 will be tabbed in order of definition after all other fields have been navigated. While not explicit in the specification, fields with negative **TABINDEX** values are skipped. Disabled fields will not be tabbed at all, which is defined in the specification. The following example demonstrates the use of the tabbing index with form elements:

```
<!DOCTYPE HTML PUBLIC "-//W3C//DTD HTML 4.0 Transitional//EN">
<HTML>
<HEAD>
<TITLE>Tab Example</TITLE>
</HEAD>
<BODY>

<FORM>
```

```
<INPUT TABINDEX="0" TYPE="text" NAME="field1"
       VALUE="tabbed after set fields"><BR>
<INPUT TABINDEX="1" TYPE="text" NAME="field2"
       VALUE="first field"><BR>
Check me:
<INPUT TYPE="CHECKBOX" NAME="field3" TABINDEX="4"><BR>
<INPUT TABINDEX="-2" TYPE="text" NAME="field4"
       VALUE="skip this field"><BR>
<SELECT TABINDEX="10" NAME="field5">
   <OPTION>Choice 1
   <OPTION>Choice 2
</SELECT><BR><BR>
<INPUT TABINDEX="3" TYPE="submit" VALUE="Submit">
</FORM>

</BODY>
</HTML>
```

TABINDEX is supported in Internet Explorer 4.*x* and beyond. It is not supported in older browsers or Netscape 4.*x* browsers. However, browsers will just default to their normal form navigation, so it is fairly safe to use this attribute.

Suggestion: Add TABINDEX attributes to improve form navigation.

First-Field Focus

For efficient form use, the user should be able to quickly use the keyboard to enter data in the form. While the TAB key can be used to quickly move between fields, you should notice that most browsers will not focus the first field by default, and the user may be forced to click the field before starting keyboard entry. Using JavaScript, it is fairly easy to focus the first field in a form. This should improve form fill-out in a subtle but noticeable way.

Suggestion: Focus the first field of a form page immediately.

The example presented here shows a short JavaScript associated with the **onload** event-handler attribute for the **<BODY>** that focuses a form field:

```
<!DOCTYPE HTML PUBLIC "-//W3C//DTD HTML 4.0 Transitional//EN">
<HTML>
<HEAD>
<TITLE>Focus First Field</TITLE>
</HEAD>
```

```
<BODY onLoad="window.document.testform.firstname.focus()">

<FORM NAME="testform">
First Name:
<INPUT TYPE="text" NAME="firstname" SIZE="30" MAXLENGTH="30">
<BR>
Last Name:
<INPUT TYPE="text" NAME="lastname" SIZE="30" MAXLENGTH="30">
<BR>
</FORM>

</BODY>
</HTML>
```

Keyboard Shortcuts

HTML 4.0 introduces the use of the **ACCESSKEY** attribute for many elements, including form elements. The access key can be used to set an accelerator for a field so that the user can access the field using a key combination—usually ALT, the defined access key. Note that the actual key combined with the defined accelerator may vary based on the underlying system. For example, Macintosh users may use CMD instead of ALT to activate accelerators. Regardless of the key combination, the syntax of the accelerator is the same. For example,

```
<INPUT TYPE="text" SIZE="40" ACCESSKEY="n" NAME="username">
```

sets the letter "n" as the accelerator for the field. In a browser such as Internet Explorer that recognizes this attribute, the key combination ALT-N will move the cursor to the field immediately. All other browsers will just ignore the key combination.

Note *Avoid using the **ACCESSKEY** attribute on the **<LABEL>** element. In many browsers, it will not focus the associated field.*

One potential problem with access keys is making sure to let the user know exactly what key combinations are used to access fields. In traditional GUI interfaces, the letter of a choice is underlined to indicate an accelerator key. For example in File the "F" key is used to access the menu. While this could be used on the Web, there may be some concern that the user will consider the underlined letter a link. Hopefully, given the context of the underline and the lack of color, the user will not jump to this conclusion. However, because of this potential concern, it may be OK to indicate accelerators in another fashion such as reversing them out.

The best approach to indicating accelerators is to use a style sheet. For example, you might define a class accesskey in a style sheet using a rule like

```
.accesskey    {text-decoration: underline;}
```

and then reference it later on in the form using a **<SPAN>** tag around the particular letter being used as the accelerator:

```
<SPAN CLASS="accesskey">N</SPAN>ame:
```

Using style sheets will allow you to experiment easily with different styles, and will also allow easy removal of the key indications when a browser doesn't support the **ACCESSKEY** attribute. It is very important to turn off the key indication, as it would frustrate a user greatly to see an indication of a keyboard shortcut and not have it work. At the time of this book's writing, only Internet Explorer supported the **ACCESSKEY** attribute. Using a little JavaScript to add the style sheet to the **<HEAD>** section of the HTML document as shown here would reduce the problem of having older browsers show the accelerator indication:

```
<!-- Use this in the HEAD section of the document only -->
<SCRIPT LANGUAGE="JavaScript1.2">
<!--
if (document.all)  // must be IE
{
 document.write("<STYLE>");
 document.write(".accesskey    {text-decoration: underline;
   font-weight: bold;}");
 document.write("</STYLE>");
}
//-->
</SCRIPT>
```

Another potential problem with accelerator keys besides browser support is accidentally masking or even overriding browser accelerator keys. Normally, a browser like Internet Explorer uses key shortcuts to access its primary menus. What would happen when you assign one of these preassigned letters to a form field? Well, either it wouldn't work and the menu would pop down from the browser instead, or you would kill the default action of the accelerator key in favor of your form. The user may be used to pressing "F" to access the File menu on their browser and become highly annoyed.

Rule: Do not override or mask browser accelerator keys.

Table 12-2 shows the current mappings for Internet Explorer and Netscape. Make sure to look carefully in your browser to see if mappings have changed before using a particular letter as an accelerator.

Key	Mapping	Notes
F	File menu	
E	Edit menu	
C	Communicator menu	Netscape only
V	View menu	
G	Go menu	
A	Favorites menu	Internet Explorer only
H	Help	

Table 12-2. *Common Browser Key Bindings*

Given the potential problems with accelerators, one might wonder if there is really any point to using them. The reality is that for a single-time-visit form, the benefit of accelerators is somewhat limited. A user will probably not be used to the form enough to use the shortcuts. However, for forms that a user must fill in frequently—for example, within an intranet or Web application—accelerators could really improve the user's ability to fill things out. Moving the hand from the keyboard to the mouse does take time. For fast form fill-out, accelerators are very useful.

Suggestion: Use accelerator keys for forms that will be used repeatedly.

ToolTips and Form Fields

A ToolTip can be set to provide a small amount of information about the meaning of a particular form field, or even instructions on its use. ToolTips can be set most easily using the **TITLE** attribute for the various HTML form elements. For example, the HTML markup

```
<FORM>
Phone Number:
<INPUT TYPE="TEXT" SIZE="10" NAME="phone"
            TITLE="Enter your phone number without dashes">
</FORM>
```

would render something like the image shown here when the user put their mouse over the field.

Phone Number: 3582702086

Enter your phone number without dashes

Providing extra information about a field using a ToolTip is an easy way to improve form use. Be careful, however, not to put critical information in the ToolTip in case the user has a browser that will not display them.

Suggestion: Use ToolTips to provide extra information about field use and format.

It is possible to use some JavaScript to simulate a ToolTip in other browsers or to provide information in the browser's status bar instead.

Status Messages

Besides using ToolTips, it may be useful to utilize the status bar to provide information to the user on the meaning and use of various form fields. While the status bar may not be in the primary area of focus for the user, unlike the ToolTip, it is not transitory and can be set to display as long as the field is in focus. For example, notice the status bar messages in the example here and how it relates to the field currently focused.

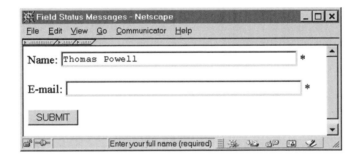

A sample script to use is provided here for use in any form—just alter the values passed to the setStatus function in each form field and include the script in the **<HEAD>** section of your page:

```
<!DOCTYPE HTML PUBLIC "-//W3C//DTD HTML 4.0 Transitional//EN">
<HTML>
<HEAD>
<TITLE>Field Status Messages</TITLE>
<SCRIPT>
<!--
function setStatus(msg) { window.status = msg;}
//-->
</SCRIPT>
</HEAD>
<BODY>
```

```
<FORM>
  Name:
  <INPUT TYPE="TEXT" SIZE="40" NAME="name"
        TITLE="Enter your full name (Required field)"
        onFocus="setStatus('Enter your full name (required)')"
        onBlur="setStatus('')"> * <BR><BR>

  E-mail:
<INPUT TYPE="TEXT" SIZE="40" NAME="email"
TITLE="Enter a complete well formed email address (required)"
onFocus="setStatus('Enter a complete well formed email address
(required)')"
        onBlur="setStatus('')"> * <BR><BR>

  <INPUT TYPE="SUBMIT" VALUE="SUBMIT">
</FORM>
</BODY>
</HTML>
```

Suggestion: Use the status bar to provide messages about field use.

Form Field Help

Given all the problems with form fill-in, it is obviously just a plain good idea to provide help wherever possible. While some browsers do provide online help integration that can be triggered with the F1 key, most users are unaware of this possibility. Besides ToolTips and status messages (discussed previously), the easiest way to provide help is simply to write the help information near the field in question or provide a link or icon indicating help is available, as shown here.

Suggestion: Provide a help button near complex form fields for context-sensitive help.

RETURN Keys and Forms

The use of the RETURN key with Web forms is rather troublesome. Sometimes, hitting the RETURN key will cause the form to submit wherever the user is within the form. In a fair number of browsers, this is the action. However, this is not always the case. Some browsers will not submit a form when the RETURN key is pressed unless the form is composed of a single text field.

 Do not assume that a RETURN press will submit a form.

Many users would like to submit a form by pressing the RETURN key, but generally only at the end of the form. Using JavaScript, it is possible to create a hack that makes forms act consistently from browser to browser. The basic idea is that the form elements are in two separate forms. The first form contains the majority of the elements and the second contains the last element that, after hitting RETURN, should cause the form to submit. When the submission is triggered, the form fields from the first form are copied and sent. The script here illustrates this script in action:

```
<!DOCTYPE HTML PUBLIC "-//W3C//DTD HTML 4.0 Transitional//EN">
<HTML>
<HEAD>
<TITLE>Form Enter Key Hack</TITLE>
<SCRIPT LANGUAGE="JavaScript">
function duplicateFields() {
  for (var i = 0; i < document.topForm.elements.length; i++)
    document.bottomForm.elements[i].value =
document.topForm.elements[i].value;
}
</SCRIPT>
</HEAD>
<BODY>
<FORM NAME="topForm">
First Name: <INPUT TYPE="TEXT" NAME="firstnametemp" VALUE=""><BR>
Last Name: <INPUT TYPE="TEXT" NAME="lastnametemp" VALUE=""><BR>
</FORM>
<FORM NAME="bottomForm" onSubmit="duplicateFields()" ACTION="">
<INPUT TYPE="HIDDEN" NAME="firstname" VALUE="">
<INPUT TYPE="HIDDEN" NAME="lastname" VALUE="">
Phone: <INPUT TYPE="TEXT" NAME="phone" VALUE=""><BR><BR>
<INPUT TYPE="SUBMIT" NAME="Submit" VALUE="SUBMIT">
</FORM>
</BODY>
</HTML>
```

While use of this script does require JavaScript, with some careful sensing and use of the **<NOSCRIPT>** it should be possible to create a fully backward-compatible implementation of this workaround. Before adding this script to your site, consider that unless there is heavy usage on a particular form, it may not be appropriate to go to such lengths to improve form usage in such a subtle manner.

Form Validation

A key aspect of usable forms is helping people to not make mistakes. One of the easiest ways to do this is to check the contents of the forms before the user submits them. This is called *form validation* and can be performed both using a client-side technology like JavaScript or a server-side technology. While a server-side technology may not rely on any particular browser capability, designers should add client-side validation to pages since they will appear more responsive to a user and avoid the round-trip time to the server.

Rule: Validate forms from the client side when possible.

However, consider that the user may not have JavaScript or a similar technology that is useful for client-side validation. In this case, you must rely on server-side checks. In order to get the best of both worlds, consider adding a hidden form field to a form that indicates the state of validation. For example,

```
<INPUT TYPE="HIDDEN" NAME="validated" VALUE="false">
```

would be used to indicate the state of the form. If the form could be validated using JavaScript, the last task to do before submission would be to change the value of the hidden field to true. On the server side, the program to deal with the form data would then look at the field value to determine if validation were required or not. When using this technique, we keep from doing double the work and are very safe to always check if a page is really validated or not.

Rule: Always provide backup validation on the server side.

A big question with form validation is when to actually validate the fields. Many people wait until the very end when the user presses the submit button to check for mistakes. An error is presented, the user corrects it and moves to press the submit button. The process repeats until all the errors are removed from the form. It would actually be better to try to correct the errors either all at once or as the user moves from field to field in the form since it would reduce the amount of trial and error for the user.

Suggestion: Try to validate as people type, using masking, or as they move from field to field.

The only downside to validating as users go along is that if a user is doing a quick head-down fill-in of a form, they may prefer to not be interrupted until they have finished. You may want to consider this when dealing with validation on frequently used forms. Regardless of when errors are caught in a form, it is very important to provide a clear indication of what the errors are and how to correct them.

> **Rule: During form validation, provide a clear indication of what fields are in error and how to correct the error.**

A subtle nuance that can greatly improve the validation experience for the user is to bring focus to a field in error. This allows the user to quickly correct the error vs. having to remember which field was in error and scroll back through the form looking for the field in question.

> **Rule: Bring immediate focus to fields in error.**

Field Masks

Using JavaScript, it is possible to limit the type of data that is entered into a field as it is typed. This goes along with the idea of catching errors as they happen rather than waiting for validation later on. For example, the following script could be used in Internet Explorer or Netscape 4.*x* or better to limit a field to only numeric characters:

```
<!DOCTYPE HTML PUBLIC "-//W3C//DTD HTML 4.0 Transitional//EN">
<HTML>
<HEAD>
<TITLE>Numerics Only Demo</TITLE>
<SCRIPT>
<!--
function numbersOnly(field, event) {
var key,keychar;

 if (window.event)
   key = window.event.keyCode;
 else if (event)
   key = event.which;
 else
   return true;

keychar = String.fromCharCode(key);

if ((key==null) || (key==0) || (key==8) ||
   (key==9) || (key==13) || (key==27) )
   return true;
```

```
else if ((("0123456789").indexOf(keychar) > -1))
  return true;
else
  return false;
}
//-->
</SCRIPT>
</HEAD>
<BODY>
<FORM NAME="testform">
Robot Serial Number:
<INPUT TYPE="TEXT" NAME="serialnumber" SIZE="10" MAXLENGTH="10"
    ONKEYPRESS="return numbersOnly(this, event)">
</FORM>
</BODY>
</HTML>
```

The benefit of masking a field is, obviously, that it avoids having to do heavy validation later on by trying to stop errors before they happen.

Suggestion: Mask text fields to limit the type of characters entered.

Another possible way to have users avoid making mistakes besides masking a field is not letting them edit a field at all if it shouldn't be modified. Through HTML or scripting, it is possible to disable a field or set its value to read only.

Disabling Fields

A disabled form field should not accept input from the user, is not part of the tabbing order of a page, and is not submitted with the rest of the form contents. The operation of the HTML 4 attribute **DISABLED** as shown here:

```
<INPUT TYPE="TEXT" VALUE="Can't Touch this" NAME="fieldname" DISABLED>
```

would be all that's necessary to disable a field under an HTML 4.0–compliant browser. A browser rendering of a disabled field is usually to "gray out" out the field. It is always a good idea to disable labels as well, either manually with a style sheet or with the **DISABLED** attribute.

A scripting language would have to be used to turn disabled fields on and off, depending on context. The following markup shows how this might be used, and works in Internet Explorer browsers:

```
<!DOCTYPE HTML PUBLIC "-//W3C//DTD HTML 4.0 Transitional//EN">
<HTML>
<HEAD>
<TITLE>Disabled 1</TITLE>
</HEAD>
<BODY>
<FORM NAME="myform">

Color your robot?  
Yes <INPUT TYPE="radio" NAME="colorrobot" VALUE="yes" CHECKED
onClick="myform.robotcolor.disabled=false;
robotcolorlabel.style.color='black'">
No <INPUT TYPE="radio" NAME="colorrobot" VALUE="no"
onClick="myform.robotcolor.disabled=true;
robotcolorlabel.style.color='gray'">
<BR><BR>

<LABEL ID="robotcolorlabel">
Color:
<SELECT NAME="robotcolor">
   <OPTION SELECTED>Silver
   <OPTION SELECTED>Green
   <OPTION SELECTED>Red
   <OPTION SELECTED>Blue
   <OPTION SELECTED>Orange
</SELECT>
</LABEL>
</FORM>
</BODY>
</HTML>
```

Unfortunately, the previous example does not work in Netscape or other browsers that lack full HTML 4 support and vary in their scripting capabilities. The use of this field does not degrade well, as shown in Figure 12-18.

Using JavaScript, it is possible to create a more backward-compatable disabling feature as shown next, but it is a less-than-ideal approach. In this case, when the field is disabled, it is reset automatically when the user tries to change it. Also note that the data will be passed in no matter if it is disabled or not, so a hidden form field is added that can be relayed to the server to indicate if the field was disabled so it can be ignored. This script should work well in all JavaScript-aware browsers, but do note it

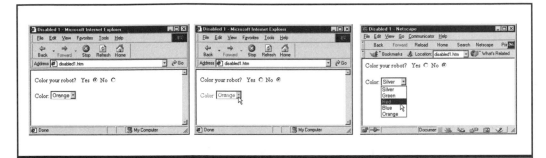

Figure 12-18. *Disabled fields do not degrade well*

does not change the appearance of fields when they are disabled and does in some sense let the user make a mistake—a less-than-ideal solution to say the least.

```
<!DOCTYPE HTML PUBLIC "-//W3C//DTD HTML 4.0 Transitional//EN">
<HTML>
<HEAD>
<TITLE>Disabled 2</TITLE>
</HEAD>
<BODY>

<FORM NAME="myform">

Color your robot?  
Yes <INPUT TYPE="radio" NAME="colorrobot" VALUE="yes" CHECKED
onClick="document.myform.robotcolordisabled.value='FALSE'">
No <INPUT TYPE="radio" NAME="colorrobot" VALUE="no"
onClick="document.myform.robotcolordisabled.value='TRUE'">
<BR><BR>

<INPUT TYPE="HIDDEN" NAME="robotcolordisabled" VALUE="FALSE">

Color:
<SELECT NAME="robotcolor"
onFocus="currentSelect=document.myform.robotcolor.selectedIndex"
onChange="if (document.myform.robotcolordisabled.value == 'TRUE')
{document.myform.robotcolor.selectedIndex=currentSelect;
alert('Field is disabled') }">
    <OPTION SELECTED>Silver
```

```
    <OPTION>Green
    <OPTION>Red
    <OPTION>Blue
    <OPTION>Orange
</SELECT>

</FORM>
</BODY>
</HTML>
```

If possible, it is better to redesign a form so it does not rely on a disable function, but if required, disabling can be accomplished by use of the HTML 4 disabled attributes and JavaScript that either hides a field or clears its value if it is disabled.

Suggestion: Disable or hide fields that are not necessary in a particular context.

Read-Only Fields

Text fields can also be set not only to a disabled state, but also to read only. A read-only text field can be clicked on but not changed. Unlike disabled fields, the values of a read-only field are submitted to the server when a form is submitted. Under HTML 4, it is easy to set a text field to this state simply by including the **READONLY** attribute like so:

```
<INPUT TYPE="text" NAME="readonlyfield" VALUE="Can't touch this!?" READONLY>
```

Like the disabled feature of HTML 4, read only does not degrade well as older browsers will simply ignore the **READONLY** attribute they don't understand, leaving the field modifiable. Using JavaScript, it is pretty easy to simulate the idea of read only simply by blurring a read-only field, as shown, as a user tries to select it. The example shown here demonstrates this in action:

```
<!DOCTYPE HTML PUBLIC "-//W3C//DTD HTML 4.0 Transitional//EN">
<HTML>
<HEAD>
<TITLE>Readonly</TITLE>
</HEAD>
<BODY>

<FORM NAME="myform">

Change standard name of robot?  
Yes <INPUT TYPE="radio" NAME="colorrobot" VALUE="yes" CHECKED onClick="robotnamereadonly=false">
No <INPUT TYPE="radio" NAME="colorrobot" VALUE="no"
```

```
onClick="robotnamereadonly=true;document.myform.robotname.value=
'Robby'">
<BR><BR>
<SCRIPT>
<!--
robotnamereadonly=false;
//-->
</SCRIPT>
Name: <INPUT TYPE="text" NAME="robotname" VALUE="Robby" SIZE=
"20" MAXSIZE="20"ONFOCUS="if (robotnamereadonly) this.blur()">

</FORM>
</BODY>
</HTML>
```

From a usability point of view, read-only fields are poorly indicated to the user. The user should be better informed of a field's read-only status.

Suggestion: When setting fields to read only, change appearance or alert the user to the status of the field.

Default Data

Even after applying every usability improvement in this chapter, filling out a form can still be an arduous process for a Web user. Consider how many forms and fields you are asked to fill out during a few-hour browsing session before adding more questions. One simple thing that can be done is to provide default data that is likely to be used by users. For example, if most users order only a single item, why not fill out the quantity field this way automatically? This is easily done using the **VALUE** attribute for a field.

```
Quantity: <INPUT TYPE="TEXT" NAME="quantity"
          SIZE="2" MAXLENGTH="2" VALUE="1">
```

Suggestion: Provide defaults and always set values to the most likely entry.

Of course, users will not always enter the same data, so defaults are not going to help all the time. If data is stored about a user, it might be possible to populate fields with data the user has entered before. Many e-commerce sites already remember common data about a user, including address, shipping preferences, and credit card number, and may fill out the form in advanced for a user. Of course, the data storage and complexity required for such personalization may be beyond some sites. Fortunately, newer browsers, such as Internet Explorer 5, provide autocompletion facilities for form fields, which should speed up data entry significantly.

Internet Explorer AutoComplete

An important form-use improvement introduced by Internet Explorer 5 is called AutoComplete. The concept of AutoComplete is to help users fill out forms by providing a pick list of previously used values for similar form names, or even relating the information in their personal data profile or vCard to form fields.

For users to fully enjoy AutoComplete features for forms, they must enable them. In IE 5, select Internet Options on the Tools menu, select the Content tab, and then click the AutoComplete button. Users might also want to fill out their personal information by selecting the My Profile button on the same dialog. Once AutoComplete is enabled, the browser should provide a pick list for text fields when the user either presses the DOWN ARROW key or the characters they are typing match a previously entered value for a similar field, as shown here:

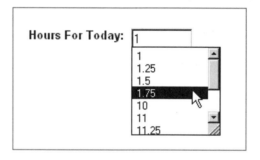

From an HTML perspective, there are a few things that are important to know about AutoComplete. First, on some fields you may want to disable AutoComplete for privacy reasons. You can set an attribute called **AUTOCOMPLETE** to off in either the **<FORM>** or the **<INPUT>** tag:

```
<FORM AUTOCOMPLETE="off"> ... </FORM>
```

or

```
<INPUT TYPE="password" AUTOCOMPLETE="off"
       NAME="supersecret">
```

Turning the attribute on will provide no benefit, as the user must enable AutoComplete in the first place. The key to using AutoComplete is to make sure to use field names similar to those of other sites out there on the Internet. The browser first presents information from previously completed form fields, and it also looks at a common name list drawn from popular Web sites. In short, if you use the same field names, the user will be prompted to reuse data. This means that you need to make sure that you name fields with simple common names like firstname, lastname, address, city, state, zip, and so on.

Suggestion: Name your field names with simple common names to take advantage of browser AutoComplete features.

Besides using common values, AutoComplete may pull information automatically from a user's vCard schema as set in the Profile Assistant. Many users have begun to use profiles such as those provided by a vCard to provide the equivalent of an electronic business card. To focus on accessing the user's profile information, use the **VCARD_NAME** attribute in the form fields. For example, to allow someone to automatically fill in form data from their vCard profile, you might have an **<INPUT>** tag like this:

```
<INPUT TYPE="text" SIZE="40" NAME="company"
       VCARD_NAME="vCard.Company">
```

Of course, it is important to associate the correct vCard field with each field in your form, Table 12-3 provides the values for the **VCARD_NAME** attribute categorized by the type of the information.

General Info	Home Info	Business Info
vCard.FirstName	vCard.Home.StreetAddress	vCard.Company
vCard.MiddleName	vCard.Home.City	vCard.Department
vCard.LastName	vCard.Home.State	vCard.Office
vCard.DisplayName	vCard.Home.Country	vCard.JobTitle
vCard.Gender	vCard.Home.Zipcode	vCard.Business.StreetAddress
vCard.Email	vCard.Home.Phone	vCard.Business.City
vCard.Homepage	vCard.Home.Fax	vCard.Business.State
vCard.Notes		vCard.Business.Zipcode
		vCard.Business.Country
		vCard.Business.Phone
		vCard.Cellular
		vCard.Pager
		vCard.Business.Fax
		vCard.Business.URL

Table 12-3. *VCARD_NAME Values by Category*

Before concluding this chapter, let's take a brief look at some of the very advanced GUI ideas that are staring to be applied on Web sites.

Advanced Web GUI Features

With careful use of JavaScript, it is possible to create a variety of advanced GUI features, many of which are used for navigation purposes. For example, a cascading menu that triggers page loads could be used to create a sitewide navigation bar as shown in Figure 12-19.

The use of such a navigation bar flattens the site by reducing the number of clicks a user has to make to get to a particular page. However, it also makes a site look more and more like a typical GUI application. Adding a navigation bar to a site isn't difficult, but the code is far too complex to present here. Interested readers are directed to the numerous online tutorials at http://www.webreference.com/dhtml/hiermenus/ to learn about adding menus to their site. The code used in Figure 12-19 that shows the context of how this menu might be used in the DemoCompany site can be found at http://www.webdesignref.com/chapter12/hiermenu.htm.

Tree Navigation

Another GUI navigation facility is the use of tree controls or expandable/collapsible outlines for navigating a site. This is shown here.

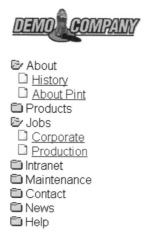

Sometimes, tree navigation controls use a folder/document icon pair, while other times they use arrows or plus and minus signs. Regardless of the form, there should be a distinction between an option that is open and one that is closed.

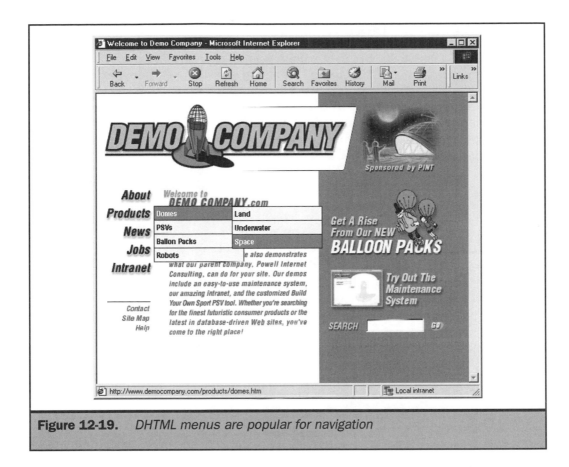

Figure 12-19.   *DHTML menus are popular for navigation*

Rule: When using a tree control, make sure that open and close states are distinct.

Another consideration with tree-style navigation is making sure that it does
not get too deep. While this feature may reduce the number of clicks to navigate a
site tremendously, the amount of scrolling that may occur for a large number of
items—both left to right, as well as up and down—could make the control difficult
to use. Make sure to consider how far the control could expand.

*Beware of using tree or outline controls on very deep lists as the user may lose their
place or the control may scroll too far rightwards.*

Like the previous example, the code for tree-style navigation can be found
in numerous places online, including http://www.webdesignref.com/
chapter12/outline.htm.

ELEMENTS OF PAGE
DESIGN

Tabbed Dialogs

Using DHTML, it is possible to create a tabbed dialog as shown in Figure 12-20.

In GUI applications, a tabbed dialog is commonly used in very complex dialog boxes, and thus its use isn't always favored. However, on the Web, there may be some use for this style of interface because in some implementations all the contents of each tab are loaded before display, which makes the interface appear very responsive. The example for the tabbed dialog can be found online at http://www.webdesignref.com/chapter12/tabbeddialog.htm.

Sliders

A slider is a relatively rare GUI interface element mostly found in color-adjustment dialogs. It is possible, using JavaScript, to build a slider as shown in Figure 12-21.

Often sliders are used to move through a large, continuous range of values. Because of this, it may be difficult for users to set exact values. Very often a text field that can be filled in directly is associated with a slider.

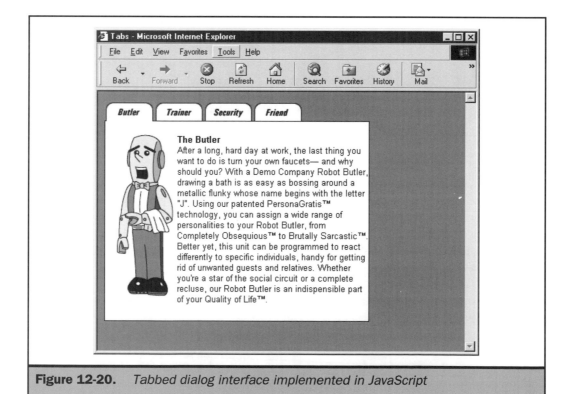

Figure 12-20. *Tabbed dialog interface implemented in JavaScript*

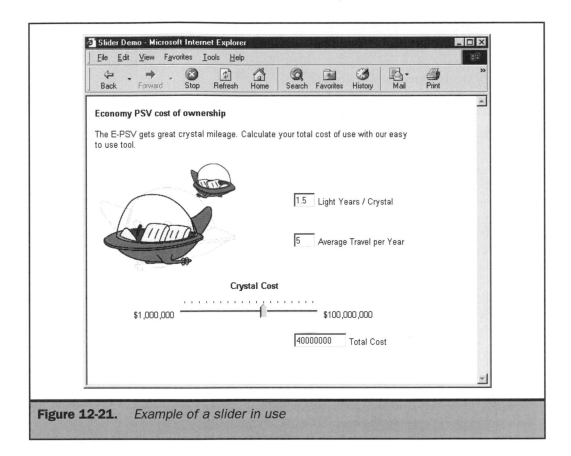

Figure 12-21.   *Example of a slider in use*

 Add a text box near a slider to show a selected value and allow a user to set the value of the slider directly.

Another potential downside to sliders is that it is often difficult to position directly to a particular value. The text box helps quite a bit, but often tick marks or other labels are used to indicate increments or useful stopping points for the slider.

 Use ticks to indicate major selection points in a slider.

Context Menus

The last advanced GUI facility is the use of the context menu. Since the introduction of Internet Explorer 5, the single-mouse-button barrier has been broken. Now, with scripting, it is possible to sense when to click on the right mouse button and perform some actions, such as creating a context menu or even suppressing the use of the menu.

Some designers, hoping to make it difficult for people to steal their images, have resorted to putting a line like this in their **<BODY>** element. However, turning off JavaScript or using an older browser easily thwarts this approach. An example of how a custom context menu could be created in shown in Figure 12-22.

When Web Applications Are Just Applications

The previous section indicates that the gap between what is possible in a Web site using standard technology like JavaScript, CSS, and HTML and a desktop application is narrowing all the time. In fact, if you consider what could be done using Java, ActiveX, or even Flash, it is pretty much possible to simulate any GUI feature known. When compatibility problems become less prominent, the difference between what is considered a Web application interface and what is just a plain application will somewhat blur. Already, many Windows applications are capable of accessing Internet facilities and Web applications are acting like desktop applications. Once the gap is closed, the need for designers to be more aware of standard GUI interface conventions may become crucial. However, until the time that the two meet, it is important to try to integrate conventions. When using object technologies like Java or ActiveX, avoid building an application interface within a Web page.

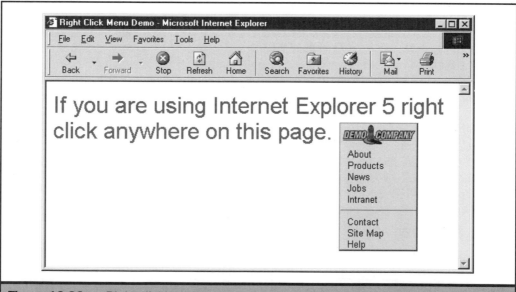

Figure 12-22. *Right-clicking exposes a custom context menu*

Take a DemoCompany-designed page. Then splice out the middle of it and put a Java applet in there that has menus and such. You might want to find a Java applet for an office-style application online and splice it in using Photoshop. You don't have to make it work.

The real problem with mixing GUI and Web design in such a manner is that you create two different contexts for a user to worry about. Consider that the operating system has an interface style, then the browser introduces its own interface, and within that a Web site is displayed with yet a third interface operation. Does it make sense to add a fourth-level interface to that mix? Probably not.

Rule: Avoid mixing complex GUI interfaces within included binaries such as Java applets with Web page interfaces.

Summary

Web sites often do utilize interface conventions common to graphical user interface (GUI) design theory. Some ideas, such as double clicking or drag-and-drop, have yet to really see much use on the Web, but more and more, the Web is starting to look like a GUI application—particularly when used within intranets. Web designers must understand both the traditions of GUI design as well as what is reasonable to implement using core HTML technologies like HTML, CSS, and JavaScript. Forms, in particular, stand to benefit greatly from GUI principles. With some work and the use of a technology like Java, a designer could turn a Web site into something that looks just like a desktop application—but should they? Web sites do have their own design aesthetics, as discussed in previous chapters, and strictly applying GUI layout and conventions from a Windows application might actually result in an unusable site. For now, designers do have to struggle through with what the technologies provide. The next chapter will present a complete discussion of the technologies used in Web design as well as some of their design and use limitations.

ELEMENTS OF PAGE DESIGN

The Complete Reference

Web Design

Part IV

Technology and Web Design

The Complete Reference

Web Design

Chapter 13

Web Technologies and Their Effect on Web Design

The medium of the Web heavily influences what is possible in design. Unfortunately, far too many designers are not adequately schooled in Web technology and make unnecessary mistakes when implementing sites. The Web is a basically a client/server environment, with three components to the medium: the client side, the server side, and the network. Each will be discussed in turn, but first we should isolate the core client-side technologies in use on the Web. The first technology is the Web browser, which renders Web pages. Almost inseparable from the browser is HTML, the glue that binds disparate page elements together into a more or less comprehensible whole. Finally, CSS is becoming an increasingly vital technology for a growing number of sites. Eventually, other markup technologies, like XML, may influence Web design—but for now the core technologies are fairly stable. Client-side technologies like JavaScript, often in the form of Dynamic HTML (DHTML), are also particularly important in modern Web pages. However, client-side technologies often come with unwanted side effects. Tried and true server-side programming, including CGI programs, should not immediately be dismissed in favor of client-side interactivity. The technology and use of multimedia is also important to understand, as browsers vary greatly in their support for animation, audio, and video. Chapter 14 will deal with how the network and server affect the delivery of a site to the user.

Web Technology Problems:
The Bucket of Ice-Cold Water

Any designer who has tried to build a Web site has occasionally been doused by a bucket of cold water known as "Web technology problems." Web technologies don't make it easy for designers to realize their vision. Building Web sites can be frustrating because the technology used to build pages changes rapidly, is not always fully defined, and may be implemented improperly by browser vendors. Since the Web was popularized, the base markup technology, HTML, has been redefined significantly four times: 2.0, 3.2, 4.0, and now XHTML. This isn't counting abortive specifications like HTML 3.0 and the numerous proprietary efforts made. Other technologies such as Java or JavaScript have changed—maybe even more significantly—in a shorter period of time. Browser vendors have pretty much kept a schedule of releasing a major new release of a browser every year, chock full of new features—and new bugs.

The problems are there, but not everyone sees them or wants to admit to seeing them. This may actually be a blessing in disguise. For kicks, turn off your JavaScript, change your font size, use a nonstandard browser, and browse the Web. Watch as large company sites and some of the most award-winning designer-oriented sites fall apart, catastrophically in some situations. Designers who claim that technology considerations are not significant to their work have either hidden their heads in the proverbial sand, or else truly do not care about designing for users, the Internet environment, or the implications of communication in the Web medium. Web design must encompass technical design or it will fail.

The lack of stable and well-supported technologies to build sites with is very troublesome. Some developers are very quick to adopt the latest and greatest technology release only to discover huge bugs and gaping specification support holes in browsers. Users often pay the price when faced with exclusionary site designs with splash pages telling them to upgrade their browsers or download a new plug-in technology. On the other hand, if we are completely open to all users, we might be forced to create a site that takes no chances with technologies, a site that is limited to simple HTML and server-side programming technologies. Users may not find a site utilizing such technologies motivating or interesting. Some usability experts will bemoan the use of bleeding-edge technologies, but the reality is that the trade-off is that of function. If a new technology can be implemented properly, and provides an exciting enough new technology, users will probably deal with the downsides. Only use bleeding-edge technologies when there is a very good reason to.

Rule: Do not use bleeding-edge Web technology without good reason.

While Web technology can make designing Web sites difficult, the standard and relatively open technologies being used online have created a development environment that has never been seen before. In the past, creating an application that could be accessed by literally millions of people around the world on a variety of platforms was nearly impossible. Today, even relatively novice developers do it all the time. The rest of the chapter will briefly present the core Web technologies in use. A few of the core technologies that all designers should understand regardless of technical sophistication—HTML, CSS, and JavaScript—will be discussed in more depth. The main purpose of this chapter is not to teach designers all the intricacies of each technology, but to present each technology's role in the larger picture of the Web, and how each affects Web design. Tips and suggestions for use will also be presented for each technology discussed. Readers looking for detailed tutorials should first access the resources page online at http://www.webdesignref.com/resources to see lists, books, and tutorials available for more in-depth study.

Browsers

The first aspect of Web technology to consider is the browser. The Web browser is the interpreter of our Web sites. It is very important to understand the Web browser being supported and what capabilities it has. The two most common browsers at the time of this book's publication are Microsoft's Internet Explorer and Netscape's Communicator (Navigator). While these two browsers account for most users accessing public Web sites, there are numerous other versions of browsers in use. The exact figure for browser usage at public Web sites varies all the time, and is tracked by sites such as http://statmarket.com, which draw usage samples from thousands of sites.

The problem with published browser usage reports is that they don't necessarily consider your browsing audience. Consider a site that publishes Macintosh software; its browser usage pattern might actually show a fair number of users with CyberDog, a Macintosh-specific browser that has a notable number of rabid followers. However, most sites probably wouldn't consider CyberDog something to even think about. Depending on your users, the types of browsers will vary. Some sites find that Web TV is important to them because they cater to senior citizens; other sites find video game console browsers important because they cater to young gamers. Finally, some sites may find text-only access using personal digital assistant or cell phone browsers a growing population. The point is that assuming that just because statistics for a collection of large or small sites favor a particular browser, it doesn't necessarily follow that your site will exhibit the same browser usage patterns—though it is pretty likely. Look at your own log files to determine browser usage patterns. If you are building an intranet site you might not even have to look at your logs to understand what browsers are in use.

> **Rule: Beware of relying on published browser usage figures; track actual browser usage on YOUR site.**

Now, given a mix of browsers that favors the top two vendors with a smattering of other browsers, the question arises: how should the site be designed? One possibility is to look at the various browsers and their capabilities and design for some common set of features. First consider the browsers discussed in Table 13-1.

Considering the variation between browsers, the common ground isn't terribly advanced. The safest design platform seems still to be what Netscape 3.x supports, though more and more designers are trying to design for 4.x generation browsers. The only problem with moving to the next generation is that the gap between what Netscape 4.x supports and Internet Explorer 4.x and beyond support is rather large. Because of this, sites are starting to significantly favor Internet Explorer. Netscape's Mozilla project suggests that an improved browser platform may be around the corner, but regardless there will not be an overnight adoption of browsers around the Web. As the installed base increases, the time to embrace new technologies will increase. Because of this, public sites should consider developing for at least one, if not two, generations behind the current release of a browser. Notice that even more than four years after the release of 2.x-generation browsers, many public sites still account for them in their design, and some sites even deal with 1.x generation browsers well.

Tip	*Consider developing for at least the last two, if not three, versions of a browser to account for slow upgrades.*

It is easy to be overwhelmed with potential browser considerations even if just dealing with the major browsers' most recent versions. Consider, for example, the number of Netscape browsers in the 4.x generation listed in the following table. At the time of this writing, there were 15 major versions of the 4.x generation alone and

Browser	Version	HTML Version Support	JavaScript	CSS	Programming	Comments
Internet Explorer	3	HTML 3.2 + extras	JavaScript 1.0	Somewhat	Helper apps, ActiveX controls, Netscape plug-in compatibility, Java, VBScript	Some corporate and slow upgraders still use this version. Good possibility to target this browser for a fallback version of a site.
Internet Explorer	4	HTML 4 + extras	JavaScript 1.1 + extras	Yes	Helper apps, ActiveX controls, Netscape plug-in compatibility, Java, VBScript	IE 4's main advances were in CSS support and improved JavaScript. IE 4 was the first browser to support pages that could be significantly manipulated after page load using JavaScript and relying on the Document Object Model, or DOM.
Internet Explorer	5	HTML 4 + extras	JavaScript 1.2 + extras	Yes	Helper apps, ActiveX controls, Netscape plug-in compatibility, Java, VBScript	IE 5 mostly refines the features provided in HTML 4, though it does begin the use of client-side XML.

Table 13-1 *Common Browser Versions and Characteristics*

Browser	Version	HTML Version Support	JavaScript	CSS	Programming	Comments
Internet Explorer	5.5	HTML 4 + extras	JavaScript 1.2 + extras	Yes	Helper apps, ActiveX controls, Netscape plug-in compatibility, Java, VBScript	IE 5.5 continues to refine the basic ideas presented in IE 4 and 5 with enhancements to style sheet support and XML.
Netscape	1.x	HTML 2 + extras	No	No	Helper apps	No frames, (good example of a worst-case graphical browser).
Netscape	2.x	HTML 2 + extras	JavaScript 1.0	No	Helper apps, plug-ins, Java	No background color on table cells. Java implementation buggy. JavaScript limited to simple form validation. Fallback browser.
Netscape	3.x	HTML 3.2	JavaScript 1.2	No	Helper apps, plug-ins, Java	Rollover buttons become possible, Java more stable. Fallback browser.

Table 13-1 *Common Browser Versions and Characteristics (continued)*

Browser	Version	HTML Version Support	JavaScript	CSS	Programming	Comments
Netscape	4.x	HTML 4 + extras	JavaScript 1.2, 1.3	Yes	Helper apps, plug-ins, Java	Limited DHTML support, primarily limited to object movement and visibility. CSS support buggy, suppressed JavaScript error messages, automatic installation of plug-ins introduced. Popular browser.
Mozilla (the upcoming Netscape)	N/A	HTML 4	JavaScript	Yes	Helper apps, plug-ins, Java	Though still an early development browser, Mozilla shows significant standards support for HTML, CSS, the DOM, and XML.

Table 13-1   *Common Browser Versions and Characteristics* (continued)

more than 200 other different potential Netscape variations—primarily older versions or beta releases—floating around the Web, all with different capabilities and bugs.

Netscape 4.x Generation Variations

4.0	4.5	4.6	4.7
4.01	4.51	4.61	4.71
4.02			4.72
4.03			
4.04			
4.05			
4.06			
4.07			
4.08			

Of course, Netscape isn't the only browser vendor, and there are slight upgrades made to Internet Explorer as well. The only point to make here is that browsers are moving targets. Every release has new features and different bugs. Just because someone is using a 4.x-generation browser doesn't guarantee a site will work the same under the same version on another platform or under an interim release. Sorry, but Netscape 4 or Internet Explorer 4 on Windows won't work the same on Macintosh and NT. Even different interim releases like 4.03 and 4.5 may exhibit significant differences in page rendering and bugs. Add in the continual use of half-done beta browsers and you have a recipe for disaster. Pages often won't render correctly, and errors will ensue. Users, unfortunately, won't always place blame correctly. A small layout problem may be interpreted as the designer screwing up, not the browser vendor releasing a poorly tested product.

Rule: Users often don't blame browsers for simple errors—they blame sites.

So what's a developer to do? First, make sure you know what's going on. Keep up with the latest news in browsers at sites like www.browserwatch.com. In particular, watch out for beta and interim releases. They are often the most dangerous, and users will not consider a 4.7 and 4.71 to be significantly different.

 Be careful of features in beta and interim releases of browsers.

The next thing to consider is exactly what browsers you need to be aware of. This is a question of the browsers used by the site's audience, so look to your log files. In general, public sites should be as browser agnostic as possible, while private sites like intranets may be designed specifically for a single browser. Designers should be aware of the browser families listed in Table 13-2. Users interested in development for noncomputing platforms may also find Palm (http://www.palm.com/devzone/) or cell phone simulators (http://www.phone.com/developers) very useful.

Browser	URL	Comments
Internet Explorer	http://www.microsoft.com/ie	Consider having the last three versions of this popular browser.
Netscape Communicator	http://www.netscape.com/browsers/	With so many versions available, consider using the last version of each major release: 4.7, 4.6, 4.5, 4.0x, 3.x, and 2.x.
Mozilla	http://www.mozilla.org	Netscape's project to build a 5.x or 6.x generation browser should eventually bear fruit, but until then keep an in-development copy around to test standards.
Opera	http://www.operasoftware.com	This fast standards-aware browser is becoming very popular and may be a strong third choice for some users.
America Online	http://webmaster.aol.com	Not a Web browser per se, but the use of Web browsers under AOL is often very troublesome. Developers should look at public sites under AOL very carefully.
WebTV	http://developer.webtv.net	The simulator shows the restrictions of the WebTV television-viewing environment.

Table 13-2. *Useful Browsers for Testing Purposes*

Browser	URL	Comments
Lynx	http://lynx.browser.org	Useful to test Lynx to understand text-only rendering.
Amaya	http://www.w3.org/Amaya/	Not a realistic browser for users, but the W3C's test browser often implements interesting standards features before commercial browsers. Useful for experimenting with specifications. Avoid for realistic testing.

Table 13-2. *Useful Browsers for Testing Purposes* (continued)

Beyond the leading browsers, consider testing with standards-oriented browsers as well as text-only or alternative environment access browsers.

Given the number of browsers available and the significant difficulties involved in testing literally dozens of different configurations just to ensure a site renders under common viewing environments, some authors are quick to author for a particular browser version or to indicate that a particular vendor's browser is the preferred viewing platform. Many sites that do this exhibit a browser badge on the site. If a particular browser is required, do not blatantly advertise it on the home page as many sites do. It simply announces that you practice exclusionary development.

Do not advertise favored browsers blatantly on a home page.

It is possible, instead, to detect to see if a user is not using the appropriate browser and direct them to a special page for more information, or to even build a page that fits their browsing environment.

Browser Detection

Using JavaScript or even CGI programming, it is possible to detect the browser in use, since all browsers should transmit a USER_AGENT value when requesting a page. The following script simply prints the value of the browser name and version values onscreen:

```
<!DOCTYPE HTML PUBLIC "-//W3C//DTD HTML 4.0 Transitional//EN">
<HTML>
<HEAD>
<TITLE>Browser Detect Example</TITLE>
</HEAD>
<BODY>
<SCRIPT LANGUAGE="JavaScript">
<!--
var browserName = navigator.appName;
var browserVersion = parseFloat(navigator.appVersion);
document.write("Your browser is ", browserName, " ",
browserVersion, ".");

// -->
</SCRIPT>
<NOSCRIPT>
Sorry, I can't detect your browser without JavaScript.
</NOSCRIPT>
</BODY>
</HTML>
```

Using a script like this, it would be possible to then create conditional pages based on the browser hitting the page. Consider the fact that, by using JavaScript, it is possible to send a user to a different page, such as index4.htm, automatically if they are using 4.x generation or better browser, as shown here:

```
<!DOCTYPE HTML PUBLIC "-//W3C//DTD HTML 4.0 Transitional//EN">
<HTML>
<HEAD>
<TITLE>Browser Detect Example 2</TITLE>
```

```
</HEAD>
<BODY>
<SCRIPT LANGUAGE="JavaScript">
<!--
var browserName = navigator.appName;

if ((browserName == "Microsoft Internet Explorer") ||
 (browserName == "Netscape"))
 majorBrowser = true;
else
 majorBrowser = false;

var version = parseFloat(navigator.appVersion);

if (majorBrowser && (version >= 4))
 location = 'index4.htm';

// -->
</SCRIPT>

3.0 version here

</BODY>
</HTML>
```

However, there are a few problems using browser detection this way. First, you have to make sure the script can even be executed. Because of this, you may want to do some basic browser detection using server-side technologies.

Suggestion: To ensure success, use server-side detection for basic browser profiling.

Regardless of where the detection is done, the fundamental problem with this approach is that you have to be a browser capabilities expert. Given the number of browsers out there, this can be rather troublesome. Fortunately, it is becoming easier and easier to deal with this. First of all, programming the detection code yourself isn't necessary; instead, you can rely on a server-side program like BrowserHawk (http://www.browserhawk.com) to figure out what kind of browser is hitting your site. Second, given the common need for designers to know what capabilities a user has, Microsoft introduced client capabilities detection in Internet Explorer 5. The markup shown here demonstrates this idea:

```
<HTML XMLNS:IE>
<HEAD>
<TITLE>Browser Detect 3</TITLE>
<STYLE>
<!--
@media all { IE\:clientCaps {behavior:url(#default#clientCaps)}
}
-->
</STYLE>
</HEAD>
<BODY>
<IE:clientCaps ID="oClientCaps" />
<SCRIPT>
<!--
document.write("<H2>Screen Capabilities</H2>");
document.write("Screen Height: " + oClientCaps.height + "<BR>");
document.write("Screen Width: " + oClientCaps.width + "<BR>");
document.write("Available Height: " + oClientCaps.availHeight + "<BR>");
document.write("Available Width: " + oClientCaps.availWidth + "<BR>");
document.write("Color Depth: " + oClientCaps.colorDepth + "bit<BR>");
document.write("<H2>Browser Capabilities</H2>");
document.write("Cookies On? " + oClientCaps.cookieEnabled + "<BR>");
document.write("Java Enabled? " + oClientCaps.javaEnabled + "<BR>");
document.write("<H2>System and Connection Characteristics</H2>");
document.write("Connection Type: " + oClientCaps.connectionType + "<BR>");
document.write("CPU: " + oClientCaps.cpuClass + "<BR>");
document.write("Platform: " + oClientCaps.platform + "<BR>");
document.write("<H2>Language Issues</H2>");
document.write("System Language: " + oClientCaps.systemLanguage + "<BR>");
document.write("User Language: " + oClientCaps.userLanguage + "<BR>");
// -->
</SCRIPT>
</BODY>
</HTML>
```

A rendering of this example in Internet Explorer 5, as shown in Figure 13-1, shows that nearly every bit of information necessary to customize a site for a user is easily found.

While IE5 makes life easier, with the proper amount of scripting it has been possible to detect browser capabilities since Netscape 3. Unfortunately, because of the difficulty, few have really spent the time to do it well. Instead, users have been locked out of sites, or designers have relied on self-profiling schemes where the user is asked to make a choice where a wrong choice may result in a poor viewing experience, as shown in Figure 13-2.

Rule: Profile technical capabilities if possible, or assume the worst if you can't.

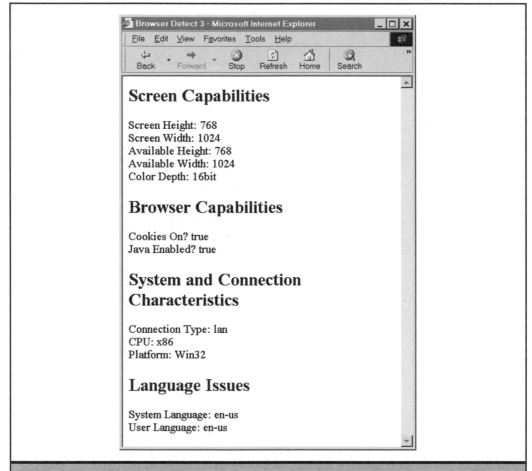

Figure 13-1. *Browser capability detection is becoming easier*

Being able to sense for user capabilities is integral to building pages custom tailored for the user, but carefully consider the implications of doing this. Parallel sites for different browsers may have to be maintained, or a great amount of conditional code will need to be used in a page. Before running out and stealing, buying, or developing browser-sensing scripts to build custom pages for different user profiles, it is worth reflecting on the long-term costs of such sensing. At the least, you will be taking on an exceptional amount of sensing code, and perhaps will have nothing different to offer. If you do go to the effort of building alternative pages, how much is enough? Taken to extremes, one could imagine a dozen different versions of a site running in parallel. This is a maintenance nightmare. And we haven't even touched on whether to use client-side or server-side technologies.

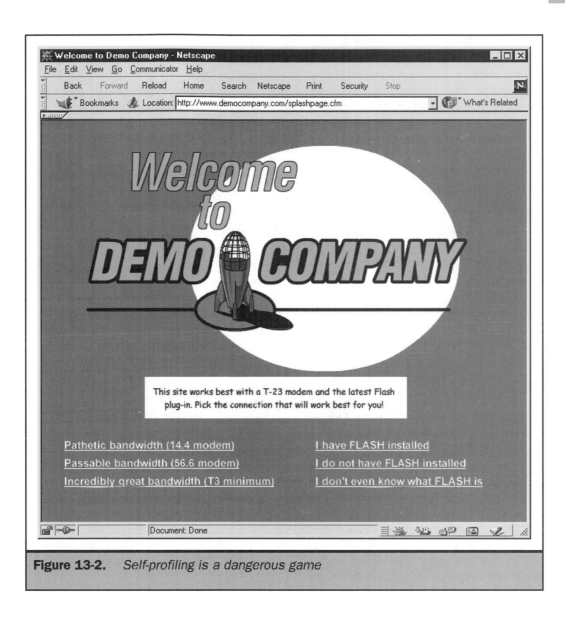

Figure 13-2.   *Self-profiling is a dangerous game*

With that in mind, consider using a script following this logic, regardless whether it be client-side JavaScript or a server technology:

```
If (browser CSS capable)
 Use linked style sheet and absolute positioning
Else
 Use tables
```

It would be possible to build the page based upon these conditions and dynamically write out code. Unfortunately, many different aspects of a page might have to be written in this manner. CSS, JavaScript, and component technologies like Netscape plug-ins are the most troublesome aspects of Web technology, and often need such conditional code. However, even HTML might occasionally need to be dynamically generated. At this point, the metaphor of a "page" fails to accurately represent what appears in the browser window. Any relation between a Web page and a print page has disappeared. Web pages that are this dynamic are truly programs.

HTML

Despite being the base technology on which Web pages are built, HTML is actually poorly understood by most of its practitioners. Many commercial editors produce illegal code, and tutorials and books on the subject contain significant falsehoods. The reason for this is that the rules of HTML are not enforced, which leads to complacency on the part of developers. Web browsers are the root of the problem. Browsers are permissive in what they allow to render. In fact, just about anything renders. Go ahead and invent a new element, like so:

```
<BOGUS>What happens?</BOGUS>
```

The browser isn't going to complain when it sees this. Browsers aren't going to complain if you don't follow the rules. Forgot to quote your attributes? No problem. Close tags not used? No big deal. Syntax is not enforced, and when browsers read pages that have errors, they will make assumptions on how to fix flawed markup or just plain ignore things they don't understand. This environment has led developers to take a loose browser-focused approach to building Web pages. Unfortunately, HTML does have rules, and when they aren't followed, bad things can and do happen. HTML serves as the foundation of a Web page—if you build on top of shaky foundation, things are bound to fall down sooner or later.

HTML Has Rules?

Hypertext Markup Language (HTML) is a very structured markup language that is used to build Web pages. A markup language such as HTML is simply a collection of codes, called *elements*, which are used to indicate the structure and often the format of a document. A Web browser that renders the document interprets the meaning of these codes to figure out how to structure or display a document. Elements in HTML consist of alphanumeric tokens within angle brackets, such as **<B>**, **<HTML>**, **<IMG>**, and **<HR>**.

Most elements consist of paired tags: a *start tag* and an *end tag*. The start tag is simply a mnemonic symbol for the element surrounded by angle brackets. For example, the symbol for bold text is **B** and its start tag is **<B>**. An end tag is identical to a start tag, except that the symbol for an end tag is preceded by a forward slash: **</B>**. An element's instruction applies to whatever content is contained between its start and end tags:

```
<B>This text is bold.</B> This text is not.
```

While most tags come in pairs, exceptions exist. Some elements don't require an end tag because they don't enclose content. These elements are referred to as *empty elements*. One example is the break element, **
, which indicates a line break. Finally, for some elements, such as the paragraph element, **<P>, an end tag is optional, so

```
<P>This is okay.
<P>This is a better way.</P>
```

are both valid. Use of optional tags in HTML is highly encouraged.

An HTML start tag can sometimes contain attributes that modify the element's meaning. Attributes within a tag's brackets must be separated from the element's name by at least one space. Some attributes indicate an effect simply by their existence. An example is adding the **COMPACT** attribute to the ordered list element: **<OL COMPACT>**. Other attributes indicate a modification to the tag by assigned values. For example, **<OL TYPE="i">** assigns the bullet type of an ordered list to lower Roman numerals. An element may contain multiple attributes if those attributes are separated by at least one space, as in **<OL COMPACT TYPE="i" START="3">**. The order of the attributes with a start tag is not fixed, but some HTML authors like to group attributes by meaning, sort attributes alphabetically, or use some other combination of rules.

The HTML specification also defines the type of content that an element can enclose. This is known as an element's *content model*. The content that may be enclosed by an element may include other elements, text, a mixture of elements and text, or nothing at all. For example, the **<HEAD>** element provides general information about an HTML document. Its content model allows it to contain only a small number of related elements, such as **<TITLE>** and **<META>**. The content model for the bold element, **<B>**, allows it to enclose text and some elements, such as the one for italic, **<I>**, but not others, such as **<HEAD>**. The content model clearly indicates that HTML is actually a very structured language, despite how it is often coded.

A complete HTML element is defined by a start tag, an end tag (where applicable), possible attributes, and a content model—in other words, the types of content that the tag can contain. Figure 13-3 shows an overview of the syntax of a typical HTML element.

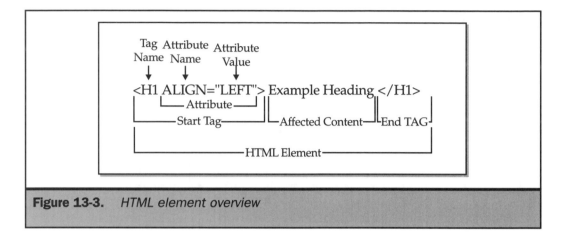

Figure 13-3.   *HTML element overview*

The actual syntax of HTML is very well defined by a document type definition (DTD). In fact, all files should begin with a **<!DOCTYPE>** declaration, which is used to indicate the particular version of HTML being employed in a page. Table 13-3 shows the most common HTML DTD indicators. You might recall noticing them at the top of the source of many Web pages.

Version	<!DOCTYPE> Declaration	Comments
2.0	<!DOCTYPE HTML PUBLIC "-//IETF//DTD HTML//EN">	This version of HTML is equivalent to what is supported by early versions of Netscape and many presentation features of HTML that developers rely on. Few sites use strictly HTML 2.0 given its limited capabilities.
3.2	<!DOCTYPE HTML PUBLIC "-//W3C//DTD HTML 3.2 Final//EN">	This version of HTML is similar to what is supported by 3.*x*-generation browsers. Many of the acceptable browser-introduced proprietary tags were adopted for this version of HTML.

Table 13-3.   *Common HTML DOCTYPE Declarations*

Version	<!DOCTYPE> Declaration	Comments
4.0 Transitional	<!DOCTYPE HTML PUBLIC "-//W3C//DTD HTML 4.0 Transitional//EN" "http://www.w3.org/TR/REC-html40/loose.dtd">	The transitional version of HTML 4.0 is roughly equivalent to what 4.*x*-generation browsers support. However, no single browser at the time of this book's writing is fully HTML 4.0 compliant despite the specification having been out for approaching three years. The transitional form of HTML 4 preserves most of the presentational markup aspects commonly employed by Web designers.
4.0 Frameset	<!DOCTYPE HTML PUBLIC "-//W3C//DTD HTML 4.0 Frameset//EN">	The frameset DTD is an auxiliary definition to deal with the use of frames in a document. It only defines the frame syntax and otherwise relies on the transitional DTD.
4.0 Strict	<!DOCTYPE HTML PUBLIC "-//W3C//DTD HTML 4.0//EN">	The strict version of HTML 4 removes nearly all the presentation-oriented markup elements in favor of using CSS for page formatting. This greatly simplifies the language, but it forces the developer to rely on CSS that is not properly supported in 4.*x*- and even 5.*x*-generation browsers.
4.01 Transitional	<!DOCTYPE HTML PUBLIC "-//W3C//DTD HTML 4.01 Transitional//EN">	A minor update release of the 4.0 specification that addresses errors and oversights in the original release.

Table 13-3.   *Common HTML DOCTYPE Declarations* (continued)

Version	<!DOCTYPE> Declaration	Comments
4.01 Frameset	<!DOCTYPE HTML PUBLIC "-//W3C//DTD HTML 4.01 Frameset//EN">	The update release of the frameset auxiliary DTD.
4.01 Strict	<!DOCTYPE HTML PUBLIC "-//W3C//DTD HTML 4.01//EN">	A minor update release of the 4.0 strict specification that addresses errors and oversights in the original 4.0 specification.
XHTML 1.0 Transitional	<!DOCTYPE html PUBLIC "-//W3C//DTD XHTML 1.0 Transitional//EN" "DTD/xhtml1-transitional.dtd">	The XHTML 1.0 version of the HTML 4 transitional specification.
XHTML 1.0 Strict	<!DOCTYPE html PUBLIC "-//W3C//DTD XHTML 1.0 Strict//EN" "DTD/xhtml1-strict.dtd">	The XHTML 1.0 version of the HTML 4 strict specification.
XHTML 1.0 Frameset	<!DOCTYPE html PUBLIC "-//W3C//DTD XHTML 1.0 Frameset//EN" "DTD/xhtml1-frameset.dtd">	The XHTML 1.0 version of the HTML 4 frameset specification.

Table 13-3.　*Common HTML DOCTYPE Declarations* (continued)

Note　*On occasion, you may see other HTML doctype indicators, notably one for the 3.0 standard that was never really adopted in the Web community.*

The doctype defines HTML syntax very carefully. Making sure that a document complies with the indicated doctype—basically, that it follows the rules—is called validation. First, let's consider the rules of HTML.

HTML Rules

HTML does have some rules even in its standard form. Unfortunately, these "rules" really aren't rules, but mere suggestions. Most browsers pretty much let just about anything render. However, under XHTML, these rules will be enforced, and incorrect documents will not be allowed to render. Most HTML, whether created by hand or a tool, generally lies somewhere in between strict conformance and no conformance to the specification. Let's take a brief tour of some of the more important aspects of HTML syntax.

HTML Documents Are Structured

All HTML documents should follow the same basic format and include a doctype indicator, the **<HTML>** element, the **<HEAD>** element, the **<TITLE>** element, and the **<BODY>** element. The only variation should occur when a **<FRAMESET>** is used in place of the **<BODY>** element. A basic HTML template would then look something like this:

```
<!DOCTYPE HTML PUBLIC "-//W3C//DTD HTML 4.0 Transitional//EN">
<HTML>
<HEAD>
<TITLE>Title goes here</TITLE>
</HEAD>
<BODY>
...Page content goes here...
</BODY>
</HTML>
```

What's interesting is that, despite this obvious inclusion of these important tags by both editors and Web designers, not as many documents as would be expected actually use them. An analysis by researchers from University of California in late 1995 of over 2.6 million Web pages revealed that only 92 percent of pages contained the **<TITLE>** element, 61 percent the **<HEAD>** element, 69 percent the **<BODY>** element, and (surprisingly) a mere 59 percent contained the **<HTML>** element. Hopefully, this rate has changed since developers have become more familiar with HTML and more sophisticated tools have been adopted.

HTML Is Not Case Sensitive

The following markup examples are all equivalent:

```
<B>Go boldly</B>
<b>Go boldly</b>
<B>Go boldly</B>
<b>Go boldly</B>
```

Developers are highly opinionated on how to case elements. Some designers point to the ease of typing lowercase tags as well as the upcoming favor of XHTML for lowercase elements as a reason to go all lowercase. Other designers point out that, statistically, lowercase letters are more common than uppercase, so keeping tags in all uppercase makes them easier to pick out in a document—thus making its structure more clear to someone doing hand markup. Of course, if tools correctly generated all HTML markup, nobody would care, but for now the key is consistency. Choose uppercase or lowercase and stick to it. Fortunately, if you change your mind, most HTML editors and maintenance tools can instantly change case.

Suggestion: Pick a casing style for HTML and stick with it.

With the rise of XHTML, lowercasing will become the published style. If hand coding continues, it may be difficult to push this, but if XHTML does come to pass, designers should be consistent and use lowercase.

One interesting aspect of HTML's case sensitivity is that while HTML element names and attribute names are not case sensitive, this doesn't mean everything isn't case sensitive. For example, consider **<IMG SRC="test.gif">** and **<img src="test.gif">**. These are both equivalent since the **<IMG>** element and the **SRC** attribute are not case sensitive. However, attribute values may be case sensitive, particularly where URLs are concerned. So, **<IMG SRC="test.gif">** and **<IMG SRC="TEST.GIF">** are not necessarily referencing the same image. When referenced from a UNIX system where filenames are case sensitive, these are two different files, while on an NT system where filenames are not case sensitive, these are the same files. This is a common problem and will keep a site from easily being transported from one site to another.

Suggestion: Be careful with casing of attribute values, particularly with filenames.

HTML Is Sensitive to a Single White-Space Character

Browsers will collapse white space between characters down to a single element. Consider the markup:

```
<B>T e s t o f s p a c e s</B><BR>
<B>T   e   s   t   o f   s p a c e s </B><BR>
<B>T
e s
t o f s p            a c e s</B><BR>
```

As shown below, all the spaces, tabs, and returns are collapsed to a single element.

T e s t o f s p a c e s
T e s t o f s p a c e s
T e s t o f s p a c e s

Under some situations, HTML treats white-space characters differently. For example, in the case of the **<PRE>** element, white space is not ignored. Also, white space is preserved within the **<TEXTAREA>** element when setting default text for a multiline text entry field.

Because browsers will ignore most white space, HTML authors often format their HTML documents for readability. However, the reality is that browsers really don't care one way or another. Because of this, some sites have adopted an idea called "HTML crunching." Crunched HTML documents have white space removed, comments stripped, and elements reduced to minimal form. Consider the effects of HTML crunching as illustrated in Figure 13-4.

For complex files, crunching can improve file size significantly. However, when using tools to automatically crunch markup, always test carefully as crunched files do not always render as intended. Pointers to some HTML compression utilities can be found at http://www.webdesignref.com/resources.

Crunch large HTML files by removing white space and other unused space in order to reduce download, but be sure to test for rendering differences.

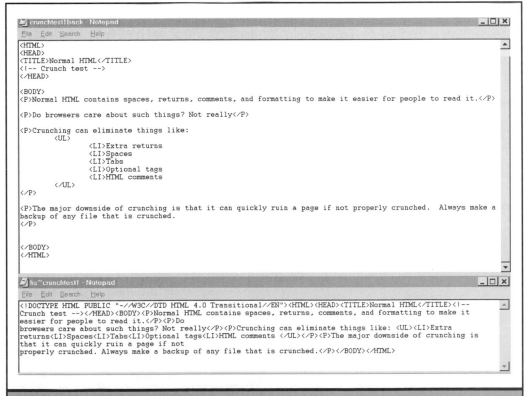

Figure 13-4.   *Crunched HTML reduces file size*

TECHNOLOGY AND WEB DESIGN

Subtle errors tend to creep into HTML files where white space is concerned; be especially careful with spacing around **<IMG>** and **<A>** elements. For example, consider the markup here:

```
<A HREF="http://www.democompany.com">
<IMG SRC="democompany.gif" WIDTH="221" HEIGHT="64"
BORDER="0" ALT="Demo Company">
</A>
```

Notice the return character after the **<IMG>** element just before the **</A>** tag that closes the link. Under some browsers, this will result in a small little "tail" to the image, often termed a tick, as shown here.

Gap in HTML code can cause a "tick" around linked images.

Some browsers will fix the tick problem and others won't. What's interesting is that the browsers with the tick are actually interpreting the HTML specification properly. Consider that if you had a link like

```
<A HREF="http://www.democompany.com">Visit Demo Company</A>
```

you would expect the space between words to be underlined, so why wouldn't other white-space characters be underlined as well? Many of the recent versions of browsers eliminate ticks by making assumptions, but at what cost?

The last aspect of spacing to consider is the use of the nonbreaking space entity, or ** **. Some might consider this the duct tape of the Web—useful in a bind when a little bit of formatting is needed or an element has to be kept open. While the ** ** entity can be used in many useful ways, such as keeping empty table cells from collapsing, designers should avoid relying on it for significant formatting. While it is true that markup like

```
      Look, I'm spaced!
```

would space in some text, the question is, exactly how far? In print, using spaces to format is dangerous and things rarely line up. It is no different on the Web.

Tip: Avoid using   to create significant spacing in layouts.

HTML Supports a Content Model

HTML supports a strict content model that says that certain elements are supposed to only occur within other elements. For example, markup like

```
<UL>
   <P>It's simple to break the content model!</P>
</UL>
```

which is often used for simple indentation, actually breaks the HTML content model. The **<UL>** element is only supposed to contain **<LI>** elements. The **<P>** element is not allowed in this context. A strict validator will indicate the above markup as an error. The problem here is that the content model is showing HTML's real role as a structural language rather than a presentation language where designers rely on the default rendering of elements like **<UL>** for layout.

HTML Elements Should Close Unless Empty

Some HTML elements have optional close tags. For example, both of the paragraphs here are allowed, though the second one is better:

```
<P>This isn't closed
<P>This is</P>
```

A few tags like the horizontal rule **<HR>** or line break **
** do not have close tags since they do not enclose any content. These are considered empty elements and can be used as is. However, for elements with optional close tags, some confusion can arise. Consider the following:

```
<P><P><P>
```

Does this produce numerous blank lines? No, since the browser minimizes the empty **<P>** elements. Notice how some HTML editors output markup like

```
<P> </P><P> </P><P> </P>
```

to deal with this. This is a misuse of HTML. Multiple **
** elements should have been used instead to achieve line breaks.

HTML Elements Should Nest

A simple rule says that HTML should nest, not cross; thus this code is incorrect:

```
<B><I>Crossed tags equal poor coding.</B></I>
```

This code, however, is correct:

```
<B><I>Properly nested tags equal good coding.</I></B>.
```

Breaking this rule seems harmless enough, but it does introduce some ambiguity if tags are automatically manipulated with a program. Under XHTML, nesting is mandatory.

HTML Attributes Should Be Quoted

While it is true that simple attribute values do not need to be quoted, not doing so can lead to trouble with scripting. For example,

```
<IMG SRC=bozo.gif HEIGHT=10 WIDTH=10>
```

would work fine in most browsers. Not quoting the **SRC** attribute is troublesome, but should work. But what would happen if the **SRC** attribute were manipulated by JavaScript and changed to "bozo 2.gif", complete with a space? This could cause a problem. Furthermore, XHTML does enforce quoting, so all attributes should be quoted like so:

```
<IMG SRC="bozo.gif" HEIGHT="10" WIDTH="10">
```

While it doesn't matter if single or double quotes are used, be consistent. Be particularly careful when adding in JavaScript. For example,

```
<INPUT TYPE="BUTTON" VALUE="PRESS ME" onClick="alert('Hello there!')">
```

and

```
<INPUT TYPE='BUTTON' VALUE='PRESS ME' onClick='alert("Hello there!")'>
```

are both okay since quotes are used properly. If, however, you utilize the same quotes in JavaScript like

```
<INPUT TYPE="BUTTON" VALUE="PRESS ME" onClick="alert("Hello there!")">
```

and

```
<INPUT TYPE='BUTTON' VALUE='PRESS ME' onClick='alert('Hello there! ')'>
```

an error will result. Escaping the quotes within JavaScript could solve the problem, but it is probably just easier to quote things using a consistent style.

Be careful with quoting when HTML intersects with JavaScript.

Browsers Ignore Unknown Attributes and Elements

For better or worse, browsers will ignore unknown elements and attributes, so

```
<BOGUS>this text will display on screen</BOGUS>
```

and an element like

```
<P ID="myPara" OBVIOUSLYBOGUS="TRUE">will also render fine.</P>
```

are both interpreted by a browser.

Validation

HTML files should be validated, no matter how they are created. Validation involves checking an HTML file to ensure that it meets the HTML specifications and rules previously discussed. Few tools actually create HTML markup completely correctly; when building HTML files by hand it is easy to make a mistake. Many popular Web editors offer built-in validation. Online validation is also possible using a site like http://validator.w3.org. The CSE Validator (http://www.htmlvalidator.com) is probably the best stand-alone HTML validator available. To understand the benefits of validation, consider the HTML shown here. This example has numerous errors, including proprietary attribute usage, missing quotes, bad nesting, tags used in inappropriate ways, and tags that aren't closed:

```
<!DOCTYPE HTML PUBLIC "-//W3C//DTD HTML 4.0 Transitional//EN">
<HTML>
<HEAD>
<TITLE>Messed <B>Up!</B></TITLE>
</HEAD>
<BODY BGPROPERTIES="fixed">

<H1 ALIGN="center">Broken HTML
<HR>
<UL>
<P>Is this <B><I>correct</B></I>?<BR>
<A HREF=HTTP://WWW.DEMOCOMPANY.COM>
Visit DemoCompany</A>
<PRE>
Should we do <B>this?</B>
   How about entities &copy; ?
</PRE>
```

```
</UL>
</BODY>
<HTML>
```

Running the page through a validator catches all the errors, as shown in Figure 13-5.

The benefits of validation can't be understated. Remember that HTML will serve as the foundation of a Web page. Other technologies like JavaScript and CSS rely on HTML to be well formed, so it is best to have it as errorproof as possible.

Rule: Validate all HTML pages.

Validation helps, but it is still important to understand the syntax of HTML. Further information on the syntax of HTML can be found at the W3C (http://www.w3.org/MarkUp/) as well in the companion book *HTML: The Complete Reference*, also by this author. While all these "rules" don't seem to matter, the introduction of XHTML could change things significantly.

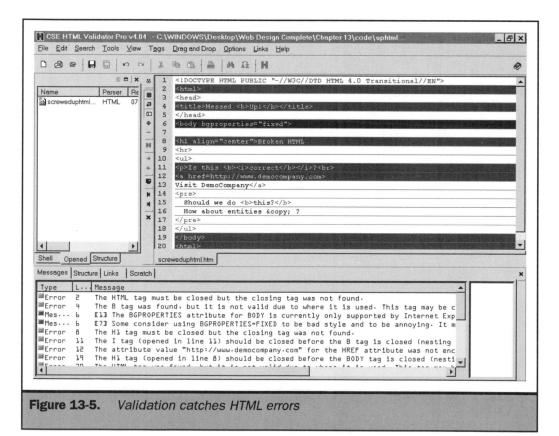

Figure 13-5. *Validation catches HTML errors*

XHTML

The new version of HTML called XHTML became a W3C Recommendation in January 2000. XHTML is a reformulation of HTML using XML that attempts to change the direction and use of HTML to the way it ought to be. So what does that mean? In short, rules now matter. In the past, you could feed your browser just about anything and it would render. XHTML ends all that. Now if you make a mistake, it matters significantly. The page won't render at all. Fortunately, the rules are pretty simple; they were already covered pretty much in the previous sections. Briefly, they include things like:

- You must have a doctype indicator and conform to its rules. <!DOCTYPE html PUBLIC "-//W3C//DTD XHTML 1.0 Transitional//EN" "http://www.w3.org/TR/xhtml1/DTD/xhtml1-transitional.dtd">.

- You must have <html>, <head>, and <body>.

- <title> must come first in the <head> element.

- You have to quote ALL your attributes, even simple ones like <p align=left>.

- You must nest your tags properly, so is ok, but is not.

- You cannot omit optional close tags, so <p> cannot stand alone; you must have <p> and </p>.

- Empty tags must close, so tags like <hr> becomes <hr />.

- You have to lowercase everything.

There's more, but this is most of them. See the XHTML specification (http://www.w3.org/TR/xhtml1/) for all the rules. Except for a few changes in syntax like the empty tag changes and the forced lowercase, just do your HTML correctly (as you should have done before). A typical XHTML document wouldn't look that dissimilar to an HTML one, as shown here:

```
<?xml version="1.0" encoding="UTF-8"?>
<!DOCTYPE html PUBLIC "-//W3C//DTD XHTML 1.0 Strict//EN"
"DTD/xhtml1-strict.dtd">
<html xmlns="http://www.w3.org/1999/xhtml" xml:lang="en" lang="en">
<head>
<title>Title here</title>
</head>
<body>
Content here
</body>
</html>
```

While XHTML doesn't appear to be a big deal, it is. Enforcing rules is going to cause problems, and most pages will have to be restructured somewhat. So the big question then rears its head: will this really come to pass? If it does, XHTML will probably not sweep the Web in a short period of time. In some sense, the technology should be a big deal, since the payoff of well-formed HTML, actually XHTML, is huge—easier document conversion, improved editors that can generate clean markup, a continued movement towards the separation of Web page presentation from structure, and even automated extraction of content since pages can be precisely parsed. Yet what will happen when the first XHTML-enforcing browser is released and it doesn't render 99 percent of the pages on the Net? Most likely, browsers will include some old markup compatibility mode. Designers aren't getting away from old HTML anytime soon. You might call HTML the DOS of the Web, always lurking around some place. However, moving to XHTML is not difficult and the benefit is great. With careful formatting, normal Web pages can be written to conform to XHTML. Tools like HTML Tidy (http://www.w3.org/People/Raggett/tidy/) and editors should make the job easier for both creating new documents and migrating old ones.

Suggestion: Consider conforming to XHTML today to futureproof Web pages.

HTML for Presentation

Another concern for designers is that XHTML and the introduction of CSS (discussed in the next section) encourage a different way of building pages. In the past, HTML has been used for laying out pages. Unfortunately, HTML is not really designed with layout in mind, and designers have struggled to force layouts. A variety of techniques have been used to try to overcome HTML's layout limitations, including:

- HTML tricks and misuse, using invisible pixels and ** **
- Using proprietary browser-specific elements
- Tables
- Putting most layout and content in images
- Binary formats like Flash to avoid HTML entirely

All these approaches have significant problems. Using browser-specific elements obvious only works when the user has the appropriate browser. Putting layout and text entirely within images is not download friendly, accessible for those who can't see images, easy to update, or properly scalable to different resolutions. While file formats like Flash solve the scaling problem, they are not too accessible and are still unfriendly, download-wise. Furthermore, updating a site with content in image format is not easy. The use of trick HTML is very popular, but it requires extreme care on the designer's part since not all browsers support the various workarounds in the same manner.

Layout using HTML tables is probably the only reasonable solution, but it produces excessive markup that can be difficult to update.

At its heart, HTML is supposed to be a logic-oriented language to structure documents. When using an element like **<H1>**, we aren't saying make an object big; we are saying it is a headline. How the browser decides to present things is determined separately. Even a tag as simple as **<P>** that defines a paragraph says nothing about whether blank lines should be used after paragraph, how many blanks should be used, or if the paragraph should be indented. Consider something as simple as formatting a paragraph to be indented 100 pixels. Using traditional HTML for presentation, you might have something like the following:

```
<!DOCTYPE HTML PUBLIC "-//W3C//DTD HTML 4.0 Transitional//EN">
<HTML>
<HEAD>
<TITLE>HTML for presentation</TITLE>
</HEAD>
<BODY>
<TABLE BORDER="0" CELLPADDING="0" CELLSPACING="0">
<TR>
<TD WIDTH="100"> </TD>
<TD><P>I am a paragraph and I am indented around 100
        pixels.</P></TD>
</TR>
</TABLE>
</BODY>
</HTML>
```

Using CSS, you would have the following:

```
<!DOCTYPE HTML PUBLIC "-//W3C//DTD HTML 4.0 Transitional//EN">
<HTML>
<HEAD>
<TITLE>CSS for layout</TITLE>
<STYLE><!-- #para1    {position: relative; left: 100px;} --></STYLE>
</HEAD>
<BODY>
<P ID="para1">I am a paragraph and I am indented around 100 pixels.</P>
</BODY>
</HTML>
```

Notice that the HTML in the second example is much simpler. The presentation and the structure of the document have not been mixed together. This will provide significant benefits, as discussed in the next section.

CSS

HTML was originally designed as a structural language, but somewhere along the way it became a tool for presentation as well, with support for fonts, colors, and other visual concerns. Cascading style sheets (CSS) offer a separate means of controlling the display of Web pages, with the intent of restoring HTML to its original structural purpose.

By separating the structure of a page, as defined in HTML or XML, from its look, a variety of benefits can be achieved. First and foremost, it becomes possible to more easily present a different look for the page, depending on user preferences or browsing conditions. By removing presentation-style markup from a page, such as excessive table use or trick HTML, HTML pages tend to be smaller and easier to update. Furthermore, the HTML becomes simpler and more logic-driven. Update of the look and feel of a page using CSS, when properly used, is much simpler than updating HTML, as it is possible to modify the look of a site from a single site-wide style sheet. In theory, CSS has so many obvious benefits that it should always be used.

Rule: Separate HTML structure from presentation, where possible, using CSS.

The reality is that very often CSS cannot be used because of poor browser implementation and a lack of support for written standards. For example, notice the rendering differences of the test document under Netscape and Internet Explorer as shown in Figure 13-6. Some of the CSS rules work in only one browser or the other, and even when both browsers support a property, presentation is often significantly different. Sites like http://style.webreview.com attempt to track the moving target of browser CSS support.

In the future, browsers should support CSS properly, but for now developers should be aware of CSS implementation problems. If you want to see the rendering of the test document in your browser, visit http://www.webdesignref.com/chapter13/csstest.htm.

Rule: Test CSS rules very carefully.

There is a great deal to know about CSS, and new features are being added all the time. CSS1, the first style sheet specification, defines more than 50 properties, and CSS2 defines over 50 more. Very importantly, CSS2 incorporates the positioning facilities that were often dubbed CSSP (supported in the 4.*x* generation of browsers and beyond). A new version called CSS3 plans on further developing the presentation capabilities as well as integrating better with other technologies, including scripts and vector-based graphics. Table 13-4 provides a quick summary of the various CSS specifications that can be found at http://www.w3.org/style.

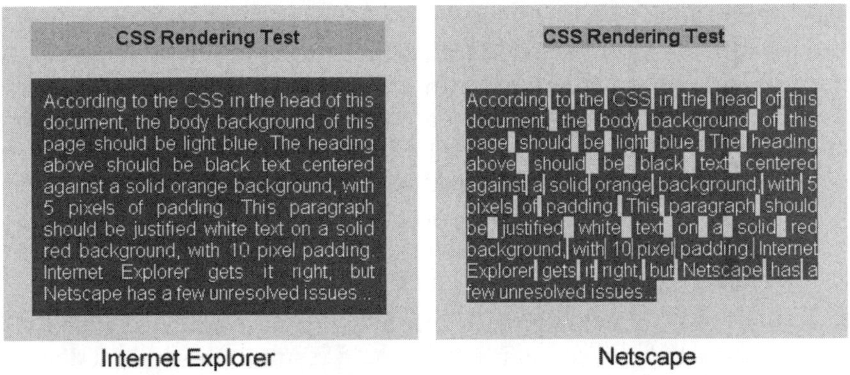

Figure 13-6.   *Significant bugs and rendering differences exist between browsers*

Version	Overview of Features
CSS1	Text handling, including fonts, sizing, style, and spacing Background and colors Margins, borders, and padding control of objects List styles
CSS2	Printing specific features Aural renderings Downloadable fonts Positioned elements (CSSP) Table support Support for CSS with XML Some interface control such as cursor display Limited behaviors such as hover effects on links
CSS3	Support for vertical running text Multicolumn layout facilities Increased support for associating behaviors and styles Integration with graphics, color, and font technologies

Table 13-4.   *CSS Versions Overview*

TECHNOLOGY AND WEB DESIGN

CSS Usage

Recall from the previous section that HTML is the underlying foundation of a Web page. In fact, style sheets rely directly on the proper use of HTML or XML elements. CSS does not replace HTML; it is a separate technology that binds directly to HTML tags. Binding an HTML element to a style specification is very simple; it consists of an element, followed by its associated style information within curly braces:

```
element {style specification}
```

Suppose that you want to bind a style rule to the **<H1>** element so that a 14-point Arial font is always used. The following rule would result in the desired display:

```
H1 {font-family: Arial;
    font-size: 14pt;}
```

In general, a style specification or style sheet is simply a collection of rules. These rules include a *selector*—either an HTML element, a **CLASS** attribute, or an **ID** attribute—which is bound to a style *property* such as **font-family**, followed by a colon and the value(s) for that style property. Multiple style rules may be included in a style specification by separating the rules with semicolons.

Style information may be included in an HTML document in any one of three basic ways. You can link to an outside style sheet, or you can import one. You can embed a document-wide style in the head of an HTML document. And, you can apply inline style to specific elements.

External Style Sheets

An external style sheet is a plaintext file containing style specifications for HTML tags or classes, saved with the extension .css. The following style rules might be found in a file called corporatestyle.css, which defines styles for a large Web site:

```
BODY {font: 10pt;
      font-family: Serif;
      color: black;
      background: white;}

P {text-indent: 0.5in;
   margin-left: 50px;
   margin-right: 50px;}
```

An HTML file that uses this style sheet could reference it by using the **<LINK>** tag within the **<HEAD>** element of the document:

```
<HTML>
<HEAD>
<TITLE>Style Sheet Linking Example</TITLE>
<LINK REL="STYLESHEET" HREF="corporatestyle.css"
TYPE="text/css">
</HEAD>
<BODY>
This page uses the linked style
</BODY>
</HTML>
```

Style sheets can be linked from any location. When using local style sheets, designers should set up a central directory to store style definitions.

 Keep all your style-sheet documents in a central styles directory.

A remote style sheet could also be referenced using a URL, such as http:// www.democompany.com/styles/corpstyle.css. Designers should be careful not to rely on remotely hosted style sheets that may move or incur a download delay.

Web designers should always try to use external style sheets, particularly if styles are going to be similar from page to page. An external style sheet facilitates updating and is more bandwidth friendly than document-wide styles (to be discussed next), since a browser can cache an external CSS file.

Suggestion: Use external style sheets whenever possible.

Embedding Style

The second way to include an external style sheet is to embed it. When you embed a style sheet, you write the style rules directly within the HTML document. Document-wide style is a very easy way to begin using style sheets. It involves using the **<STYLE>** element placed within the **<HEAD>** element of an HTML document. You enclose the style rules within the **<STYLE>** and **</STYLE>** tag pair and place this pair within the head section of the HTML document. Because multiple forms of style sheets may be included (beyond the standard CSS format), you should still include the **TYPE** attribute to indicate which format of style sheet you are using, regardless of the browser's support for other style-sheet technologies. You can have multiple occurrences of the **<STYLE>** element within the head of the document, and you may even import some styles, link to some style rules, and specify some styles directly.

One concern with embedded style sheets is that not all browsers understand style information. To avoid problems, comment out the style information by using an HTML comment, such as **<!-- -->**, so that the style rules aren't displayed onscreen or misinterpreted by older browsers.

Rule: Always comment out style rules to avoid interpretation by older browsers.

A complete example of a document-wide style sheet, including using comments to hide rules from older browsers, is shown here:

```
<HTML>
<HEAD>
<TITLE>Document-Wide Style Sheets</TITLE>
<STYLE TYPE="text/css">
<!--
BODY {background: white;
 margin-left: 1in;
 margin-right: 1.5in;}

H1 {font-size: 24pt;
 font-family: sans-serif;
 color: red;
 text-align: center;}

P {font-size: 12pt;
 font-family: Serif;
 text-indent: 0.5in;
 color: black;}
-->
</STYLE>
</HEAD>
<BODY>
. . .Content affected by style sheet . . .
</BODY>
</HTML>
```

Inline Style

Finally, style information can be added to individual HTML elements using the **STYLE** attribute, which is available for nearly every HTML element. This short example shows how to apply a style to an **<H1>** element using an inline style sheet:

```
<H1 STYLE="font-size: 48pt;font-family: Arial; color: green;">Style
Test</H1>
```

This sort of style information doesn't need to be hidden from a browser that isn't style sheet aware, because browsers ignore any attributes that they don't understand.

CSS in Practice

Using CSS in Web pages can be tricky when considering that older browsers do not support it at all. Many of the newer browsers have incomplete implementations, and vary greatly even when they support the same properties. The first thing to consider is the relationship between CSS and HTML. HTML elements do have default renderings and are supposed to be used to designate the logical meaning of some content. If you are simply looking to create a look for a particular section of a document, you should become comfortable with the **<DIV>** and **<SPAN>** elements.

When applying style to a fairly large portion of a document, say to several paragraphs, use the **<DIV>** element:

```
<DIV STYLE="background: lightblue; font-weight: bold; color: black;">
<P>This paragraph is highlighted in blue.</P>
<P>So is this one.</P>
<P>Not to mention this final paragraph...</P>
</DIV>
```

To provide style information just for a few words or letters, use the **<SPAN>** element:

```
<P>Calling out <SPAN STYLE="background: yellow; font-weight: bold;
color: black">special sections of text</SPAN> isn't hard with SPAN</P>
```

Be careful when using HTML elements and style sheets. They can be used both in a positive and negative manner. Hopefully, logical elements are primarily used, and CSS is used to apply appearance, as in this code:

```
<P STYLE="line-height: 200%; font-size: 12pt;">Logic and look are
separate here.</P>
```

However, it is also possible to create some difficult-to-understand markup when combining more physical elements with CSS:

```
<B STYLE="font-weight: normal; font-style: italic;">What's going on
here!?</B>
```

TECHNOLOGY AND WEB DESIGN

While the previous example is unlikely and not encouraged, it does point at the potentially messy intersection between using HTML for layout and using CSS. At times, it tends to be an all-or-nothing situation, such as when using positioned elements in CSS. Using CSS, it is easy to place an object anywhere you like on the screen. Consider the HTML markup shown here:

```
<!DOCTYPE HTML PUBLIC "-//W3C//DTD HTML 4.0 Transitional//EN">
<HTML>
<HEAD>
<TITLE>CSS Positioning</TITLE>
<STYLE>
<!--
#region1    {position: absolute;
              top: 100px; left: 100px;
              height: 100px; width: 100px;
              background-color: #3399ff;}

#region2    {position: absolute;
              top: 120px; left: 200px;
              height: 100px; width: 100px;
              background-color: #cc3300; }

#region3    {position: absolute;
              top: 100px; left: 300px;
              height: 100px; width: 100px;
              background-color: #3399ff; }

#textregion {font-family: Arial;
              font-size: 25px;
              position: absolute;
              top: 140px; left: 105px;
              color: White; }
-->
</STYLE>
</HEAD>
<BODY>
<DIV ID="region1"> </DIV>
<DIV ID="region2"> </DIV>
<DIV ID="region3"> </DIV>
<DIV ID="textregion">Behold the power of CSS!</DIV>
</BODY>
</HTML>
```

The previous example will position three regions and overlay text on it in a properly aware CSS browser. Of course, under older browsers or those that don't support CSS properly, the rendering will be dramatically different, as shown in Figure 13-7.

As shown in Figure 13-7, when positioning isn't supported, the difference can be dramatic. Under older browsers, the layout completely fails; even under some modern browsers, the layout is significantly altered. Because of the problems with CSS support, designers should use script to detect the browser in use, or rely on an older technology like tables, unless only compatible CSS browsers hitting the site can be guaranteed.

Suggestion: Avoid relying solely on style sheets for layout unless non-CSS-compliant browsers can be limited or detected and dealt with.

Another possibile way to include CSS in a page is to depend on it less. Consider setting double spacing in a page using a CSS property. If the browser picks it up, great;

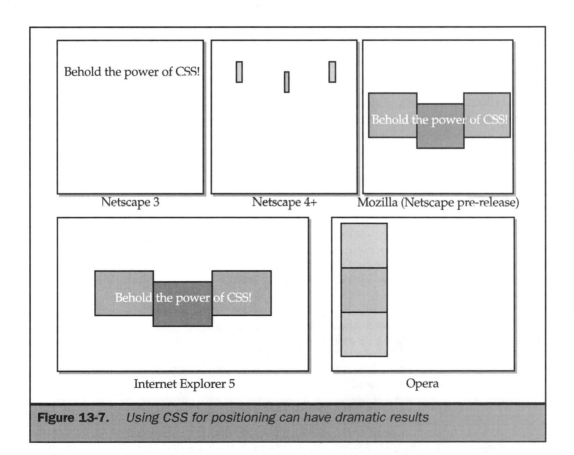

Figure 13-7.   *Using CSS for positioning can have dramatic results*

if not, users won't know what they are missing. Consider overloading HTML presentation elements like the **<FONT>** element. For example, try to set text size to around 22 points. You can come close with HTML browsers, and get it just right in CSS browsers, like so:

```
<FONT SIZE="5" STYLE="font-size: 22pt">HTML comes close,
    CSS hits it right on!</FONT>
```

A variety of CSS properties like font sizing can be used for CSS-oriented browsers, and HTML can be used for older ones.

Suggestion: Use CSS to overload HTML presentation elements like <FONT>.

The reality is that things aren't always as clean as the previous example suggests. Browser implementations are buggy and incomplete. JavaScript can be utilized to avoid these problems. For example, consider sensing to add a style sheet with Microsoft-compatible rules or one with Netscape-compatible rules using a script like the following in the **<HEAD>** of a document:

```
<SCRIPT>
<!--
if (document.all)
 document.write('<LINK REL="STYLESHEET" HREF="ms.css">');
else
 if (document.layers)
 document.write('<LINK REL="STYLESHEET" HREF="nav.css">');
//-->
</SCRIPT>
```

JavaScript can be used to create solutions for some CSS problems, but the reality is that there are still many open issues. Designers need to stay on top of CSS and use it carefully. Sites like http://style.webreview.com/ provide a great overview of browser compatibility. Tools also can be helpful creating quality Web documents that work in all browsers.

Authoring HTML/CSS Pages

What's interesting about HTML is that, quite often, Web designers are more concerned with how they create HTML and CSS documents than how well they do it or how appropriate their method of creation is. There are pros and cons to every method of page creation, from hand editing of markup to the latest WYSIWYG editor. Each of the basic methods and some of its pros and cons are presented in Table 13-5.

The reality of creating HTML documents is that there are occasions to use nearly every approach. For example, making a quick change of a single tag is often fastest in

Method	Example	Pros	Cons
By hand	Coding pages with Notepad	+ Great deal of control over the HTML + Can address bugs and new HTML elements or CSS properties immediately	– Slow – Error prone – Requires intimate knowledge of HTML elements and CSS properties – No direct visual representation
Translation	Save document from another tool like Microsoft Word	+ Quick + Simplifies conversion of existing documents	– Produced HTML is often problematic – Still requires editing to add links and clean up problems
Tagging Editor	Using HomeSite	+ Great deal of control + Faster than hand editing + Provides help addressing errors and writing structured HTML or correct CSS	– Slow – Requires intimate knowledge of HTML and CSS
WYSIWYG Editor	Using FrontPage	+ Work directly on visual representation of page + Requires no significant knowledge of HTML or CSS	– Often generates incorrect HTML or CSS – Precise control of layout often requires direct markup editing

Table 13-5.   *Methods of HTML and CSS Creation*

a pure-text editor. Saving out large existing print documents might make sense using a translator. Precision coding of an HTML template might be best performed within a tagging editor. Building a modest site in a visual manner is easily done using a WYSIWYG editor. Always consider the applicability of the tool to the job before marrying it.

Suggestion: Create HTML and CSS documents in the most suitable manner, rather than relying on only one tool or approach.

The tools change all the time, but at the time of this writing the HTML tools mentioned in Table 13-6 are popular. Certainly many tools exist—all with their own

Product	Platform(s)	URL	Comments
Dreamweaver	Windows Macintosh	http://www.macro media.com/ or www.dreamweaver.com	A good visual design tool that balances WYSIWYG design capabilities with code editing. Strong CSS and DHTML support.
HomeSite	Windows	http://www.allaire. com/homesite	A top-notch text editor for HTML professionals. Poor visual support, but incredible code and markup handling. Its sister product, Cold Fusion Studio, adds in even greater support for dynamic site-building technologies.
GoLive	Macintosh Windows	http://www.adobe. com/products/golive/	Very popular amongst the Macintosh set, this tool has a visual designer-oriented interface. Some generated markup problems have limited its popularity with strict standards developers.
FrontPage	Windows	http://www.microsoft. com/frontpage	Popular with the small developer and internal corporate development crowds. It has improved greatly, but still has a reputation for generating bad or too Microsoft-specific pages.

Table 13-6.   *A Selection of Popular HTML Development Tools*

features and benefits—but given their use at large-scale Web firms, the combination of Dreamweaver and HomeSite is suggested for professional developers. An updated "short list" of some of the popular tools will be kept online at http://www.webdesignref. com/resources.

Regardless of how HTML documents are constructed, special care should be taken. First, consider putting in comments at the start of HTML documents indicating important information about the document, the author, and so on. For example, the following HTML document shows how comments could be used in the **<HEAD>** to inform document maintainers about the document:

```
<HTML>
<HEAD>
<TITLE>DemoCompany Announces Butler 1.0</TITLE>
<!--
Document Name: Butler Robot Press Release

   Description: The press release announcing the newest Robot Butler
                in the Demo Company family.

   Author: Thomas A. Powell (tpowell@democompany.com)

   Creation Date: 5/15/99
   Last Updated: 1/5/00

   Comments: Used SuperDuperEdit 7.0 to build the page.
-->
</TITLE>
<BODY>
...
</BODY>
</HTML>
```

Suggestion: Use comments in HTML documents.

Supplementary document information can also be stored in **<META>** tags or within a database. However, comments will do in a pinch, and are useful just to let future developers know about complex features in a page. The only downside of HTML comments is that end users can see them if they view your source code, so be careful not to leak too much information.

Tip *Avoid telling end users too much in HTML comments.*

Some designers suggest using comments that are stripped out before page delivery. For example, in a ColdFusion environment comments using three dashes <!--- and ---> will be stripped before delivery.

One of the best approaches when authoring HTML pages is not to think about pages, but about templates. Why make ten different press releases when a single press release template can be created and modified? Unfortunately, many tools and design books alike tend to take a page-at-a-time approach. Avoid this and create generic templates. Using a template will speed up development and make resulting pages more consistent in style and structure.

Suggestion: Create and use page templates.

Some designers are hesitant to use templates, thinking that it limits design possibilities. But templates don't take the creativity out of design. Using templates takes much of the tedium out of building sites, leaving the designer more time to design. Generally, if a designer follows the rules of consistency and usability, there really are no restrictions imposed by templates.

The concluding suggestion for HTML document construction is the most contentious of all for some designers—to use an .htm or .html file extension? There is some benefit to using .htm since it is slightly more transportable, but the reality is that it really doesn't matter. The only thing is to be consistent. It is sad, but somewhat amusing, to watch developers struggle with files called index.htm and index.html in the same directory and not understand why changes are showing up. Save yourself the aggravation and be consistent in whatever you choose.

Rule: Be consistent in HTML file naming—choose .htm or .html and stick to it.

XML

HTML isn't perfect, but it works pretty well—particularly if you consider the millions of documents created by people all over the world with varying markup knowledge levels. Yet HTML does have two major weaknesses—it does not enforce rules, and it is not extensible.

As mentioned earlier, browsers do not strictly enforce HTML rules. While this makes it easy for mere mortals to author documents, it makes it difficult for programs to read our inconsistent results. This could have serious ramifications if structure were important. Imagine if you authored an electronic invoice in HTML to send to a customer. The customer might write a program to read the invoice and automatically submit the appropriate information to their accounts payable system. However, their program would have to assume a particular structure for the document. What happens, then, if you or your editor changes the structure of the HTML invoice? Obviously, the client's program breaks. Even without changing structure, just the loose imprecise nature of HTML could make pulling apart the document a difficult chore.

The second problem with HTML is that it's not extensible. In other words, we can't define our own elements. Consider again the idea of the electronic invoice. If a tag were defined called **<TOTAL>**, it would be pretty easy to parse the document and find the amount owed. A whole range of tags could be defined for the invoice language, including **<ADDRESS>**, **<RATE>**, **<DESCRIPTION>**, **<HOURS>**, **<TAX>**, and so on. We might get so excited about our language that we named it IML for Invoice Markup Language. We could even create a simple document in our language, like

```
<?xml version="1.0"?>
<INVOICE>
 <TITLE>Invoice</TITLE>
<CUSTOMERINFO>
<NAME>DemoCompany</NAME>
 <ADDRESS>
<STREET>2105 Garnet Ave., Suite E</STREET>
<CITY>San Diego</CITY>
<STATE>CA</STATE>
<ZIP>92109</ZIP>
</ADDRESS>
</CUSTOMERINFO>

<SERVICES TYPE="CONSULTING">
 <DESCRIPTION>Jabbering about things</DESCRIPTION>
<RATE>250.00</RATE>
 <HOURS>3</HOURS>
<TOTAL>750.00</TOTAL>
</SERVICES>
</INVOICE>
```

and name it invoice1.xml. This document would actually even render as something in an XML-aware browser like Internet Explorer 5, as shown in Figure 13-8.

Of course, two questions probably immediately are raised after looking at Figure 13-8. First, how do you define these tags? Second, what's the point of this rendering? First, let's address the tags. To create elements, just make up any element and attribute names that meaningfully represent the domain that you want to model.

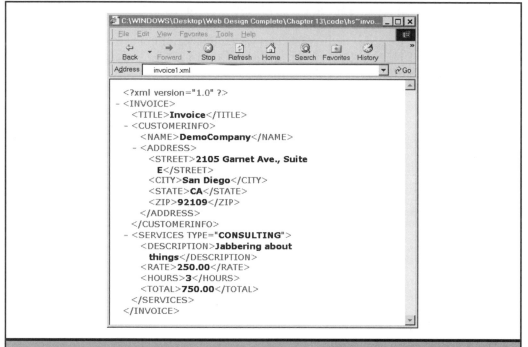

Figure 13-8. *Well-formed XML example rendering*

Does this mean that XML has no rules? No. It has rules, but they are few, simple, and relate only to syntax:

- *All elements must be properly nested*, just like well-written HTML. For example,

  `<OUTER><INNER>nesting is good</INNER></OUTER>`

  is correct, while this isn't:

  `<OUTER><INNER>crossing is bad</OUTER></INNER>`

- *All attribute values must be quoted.* In HTML, quoting is good authoring practice, but it is required only for values that contain characters other than letters (A–Z, a–z), numbers (0–9), hyphens (-), or periods (.). For example, under XML,

  `<BLASTOFF COUNT="10">`

  is correct, while this isn't:

  `<BLASTOFF COUNT=10>`

- *All elements with empty content must be self-identifying*, by ending in "/>" instead of the familiar ">." An empty element is one such as the HTML **
, **<HR>, or **<IMG>** elements. In an XML-like language like XHTML, these would be represented, respectively, as **
, **<HR/>, and **<IMG SRC="test.gif" />**.

- *All elements must be cased consistently.* If you start a new element such as **<INVOICE>**, you must close it as **</INVOICE>**, not **</invoice>**. Later in the document, if the element is in lowercase, you actually are referring to a new element known as **<invoice>**. Attribute names are also case sensitive.

- *A valid XML file may not contain certain characters that have reserved meanings.* These include characters such as **&**, which indicates the beginning of a character entity like ** **, or **<**, which indicates the start of an element name such as **<SUNNY>**. These characters must be coded as **&** and **<**, respectively, or may occur in a section marked off as character data.

These rules are more important here in XML than they are in HTML. In the case of our invoice language, a simple typo like forgetting to close a tag causes the browser not to render the page at all as shown in Figure 13-9.

A document constructed according to the previous simple rules is known as a *well-formed document.* Syntax is fine and well and must be carefully followed, but these tags don't really have any meaning. To make this a valid document, we have to define the rules of our particular invoice language by writing a document type definition

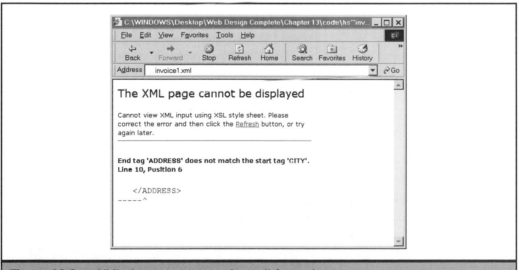

Figure 13-9.   *XML documents must be well formed*

(DTD). A DTD defines how a language can be used by indicating what elements can contain what other elements, the values of attributes, and so on. A simple DTD to define a grading language for elementary school children is shown here:

```
<!-- Grades DTD -->
<!ELEMENT  GRADES  (STUDENT+)>
<!ELEMENT  STUDENT (COURSE+)>
<!ATTLIST  STUDENT  NAME  CDATA  #REQUIRED
           SEX  (M|F)  #REQUIRED
           LEVEL  (1|2|3|4|5|6) #REQUIRED>

<!ELEMENT   COURSE EMPTY>
<!ATTLIST  COURSE TITLE  CDATA  #REQUIRED
           GRADE  (PASS|FAIL) #REQUIRED>
```

This DTD file named grades.dtd would be referenced by an XML file such as the one shown here:

```
<?xml version="1.0"?>
<!DOCTYPE GRADES SYSTEM "grades.dtd">
<!-- the document instance -->

<GRADES>
<STUDENT NAME="THOMAS" SEX="M" LEVEL="3">
   <COURSE TITLE="MATH" GRADE="PASS" />
   <COURSE TITLE="ENGLISH"  GRADE="FAIL" />
</STUDENT>

<STUDENT NAME="SYLVIA" SEX="F"  LEVEL="1">
   <COURSE TITLE="MATH"  GRADE="PASS" />
   <COURSE TITLE="ART" GRADE="PASS" />
</STUDENT>
</GRADES>
```

The example would now not only be syntactically checked, but we could validate the document against the DTD. If this last example leaves you wondering why you would ever want to define your own language, it should. There are certainly many reasons to define a language, but there also many reasons not to. In fact, with everyone going around defining languages, we could easily turn the Web into a modern-day equivalent of the story of the Tower of Babel—HTML cast aside in favor of languages that many organizations don't know or agree upon. Regardless, writing DTDs really should not be put in the hands of everyone. Most should be more concerned with using a language rather than defining their own. Already many useful languages such as Channel Definition Format (CDF), used to create push channels in Microsoft browsers (http://www.w3.org/TR/NOTE-CDFsubmit.html); SMIL (Synchronized Multimedia Interchange Language), used to create presentations and supported by RealPlayer (http://www.w3.org/TR/REC-smil/); WML (Wireless Markup Language), the primary cellular language (http://www.wapforum.org); and many other XML-based languages are in fairly widespread use.

Suggestion: Try to rely on standard XML languages rather than in-house-developed languages.

The fact of the matter is that XML from a designer's point of view is like concrete in the mind of an architect. You use it to build things, but you don't play around in it or wonder about its chemical composition.

The second question that should be considered about XML is what do you do with it? It doesn't seem to look like much in a browser. That's true, but we could convert it into HTML or even attach a style sheet to it. Consider the style sheet here called invoice.css:

```
INVOICE         {font-family: Arial; font-size: medium;}
TITLE           {text-align: center; text-decoration: underline;
                {display: block; font-size: x-large;}
CUSTOMERINFO    {text-align: right;   display: block;}
NAME            {font-size: smaller; font-weight: bold;
                 display: block;}
ADDRESS, CITY   {display: block;}
STATE, ZIP      {display: inline;}
SERVICES        {text-align: left; position: relative; top: 50px;
                 background-color: EEE88A; display: block;
                 border: solid;}
DESCRIPTION {position: absolute; left: 20%; font-style: italic;}
RATE        {position: absolute; left: 50%; font-family: Courier;}
TOTAL       {position: absolute; left: 80%; color: green;
             font-weight:bold}
```

This could be associated to the XML file invoice.xml with a simple statement like the following:

```
<?xml-stylesheet href="invoice.css" type="text/css" ?>
```

In a browser supporting both CSS and XML, the page would begin to take shape as shown in Figure 13-10.

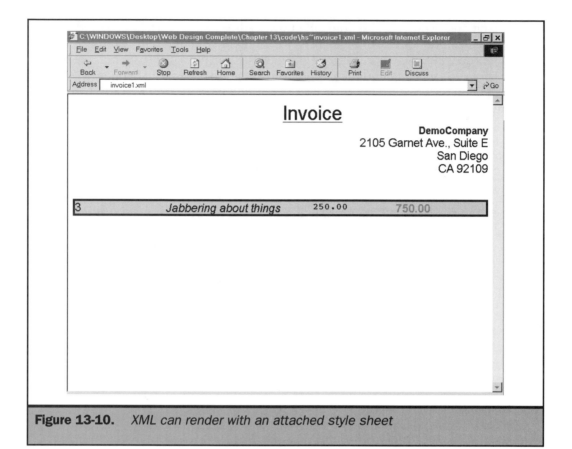

Figure 13-10.   *XML can render with an attached style sheet*

> **Note**   *This style sheet will have rendering issues. There are shortcomings in the approach taken and the use of CSS in this fashion, but it does show something could be rendered without changing it into HTML, which is not the ultimate goal in the far future.*

This last example explicitly shows the idea of separation of logic and presentation as alluded to by HTML. However, what's going to happen in older browsers? Absolutely nothing. For now, client-side XML doesn't make sense. Even later, one wonders if it will make sense. The major benefit of XML, in reality, probably won't be as a client-side language but as a server-side one. What XML will eventually bring is the power to make data more regular and more specific to particular applications or industries. With improved structure, migrating Web data to and from databases, exchanging documents with other parties, and navigating large collections of documents could get significantly easier because documents will follow a rigid structure. XML's rule enforcement should allow data interchange between many organizations, making the example of an automated invoice exchange system a reality and signal a move away from just publishing documents but writing programs to handle them.

Suggestion: Use XML as a neutral storage format and for exchange.

Programming and Web Design

While technologies like HTML, CSS, and XML can be used to improve the structure and presentation of Web pages, the fundamental approach taken by many designers with these technologies is a static document-centric one. The reality is that the Web can be made much more interactive. Web sites are becoming more and more software-like as time goes on. Unfortunately, some designers seem to think the increased focused on programming will regulate them to mere front-end implementers. While it is true that in many cases it would probably be best to leave programming to those who love it, designers should try to understand Web programming technologies as much as possible. Remember that we must truly know our medium in order to design properly for it.

Understanding the basic idea of adding programming to a site isn't hard, but it is easy to get overwhelmed by the number of technologies to choose from, particularly if you assume that each is very different. The reality is that Web programming technologies can be grouped into two basic groups: client-side and server-side. Client-side technologies are those that are run on the client—generally within the context of the browser, though some technologies like Java applets or ActiveX controls may actually appear or truly run beyond the browser (and Helper applications do so implicitly). Of course, programs can run instead on the server, and thus are dubbed server-side programming. Table 13-7 presents the general programming choices available to Web developers, while Figure 13-11 shows the relationship of all programming technologies.

The challenge of Web-based programming is making sure to choose the right technology for the job. More often than not, designers are quick to pick a favorite technology—whether it is JavaScript, ColdFusion, or Java—and use it in all situations. The reality is that each technology has its pros and cons. In general, client-side and

Client Side	Server Side
Helper applications	CGI scripts and programs
Plug-ins	Server API programs (ISAPI/NSAPI)
ActiveX controls	Java servlets
Java applets	Server-side scripting
Scripting languages	Active Server Pages
JavaScript	ColdFusion
VBScript	PHP
Dynamic HTML	

Table 13-7.   *Web Client-Side and Server-Side Programming Options*

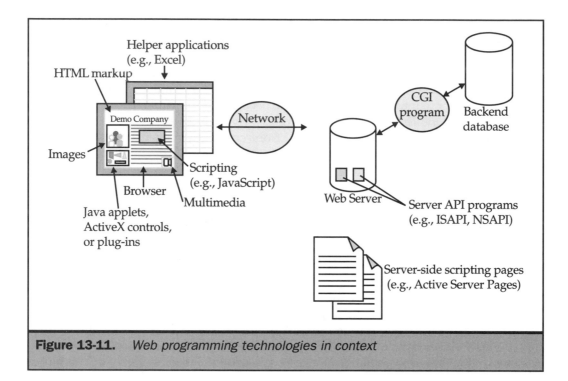

Figure 13-11.   *Web programming technologies in context*

server-side programming technologies have characteristics that make them complementary rather than adversarial. Consider, for example, the situation of adding a form to a Web site to collect data to save in a database. It is obvious that it would make more sense to check the form on the client side to make sure that the user entered the correct information since it would not force a network round-trip to the server just to check the input data. Client-side programming would make the form validation more responsive and frustrate the user less. On the other hand, putting the data in the database would be best handled by a server-side technology given that the database would be located on the server side of the equation. The reality is that each general type of programming has its place, and a mixture is often the best solution.

> **Rule: Consider using both client- and server-side technologies in a site rather than one or the other.**

Server-Side Programming

Server-side programming comes in many flavors, including CGI scripts, server-API programs like NSAPI and ISAPI programs as well as Java servlets, and server-side scripting environments such as Microsoft's Active Server Pages and Allaire's ColdFusion. Each technology has is its own pros and cons, but all forms of server-side programming share one common quality—control. The server is really the only part of the client/server equation that the developer has real control over, and we can carefully dictate how a server-side program will run. Server-side programs don't rely to any major degree on client-side variations, so in theory a site using interactivity running on the server can deliver pages to any type of browser. Notice that, despite a great deal of hype about client-side technologies, most of the extremely high-traffic sites rely to a great degree solely on server-side technology to develop interactive elements. Of course, the major downside of server-side programming is speed. Because all the interactivity takes place on the server, the user may perceive delays because of server response time limitations or network round-trip time.

Rule: Carefully monitor responsiveness of server-side technologies.

Server-side programs must be carefully designed to avoid responsiveness issues and to ensure that they can handle the volume of users who may access the site. Numerous examples of sites faltering under enormous user loads show how difficult it is to plan for the capacity of sites. However, it is possible to do. If you know that a typical page takes two seconds to build and is 50K in size, you can actually calculate things like the number of simultaneous users that can be handled with 1 Mbps of bandwidth.

Rule: Create a capacity plan when using server-side technologies.

Capacity plans are not trivial, and they do reveal that it often takes a great deal of hardware and bandwidth to service users. A more detailed discussion of delivery requirements is presented in the next chapter; for now, let's take a brief tour of each of the server-side programming technologies commonly used in sites.

CGI Programs

The oldest version of server-side programming is the Common Gateway Interface (CGI) program. A CGI program is a program written to conform to a standard way of passing data into an external program through the use of HTTP methods (GET and POST) and environment variables, and passing any results back with the appropriate HTTP headers in a format the browser can understand (such as HTML). CGI programs can be written in any language that can be used on the server executing the program. Commonly, CGI programs tend to be written in PERL, given the language's excellent string capabilities and Web support. However, there is no reason that a CGI program couldn't be written in C/C++, Visual Basic, Pascal, Java, Cobol, or even Fortran.

Write CGI programs in a language that is fast, portable, and appropriate for the server running the program and the programmer writing and maintaining it.

CGI programs have long suffered the stigma of being considered slow. Part of this can be attributed to writing CGI programs in relatively slow interpreted languages like PERL. A simple rewrite or compilation of a PERL program, or the use of a special CGI acceleration module, might substantially improve performance.

Suggestion: To improve CGI execution, consider compiling or rewriting heavily used programs.

However, CGI programs will generally always incur some performance hit because they are generally run in a separate memory space from a Web server and may incur operating system launch overhead since a single instance of a CGI program may be started for every single user. The only way around this problem is to consider using a server-side program written to run within a Web server directly. See the next section entitled "Server APIs" for more information on this.

Server-side programs may have special security considerations. Since CGI programs are run on the server and are often simple scripts, they are targeted for exploitation. Traditionally, Web developers have been conscious of the potential for exploitation and have tried to limit the use of CGI programs to a single directory called cgi-bin. Following this convention is a good way to keep track of CGI programs.

 Follow the cgi-bin directory convention and keep your CGI programs in a single place for security and management purposes.

There really isn't anything particularly special about CGI programs, and the truth is that most CGI programs are relatively simple to build and are commonly available online. Consider, for example, how many people want to add a guest book, online auction, or form to look up information in a database. Surely this is not unique to your site. This brings up the famous buy vs. build question. Always make sure to investigate sites like http://www.cgi-resources.com for pointers to prewritten CGI programs. However, if speed, security, or reliability is an issue and you find CGI programming mystical, hire a professional programmer.

 Try to use existing CGI programs for common tasks, but be careful about quality and security.

Server APIs

To avoid CGI performance bottlenecks, writing programs that are tightly bound to the actual Web server via a server API is possible. Netscape servers offer the API (application programming interface) called NSAPI, and Microsoft appeals to

Windows developers with its own API, called ISAPI. Apache servers provide Apache modules. A technology called Java servlets exists that tries to take the server- and platform-specific nature out of the equation, but the reality is that all these approaches have a trade-off between speed and portability. These API programming solutions provide performance improvements over CGI by supporting tight integration with the actual Web server. In some sense, server API solutions are analogous to plug-ins on browsers. Because of the tie-in at the server level, applications written using server APIs can access core server functions such as authentication, access control, and fast access to database or back-end services.

 Use server API programs for site-critical high-performance tasks.

The reality of server-side API programs is that they are often too complex or expensive for many development projects. If improperly created, buggy API programs can bring down an entire Web server, while a bad CGI would just take up processing time. Server API-oriented solutions are obviously faster and, if well developed, more robust, but the difficulty of developing such applications makes them unrealistic for many Web professionals. Furthermore, developing software for a particular server API will lock the application into that particular server platform. Code may need to be rewritten to ensure compatibility if a new server is used.

Server-Side Scripting

Often dubbed "server-parsed HTML" or "server-side scripting," this form of server programming attempts to more closely associate programming with Web pages, and do so in a simple manner that runs relatively fast. The idea of server-side scripting is to create special HTML files or templates that contain a mixture of script and HTML that is read by the server when requested. The server then parses the page and outputs the resulting HTML file. Figure 13-12 overviews this process.

There are many server-side scripting environments. The three most popular are probably ColdFusion (http://www.allaire.com), PHP (http://www.php.net), and Active Server Pages (http://msdn.microsoft.com). Many exist, but the main difference is syntax. The actual benefits of one technology over another are generally minor, so the choice between them is somewhat a question of personal preference. All suffer from relatively slow execution speeds vs. more advanced server-side programming like server APIs. The trade-off is that the technology is relatively simple. Many designers like ColdFusion for its simple syntax, while programmers sometimes prefer other technologies.

 Consider ColdFusion if you want to do some simple server-side programming.

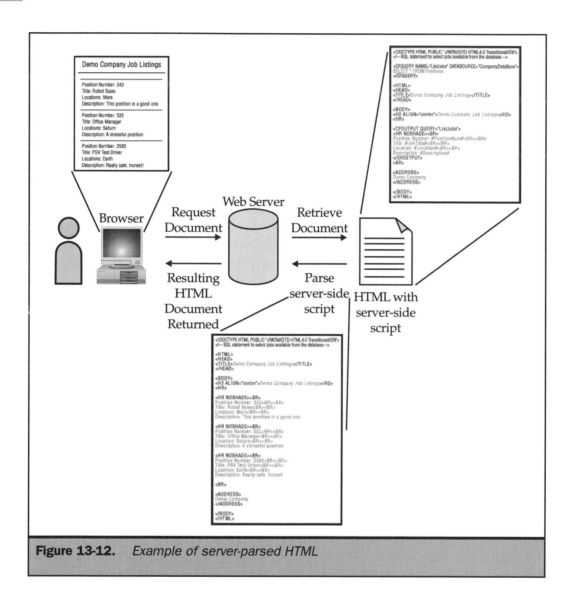

Figure 13-12.   *Example of server-parsed HTML*

Usability and Server-Side Programming

As already mentioned, the main problem with server-side programming usability-wise is that it tends to not be as responsive as client-side technology since a network request has to be made every time the user wants to do something. However, for this reduction in speed we gain a huge improvement in reliability. From a usability standpoint, it might be better to be a little slower rather than show error messages all the time. However, one other usability problem with server-side programming does rear its ugly head: the complex URLs, as shown here.

Address	http://www.democompany.com/products/pdproductdetail.cfm?keyProduct=1360&robot=Butler&color=green ▼

Users are often confused by these URLs that look big and scary—and are certainly not easy to type in. Recall that users use URLs to understand where they are. It may be better to hide these complex addresses, particularly because they change all the time. What's interesting is that, in many instances, relying on the POST method rather than the GET method to pass data between pages could hide these URLs. In some situations, it may not be possible to do this, but frames could be utilized to show a different URL in place of the complex one. Designers should at least consider if URLs could be cleaned up.

Suggestion: Using server-side technologies with complex URLs may confuse users.

Client-Side Programming

The major drawback of server-side programming is speed. Programs executed "client side," however, appear to be quite fast to a user in most cases. It makes sense why if you consider that no network round-trip is required to show the result of some action. Of course, client-side programming does come with one serious drawback—a lack of control. For example, when designing public Web sites, it is hard to say exactly what kind of users are going to hit a site. What browser is being used, what features are turned on, and what kind of processor the user has are all questions that are not always easy to answer. Even with browser sensing, client side programming does leave things more up to chance. There is always that one user who doesn't want to play by the rules, who wants to use alpha-level software, turn off their scripting support midvisit, or modify their browser in some unpredictable way. Client-side programming often won't be able to recover from such changes because it relies on the browser for more than mere display of data. Because of this, client-side programming doesn't always work. The best approach is to assume that it will work but to account for it not working by providing some fallback state. Consider form validation again. Go ahead and check the form client side, but if it needs to be checked once it reaches the server, do the check again.

Rule: Provide a fallback state for all client-side programming technologies.

The idea of always accounting for the problems will be presented again and again throughout this chapter. For now, let's take a look at each of the possible client-side technology choices in turn.

Helpers

One approach to client-side programming comes in the form of programmed solutions like helper applications. In the early days of the Web—around the time of Mosaic or Netscape 1.*x*—browsers had limited functionality and support for media beyond HTML. If new media types or binary forms were encountered, they had to be passed to an external program called a "helper application." Helper applications generally run outside the browser window. An example of a helper application would be a compression or archive tool like WinZip, which would be launched automatically when a compressed file was downloaded from the Web. Helpers are often problematic because they are not well integrated with the browser and lack methods to communicate back to the Web browser. Because the helper was not integrated within the Web browser, external media types and binaries could not be easily embedded within the Web page. Lastly, helper applications generally had to be downloaded and installed by the user, which kept many people from using them.

The idea of a helper application is rather simple: it is a program that the browser calls upon for help. Any program can be a helper application for a Web browser, assuming that a MIME type can be associated with the helper. When an object is delivered on the Web, HTTP header information is added to the object indicating its type. This information is in the form of a MIME type. For example, every Acrobat file should have a content type of application/pdf associated with it. When a browser receives a file with such a MIME type, it will look in its preferences to determine how to handle the file. These may include saving the file to disk, deleting the file, or handing the file off to another program such as a helper or browser plug-in. With MIME types and helpers, a developer can put Microsoft Word files on their Web site; users may be able to download them and read them automatically, assuming they have the appropriate helper application. Figure 13-13 overviews the basic way helper applications operate.

Oddly, helper applications are not used as much as they could be. Consider, for example, the use of HTML on an intranet. Within an organization, data may often be created in Microsoft Word or Excel format. While it is possible to easily translate such information into HTML, why would you want to? HTML is relatively expensive to create, often difficult to update, and may limit the quality of the document's presentation. The main reason that documents are put in HTML is that they can be ubiquitously read, meaning we don't have to rely on users having a particular application other than a Web browser to read our document. However, in an intranet this probably isn't an issue. In fact, it might be easier to create helper mappings on every system within a corporation rather than to reformat documents in HTML.

> **Suggestion: Rely on helper applications when translation to a native Web form is impractical.**

Plug-Ins

Plug-ins were introduced by Netscape in Navigator 2 and have limited support in other browsers like Opera or Internet Explorer, which relies more on ActiveX controls. Using plug-ins addresses the communication and integration issues that plagued helper applications. Recall that helper applications are not integrated into the design of a Web

1. Browser checks lookup table mapping MIME to action.

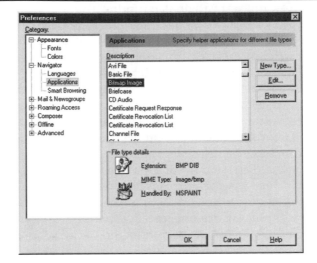

2. If no action, browser prompts user.

3. Pass to helper application if set up to do so.

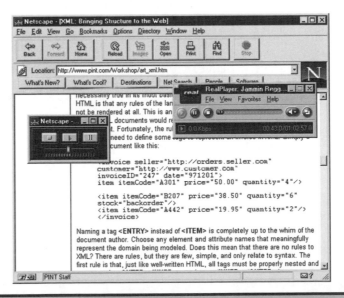

Figure 13-13.   *Overview of helper use*

page; rather, they appear in a separate window and may not be able to communicate well with the browser. However, plug-ins are components that run within the context of the browser itself, and thus can easily be integrated into the design of a page and communicate with the browser through technologies like JavaScript.

The plug-in approach of extending a browser's feature set has its drawbacks, however. Users must locate and download plug-ins, install them, and even restart their browsers. Many users find this rather complicated. Netscape 4 offers some installation relief with self-installing plug-ins and other features, but plug-ins remain troublesome. To further combat this problem, many of the most commonly requested plug-ins, such as Macromedia's Flash, are being included as a standard feature with Netscape browsers. The standard plug-ins that are primarily geared towards media handling and include Macromedia Flash and Shockwave, Adobe Acrobat, RealVideo, RealAudio, and simple download-and-play multimedia technologies like LiveAudio and LiveVideo. If plug-ins are considered, focus on the popular ones first given the installation hassle you'll put the user through.

> **Suggestion: Focus on using only the more popular plug-in technologies unless automatic installation can be performed.**

However, even if installation were not such a problem, unfortunately, plug-ins are not available on every machine; an executable program, or binary, must be created for each particular operating system. Because of this machine-specific approach, many plug-ins only work on Windows 95/NT. A decreasing number of plug-ins work on Windows 3.1, Macintosh, or UNIX. Finally, each plug-in installed on a system is a persistent extension to the browser and takes up memory and disk space. There really is a limit to how many modifications a user will be able to reasonably add to their browser.

The main design benefit of plug-ins is that they can be well integrated into Web pages. They may be included by using the HTML elements **<EMBED>** or **<OBJECT>**. Typically, the **<EMBED>** syntax is used, but the **<OBJECT>** syntax is the preferred method and will eventually supplant **<EMBED>** completely. In general, the **<EMBED>** element takes an SRC attribute to specify the URL of the included binary object. **HEIGHT** and **WIDTH** attributes often are used to indicate the pixel dimensions of the included object, if it is visible. To embed a short audiovideo interleaved (AVI) format movie called welcome.avi that can be viewed by the Netscape LiveVideo plug-in (generally installed with Netscape 3.x- and 4.x-generation browsers), use the following HTML fragment:

```
<EMBED SRC="welcome.avi" HEIGHT="100" WIDTH="100">
```

The **<EMBED>** element displays the plug-in (in this case, a movie) as part of the HTML document in a rectangular area of the page (shown in Figure 13-14).

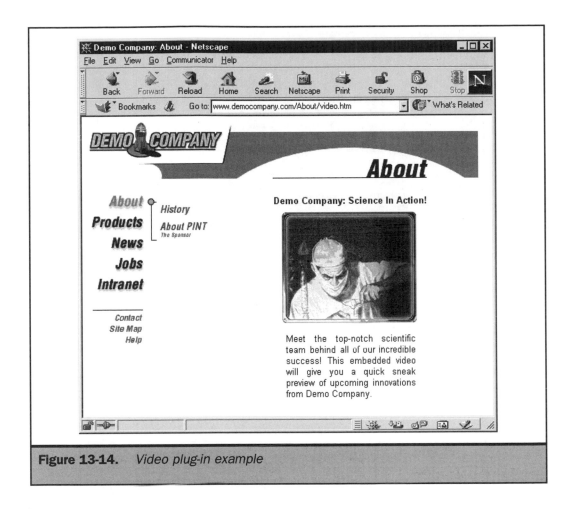

Figure 13-14. *Video plug-in example*

TECHNOLOGY AND WEB DESIGN

> **Note** *Although plug-ins can appear anywhere in a Web page, special limitations apply to plug-ins within positioned areas using style sheets.*

A browser may have many plug-ins installed. To check which plug-ins are installed in Netscape, the user may enter a strange URL, such as about:plugins, or look under the browser's Help menu for an entry that reads "About Plug-ins." The browser will show a list of plug-ins that are installed, the associated MIME type that will invoke each plug-in, and information as to whether that plug-in is enabled. Figure 13-15 shows an example of the plug-in information page under Netscape. Note that this will not work under Internet Explorer.

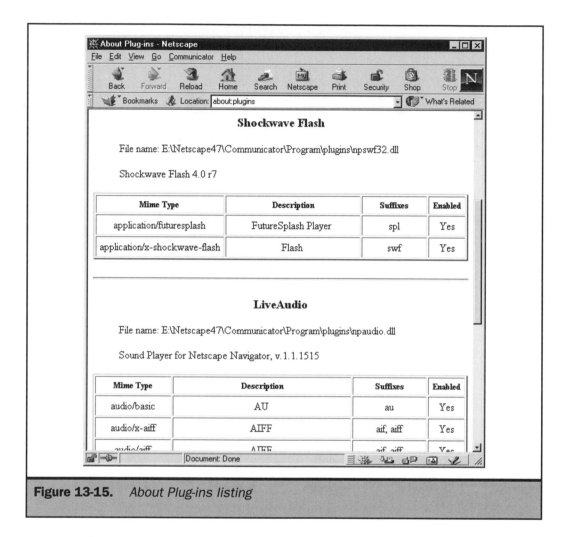

Figure 13-15. *About Plug-ins listing*

The obvious problem is what to do in case users don't have plug-in capability or are missing the appropriate plug-in. First, consider the user of the **<NOEMBED>** element to deal with nonplug-in capable users, as shown here:

```
<EMBED SRC="welcome.avi" HEIGHT="100" WIDTH="100">
<NOEMBED>
   <IMG SRC="welcome.gif" ALT="The history and philosophy of
Demo Company is both humorous and mysterious.">
</NOEMBED>
```

In this case, a browser not aware of the **<EMBED>** syntax would skip the first element and utilize the **<IMG>** element. In the case of the browser not supporting images, it would then even display the **ALT** attribute. With careful coding, it is possible to fall back to an acceptable state in nearly every situation.

Suggestion: Use the <NOEMBED> syntax with plug-ins.

The second situation is a little harder to deal with. In the case that the use has a browser that can support plug-ins but just does not have the needed plug-in, we need to use some scripting to sense for support and deal with the situation. For example, Flash can save out a detection script that can check to make sure that a plug-in is installed and write out the **<EMBED>** syntax only if it is detected. An example of such a detection script is shown here:

```
<SCRIPT LANGUAGE="JavaScript">
<!--
var plugin = (navigator.mimeTypes &&
navigator.mimeTypes["application/x-shockwave-flash"]) ?
navigator.mimeTypes["application/x-shockwave-flash"].enabledPlugin : 0;

if ( plugin &&
parseInt(plugin.description.substring(plugin.description.indexOf(".")-1)) >=
4 ) {
    document.write('<EMBED src="Movie1.swf" quality=high bgcolor=#FFFFFF ');
    document.write(' swLiveConnect=FALSE WIDTH=550 HEIGHT=400');
    document.write(' TYPE="application/x-shockwave-flash"
PLUGINSPAGE="http://www.macromedia.com/shockwave/download/index.cgi?P1_Prod_
Version=ShockwaveFlash">');
}
//-->
</SCRIPT>
```

Of course, what should be done if the plug-in isn't found to display the Flash animation? First, try to present an alternative such as an animated GIF. Second, try to either automatically install the plug-in or, at the very least, offer assistance on obtaining and installing the required technology. Avoid blatant advertising for plug-ins on a home page—just try to carefully redirect users to the appropriate download pages if (and only if) they need it.

Rule: Provide installation assistance for plug-ins and helpers.

The main downside of plug-ins is the barrier to entry they create because of installation and system requirements. If installation can be improved, designers will be able to rely more and more on the technologies provided.

ActiveX

ActiveX (http://www.microsoft.com/activex), which is the Internet portion of the Component Object Model (COM), is Microsoft's component technology for creating small components, or controls, within a Web page. ActiveX is intended to distribute these controls via the Internet to add new functionality to Internet Explorer. Microsoft maintains that ActiveX controls are more similar to generalized components than to plug-ins, because ActiveX controls can reside beyond the browser—even within container programs such as Microsoft Office. ActiveX controls are similar to Netscape plug-ins insofar as they are persistent and machine specific. Although this makes resource use a problem, installation is not an issue: the components download and install automatically.

Security is a big concern for ActiveX controls. Because these small pieces of code could potentially have full access to a user's system, they could cause serious damage. This capability, combined with automatic installation, creates a serious problem with ActiveX. End users may be quick to click a button to install new functionality, only to accidentally have their hard drives erased. The potentially unrestricted functionality of ActiveX controls creates a gaping security hole. To address this problem, Microsoft provides authentication information to indicate who wrote a control, in the form of code signed by a certificate, as shown by the various dialogs in Figure 13-16.

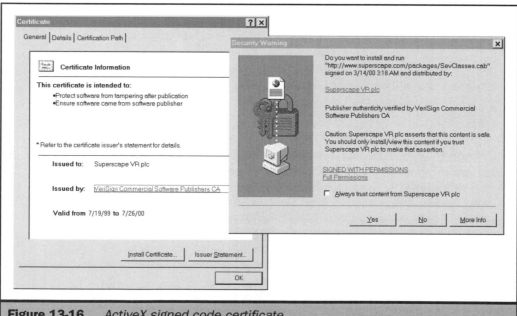

Figure 13-16.   *ActiveX signed code certificate*

Certificates only provide some indication that the control creator is reputable. They do nothing to actually prevent a control from doing something malicious. That's up to the user to understand. Safe Web browsing should be practiced, by accepting controls only from reputable sources.

Adding an ActiveX control to a Web page requires the use of the **<OBJECT>** element. For example, this markup is used to add a Flash file to a page:

```
<OBJECT classid="clsid:D27CDB6E-AE6D-11cf-96B8-444553540000"
 codebase="http://active.macromedia.com/flash2/cabs/
swflash.cab#version=4,0,0,0"
 ID="Movie1" WIDTH="550" HEIGHT="400">
 <PARAM NAME="movie" VALUE="Movie1.swf">
 <PARAM NAME="quality" VALUE="high">
 <PARAM NAME="bgcolor" VALUE="#FFFFFF">
  Sorry you don't have ActiveX
</OBJECT>
```

However, what appears in a browser with ActiveX? In this case, just a short message indicating the user doesn't have ActiveX. The reality is that the page should also provide options for other technologies such as plug-ins, or even images, before giving a failure message. The following example demonstrates how that could be done for Flash. Notice how all issues are dealt with: ActiveX, plug-ins, no plug-ins, no scripting, and even no images on.

```
<!DOCTYPE HTML PUBLIC "-//W3C//DTD HTML 4.0 Transitional//EN">
<HTML>
<HEAD>
<TITLE>Flash Demo</TITLE>
</HEAD>
<BODY BGCOLOR="#FFFFFF">
<OBJECT classid="clsid:D27CDB6E-AE6D-11cf-96B8-444553540000"
 codebase="http://active.macromedia.com/flash2/cabs/
   swflash.cab#version=4,0,0,0"
ID="Movie1" WIDTH="550" HEIGHT="400">
 <PARAM NAME="movie" VALUE="Movie1.swf">
 <PARAM NAME="quality" VALUE="high">
 <PARAM NAME=bgcolor VALUE="#FFFFFF">

<!-- here is the detection for plug-in for Netscape -->
 <SCRIPT LANGUAGE="JavaScript">
<!--
```

```
var plugin = (navigator.mimeTypes && navigator.mimeTypes
["application/x-shockwave-flash"]) ? navigator.mimeTypes
["application/x-shockwave-flash"].enabledPlugin : 0;
if ( plugin &&
 parseInt(plugin.description.substring(plugin.description.
indexOf(".")-1)) >= 4 ) {
    // Check for Flash version 4 or greater in Netscape
    document.write('<EMBED src="Movie1.swf" quality=high
    bgcolor=#FFFFFF ');
    document.write(' swLiveConnect=FALSE WIDTH=550 HEIGHT=400');
    document.write(' TYPE="application/x-shockwave-flash"
PLUGINSPAGE="http://www.macromedia.com/shockwave/download/
index.cgi?P1_Prod_Version=ShockwaveFlash">');
} else if (!(navigator.appName && navigator.appName.indexOf
("Netscape")>=0 && navigator.appVersion.indexOf("2.")>=0)){
    // Netscape 2 will display the IMG tag below so don't write
an extra one
    document.write('<IMG SRC="Movie1.gif" WIDTH=550 HEIGHT=400
    BORDER=0>');
}
//-->
</SCRIPT>
<NOEMBED>
<IMG SRC="Movie1.gif" WIDTH="550" HEIGHT="400" ALT="Flash Rules!">
</NOEMBED>
<NOSCRIPT>
<IMG SRC="Movie1.gif" WIDTH="550" HEIGHT="400" ALT="Flash Rules!">
</NOSCRIPT>
</OBJECT>
</BODY>
</HTML>
```

While this script may look complicated, it can be generated automatically, and once a single detection script is written it could be reused in many situations. Don't avoid this script or ActiveX because of complexity or security. Within intranets, the security concerns may not be a big issue, and on public sites ActiveX can be used safely to utilize many component technologies such as Macromedia Flash. However, like plug-ins in Netscape, make sure not to be exclusive to Microsoft browsers.

Rule: If ActiveX is used on a public site, make sure to provide alternatives for Netscape or other browsers.

Also, consider that many users will be paranoid about the potential security hazards involved in using ActiveX. Make sure that you provide information on changing security levels and exactly what your ActiveX control is doing.

Suggestion: Be clear and honest with users about security issues related to object technologies.

Java

The main downside of component technologies like Netscape plug-ins and ActiveX controls is that they are platform specific. Unfortunately or fortunately, depending on how you look at it, not every user runs on Windows or even Macintosh. How do we deal with cross-platform issues? Well, one way is to make a new platform that is common to all systems—and this is the idea of Java.

Sun Microsystems' Java technology (http://www.javasoft.com) is an attractive, revolutionary approach to cross-platform, Internet-based development. Java promises a platform-neutral development language, somewhat similar in syntax to C++, that allows programs to be written once and deployed on any machine, browser, or operating system that supports the Java virtual machine (JVM). Web pages use small Java programs, called *applets,* that are downloaded and run directly within a browser to provide new functionality.

Applets are written in the Java language and compiled to a machine-independent byte code in the form of a .class file, which is downloaded automatically to the Java-capable browser and run within the browser environment. But even with a fast processor, the end system may appear to run the byte code slowly compared to a natively compiled application, because the byte code must be interpreted by the JVM. This leads to the common perception that Java is slow. The reality is that Java isn't necessarily slow, but its interpretation can be. Even with recent just-in-time (JIT) compilers in newer browsers, Java often doesn't deliver performance equal to natively compiled applications.

Rule: Consider end-user system performance carefully when using object technologies like Java.

Even if compilation weren't an issue, current Java applets generally aren't persistent; they may have to be downloaded again in the future. Java-enabled browsers act like thin-client applications, because they add code only when they need it. In this sense, the browser doesn't become bloated with added features, but expands and contracts upon use.

Adding a Java applet to a Web page is relatively easy and can be done using the **<APPLET>** or **<OBJECT>** element, though **<APPLET>** is preferred for backward compatibility. If, for example, we had a .class file called helloworld, we might reference it with the following markup:

```
<APPLET CODE="helloworld.class"
        HEIGHT="50" WIDTH="175">
<H1>Hello World for you non-Java-aware browsers</H1>
</APPLET>
```

In the preceding code example, between **<APPLET>** and **</APPLET>** is an alternative rendering for browsers that don't support Java or the **<APPLET>** element, or that have Java support disabled.

The basic idea of how Java is utilized is shown in Figure 13-17.

Security in Java has been a serious concern from the outset. Because programs are downloaded and run automatically, a malicious program could be downloaded and run without the user being able to stop it. Under the first implementation of the technology, Java applets had little access to resources outside the browser's environment. Within Web pages, applets can't write to local disks or perform other harmful functions. This framework has been referred to as the *Java sandbox*. Developers who want to provide Java functions outside of the sandbox must write Java applications, which run as separate applications from browsers. Other Internet programming technologies (plug-ins and ActiveX) provide little or no safety from damaging programs.

Oddly, Java developers often want to add just these types of insecure features, as well as such powerful features as persistence and interobject communication. In fact, under new browsers, extended access can be requested for signed Java applets. (A *signed applet* enables users to determine who authored its code, and to accept or reject the applet accordingly.) This is very similar to how ActiveX is implemented. If desired, Java applets can securely request limited disk access, limited disk access and network usage, limited disk read access and unlimited disk write access, and unrestricted access. Users downloading an applet that is requesting any enhanced privileges are presented with a dialog box that outlines the requested access and presents the applet's credentials in the form of its digital signature. The user can then approve or reject the applet's request. If the user doesn't approve the request, the applet may continue to run, but it can't perform the denied actions.

The reality of Java as far as a Web designer is concerned is that it really isn't useful on public sites. The truth is that there are so many different Java virtual machines in browsers that the idea of "write once, run everywhere" has been turned into "write once, debug everywhere." The major benefit of Java applets just isn't there. Designers should need no proof other than the fact that major sites that relied on Java applets have long since removed them in most cases. However, within intranets, on the server side in the form of Java servlets, or with very careful coding, Java applets can be used. The complexity of Java, though, has often locked designers out, leaving much of the interface design strictly to programmers. The major downside is that often the

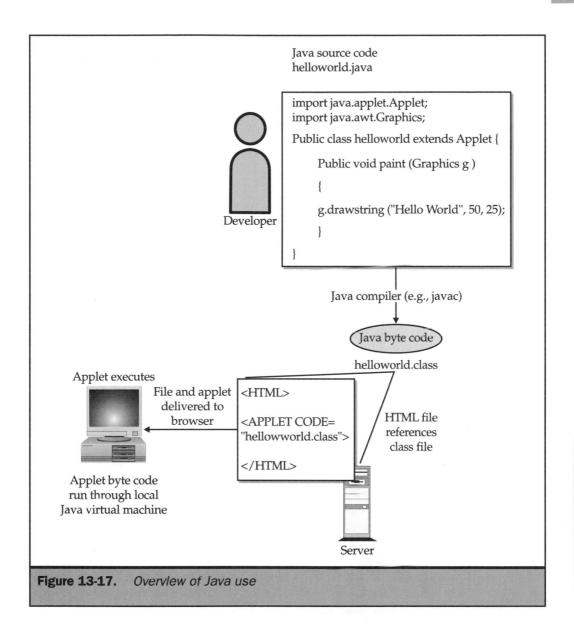

Figure 13-17.   *Overview of Java use*

programmers end up building a typical GUI application within a Java applet and then deliver it via a Web page. As discussed in the previous chapter, this really isn't what the Web was supposed to be about.

Suggestion: Avoid building GUI interfaces within Web site interfaces using a binary technology like Java or ActiveX.

Integration is always the key. Programming should be used to quietly breathe life into a page, not to supersede it entirely with something new or force the user to wait or jump through hoops. Oftentimes, simple tasks like creating a scrolling news ticker will be created in Java, forcing the user to look at a gray box for 20 seconds—when it could easily have been done in JavaScript. Again, recall the idea of choosing the correct technology for the job.

JavaScript

JavaScript is a scripting language originally developed by Netscape and supported by Microsoft browsers in the form of JScript, a clone language used in Internet Explorer. The language was turned over to the international standards body *European Computer Manufacturers Association (ECMA)*, which announced during the summer of 1997 the approval of ECMA-262, or ECMAScript, as a cross-platform Internet standard for scripting. Browser vendors generally comply with the specification, but will still use the commonly recognized JavaScript name.

As a scripting language, JavaScript is meant to be easy to use, noncompiled (interpreted), and useful in small chunks. This sets it apart from Java and other languages that might be used on the Internet, which tend to be compiled and relatively hard to master for the nonprogrammer. The syntax of JavaScript is somewhat like C or Java with PERL-style regular expression handling, and the language has basic object-oriented capabilities. JavaScript is not, however, a true object-oriented programming language, and retains features (such as weak typing) that are common to simple scripting languages.

JavaScript is useful for small jobs, such as checking form data, adding small bits of HTML code to a page on the fly, creating small embellishments such as rollover buttons (as discussed in Chapter 6), and performing browser-, time-, and user-specific computation. JavaScript is also a powerful means of controlling events in browsers and accessing the HTML elements themselves for manipulation through something called the Document Object Model, or DOM for short. This advanced use of JavaScript is often dubbed Dynamic HTML or DHTML. The reality is that this is just JavaScript and should not really be distinguished in any special way. Though following the DHTML philosophy, it is easy to see the important potential function of JavaScript to act as the glue between different technologies, such as CSS, HTML, plug-ins, Java applets, and so on. Even without this, JavaScript is a core Web technology that designers are encouraged to understand well.

Tip   *Designers looking to understand Web programming should start with JavaScript.*

An example of JavaScript code being used to greet the user is shown here; a rendering of the script in action is shown in Figure 13-18.

```
<!DOCTYPE HTML PUBLIC "-//W3C//DTD HTML 4.0 Transitional//EN">
<HTML>
<HEAD>
<TITLE>JavaScript Example</TITLE>
<SCRIPT LANGUAGE="JavaScript">
<!--
 function Greet()
 {
    alert("Hello user! Welcome to JavaScript.");
    }
//-->
</SCRIPT>
</HEAD>
<BODY>
<H1 ALIGN="CENTER">First JavaScript Example</H1>

<DIV ALIGN="CENTER">
<FORM>
    <INPUT TYPE="BUTTON" VALUE="Press Me" onClick="Greet()">
</FORM>
</DIV>
<SCRIPT>
<!--
document.write("Last modified on: "+document.lastModified);
//-->
</SCRIPT>
</BODY>
</HTML>
```

This is a simple example of how JavaScript may be included in an HTML file. The Form button triggers the function called **Greet()**, which greets the user. The event-handler attribute **onclick** is used to tie the HTML to the JavaScript that is contained in the head of the document within the **<SCRIPT>** element. The **<SCRIPT>** element at the bottom shows the use of an immediate script that is executed no matter what the user does.

While this example is very easy, remember that it is also a trivial example; this is a real programming language that has many nuances. For more information on

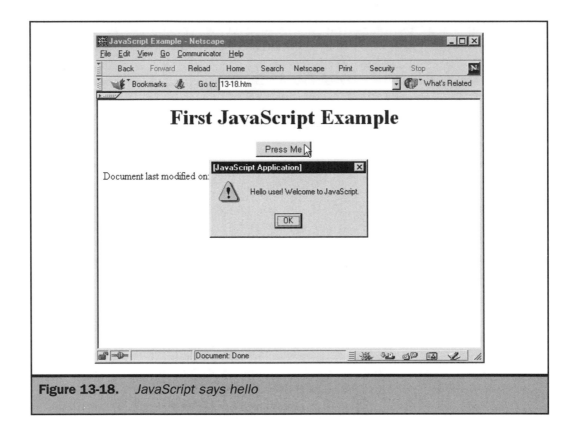

Figure 13-18.   *JavaScript says hello*

learning JavaScript, visit Netscape's developer site at http://developer.netscape.com/. Information about Microsoft's implementation of JavaScript, called JScript, can be found at http://msdn.microsoft.com/scripting/. For now, let's discuss some issues that are helpful for designers to understand.

JavaScript Versions

During its short lifetime, JavaScript has undergone many changes. Not all browsers support it to the same degree, if at all. JavaScript has a few major dialects, including JavaScript 1 (=Netscape 2.*x*), JavaScript 1.1 (=Netscape 3.*x*), and JavaScript 1.2 (=Netscape 4.*x*). JScript in Internet Explorer 3 is approximately equivalent to JavaScript 1; it doesn't support JavaScript 1.1 features, such as dynamic image replacement. Internet Explorer 4 appears to support JavaScript 1.1, but with a richer object model, and is able to modify page elements at will. Finally, there is the ECMAScript standard. Table 13-8 summarizes the versions of JavaScript.

The reason designers need to be aware of all these versions is that each varies in what it can do. For example, if you code for Netscape 4, it probably won't work in

Browser	JavaScript Support
Netscape Navigator 2.*x*	JavaScript 1
Netscape Navigator 3.*x*	JavaScript 1.1
Netscape Navigator 4–4.05	JavaScript 1.2
Netscape Navigator 4.06, 4.5*x*	JavaScript 1.3
Internet Explorer 2.*x*	None
Internet Explorer 3.*x*	JScript (JavaScript 1)
Internet Explorer 4.*x*	JScript (JavaScript 1.1)
Internet Explorer 5.*x*	JScript (JavaScript 1.2)

Table 13-8.   *JavaScript Support by Browser Release*

older browsers or maybe even Internet Explorer 4! The point here is to simply be aware of the multiple versions of the language and try to find the neutral ground if possible.

Suggestion: Make sure to test to see if a script works in all versions of the language.

Fall-Through Script

One way to deal with different versions of JavaScript is to utilize the **LANGUAGE** attribute of the **<SCRIPT>** element. Script-aware browsers will ignore the contents of **<SCRIPT>** tags they do not understand. Because browsers act this way, it is possible to create multiple versions of a script for varying versions of the language, as you can see here:

```
<SCRIPT LANGUAGE="JavaScript">
Netscape 2.0 version here
</SCRIPT>

<SCRIPT LANGUAGE="JavaScript1.1">
Netscape 3.0 version here
</SCRIPT>

<SCRIPT LANGUAGE="JavaScript1.2">
Netscape 4.0 version here
</SCRIPT>
```

Object Detection

Fall-through code isn't the best way to do things. In some cases, it is just better to check to see if it is possible to do something. For example, you might be interested in checking to see if it is possible to do rollover buttons. Netscape 3 browsers and beyond, as well as Internet Explorer 4 and beyond, can all do rollovers, so you might be tempted to use browser sensing to decide if rollovers should be activated. Unfortunately, what happens if a new browser comes out, say SuperBrowser 1.0, that supports rollover capability but doesn't match in name or version to the other rollover-capable browsers? Well, your code simply won't work. Rather than knowing everything about what browsers support what versions of JavaScript, it is probably just better to detect for capabilities by checking if the appropriate object is available. For example, a script here would check to see if your browser could support rollover images by simply looking to see if the image object is defined:

```
<SCRIPT>
if (document.images)
 alert("Rollovers possible")
else
  alert("Sorry no rollovers");
</SCRIPT>
```

Rule: Utilize object, method, and version checks in all scripts.

Of course, checking for object existence assumes that scripting is even on. It is also possible to deal with a browser with scripting off.

Dealing with Nonscript-Aware Browsers

There are two ways to deal with nonscript-aware browsers:

- Using comments to mask out scripting commands
- Using the **<NOSCRIPT>** element

Consider what would happen in a browser that didn't understand script when the markup below is encountered:

```
<SCRIPT>
if (document.images)
 alert("Rollovers possible")
else
  alert("Sorry no rollovers");
</SCRIPT>
```

The nonscript-aware browser would ignore the **<SCRIPT>** tag and simply print the code onscreen. To avoid this problem, make sure to comment out the script code. To deal with a browser that doesn't support script (or script was turned off), you would need to use the **<NOSCRIPT>** element to present alternative markup. This short example shows how both techniques could be used:

```
<SCRIPT>
<!--
if (document.images)
 alert("Rollovers possible")
else
  alert("Sorry no rollovers");
//-->
</SCRIPT>
<NOSCRIPT>
      Sorry you have no JavaScript thus no rollovers.
</NOSCRIPT>
```

Rule: Comment out scripts and use a <NOSCRIPT> element to deal with nonscript-aware browsers.

Error Catching in JavaScript

Even if we deal with different script versions and browsers that don't support script, there are bound to be errors that happen in a page. Users are probably all too familiar with messages like the ones shown here popping up every second.

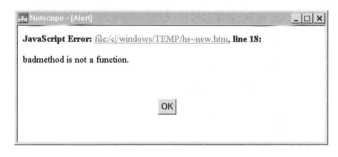

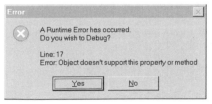

Script errors are so significant that, by default, Netscape suppresses them to a console. The only clue that something has gone wrong is a small message like this one in the status bar.

Of course, if you do actually access the JavaScript console, you'd eventually see the same errors.

The fact of the matter is that errors will occur. It is probably better to handle them gracefully rather than let the browser do so. The following short example shows the inclusion of a custom error handler:

```
<!DOCTYPE HTML PUBLIC "-//W3C//DTD HTML 4.0 Transitional//EN">
<HTML>
<HEAD>
<TITLE>Errors Happen</TITLE>
<SCRIPT LANGUAGE="JavaScript">
<!--
function errorHandler(message, url, line) {
  alert("Sorry an error has occurred!");
  return true;
}
```

```
window.onerror = errorHandler;
 // -->
</SCRIPT>
</HEAD>
<BODY>
<H2 ALIGN="CENTER">Press to trigger an error</H2>

<FORM>
<INPUT TYPE="BUTTON" VALUE="PRESS ME" onClick="Bomb()">
</FORM>
</BODY>
</HTML>
```

Note *Internet Explorer 5 has adopted new syntax for error handling that does not act in a standard way. This example will only work under IE4 or Netscape 4 browsers, and is meant only to illustrate the idea of error catching.*

As mentioned in the previous chapter, it would be possible to customize the error dialog to even fit with the design of the site.

Rule: Always add an error handler for JavaScripts.

Linked Scripts

Interestingly, on the Web, designers are repeating the mistakes of the past with JavaScript. Consider how many pages include a massive amount of script code directly within the HTML markup. Just like combining structure and style, as we did with HTML, only to later try to remove it with CSS, the same is being done with scripts. Yet there is no reason to. It is easy to separate scripts out in external .js files, like so:

```
<SCRIPT SRC="formvalidation.js"></SCRIPT>
```

External scripts have many benefits. First, obviously, it makes it easier to update HTML and scripts separately. Secondly, it does hide script from older browsers. Third, it allows browsers to cache the script so it doesn't have to be downloaded over and over again. Yet despite these benefits, linked scripts are hardly used. While there were some initial compatibility considerations using linked scripts, it is possible to use them today without too much worry.

Suggestion: Use linked scripts rather than inline ones when possible.

Like style sheets, it is probably a good idea to keep all the JavaScripts for a site in a central location such as a /scripts directory. This is just a matter of good style.

JavaScript Style

Like HTML, JavaScript often suffers from a serious lack of coding quality.
Many JavaScripts do not exhibit a clean coding style. For example, many
scripts lack meaningful variable names, choosing a name like "nw" instead of
"navigationwindow." Of course, this may be for download speed, but oftentimes
it seems to be sloppy coding more than anything else. In short, try to pick a good
JavaScript coding style and stick with it. Use meaningful, descriptive names for
items. You might want to borrow from the programming conventions, some of
which are borrowed from the Java Language shown in Table 13-9, when writing
JavaScripts.

Rule: Practice good coding standards and consistent style in JavaScripts.

Program Structure	Comment	Examples
Variables	Fully lowercase and use nouns. Scope variables using the **var** command to avoid making all variables global.	`var car = "BMW";` `browserversion = 4;`

Functions	Use verbs or phrases containing verbs and mix case the name. Pass values as parameters and use return to avoid excessive manipulation through global variables.	`function`
		`openNewWindow(url,`
		`windowname)`
		`{`
		`    window.open(url,`
		`windowname,`
		`"toolbar=0,location=0,`
		`width=615,height=440");`
		`}`
		
		`function`
		`calculateTotal(value1,`
		`value2 )`
		`{`
		`return ((value1 +`
		`value2)*100);`
		`}`

Table 13-9. *A Few JavaScript Style Suggestions*

Program Structure	Comment	Examples

Class	Though classes are special cases of functions, make sure to indicate them as a class when they are objects by capitalizing them.	`function PushButton( )`
		
		`function Car()`

Comments	Utilize comments to explain how to use scripts or explain difficult ideas.	`/* Function openWindow`
		`creates a chromeless`
		`window named as the`
		`value of the name`
		`parameter with the value`
		`of the URL parameter`
		`loaded in it. */`
		
		`total //x+y`

Semicolons	Terminate all statements with semicolons.	`string1="line1";` `string2="line2";`

Table 13-9.   *A Few JavaScript Style Suggestions* (continued)

Crunched JavaScript

The addition of JavaScript to HTML documents can result in very long documents. As with HTML, it is possible to crunch JavaScript. For example, returns can be eliminated from statements if semicolons are used. Consider that in JavaScript, the following are equivalent:

```
docment.write("Hello ")
document.write("world!");
```

and

```
document.write("Hello);document.write("world");
```

Of course, if you don't use semicolons, crunching can ruin a script.

"Crunch" large scripts, but beware of semicolon problems.

It is also possible to utilize shorthand notations to further crunch files. For example, some JavaScript authors prefer

```
(quantity > 10) ? alert("You get a discount!") : alert("Sorry, no
discount.");
```

to

```
if (quantity > 10)

  alert("You get a discount!");
else
  alert("Sorry, no discount.");
```

though both are equivalent. Some coders may even begin to rename variables like quantity to simple single letters like q. Be careful—you can take crunching so far as to create unreadable code!

Using JavaScripts

Writing JavaScript doesn't have to be difficult, but it should be done in a very conservative manner. Like all forms of client-side programming, there is a lot of room for things to go wrong. Always try to account for new browser versions, browsers with their script off, and just the plain unforeseen. Remember, if we are going to fail, we should at least fail gracefully. If you don't plan on becoming a JavaScript programmer, it is still possible to add script to pages by visiting tutorial and script library sites like www.webreference.com/js and www.dynamicdrive.com. Just make sure you are careful when you add it to your pages and have a programmer look over what you've done.

Before moving on to multimedia programming considerations, the loaded issue of cookies should be discussed. Make sure to pay attention, since invariably you'll have to explain more than a few times what cookies are to concerned colleagues or clients.

Cookies

A *cookie* is a small amount of information sent by a Web server that is stored on a user's system for later retrieval. The main purpose of a cookie is to save information for later. The major use of cookies is to store user identification and passwords so the users don't have to always retype them back in. Another common use of cookies is to store any preferences you may set when you access a site. From a programming point of view, cookies are used to solve the state-management problem. Basically, the state problem relates to the idea that servers don't remember a user from one visit to the next, so cookies are need to create features such as shopping baskets that last across multiple visits. Other state preservation forms, such as hidden data within forms or complex URLs, can be used *within* visits, but *between* visits cookies are really the only possible solution.

Many users are absolutely paranoid about cookies. The reality is that they really aren't anything more than a small string of information. If you look for cookies on your hard drive, you will probably come across a filed called cookies.txt in your browser folder, or even a whole directory of cookie text files, generally in C:\Windows\Cookies. Taking a look at an individual cookie, you might see something like this:

```
.google.com    TRUE  /  FALSE   2147368374   ID   112005d255531c2c
```

This particular cookie is associated with the Google search engine. What it is used for, one can't be quite sure. However, in general, the purpose of a cookie is simply to act somewhat like a Web laundry ticket. It allows the user to pick up the items in their shopping cart, keep their preferences set, and so on. In and of itself, the cookie doesn't say much about a user. Like a laundry ticket, it is just a code number. However, when associated with user-provided information, it is possible to build a profile about the user. The fear of tracking through cookies has led to some pretty serious worries on the part of users. In reality, cookies are relatively harmless if they can't be associated with personal information. Despite any claims to the contrary, a cookie cannot be used to retrieve data from a user's hard drive other than the value of the cookie itself. The cookie can't steal sensitive information such as a user's e-mail address or browser preferences. However, again, a cookie can be used to track users. Oftentimes, this is used to display banner ads to users or show them products that may appeal to them based on past browsing habits. Some users do not like the fact they are so carefully tracked and will disable their cookies. To avoid this, and to try to instill some trust with users, designers are encouraged to be honest with users about cookie use within sites.

Suggestion: Inform users what cookies are used for in an easily found privacy policy or usage statement.

Because users may have their preferences set to warn about cookies being issued, you do not want to bug them too much. Consider trying to use a single cookie on your site to track the user and provide state-preservation features. Issuing multiple cookies can be a nuisance for the user who has to accept each and every one.

Suggestion: Avoid issuing multiple cookies.

Of course, some people are just going to reject cookies outright. If at all possible, provide another way for users to access your site without cookies. If this is not possible, at least gracefully fail and indicate to the user that they will not be able to use your site if they are going to be so paranoid.

Suggestion: Provide an alternative for users unwilling to accept cookies.

Note   *Weblink: For more information on cookies, visit http://www.cookiecentral.com.*

The final topic of this chapter concerns multimedia within Web pages. Though not always natively supported within browsers, animation, sound, and video are becoming more and more popular. This next section presents only a very basic overview of some of the technologies available. Like all the other technologies presented in this chapter, explicit details beyond simple syntax would constitute a book equal in size to this one.

Multimedia in Web Design

As the Web moves away from a print design background, it has continued to become more and more multimedia-driven. Many sites use animation, and audio and video are becoming popular as well. However, while multimedia may improve the presentation of a site, it often comes with significant bandwidth and technology restrictions. Designers should first consider if the addition of multimedia elements will actually improve the user's ability to understand information or make the experience of visiting the site more pleasing. If not, it really shouldn't be included. Secondly, how the multimedia elements should be added is very important. Designers should stick to common technologies lest they create a barrier to entering a site. The following sections will briefly discuss the various multimedia additions that could be made to a site, their best use, and the most common forms of implementation.

Animation

A little animation can spice up a Web page a great deal. Animation on the Web is used for many things: active logos, animated icons, demonstrations, and short cartoons. There are a variety of animation technologies available to Web designers. Some of the most common animation approaches include animated GIFs, Flash and Shockwave, and DHTML animations. Other animation possibilities also exist—notably, Java-based animations and older animation techniques such as server push are still possible, but the field has narrowed significantly and few older or proprietary animation formats are actually worth exploring. Table 13-10 details the animation choices commonly used and provides some comments about each.

Animation is often used in splash pages or in an advertising banner and is a good way to pique someone's curiosity. In some sense, animation is used to signal "look at me" to the user. Of course, while animation can grab the user's attention, it can easily

Animation Technology	Comments
Animated GIFs	Animated GIFs are the simplest form of animation and are supported natively by most browsers. Looping and minimal timing information can be set in an animated GIF, but complex animation is beyond this format's capabilities. Further information on this format can be found in Chapter 11.
DHTML	DHTML (JavaScript) can be used to move objects around the screen. However, DHTML-based animation tends to be choppy and is not suggested for anything beyond simple button rollover effects, as discussed in Chapter 6, and scrolling text effects. Dreamweaver (http://www.dreamweaver.com) can add DHTML-based path animations easily to pages.
Flash	Macromedia Flash (http://www.macromedia.com/flash) is the leading format for sophisticated Web-based animations. Flash files are very compact, and most users have Flash preinstalled on their system. Flash does support some limited programming facilities, but often will have to be augmented with JavaScript. Complex interactivity associated with an animation may be better left to Shockwave or Java.
Shockwave	Shockwave files are compressed Macromedia director files. Their main benefit over Flash is simply that they support complex scripting. However, they can be significantly larger than Flash files.
Java	While Java can be used for animation, it is not suggested. The only major benefit of Java-based animations is that they can be created on the fly based on a complex calculation. The only major use for Java in this sense might be animations created client-side based on user inputs. Java might be used for a simulation or animated graphing application. Java, of course, is relatively complex, and is overkill for simple animations.

Table 13-10. *Web Animation Choices*

be overused. Consider, for example, two very animated banner advertisements on the same page. How will the user be able to focus on one banner ad if another one continues to signal them? While the user's ability to tune out sensory input, as discussed in Chapter 3, is great, competing animations will likely distract the user and literally cause their eyeballs to bounce like ping-pong balls.

Rule: When trying to draw attention, avoid competing animations.

While it may be possible to get a user to notice animations, after a while they will probably tune them out or get annoyed. Because of this, continuously looped animation should be avoided.

Rule: Avoid continuously running animation loops.

What's interesting is that many designers often use animation for the sake of gratuitous flash or attraction, but they forget that animation is also an effective means to illustrate important points. Imagine that you want to demonstrate your new image-enhancement program. An animated demonstration of its effects would be far more impressive than two static "before and after" pictures sitting side by side. It is important to work the animation into the functionality of your site, preferably during the design phase of a project.

Sound

The latest audio technologies on the Internet cover a lot of ground, from traditional download-and-play systems in a variety of formats to *streaming audio,* which plays close to real time. Surprisingly, the most advanced technologies, and the most popular, may not be the best solution.

Digital Audio Basics

This section provides a very brief overview of digital sound. Digital sound is measured by the frequency of *sampling,* or how many times the sound is digitized during a specific time period. Sampling frequencies are specified in kilohertz (kHz), which indicate the sound sampling rate per second. CD-quality sound is approximately 44.1kHz, or 44,100 samples every second. For stereo, two channels are required, each at 8 bits; at 16 bits per sample, that yields 705,600 bits of data for each second of CD-quality sound. In theory, the bits of data on a CD could be delivered over the Internet, creating high-quality music at the end user's demand. In reality, transmitting this amount of data would take nearly half a T1 network's bandwidth. Since this type of bandwidth is not available to the average Web user, another approach is needed.

One approach is to lower the sampling rate when creating digital sound for Web delivery. A sampling rate of 8kHz in mono might produce acceptable playback results for simple applications, such as speech, particularly considering that playback hardware often consists of a combination of a simple sound card and a small speaker. Low-quality audio requires a mere 64,000 bits of data per second, but the end user still has to wait to download the sound. For modem users, even in the best of conditions, each second of low-quality sound takes a few seconds to be delivered, making continuous sound unrealistic.

Audio-File Formats and Compression

Audio files can be compressed to reduce the amount of data being sent. The software on the serving side compresses the data, which is decompressed and played back on the receiving end. The compression/decompression software is known together as a *codec*. Just like image formats, audio compression methods are either lossy or lossless. *Lossy* data compression doesn't perfectly represent what was compressed, but is close enough given the size savings. Because *lossless* compression techniques guarantee that what goes in one end comes out the other, most techniques can't compress files to any significant degree. Compression always involves a trade-off between sound quality and file size; larger file sizes mean longer download times.

When dealing with sounds, you don't really select different forms of compression. You select file formats. Many standard file formats are available, as shown in Table 13-11.

File Format	Description
WAV	Waveform (or simply *wave*) files are the most common sound format on Windows platforms. WAVs may also be played on Macs and other systems with player software.
MPEG (MP3)	Motion Pictures Experts Group format is a standard format that has significant compression capabilities. MPEG level 3 or MP3 files are very commonly used for distribution of music on the Web. However, due to the size, MPEG files are generally downloaded completely before playback.
RealAudio (.rm)	RealAudio is the predominant streaming technology currently in use on the Web. It requires a proprietary player, but basic versions of the player are available free.
MIDI	Musical Instrument Digital Interface format is not a digitized audio format. It represents notes and other information so that music can be synthesized. MIDI is well supported and files are very small, but it is useful for only certain applications due to its sound quality when reproduced on PC hardware.

Table 13-11.   *Common Web Audio Formats*

TECHNOLOGY AND WEB
DESIGN

File Format	Description
AU	Sparc-audio, or u-law format, is one of the oldest Internet sound formats. A player for nearly every platform is available.
RMF	Rich Music Format as supported by Beatnik (www.beatnik.com) is a compact high-quality primarily download-and-play audio format growing in popularity.
AIFF	Audio Interchange File Format is very common on Macs. Widely used in multimedia applications, it is not very common on the Web.

Table 13-11.   *Common Web Audio Formats* (continued)

Simple Web Audio

Sound on the Web was initially available only in "download-and-play" format, which obliged users to download sounds completely before they could play them. This takes up valuable hard drive space, even if a user wants to hear only the first few seconds of a file. Sounds must be degraded significantly in this situation, which may not be acceptable for content that requires flawless playback. Even at very low sampling rates, these sounds must be fairly short to spare impatient users the agony of prolonged download times. Download time can be reduced by creating smaller audio files, which only accentuates the drawbacks of this method.

Using HTML, the simplest way to support the download-and-play approach is by linking to a sound file and letting another application deal with it, such as a helper or plug-in. If no helper or plug-in is configured, the user is prompted to deal with the sound. For example, to link to an audio file in WAV format, insert a link like this:

```
<A HREF="democompanyjingle.wav">Demo Company's Corporate Jingle
(7 second WAV - 180K)</A>
```

When using the download-and-play approach, it is wise to put the decision to download the file in the hands of users. Inform them about the file format and size, so that they have some indication of how long the download will take. Another helpful bit of information might be how long the sound is going to be.

Suggestion: When linking to informational sounds such as speeches or audio broadcast excerpts, always indicate the length, format, and size of the sound file.

Download-and-play–based audio delivery is recommended where a quick bit of sound is required. Probably the best bet for a brief dash of sound in a page is using a WAV file. While a WAV file does not offer a high degree of compression, support for sound files in this format is generally common in browsers or is provided via standard helper applications and plug-ins.

Suggestion: For download-and-play delivery, use WAV for low-quality music, sound effects, or speech.

MIDI (Musical Instrument Digital Interface) files are also commonly used for download-and-play applications. Unlike other audio formats, MIDI files describe the music or sound and then rely on the playback device to reproduce the sound or instruments described in the file. In some sense, a MIDI file is similar to a vector image format that has to be rendered on a local browser. Like a vector image, the image benefit of MIDI files is that they are extremely compact. Whole songs lasting literally minutes can be represented in a few dozen kilobytes when saved in MIDI format.

Suggestion: Use MIDI files with long background-music files, particularly when bandwidth is at a premium.

The major downside with MIDI is that it must be played back on the end user's system using their equipment. An end user's sound card may have the music synthesis capability of a cheap electronic keyboard, making the included MIDI sound detract from the seriousness of the content presented.

 When using MIDI files, consider that the playback device will greatly affect what the user hears.

While MIDI is appropriate for the low end, MPEG—particularly MPEG level 3 (MP3)—is really the only choice for high-quality playback (especially music).

Simple Audio in Practice

Both Microsoft and Netscape browsers should provide limited sound support built in for download-and-play WAV and MIDI files. Netscape uses its LiveAudio plug-in, and Microsoft Internet Explorer uses its proprietary **<BGSOUND>** tag.

Both browsers also support MIDI sound. For example, to set LiveAudio to include a sound called "test.wav" and a panel to control the sound, use the following HTML fragment:

```
<EMBED SRC="test.wav" HEIGHT="60" WIDTH="144">
```

Including the **HEIGHT** and **WIDTH** values is important; otherwise, the browser may clip the console. The default size for the LiveAudio control is 60 pixels high and 144 pixels across. Other control styles have different default sizes. If you want to create a background sound for a page, you may find this line more appropriate:

```
<EMBED SRC="test.wav" HIDDEN="TRUE" AUTOSTART="TRUE">
```

Although Netscape's LiveAudio isn't an official standard by any means, it is common enough that it could be used carefully within a Netscape environment. In a most basic form, it is also possible to support both Netscape and Microsoft browsers with LiveAudio itself or with Microsoft-specific elements, such as **<BGSOUND>**.

```
<EMBED SRC="test.wav" HIDDEN="TRUE" AUTOSTART="true">
<BGSOUND SRC="test.wav" LOOP="2">
```

In this case, Internet Explorer should ignore the first statement, while Netscape should ignore the second. When dealing with other forms of technology, it is preferable to use JavaScript to control which form is inserted into the document. With both forms of sound support enabled, conflicts can occur, so page authors are advised to test their documents thoroughly.

Streaming Audio

Proprietary audio formats like RealAudio offer one thing that many "standard" digital audio formats lack: the possibility of *streaming data*. As a rule of thumb, a 28.8-Kbps modem user receives approximately 2K of data per second. If one second of sound could be represented in 2K, and the data could get to the end user at a rate of 2K every second, then the data would effectively *stream*, or play in real time. Streaming seems to make a whole lot of sense. Why wait for an hour-long speech to download before playing when you care only about the current second of data being listened to? Streamed data doesn't take up hard-drive space, and it opens up random access to any position in an audio file. However, streaming audio has a few potentially serious drawbacks. First, to compress audio far enough for streaming, you have to sacrifice a certain degree of sound quality. Second, the Internet protocols themselves do not readily support the requirements of streaming.

As you may know, the Internet is frequently subject to bursts and traffic delays. Here are a couple of key points to remember. The TCP/IP protocols used on the Internet were designed for robustness and scalability. The Internet is a packet-switched network that breaks up data into little chunks and sends them separately, to be reassembled at the other end. Because these packets may be lost along their journey or arrive out of order, the Transmission Control Protocol (TCP) guarantees the integrity of the data. This way, many users can share a fixed circuit that allows for economies of scale. However, packet-switched networks have one serious problem—they can't guarantee delivery time without special modifications. This makes streamed audio, video, and other "real time" applications on packet-switched networks very difficult. In fact while many protocols and assumptions are made to improve the likelihood of streaming sound working properly most of the time, the awful reality is that it doesn't always work. Fight it if you like, but consider the following rule from the next chapter before relying too greatly on the quality of streaming media.

> **Rule: Predictable and error-free delivery of real-time data on the Internet cannot be guaranteed with today's protocols and usage.**

The streaming-media discussion is presented in more depth in Chapter 14, but don't let the downsides discourage you from adding sound to your site. Interested readers are directed to http://www.real.com to download the latest encoding and serving software.

Usability and Audio Files

Adding sound to a Web site shouldn't be an infuriating experience for Webmasters or Web users. The first thing to consider is not putting something very important *only* in audio form. Remember, not every user will have speakers on their computer or be in an environment were sound can or should be heard.

> **Suggestion: Don't assume audio support. Always provide alternative forms of access for important audio-based content such as a text transcript.**

Even when a user can hear audio, do they necessarily want to? Consider well the business user hitting a site only to have some theme music play in the background, letting everyone know what he or she is doing.

When sound is used—particularly if it is continuous—make sure you provide an easy way for the user to turn it off. A common sound toggle button should be used, and would look something like this.

> **Rule: Always allow a user to turn off continuously playing sounds.**

Like other technologies, it might be better to use a simple download-and-play sound format built into a browser rather than making a user jump through hoops installing special plug-ins for proprietary audio forms or streaming data. However, if downloading sounds, make sure not to make users wait too long. Try to compress files further by following the following basic rules of thumb:

- Reduce the length of the sound file.
- Reduce the number of channels.

TECHNOLOGY AND WEB
DESIGN

- A mono audio file will be half the size of a stereo file.
- Reduce the sampling rate.

While this reduces the quality of the sound, 8khz should be acceptable for voice and 22khz may be acceptable for music.

Even with compression, the size of audio files is going to get so large that they will not be effective for many users. Once we add full-motion video to the mix, things are only going to get worse.

Video

The holy grail of Internet multimedia is certainly high-quality, 30-frames-per-second real-time video. Many companies are working toward the idea of television on the Web, but most of their solutions just don't work well within the bandwidth limitations faced by the average Internet user. Sooner or later, video will be used extensively on Web pages—but what Web video technology, if any, is appropriate for the job, and how can video be accessed via HTML? The latest Internet video technologies range from low-quality streaming audio with an occasional picture to traditional download-and-play systems for a variety of file formats. As with audio, the most popular technologies—and the most advanced—may not offer the best solutions for simple Web video needs.

Digital Video Basics

Digital video is measured by the number of frames per second of video, and by the size and resolution of these frames. The total size requirement for video is huge, particularly if you want NTSC (TV quality) video. A 640 × 480 image with 24 bits of data representation for color and a frame rate of 30 frames per second takes up a staggering 27MB per second—and that's without sound. Add CD-quality audio (705,600 bits of data for each second of data) and the file size increases proportionately. In theory, the bits of data necessary to deliver TV-quality video could be transmitted over the Internet, creating the long-sought-after interactive TV. In the real world, transmitting this amount of data generally isn't feasible, even after compression.

One approach to video on the Internet is breathtakingly simple: just don't do it. A simple frame of movement every once in a while or a static picture with continuous audio can provide the illusion required for simple "talking head" applications. Frame rates and image size can be reduced enough to make download sizes seem plausible, but even a simple slide show with audio narration is nearly impossible to do in real time without compression.

Suggestion: Avoid video use unless the message is improved in this medium.

Video-File Formats and Compression

Like audio files, video files can be compressed to reduce the amount of data being sent. Because of the degree of compression required by video, most video formats use a lossy approach that involves a trade-off between picture/sound quality and file size. Like audio, numerous formats are supported for Web-based video, including AVI, QuickTime, MPEG, RealVideo, and ASF. Table 13-12 presents a brief overview of the various Web video formats.

Video Format	Description
AVI	Audio Video Interleave. The video for Windows file format for digital video and audio is very common and easy to specify. A growing number of video files in AVI format are being used on the Internet, but file size of AVI is significant. Both Netscape and Internet Explorer are capable of dealing with AVIs easily.
MOV (QuickTime)	MOV is the extension that indicates the use of Apple's QuickTime format. Probably the most common digital video format, it continues its popularity on the Internet. QuickTime has a strong following in the multimedia development community. Various codecs and technology enhancements make QuickTime a strong digital video solution.
MPEG	Motion Picture Experts Group video format is generally considered the standard format for digital video. Although compression and image quality of MPEG files are impressive, this format can be difficult to work with at times.
ASF	Microsoft's Advanced Streaming Format is delivered using their NetShow, now called Windows Media server technology. A rising competitor to RealVideo, ASF files are high quality and commonly supported by Internet Explorer browsers.
RM	RealVideo is the current leader in streaming video technology at the time of this writing. RealVideo files can be saved at a variety of quality levels, depending on end-user bandwidth availability.

Table 13-12.   *Common Web Video Formats*

For download-and-play delivery, AVI and QuickTime are the safest formats for short video clips. MPEG is a good choice for extremely high-quality playback. AVI and QuickTime files are commonly supported via helper applications. They're even supported natively by many modern Web browsers in a download-and-play style. In terms of browser support, it is difficult to come up with a best bet for simple Web video. Netscape 3 and Internet Explorer 3 and beyond all support AVI in their Windows incarnations, but Macintosh users don't even get a consolation prize. For QuickTime, Internet Explorer and Netscape for Windows users without QuickTime installed on their operating systems are left out in the cold. AVI apparently might be less of a problem, but the size and synchronization quality of AVI video files makes the format far from ideal. For anything larger than a few seconds or used outside an intranet environment where bandwidth is more plentiful, designers should stick with a streaming video approach using RealVideo or Microsoft's ASF format (despite the fact that it is even less likely to work perfectly than streaming audio). Interested readers should visit the developer areas of Real (http://www.realnetworks.com/devzone/) and Microsoft (http://msdn.microsoft.com/windowsmedia/) for up-to-date information on syntax to add video to pages, production tools, and servers required to deliver Web-based video.

Even with better integration of video into a Web page, compression and performance guarantees will be the key points—unless the bandwidth problem is resolved. More exotic compression technologies, such as fractal or wavelet video compression, will certainly become more commonplace as people struggle to stream the smallest files to users and provide the closest semblance to the holy grail of Web television. The Internet, however, is a difficult place to broadcast information. With single sites as video stream sources, latency will make streaming to distant users impossible, regardless of how much compression is used. Content distribution services allowing European users the same access to video clips as users in North America or Asia are growing rapidly, allowing for quality real-time broadcasting of video on the Internet. However, access to these services, for the time being, will remain restricted to the select few who can afford it. In the case of video, it is obvious that delivery is a very significant issue. As the Web matures and users become less patient with slow-loading sites, delivery will become more of an issue—even for sites without multimedia.

The next chapter continues the investigation into Web technology with an in-depth look at serving and network issues.

Summary

Building Web pages can be challenging since Web technologies are immature and everchanging. Designers are encouraged to fully investigate the strengths and weaknesses of each technology before using it online. In particular, don't rely on tools to solve all problems. Unfortunately, as with software, both browsers and Web editors have bugs like any other program. To combat potential execution problems, a developer should be intimately familiar with core Web technologies like HTML and CSS. Programming facilities also will be added to Web pages, and designers are encouraged not to focus on just client-side programming using JavaScript or server-side programming using CGI or parsed solutions such as ColdFusion. The reality is that every tool in the developer's toolbox has its use—rely solely on one, and problems will probably ensue. Like programming, multimedia also has its place on the Web, but technological limitations do restrict its use at times. Unfortunately, the delivery of advanced technologies—particularly multimedia—may be the limiting factor over time, even once browsers support everything correctly. The next chapter investigates the delivery of Web sites and the effect of networks and servers on Web design.

TECHNOLOGY AND WEB DESIGN

The Complete Reference

Web Design

Chapter 14

Site Delivery and Management

667

D elivering a site to a user is just as important as building the site. A site's usability is heavily influenced by its responsiveness, which has a direct impact on the end user's overall feeling about the site. Most designers are painfully aware of the need for speed. Even so, designers often focus on a few aspects of a Web site, such as image-file size or end-user connection rate, to explain why a site is slow. The actual cause of the delay may not be so obvious. Speed may be dictated by a multitude of things, including network effects like traffic, protocol issues, server issues, and site content. Designers will have to address all aspects of delivery, because the end user is not going to split out the individual components of transmission, but will consider the site as a single system. Even when it is delivered properly, running a Web site can be challenging and time-consuming. There is always something for the Webmaster to do: content must be maintained, broken links repaired, and the site monitored for availability. One interesting aspect of site maintenance is usage analysis. On the Web, it is possible to understand what users do when they visit our sites by analyzing log files. We can use knowledge to better design our sites, but collecting such usage data brings up concerns of privacy. This chapter will provide an overview of the delivery and maintenance of Web sites, with a focus on demonstrating how this can influence site design.

The Importance of Delivery

Unfortunately, delivery issues are often only contemplated after a Web site has been designed and built. In many cases, the budget for the site doesn't significantly consider delivery costs, and so corners are cut. This is like spending big money to design and print a corporate brochure, only to have it delivered via third-class postal mail because no funds were left after design and printing. The effect of the brochure would be severely diminished by its slow arrival. Delivery of Web sites is even more critical, particularly given the rise of task-oriented Web sites or e-commerce sites, where any delay may be the difference between a successful sale and a lost one.

While designers may admit that users don't like slow sites, they tend to focus only on a few aspects of what makes a site slow. Consider that users will not be able to distinguish which aspect of site delivery is causing a page to load slowly. They are going to view it as a slow site, whether or not the graphics were optimized properly. Too much emphasis on optimizing file size, and not enough attention to servers, network choice, and even the characteristics of the medium itself, is a common mistake made by Web site designers. Consider all the possible reasons a site may be slow, as illustrated in Figure 14-1.

While there are numerous potential problems to consider when delivering a site, the one inescapable fact is that, eventually, data will have be transferred. Whether you download now or download later, you eventually have to do it. From the user's perspective, how much data is downloaded doesn't really matter; it only matters how responsive the site is. The user only counts the seconds on their watch, not the number

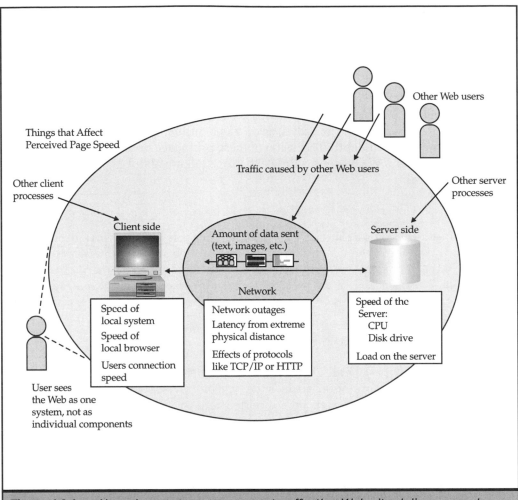

Figure 14-1.   *User does not see components affecting Web site delivery speed*

of bytes delivered. How much data comes down doesn't matter to the end user. Furthermore, if you are using huge graphics by downloading them during the idle moments, the user certainly won't care.

Rule: The amount of bytes delivered to create a page is not as important as how fast the user perceives the page to be.

The bottom line is keeping the user happy. If your design requires a great deal of bandwidth, has many individual requests, or requires real-time delivery, you may have to shelve it. Always respect the medium of the Web. Just as a print designer understands that ink may bleed on paper, the Web designer should understand the nature of the network and servers used to deliver their creations.

Web Protocols

The Web is built upon protocols whose characteristics affect Web page delivery. We should attempt to understand the basics, as they may influence the way pages are built. This is by no means an in-depth discussion of these protocols, but serves to present basic facts about them. We'll spend a little extra time talking about HTTP since it is so integral to the Web.

HTTP

Hypertext Transfer Protocol (HTTP) is the basic application-level network protocol used to coordinate the exchange of data to and from a Web server and a browser. The protocol is a very simple request/response protocol designed primarily to deliver static content. The basic idea of the protocol is that a browser will request a page from a server using a request such as

```
GET /products/index.htm HTTP/1.1
```

and then provide any parameters, if required. A complete request from a browser tells all sorts of interesting information, such as the type of browser being used, the language being used, the character sets supported, and so on. An example of a complete request is shown here:

```
GET /products/index.htm HTTP/1.1
    Connection: Keep-Alive
    User-Agent: Mozilla/4.0 (compatible; MSIE 5.01; Windows 98)
    Accept: application/x-comet, image/gif, image/x-xbitmap,
            image/jpeg, image/pjpeg, */*
    Accept-Language: en-us
```

As mentioned in previous chapters, this information can be used to determine a user's environment and dynamically configure a page to match their native language or browser.

 Most of the header data passed by a browser is completely harmless, but some users may actually go through the trouble of hiding the user agent. This does nothing but limit their ability to receive customized pages.

Once a complete request has been made to the server, it will then answer with its own code. "404 Not Found" is a common server response seen when a requested page does not exist. If things are going well, a response like

```
HTTP/1.1      200 OK
```

with a bunch of other header information following is returned, as shown here:

```
HTTP/1.1 200 OK
Date: Tue, 18 Jan 2000 02:37:58 GMT
Server: Apache/1.3.4 (Unix)
Last-Modified: Tue, 12 Oct 1999 21:04:18 GMT
Content-Length: 7947
Connection: close
Content-Type: text/html

<HTML>

... HTML document follows...

</HTML>
```

One particular header to pay attention to is the content-type header. This header indicates the MIME type of the data to be passed back. A MIME type is comprised of two parts: a data type and subtype separated by a slash, as shown here:

```
Content-type: type/subtype
```

The type is set to a general data type such as image, audio, text, video, application, multipart, message, or extension-token. The subtype gives a more specific detail about the type of data, like if it is a GIF image or an HTML file. A few sample MIME types are listed here:

text/html	image/gif
text/xml	audio/x-wav
video/quicktime	application/x-shockwave-flash
video/x-msvideo	application/x-zip-compressed

Once a browser receives the reply, it will look at the content-type header to determine how to handle the request. For example, the lookup table for Netscape Communication 4.x–generation browsers is shown here.

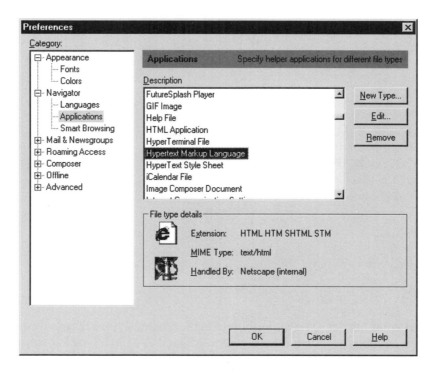

Notice that in the case of the example, the type is text/html and the actual HTML document is passed back after all the headers are finished. The dialog indicates that the browser itself will handle the file internally. Also notice that the browser indicates that it recognizes the file extensions .html, .htm, .stm, and .shtml as HTML files. However, other file extensions seem to appear as normal HTML when they are viewed online. The MIME type is the key to why a file with an extension like .cfm, .asp, .jsp, and so on is treated as HTML by a Web browser when delivered over a network, but if opened from a local disk drive is not read properly. The reason is that these extensions often are associated with dynamically generated pages that are stamped with the HTML MIME type by the server; when reading off the local drive, the browser relies instead on the file extension like .htm to determine the contents of a file. If a browser attempts to read a file that it is unsure about, either because of file extension or MIME type, it should respond with a dialog like the one shown here as Netscape does.

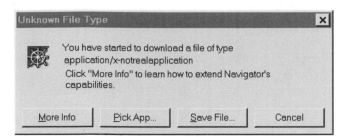

What's very interesting is how Internet Explorer prompts the user to immediately save data if the MIME type is not understood, as shown by this dialog.

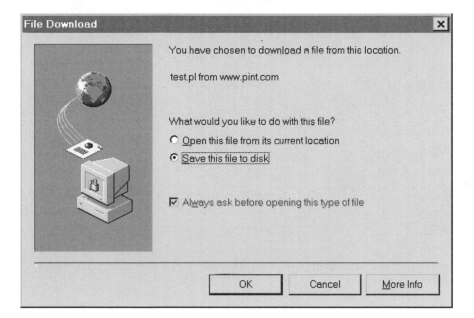

Normally, Web pages are delivered properly, so these dialogs are not seen. The browser would first read the HTML being delivered and then retrieve any other objects, such as GIF images, sound files, Flash files, Java applets, etc., that are associated with the page. Each object would result in another request to the server. If the browser encountered something like

```
<IMG SRC="images/logo.gif" HEIGHT="100" WIDTH="200"
    ALT="Demo Company">
```

it would then form a request like

```
GET /images/logo.gif HTTP/1.1
    Connection: Keep-Alive
    User-Agent: Mozilla/4.0 (compatible; MSIE 5.01;
                Windows 98)
    Accept: application/x-comet, image/gif, image/x-xbitmap,
            image/jpeg, image/pjpeg, */*
    Accept-Language: en-us
```

The server would then respond with a similar answer as before, but this time indicating that a MIME type of image/gif is being returned, followed by the appropriate form of binary data to make up an image as demonstrated here:

```
HTTP/1.1 200 OK
Date: Tue, 18 Jan 2000 04:41:15 GMT
Server: Apache/1.3.4 (Unix)
Last-Modified: Wed, 13 Oct 1999 23:37:38 GMT
Content-Length: 28531
Connection: close
Content-Type: image/gif

GIF87a—'  'æ÷ÿïÿÿÆï÷÷ÒÒÖ÷ïïõñî½Öïïïèñ½ïèóÆçã¿Æçõ½çç÷áß´µçÞï–çÝç½
Þñ¥çß÷´Þï–ÞÞÖä¥Ü÷œÞÖï°Õç"ÞÏ®ŒÞÖï™×÷"ÖÇµŒÖÆ–„ÖÆ–{ÖÅÓsÖ½–½½¥À½œsÎ½
¥¿¹●kÎÎµ¥¬–●yµÏ©¨<¥¥¥ ¡–œ>Œ¥●{""‡'●
X
<●^ŒŒ{„Œ{j●¢„„s,●„'}l●●{„{s‚fT{{s●zjq|~|eUmogKvŠ●]QljZckZoe
PfegccZccRZcRX
… binary file continues …
```

Consider that with the MIME type set properly, it is literally possible to serve any object. Designers often avoid serving custom forms of data beyond HTML or common media types like GIF, JPEG, or WAV because of unfamiliarity with the MIME-type configuration possibilities on client and server.

 Consider adding a MIME type to handle a proprietary information format rather than convert it to HTML, particularly on an intranet.

That's really all there is to HTTP. First, the browser makes an HTTP request, and the server responds in the appropriate fashion with MIME type attached. This cycle repeats as each of the individual elements that makes up a page is requested. Interested readers should reference the chapter on site delivery in the companion book *HTML: The Complete Reference* (Osborne/McGraw-Hill, 1999) for a full discussion of HTTP headers and methods. Even with all the extra details added in, the HTTP protocol is really quite simple, and that's what causes many of its problems.

Protocols and Web Design

While HTTP isn't really the most sophisticated or fastest network protocol, it is well understood by all browsers in use. The simplicity of this request/response application causes some potential problems, particularly when mixed with other protocols such as Transmission Control Protocol (TCP). The first thing to consider is that the HTTP protocol requests each object within a Web page separately. Consider an HTML page with eight images. There is one request first, for the HTML, followed by eight more requests for the images. There may even be an extra request at the beginning if the URL is partially formed like http://www.democompany.com/products and has to add the trailing slash and be directed to an index file. With nine or ten separate requests, there is bound to be some extra overhead added, as opposed to a single request for all the objects at once. Consider this carefully when building a page. Say that one page has a single large image nearly 75KB in size, while another has ten images totaling 60KB. While the total bytes to be delivered would suggest that the second page should be faster, the first page may actually download quicker as far as the user is concerned.

> **Suggestion: Try to keep the number of unique individual objects in a page small to reduce the number of HTTP requests.**

While there will always be overhead associated with individual requests, the HTTP 1.0 protocol was notorious for its inefficiency—particularly when paired with the congestion-avoidance features of the lower-level TCP used to control the transmission of data from browser to Web server. TCP uses a variety of techniques, such as slow start and backoff once traffic is encountered, to keep networks from clogging up. Users certainly notice the slow-start facility of TCP when downloading large files, since the download speeds keep increasing until it reaches a plateau. The problem with congestion avoidance is significant when considering the size of typical Web objects, which are often less than 20KB. Given the small size of Web objects, most connections never reach the full potential of the connection given the slow-start facility. This is one of the reasons that a single image at 100KB may beat a few images totaling 80KB, particularly on a fast connection. Notice that when using a high-speed connection, such as a cable modem or leased line, that the improved bandwidth doesn't make as much of a difference on typical sites as it does when downloading large files or accessing sites that use large binary formats like Macromedia Flash. The reason is partially the network protocols being used. Typically, sites being accessed by users with slow connections find splitting up files into multiple pieces better than delivering large files. It goes back to usability: keep the users happy with a little bit at a time. However, a high-speed user may find sites with a few large images to be more responsive.

Designing for high-speed connections and low-speed ones is not just about the size of the objects that can be delivered, so always design with the type of connection in mind—not just the amount of data to transfer.

> **Suggestion: Match data types, number of items, and size of data items to be delivered to the speed of the user's connection.**

HTTP is considered a stateless, connectionless protocol because it doesn't maintain a constant connection between the browser and server. As discussed in previous chapters, the stateless nature of HTTP also presents significant challenges—particularly to interactive Web sites—since it can be difficult to preserve information from page load to page load. Cookies, extended path information, and hidden form fields are all used to deal with this limitation. By its nature, HTTP does not make this easy; designers should make sure to implement complex interactive sites carefully, and in such a way that they are not overly optimistic about the presence of a particular technology such as cookies. However, don't consider the stateless, connectionless nature to be a serious flaw with HTTP; it is exactly these characteristics that allow Web servers to service numerous users simultaneously, because the overhead of a connection does not have to be maintained.

TCP and Real-Time Data

An interesting aspect of the TCP protocol that is not well considered by many Web designers is the protocol's inability to efficiently deal with real-time data. If you've used the Internet for any period of time, you've encountered occasional delays. The network is "bursty" by nature. The TCP/IP protocols used on the Internet were designed this way for robustness and scalability. The Internet is a packet-switched network that breaks data up into little chunks and sends them separately, to be reassembled at the other end, because these packets may be lost along their journey or arrive out of order. However, the Transmission Control Protocol, or TCP, solves this problem with retransmission and proper assembly of data packets that guarantees the integrity of the data. This way, many users can share a fixed circuit, which allows for economies of scale.

Packet-switched networks have distinct advantages over circuit-switched networks like the telephone system. If your connection is cut off during a phone call, you have to redial. If there are already too many calls going across a circuit, you get a busy signal. When a packet-switched network like the Internet faces increased traffic and failing connections, it just slows down and reroutes (although servers and overloaded Internet providers can create the equivalent of a busy signal). However, most packet-switched networks like the Internet have one serious problem—they cannot guarantee delivery time without special modifications. This makes streamed audio, video and other "real-time" applications difficult on packet-switched networks.

Packet-switched networks can be augmented with protocols like RTP (Real Time Transport Protocol), RTSP (Real Time Streaming Protocol), and RSVP (Resource

Reservation Protocol), which help format or even control the delivery of time-sensitive data over the Internet. However, some of these ideas—particularly the idea of being able to reserve bandwidth—are not well supported yet, and introduce economic considerations. For example, how would you charge or limit bandwidth reservations? Wouldn't a user always want maximum bandwidth? True real-time delivery protocols are still in development, so another approach to real-time data on the Internet is necessary.

The current approach to real-time data on the Internet is really just an assumption—you hope the end user has the end-to-end bandwidth to receive the file in real time. For example, consider a user with a 14.4Kbps modem. On average, we predict the user can receive about 1KB per second. If we can compress one second of audio down to 1KB, we could deliver it to the end user and have the sound play in real time. Whatever the bandwidth, from 14.4Kbps to T1, an assumption like this is made. When the assumption holds, the sound can be streamed effectively. However, when the assumption doesn't hold, there are glitches, and the sound may drop out. If you get too much dropout, the user turns off the audio stream. One way to avoid dropout is to buffer data. This process gives you a head start by preloading a certain amount of data in a buffer so that rough spots can be overcome. An initial buffering delay of 10 or 15 seconds is acceptable for long audio clips; buffering short sounds is counterproductive. Many Internet audio solutions use a combination of significant compression, buffering, and the bandwidth assumption to achieve streaming.

The bottom line is that there is really no way to guarantee that bandwidth will be available. Traffic conditions on the Internet are unpredictable. Even worse, the base Internet protocols like TCP were never designed to provide the guarantee of delivery time in the first place. About the only thing to do is to make conservative estimates of available bandwidth, minimize the path between server and client so latency is reduced and there are fewer points of failure, and hope for the best. However, assuming that radio- or television-quality delivery of audio or video over today's Internet is possible is a naïve assumption that does not consider the medium. Will reliable high-quality real-time data transmission be possible in the future? Probably, particularly with new protocols and improved network infrastructure, but for now designers should consider the limitations of real-time data before relying too greatly on it.

> **Rule: Predictable and error-free delivery of real-time data on the Internet cannot be reliably guaranteed with today's protocols and usage.**

Domain Names Issues

Never underestimate the power of a good domain name. Many sites have an easy-to-remember (and type) domain name to at least partially thank for their success. Some sites have even found that having a domain name like "cheaptickets" or some generic expression is a good way to attract customers. However, beyond the marketing aspects, domain names should be well thought-out, as some Web users can become confused on how to actually address a site.

Today, sites are addressed by Uniform Resource Locator or URL. URLs can be troublesome for some users as they contain a multitude of colons, slashes, and protocol names that may be confusing to the novice. For example, the actual full URL syntax is

```
protocol://siteaddress/directory/file
```

A minimal URL for a machine called www.democompany.com would be http://www.democompany.com/, which tells a browser to access the root directory of a machine called www.democompany.com using the HTTP protocol and return the directory listing or the index file of the directory. However, many end users have become accustomed to just entering in the URL without the trailing slash, or even without the http indication. While this is okay since modern browsers and servers rectify this issue, you must be careful in dealing with a new URL form. Many sites now are using URLs like http://democompany.com or just democompany.com if the user doesn't specify the protocol. A browser will not fix this issue; a domain name mapping must be set up to force this. Traditionally, the nonspecified machine name for a domain mapped to a router for the domain, but given the rise in importance of Web services, many sites opt to map this simplified address to the Web server. Some designers also promote the use of "web" along with "www" as the machine name for a site. Given the ease of having multiple names for a single machine, designers are encouraged to use the www, web, and simplified domain form. In short, as many similar names and near-miss names should be set up as possible, particularly if the site has a domain that is hard to type.

Suggestion: Provide numerous domain name forms for a site.

In the future, domain names may change. We may see a rise in popularity of both new domain name forms as well as unique addresses, often generically referred to as Uniform Resource Names, or even keyword-based navigation directly from within a browser. Whatever the form of address, it is important to consider that it addresses an important part of getting the user to find and continue to use a site.

Web Address Trickery

Some sites utilize Internet Protocol (IP) addresses or encoded URLs rather than domain names, often to mask their identity. For example, notice that URLs are often displayed in a special form called URL encoded, where special or problematic characters such as spaces and even slashes are translated into special codes. This translation is often seen in the URL of a CGI program using the GET method or a search engine. For example, try running a query for "Robert O'Reilly's Robot Repair Shop." Many search engines will show a query string in the URL like

```
http://www.fakesearchengine.com/run-search.cgi?query=
Robert+O%27Reilly%27s+Robot+Repair+Shop
```

Notice that, in the encoding, spaces were converted to plus signs, and special characters such as apostrophes were translated to a value like %27. This format, which may appear cryptic, is a highly regular format called URL encoded. The basic idea is to encode characters that would be unsafe as part of a URL in another format, such as hex values or plus signs. Because browsers should have no problem decoding URL-encoded addresses, some less scrupulous Web users—particularly people who send a great deal of junk mail—attempt to mask their identity with an encoded URL. For example, www.democompany.com would appear as

```
http://%77%77%77.%64%65%6D%6F%63%6F%6D%70%61%6E%79.%63%6F%6D
```

Some sites instead might just utilize a simple IP address like

```
http://206.252.142.209
```

While valid, neither of these address forms is as good as a real domain name, particularly since the mysterious encoding may suggest to the end user that some sort of funny business is going on. So don't use things like this in links or play other encoding games, and be very wary of those people who do.

Domain Name Service

The Web's reliance on the domain name service should be strongly considered by all Web publishers. When a user types in a URL like http://www.democompany.com, the address www.democompany.com must first be translated into the underlying IP address before a request can be made. The first time a user accesses a particular site, there can be a substantial delay (on the order of a few seconds) to perform the name translation. Users notice this delay by the messages shown in the browser status bar like the one shown here.

Connect: Looking up host: www.democompany.com...

For slow connections or uncommonly accessed hosts, the initial lookup may time-out and force the user to look up the host again. If the domain name server that does the translation is down, the site will be effectively down unless the user somehow knows the underlying IP address of the site. Because of the heavy reliance on domain name service, a site should have multiple domain name servers that are geographically and network dispersed to improve the likelihood that at least one server is available and responsive. While domain name translation requests are small, the servers should also be designed for responsiveness.

Suggestion: Make sure that domain name service for a Web site is fast and robust.

While the Web server may be a critical component in the delivery of a Web site, don't forget: if the user can't get to the server, no one will care how fast it is.

Web Servers

To many, Web servers seem mystical. In reality, a Web server is just a computer running a piece of software that fulfills HTTP requests made by browsers. In the simplest sense, a Web server is a just a file server, and a slow one at times. Consider the operation of a Web server resulting from a user requesting a file, as shown in Figure 14-2. Basically, a user just requests a file and the server either delivers it back or issues some error message, such as the ubiquitous 404 not found message.

However, a Web server isn't just a file server, because it can also run programs and deliver results. In this sense, Web servers could also be considered application servers—if occasionally simple or slow ones.

Recall from earlier in the chapter that the user will not be able to break out the individual components of Web delivery. If a site is slow, users often don't know why. It could be the network, it could be the server, or it might even be their own system. Designers should always try to improve the user's perception of a site, and thus should strive to control what *can* be controlled—namely, the server and its connection out to the Internet. Let's consider each in turn.

Web Server Components

A Web server is composed of both hardware and software. The primary operation of a Web server is to copy the many (generally small) files making up a Web page from disk to network as fast as possible for numerous simultaneous users. A secondary mission is to run programs for numerous individuals and deliver their results as fast as possible. Given these requirements, consider the hardware requirements of a Web server shown in Table 14-1.

Suggestion: Don't skimp on Web server hardware and focus on systems with high-speed hard drives, a great deal of memory, and good network interfaces.

Beyond getting the best hardware you can afford, it is important to consider that the operating system running on the hardware is going to have a great effect on the speed of the Web server, as well as the server and development-software options available. In general, given that Web servers have to deal with multiple requests at once and need a rich set of development options, most developers tend to use either Windows NT or some variant of UNIX, including Linux, for their operating system.

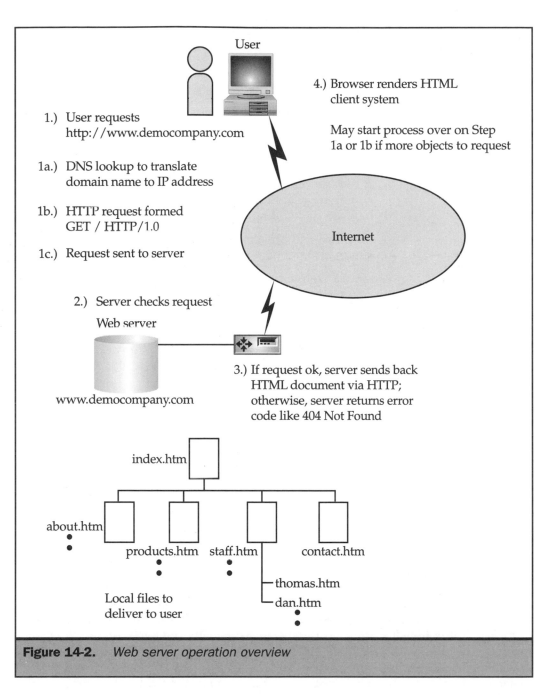

Figure 14-2.   *Web server operation overview*

Table 14-2 presents the major operating-system choices as well as some of the issues in using them for Web serving.

Hardware Component	Considerations
Processor	While a fast processor seems key to a fast Web server, the reality is that computational requirements of a Web server are limited. Multiple processors may be more useful than a single fast processor when dealing with numerous requests made on a server.
Memory	A Web server may need a large amount of RAM to hold numerous individual processes running CGI programs for users or fulfilling file requests.
Bus	Web data will constantly move from disk to memory to network. Don't limit the data path with a slow bus.
Disk drive	Since a Web server's primary task is delivering files to a user, a high-speed disk drive that is kept optimized is a primary goal. Spend extra on drives with high-speed adapters such as SCSI-3.
Network interface	Once files are retrieved from disk, they are delivered back to the user via the network. Don't limit a server by its network interface card. Consider Fast Ethernet or better. For high-volume servers, multiple network interfaces may be mandatory.
Other	Most other aspects of a Web server have little bearing on the delivery of a site. However, some peripherals such as tape drives or other backup storage facilities are mandatory for site maintenance.

Table 14-1. *Web Server Hardware Issues*

While Table 14-2 presents a good overview of some of the issues faced when choosing one operating system over another for a Web server, the decision may often be made due to familiarity or personal taste. While one person may argue about the merits of UNIX, introducing a UNIX server into an environment with heavy Macintosh investment would be foolish. The bottom line is to always remember suitability and total cost over time. A relatively low traffic site for a school might do well on a Macintosh. A Windows NT system might make a great departmental server in a corporation that favors Windows systems. A Linux system might appeal to a technical-minded individual looking to avoid spending money on hardware and software, and a high-end Sun server running Solaris might be appropriate for a large e-commerce venture. Some sites may find that a server-appliance that does not expose operating-system issues may also be appropriate

Operating System	Pros	Cons
UNIX	Tends to run on fast hardware such as UltraSparc and Alpha systems Very flexible development environment High-end applications and servers are available	Can be complicated to use and difficult to set up and maintain Labor costs may be high Buy-in costs for hardware and software are relatively high
Windows NT	Runs on both high- and low-end hardware Many servers and development tools available Basic administration is simple	May require multiple servers for high-volume sites Advanced administration may rival UNIX in difficulty Guaranteeing server stability can be troublesome
Linux	Available on low-end equipment Cost is low Many servers and development tools available	Can be complicated to use and difficult to maintain Lacks volume of commercial software support found with mainstream UNIX systems like Solaris
Windows 95/98	Easy to run Low equipment costs Inexpensive software	Not a multiuser environment Not as robust as NT or UNIX for server applications Selection of Web software is limited compared to Windows NT or UNIX variants Security concerns can be significant
Macintosh	Easy to run and administer Low equipment costs Inexpensive software	Not a multiuser environment Selection of Web software is limited compared to Windows or UNIX Often not as robust as NT or UNIX for serving

Table 14-2.   *Operating Systems and Web Serving Considerations*

if maintenance is a significant concern. The point is always to choose an operating system for a server based on the practicality of performance, development, and long-term maintenance characteristics of the OS.

> **Suggestion: Don't choose an operating system for a Web server solely based on popularity; consider total cost of ownership and suitability for development and long-term maintenance.**

Web Server Software

Once hardware and operating system are selected, it is time to consider which Web server package to use. Only a few years ago, there were only two major Web servers available: NCSA's httpd server for UNIX and CERN's httpd server for UNIX, both free servers that required fairly significant knowledge of UNIX and programming to use and develop for. Today, there are dozens of different Web servers—both commercial and freeware—available on a variety of machines. Rather than considering all Web servers in your decision, it might be wise to look at the most common Web servers used. Based on surveys and analysis of reachable servers on the Internet, the following are considered to be some of the most common Web servers used, though their exact market percentage is a topic of hot debate. The major Web servers include:

Apache	WebSite
Microsoft's IIS	WebStar
IPlanet servers (formerly Netscape)	Domino

Each of the popular Web servers is discussed next. This should by no means be considered as approval of these products, but rather just a synopsis of each product and some of its known characteristics.

Weblink: Serverwatch (www.serverwatch.com) provides links and reviews of most of the popular Web servers available.

Apache (http://www.apache.org/)

A descendant of NCSA's httpd server, Apache is probably the most popular Web server on the Internet, at least as far as public Web sites are concerned. Apache's popularity stems from the fact that it is free and fast. It is also very powerful, supporting features like HTTP 1.1, extended server-side includes (SSIs), a module architecture similar to NSAPI/ISAPI, and numerous free modules that perform functions such as server-based Perl interpretation. However, Apache is not for everyone. The main issue with Apache is that it isn't a commercial package. Some firms are hesitant to run their mission-critical systems on a user-supported product. However, as with operating systems like Linux, various third parties offer commercial support for Apache. Another potential limiting factor for Apache is that the system currently is mainly for UNIX. Although there is a port of Apache to Windows 32-bit systems, as well as one for the Macintosh OS X environment, the server is optimized for popular UNIX and Linux variants. The lack of heavy NT support may limit the use of Apache within many Windows-centric enterprises. Probably the most troublesome aspect of Apache for some developers is that it might require modification of configuration files or even compilation in order to install properly. If you like to tinker or desire speed, have a UNIX system, and don't have a lot of money, then Apache might just be for you. You'll be in good company: some of the largest Web sites on the Internet swear by this product.

Note *For Web trivia buffs, the name "Apache" is derived from the description of the software as a patched version of NCSA. Think "a patchy NCSA server."*

Microsoft Internet Information Services (http://www.microsoft.com/iis/)

IIS is Microsoft's server for Windows NT. Windows 95/98 also supports a similar but much less powerful version of IIS called the Personal Web Server (PWS). While PWS is certainly popular, of the two, most organizations favor IIS. One very important aspect of IIS is that it is very tightly integrated with the Windows NT environment. In fact, today it is hard to distinguish IIS as a stand-alone service within Windows 2000. Unfortunately, being so Windows NT specific is also considered one of the problems with IIS. Because of hardware and clustering issues, IIS hasn't proved quite as scalable as some UNIX-based servers. With new Microsoft clustering technologies and integration with a transaction processor, this scalability problem is likely to change. For an intranet environment—particularly one with heavy Microsoft investment—it is difficult to beat the features offered by IIS—particularly its integration with other Microsoft products such as the SQL Server database. The price for IIS is currently a major positive point for the software—it's freely bundled with the operating system.

iPlanet: Severs Formerly Known as Netscape (http://www.iplanet.com)

iPlanet, the new software concern born of the Sun-Netscape alliance formed after the merger between Netscape and AOL, has a larger number of Web servers. These servers continue Netscape's long history of supporting high-end Web and application servers running on most major variants of UNIX (Solaris, SunOS, AIX, HP-UX, Digital UNIX, and IRIX) as well as Windows NT. The servers are well developed, as they represent more than four generations of software releases. The servers are also very developer friendly and powerful, with support for databases and directory services, content management, HTTP 1.1, and a variety of other features. If you are in a cross-platform or UNIX environment and you are looking for commercial-quality Web serving solutions, then consider using iPlanet servers.

WebSite (http://website.ora.com/)

A very easy-to-use Web server for Window 95/98 and Windows NT, O'Reilly's WebSite is one of the few robust Web servers available for Windows 95/98. Though some suggest WebSite lacks the performance of Netscape or Microsoft servers running on more powerful systems, WebSite is considered one of the easiest servers to install and administer. Furthermore, the system provides many nice development features such as a special server-parsed language called iHTML. For intranets or sites that don't need the performance of high-end Windows NT or UNIX systems, WebSite is a great choice.

WebStar (http://www.starnine.com/)

The most popular Web server for the Macintosh was originally based on MacHTTPD. WebStar integrates well with the Macintosh. It supports AppleScript and other Macintosh-specific tools. The system supports UNIX-style CGI programs, a Java virtual machine for server-side Java, and extended SSI, and has solid security features. The performance of WebStar often leaves much to be desired, though it is improving and is probably more than adequate for intranets or small Web sites. Many developers favor running UNIX shells on top of Macintosh to run Apache. The Mac OS X, in fact, also supports Apache.

Lotus Domino (http://www.lotus.com/domino)

Domino is an example of the collision between traditional Web serving and messaging and groupware. Domino runs on Windows NT, variants of UNIX, and even large IBM systems such as AS/400s, and is often used in corporate intranet and extranet environments where workflow and integration with messaging and backend system may be more important than raw Web serving performance. Designing Web pages within the Domino environment can be somewhat restrictive because of the template approach Domino takes. However, it is possible to integrate Domino with other servers, including IIS, to provide raw HTTP facilities.

There are numerous Web server software choices. Remember that different packages will have different performance characteristics. Using the same hardware, one Web server software package may far outperform another. When planning to build a Web server, start either from the hardware and build up, or start from the particular software and build down, picking the best possible hardware. If you make good software and hardware choices, the performance of the site can be significantly improved. Always try to base your choices on usage requirements, such as target number of simultaneous users or requests per minute or second. Once the requirements of the site have been carefully determined, it is possible to best choose how to serve a site.

Web Server Location

The second half of the Web serving equation is where the Web server will live. The choice is whether to have a server at your own location or at another location offsite, such as at an Internet service provider or hosting vendor. Choosing whether to run your own server or outsource the server and maintenance to a third party can be a complex question, but regardless you should always try to put the server close to users. The reason for this is that by minimizing the network path between a server and a user, you minimize the possibility of problems caused by the network.

Rule: Always strive to minimize network distance between a site and its users.

For an intranet, it is pretty obvious that the server should be on your local network. But what about for an external site? Many people prefer to host their own site, which requires a full-time connection to the Internet. However, is the server as close as it could be to the end users? Furthermore, will a locally hosted site provide enough bandwidth for users? Having enough bandwidth available can be important for mission-critical Web sites. Regardless of server bottlenecks, a mere fractional-T1 or full-T1 leased line might not provide enough bandwidth to deal with the bursty nature of Web access. However, installing multiple T3 leased lines just to deal with the occasional flash crowd that may swamp a site seems wasteful given the significant investment required. Rather than bringing bandwidth to the server, why not move the server to the bandwidth? Even if bandwidth is not an issue, there may be some issues of network closeness. It is unlikely that you'll be able to install leased lines to multiple different connectivity providers. Even if you can, your site will still be more hops away from central exchange points than the providers you may purchase bandwidth from.

Another motivation for not placing an external Web server locally is the security implications. Many companies are still very afraid of the security problems associated with the Internet. Firewalls and security policies can help, but if a public Web server is located on the firm's LAN, allowing Web viewers to access it is similar to asking potential robbers to come knock on your door. Putting public-use information on outsourced Web servers keeps casual intruders away from a firm's network access point and allows stronger security policies to be put into place at the corporate firewall.

Facilities are often an overlooked aspect of locating a Web server. Does your own location provide a safe environment for a server? Are power systems highly reliable, with backups in place? Is the building secure and staffed twenty-four hours a day, seven days a week? Is there a computer-safe fire-suppression system? The cost of providing the physical and personnel facilities necessary for a high-end Web site should not be underestimated.

Don't automatically assume that placing a Web server at another location such as a Web hosting vendor is the only way to go. Certainly the network and services provided by hosting vendors can exceed local hosting, but you give up security and control. If you need to provide access to highly sensitive data, you may find that outside vendors do not provide the comfort level you desire. Furthermore, outside vendors are by their nature outside. They may promise to do their best to protect your system from harm and provide quality support, but some people want the control of doing it themselves. Finally, if the requirements for a site are minimal and the infrastructure is in place, it just may not be cost effective to outsource site delivery.

Suggestion: Choose to host your own Web site when security or control is a primary concern.

Outsourcing Web Hosting

As Web sites become more critical to the information infrastructure of companies, there is a growing need to provide high-quality, high-availability solutions. For example, a business selling something only online can't afford to have its site go down at all. The serving of a site to an e-business is as critical as power and telephone services would be to a traditional business. This trend might be termed the "utilization" of the Web, as some may consider the health and delivery of their Web site as important as utility. However, given that the site must be run in a very efficient and reliable manner, firms quickly discover that it is in fact quite expensive for companies to develop in-house the talents and facilities to run a mission-critical Web site. Because of this fact, many firms have decided to outsource their Web facilities. Web server outsourcing comes in many flavors, but many of the differences revolve around two factors. The first differentiating factor is if you are sharing a machine with other sites. The second is whether or not the machine being used is owned and managed by you or the outsource vendor. Each type of service will be discussed in turn, with special focus on their pros and cons.

Shared Hosting

The most basic form of hosting or shared hosting ranges from free Web space added to other services or in exchange for advertisement placement to high-end application service providers (ASPs). At the low end, many Internet service providers will provide a directory on one of their Web servers with a few megabytes of disk space and possibly access to a few shared tools that can be used on your Web site, such as simple form handling scripts, counters, or message boards. Usually, the URL for a site like this is of the form http://www.isp.net/~enduser or http://www.isp.net/enduser. The hosting service lacks any customization like your domain name (yourname.com), and may impose limits on traffic delivered or programming tools that can be used. The upside to these types of services is that they are often free and may be included in the cost of your Internet connection. There are also many vendors who will provide free Web serving in exchange for personal information for marketing purposes, or if you agree to show banner advertisements they book on your Web site. While these services are appealing to home users or those looking to put up a site for fun, most will prefer other forms of shared hosting.

Shared host services that provide a domain name (www.*yourname*.com), often called a *virtual server*, generally are not free. These services also provide improved development facilities like your own cgi-bin directory, statistical reports on site traffic, and other useful features, including shopping-cart facilities. The costs for virtual server accounts on a shared system usually start around $20 or more per month. However, costs vary greatly, and the more bandwidth your site consumes or the more special requests you have, the higher it may cost—even if the machine is not dedicated to you. In fact, with complex shared hosting services, where you may have access to content-management systems or e-commerce facilities, the cost can literally skyrocket to hundreds or even thousands of dollars per month.

The major downside of shared Web hosting is that it involves using the shared server facilities of a hosting vendor. This means that the site will share Web server resources and bandwidth with other hosted sites. Server responsiveness may be significantly affected because of other hosted Web sites, particularly if those sites become popular. Furthermore, many customers are wary of sharing a server with others, because security often cannot be guaranteed on these shared systems. Despite its drawbacks, shared hosting is very popular—mainly due to price.

Dedicated Hosting

Because of the downside of sharing a server with others—most notably security and control—many people opt to use a dedicated server. Dedicated servers are advantageous because you can customize your server greatly with whatever tools or programs you like; they are not affected by other sites as much. However, the trade-off is cost. Dedicated servers tend to be more expensive.

There are two forms of dedicated server hosting. The first is where the outsource vendor owns and maintains the equipment. This may be called *fully managed* or *dedicated hosting*. The other is where you own and may even be responsible for maintaining your server. This is usually called *co-location*. With co-location, the vendor provides space at their facility, electrical power, a network connection, a certain amount of bandwidth, and very limited system management for your server (like rebooting it if it crashes or maybe doing tape backups). Co-location is generally cheaper than fully managed services, but for those who don't want to be bothered with the details of Web site delivery, co-location is not as great a deal as it might seem.

Dedicated hosting solutions are very attractive to those who want control, security, and power, but don't want to deal with many of the day-to-day issues of running a Web server. The major downside of these solutions is price. Services-provided, top-tier vendors such as Exodus (www.exodus.net) and AboveNet (www.above.net) might run many thousands of dollars per month based on the equipment and bandwidth required as well as any services added, such as security monitoring or sophisticated hosting requirements like mirroring a site at multiple locations. However, if a business really relies on robust fast Web site delivery, many of these vendors are a bargain even at what appears to be a high price. Consider the actual cost of maintaining a telephone-company-grade equipment room filled with servers connected to numerous Internet providers being monitored twenty-four hours a day, seven days a week by capable system and network administrators, and you'll see that the cost may be well worth it. Consider that some of the largest content, search-engine, and e-commerce sites don't run their own servers, and you'll se that considering an outside hosting vendor is a good idea.

Companies looking to save money on Web delivery may find outsourcing very attractive, but some flexibility and security may have to be sacrificed. With less-experienced hosting companies, this lack of control can be disastrous, resulting in hidden costs or problems with reliability. Those who want more control over their Web services should consider co-location or running their own servers locally.

Weblink: *Links to commercial hosting vendors can be found at*
http://www.webhostlist.com.

Managing Web Servers

Once a Web server is installed and successfully delivering content to users, there are a great number of maintenance tasks that should take place. Servers must be continually monitored for availability, performance, and security. Checking availability might be simply a matter of utilizing a tool to "ping" the server every few minutes by sending it a small data packet to see if it is alive. However, such simple checking doesn't ensure that the server is working—just that it is reachable on the network. More sophisticated server monitoring actually requests a page on a site, and may even look for some key phrase or element to make sure that the page is completely formed. Make sure your hosting vendor provides such monitoring facilities for your site. If not, consider purchasing a tool such as WebTrends Enterprise Edition (www.webtrends.com), as shown in Figure 14-3, that includes site monitors and alarms.

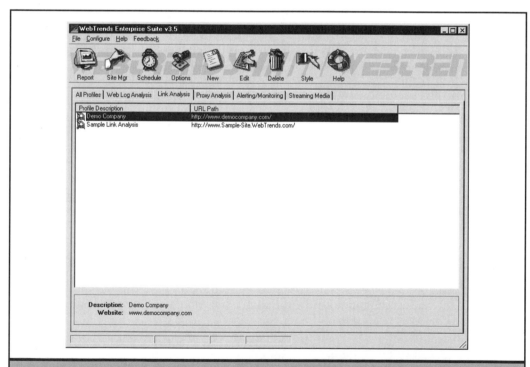

Figure 14-3.   *WebTrends Enterprise provides basic site-monitoring facilities*

However, consider that a monitoring tool only shows availability of your server from a particular location. You may want to test the reliability and availability of your network connection to other locations on the Internet. The best way to do this is to employ a site-monitoring service that can test your site from multiple locations online.

Suggestion: Utilize a monitoring tool or service to ensure that your site is constantly available to users.

The responsiveness of the server should also be carefully monitored. While a server may not necessarily crash, it can become so overloaded that it is effectively unusable. Make sure that the load on a server is carefully monitored as well.

Web Server Security

With the rise of e-commerce on the Web, monitoring site security has become paramount. A lax attitude towards security leads to intrusion by hackers, crackers, or whatever term—probably derogatory—that you wish to use to describe an unsavory character who compromises your site. Why people decide to intrude into other people's sites ranges from simple curiosity to malicious or criminal intent. Consider that people *do* attempt to enter into a site to steal credit cards or other valuable information, as well as to undermine the reputation of a firm by posting profane or incorrect information to the site. A great number of people point to the fact that many intrusions do not result in significant damage as some indication not to worry too much about it. However, that is a naïve viewpoint that will be less tolerated as more and more businesses begin to do business on the net and damaging intrusions continue to happen. In the "real world," casual intrusion into a store in the middle of the night by an individual who claims they are doing this just to see if they can is just plain illegal. It is unlikely that a defense like "the locks should have been stronger" or even "they should have locked the door" will satisfy any sane jury. Regardless of your take on the hacking/cracking issue, site owners should still take precautions and attempt to fortify their site against unauthorized access. In order to do so, you must first consider the methods of intrusion employed. A few of the common intrusion techniques are briefly summarized in Table 14-3.

To combat some of these attacks, consider employing all the methods described in Table 14-4.

What's interesting about all these rules is that they must all be considered together in order to create a complete security policy. The strongest firewall in the world isn't going to keep someone out of your network if they can look through your garbage to find configuration information or simply call up and pretend to be an important executive. In some ways, security is somewhat an all-or-nothing venture if you are serious about it. Many people point to plugging the obvious holes and then not worrying about it, but when money is exchanging hands, as in the case of an e-commerce site, that is a dangerous proposition.

Method	Discussion
Password guessing	A common way sites are exploited is because system passwords are easily guessable. Cracking tools can be employed that try common passwords or even try every word in the English dictionary.
Operating system exploits	The underlying operating system may be open to exploitation because of bugs or known flaws. Once the operating system is compromised, the intruder will have the run of the site.
Spoofing	Not necessarily used for intrusion, spoofing is a technique where an intruder appears to be someone else. This may be used for intrusion when the intruder spoofs a trusted site. Spoofing can also be used for an intruder to pretend to be the site when a user is conducting a transaction.
Denial of service	A denial-of-service attack is not necessarily performed to gain access to a site. Denial of service is generally employed to cause damage or ruin reputation. Typical denial of service includes crashing the system, using up all server resources and thus locking out legitimate users, or flooding a network with bogus requests.
Social engineering	Social engineering is when an intruder attempts to trick unsuspecting site owners or associated staff members into divulging important information such as system passwords. Typically, the intruder will attempt to impersonate a trusted or important individual over the phone or email since physical deception can be difficult.
Physical compromise	Probably the least common attack form, but still important to consider, is physical intrusion of a site location, including actually stealing a system.

Table 14-3. *Typical Site-Attack Methods*

Rule: Create, implement, and test a full-site security policy that goes beyond a simple firewall.

Keeping up with security matters can be a full-time task. Numerous sites like www.cert.org issue warnings literally weekly and sites like www.rootshell.org post

Method	Discussion
Use and rotate strong passwords	Use longer, difficult-to-guess passwords. Make sure there is a limit to the life of passwords. Consider using hardware-generated passwords.
Maintain your OS	Keep operating system software up-to-date by applying all patches and upgrades.
Limit access points	Remove services that are not in common use. Limit Web servers to only providing Web services and consider removing any form of network protocol access to a server except HTTP.
Set up a firewall	Configure a firewall so as to limit network traffic. Consider using both packet-filtering and application-protocol limitations.
Use strong encryption	When transmitting sensitive data, either via email or HTTP, encrypt the information using the strongest possible ciphers allowed.
Use digital certificates	Install digital certificates from organizations like VeriSign (www.verisign.com) so that identity can be verified.
Reduce information leakage	Don't freely expose information that a hacker could utilize to figure out a hole to exploit on your system. Don't allow a remote login, even with a prompt. If you do allow remote login, at least modify any prompts returned not to indicate the variant of the software or operating system in use. Modify your HTTP server headers not to reveal the type of Web server in use. Don't reveal the type of technology used in programmed Web pages like Perl. Consider using generic file extensions like .cgi instead of language specific ones like .pl. Avoid exposing information about your network through domain name services. Avoid naming systems in such a way as to reveal their operating system (e.g., solaris1.democompany.com). Modify your WHOIS record not to include personnel information that can be used in social engineering attacks.
Employ physical security	Limit physical access to important servers. Destroy sensitive documents, including documents that detail network or server configurations.

Table 14-4.   *Common Site-Protection Methods*

any and all exploits for all to see. So, consider that any person interested in cracking a system will have little problem finding sites that detail how to exploit common system holes. Because of the constant vigilance required to maintain secure systems, you may consider hiring an outside firm that specializes solely in security to audit your site and plug any exploitable holes.

Other Web Server Management Duties

Beyond ensuring the performance, availability, and security of a server, a Webmaster must often perform tasks such as hardware and software upgrades as well as back up the server software and site on a regular basis. Backups may be performed both to offline storage like a DAT tape and to hot spare servers when any downtime could be detrimental. What's interesting is that given the focus on availability, security, and routine system tasks, a Webmaster may spend much of their time acting as a traditional system or network administrator—just with a focus on Web services. Of course, other organizations may consider the Webmaster the individual responsible less for the maintenance of the Web server itself than for the content of the site. Certainly content management is a key aspect to Web site management, but it does intersect with traditional system-administration duties once usage analysis is considered. Certainly the line between system, network, and content management blurs on occasion.

Content Management

Maintaining content is just as important as maintaining the server itself. Large sites or those with numerous contributors will quickly degrade if special care is not taken. First, make sure there is a set policy for naming files. For example, consider avoiding using special characters such as underscores (_) in filenames, because it will be difficult for users to notice them in the address line of a browser. Instead of robot_butler.htm, consider robot-butler.htm or just robotbutler.htm.

> **Suggestion: Avoid using underscores in filenames. Consider using dashes or no space between words.**

However, be careful with using filenames like RobotButler.htm or even capitalizing directories. The domain aspect of a URL is not case sensitive and the user may not be consistent in their use of case. Also, some servers such as UNIX systems are case sensitive, while others like NT are not, so moving sites between the systems could be troublesome. Always use lowercase to avoid such problems.

> **Suggestion: Do not use mixed or uppercase letters in file or directory names.**

Set a file-extension policy and stick to it. Shorter extensions are generally better if you just consider the extra characters to type, as well as the fact that some older systems prefer three-character extensions. However, regardless of your take on .htm vs. .html, pick one and be consistent.

Rule: Pick either .htm or .html as a file extension and stick with it.

Consider even limiting filename length, or even using consistent naming schemes. For example, some files may include dates in them, such as press releases. Consider that pr021299.htm and pr010500.htm could reference press releases on 2/12/1999 and 01/05/2000, respectively.

Make sure to use the same care with directories as you do with files. Pick short, easy-to-type and -spell directories in all lowercase letters that lack special characters. Also, consider using common directory names to hold site assets. Table 14-5 details a few common directory names and their usual contents.

Probably the hardest part of dealing with site content is all the changes that are made. When many people are working on a site, it is easy for conventions to be overlooked and for simple errors to be introduced. To reduce the possibility that content degrades, first carefully limit who can make changes to a site. Second, resist the desire to fix site problems or add content on a moment's notice. It is far better to make regular updates, such as once a day or once a week. This allows backups to be made and provides a stable base to roll back to in case problems are introduced.

Suggestion: Do not update on demand. Create a regular update schedule.

Directory Name	Contents
/cgi-bin	The traditional location for executable programs on a Web server, particularly CGI programs.
/scripts	Contains scripts for the site, including JavaScripts, CGI scripts, and server-parsed languages like Cold Fusion or Active Server pages. Occasionally, the directory may be named after the type of script stored—for example, /js or /javascripts for linked JavaScript files.
/styles or /css	Should contain any linked style sheets used on a site.
/images	Contains all site images, including GIFs, JPEGs, and PNG files.
/video	Contains video assets—primarily nonstreamed video clips.
/audio	Contains audio assets—primarily nonstreamed audio files.
/pdfs	Contains PDF files such as a library of datasheets.
/download or /binaries	A central location for any programs or software distributions that are to be downloaded from the site.

Table 14-5. *Common Site-Directory Names*

If a site is heavily updated, consider employing a content-management tool. A simple source-code control system can be used. A source-code control system will provide an audit trail and rollback facilities, and will force site contributors to check out pages to make changes to them. More powerful content-management systems that include easy-to-use, browser-based front ends, including form-based page editing, can be built or purchased. The DemoCompany site (www.democompany.com) itself uses such a tool, as shown in Figure 14-4. Interested readers who have not experienced content-management systems are encouraged to try this system. More complex systems such as Vignette's StoryServer (www.vignette.com) provide even more advanced capabilities and are used to run complex Web sites, particularly heavily updated sites like news sites.

Regardless of the methodology used to control the update of a site, one rule cannot be stressed enough. Never work directly on a live site. Consider that users may see your changes as they happen, and even see pages in half-finished form. Furthermore,

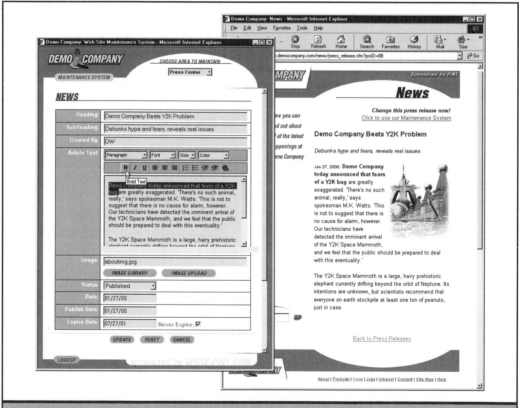

Figure 14-4. *DemoCompany's homegrown content-management system*

if any serious blunder is made, it may be difficult to recover from if the live site is being edited directly.

Rule: Do not work directly on a live site!

Rather than working on a live site, consider using a three-site architecture as illustrated in Figure 14-5. First, set aside a development server where a copy of the site is kept, and major changes and programming features can be added and tested. Second, create a staging server with an exact duplicate of the published site. The staging server is where changes are made and tested. Lastly, a production server should be utilized to actually hold the site being delivered. Changes should only be made on the development or staging site, which is later synchronized with the production server.

Even with careful planning, errors are bound to creep in. In fact, some things may even be beyond your control, such as the availability of external servers you link to. Because of the potential for broken links, a link-checking tool should be utilized often.

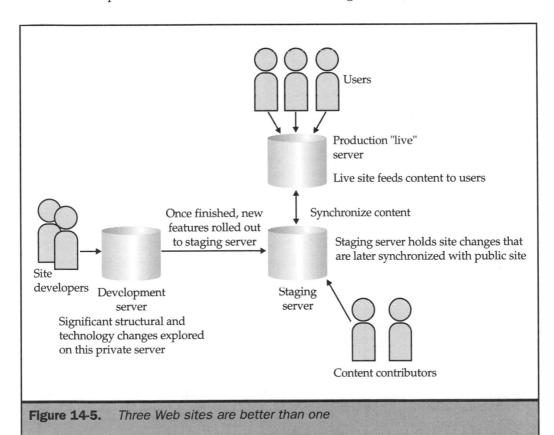

Figure 14-5.   *Three Web sites are better than one*

However, beware of just running link checking on a huge site and then trying to correct all the errors at once. It may be wiser to check sections of the site on a rotating basis. For example, every day a different part of the site tree might be examined and any broken links repaired.

Rule: Check site links constantly.

Besides link checking, it is important to continually check the quality of site content. Tools can be used, such as LinkBot (www.linkbot.com), that look for common site-quality problems such as slow-loading pages, spelling errors, or poor HTML, but nothing beats the human eye for spotting content problems. Focus particularly on page details such as copyright information, page titles, and text sizing. Subtle differences can mean the difference between a positive user visit and a negative one. One good way of finding problems is to actually print pages and look them over carefully.

Suggestion: Check regularly for page details including spelling, legal terms, and font usage. Perform a print test if necessary.

While careful checking will ferret out many problems, errors will still occur in most sites. Make sure that users have a form or email address to use to send in any found errors. Sites should always consider the address webmaster@yourdomainname.com as a default address published for users to send problems to.

Suggestion: Provide the address webmaster@yourdomainname.com for users to contact you with suggestions and error reports.

Even if users don't tell you where your errors are, looking at the way users browse a site by examining access logs may provide valuable clues to sections that should be examined further.

Usage Analysis

A very important task in managing a Web site is analyzing site traffic. Many sites use very simple measurements, such as page counters showing the number of visitors, to monitor usage. Acting like some sort of online equivalent showing the number of visitors served, the true benefit of these counters is unknown. Consider first that a visitor to the site may make a determination to stay or go based on the counter. If the counter shows only a few visitors have ever been to the site, they may assume there is nothing there and just leave. The counter, of course, is under complete control of the designer, and the number of visitors showing can be adjusted. If you decide to roll your counter to a much higher number, you may still have problems, as the user may believe the counter to be misleading—which could cast suspicion on the accuracy of the site's content. The bottom line is the user doesn't need to know how many people are visiting your site. Furthermore, visitor counters are not found on most high-quality sites, and many users may feel that a site with one is amateurish.

Suggestion: Do not put a visible page counter on your site.

Rather than counters to understand site usage, you should rely on server log files as they show what users actually look at in a site and can be used to glean important information about site usage and success. For example, by analyzing a log file you can see which files users read and which they do not. From this information, you might decide to promote heavily used pages closer to the top of the site or prune older pages from the site. Managing log files is not difficult, but it does require some planning to deal with them properly, and they must be analyzed carefully so as not to jump to false conclusions about a site. If you decide you'd rather not keep statistics, there are numerous services that will monitor your site traffic for you—for example, HitBox (www.hitbox.com).

Regardless who does the collection or what kind of server is used, log files are fairly similar. Web servers generally provide two basic logs: the access log and the error log. There may also be a referrer log, which records users following links from other sites to your site, and an agent log, which records information about the user agents (usually browsers) that are accessing the site. Often, the referrer information and user-agent information is recorded in the access log as well. The most common format of access log is called appropriately the *common log format*. The format of the common log format is

```
Host    identd  authenticated-user  [Time of request]
        "request made"  result-code  bytes-transferred
```

Each field in a typical common log is explained in Table 14-6.
A few examples entries from an access log are shown here:

```
206.251.142.45 - - [22/Jan/2000:19:29:09 -0800]
            "GET /badfile.htm HTTP/1.0" 404 222
sj.ix.netcom.com - - [22/Jan/2000:19:29:12 -0800]
            "GET / HTTP/1.1" 200 7947
sj.ix.netcom.com - - [22/Jan/2000:19:29:13 -0800]
            "GET /images/about.gif HTTP/1.1" 200 506
sj.ix.netcom.com - - [22/Jan/2000:19:29:14 -0800]
            "GET /images/staff.gif HTTP/1.1" 200 580
sj.ix.netcom.com - - [22/Jan/2000:19:29:14 -0800]
            "GET /images/products.gif HTTP/1.1" 200 620
phoenix.goodnet.com - lsw [22/Jan/2000:19:40:50 -0800]
            "GET /images/whatsnewtop.gif HTTP/1.1" 200 874
```

The example entries show bad requests, a series of requests that constitute a full page, and an entry that was authenticated. Given that every single individual object requested on a site is recorded, log files become enormous relatively quickly. Log-file information should be cut into manageable chunks for analysis.

Field	Description	Examples
Host	The address of the client making the request. Oftentimes, this is just an IP address since domains may not be resolved until later on.	192.102.249.5 pc1.fakedomain.com
identd	The information returned by identd. If this is not used, a dash is recorded instead.	-
Authenticated user	This field indicates any username sent for authentication. A dash is found if no user challenge was issued.	- bigboss
Time of request	This field indicates the time the request was made. It should be in the form DD/Mon/YYYY:hh:mm:ss –GMT where *DD* is the day, *Mon* the month, *YYYY* the year, *hh* the hour on a 24-hour clock, *mm* minutes, *ss* seconds, and *–GMT* the offset from Greenwich mean time.	[22/Jan/ 2000:13:52:54 -0800]
Request made	This is the actual HTTP request made by the client.	"GET /products/ robotbutler.htm HTTP/1.0"
Result code	This is the HTTP numeric status code returned by the server indicating the success or failure of the request made.	200 404
Bytes transferred	This field records the number of bytes sent back to the requesting client.	2358

Table 14-6. *Access-Log Fields*

Tip *Split logs on a regular basis such as daily, weekly, or monthly to avoid log files getting unwieldy.*

Once a log file is generated, it should be periodically analyzed. Many software packages exist that can be used to batch analyze Web server logs. Many of these packages can be automated to fetch log files and run reports at a specified time. For example, WebTrends (www.webtrends.com) Log Analyzer, as shown in Figure 14-6, is a particularly popular log-analysis package.

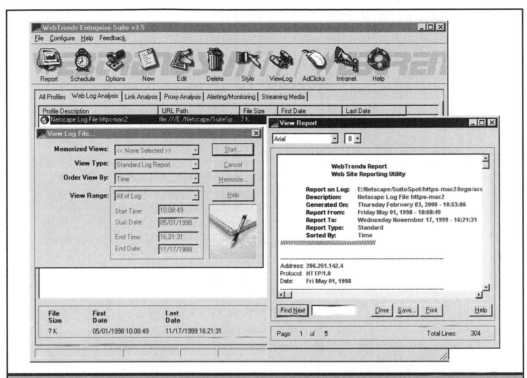

Figure 14-6.   *WebTrends presents an easy-to-use log-file analyzer*

One important consideration when choosing a log-file program is whether or not the usage data is stored in a database. Some lower-end analysis programs will simply read a log file and create a report. If you desire to see a different report, the entire log file must be reread. For quick and dirty analysis, such batch log file analysis is probably adequate, but many designers will want to investigate results dynamically and may want to run comparisons over long time periods. Sites with more than a few thousand visitors per month should consider using a database-enabled log analyzer and save statistical data over time in a data warehouse. However, the amount of usage data a site collects grows quickly, so think carefully about how much data is really necessary to save. Also, if your site gets a reasonable amount of traffic, you should actually consider dedicating a machine solely to process and analyze log files. Sites with large volumes of traffic find that keeping up with usage is very difficult, and they are forced to try to process log data in real time because most of the time that will be mandatory to offload the server—particularly if usage analysis is going to be performed in real time.

Analyzing Site Usage

The ultimate purpose of saving log files is to process them and create reports to understand site usage. Statistical-analysis programs can generate fancy reports showing various aspects of site use. An example report is shown in Figure 14-7. This sample report can be found online at http://www.webdesignref.com/chapter14/samplereport.htm.

While log analysis reports often contain pretty graphs and charts that look useful, a significant problem is that little meaning is often distilled from the reports. In fact, far too often Web site managers focus too much on gross-usage statistics, such as total page views, or concentrate on general trends rather than trying to understand what is actually happening on the site. Oftentimes, without close inspection, such metrics can be misleading. For example, are all the visits to a site a single visitor or multiple visitors? Are pages being reloaded? Are the page views coming from your own organization being filtered out? There is much more to measuring the use of a site than looking at the number of pages viewed. Consider performing the tasks listed in Table 14-7 when looking at log analysis reports.

Remember, one of the major reasons to look at a log file is to study how users actually use a site. Remember that these are real users with real goals, so try to

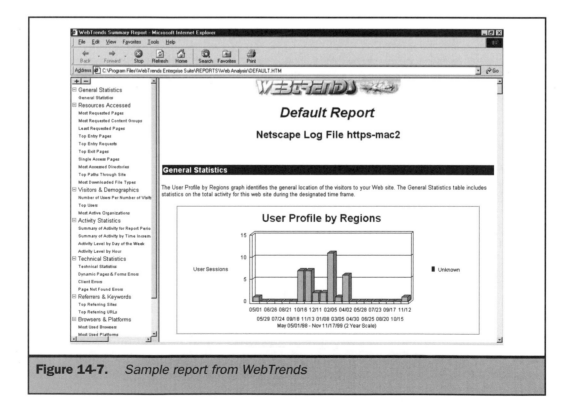

Figure 14-7.   *Sample report from WebTrends*

Task	Purpose of Task
Look for entry points	Determine where users enter a site. If users are not entering through the home page, then how are they entering the site? The users may have bookmarked the site or are search engines deep linking to pages within the site.
Look for exit points	Which pages are users commonly viewing last? Are these pages valid exit points at the conclusion of a typical task or are users bailing out of a site visit midstream?
Find common paths	What paths did users take through a site? Did these paths lead to valid conclusion pages? Are these paths efficient, or could the number of clicks be reduced?
Look at average visit length	While the time of the visit may be difficult to determine exactly, at least look at the numbers of pages viewed and the time estimate. Make sure to consider if the length of time is reasonable. Don't assume the longer the visit, the better. A visitor may just want to get a particular piece of information and leave.
Look for domain and user spikes	Look to see which domains and users visit the site frequently. Take particular note of surges of domains or users. It may be related to a particular event. Be careful to filter out local users, as an organization tends to be its own heaviest visitor.
Look for single-visit or multivisit trends	Determine if site users are inclined to visit the site frequently or not by looking for return visits. If the site is geared towards heavy return visitation, attempt to track individual users with cookies.
Watch for day and time patterns	When do users visit the site? Is the site a night or day site? Is it heavily used during the week or on the weekend? Business sites often find their logs closely match business hours, while entertainment sites may show heavier use at night. Look for the heaviest traffic periods and try to understand the reason. It may be just that it is the time of day or week that the most users are likely to use the site, or it may be related to events that happened on the site such as a new software release or the posting of an earnings report.

Table 14-7.   *Common Tasks to Perform During Log-Report Inspection*

Look for language and geography patterns	Look to see if users from foreign countries are using the site. Consider language changes or localization if heavy usage is found.
Look at browser usage	Look at the types of browsers using the site. Optimize the site for use by the most common browsers, but account for limitations of uncommon browsers seen in the log file.
Look for referring sites	Determine how users reach the site. If referring links are followed, backtrack and see what sites are pointing to yours. Keep a database of referring sites, particularly if links are paid for, to judge cost per visit.
Look at search-engine keywords	If users are utilizing search engines to reach the site, make sure to monitor which keywords they are using to find the site.
Look for errors	Make sure to look at the error log and look for 404 page requests, server response problems, and any other errors that might have occurred.

Table 14-7.   *Common Tasks to Perform During Log-Report Inspection* (continued)

determine what they are trying to accomplish at the site. Measuring the success or failure of visits is particularly important. It may be better to first focus on the number of software demos downloaded, forms submitted, products purchased, and so on, rather than focus on the number of pages viewed.

> **Rule: Analyze your log files carefully, and use them to improve a site or measure its effectiveness.**

Log analysis can also be used to show the economic effectiveness of a site. For example, an e-commerce site might measure the number of visitors per sale, the number of page views per sale, the number of bytes delivered per sale, and so on. In fact, for e-commerce sites, it is wise to consider visitation costs as related to sales. Remember, delivery of sites is not free, so it is important to try to understand the cost of each visit.

When log analysis is used carefully, it is also possible to understand the effectiveness of site-promotion techniques. For example, consider the placement of a magazine advertisement for a new product. Rather than promoting the standard URL for an organization like www.democompany.com, use a special URL like www.democompany.com/robot/magad, or something less obvious like www.democompany.com/robot4, where each advertisement has a URL with a different number at the end. Some organizations even create special URLs like robot.democompany.com, or even full sites like www.robotbutler.com, often termed *microsites*, that can be associated with a particular site promotion. Regardless of just using a special URL and redirecting the user or creating a whole new site, a unique entry point can be monitored in the log files to determine the effectiveness of the advertisement. Furthermore, the entry page can be created to be more contextually appropriate to the advertisement, as shown in Figure 14-8.

Tip   *When providing site addresses to the public, set up special entry URLs to track usage and provide more focused information to users.*

While log files can be used very effectively to understand site use, don't fall into the trap of thinking the logs tell the whole story. A log file isn't going to say if a user enjoys a visit to a site or finds it confusing. For example, a user may get to a particular page in the shortest number of clicks, but may have guessed or been forced to very carefully read information in order to do so. Analyzing log files does not remove the need to talk to users. You should still solicit comments from users and even hold surveys to determine user satisfaction.

Rule: Do not rely solely on log files to understand a site's effectiveness. You still have to talk to the site's users.

Also, because of assumptions made by log-analysis software as well as the people analyzing the files, it is very easy to jump to incorrect conclusions. This is further compounded by network and protocol effects, which may taint log data.

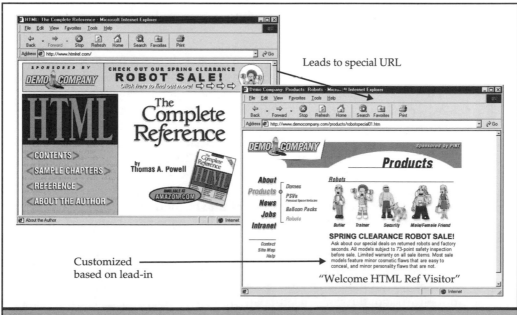

Figure 14-8.   *It is often better to push users to specific URLs or sites*

Accuracy of Logs

Be careful when looking at log files not to infer too much. For example, the domain name or IP address of a user requesting a page is recorded in the log files. Some people are tempted to relate the domain name to the physical location of the organization that holds the domain name. This could then be used to understand what geographical regions people are coming from. However, the Internet isn't as geographically sensitive as many people might think. For example, if a user is coming from aol.com, that says nothing about where they are physically located. In fact, relating domain names to geographical locations will make you believe that California and Virginia account for the majority of a public site's traffic. The problem here is that many large Internet connectivity vendors are based in these regions and their domain names show this. Furthermore, don't assume that just because a user comes from a .com domain that they are in the United States. Many foreign firms use the shorter domain names as well.

Another problem with log accuracy is related to network and protocol issues. Remember that HTTP is a stateless and connectionless protocol. Because of this, it is very difficult to tell how long a user visit lasts. For example, consider that a user requests the home page at a particular moment in time. A minute later, they click on a link to visit a subpage, and then they leave by shutting down their system or entering a URL of another site directly in the browser. Question: How long was the visit? You can't really tell. The user may have lingered on the subpage for ten seconds, ten minutes, or even ten hours. You can't see them leave. You just know they didn't view any more pages in your site. Most statistics-analysis packages make an assumption to end a particular visit after so many minutes of inactivity. Tune the package to use a longer amount of time as its assumption, and your reports will suddenly show longer visitation times.

Consider the effect of network consideration such as dynamic IP addresses and proxy servers on log accuracy. Many users access the Internet from a machine that is given a new IP address dynamically each time it connects to the Internet. If you measure visitors by their IP address, you may easily overreport the number of unique visitors when dynamic IP addresses are issued. Furthermore, when a proxy cache is used, you may see only a single visitor rather than numerous ones because all users appear to come from a single IP address. It is possible to get around some of these issues by handing out a cookie to the user. The cookie can be used to identify the user, and will identify them uniquely regardless of what IP address they are coming from. Unfortunately, users may not accept cookies and may become suspicious of the amount of tracking going on. While it is important to track users to understand their likes and dislikes, it is also important not to appear to be monitoring them too closely. Privacy is a growing concern for users and is discussed in the next section. However, before discussing this, consider the implication of site-usage accuracy.

Some readers may be familiar with the expression, "There are lies, damn lies, and then there are statistics." It is true that it is easy to be misled by site-usage statistics, particularly when assumptions like an IP address equals a user are made. As long as the assumptions are kept the same, useful patterns can be determined. The only real danger with site-usage analysis is when the unscrupulous designer learns that it is easy to modify or even create results. Far too often it seems sites strive to show heavy usage, and in some cases may misrepresent it. Some play word games, talking about "hits" rather than page views. A hit is simply a request for an object in a page. If a page has nine images in it, it produces ten hits or more—one for the page itself and nine for the images. If you want to look like you have a lot of traffic, put many small objects in every page and talk about your hits. Others have even gone so far as to create results by either writing a program to browse a site or by paying people to click on sites. In fact, creating realistic-looking usage data complete with unique IP addresses is far easier than you think. It is no wonder that advertisers are hesitant to pay for mere banner views, and prefer paying for clicks or results. This type of trickery does nothing but hurt the industry. Legitimate sites already have begun relying on third-party auditing to verify usage for advertisers and other concerned parties. The idea of "faking it until you make it" traffic wise is a dangerous game that no site should play.

Privacy

What is done with data collected from a user visit can be just as important as the delivery of the site itself. As more and more users begin to rely on the Web for day-to-day business and personal tasks, the issue of privacy grows in importance. Many users, particularly novice users, are worried about being tracked by sites, and may not want to transmit a credit card number over the Web for fear of interception. While some of these fears are certainly not warranted, Web designers should never quickly dismiss user concerns, as this would go against the very nature of user-centered design.

First, consider the user's fear of privacy related to tracking their online movements. Indeed, sites do track users both openly and legitimately through log files, and occasionally they do so surreptitiously using cookies or even HTML tricks. While cookies may be useful to rectify various environment problems such as the stateless nature of HTTP or dynamically assigned IP addresses, they are indeed used to track the user to some degree. Now, how you decide to utilize the information collected will vary, but it is important to inform the user of what is collected and what it is used for. A privacy policy should be written that overviews the collection and usage of sensitive information. Organizations like TRUSTe (www.truste.org) will help sites create a privacy policy. However, enforcement of policy is problematic, and users are still wary of sites—even those that may have been audited by organizations such as TRUSTe. Recall the rule from Chapter 9.

> **Rule: If sensitive or personal information is collected, provide an easily accessible and understandable privacy statement.**

The crux of online privacy really gets back to control. Should the user be in control of their online personal information and know what is being collected about them and what is stored in various databases, or should Web sites be able to freely collect and trade information about users? Unfortunately, at least in the United States, the power to regulate personal information is not truly in the hands of users. Even when it comes to credit reports, consider how difficult it can be to obtain and correct your own credit report. Now consider how damaging incorrect entries can be on your report when trying to apply for a home loan. The Web brings this to a whole new level.

Sites can and do develop profiles on users and use these profiles to try to market more selectively to them. In some situations, sites may even sell or trade user profile information with others. In fact, the degree of personal information that can be obtained online is quite scary. A recent news story detailed how a boy with a high-school crush gone wrong used the Web to obtain and post information about the whereabouts of his obsession. He eventually found and murdered the girl. However, don't leap to conclusions about the evils of the Internet. The medium itself does nothing. Consider that few stories run discussing how people used the telephone to plan a crime, which is certainly done frequently. The key to improving the Web is to make sure to apply common sense to its usage and consider or even monitor carefully what is consumed.

Content Concerns

Like privacy, the delivery of data and interaction with a user is not just a technical matter. It includes feelings and beliefs about the acceptability of content. Many parents, and now even employers, are concerned with the content that is easily available online. It seems that far too often children are able to easily find less-than-desirable material such as hateful sites or hardcore pornographic material online, and consume this information without their parents' knowledge. Of course, much of the blame can be placed on parents, who may not carefully monitor what their children are doing and interact with them in a positive way to warn them about such sites.

While what constitutes unacceptable will certainly vary from individual to individual, few will argue that there are not at least a few sites that should be kept away from children, if possible. Of course, deciding what is acceptable and what is not should not be strictly determined and enforced by a third party—particularly the government—since this would inhibit freedom of speech and introduce censorship. However, parents, teachers, and even employers should have the tools to help monitor and control content usage where acceptable. Site filtering is probably the most common technique employed. The basic idea with site filtering is that special filtering software looks first for a content rating before allowing a page to be loaded. If the content is deemed acceptable, it is presented to the user; if not, it is rejected. From a site-delivery aspect, the key concern about content acceptability is making sure that content that is unacceptable is clearly marked as such and, conversely, that acceptable content is not mislabeled or not labeled at all so that it is filtered.

The W3C has proposed the Platform for Internet Content Selection, or PICS (http://www.w3.org/pub/WWW/PICS/), as a way to address the problem of content filtering on the Web. The idea behind PICS is relatively simple. A rated page or site will include a **<META>** element within the head of an HTML document. This **<META>** element indicates the rating of the particular item. A rating service, which can be any group, organization, or company that provides content ratings, assigns the rating. Rating services include independent, nonprofit groups such as the Recreational

Software Advisory Council (RSAC) (http://www.rsac.org), which already implements a rating system for video games. The rating label used by a particular rating service must be based on a well-defined set of rules that describes the criteria for rating, the scale of values for each aspect of the rating, and a description of the criteria used in setting a value.

To add rating information to a site or document, a PICS label in the form of a **<META>** element must be added to the head of an HTML file. This **<META>** element must include the URL of the rating service that produced the rating, some information about the rating itself (such as its version, submitter, or date of creation), and the rating itself. Many rating services, such as RSACi, the Internet rating system from RSAC, allow free self-rating. Filling out a form and answering a few questions about a site's content is all that is required to generate an RSACi PICS label. After you complete and submit the questionnaire, you receive a page or email containing the appropriate meta information, which can then be placed in the head of your HTML documents. An example of a PICS label in the form of a **<META>** tag using the RSACi rating is shown here:

```
<META http-equiv="PICS-Label"
content='(PICS-1.1 "http://www.rsac.org/ratingsv01.html"
l gen true comment "RSACi North America Server" for
"http://www.democompany.com" on "2000.01.31T03:52-0800" r
(n 0 s 0 v 0 l 0))'>
```

Under the RSACi rating system, information is rated based on nudity, sex, violence, and language on a scale of 0 to 4 with 0 being harmless and 4 being the most extreme form of each criterion. In the previous case, nothing was offensive so the site received 0 on all accounts. Now remember that when filtering, software reads a file that contains a rating, then it determines whether the information should be allowed or denied. Very strict filtering environments may deny all sites that have no rating, so sites with a broad audience are encouraged to use ratings to avoid restricting readership.

Filtering technology that supports PICS is beginning to achieve widespread acceptance and use. For example, Internet Explorer already includes PICS-based rating filtering, as shown in Figure 14-9.

Of course, the technology itself can't cure the problem. Trust in a particular ratings system is a major stumbling block in adoption of the filtering idea. Even when trust is gained, if the rating system seems confusing or arbitrary, its value is lowered. In the real world, Hollywood's MPAA movie-rating system has a single value of G, PG, PG-13, R, or NC-17 for each movie. The assignment of a particular movie rating is based on many factors that often seem arbitrary to casual observers. When considering movies, parents may wonder how scenes of a dinosaur ripping a person to shreds merits a PG or PG-13 rating, while the use of certain four-letter words indicates an R rating. Certainly similar situations occur on the Internet. Because of the imprecise nature of ratings, the topic is a loaded one, both off and on the Internet. Be careful not to inadvertently cause problems for your site by not rating it, particularly if the content could be construed unacceptable by some users.

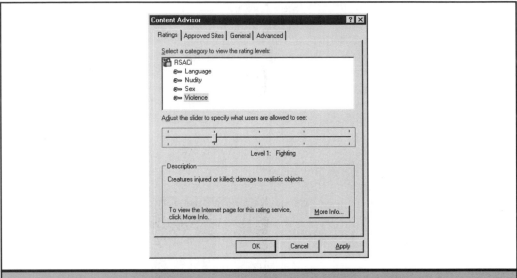

Figure 14-9.   *PICS rating support under Internet Explorer*

Rule: If your content is in any way questionable, have it PICS rated.

Summary

Speedy site delivery is very important because the user's feeling about a site is heavily influenced by its responsiveness. When optimizing sites for speed, make sure to consider all aspects of delivery, including the protocols, the servers, and network location. When building a Web server, make sure to first consider the site's delivery requirements and then choose the hardware, operating system, and server software to match. Hosting choices should also be carefully considered, and outsourcing should be considered a viable option for many sites. Once the site is being delivered, make sure to monitor it carefully. Site maintenance will not only have to be performed on server hardware and software, but on the content itself. Analyzing log files and checking for broken links is an important aspect of proper site maintenance. However, always consider that delivering sites to a user is akin to having a conversation with them, and the issue of security, privacy, and acceptability of the content being delivered will certainly come up. Site delivery is a key aspect of site design and should not be an afterthought. In fact, as the Web becomes more and more interwoven in the daily lives of users, proper site delivery and use become more critical. The future of the Web suggests that many Web sites will be as critical to users as water, power, or the telephone, making information the fourth utility. The next chapter explores the trends that Web designers will most likely face in the coming years.

The Complete Reference

Web Design

Part V

Future Directions

The
Complete
Reference

Chapter 15

The Future of
Web Design

What does the future hold for Web designers? Will the skills of today become obsolete, turning Web professionals into the digital age's equivalent of movable typesetters? Probably not, although designers who have made their living only by knowing a variety of HTML **<TABLE>** tag tricks may find their skills much less in demand in the near future. While exact predictions are difficult, some trends seem pretty likely. It is likely that the underlying Web technologies will change somewhat, but there will certainly be a path from where we are today to the future. Big trends such as the rise of broadband access, the use of non-PC devices to access the Web, and the continued explosion of content and commerce online will send shock waves throughout the profession of Web development. It is also very likely that these trends will continue to foster the growth of the Web lifestyle, which will certainly make Web design and development services even more critical than they are today.

The Near Future

Predicting the future can be difficult. The far future is usually a safe bet to talk about, partially because by the time it arrives it is difficult to verify claims made. In the case of the far future of the Internet and Web—say in 25 years or more—most pundits predict that access will become nearly ubiquitous. High-speed data services will be available to a large portion of the developed world, both in fixed and mobile forms, and a variety of interfaces—including voice command, handwriting, and potentially even biomechanical—will be possible. As in a popular science-fiction show, you'll probably be able to move around the real world and interact with the virtual one at nearly the same time. Interaction with information may be possible via voice interfaces that remotely control your home- or business-based system, and your very environment—both offline and online—will adapt to your needs and habits. However interesting this far-off future world may sound, thinking too much about its effects isn't terribly useful in a practical hands-on book like this one. The path to the future is going to be a long one. Most people are probably interested more in what's going to happen in the near term.

What will happen in the very near term isn't always easy to predict, but a few things seem fairly evident. I'll focus on a few that are important to the Web developer before talking about larger trends that could significantly change the way sites are developed.

The Legacy of HTML

Like it or not, HTML will still be around in the next few years, if not for the foreseeable future. Like the DOS operating system, HTML won't be easy to shed. It will probably be lurking around underneath sites in some form or another for a long time to come.

Prediction: HTML will still be around in some form or another for a great while.

Consider the amount of content in HTML form. Changing over to another format would be a massive undertaking that would take years. However, in its current form HTML is not adequate to serve the growing needs of the Web. HTML is very often malformed, and browsers are lax in complying to or enforcing standards. Because of the permissive nature of browser rendering—literally anything thrown at them— designers and Web editors have had little reason to write correct HTML. However, without standards it is difficult to automatically generate and parse HTML files accurately. Furthermore, to deal with ambiguity of markup usage, browsers often make assumptions. Consider that these assumptions vary; the meaning and rendering of HTML that truly serves as the foundation of a Web page is shaky indeed.

The largest problem with HTML is that it is misused as a presentation technology. The idea behind HTML markup is really to separate the meaning of content from its eventual presentation. Consider how the tag **<B>** says how content looks while the tag **<STRONG>** really says more what it is—in this case, something that is more important. Paragraphs **<P>**, Headings **<H1>**, and nearly every HTML tag you can think of really are more logical in flavor than physical. How big does an **<H1>** heading render under a browser like Internet Explorer? What about on a PDA or cell phone browser? While the physical-minded HTML layout approach that most WYSIWYG editors push may appear to work in most browsers, control is rather limited in HTML. Even if there were only a single browser in use, with the proliferation of alternate viewing environments like cell phones, the HTML approach to layout isn't going to work. In fact, forcing HTML to be a presentation language creates bulky markup laden with table tags and a variety of tricks and misused tags.

A better approach is to utilize cascading style sheets (CSS) for layout while relegating HTML to document structuring. While it seems that every year CSS is predicted to be the next big thing, it is starting to make inroads—mostly because CSS affords the designer a great deal of control over page layout. Fortunately, CSS does not bind so tightly to content like HTML layout can, which makes it easy to apply a different style-sheet look depending on the situation. Browser vendors have been slowly creeping towards full CSS support since primarily the 4.x releases, though Internet Explorer had some CSS support even in its 3.x version.

Prediction: CSS will eventually be commonly used, relieving HTML of its presentation duties.

A missing component of layout is the inclusion of fonts. Both Microsoft and Netscape introduced the use of downloadable fonts. So far their use has been rather limited, partially due to bugs as well as well as limited publicity about the availability of font technology. However, downloadable fonts should be used within sites as they avoid the designer's having to rely on saving custom text layouts as graphic images that do not scale and incur download delays.

Prediction: Downloadable fonts will become commonplace.

As layout requirements continue to increase and HTML is relegated to basic document structure, it is unlikely that developers will continue to hand edit HTML. If strict enforcement of HTML syntax happens through the adoption of XHTML, it will be far easier to create Web editors that produce clean markup, thus eliminating the need for hand editing. Certainly there will continue to be those who prefer to get directly into the markup. There will also be for a need for hand tagging by programmers who are generating markup from programs. As editors improve, CSS gains acceptance, and HTML is simplified and cleaned up, the need to modify HTML directly will become less and less important.

Prediction: Hand editing of HTML will become less commonplace as HTML becomes more structured and rules are enforced.

Mixing It All Up

One of the big problems with Web pages is that structural markup, presentation, and business logic—often in the form of script code—is often all jumbled together in one big mess. In many Web pages HTML is used heavily for formatting, CSS is added in directly to tags using the **STYLE** attribute, and scripts are placed all over the document and even within tags through the use of event-handler attributes like onClick or onMouseover. For example, consider the following markup that works in Internet Explorer.:

```
<!DOCTYPE HTML PUBLIC "-//W3C//DTD HTML 4.0 Transitional//EN">
<HTML>
<HEAD>
<TITLE>Mixed Up</TITLE>
</HEAD>
<BODY BGCOLOR="black" TEXT="white">

<P ALIGN="center" STYLE="font-size: 18pt; line-height: 200%"
onMouseover="this.style.backgroundColor='orange'"
onMouseout="this.style.backgroundColor='black'">
I'm all mixed up!</P>

</BODY>
</HTML>
```

In this particular situation, HTML is combined with style sheets and scripting in such a way that it is difficult to update one item without considering others. Rather than combining this all in one file, it is possible to separate the content out into separate linked files. For example:

```
<!DOCTYPE HTML PUBLIC "-//W3C//DTD HTML 4.0 Transitional//EN">
<HTML>
<HEAD>
<TITLE>Not So Mixed Up</TITLE>
<LINK REL="stylesheet" HREF="externalstylesheet.css">
</HEAD>
<BODY>
<P ID="para1">I'm all mixed up!</P>

<SCRIPT SRC="linkedscript.js"></SCRIPT>
</BODY>
</HTML>
```

Then the linked style sheet (externalstylesheet.css) sets the look of the page, like so:

```
BODY      {background-color: black;
           color: white;}

#para1    {text-align: center;
           font-size: 18pt;
           line-height: 200%;}
```

while the linked script (linkedscript.js) makes the paragraph light up when the user rolls over it:

```
function goOrange()
 {
  para1.style.backgroundColor='orange';
 }

function goBlack()
 {
  para1.style.backgroundColor='black';
 }

para1.onmouseover = goOrange;
para1.onmouseout = goBlack;
```

The benefit to this approach is that we have separated all the components so they can be easily maintained as well as interchanged between pages. Recall the pyramid analogy that contains form, function, content, and purpose. Different individuals often handled each aspect of Web design in this analogy. By separating out the components of a Web page, it is much easier to modify complex pages. This is a simple application of modular design as found in complex software systems.

Prediction: Strict separation of structure, logic, and presentation of Web content will become more important.

The individual components of a Web page will eventually have to be brought together. Figure 15-1 shows a possible relationship between the aspects of a typical Web page.

Page elements may have to be stored and sorted, and output based upon various user criteria. Page elements may be changed all the time, so it is important to carefully manage site assets—typically using a database. According to traditional hypertext theory, the heart of any hypertext system is a database. Sites with any degree of complexity will find that using a database is mandatory.

Prediction: Databases will continue to store a large amount of Web content.

The benefit of separation of content from its eventual output form cannot be understated. Imagine storing a site's content in a central data repository and then dynamically creating pages for a variety of different output environments based upon user actions. This is possible with a database and good separation of content, structure, style, and logic, as illustrated in Figure 15-2.

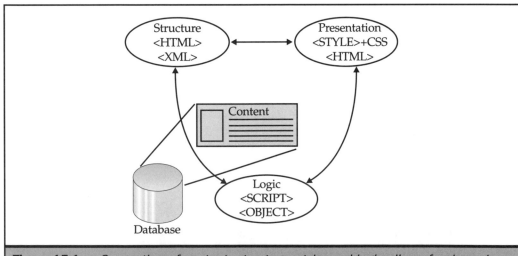

Figure 15-1. *Separation of content, structure, style, and logic allows for dynamic pages*

XML: Good for Everything or Good for Nothing?

XML (www.w3.org/XML) would appear to provide many of the benefits mentioned in the previous section. However, don't run out and dump a database in favor of XML documents. The reality of XML is that it deals with structure of content, not storage. For example, you may decide to store your site's pages natively in XML rather than in a database. Now, if a user wants to search for an item in a particular page in the site, how quickly can it be found? If there are 1,000 pages in no particular order, the best case is that you find something in the first page and the worst case is you have to look through every single page. On average, you'll probably have to look through at least half the pages to find what you are looking for. To speed the process, you may try to sort the pages or provide some form of index. However, this is exactly what a database provides. Databases provide facilities for quickly searching data, maintaining data, providing security, and so on. A flat file system filled with XML files will not provide this benefit.

The downside of databases is that their content cannot be easily shared at times. If you store invoices in your accounting database, it would be nice to automatically ship the invoice to a customer and have it quickly merged into their accounts payable

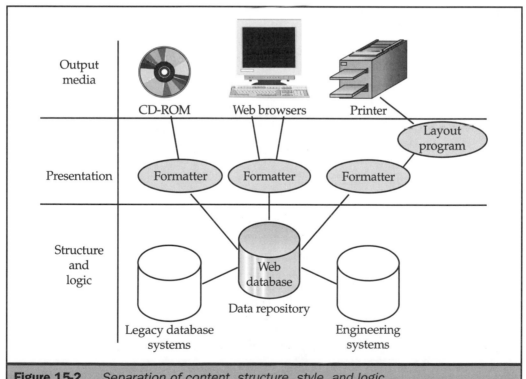

Figure 15-2.   *Separation of content, structure, style, and logic*

database. Of course, exchanging data between two very different systems may be difficult. The fields on your invoice may not directly match fields in the payment system in name and format. In order to smooth the exchange of data from one system to another, a neutral data format could be adopted. XML provides just the tools to define such a language.

Prediction: XML languages will be well accepted as neutral interchange languages.

Beyond data exchange, XML may be slow to be adopted for many reasons. First of all, browser rendering of raw XML is not widely supported. Even if it is, XML languages may not be well understood by the document-authoring community. The explosion of numerous XML-based languages could be the modern equivalent of the Tower of Babel, fragmenting the Web into numerous specialized languages that only small groups of practitioners actually understand. A further problem is that many commercial organizations may be hesitant to use languages they did not invent. If one company in the oil industry creates a language they call SGOML (Standard Gas and Oil Markup Language), would other firms be willing to adopt it? Maybe. But they might not adopt it, out of fear that by using a language they didn't define, they may suffer some competitive disadvantage. Firms might prefer instead to wait for a neutral language to be defined and set by a standards body. The bickering between concerned parties when defining an XML language and the hesitation to use another organization's language should not be underestimated. Within the SGMOL community, the human factor has significantly hampered the use of many languages.

Prediction: The uptake of XML will be slow, and the hurdle for adoption will be agreement between users.

While XML-based languages will become very important in the future, never underestimate the power of HTML itself. It is well known and has a huge installed base of users. Users are really the key to the success of a language, as well as that of a Web site itself.

Users Rule

A prediction that can be made with near certainty is that, in the near term, sites will continue to have to retain a serious focus on user demands. In a startup environment with many choices, users certainly don't have to put up with sites that don't meet their needs. The user's ability to move away from a site providing a confusing interface or slow access is nothing more than a single click of the mouse. Throughout this book we have focused on making sure to always keep users well in mind when designing sites. This concept will continue to grow in popularity as sites become more integral to daily life.

Prediction: User-centered design will continue to be paramount.

Do not assume, however, that the future of the Web is an online utopia where users always get their way. Consider that once a site reaches a critical mass of users, or offers a service that makes it difficult for the user to move to another vendor, it may start to pay as much attention to users as it did as a startup. For example, many portal sites strive to create "sticky" content and services that make it difficult for a user to move to a competitor. Consider the user who keeps personal calendar, contact, and bill-payment information in a particular portal page. If that site stumbles a bit in its customer focus, the user may put up with it because of the difficulty of moving to another site. Sites will strive to create features like this to retain customers. Some of these ideas may go against the theory of user-centered design. Always remember that the aspects of the Web design pyramid are at odds with each other at times; in this case, purpose and economics may go somewhat against user desires. No single aspect of Web design theory will dominate in all situations.

Rise of Broadband

One of the trends that many predict will greatly change Web design is the rise in popularity of broadband access. Already many users in the United States and other countries with well-developed telecommunications infrastructure have relatively high-speed access through ISDN, DSL, satellite, or cable modem. With relatively rapid adoption, a fairly large number of users should have bandwidth in the range of 500 Kbps, or even far greater, in the next few years. With all the available bandwidth, one would assume that Web sites would become much more visual. That's true. Larger graphics, audio, video, and animation are much more easily downloaded over a high-speed connection, but as the experience becomes richer, don't assume that users' expectations won't grow as well. Designing with download in mind will continue to be an issue for the near future.

Prediction: Broadband access will increase multimedia usage, but download will still be an issue.

While download will be an issue, it will still be possible to build much richer interfaces than those used today. Animation will continue to rise in popularity, primarily in the Flash (www.macromedia.com/flash) format. Audio and video will also rise in popularity. In some situations, Web interfaces may begin to resemble CD-ROM–style interfaces. However, consider that there is a limit to the benefit of very rich buttons complete with animation and sound effects. Most of the newly acquired bandwidth should be used to deliver improved content rather than to provide sophisticated animation effects for interface elements.

To really see the benefit of improved bandwidth, designers may have to consider pacing site delivery better. With more bandwidth, you should deliver a sizable chunk of information for the user to consume. Trying to continuously dish out small amounts of information at a time will not provide the degree of responsiveness that users would expect from a high-speed connection, particularly since network protocols or server load issues may erase some of our gains here.

> **Prediction: Interfaces should become more responsive and richer with broadband, but the bulk of bandwidth will be used for content.**

Despite the rise of bandwidth, some content won't make sense animated, or in audio or video form. Text will continue to be the primary content form of the Web for the foreseeable future. Even as multimedia is used more and more, text will have a renaissance of sorts as developers realize that it is not as bandwidth sensitive and can be utilized in a multitude of environments. For example, text could be converted to speech, stripped of layout, and delivered to a PDA, laptop, or cell phone easily.

> **Prediction: Simple text will continue to be an important content form because of its flexibility.**

Non-PC–Based Web Access

The rise of non-personal computer–based Web access is almost assured. Already there are legitimate examples of this. For example, television and the Web have achieved a modicum of integration with the rise of set-top boxes such as WebTV (www.webtv.net). WebTV presents a much different design environment than traditional PC usage. First, the environment of consumption is much different. Television users may sit far away on a couch and use a remote control or keyboard to interact with the Web. Also, the user may find that they can consume much less text on screen because of the lower resolution of televisions and the fact that text must be larger to be easily read. Users may not print or save documents as much when using a television access device. Users may browse the Web in a more social setting; in fact, a family might look at information together. Lastly, the Web may be integrated with television programming so the user can access information about a show as they watch it.

Besides WebTV there are numerous other examples of viable non-PC–based viewing environments. Already some video game consoles such as Sega Dreamcast (www.dreamcast.com) offer Web access via a modem using an embedded Web browser (www.planetweb.com). Continued integration between game consoles is likely since gamers find browsing the Web useful to read about games as well as to find opponents to chat with or challenge. Beyond game consoles, network appliances ranging from limited computer-like systems to Web-enabled home phones have started to appear. However, these devices have yet to come close to the relatively modest penetration that WebTV and Web-enabled games have achieved. It is possible, however, that these new appliances will meet with some success, particularly if geared for specific tasks or targeted to markets that lack personal computers.

From the Web design point of view, the rise of non-PC–based Web viewing presents some interesting challenges. Most of these devices may have interfaces that do not support excessive typing or mouse movement. Furthermore, users accessing the Web with such appliances may have a less preconceived notion about how things work and may have very different goals than typical computer users. With such users coming onto the Web in increasing numbers, Web designers should well consider that the "rules" presented may change dramatically.

Prediction: Non-PC–based Web browsing will grow and require different interface design considerations.

Browsers Become Commodity

For some, this prediction is a sad one. It is very likely that future Web users will care much less about their browsers than users do today. Few people really get terribly worked up about the brand of their television. The set itself, while important, is not the primary focus to the viewer: the shows are. Of course, if the set breaks that might be a different story.

For the next generation of Web users, browsers will become less important as they fade into the background. Already the browser is becoming heavily integrated into the operating system in the case of Windows. In the case of many networked information efforts such as the Java platform, the browser is in some sense becoming the operating system. Regardless of which idea wins, the browser will become more of a commodity piece of software. Even more importantly, the user may stop paying attention to the browser.

Prediction: Browsers will be less of a focus.

While browsers may become less of a focus to the user, this doesn't mean that the Web designer will have less to worry about. On the contrary, the designers will have to make sure that they do nothing to bring attention to the browser itself. In the WebTV environment, the browser is somewhat transparent to the user. In a Windows Active Desktop setup, the entire environment is in some sense using a browser. As the integration becomes tighter and tighter, we can't rely on particular browser customizations, nor will we want to bring the user's attention back to the browser. Better to keep them focused on the site's content.

Untethered Web Access

A fairly easy prediction to make is that the Web will go on the move. Wireless networks provide the possibility for people to take the Web where they go, rather than have users feel they have to come to the Web. Already local area networks have been enabled for wireless access, and some have begun to use laptops in a roaming fashion. In limited regions, roaming access for laptops is also possible; see www.ricochet.net for an example of a wireless access service.

Web-enabled cell phones also offer the opportunity for people to take the Web with them. However, a cell phone provides a significantly different way to access the Web than a computer. The screen size of a laptop is small, and the input interface may be awkward, often using some form of roller, extra keys, or the numeric keypad itself.

Cellular networks tend to have coverage and reliability issues, and bandwidth is limited, though that is changing rapidly.

Personal digital assistants (PDAs) like Palm Pilots and Windows CE devices can also be used to access the Web in a wireless fashion. The screen size of a PDA is usually much better than a cell phone, but at best it tends to be less than half or even a quarter the resolution of the most limited notebook computers. Input on PDAs can be a limiting factor for Web access because they often use a small keyboard or rely on handwriting recognition.

Web access is also being promoted within vehicles. Automobile-based browsing is wireless and generally is touch-screen or voice activated. Focus can be a large issue for in-car Web access. Interaction may be limited primarily to on-demand directions, news, and communication alerts. Screen size may not be an issue, but the viewing environment of all forms of out-of-office browsing, including the car, may be hampered by less than ideal lighting conditions.

The mobile Web will not be used for casual browsing, but will instead be focused upon time- and location-sensitive information such as driving directions, nearest ATM machine, important messages, weather, and traffic conditions.

Prediction: Wireless Web access will focus on location- and time-sensitive information.

Non-PC browsing environments will probably focus more on consumption than on entry. Initially, most mobile devices will focus on retrieval of information rather than input because traditional text input, particularly, could be difficult with these devices. Also, the environment of use will probably not facilitate careful composition of data. Handwriting, voice control, and even simple icon-driven touch screens may be the preferred way that people access the wireless Web. Small keyboards may also be used, but probably more when people stop to interact with the device.

Because of limited bandwidth and screen size, Web sites will have to be streamlined to deal with mobile users. It is unlikely that sites will be able to be filtered through some sort of translation server. Even if the syntax of Web pages could be reformatted from HTML or XHTML to a language like Wireless Markup Language (WML) cleanly, there is a question of relevance. A wireless user may not need much of the information provided to computer-based users. Because of the design requirements, special wireless or PDA-geared Web sites will be developed. Already, numerous development firms like Dokoni (www.dokoni.com) have begun to focus on this emerging market. Consider the radically different design considerations in Figure 15-3 and you'll see why.

A major challenge with the mobile Web design is that designers have to be aware that the Web and real life are now much closer. No longer will we necessarily bring users into the Web; rather, they will bring the Web into their lives more often. Web sites will have to have "transparent integration" into larger tasks such as taking a trip to the store. Once the Web goes mobile, it touches the "real world" more directly, which leads to the Web lifestyle discussed later in the chapter.

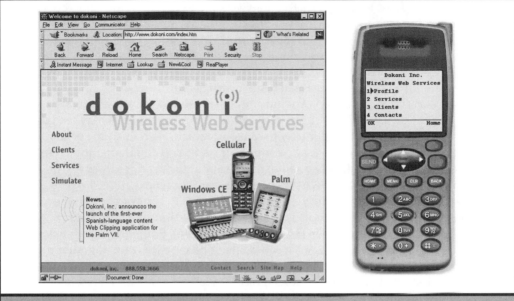

Figure 15-3.   *The two faces of a wireless Web firm*

Effects of Community

While some may believe that the concept of community on the Web is overrated, it can be very important. Community brings personality to the Web. Rather than interacting with soulless content, users can interact with each other. People with similar interests can link their sites, chat, and exchange information. A simple form of Web community, called Web rings (www.webring.com), allows users to join a group of Web sites on a similar subject. A user who visits the site will find a navigation system that will link them to other sites in the ring, like the one shown here:

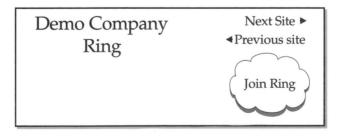

The major benefit of Web rings is that they link related content together, creating a path for users interested in a particular subject. Using community for navigation is an interesting idea that follows the basic idea of "birds of a feather flock together." While searching for information on a particular subject such as astronomy, we might be interested in visiting sites that other users visited. Alexa (www.alexa.com), as well as the browsers themselves, provides related site features that show what links may be related to the current page viewed or what sites users tended to visit afterwards.

While providing related link information from user browsing habits may lead users on a path to good information, it is very easy to cause a problem with this type of community navigation. If you visit a more successful competitor's site, you could attempt to create a related link to your own site. In some sense, this is similar to "beating down the grass" to create a path for animals to run down when you are herding them.

More advanced Web community systems allow users to chat or comment on sites as they visit them. Popular tools at the time of this writing include Gooey (www.gooey.com) and Third Voice (www.thirdvoice.com). Some tools such as PowWow (www.powwow.com) even allow users to browse the Web together in groups. What is interesting about many of these tools is how some users have used them to create the equivalent of electronic graffiti by posting negative comments on the home pages of sites they don't like.

Digital communities, like real communities, need monitoring, so site designers will have to understand how to become good citizens. Designers will also have to come to grips with the fact that users are able to interact with site content and make comments whether they like it or not. Over time, restrictions on anonymous postings may be erected and sites informed about postings made on their site that they may not be able to see.

Community won't stop at linking, postings, and limited group interaction. As we combine the Web and chatting environments, particularly graphic environments, we will eventually see the rise of virtual environments such as the one shown in Figure 15-4.

While in the beginning many online environments will be focused on entertainment, over time community will continue to affect commercial organizations. Sites like Amazon.com already have found community facilities successful for improving customer satisfaction.

Content Overload Issues

One of the best qualities of the Web is the wide range of content available. The amount of content on the Web will certainly continue to grow. Unfortunately, having so much content can be a problem. In many ways, the Web is really composed of numerous "islands" of well-organized, useful data in a vast ocean of uncategorized, suspect, and even hazardous information. A key part of a Web designer's job is to chart safe paths through information. A great deal of this book has been devoted to discussing how to

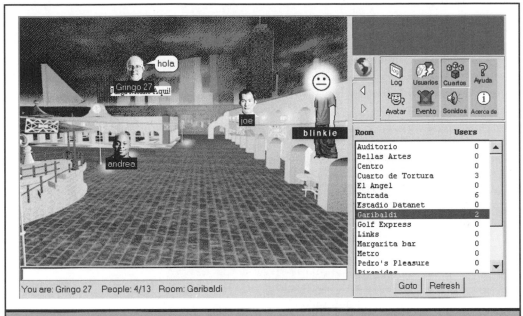

Figure 15-4. *Graphic chat points to the future of Web communities*

improve way-finding. Unfortunately, we are only able to dramatically affect navigation and content issues within sites under our own control.

What methods will be utilized to help users find their way around the Web at large or within very large Web sites? First, consider the continued reliance on human guides. Experts will filter content for others, including providing ratings, acting as guides, or even holding tours for others. Search engines will continue to improve, but gains will not be as significant as some might believe. A challenge for search engines will be to make sense of the rising tide of non-textual information. Visualization might be used to make sense of large pools of data, but probably won't be used as a generalized browsing paradigm by most users. A variety of graphical interfaces have been tested that put a visual interface on large data sets, including Web sites, to allow users to observe trends and even find information more easily. Cartia (www.cartia.com) uses a topology map-style interface to chart information as shown in Figure 15-5, which maps technology news stories.

Another popular form of visualization uses a hyperbolic tree. Often, such visualizations are used to show the topics in a site and may even be used as a site map. Figure 15-6 shows a hyperbolic tree for the DemoCompany site prepared with software from inxight (www.inxight.com).

FUTURE DIRECTIONS

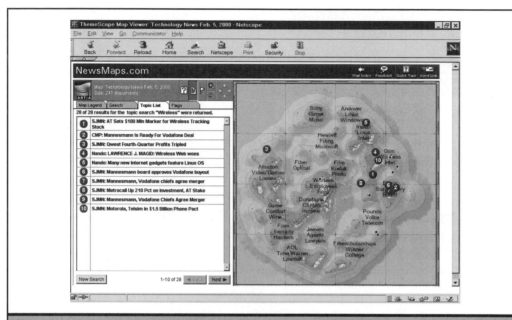

Figure 15-5.   *Related articles are shown to be visually close to each other*

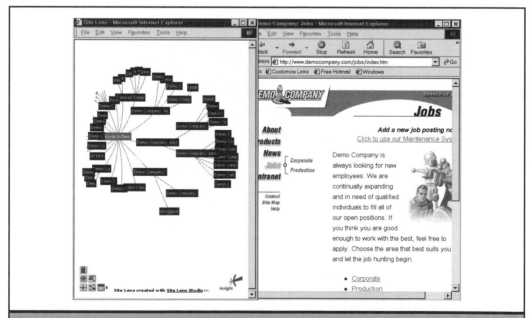

Figure 15-6.   *Hyperbolic trees can be used to visualize site structure*

Numerous other forms of visualization are possible, but the reality is that it often gets in the way of users—unless the user's primary purpose is to look for patterns in a set of Web pages or to analyze a large body of information looking for trends.

Prediction: Visualization interfaces will be limited to data set analysis and will not be used for navigation by most users.

Agents

It is better to use a program rather than a person to perform repetitive tasks and wade through large amounts of information. Much has been said about the use of autonomous agents or bots—short for robots—on the Internet. The thought is that eventually bots could be written that could act on the behalf of users. For example, you could have a bot watch your stock portfolio and make trades when certain conditions are met. Today, bots are relatively simple and are capable of performing basic tasks like price comparisons, link checking in sites, automatic retrieval of news articles, and so on. Botspot (www.botspot.com) provides information on and links to many of the bots that are available. However, for bots to be really successful they will probably have to have a social interface of some sort so they are easy to command and have some limited form of intelligence. Already Microsoft has developed software that allows the production of social agents, as shown in Figure 15-7.

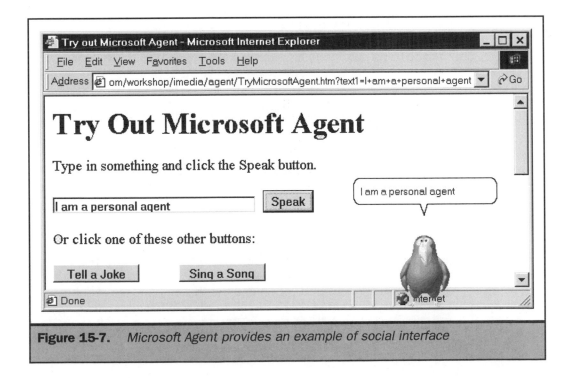

Figure 15-7.   *Microsoft Agent provides an example of social interface*

FUTURE DIRECTIONS

Do not assume just because an agent or bot has a social interface that it has any reasonable amount of intelligence. In fact, it is unlikely that you would want to trust an agent to perform purchasing tasks for you or other things without being very careful to tell it exactly what you want to do. Remember that without real artificial intelligence an agent will lack common sense. Ask an agent to buy a plane ticket for a far-off land, and it may find the cheapest one, but it may not consider that the airline has a horrible reputation amongst fliers.

Prediction: Bots will be useful in the near future for basic tasks, but an agent with any significant intelligence is far off.

A Web designer should assume that in the future some of their users might visit a site in proxy using an agent. This may mean that the site will have to be designed so that an agent can easily find the information it is looking for. Agents won't need graphics and instructions. However, agents do need very regular data. For bots to be useful, there will have to be an increase in the use of structured data on the Web.

The Web Lifestyle

The most important trend of all is the continued "colonization of the Web." Many users are beginning to live more and more online, intertwining their real lives with their virtual ones. While they can't really live online in the real sense yet, many people have already begun to rely significantly on the Web for accomplishing tasks in their daily life, from checking bank statements to making dinner reservations. Online commerce continues to boom, and users have started to adopt a Web lifestyle.

The Web lifestyle is one where the user expects the Web to act the way they want it to. Customization continues, and the idea of WYSIWYW (What You See Is What You Want) presented in Chapter 1 is alive and well. Users will expect sites to respond to their needs and to work consistently. They will expect sites to react to their location, their language, their technology, and their preferences. Those practicing the Web lifestyle will not like to use sites that are not designed for the WYSIWYW philosophy. These users will also be particularly critical of sites that are not well-designed, are not easy to use, or have delivery problems.

Prediction: Users practicing a Web lifestyle will become even more impatient and less forgiving of Web sites.

For designers, the rise of Web lifestyle means that it's time to get very serious about Web development. For example, consider video on the Web compared to television. Television shows are delivered consistently with a high degree of quality every day. What about Web-based video? The Web lifestyle will not allow for so many glitches. Best practices need to be applied to Web development. Because of this, there will continue to be a separation of tasks and movement away from the "jack of all trades" Webmaster. However, if you are a designer who does a little bit of everything, don't despair. While the industry will certainly change, it will grow dramatically in size and become more formalized.

Summary

Accurate predictions are difficult, but many trends in the Web industry seem pretty likely. Some technologies may change, but many of today's technologies like HTML are probably going to be around for a while. Even when tools and technology finally do change, many of the techniques will stay somewhat the same—the focus will continue to be the user. Users will increase their demand for quality high-impact Web sites. While bandwidth will certainly increase, improved access to fast connections will also cause users to want more and more. And while some sites may utilize richer and richer forms of multimedia, the need for text and alternative renderings of sites will grow significant as users begin to use devices other than traditional personal computers to access the Web. In particular, the growth of mobile Web applications will bring many challenges to Web design having to do with the relationship of Web-based information to a user's location. There will continue to be an explosive growth of content and commerce online, but with this growth some users may feel they are drowning in information. Visualization tools, search engines and autonomous-agent software may provide some relief as well. However, good old human categorization may offer the best way to separate the wheat from the chaff online. As more and more users utilize the Web, communities will continue to be important. Finally, users will begin to rely more and more on the Web, eventually adopting a Web lifestyle. However, the coming generations of Web users will be less and less forgiving of Web sites they rely on. The Web design industry will certainly mature to meet the new requirements, and those designers and developers who lay the foundation for future online communities truly will be living up to the title "Information Architect."

The Complete Reference

Part VI

Appendixes

The Complete Reference

Web Design

Appendix A

Core Web Site Design Principles

Throughout *Web Design: The Complete Reference*, key concepts have been summarized as Web design Rules, Suggestions, and Premises. Useful Definitions have also been provided when necessary. This appendix collects all of these in one place, grouped by chapter, to give the reader a chance to quickly review the basic ideas of this book.

Introduction to Web Design

These rules from Chapter 1 summarize some essential concepts for effective Web design. The slogan WYSIWYW (What You See Is What You Want) is presented as a possible change to traditional GUI design principles adopted to the Web.

Rule: YOU are NOT the USER.

Rule: USERS are NOT DESIGNERS.

Rule: Design for the common user, but account for differences.

Rule: A site's execution must be close to flawless.

Rule: Know and respect the Web and Internet medium constraints.

Rule: Web sites should respect GUI principles where appropriate.

Rule: Navigation is only a means to an end result.

Rule: Visuals will heavily influence the user's initial perception of a site's value.

The Web Design Process

These rules and suggestions from Chapter 2 focus on the importance of developing and sticking to a process when approaching Web design.

Suggestion: Always collect content before design if at all possible.

Rule: Visual Design should proceed in a top-down fashion from home page to sub section pages and, finally, to content pages.

Suggestion: Always consider the bordering effect of the browser window when developing visual composites.

Rule: Don't marry your design prototypes. Listen to your users and refine your designs.

Rule: Sites always have bugs, so test your site well.

Rule: Testing should address all aspects of a site, including content, visuals, function, and purpose.

Rule: User test is the most important form of testing and should be performed last.

Rule: Site development is an ongoing process—plan, design, develop, release, repeat.

Designing for Users

These rules, suggestions and definitions from Chapter 3 emphasize the importance of considering your target audience—the actual users of the site—when designing for the Web.

Definition: Usability is the extent to which a site can be used by a specified group of users to achieve specified goals with effectiveness, efficiency, and satisfaction in a specified context of use.

Rule: There is no absolute idea of what constitutes a usable site. Usability will vary as much as the users accessing the site.

Rule: Usability depends on the medium of consumption.

Rule: Usability depends on the type of site as well as the user's familiarity with it.

Rule: Usability and user satisfaction are directly related.

Rule: Browsers do not use sites, people do.

Suggestion: There are no generic people. Always try to envision a real person visiting your site.

Suggestion: Avoid using text, graphics, and backgrounds of similar hue.

Suggestion: Avoid combining text, graphics, and backgrounds of similar saturation.

Rule: Keep contrast high. Avoid using text, graphics, and background of similar lightness.

Suggestion: Avoid using busy background tiles.

Rule: Make sure colors that are meant to distinguish items like links are significantly different in two ways, such as hue and lightness.

Rule: Users try to maximize gain and minimize work.

Rule: Recognition is easier than recall, so don't force users to memorize information.

Rule: Do not make visited links the same style or color as unvisited ones, as it forces the user to memorize where they have been.

Suggestion: Since it is easier to remember visuals, make pages that will be remembered as visually different from the rest.

Suggestion: Limit groups of similar choices such as links to 5–9 items.

Suggestion: Aim for memorization of only three items or pages sequentially.

Rule: When response times such as page loads take more than 30 seconds, try to provide your own feedback to the user such as a load-time progress bar.

Rule: Time matters more to a user than bytes delivered.

Suggestion: Improve Web page response time by taking advantage of user "think time" with preloading.

Suggestion: Use preloading on a linear progression of pages.

Suggestion: Make page elements obviously different if they are different.

Suggestion: Limit page noise and segment page objects so that they don't compete so much visually that the user is unable to focus on what they are interested in.

Rule: Sensory adaptation does occur on the Web. If you want a user's full attention, you'll have to vary things significantly and often.

Rule: Try to optimize keyboard access for all pages in a site, not just form pages.

Rule: Minimize mouse travel distance between successive choices.

Rule: Minimize mouse travel between primary page hover locations and the browser's Back button.

Rule: Make clickable regions large enough for users to move to them quickly and press them accurately.

Suggestion: Always remember that you need to bring a site into the user's world, not the other way around.

Rule: Account for the characteristics of the probable environment in which the user will access a site.

Suggestion: Aim to create an adaptive Web site that meets the requirements of novices, intermediates, and advanced users.

Suggestion: Design for the intermediate user if an adaptive Web interface is not possible.

Rule: Users bring past experiences with the world, software, and the Web to your site. Make sure your site meets their expectations.

Rule: Do not stray from the common interface conventions established by heavily used sites.

Suggestion: Perform user testing early and often.

Suggestion: When performing even an informal usability test, avoid talking too much or guiding the user.

Suggestion: Do not use usability concerns as a way to avoid or eliminate visual, technological, or economic aspects of a site.

Suggestion: Practice "Las Vegas" Web design. Provide the user with a pleasant experience complete with perks and the illusion of unlimited choices, but control the situation strictly at all times.

Site Types and Architectures

These rules, suggestions, definitions and premises from Chapter 4 are concerned with defining and understanding the many types of Web sites and site structures that can be worked with.

Premise: A Web site's logical structure is more important to a user than its physical structure.

Rule: Do not expose physical site file structure, when possible.

Rule: A site's logical document structure does not have to map to directly match physical structure.

Suggestion: Aim for a site click depth of three.

Suggestion: Aim for positive feedback indicating progress towards a destination every click, with a maximum of three clicks without feedback.

Suggestion: Even for wide site structures, consider a range of 25–81 links per page when page links are ideally clustered.

Premise: The more important the page, the more redundant links should be provided to it.

Suggestion: Redundant links in a site should be no more than 10–20 percent of a page's total exit links.

Premise: The overriding purpose of any commercial site is to serve the user in a way that hopefully benefits the company either directly or indirectly.

Premise: Entertainment sites may find novelty or surprise more useful than structure or consistency.

Premise: Novice users prefer sites with predictable structure and may put up with extra clicks or a lack of control to achieve a comfortable balance.

Premise: Power users or frequent site users want control and will favor structures that provide more navigation choices.

Navigation Theory and Practice

These rules, suggestions and definitions from Chapter 5 approach the important issue of Web site navigation both from a theoretical and a practical standpoint and how it effects usability.

Rule: Use simple and memorable URLs to improve navigation.

Rule: Do not hide URLs—complex or simple—unless you are trying to keep people from direct linking.

Rule: Use consistent and explicit page labels for all pages in a site.

Rule: Site wide labeling icons or words such as the organization name or logo should always return a user to the home page of the site when clicked.

Suggestion: Button states should be considered a secondary form of page label and the selected state should always be subdued, not prominent.

Suggestion: When using color-coding to imply section location, make sure the colors used are significantly different from each other.

Suggestion: Do not go so overboard with theme-based location hints that you fall into a designer-defined metaphor.

Suggestion: Do not attempt to mimic the browser history mechanism with links.

Rule: Avoid links named simply "Back." Always explicitly indicate where a back link will go.

Rule: Avoid creating pages that cannot be backed out of easily using the browser Back button.

Rule: Users remember their start page as a permanent landmark and the home page of a visited Web site as a semi-permanent landmark. Because of this, these pages should be stable in their presentation but look noticeably different than other pages visited.

Suggestion: Don't hide a destination choice from a user unless the link is less important or clutter forces sacrifices.

Suggestion: Avoid placing primary navigation on the far right of the screen.

Suggestion: Home pages or other landmark pages should consider using center-oriented navigation to distinguish themselves from other pages in a site.

Rule: Placement of navigation should be consistent within a page layout.

Rule: Navigation should be consistent and elements should exhibit stability in position, order, and contents.

Suggestion: When separating navigation choices by position onscreen, understand that four locations is a hard barrier.

Suggestion: Navigation-oriented pages should fit vertically within the screen whenever possible, as should primary navigation in all other types of pages.

Suggestion: Minimize the distance between primary site navigation buttons and the Back button.

Suggestion: Always attempt to limit mouse movement between subsequent navigation items.

Suggestion: Avoid using frames for layout. Use them for navigation.

Suggestion: When using frames, make smaller frames control larger adjacent frames.

Suggestion: Do not turn off frame resizing and scrolling unless resolution is very well accounted for.

Suggestion: Do not make a remote the mandatory form of navigation.

Rule: Limit scrolling and mouse travel in navigation as much as possible.

Rule: Consider a maximum of three page loads before a result.

Linking: Text, Buttons, Icons, and Graphics

These rules and suggestions from Chapter 6 examine the many ways to create links in a Web site.

Suggestion: Occasionally provide some unstructured links within document text to promote exploration and thought.

Suggestion: Always provide textual links at the bottom of pages when using long pages or pages with graphical buttons.

Suggestion: When using image maps, always provide a secondary navigation form such as text links.

Rule: Never completely remove visited link indication.

Rule: Avoid changing link colors.

Rule: Avoid underlining non-linked text in Web documents—use italics or bold instead.

Suggestion: Avoid automatically turning off link underlining. If you do, add another link indicator form.

Suggestion: Avoid using ellipses in links, as they are generally redundant.

Suggestion: Graphical buttons should have at minimum an unselected and selected state. Over states and press states should be considered optional.

Suggestion: Provide good labels indicating the form of the content. Consider using icons to show content types.

Suggestion: Make sure to indicate if the link will jump them within a page, within a site, or to an external site. Don't hide the URL, in case the user can deduce the answer from it.

Suggestion: Indicate an external link by exposing the URL or using an icon. Indicate file size if triggering a download.

Suggestion: Use an icon or symbols, or issue an alert dialog before the link.

Suggestion: Avoid changing visited link colors.

Suggestion: Add the last modification date to show update times and, where necessary, use a New icon.

Suggestion: Use an alert, or warn with an obvious label.

Suggestion: When using status bar messages, consider providing URL information with the text when linking externally.

Rule: Broken links should be considered catastrophic failures.

Suggestion: Avoid automatic redirects for 404 errors.

Search and Design

These rules and suggestions from Chapter 7 examine the concept of designing a site in a way that is optimized for search.

Rule: Utilize past user experience with search engines by using similar layout and labeling in local search facility design, but avoid imitating aspects of public search engines that deal with the uncontrollable nature of public Web sites.

Rule: Do not design pages solely to attract search engines as, ultimately, pages are for people.

Rule: If a site is filled with regular formatted data, very complex to digest data, or contains more than 100 pages, include a local search engine.

Rule: If a site caters to power users or frequent return visitors, provide a search facility.

Suggestion: When search is available in a site, include a search button or field on all pages.

Rule: A search form as well as the result pages must match the look and feel of a site.

Rule: A search form should match the content being searched.

Suggestion: Primary search text boxes should be about twice as big as secondary search text boxes.

Suggestion: It is better to limit search to a topic, category, or idea rather than a section of a site.

Rule: Advanced search facilities must provide instructions and examples.

Rule: Result pages should provide as much information as possible so users can decide what items to peruse further.

Rule: The format of the search results should fit the data that is being returned.

Rule: Negative search result pages must include information on why a query failed, and, potentially, how to fix the query.

Page Types and Layouts

These rules and suggestions from Chapter 9 consider aspects of pages and page layouts, from screen size to function-specific pages.

Rule: Set the size of the page to fit the purpose and the content at hand.

Rule: Avoid wide pages, particularly those that cause rightward scrolling.

Rule: Try to keep important items such as primary navigation in the first screen.

Suggestion: Be aware of the screen "fold," and try to hint at content beyond the first screen.

Rule: Avoid resolution entry restrictions for sites if at all possible.

Rule: When designing for WebTV, consider a hard and fast page width of 544 pixels.

Suggestion: If designing with assumed screen sizes, be conservative and give yourself a slop factor of as much as 10 percent of the available region.

Suggestion: Allow the user to stretch or shrink pages at will. Do not force pages to fill to an available resolution unless layout will be lost without the size increase.

Suggestion: When using fixed page sizes, make sure to center your page to reduce the perception of empty space on larger displays.

Suggestion: Avoid using stretchable designs on pages with little content.

Suggestion: Try to fit content vertically within 3–5 screens, if possible.

Suggestion: Either control page margins or account for their variation with some layout slop factor.

Suggestion: Provide an obvious link to quickly skip a splash page.

Rule: A home page should set the visual and navigational tone of a site.

Rule: A home page should load fast, but be dramatic enough to encourage interest.

Rule: A home page should clearly indicate what's inside a site.

Suggestion: A home page should provide informational value and an obvious indication of site change if change is occurring.

Suggestion: If a particular subpage is a landmark or common entry page such as a "section home page" make it visually distinctive.

Rule: Subpages should follow the style and navigation of the home page, at least in spirit.

Suggestion: Make FAQ pages a single document so they are easily printable, if they are of a reasonable length.

Suggestion: Provide a link back to the top of the document or to the list of the questions at the end of every answer.

Suggestion: Consult a legal professional for drafting or inspection of any legal terms used.

Suggestion: Add a last modification indication to pages.

Rule: If sensitive or personal information is collected, provide an easily accessible and understandable privacy statement.

Rule: Full contact information should be available within one click of any page on a site; minimal contact information such as an email address should be included on every page.

Suggestion: Inform users that printed pages will be different than what is seen onscreen or show the print version directly.

Suggestion: Use Acrobat PDF files for highly complex information that needs to print perfectly such as data sheets, technical drawings, and complex financial or mathematical information.

Suggestion: Clearly indicate Acrobat files with text and an icon, and provide information on using these files.

Rule: Provide an obvious conclusion page for a task.

Suggestion: Provide a way back to the site from an exit page.

Rule: Let users leave in peace. Avoid "please don't go" or "last chance" pop-up windows.

Suggestion: When using text-oriented design, consider providing navigation bars as well as contextual links.

Suggestion: Consider using a text design philosophy on sites where download speed or display flexibility is paramount.

Suggestion: Avoid using metaphor design on sites geared toward expert users or heavy repeat use.

Suggestion: Avoid unconventional or very artistically oriented interfaces designs on task-driven or frequent-use sites.

Suggestion: Use header-footer design for content-focused sites, particularly when wide content is common.

Rule: Strive always in Web design to be the same, but different.

Text

These rules and suggestions from Chapter 10 offer ideas to guide your usage of text on the Web and covers topics ranging from the use of particular fonts to writing for Web readability.

Rule: Increase line height to improve online text readability.

Suggestion: Create a type hierarchy by varying text color, size, style, and position to improve page usability.

Rule: The details of a site may heavily influence the take-away value.

Suggestion: Avoid anti-aliasing small text.

Suggestion: Consider three fonts per page: one for page labels and headlines, one for body text, and one for navigation.

Rule: Columns of text in Web pages should never wrap up and down.

Rule: Navigation-focused pages generally require less text white space than consumption pages.

Rule: Always use white space to complement the use of information.

Suggestion: Be careful of using words that have alternate Web meanings.

Colors, Images, and Backgrounds

These rules and suggestions from Chapter 11 focus on the use of color and images on the Web, from basic font coloring, through background images, to advanced uses of CSS with colors and images.

Rule: To ensure the appropriate color is produced, always use a hexadecimal value over a named color except in the case of basic colors like white, black, red, and so on.

Suggestion: To safely break the 216-color barrier, use pre-dithered patterns or so-called hybrid colors.

Suggestion: Due to poor cross-browser support, avoid using the <BASEFONT> element to set font values in a document—especially where colors are concerned.

Rule: Always store your images in a separate directory.

Rule: Name your images in a logical fashion that groups them by purpose or usage.

Rule: You can't use the <IMG> tag without the SRC attribute.

Suggestion: ALT text should reinforce the meaning of significant images; if an image does not convey essential meaning, leaving the ALT value blank is better than cluttering the page with unnecessary ToolTips.

Rule: Always use the HEIGHT and WIDTH attributes with the <IMG> tag.

Rule: Never use the HEIGHT and WIDTH attributes to resize images with HTML. If a smaller version of an image is needed, create a smaller version of the image and use HEIGHT and WIDTH correctly.

Rule: Always set an image's BORDER attribute to zero unless you have a specific design reason to do otherwise—and remember that linked images with no BORDER attribute will render with colored borders by default.

Suggestion: Limit graphics formats in Web pages to JPEG and GIF until other formats become generally supported.

Suggestion: Don't rely solely on color as a cue in links and informational graphics.

Rule: when creating layouts with cut-up images and tables, make sure that WIDTH and HEIGHT values for images and table cells always add up appropriately.

Rule: For cut-up images and tables to work together properly as layouts, always set the table's CELLPADDING and CELLSPACING values to zero.

Suggestion: Do not make a background tile a very small height or width (e.g. 1–2 pixels) as an annoying monitor flashing effect may result.

Building Interactivity Using GUI Features

These rules and suggestions from Chapter 12 consider Web design in light of GUI (graphical user interface) principles that have been long established in the field of software design. Many of these ideas have already become the common conventions behind good Web design.

Suggestion: Provide a useful service that is difficult to transfer between sites to improve site "stickiness."

Suggestion: Provide online documentation (or, in some cases, printed documentation), but don't rely on the user accessing it.

Suggestion: Avoid modification of the appearance of the user's primary browser window.

Rule: When using full-screen window, inform the user how to exit or provide a close button.

Suggestion: Do not go full screen without asking the user first.

Rule: Do not create general modal windows. Reserve modality for alerts, prompts, and confirmation windows.

Suggestion: Use alerts to inform the user of important issues, not general information.

Suggestion: Use a confirmation dialog to verify the execution of an irreversible or important task such as form submission.

Suggestion: Use prompt dialogs only to ask a user to provide a short word or numeric answer to a simple question. Do not ask questions that would result in a multiple-line answer.

Suggestion: Set the length of text fields to reasonably fit data being provided.

Rule: Always set your MAXLENGTH for a text form field.

Rule: Only allow a text field to scroll rightwards when there is a premium on screen real estate and the data to be entered is larger than the available screen region.

Rule: Never allow password fields to scroll.

Rule: Limit the length of password fields to match password sizes.

Rule: Do not use default values with password fields.

Rule: Set text wrapping in multiline text regions.

Suggestion: Consider vertically aligning related check boxes to decrease mouse travel.

Rule: Always check an initial radio button by default.

Rule: Use radio buttons for yes/no questions rather than pull-down menus or check boxes.

Suggestion: Avoid more than eight items in a radio group.

Suggestion: Use pull-downs if more than eight items are in a selection of one-choice-of-many to save screen real estate, as stated by this rule.

Rule: Do not use radio buttons for navigation.

Suggestion: Avoid changing the display of single-choice pull-down menus with the SIZE attribute.

Rule: Make the result of navigation pull-down clear by context, labels, and possibly a trigger button.

Rule: Make sure pull-down navigation degrades gracefully when JavaScript is off.

Rule: If a go button is shown onscreen with pull-down navigation, make sure the user can actually click it.

Rule: Reset a pull-down when users back out of a page as well as when they select separator items.

Suggestion: Avoid scrolled lists if you expect alternative browsing environments; use check boxes instead.

Rule: When using scrolled lists, make sure to provide some form of instructions for novice users on how to select multiple items.

Suggestion: Do not use default form-style push buttons for navigation; instead, reserve them to cause actions.

Rule: Provide a confirmation on a form reset button to avoid accidents.

Suggestion: Consider moving your reset button away from the submit button.

Rule: Provide a final chance before submitting important information or starting a difficult-to-reverse action.

Suggestion: Keep the submit button at the bottom of the form, either in the center or on the left side.

Suggestion: Provide a degradable state for image buttons with scripting or images off.

Suggestion: Generally, lay out form elements up to down, but consider left to right based on the context of the information being asked for.

Suggestion: Consider keeping table borders on when formatting table elements as they help associate labels and fields.

Suggestion: Imitate real-world forms directly if users are very used to filling them out; otherwise, focus on reducing the amount of data entry.

Rule: Make forms keyboard friendly.

Rule: Limit mouse travel between form elements.

Rule: Label all required fields carefully using an asterisk or the word *"required."*

Suggestion: Add TABINDEX attributes to improve form navigation.

Suggestion: Focus the first field of a form page immediately.

Rule: Do not override or mask browser accelerator keys.

Suggestion: Use accelerator keys for forms that will be used repeatedly.

Suggestion: Use ToolTips to provide extra information about field use and format.

Suggestion: Use the status bar to provide messages about field use.

Suggestion: Provide a help button near complex form fields for context-sensitive help.

Rule: Validate forms from the client side when possible.

Rule: Always provide backup validation on the server side.

Suggestion: Try to validate as people type, using masking, or as they move from field to field.

Rule: During form validation, provide a clear indication of what fields are in error and how to correct the error.

Rule: Bring immediate focus to fields in error.

Suggestion: Mask text fields to limit the type of characters entered.

Suggestion: Disable or hide fields that are not necessary in a particular context.

Suggestion: When setting fields to read only, change appearance or alert the user to the status of the field.

Suggestion: Provide defaults and always set values to the most likely entry.

Suggestion: Name your field names with simple common names to take advantage of browser AutoComplete features.

Rule: When using a tree control, make sure that open and close states are distinct.

Rule: Avoid mixing complex GUI interfaces within included binaries such as Java applets with Web page interfaces.

Web Technologies and Their Effect on Web Design

These rules and suggestions from Chapter 13 take a closer look at the underlying technologies of the Web and how they impact design.

Rule: Do not use bleeding-edge Web technology without good reason.

Rule: Beware of relying on published browser usage figures; track actual browser usage on YOUR site.

Rule: Users often don't blame browsers for simple errors—they blame sites.

Suggestion: To ensure success, use server-side detection for basic browser profiling.

Rule: Profile technical capabilities if possible, or assume the worst if you can't.

Suggestion: Pick a casing style for HTML and stick with it.

Suggestion: Be careful with casing of attribute values, particularly with filenames.

Rule: Validate all HTML pages.

Suggestion: Consider conforming to XHTML today to future-proof Web pages.

Rule: Separate HTML structure from presentation where possible, using CSS.

Rule: Test CSS rules very carefully.

Suggestion: Use external style sheets whenever possible.

Rule: Always comment out style blocks to avoid interpretation by older browsers.

Suggestion: Avoid relying solely on style sheets for layout unless non-CSS-compliant browsers can be limited or detected and dealt with.

Suggestion: Use CSS to overload HTML presentation elements like <FONT>.

Suggestion: Create HTML and CSS documents in the most suitable manner, rather than relying on only one tool or approach.

Suggestion: Use comments in HTML documents.

Suggestion: Create and use page templates.

Rule: Be consistent in HTML file naming—choose .htm or .html and stick to it.

Suggestion: Rely on standard XML languages rather than in-house-developed languages.

Suggestion: Use XML as a neutral storage format and for exchange.

Rule: Consider using both client- and server-side technologies in a site rather than one or the other.

Rule: Carefully monitor responsiveness of server-side technologies.

Rule: Create a capacity plan when using server-side technologies.

Suggestion: To improve CGI execution, consider compiling or rewriting heavily used programs in another language.

Suggestion: Using server-side technologies with complex URLs may confuse users.

Rule: Provide a fallback state for all client-side programming technologies.

Suggestion: Rely on helper applications when translation to a native Web form is impractical.

Suggestion: Focus on using only the more popular plug-in technologies unless automatic installation can be performed.

Suggestion: Use the <NOEMBED> syntax with plug-ins.

Rule: Provide installation assistance for plug-ins and helpers.

Rule: If ActiveX is used on a public site, make sure to provide alternatives for Netscape or other browsers.

Suggestion: Be clear and honest with users about security issues related to object technologies.

Rule: Consider end-user system performance carefully when using object technologies like Java.

Suggestion: Avoid building GUI interfaces within Web site interfaces using a binary technology like Java or ActiveX.

Suggestion: Make sure to test to see if a script works in all versions of the language.

Rule: Utilize object, method, and version checks in all scripts.

Rule: Comment out scripts and use a <NOSCRIPT> element to deal with nonscript-aware browsers.

Rule: Always add an error handler for JavaScripts.

Suggestion: Use linked scripts rather than inline ones when possible.

Rule: Practice good coding standards and consistent style in JavaScripts.

Suggestion: Inform users what cookies are used for in an easily found privacy policy or usage statement.

Suggestion: Avoid issuing multiple cookies.

Suggestion: Provide an alternative for users unwilling to accept cookies.

Rule: When trying to draw attention, avoid competing animations.

Rule: Avoid continuously running animation loops.

Suggestion: When linking to informational sounds such as speeches or audio broadcast excerpts, always indicate the length, format, and size of the sound file.

Suggestion: For download-and-play delivery, use WAV for low-quality music, sound effects, or speech.

Suggestion: Use MIDI files with long background music files, particularly when bandwidth is at a premium.

Rule: Predictable and error-free delivery of real-time data on the Internet cannot be guaranteed with today's protocols and usage.

Suggestion: Don't assume audio support. Always provide alternative forms of access for important audio-based content such as a text transcript.

Rule: Always allow a user to turn off continuously playing sounds.

Suggestion: Avoid video use unless the message is improved in this medium.

Site Delivery and Management

These rules and suggestions from Chapter 14 provide an overview of site delivery issues as they impact Web design, and the importance of designing sites with site management in mind.

Rule: The amount of bytes delivered to create a page is not as important as how fast the user perceives the page to be.

Suggestion: Try to keep the number of unique individual objects in a page small to reduce the number of HTTP requests.

Suggestion: Match data types, number of items, and size of data items to be delivered to the speed of the user's connection.

Rule: Predictable and error-free delivery of real-time data on the Internet cannot be reliably guaranteed with today's protocols and usage.

Suggestion: Provide numerous domain name forms for a site.

Suggestion: Make sure that domain name service for a Web site is fast and robust.

Suggestion: Don't skimp on Web server hardware and focus on systems with high-speed hard drives, a great deal of memory, and good network interfaces.

Suggestion: Don't choose an operating system for a Web server solely based on popularity; consider total cost of ownership and suitability for development and long-term maintenance.

Rule: Always strive to minimize network distance between a site and its users.

Suggestion: Choose to host your own Web site when security or control is a primary concern.

Suggestion: Utilize a monitoring tool or service to ensure that your site is constantly available to users.

Rule: Create, implement, and test a full-site security policy that goes beyond a simple firewall.

Suggestion: Avoid using underscores in filenames. Consider using dashes or no space between words.

Suggestion: Do not use mixed or uppercase letters in file or directory names.

Suggestion: Do not update on demand. Create a regular update schedule.

Rule: Do not work directly on a live site!

Rule: Check site links constantly.

Suggestion: Check regularly for page details including spelling, legal terms, and font usage. Perform a print test if necessary.

Suggestion: Provide the address webmaster@yourdomainname.com for users to contact you with suggestions and error reports.

Suggestion: Do not put a visible page counter on your site.

Rule: Analyze your log files carefully and use them to improve a site or measure its effectiveness.

Rule: Do not rely solely on log files to understand a site's effectiveness. You still have to talk to the site's users.

Rule: If you are collecting sensitive data online, post a privacy policy or statement in an obvious place on the site.

Rule: If your content is in any way questionable, have it PICS rated.

The Future of Web Design

These predictions and rules from Chapter 15 provide a look ahead into the near future of the Web. Some may eventually prove to be wrong, but odds are most of them will be useful to consider.

Prediction: HTML will still be around in some form or another for a great while.

Prediction: CSS will eventually be commonly used, relieving HTML of its presentation duties.

Prediction: Downloadable fonts will become commonplace.

Prediction: Hand-editing of HTML will become less commonplace as HTML becomes more structured and rules are enforced.

Prediction: Strict separation of structure, logic, and presentation of Web content will become more important.

Prediction: Databases will continue to store a large amount of Web content.

Prediction: XML languages will be well-accepted as neutral interchange languages.

Prediction: The uptake of XML will be slow, and the hurdle for adoption will be agreement between users.

Prediction: User-centered design will continue to be paramount.

Prediction: Broadband access will increase multimedia usage, but download will still be an issue.

Prediction: Interfaces should become more responsive and richer with broadband, but the bulk of bandwidth will be used for content.

Prediction: Simple text will continue to be an important content form because of its flexibility.

Prediction: Non-PC–based Web browsing will grow and will require different interface design considerations.

Prediction: Browsers will be less of a focus.

Prediction: Wireless Web access will focus on location- and time-sensitive information.

Prediction: Visualization interfaces will be limited to data set analysis and will not be used for navigation by most users.

Prediction: Bots will be useful in the near future for basic tasks, but an agent with any significant intelligence is far off.

Prediction: Users practicing a Web lifestyle will become even more impatient and less forgiving of Web sites.

Rule: The site's take away value is influenced by visuals, content, technology, usability, and goal accomplishment.

Rule: There is no form of "correct" Web design that fits every site.

Rule: Control should be given or at least appear to be given to the user.

Slogan: What You See Is What You Want (WYSIWYW).

The Complete Reference

Web Design

Appendix B

Sample Site-Evaluation Procedure

751

Evaluating a Web site is a very common task in Web development. When you are working on a site redesign, it is important to get a handle on the site's current strengths and weaknesses even though performing a site evaluation does not always involve a redesign. It can be useful to occasionally evaluate a site just to make sure you haven't missed anything. This appendix describes a basic method for site evaluation that will help guide Web developers looking at a site, and also includes a sample Site Evaluation form that you could use as a template. However, be careful not to look at this procedure as foolproof. The person running the evaluation can easily skew results. A person who is unfamiliar with the site being evaluated may pick out different things than someone who knows the site intimately.

This appendix presents each of the areas of a site that should be evaluated, along with an approach to testing each area. A sample form is included, and it's filled out with possible answers to illustrate the testing procedure, using www.democompany.com as the sample site. The appendix concludes with a blank form that can be used for your own testing. This form is available online at www.webdesignref.com/appendixB/evaluation.

Before you conduct a site analysis using the tips provided in this appendix, consider that this evaluation method is for designers. User testing should be performed in a totally different manner. A brief discussion about user testing is located at the end of this appendix. Remember that the answers to the questions in this evaluation method do not completely prove or disprove the effectiveness of a site. Be particularly careful when evaluating sites where you must make assumptions about purpose, audience, creation method, and so on. Without this information, the test taker will need to make assumptions in order to complete the evaluation. If these assumptions are incorrect, the associated conclusions could be equally incorrect. In short, use a site evaluation to help find positive or negative aspects of a site, but don't immediately assume that your site review will necessarily come to the same conclusions as someone else's evaluation.

Starting the Evaluation

When you begin an evaluation, it is important to stop and record some basic information. For example, note the URL of the site you are to evaluate, the date, the time, the person conducting the evaluation, and the reason for the evaluation. When you begin the evaluation you should block out some time to do the evaluation continuously; otherwise, it could adversely affect your impressions. Consider recording your end time to get an idea of how long it took to reach your conclusions.

Before you start the actual evaluation, stop and write down your first reaction. Hopefully, you aren't so familiar with the site that the first impression is tainted. If you are very familiar with the site, you might want to get a few other people, show them the site, and ask what they think on a scale from 1 to 5 (where 1 is the most negative feeling and 5 is the most positive). The point here is to gauge a first impression of a site. Unfortunately, a first impression is only accurate if it is truly the first time you are looking at a site. Don't discount this part of the test. Even though a first impression may be an emotional reaction heavily influenced by visuals or environment considerations, record it and try to understand what's causing your feeling. If users coming to a site have a very positive or negative first impression, it could certainly affect their desire to go further.

Preliminary Information

Here is the kind of preliminary information your evaluation should begin with. In this section, you should record basic information about the site, such as its name, the URL of its home page, when the site evaluation was conducted, and so on.

Sample Evaluation: Basic Information

Fill out the information on this sheet:

Site name:	*DemoCompany*
URL:	*http://www.democompany.com*
Purpose of evaluation:	*Sample evaluation for Web design book.*
Evaluated By:	*Thomas A. Powell*
Date:	*March 1, 2000*
Time:	*3 PM*
First Impression: 1 (poor)–5 (excellent)	*3*
Comments:	*Clean look. Fast load. Nothing too exciting.*

Navigation Pretest

After the first impression, you should perform a few pretests. The pretests allow you to make some logical assumptions that you will later verify. The first and probably the most telling is the navigation pretest. In this test, before you use the site, look at the home page and attempt to guess which areas of the screen are clickable. You may consider printing the page and circling the hot spots. Once you have evaluated the whole page, go back and verify your intuition. You will probably find that some areas of the page do not obviously look like navigation.

Sample Evaluation: Navigation Pretest

Print the page or do not touch anything. Identify clickable areas on the screen by visual inspection, then test to see if your intuition was correct.

Number of believed clickable areas:	*19*
Actual number of clickable areas:	*19*
Accuracy:	*100%*
Comments:	*Home page identifies clickable areas rather well.*

Identity Pretest

Another useful pretest would be to take a good look at the site's home page and take a guess at who owns the site, and what kind of site it is. First try to determine what kind of organization is represented by the site. Try to determine if its primary focus is commercial, educational, governmental, entertainment, and so on. Try to be very specific and identify the exact organization behind the site if you can from your initial impression.

Sample Question: Whose site is it, anyway?

Based solely on the information presented, identify site owner and describe general type of site:
This site appears to be created by the Demo Corporation. This doesn't necessarily seem to be a real company. The true identity of the site owner is somewhat hidden on the homepage but is an organization called PINT.

Purpose Pretest

Next, consider the purpose of the site. What are users supposed to accomplish at the site? Again, stick with your first impression from the home page.

Sample Question: What is the purpose of the site?

Based upon quick inspection, identify the basic points of the site. What basic functions would it likely provide?
The purpose of the site would appear to be a demonstration of sorts based upon its name. However, the teaching or demonstration aspect of the site seems to be downplayed, making it appear that the company is serious about selling a variety of cartoonish futuristic products, which are obviously not real.

Audience Pretest

The last pretest can be very important: who is the site actually built for? For some sites—particularly those that you may not have much involvement in—performing a site evaluation may be much like an archaeologist looking at an ancient civilization's ruins. Making guesses about the purpose, use, and users of a particular aspect of a Web site will be almost as difficult to make as what an archaeologist faces when looking at a few stones from a large structure. Try to identify the site's intended user base from your initial impression.

Sample Question: What audience is this site intended for?

Based upon quick inspection, consider who the audience for the site would be.
This site would be for beginning-to-intermediate Web developers and designers looking to study the site's features as well as well as its technical details. If it were a real site, its audience would probably be the general public in the future, looking to buy a variety of consumer items like robots or space cars.

General Site Characteristics

Before you start serious evaluation of a site, it is important to get some general characteristics about the site: how big it is, how is it organized, how it is delivered, and a general idea of the kinds of areas to focus on later in the analysis. For example, if the site is a very visually oriented—one with little content or technology used, you may want to ask why this is the case, and pay special attention to the visual design details.

If the site is an e-commerce site with relatively spartan visuals, you may want to concentrate more on the technical and functional tests. Many of the statistics about a site, such as the number of pages in the site, are easily available using a tool such as Linkbot (www.linkbot.com) or

COAST WebMaster (www.coast.com). Simply use one of these maintenance tools to probe the site and it should produce a report like the one shown in Figure B-1.

Site Structure

Understanding the structure of a site is useful in numerous ways. The easiest way to visualize a site's structure is through the use of a site diagram or flowchart as shown in Figure B-2.

There are tools that can create such diagrams automatically, but you may find that it is easier just to create one by hand. When looking at site structure, make sure to look at issues such as page depth, orphaned files, and broken links. Tools such as Linkbot (www.linkbot.com) can analyze a site quickly for such problems.

Once you've clicked around the site for a while, you should have some idea of how the site is structured. Refer back to the basic site stuctures discussed in Chapter 4. More things to consider: does the site provide a diagram of its own structure? Are there broken links? And are there clear entrance/exit pages?

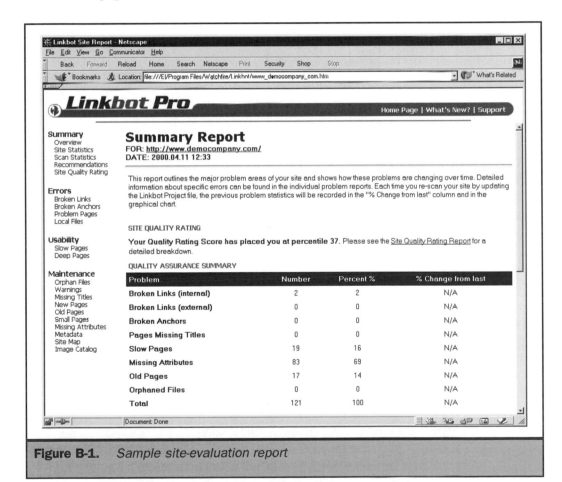

Figure B-1.   *Sample site-evaluation report*

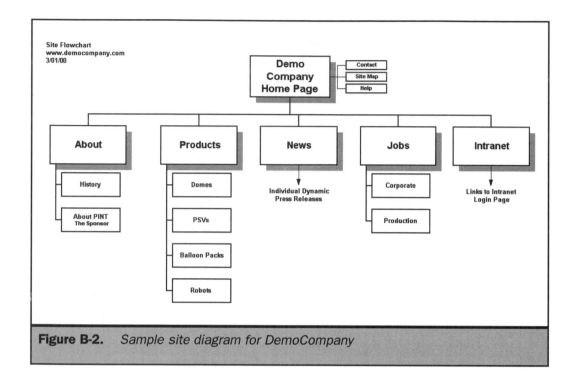

Figure B-2.   *Sample site diagram for DemoCompany*

Sample Question: What sort of structure does this site employ?

Describe the site structure:

- ❏ Linear
- ❏ Grid
- ☑ *Tree/Hierarchy*
- ❏ Mixed Tree
- ❏ Pure Web

Provide a site diagram?

- ☑ *Yes*
- ❏ No

Are there any broken links in the site?
Yes, there are 2.
If yes, are they broken links to external sites or internal pages?

- ❏ External
- ☑ *Internal*
- ❏ Both

What is the maximum page depth in the site?
(clicks from the home page)
<u>2</u>

Are there orphaned files in the site?

❑ Yes

☑ *No*

Are there clear entrance and exit pages to the site?

❑ Yes

☑ *No*

Describe:
<u>*The home page serves as a clear entrance, but there are no obvious conclusion pages other than the content*</u>
<u>*pages themselves.*</u>

Delivery

How the site is delivered is extremely important to understanding the site's usability. Users appreciate fast downloads, but as discussed in Chapter 14, speed of delivery is often influenced by many factors beyond the size of files being delivered. It is important to understand the server resources used to deliver a site, including both hardware and software used. It is also important to understand how the site is hosted. How the site eventually connects to the Internet can impact performance greatly. Using even simple network tools like ping, it is possible to determine the responsiveness of a server. Many operating systems provide this tool; for example, under Windows, access the DOS prompt and type **ping** and a host name. If you typed **ping www.pint.com** you might see something like this:

```
C:\WINDOWS>ping www.pint.com

Pinging www.pint.com [207.110.46.123] with 32 bytes of data:

Reply from 207.110.46.123: bytes=32 time=21ms TTL=245
Reply from 207.110.46.123: bytes=32 time=20ms TTL=245
Reply from 207.110.46.123: bytes=32 time=18ms TTL=245
Reply from 207.110.46.123: bytes=32 time=20ms TTL=245

Ping statistics for 207.110.46.123:
  Packets: Sent = 4, Received = 4, Lost = 0 (0% loss),
Approximate round trip times in milli-seconds:
  Minimum = 18ms, Maximum = 21ms, Average = 19ms
```

The round-trip time of data can be used to get a general sense of the responsiveness of the server. It is also possible to determine other server and network information using tools like WHOIS, traceroute, nslookup, and others. On Windows, most of these tools are either included in the operating system, can be found in the public domain, or are nicely packaged in network tools like WS_Ping ProPack (http://www.ipswitch.com/). After server and network issues, the size of the pages delivered should be considered. Most site-analysis tools will identify pages that are considered large. You can set the threshold for what is considered large, byte-wise, in most of the programs, but some consider anything over 30–50KB a large page despite the rise in popularity of faster Internet access. Theoretical download times under a variety of line speeds can also be determined with a site-analysis tool, and most Web page editors like HomeSite or Dreamweaver even provide facilities to determine page weight and download speed. However, do not rely solely on theoretical times; test the site under actual conditions if possible. Since network conditions are always changing site delivery, test results may vary greatly from moment to moment.

Site Delivery Characteristics

This area may require the use of a site-analysis tool. The purpose of this section is to evaluate how the site is delivered, and how well. Identifying the hardware and software used to host the site, the bandwidth available from the server, page sizes, and other related questions will help you get a good idea of the quality of the site's delivery.

Sample Question: What are the details of how this site is delivered to the end user?

Describe hardware used if possible:
Pentium II 400Mhz with 128MB of RAM

What operating system is used on the Web server?
Windows NT Server

What Web server software with version number is being used?
Microsoft IIS 4.0

Where is the site being hosted?

- ☑ *Internally*
- ❒ Externally

Who is the closest "upstream" Internet Service Provider from server?
ConnectNet

What is the amount of bandwidth available for the server if known or determinable?
T1

Rate the responsiveness of the server 1 (very slow) –5 (very fast)

- ❒ 1
- ❒ 2
- ❒ 3
- ☑ 4
- ❒ 5

What is the largest page in the site byte-wise?
Home Page–99KB

What is the average page size in the site?
_23KB_

What are the theoretical download times for the average and worst pages at:
Modem speeds (56Kbps) _____
ISDN (128Kbps) _____
Cable (600Kbps +) _____
DSL/T1/Ethernet (1Mbps +) _____

Are real download times similar?

☐ Yes

☑ _No_

If no, provide times for tested speeds: _____

Visuals and Layout

Evaluating the look and feel of a site can be difficult because they are often too intertwined with personal taste. However, execution of images and layout should be evaluated regardless of your personal take on a site's aesthetics. Images may not be used properly or optimized correctly. There may be color problems in the site, font-sizing issues, and page-layout problems. In many cases the page layout may not even fit the screen resolution or print correctly. Pay particular attention to testing the site under less-than-ideal conditions. In many cases, a site's layout will completely fall apart when images are turned off or font sizes modified. When doing the visual portion of a site evaluation, it is important to print out a screen capture of the evaluated page as it may change over time. Screen printouts can be marked up to then draw attention to both problem areas as well as interesting features.

Sample Visuals and Layout Questions

Now you can begin to consider design and layout issues in your evaluation. This section covers general impressions of the images and visuals used on the site, and specifics such as optimization, functionality of images, and if the layout holds up or "breaks" under various browser sizes and screen resolutions.

Sample Question: How effective/appropriate are the layout and visuals employed on this site?

Describe the visuals used in the site:
Colorful, well-contrasted, a bit garish

Do you like the visuals?

☑ _Yes_

☐ No

Why or why not?
They appeal to my complete lack of good taste.

Are the visuals purely decorative or do theyadd to the site's function or information?

- ❏ Only decoration
- ☑ *Improve function*

Print out the home page as well as a sub-page and content page. Mark up the printouts to illustrate previous answers. (See Figure B-3.)

Describe the layout of the home page:
Relatively uncluttered, good color coordination

Describe the layout of a typical sub-page:
Reasonable text area near center/right of page, with top graphics for navigation, plus subsidiary nav graphics on the left side

Describe the layout of a content page:
Pretty much same as above.

How is the screen contrast? 1 (poor) –5 (excellent)

- ❏ 1
- ❏ 2
- ❏ 3
- ❏ 4
- ☑ *5*

If bad, describe why:

Describe text size:

- ❏ Too small
- ☑ *Just right*
- ❏ Too large

Change browser text size large or smaller. Does the layout still work?

- ☑ *Yes*
- ❏ No

Resize the browser very large or very small. Does the layout still work?

- ☑ *Yes*
- ❏ No

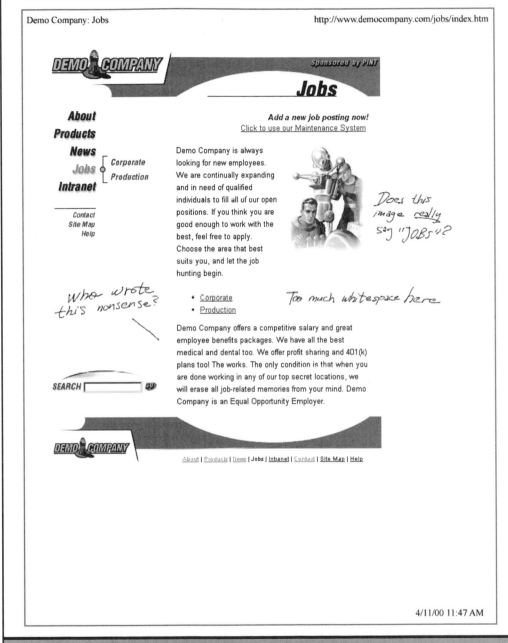

Figure B-3.   *Printed page marked up*

Is the layout static (stay the same size) or does it grow with the screen size?

- ☑ *Static*
- ☐ Stretchable

If the site has a static width does the page fit or is there right-ward scrolling at:
640 × 480?

- ☑ *Fits*
- ☐ Scrolls right

800 × 600?

- ☑ *Fits*
- ☐ Scrolls right

1,024 × 768 and greater?

- ☑ *Fits*
- ☐ Scrolls right

With respect to vertical screen size does the primary navigation fit on screen at:
640 × 480?

- ☐ Fits
- ☑ *Scrolls off*

800 × 600?

- ☑ *Fits*
- ☐ Scrolls off

1,024 × 768 and greater?

- ☑ *Fits*
- ☐ Scrolls off

Note: You may want to perform this test at resolutions other than those mentioned depending on your target platform.

Do pages print correctly?

- ☑ *Yes*
- ☐ No

What kind of images are used in the site?

- ☑ *GIF*
- ☑ *JPEG*
- ☐ PNG
- ☐ Other

Are the images generally used correctly?
(e.g., GIF for illustrations, JPEG for photos)

☑ *Yes*

❏ No

Are the images optimized properly?
(e.g., small file size, safe colors)

☑ *Yes*

❏ No

Are there image-execution problems?
(e.g., color matching, seams showing in background tiles, etc.)

❏ Yes

☑ *No*

If yes, describe:

Is ALT text used for images?

❏ Yes

❏ No

☑ *Partially*

Is the site usable without images?

❏ Yes

❏ No

☑ *Partially*

Content

The quality of a site beyond first impressions of design or technology is heavily influenced by the freshness and quality of content presented. A site's content should be appropriate in quantity, not so much that it is difficult to find appropriate information easily, but not so little that the user is left wanting more. The content should also be up-to-date and accurate. Execution issues such as spelling, grammar, and tone should also be well considered. Finally, the details of the site should be very carefully examined. Truly, with Web sites the devil is in the details. Copyright dates, trademarks, product names, and very small formatting errors are often glaring to the user and may ruin an otherwise excellent experience.

The best way to evaluate content is to do a careful screen-and-paper walk-through. Printing pages out and going over each one very carefully is probably the best way to find typos and consistency issues. However, many Web maintenance tools and even page editors can be used to spell-check pages. When looking for details, it is tough to spot everything; fortunately, some Web site maintenance tools such as COAST WebMaster (www.coast.com) could be used to search for term consistency through the use of custom rules that look for the inclusion of certain key phrases.

General-Content Statistics

As you move in deeper through the site, you will experience more of the site's content. Once you've looked at this for a while, you might wish to assess the amount and quality of the content with questions such as the following.

Sample Question: How much content is in the site, and how effective is it?

Approximate number of content pages in the site: _____
Percentage of content pages in site:
xx% (content pages / total pages) × 100 _____

Content Qualities

Is there enough detail to answer simple questions?

☑ *Yes*
☐ No

Is there enough content detail to answer complex questions?

☐ Yes
☑ *No*

Does content appear accurate and truthful?

☐ Yes
☑ *No*

If no describe what suggests this belief:
It's a fake company site.

Are there obvious misspellings in the site?

☐ Yes
☑ *No*

Are there egregious spelling errors such as misspellings in buttons or headlines?

☐ Yes
☑ *No*

Are there obvious grammar or usage errors in the site?

☐ Yes
☑ *No*

If yes, describe these errors:
(e.g., fragments, run-ons, heavy use of acronyms without explanation)
_n/a_

Describe the tone of content in the site:
(e.g. playful, business-like, serious, humorous)
The tone is playful and humorous.

Does the tone of content fit what is presented?

☑ *Yes*

☐ No

If no, describe why not:

Is content updated on the site?

☑ *Yes*

☐ No

Is update necessary?

☑ *Yes*

☐ No

Answer the following questions only if content is being actively updated.

If content requires update, is it fresh?

☐ Yes

☐ No

☑ *Partially*

On average how often does it appear the content is updated?

☐ Daily

☐ Weekly

☑ *Monthly*

☐ Yearly

☐ Other

How was freshness determined?
(copyright, label of last update, etc.)
Dates of press releases and changing job postings

Technology Usage

As discussed in Chapter 1, Web design relies heavily on technology ranging from simple markup languages to complex programming approaches. When evaluating a site you have full access to, it is possible to look not only at client-side technologies such as HTML but to examine server-side technologies such as CGI programs or databases. Unfortunately, when examining sites externally, you may be limited to looking only at technology easily viewed at the browser or the effect of technology executed on a server. For some evaluators it may be appropriate to call in a professional programmer to evaluate the quality of examined code, as glaring errors may escape those who are only familiar enough with CGI or JavaScript to use a canned script.

HTML

Because HTML serves as the bedrock of a Web site, particular focus should be paid to the accuracy and quality of HTML. Compliance to HTML standards should be examined by validating key pages in the site. Online validators such as http://validator.w3.org can be used, but readers may find stand-alone validation tools like CSE Validator (http://www. htmlvalidator.com) to be superior. Figure B-4 shows this validator in action.

Proprietary tag usage or trick HTML should be carefully noted. Inspection **<META>** tags, comments, and other small signs such as consistent page formats should be noted to help determine how HTML was created, such as with a tool or by hand. If it is possible to directly query the developer, ask which tools were used and what standards were followed. Using the following section, rate the HTML used on the site.

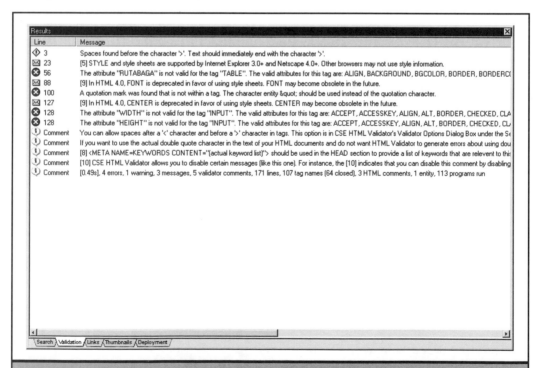

Figure B-4.   *Example of HTML validation*

Sample Question: What is the nature and quality of the HTML usage on this site?

<u>HTML</u>
Version(s) used:

- ☐ HTML 2.0
- ☐ HTML 3.2
- ☑ *HTML 4.0 Transitional*
- ☐ HTML 4.0 Strict
- ☐ XHTML
- ☐ No consistent compliance

Proprietary tag use:

- ☑ *Yes*
- ☐ No

Examples:
<u>*Used TOPMARGIN attribute for the BODY tag.*</u>

Home-page validation

- ☑ *Pass*
- ☐ Fail

Comments:

Sub-page validation:

- ☑ *Pass*
- ☐ Fail

Comments:

Style of HTML 1 (poor) –5 (excellent)
(e.g., tag case, formatting, comments, etc.)

- ☐ 1
- ☐ 2
- ☐ 3
- ☐ 4
- ☑ *5*

HTML style consistency 1 (poor/many styles) –5 (excellent/strict guidelines)

- ❏ 1
- ❏ 2
- ❏ 3
- ❏ 4
- ☑ *5*

Method of creation:

- ❏ By hand
- ☑ *Editor*
  Editor(s) used: HomeSite
- ❏ Translator (e.g. Save as…)
  From what: _____
- ❏ Dynamically created
  Method: _____

CSS

Cascading style sheets are rapidly become an important technology for presenting Web pages. CSS use provides a major benefit because it can be used to separate document structure from presentation. However, unless the site uses external style sheets, this benefit is reduced. Document-wide style sheets or inline styles are adequate, but their use should be considered less than ideal. Regardless of the method of including style rules, extreme care must be taken with CSS given all the browser bugs and rendering differences. Compliance to the CSS1 and CSS2 standards may not be as important as making sure the various CSS properties work under common browsers. Close attention should also be paid to the types of rules used and whether or not there is any problem with browsers using pages that do not support CSS. Testing with an older browser or with the CSS facilities turned off should be performed.

Using the followiing section, assess the extent and quality of CSS usage on the site.

Sample question: How much CSS is used on the site, and how effectively?

CSS
Version(s) used:

- ❏ CSS1
- ❏ CSSP (Positioning features)
- ☑ *CSS2*
- ❏ CSS3

Proprietary properties:

- ❏ Yes
- ☑ *No*

If yes, provide examples:

Do all CSS rules work correctly?

- ☑ *Yes*
- ❑ No

CSS rules inclusion method(s)

- ❑ Linked style sheet
- ☑ *Document-wide style sheet*

Inline style
Quality of rules 1 (poor) –5 (excellent)
(e.g., simplicity, style, naming)

- ❑ 1
- ❑ 2
- ❑ 3
- ☑ 4
- ❑ 5

CSS use consistency 1 (poor/many styles) –5 (excellent/strict guidelines)

- ❑ 1
- ❑ 2
- ❑ 3
- ❑ 4
- ☑ *5*

Method of creation

- ☑ *By hand*
- ❑ Editor
  Editor(s) used: _____
- ❑ Translator (e.g. Save as…)
  From what: _____
- ❑ Dynamically created
  Method: _____

Degradability (works without CSS)

- ❑ Perfect degradation
- ☑ *Degradation with subtle cosmetic differences*
- ❑ Degradation with serious differences in appearance
- ❑ Significant layout problems without CSS

XML

XML will likely be an important base-level technology for the sites of tomorrow. The reality is that its use today is mostly limited to non–browser-based communication or server-side files that are eventually translated into HTML, or into HTML and CSS. If XML is used, compatibility should be a major concern. Even when XML is used in a way that is not exclusive, make sure to investigate the language being used to determine if it is proprietary or a standard language, and if its document type is easy to understand. Nothing is worse in Web design than creating a special markup language that only a few people can understand.

Sample Question: Is XML used on the site, and how effectively?

XML
XML used?

□ Yes

☑ *No*

If yes, where is it used (client-side or server-side)?

If present, what is it used for?

□ Data storage

□ Document structure

□ Data exchange

□ For presentation using CSS or XSL

Name of XML language used: *n/a*
Proprietary language? *n/a*
DTD available? *n/a*

DTD clarity 1 (complex/confusing) –5 (simple/commented)

□ 1

□ 2

□ 3

□ 4

□ 5

Is the site usable with non–XML-aware browsers?

☑ *Yes*

□ No

If no, describe how dealt with:

Programming

As mentioned in Chapter 13, a variety of programming technologies are at the disposal of Web developers. While client-side programming technologies like JavaScript tend to be easy to include and very responsive, they often are used dangerously, causing many bugs to occur. Very commonly, a site will fail on the Internet when a simple change is made to a browser, such as turning off JavaScript support. Poor performance, error messages, and even browser crashes are unfortunately too common when client-side technologies are misused. Server-side technologies, such as CGI or ColdFusion, however, don't tend to rely as much on browser conditions and thus tend to be more robust. However, these technologies often result in less-than-stellar performance, particularly when server issues haven't been adequately addressed. Server-side technologies may be difficult to examine, although if you are not evaluating your own site, you may be limited to doing only a cursory inspection of their use.

Server-side Technology

Use the following section to evaluate the use of server-side technologies on the site, if applicable.

Sample Questions: Server-side Technology Use

<u>Server-side</u>
Are server-side programming facilities used?

☑ *Yes*

❏ No

Which ones?

❏ CGI (using Perl, C, etc.)

☑ *Cold Fusion (.cfm)*

❏ Active Server Pages (.asp)

❏ PHP (.php)

❏ Java Server Pages (.jsp)

❏ Server-APIs (ISAPI, NSAPI)

❏ Other

Describe usage of server-side technologies:
(e.g., form processing, dynamic page generation, etc.)

Describe the performance of the server application:

Describe any errors encountered:

Is a database used in the site?

☑ *Yes*

◻ No

Describe how the database is used:

Client-side Scripting: JavaScript/DHTML
JavaScript used?

☑ *Yes*

◻ No

If yes, describe uses:

How are scripts included?

◻ Directly in document

◻ Linked to external .js file

Script functions properly?

☑ *Yes*

◻ No

JavaScript version(s)
(check all that apply)

◻ 1.0

◻ 1.1

◻ 1.2

◻ 1.3

◻ Other

JavaScript style 1 (convoluted/not commented) –5 (clear/well commented)

◻ 1

◻ 2

☑ *3*

◻ 4

◻ 5

Degradable?
(works on older browsers or without scripting)

☑ *Yes*

☐ No

Note | *VBScript could be analyzed in a similar manner but is omitted for this discussion.*

Client-side Component Technology

Use the following section to evaluate the use of client-side technologies on the site, if applicable.

Sample Questions: Client-side Technology Use

<u>Java</u>
Are Java applets used?

☐ Yes

☐ No

If yes, describe how used and applet(s) name:

Degradable?
(warning messages or alternate for no Java) *n/a*

Are there functionality problems?
(e.g., errors) *n/a*

Performance problems? *n/a*

Security problems? *n/a*

<u>ActiveX</u>

Are ActiveX controls used?

☑ *Yes*

☐ No

If yes, describe how used and control(s) name:
Macromedia Flash is used on a demo.

Does the site work properly without ActiveX controls?

☑ *Yes*

☐ No

Are there functionality problems?
(e.g., errors)

   ❐ Yes

   ☑ *No*

Performance problems?

   ❐ Yes

   ☑ *No*

Security problems?

   ❐ Yes

   ☑ *No*

<u>**Netscape Plug-ins**</u>

Are Netscape plug-ins used?

   ☑ *Yes*

   ❐ No

If yes, describe how used and plug-in(s) name:
<u>*Macromedia Flash*</u>

If a plug-in is not present, is assistance provided to obtain it?
<u>*No, degrades gracefully though*</u>

Does the site work properly without plug-ins?

   ☑ *Yes*

   ❐ No

Are there functionality problems?
(e.g., errors)

   ❐ Yes

   ☑ *No*

Performance problems?

   ❐ Yes

   ☑ *No*

Security problems?

   ❐ Yes

   ☑ *No*

Cookies

For many, the use of cookies appears to be an invasion of personal privacy. The reality of cookies is that they are very useful to get around the limitations that are caused mainly by HTTP protocol. However, regardless of your personal take on cookies, it is important to understand whether a site uses them and what they are used for. Some sites may even issue multiple cookies per visit, each with different purposes. Careful inspection of cookie data can yield valuable clues to how a site works. If cookies are used, it is important to verify that the site still works with cookies off. Also, if cookies are used, a policy indicating what they are used for should be available on the site.

Use the following section to evaluate the use of cookies, if any, on the site.

Sample Question: Are cookies used on the site?

<u>Cookies</u>
Are cookies used on the site?

❒ Yes

❒ No

If yes, describe their use:

Is a privacy policy used on the site explaining cookie use?

❒ Yes

❒ No

How many cookies are set? _____

What is the format of the cookie? _____
If cookies are used does the site work with cookies support off?

❒ Yes

❒ No

Browser Support

Probably the most well-known aspect of site testing is browser support. Many discussions about site testing state simply to test in as many browsers as possible. The reality is that you should attempt to create a matrix of the various different browsers and perform the technology and layout tests within each browser individual. Oddly, you may find that there is a subtle rendering difference in each browser, as well as numerous bugs. A large matrix showing all the different versions of each browser and each operating system is the best way to conduct a browser test. Unfortunately, you may find that there are literally dozens of versions of just the 4.*x* generation of Netscape. Because of the difficulty of testing so many combinations, you may want to focus on those browsers that are known to use your site. In some cases, such as with an intranet, the browser being used may be obvious. Before guessing which browsers a site's users commonly use, however, consider accessing the log files to make sure.

Browser Issues

Use the following section to evaluate the sites compatibility with different browsers.

Sample Question: What browsers does the site work or not work with?

Browsers
Site works in Netscape?

☑ *Yes*
❏ No

What versions?
2.x to latest, with some support for 1.x generation browsers

Site works in Internet Explorer?

☑ *Yes*
❏ No

What versions?
2.x to latest

Other browsers supported?
Opera

Does site identify a browser that it does not work in?
No, though the site appears to work in nearly all modern browsers

If compatibility problems exist, are they explained in the site?

❏ Yes
☑ *No*

Navigation

Chapters 5–8 discuss site navigation. Recall that navigation is concerned with how efficiently a user can move around the site. Remember that one of the most important aspects of usable navigation is consistency. Consistency of navigation should include both the style of navigation as well as the placement of navigational elements. A navigation hierarchy should be used that clearly indicates important global navigation elements distinctly from local navigational elements. Having different-sized navigational items or placing the navigation in a different position on the screen is often effective in creating such a hierarchy. The number of navigational choices should

APPENDIXES

be considered on pages. Pages with too few choices may require a great number of clicks. However, a page laden with navigational choices may overwhelm the user. The various navigation labels should be closely inspected. The ordering, type, and even wording of labels can greatly affect the understandability of the navigation. Navigation elements—like buttons— may utilize a variety of feedback methods, such as link color, animation, or tool tips to help users understand how to use things.

General Navigation

Use the following section to evaluate general site navigation.

Sample Question: How effective is general site navigation?

<u>Navigation</u>
Placement of navigation elements:
(check one or more)

☐ Top
☐ Bottom Left
☐ Right

Consistency of navigation placement 1 (random) –5 (very stable)

☐ 1
☐ 2
☐ 3
☑ 4
☐ 5

Comments on navigation placement:

Navigation hierarchy used?

☐ Yes
☐ No

Describe:

Average number of navigation items per page: _____
Average number of navigation items per navigation cluster: _____
Are alternate forms of navigation provided?

☑ *Yes*
☐ No

Describe:
Text links on the bottom of the page, search filed, site map.

Does navigation in the site rely on the back button?

❏ Yes
❏ No

Navigation label clarity 1 (unclear) –5 (very clear)

❏ 1
❏ 2
❏ 3
❏ 4
❏ 5

Scope notes used for labels?

❏ Yes
❏ No

Tool tips used?

❏ Yes
❏ No

What is the organization of navigation labels?

❏ Alphabetical
❏ Importance
❏ Random
❏ Other

What forms of navigation feedback are employed?

☑ *Font type*
☑ *Font size*
☑ *Color*
☑ *Position*
☑ *Looks pressable*
❏ Underlined
☑ *Rollovers*
❏ Sound
❏ Other

Is the feedback useful?

☐ Yes

☐ No

Discuss:

Are link colors modified from the blue, red, and purple?

☐ Yes

☑ *No*

If yes, is the color combination logical?

How is location indicated?

☑ *URL*

☑ *Page label*

☑ *Deselected labels*

☐ Depth gauge

☐ XXXX

☐ Color

☐ Design style

Are frames used?

☐ Yes

☑ *No*

If yes, are they for navigation or layout?

Can pages be bookmarked?

☑ *Yes*

☐ No

Is there helpful information with broken links (404 errors)?

☑ *Yes*

☐ No

If yes, describe:
A custom page indicating the broken link that fits with the site design is presented. It moves the user to the site or encourages them to contact the organization.

Is there helpful information when page have been moved?

☐ Yes

☐ No

Describe:

Search

Increasingly, site users are relying more and more on search systems to locate desired content. First, determine if a search system is used on a site. If not, consider if the site would be improved with an internal search engine. When evaluating the search facility, first consider how it is accessed. Is a small search field directly included in a page or is there a separate search page? When search is included, does it fit with the design of the site? Next, consider the type of search. Is it a simple free text search or are there parameters that can be modified to refine the search? Is the search form easy to understand? Are there instructions explaining the more complicated features of the search?

Testing the search system will require you to run both positive and negative queries. First, try to run a query that will not return anything like a nonsense word. Does the negative result provide any helpful information explaining what might have gone wrong or provide other suggestions on how to get a meaningful result. Now, try to just enter nothing in a search field and see what happens. Finally, try to enter a legitimate query. Are the results reasonable? If the results are large, is it possible to refine the search? Finally, the most interesting test for the search facility is to find an interesting page or fact within the site and try to find it with the search engine. Search evaluation can be very complex. Make sure to review Chapter 7 before you do this test. You may want to print out the search page and examples of positive and negative results for detail checking.

Use the following section to evaluate the site's search capabilties, if any.

Sample Question: Does the site have a search system, and how well does it work?

<u>Search</u>
Does site have an internal search system?

❏ Yes

❏ No

If no, should one be included?

❏ Yes

❏ No

Reason:

How is search accessed?

❏ Within page

❏ Separate page

❏ Both

Search integrated with design?

☑ *Yes*

❐ No

Type of search:

❐ Free text

❐ Parametric

❐ Both

If parametric, describe search parameters:

Search forms:

❐ Simple

❐ Advanced

❐ Both

Clarity of search form 1 (poor) –5 (excellent)

❐ 1

❐ 2

❐ 3

❐ 4

❐ 5

Instructions for search form included?

❐ Yes

❐ No

Negative query provide reasonable result and help?

❐ Yes

❐ No

Positive queries provide reasonable results?

❐ Yes

❐ No

Refinement of queries easily performed?

❐ Yes

❐ No

Known item searching accuracy 1 (poor/ not found) –5 (excellent/#1 position)

☐ 1

☐ 2

☐ 3

☐ 4

☐ 5

Navigation Aids

Web sites often rely on navigation aids beyond search aids, in particular, site maps or occasionally alphabetical site indexes. Some sites may even include glossaries. A complete discussion of these types of aids can be found in Chapter 8. During evaluation, look for each navigation aid and consider its usefulness. If an aid is missing, should it be included? You may want to print out a screen snapshot of each aid for your final report. Like other printouts, it can be marked up with callouts to interesting features or problems.

Use the following section to evaluate the site's extended navigational aids (site maps, glossaries, etc.).

Sample Question: Does the site offer additional navigation aids?

<u>Site Map</u>
Site map included?

☑ *Yes*

☐ No

If no, should a site map be included?

☐ Yes

☐ No

Reason:

Method to access site map?

☐ Link on all pages

☐ Link on one or few pages

☐ Help system or search engine

What is the scope of the site map?

☐ Whole site

☐ Most pages

☐ Main sections

☐ Unknown scope

What is the format of the site map?

❏ Graphical

❏ Text

Static or dynamic site map?

❏ Static

❏ Dynamic

If static, is it up to date?

❏ Yes

❏ No

Comments on site map:

Site Index

Is a site index used?

❏ Yes

❏ No

If no, should a site index be included?

❏ Yes

❏ No

Reason:

Method to access site index?

❏ Link on all pages

❏ Link on one or few pages

❏ Help system or search engine

What is the scope of the index?

❏ All topics

❏ Main topics

❏ Unknown selection of topics

Static or dynamic site index?

❏ Static

❏ Dynamic

If static, is it up to date?

☐ Yes

☐ No

Comments on site index:

Glossary

Glossary included?

☐ Yes

☑ *No*

If no, should a site term glossary be included?

☐ Yes

☐ No

Reason:

What is the method to access glossary?

☐ Link on all pages

☐ Link on one or few pages

☐ From the help page

Number of terms in glossary: _____

Comments on glossary:

Help System

The site should contain some form of help system. Minimally clear contact information, such as a Webmaster address, should be obviously provided. Documentation online also would be useful, particularly if the site uses uncommon technology or has sophisticated navigation. Any help system provided should be obviously accessible throughout the site.

Use this section to evaluate the site's help system.

Sample Question: Does the site have a Help system? If yes, evaluate.

<u>Help</u>
Basic contact information:

❒ Yes

❒ No

Contact for Web-specific problems:

❒ Yes

❒ No

Online Help system?

❒ Yes

❒ No

Describe:

The Final Score

Now that you have evaluated many aspects of a site, consider what you would give the site as a final score. You don't have to be very scientific about your final rating; simply consider—given how much you know now about the site—whether you think it is a great site or not. Would you take away a positive, neutral, or negative feeling about the site? Consider listing out a few of the reasons that made you skew one way or another.

Final Score 1 (dislike) –5 (like a lot)

❒ 1

❒ 2

❒ 3

☑ 4

❒ 5

Key reasons for final score:
The site never broke and it illustrated many ideas ranging from database driven pages to clean simple design. The writing was funny, but it didn't really wow with me with an amazing new look or fancy new features.

Evaluation Form

A copy of a blank evaluation is provided here for you to photocopy and print if you like. If you desire an electronic copy, an Adobe Acrobat version is provided online at www.webdesignref.com/appendixB/evaluation. Modifications or format improvements to the evaluation can be returned to the author at tpowell@pint.com and will be shared with the Web design community via the book's support site.

Beyond Developer Evaluation: Log Analysis and User Test

While this evaluation process is useful to uncover many types of site problems, it is important to not limit evaluations just to inspection. Developers may be much more critical of certain types of details and they may completely miss problems commonly encountered by users. Furthermore, this form of evaluation says little about how users actually use a site. Looking at log files can provide valuable insight into how a site is used. Log files will show who is looking at a site (by IP address or domain name), what pages users commonly look at, when they look at these pages, the paths users take through a site, the links followed to get to a site, and even what kind of browsers are being used. The log file can be used in place of assumptions made during evaluation or to verify assumptions.

While log files provide a great deal of useful information, they really say very little about a user's feelings about a site. The best way to evaluate a site is to watch how users actually use a site and try to solicit feedback from them. Be careful to try to watch user's without them knowing; if you ask users to take a usability test, you may find that they pay more attention or try harder to figure things out than they would normally. Also, if you ask users to evaluate a site, don't guide them through it. If you co-pilot the users' browsing session, they may uncover only what you want them to and may not use the site as it was intended. The best way to learn about how users feel about a site is to simply try to casually observe them using the site. If you are testing a site such as an intranet, just look over their shoulder and watch how they do things. You should also ask users to provide feedback on whether or not they like a site or if they found it frustrating.

A good way to understand a site's usability is by setting up some common tasks for users to complete and watching them try to complete the task. During your own evaluation you can come up with simple tasks to perform and test yourself, but it is better to use real users for this part of a site evaluation. You can certainly be very scientific about user testing in this fashion using two-way mirrors, recorded mouse travel and keystrokes, and even monitored pauses or mistakes made by the user during a typical task. Some might go so far as to watch facial expressions or even monitor the blood pressure of the test subject. However, the result is often really the most important aspect of the test. Remember in the final analysis that whether or not users actually were successful in their mission and enjoyed the visit, will probably be the only really important thing to them. This doesn't mean that the study of usability doesn't include any reasonably measurable characteristics, it just suggests that as imperfect creatures, humans may quickly forget the difficulty of performing a task if there is a wonderful reward at the end. Readers interested in understanding more about user testing and usability, particularly the theory and practice of conducting usability tests, should visit www.useit.com and www.usableweb.com.

SITE EVALUATION WORKSHEET

PRELIMINARY INFORMATION

Site name: _____

URL: _____

Purpose of evaluation: _____

Evaluated by: _____

Date: _____

Time: _____

First Impression: *1 (poor) –5 (excellent)*

❑ 1

❑ 2

❑ 3

❑ 4

❑ 5

General Comments:

Navigation Pretest: *Print the page or do not touch anything. Identify clickable areas on the screen by inspection:*

Number of believed clickable areas: _____

Actual number of clickable areas: _____

Accuracy: _____

Comments:

Identity Pretest: *Based solely on information presented, identify the site owner and describe general type of site:*

Purpose Pretest: *Based upon quick inspection, identify the basic points of the site. What basic functions would it likely provide?*

Audience Pretest: *Based upon quick inspection, consider who the audience for the site would be:*

GENERAL SITE CHARACTERISTICS

Site Structure

Describe the site structure:

- ❐ Linear
- ❐ Grid
- ❐ Tree/Hierarchy
- ❐ Mixed Tree
- ❐ Pure Web

Provide a site diagram: *Map out the contents on the site into a flowchart*

Are there any broken links in the site?

- ❐ Yes
- ❐ No

If yes, are they broken links to external sites or internal pages?

- ❐ External
- ❐ Internal
- ❐ Both

What is the maximum page depth in the site? (*clicks from the home page*) _____

Are there orphaned files in the site?

- ❐ Yes
- ❐ No

Are there clear entrance and exit pages to the site?

- ❐ Yes
- ❐ No

Describe:

Delivery

Describe hardware used if possible:

What operating system is used on the Web server? _____

What Web server software with version number is being used? _____

Where is the site being hosted?

❑ Internally
❑ Externally

Who is the closest "upstream" Internet Service Provider from server? _____

What is the amount of bandwidth available for the
server if known or determinable? _____

Rate the responsiveness of the server *1 (very slow) –5 (very fast)*

❑ 1
❑ 2
❑ 3
❑ 4
❑ 5

What is the largest page in the site bytewise? _____

What is the average page size in the site? _____

What are the theoretical download times for the average and largest pages at:
Modem speeds (56Kbps) _____
ISDN (128Kbps) _____
Cable (600Kbps +) _____
DSL/T1/Ethernet (1Mbps +) _____

Are real download times similar?

❑ Yes
❑ No

If no, provide times for tested speeds: _____

Visuals and Layout

Describe the visuals used in the site:

Do you like the visuals?

❑ Yes
❑ No

Why or why not?

Are the visuals purely decorative or do they add to the site's function or information?

- ❒ Only decoration
- ❒ Improve function

Print out the home page as well as a sub-page and content page. Mark up the printouts to illustrate previous answers.

Describe the layout of the home page:

Describe the layout of a typical sub-page:

Describe the layout of a content page:

How is the screen contrast? *1 (poor) –5 (excellent)*

- ❒ 1
- ❒ 2
- ❒ 3
- ❒ 4
- ❒ 5

If bad, describe why:

Describe text size:

- ❒ Too small
- ❒ Just right
- ❒ Too large

Make browser text size larger or smaller. Does the layout still work?

- ❒ Yes
- ❒ No

Resize the browser very large or very small. Does the layout still work?

❏ Yes

❏ No

Is the layout static (stay the same size) or does it grow with the screen size?

❏ Static

❏ Stretchable

If the site has a static width, does the page fit or is there rightward scrolling at: 640 × 480?

❏ Fits

❏ Scrolls right

800 × 600?

❏ Fits

❏ Scrolls right

1,024 × 768 and greater?

❏ Fits

❏ Scrolls right

With respect to vertical screen size does the primary navigation fit on screen at: 640 × 480?

❏ Fits

❏ Scrolls off

800 × 600?

❏ Fits

❏ Scrolls off

1,024 × 768 and greater?

❏ Fits

❏ Scrolls off

Note   *You may want to perform this test at resolutions other than those mentioned depending on your target platform.*

Do pages print correctly?

❏ Yes

❏ No

What kind of images are used in the site?

☐ GIF

☐ JPEG

☐ PNG

☐ Other

Are the images generally used correctly?
(e.g., GIF for illustrations, JPEG for photos)

☐ Yes

☐ No

Are the images optimized properly?
(e.g., small file size, safe colors)

☐ Yes

☐ No

Are there image execution problems?
(e.g., color matching, seems showing in background tiles, etc.)

☐ Yes

☐ No

Describe:

Is ALT text used for images?

☐ Yes

☐ No

☐ Partially

Is the site usable without images?

☐ Yes

☐ No

☐ Partially

General Content Statistics

Approximate number of content pages in the site: _____

Percentage of content pages in site
(content pages / total pages) _____

Content Qualities
Is there enough detail to answer simple user questions?

❑ Yes
❑ No

Is there enough content detail to answer complex user questions?

❑ Yes
❑ No

Does content appear accurate and truthful?

❑ Yes
❑ No

If no, describe what suggests this belief:

Are there obvious misspellings in the site?

❑ Yes
❑ No

Are there egregious spelling errors such as misspellings in buttons or headlines?

❑ Yes
❑ No

Are there obvious grammar or usage errors in the site?

❑ Yes
❑ No

If yes, describe these errors (e.g., fragments, run-ons, heavy use of acronyms without explanation):

Describe the tone of content in the site (e.g., playful, businesslike, serious, humorous):

Does the tone of content fit what is presented?

❑ Yes
❑ No

If no, describe why not:

Is content updated on the site?

- ❑ Yes
- ❑ No

Is update necessary?

- ❑ Yes
- ❑ No

Answer the following questions only if content is being actively updated.

If content requires update is it fresh?

- ❑ Yes
- ❑ No
- ❑ Partially

On average how often does it appear the content is updated?

- ❑ Daily
- ❑ Weekly
- ❑ Monthly
- ❑ Yearly
- ❑ Other

How was freshness determined?
(copyright, label of last update, etc.)

TECHNOLOGY USAGE

HTML

Version(s) used:

- ❑ HTML 2.0
- ❑ HTML 3.2
- ❑ HTML 4.0 Transitional
- ❑ HTML 4.0 Strict
- ❑ XHTML
- ❑ No consistent compliance

Proprietary tag use:

❏ Yes

❏ No

Examples: _____

Home page validation:

❏ Pass

❏ Fail

Comments:

Sub-page validation:

❏ Pass

❏ Fail

Comments:

Style of HTML 1 (poor) –5 (excellent)
(e.g., tag case, formatting, comments, etc.)

❏ 1

❏ 2

❏ 3

❏ 4

❏ 5

HTML style consistency 1 (poor/many styles) –5 (excellent/strict guidelines)

❏ 1

❏ 2

❏ 3

❏ 4

❏ 5

Method of creation:

- ❏ By hand
- ❏ Editor
  Editor(s) used: _____
- ❏ Translator (e.g. Save as…)
  From what: _____
- ❏ Dynamically created
  Method: _____

CSS

Version(s) used:

- ❏ CSS1
- ❏ CSSP (Positioning features)
- ❏ CSS2
- ❏ CSS3

Proprietary properties:

- ❏ Yes
- ❏ No

If yes, provide examples:

Do all CSS rules work correctly?

- ❏ Yes
- ❏ No

CSS rules inclusion method(s)

- ❏ Linked style sheet
- ❏ Document-wide style sheet

Inline style
Quality of rules 1 (poor) –5 (excellent)
(e.g., simplicity, style, naming)

- ❏ 1
- ❏ 2
- ❏ 3
- ❏ 4
- ❏ 5

CSS use consistency 1 (poor/many styles) –5 (excellent/strict guidelines)

- ☐ 1
- ☐ 2
- ☐ 3
- ☐ 4
- ☐ 5

Method of creation

- ☐ By hand
- ☐ Editor
  Editor(s) used _____
- ☐ Translator (e.g. Save as…)
  From what: _____
- ☐ Dynamically created
  Method: _____

Degradability (works without CSS)

- ☐ Perfect degradation
- ☐ Degradation with subtle cosmetic differences
- ☐ Degradation with serious differences in appearance
- ☐ Significant layout problems without CSS

XML

XML used?

- ☐ Yes
- ☐ No

If yes, where is it used (client-side or server-side)?

If present what is it used for?

- ☐ Data storage
- ☐ Document structure
- ☐ Data exchange
- ☐ For presentation using CSS or XSL

Name of XML language used: _____
Proprietary language? _____
DTD available? _____

DTD clarity 1 (complex/confusing) –5 (simple/commented)

☐ 1

☐ 2

☐ 3

☐ 4

☐ 5

Is the site usable with non-XML aware browsers?

☐ Yes

☐ No

If no, describe how dealt with:

PROGRAMMING

Server-side Technology

Are server-side programming facilities used?

☐ Yes

☐ No

Which ones?

☐ CGI (using Perl, C, etc.)

☐ Cold Fusion (.cfm)

☐ Active Server Pages (.asp)

☐ PHP (.php)

☐ Java Server Pages (.jsp)

☐ Server-APIs (ISAPI, NSAPI)

☐ Other

Describe usage of server-side technologies?
(e.g., form processing, dynamic page generation, etc.)

Describe the performance of the server application:

Describe any errors encountered:

Is a database used in the site?

❏ Yes

❏ No

Describe how the database is used:

Client-side Scripting: JavaScript/DHTML

JavaScript used?

❏ Yes

❏ No

If yes, describe uses:

How are scripts included?

❏ Directly in document

❏ Linked to external .js file

Scripts functions properly?

❏ Yes

❏ No

JavaScript version(s)
(check all that apply)

❏ 1.0

❏ 1.1

❏ 1.2

❏ 1.3

❏ Other

JavaScript style 1 (convoluted/not commented) –5 (clear/well commented)

❏ 1

❏ 2

❏ 3

❏ 4

❏ 5

Degradable?
(works on older browsers or without scripting)

   ❐ Yes

   ❐ No

Client-side Component Technology

Java

Are Java applets used?

   ❐ Yes

   ❐ No

If yes, describe how used and applet(s) name:

Degradable?
(warning messages or alternate for no Java)   _____

Are there functionality problems?   _____
(e.g., errors)

Performance problems?   _____

Security problems?   _____

Are ActiveX controls used?

   ❐ Yes

   ❐ No

If yes, describe how used and control(s) name:

Does the site work properly without ActiveX controls?

   ❐ Yes

   ❐ No

Are there functionality problems?
(e.g., errors)

   ❐ Yes

   ❐ No

Performance problems?

❏ Yes

❏ No

Security problems?

❏ Yes

❏ No

Netscape Plug-ins

Are Netscape plug-ins used?

❏ Yes

❏ No

If yes, describe how used and plug-in(s) name:

If a plug-in is not present, is assistance provided to obtain it?   _____

Does the site work properly without plug-ins?

❏ Yes

❏ No

Are there functionality problems?
(e.g., errors)

❏ Yes

❏ No

Performance problems?

❏ Yes

❏ No

Security problems?

❏ Yes

❏ No

Cookies

Are cookies used on the site?

❐ Yes
❐ No

If yes, describe their use:

Is a privacy policy used on the site explaining cookie use?

❐ Yes
❐ No

How many cookies are set? _____

What is the format of the cookie? _____

If cookies are used does the site work with cookies support off?

❐ Yes
❐ No

BROWSER SUPPORT

Site works in Netscape?

❐ Yes
❐ No

What versions? _____

Site works in Internet Explorer?

❐ Yes
❐ No

What versions? _____

Other browsers supported? _____

Does site identify a browser that it does not work in? _____

If compatibility problems exist, are the explained in the site?

❐ Yes
❐ No

NAVIGATION

Placement of navigation elements:
(check one or more)

- ❐ Top
- ❐ Bottom Left
- ❐ Right

Consistency of navigation placement 1 (random) –5 (very stable)

- ❐ 1
- ❐ 2
- ❐ 3
- ❐ 4
- ❐ 5

Comments on navigation placement:

Navigation hierarchy used?

- ❐ Yes
- ❐ No

Describe:

Average number of navigation items per page: _____

Average number of navigation items per navigation cluster: _____

Are alternate forms of navigation provided?

- ❐ Yes
- ❐ No

Describe:

Does navigation in the site rely on the back button?

- ❐ Yes
- ❐ No

Navigation label clarity 1 (unclear) –5 (very clear)

- ❏ 1
- ❏ 2
- ❏ 3
- ❏ 4
- ❏ 5

Scope notes used for labels?

- ❏ Yes
- ❏ No

Tool tips used?

- ❏ Yes
- ❏ No

What is the organization of navigation labels?

- ❏ Alphabetical
- ❏ Importance
- ❏ Random
- ❏ Other

What forms of navigation feedback are employed?

- ❏ Font type
- ❏ Font size
- ❏ Color
- ❏ Position
- ❏ Looks pressable
- ❏ Underlined
- ❏ Rollovers
- ❏ Sound
- ❏ Other

Is the feedback useful?

- ❏ Yes
- ❏ No

Discuss:

Are link colors modified from the blue, red, and purple?

❑ Yes

❑ No

If yes, is the color combination logical?

How is location indicated?

❑ URL

❑ Page label

❑ Deselected labels

❑ Depth gauge

❑ XXXX

❑ Color

❑ Design style

Are frames used?

❑ Yes

❑ No

If yes, are they for navigation or layout?

Can pages be bookmarked?

❑ Yes

❑ No

Is there helpful information with broken links (404 errors)?

❑ Yes

❑ No

If yes, describe:

Is there helpful information when page have been moved?

❑ Yes

❑ No

Describe:

Search

Does site have an internal search system?

❐ Yes

❐ No

If no, should one be included?

❐ Yes

❐ No

Reason:

How is search accessed?

❐ Within page

❐ Separate page

❐ Both

Search integrated with design?

❐ Yes

❐ No

Type of search:

❐ Free text

❐ Parametric

❐ Both

If parametric, describe search parameters:

Search forms:

❐ Simple

❐ Advanced

❐ Both

Clarity of search form 1 (poor) –5 (excellent)

❐ 1

❐ 2

❐ 3

❐ 4

❐ 5

Instructions for search form included?

❑ Yes

❑ No

Negative query provide reasonable result and help?

❑ Yes

❑ No

Positive queries provide reasonable results?

❑ Yes

❑ No

Refinement of queries easily performed?

❑ Yes

❑ No

Known item searching accuracy 1 (poor/ not found) –5 (excellent/#1 position)

❑ 1

❑ 2

❑ 3

❑ 4

❑ 5

Navigation Aids

Site Map

Site map included?

❑ Yes

❑ No

If no, should a site map be included?

❑ Yes

❑ No

Reason:

Method to access site map?

    ❒ Link on all pages

    ❒ Link on one or few pages

    ❒ Help system or search engine

What is the scope of the site map?

    ❒ Whole site

    ❒ Most pages

    ❒ Main sections

    ❒ Unknown scope

What is the format of the site map?

    ❒ Graphical

    ❒ Text

Static or dynamic site map?

    ❒ Static

    ❒ Dynamic

If static, is it up to date?

    ❒ Yes

    ❒ No

Comments on site map:

Site Index

Is a site index used?

    ❒ Yes

    ❒ No

If no, should a site index be included?

    ❒ Yes

    ❒ No

Reason:

Method to access site index?

- ❑ Link on all pages
- ❑ Link on one or few pages
- ❑ Help system or search engine

What is the scope of the index?

- ❑ All topics
- ❑ Main topics
- ❑ Unknown selection of topics

Static or dynamic site index?

- ❑ Static
- ❑ Dynamic

If static, is it up to date?

- ❑ Yes
- ❑ No

Comments on site index:

Glossary

Glossary included?

- ❑ Yes
- ❑ No

If no, should a site term glossary be included?

- ❑ Yes
- ❑ No

Reason:

What is the method to access glossary?

- ❑ Link on all pages
- ❑ Link on one or few pages
- ❑ From the help page

Number of terms in glossary: _____

Comments on glossary:

Help System

Basic contact information:

❏ Yes

❏ No

Contact for Web-specific problems:

❏ Yes

❏ No

Online Help system?

❏ Yes

❏ No

Describe:

THE FINAL SCORE

Final Score 1 (dislike) –5 (like a lot)

❏ 1

❏ 2

❏ 3

❏ 4

❏ 5

Key reasons for final score:

The Complete Reference

Web Design

Appendix C

Fonts

T his appendix contains a quick reference to HTML and CSS coding that pertains to font display, along with a list of commonly available fonts and a discussion of downloadable fonts.

HTML: The <FONT> Element

Under the HTML 4.0 specification, the **<FONT>** element is considered transitional. Ultimately, all display issues will be handled by cascading style sheets (CSS). Until CSS support is universal, however, HTML font formatting remains an important aspect of Web design.

The **<FONT>** element has four basic attributes that are germane to this discussion: **FACE**, **SIZE**, **COLOR**, and **STYLE**.

FACE

The **FACE** attribute sets the name of the font or font family used to render text in a Web page:

```
<FONT FACE="Britannic Bold">This is important</FONT>
```

The Web browser will read this HTML fragment and render the text in the font named in the **FACE** attribute—but only for users who have the font installed on their systems. Multiple fonts can be listed using the **FACE** attribute:

```
<FONT FACE="Arial, Helvetica, Sans serif">
This should be in a different font</FONT>
```

Here, the browser will read the comma-delimited list of fonts until it finds a font it supports. Given the fragment shown above, the browser would try first Arial, then Helvetica, and finally a sans serif font before giving up and using whatever the current browser font is.

A little guesswork can be applied to take advantage of the **FACE** attribute. Most Macintosh, Windows, and UNIX users have a standard set of fonts. If equivalent fonts are specified, it may be possible to provide similar page renderings across platforms.

Fonts for Microsoft Platforms and Browsers

The following fonts are available for Microsoft browsers and systems; they are displayed in Figure C-1.

Font	Systems
Andale Mono	Windows 98, Windows 95, Windows NT (add-on)
Arial	Windows 98, Windows 95, Windows 3.1x, Windows NT 3.x, Windows NT 4.x
Arial Black	Windows 98, Internet Explorer 3, 4, & 5

Font	Systems
Arial Bold	Windows 98, Windows 95, Windows 3.1x, Windows NT 3.x, Windows NT 4.x
Arial Italic	Windows 98, Windows 95, Windows 3.1x, Windows NT 3.x, Windows NT 4.x
Arial Bold Italic	Windows 98, Windows 95, Windows 3.1x, Windows NT 3.x, Windows NT 4.x
Comic Sans MS	Windows 98, Internet Explorer 3, 4, & 5
Comic Sans MS Bold	Windows 98, Internet Explorer 3, 4, & 5
Courier New	Windows 95, Windows 3.1x, Windows NT 3.x, Windows NT 4.x
Courier New Bold	Windows 95, Windows 3.1x, Windows NT 3.x, Windows NT 4.x
Courier New Italic	Windows 95, Windows 3.1x, Windows NT 3.x, Windows NT 4.x
Courier New Bold Italic	Windows 95, Windows 3.1x, Windows NT 3.x, Windows NT 4.x
Georgia	Windows 98, IE 4 & IE5 (add-on)
Georgia Bold	Windows 98, IE 4 & IE5 (add-on)
Georgia Italic	Windows 98, IE 4 & IE5 (add-on)
Georgia Bold Italic	Windows 98, IE 4 & IE5 (add-on)
Impact	Windows 98, Internet Explorer 3, 4, & 5
Lucida Sans Unicode	Windows NT 3.x (except NT 3.0) , Windows NT 4.x
Lucida Console	Windows 98, Windows NT 3.x (except NT 3.0), Windows NT 4.x
Marlett	Windows 98, Windows 95
Minion Web (Adobe)	Microsoft lists this as one of their "core fonts," but it seems to be available (for sale) only from Adobe (http://www.adobe.com)
Monotype.com	Old version of Andale Mono, still available for Windows 3.1 and 3.11 (add-on)
Symbol	Windows 98, Windows 95, Windows 3.1x, Windows NT 3.x, Windows NT 4.x

Font	Systems
Tahoma	Windows 98, Windows 95 (add-on), Windows NT 4.x (add-on)
Times New Roman	Windows 98, Windows 95, Windows 3.1x, Windows NT 3.x, Windows NT 4.x
Times New Roman Bold	Windows 98, Windows 95, Windows 3.1x, Windows NT 3.x, Windows NT 4.x
Times New Roman Italic	Windows 98, Windows 95, Windows 3.1x, Windows NT 3.x, Windows NT 4.x
Times New Roman Bold Italic	Windows 98, Windows 95, Windows 3.1x, Windows NT 3.x, Windows NT 4.x
Trebuchet MS	Windows 95, Windows 98, IE 4 & IE5 (add-on)
Trebuchet MS Bold	Windows 95, Windows 98, IE 4 & IE5 (add-on)
Trebuchet MS Italic	Windows 95, Windows 98, IE 4 & IE5 (add-on)
Trebuchet MS Bold Italic	Windows 95, Windows 98, IE 4 & IE5 (add-on)
Verdana	Windows 98, Internet Explorer 3, 4, & 5
Verdana Bold	Windows 98, Internet Explorer 3, 4, & 5
Verdana Italic	Windows 98, Internet Explorer 3, 4, & 5
Verdana Bold Italic	Windows 98, Internet Explorer 3, 4, & 5
Webdings	Windows 98, Internet Explorer 4 & 5
Wingdings	Windows 98, Windows 95, Windows 3.1x, Windows NT 3.x, Windows NT 4.x

More information about these fonts can be found at http://www.microsoft.com/typography/fontpack/.

Fonts for Apple Macintosh System 7

The following fonts are available for Macintosh System 7; they are displayed in Figure C-2.

Chicago	Courier Regular	Geneva
Helvetica	Monaco	Palatino
New York	Symbol	Times

Andale Mono
Arial
Arial Bold
Arial Italic
Arial Bold Italic
Arial Black
Comic Sans MS
Comic Sans MS Bold
Courier New
Courier New Bold
Courier New Bold Italic
Courier New Italic
Georgia
Georgia Bold
Georgia Italic
Georgia Bold Italic
Impact
Lucida Console
Lucida Sans Unicode
M ✓ ✗ ⌐ ⌐ ▲ ▲ (Marlett)
Minion Web
Σψμβολ (Symbol)
Times New Roman
Times New Roman Bold
Times New Roman Bold Italic
Times New Roman Italic
Tahoma
Trebuchet MS
Trebuchet MS Bold
Trebuchet MS Italic
Trebuchet MS Bold Italic
Verdana
Verdana Bold
Verdana Bold Italic
Verdana Italic
▶ 🏛 ✂ ♥ ①◑▮ ? (Webdings)
✚✠ ■ ♈ ♎✠ ■ ♈◆ (Wingdings)

Figure C-1. *Font families available for Microsoft browsers and systems*

Chicago

Courier Regular

Geneva

Helvetica

Monaco

New York

Palatino

Σψμβολ (Symbol)

Times

Figure C-2. *Font families available with Macintosh System 7*

Additional fonts for Apple Macintosh System 8.x

In addition to the fonts shown above for System 7, Macintosh System 8 offers the following fonts; they are displayed in Figure C-3.

Apple Chancery   Charcoal   Hoefler Text   Skia

Apple Chancery

Charcoal

Hoefler Text

Skia

Figure C-3. *Additional font families available with Macintosh System 8*

Fonts for UNIX Systems

The following fonts are available for most UNIX systems, and they are displayed in Figure C-4.

Charter	Clean	Courier
Fixed	Helvetica	Lucida
Lucidabright	New Century Schoolbook	Symbol
Terminal	Times	Utopia

Most users may have many other fonts beyond the ones shown in the tables. Users of Microsoft Office will probably also have access to fonts like Algerian, Book Antiqua, Bookman Old Style, Britannic Bold, Desdemona, Garamond, Century Gothic, Haettenschweiller, and many others. The various browsers are also trying to make new fonts available. Under Internet Explorer 4.0, Microsoft has introduced a new font called Webdings, which provides many common icons for use on the page. Some of these icons would be useful for navigation, like arrows, while others look like audio or video symbols that could provide an indication of link contents before selection.

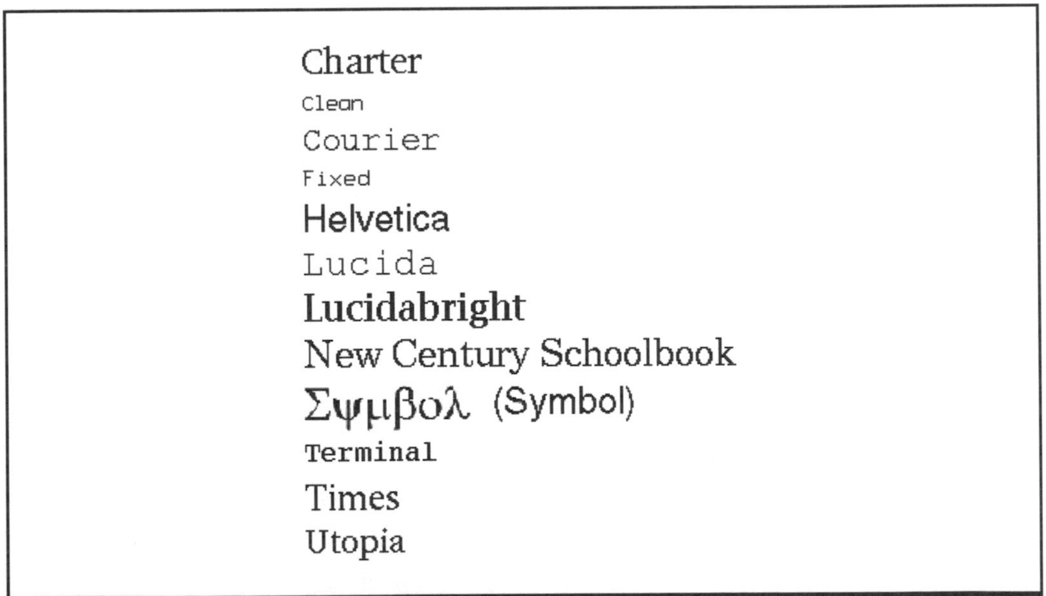

Charter
Clean
Courier
Fixed
Helvetica
Lucida
Lucidabright
New Century Schoolbook
Σψμβολ (Symbol)
Terminal
Times
Utopia

Figure C-4. *Font families available on common UNIX systems*

SIZE

The **SIZE** attribute sets the relative size of type. In a Web page, there are seven relative sizes for text numbered from 1 to 7, where 1 is the smallest text in a document and 7 is the largest. To set some text into the largest size, use **<FONT SIZE="7">**This is big**</FONT>**. By default, the typical size of text is 3; this can be overridden with the **<BASEFONT>** element discussed later in this appendix. Sizing is not exact in HTML; as a rule of thumb, however, if the user has not modified their browser settings, the size corresponds to the point sizes in Table C-1. Designers are warned that these are only guidelines; if exact point sizes are required, CSS should be used or the text made into an image.

Relative sizing with HTML is possible. For example, if the text should just be made one size bigger, the author can use an alternative sizing value such as **<FONT SIZE="+1">** instead of specifying the size directly. The + and - nomenclature makes it possible to bring the font size up or down a specified number of settings. The values for this form of the **SIZE** attribute should range from +1 to +6 and -1 to -6. It is not possible to specify **<FONT SIZE="+10">** because there are only seven sizes. If the increase or decrease goes beyond acceptable sizes, the font generally defaults at the largest or smallest size, respectively.

COLOR

Under HTML 4.0, it is possible to color a portion of text a particular color by enclosing it within the **<FONT>** element and setting the **COLOR** attribute equal to a valid color

<FONT SIZE="*n*">	Typical Point Size
1	8
2	10
3	12
4	14
5	18
6	24
7	36

Table C-1. *Typical <FONT SIZE> and Point Size Equivalents*

name like "red" or an equivalent value such as #FF0000. For more on RGB hexadecimal equivalent codes, see Appendix D. So the code

```
<FONT COLOR="red">This is important</FONT>
```

sets the text "This is important" in red, as would

```
<FONT COLOR="#FF0000">This is important</FONT>
```

<FONT> and <TABLE>

The **<FONT>** element and the **<TABLE>** element often have an undesirable interaction in browsers. The major browsers will treat the use of the **<FONT>** tag differently when it encloses a table. The markup shown here produces very different results when rendering in Internet Explorer and Netscape, as shown in Figure C-5:

```
<!DOCTYPE HTML PUBLIC "-//W3C//DTD HTML 4.0 Transitional//EN">
<HTML>
<HEAD>
<TITLE>FONTS and TABLES</TITLE>
</HEAD>
<BODY>
<FONT FACE="Comic Sans MS" SIZE="5" COLOR="GREEN">
This is text outside the table
<TABLE BORDER="1" BGCOLOR="yellow">
<TR>
<TD>This is text inside the table.</TD>
</TR>
</TABLE>
</FONT>
</BODY>
</HTML>
```

The only real solution to this problem is to enclose a **<FONT>** tag around all content within each **<TD>** element within the table as shown below:

```
<!DOCTYPE HTML PUBLIC "-//W3C//DTD HTML 4.0 Transitional//EN">
<HTML>
<HEAD>
<TITLE>FONTS and TABLES 2</TITLE>
</HEAD>
```

```
<BODY>
<FONT FACE="Comic Sans MS" SIZE="5" COLOR="GREEN">
This is text outside the table</FONT>
<TABLE BORDER="1" BGCOLOR="yellow">
<TR>
<TD>
<FONT FACE="Comic Sans MS" SIZE="5" COLOR="GREEN">
    This is text inside the table</FONT>
</TD>
</TR>
</TABLE>
</FONT>
</BODY>
</HTML>
```

While it would seem that the use of style sheets would clear up many font issues, it turns out that you will have to be very careful applying the style rules to achieve the desired results. For example, using a <DIV> that encloses text both inside and outside a table will produce the same results as the <FONT> and <TABLE> problem in current browsers. Fortunately, application of a style rule directly to the <TABLE> tag itself, or, more effectively, to the <TD> tag, will avoid having to apply font rules to each cell.

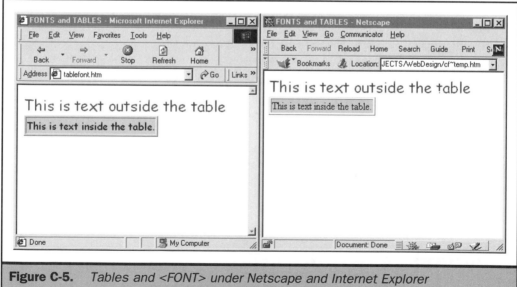

Figure C-5.   *Tables and <FONT> under Netscape and Internet Explorer*

<BASEFONT>

In some cases, it may be appropriate to change the font size, color, or face throughout an entire document. To do this, use the **<BASEFONT>** element in the <HEAD> of the document. **<BASEFONT>** supports the attributes **COLOR**, **FACE**, and **SIZE**, and should only occur once in the document. Like the **<FONT>** element, **COLOR** should be set to an RGB hexadecimal equivalent value or color name. FACE should be set to a font name or comma-delimited list of fonts. **SIZE** should be set to a size value between 1 and 7. Relative sizing for the **SIZE** attribute does not generally make any sense. To set the font of the document in red Arial or Helvetica with a relative size of 6, use **<BASEFONT COLOR="RED" FACE="Arial, Helvetica" SIZE="6">** within the **<HEAD>** element of the document.

Similar to the problem between <FONT> and <TABLE>, the <BASEFONT> tag may not affect the content of tables in the two major browsers. You will be required to manually apply <FONT> tags to each individual <TD> cell.

Fonts and CSS

Cascading style sheets (CSS) provide numerous font-oriented properties to set the family, style, size, and variations of the font used within a Web page. Style information can be applied directly to elements like **<P>** or **<FONT>** using the **STYLE** attribute:

```
<P STYLE="font-face: Arial">This text is in the Arial font.</P>
```

Combining CSS and HTML formatting can give greater control over fonts in CSS-compliant browsers, while providing backwards compatibility for older browsers:

```
<FONT FACE="Arial, Helvetica, Sans serif" SIZE="-1"
STYLE="font-size: 11pt">Newer browsers will
     display this text at 11 points.</FONT>
```

Older browsers will only use the **FACE** and **SIZE** information, but those that support CSS will override the **SIZE** attribute and set the size at 11 points.

Style information can also be set in the head of an HTML document, and assigned to specific elements, as shown in this embedded style sheet example:

```
<!DOCTYPE HTML PUBLIC "-//W3C//DTD HTML 4.0 Transitional//EN">
<HTML>
<HEAD>
<TITLE>CSS Demo</TITLE>
```

```
<STYLE>
<!--
H1    {font-face: Arial, Helvetica, Sans serif; font-size: 18pt}
P     {font-face: Times New Roman, Times, Serif; font-size: 12pt}
-->
</STYLE>
</HEAD>
<BODY>
   content to apply style to
</BODY>
</HTML>
```

CSS font properties are discussed in the following sections. For more information about CSS, see Chapter 15.

font-family

The font-family property sets the font family using either a specific font, such as Arial, or a generic family, such as sans serif. You have to quote any font family names that contain white space, such as "Britannic Bold", and you may have to capitalize font values for a match.

According to the CSS1 specification, the following generic families should be available on all browsers that support CSS1: serif, sans serif, cursive, fantasy, and monospace. When setting the font-family property, you can provide a list of names, just like the **FACE** attribute discussed above. Always provide a generic font family at the end of the font-family. To set a document-wide font, use a rule such as the following:

```
BODY    {font-family: Arial, Helvetica, Sans serif}
```

As already noted, the browser will first check for the Arial font, then for Helvetica, and finally settle on the default sans serif font if the other fonts are not available.

font-size

The font-size property sets the relative or physical size of the font. Values may be mapped to a physical point size or to a relative word describing the size. Physical point-size values include xx-small, x-small, small, medium, large, x-large, and xx-large, or a relative word, such as larger or smaller. Physical sizes also may include 48pt (point size), 2cm (centimeters), .25in (inches), or 16px (pixels). Percentage values, such as 150%, are also valid for relative sizing; negative percentages or point sizes are not allowed. A few examples are shown here:

```
P          {font-size: 18pt}
STRONG     {font-size: larger}
H1         {font-size: 200%}
```

This is a clear case where CSS provides more control options than HTML.

font-style

The font-style property is used to specify normal, italic, or oblique font style for the font being used. A few examples are shown here:

```
H1         {font-style: oblique}
H2         {font-style: italic}
P          {font-style: normal}
```

Don't try to override HTML elements with this property. Setting a rule whereby the <B> element has an italic rendering may not work. When it does, it makes for confusing markup.

font-weight

The font-weight property selects the weight, or darkness, of the font. Values for the property range from 100 to 900, in increments of 100. Keywords are also supported, including bold, bolder, and lighter, which are used to set relative weights. Some browsers may also provide keywords such as extra-light, light, demi-light, medium, demi-bold, bold, and extra-bold, which correspond to the 100 to 900 values. Because font families also include bold values, and the meaning within them varies, the numeric scheme is preferred. A few examples are shown here:

```
STRONG        {font-weight:   bolder}
H1            {font-weight:   900}
H2            {font-weight:   extra-bold}
```

Typically, the value bold is the same as 700, while the normal font value is 400.

font-variant

The font-variant property is used to select a variation of the specified (or default) font family. The only current variants supported with this property are small-caps, which displays as small uppercase letters, and normal, which doesn't do anything. A simple rule is shown here:

```
EM              {font-variant: small-caps}
```

font

The font property provides a concise way to specify all the font properties with one style rule. One attribute that is included within font is line-height, which specifies the distance between two lines of text. Each font attribute can be indicated on the line, separated by spaces, except for line-height, which is used with font-size and separated by a slash. You can use as few or as many font rules in this shorthand notation as you want. The general form of the font rule is shown here:

```
font: font-style font-variant font-weight font-size/line-height
      font-family
```

The following is an example of using a compact font rule:

```
P {font: italic small-caps 600 18pt/24pt "Arial, Helvetica"}
```

The shorthand notation does not require all the properties, so the next example is just as valid as the complete notation:

```
P    {font: italic 18pt/24pt}
```

Measurements Supported by CSS

CSS provides a wide range of measurements that can be used to determine font size, as well as line height. These units of measurement are listed in Table C-2.

Cross-Platform Sizing Issues

You should be extremely careful when using CSS measurements when you are working for very precise control. Unfortunately, the PC and the Macintosh calculate their screen text size very differently. On a PC, you will find the text to be approximately 33 percent larger than on a Macintosh. Look at Figure C-6, which shows the various standard HTML sizes for fonts from 1 to 7.

The onscreen differences for the two platforms can be very dangerous when using **<FONT SIZE="1">**. PC users may find this barely readable and the Mac users not at all with certain fonts.

Some designers may desire very great control of text size given that CSS is now available. However, the same problem with normal HTML sizes will hold in CSS. Using pixel measurement for characters may produce good onscreen results, but it will

Unit	Description	Browser Support
%	This value defines a measurement as a percentage relative to another value.	Internet Explorer 3, 4, and 5 Netscape 4 and 4.5
cm	This value defines a measurement in centimeters.	Internet Explorer 3, 4, and 5 Netscape 4 and 4.5
em	This value defines a measurement for the height of a font in em spaces.	Internet Explorer 3 (Mac only) Netscape 4 and 4.5 (incomplete)
ex	This value defines a measurement relative to a font's x-height. The x-height is determined by the height of the font's lowercase letter x.	Internet Explorer 3 (Mac only) Netscape 4 and 4.5 (incomplete)
in	This value defines a measurement in inches.	Internet Explorer 3, 4, and 5 Netscape 4 and 4.5
mm	This value defines a measurement in millimeters.	Internet Explorer 3, 4, and 5 Netscape 4 and 4.5
pc	This value defines a measurement in picas where 1pc = 12pt.	Internet Explorer 3, 4, and 5 Netscape 4 and 4.5
pt	This value defines a measurement in points where a point is equivalent to 1/72 in.	Internet Explorer 3, 4, and 5 Netscape 4 and 4.5
px	This value defines a measurement in pixels.	Internet Explorer 3, 4, and 5 Netscape 4 and 4.5

Table C-2. *CSS Measurements*

generally produce awful printouts. You can also attempt to use em measurements and write a short JavaScript to include a different style sheet based on the user having a Macintosh or PC. The PC style sheet would use a style that would be two-thirds the normal size to equalize the two systems. In short, when building pages on a PC you would multiply the PC em size by 3/2 to equal Mac em size. If you own a Mac, multiply the Mac em size by 2/3 to equal the PC em size. The reality of the Web at the time of this writing is that attempting to get such a degree of text control will be a lesson in frustration.

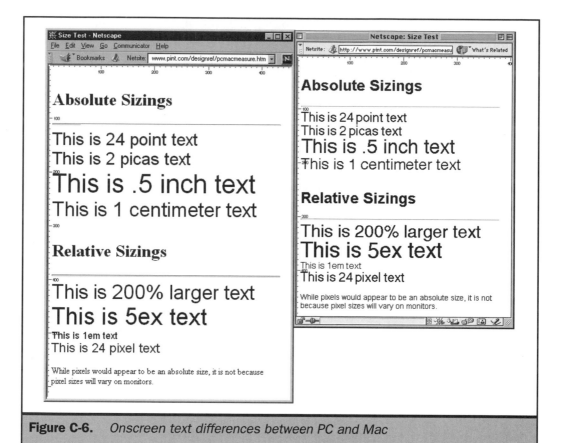

Figure C-6.   *Onscreen text differences between PC and Mac*

Downloadable Fonts

Beyond sizing issues, the best solution for fonts on the Web would be to come up with a cross-platform font that could be downloaded to the browser on the fly. Both of the major browser vendors have developed their own versions of downloadable fonts. Microsoft's solution is called OpenType (www.microsoft.com/typography). Netscape's solution, called Dynamic Fonts, is based on TrueDoc (www.truedoc.com). Note that only 4.x generation and beyond browsers support downloadable font technology.

Netscape's Dynamic Fonts

To use a dynamic font under Netscape, page authors should use the **FACE** attribute of the **<FONT>** element, or a style sheet attribute as discussed above in "Fonts and CSS," to set the font face. If the user does not have the font installed on the system, a downloadable font linked to the page can be fetched and used to render the page. To include a link to a Netscape font definition file in Portable Font Resource (PFR) format, use the **<LINK>** element by setting the **REL** attribute to fontdef and the **SRC** attribute equal to the URL where the font definition file resides. The **<LINK>** element must be found within the **<HEAD>** of the document. You will have to create a PFR file using a tool such as HexMac's Typograph (www.hexmac.com). A more complete list of tools can be found at www.truedoc.com. An example of how this element would be used is shown here:

```
<HTML>
<HEAD>
<TITLE>Netscape Font Demo</TITLE>
<LINK REL="fontdef"
SRC="http://www.bigcompany.com/fonts/ransom.pfr">
<STYLE>
<!--
.special  {font-family: ransom; color: green; font-size: 28pt;}
->
</STYLE>
</HEAD>
<BODY>
<FONT FACE="ransom">
Content rendered in the font "newfont" which is
part of the pfr file.
</FONT><BR>
<SPAN CLASS="ransom">You can use CSS rules to access
the new font as well.</SPAN>
</BODY>
</HTML>
```

Note that there may be many fonts in the same font definition file. There is no limit to how many fonts can be used on a page. Once the font is accessed, it is used just as if it were installed on a user's system. You can use either CSS or normal HTML **<FONT>** syntax to access the downloadable font.

 One drawback to the Netscape approach to dynamic fonts is that it may cause screen flashing in many versions of Netscape. This can be disorienting for the user and has somewhat limited the use of this technology.

Microsoft's Dynamic Fonts

Microsoft also provides a way to embed fonts in a Web page. To include a font, you must first build the page using the **<FONT>** element, or style sheet rules that set fonts.

When creating your page, don't worry about whether or not the end user has the font installed; it will be downloaded. Next, use Microsoft's Web Embedding Fonts Tool or a similar facility to analyze the font usage on the page. The program should create an .eot file that contains the embedded fonts. Then, add the font use information to the page in the form of cascading style sheets (CSS) style rules, as shown here:

```
<HTML>
<HEAD>
<TITLE>Microsoft Font Test</TITLE>
<STYLE TYPE="text/css">
<!--

  @font-face {
font-family: Ransom;
font-style:  normal;
font-weight: normal;
src: url(fonts/ransom.eot);
}

  .special {font-family: Ransom; color: green; font-size: 28pt;}
-->
</STYLE>
</HEAD>
<BODY>
<FONT FACE="Ransom" SIZE="6">Example Ransom Note Font</FONT><BR>
<SPAN CLASS="special">This is also in Ransom</SPAN>
</BODY>
</HTML>
```

Notice how it is possible to use both typical style sheet rules like a **CLASS** binding as well as the normal **<FONT>** tag. A possible rendering of font embedding is shown in Figure C-7.

As in the Netscape approach, you must first create a font file and reference it from the file that uses the font. It may be useful to define a fonts directory within your Web site to store font files, similar to storing image files for site use.

The use of the **@font-face** acts as a pseudo element that allows you to bring any number of fonts into a page. For more information on embedded fonts under Internet Explorer, and links to font file creation tools like Web Embedding Font Tool (WEFT), see the Microsoft Typography site (www.microsoft.com/typography).

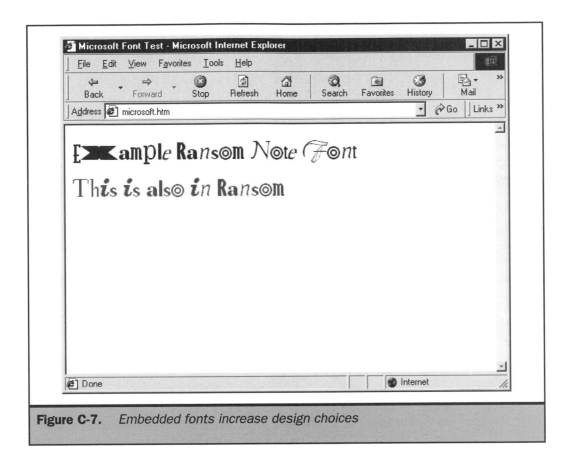

Figure C-7. *Embedded fonts increase design choices*

Note *It is possible to provide links to both Microsoft and Netscape font technology in the same page. This really adds only one line or a few style rules as the rest of the document would continue to use the same <FONT FACE=""> statements. TrueDoc technology also supports an ActiveX control to allow Internet Explorer users to view their style of embedded fonts.*

The
Complete
Reference

Web
Design

Appendix D

Color Reference

The following table lists all the color names commonly supported by the major browsers (Netscape 3.0 and above, Internet Explorer 3.0 and above, and WebTV). Sixteen colors (aqua, black, blue, fuchsia, gray, green, lime, maroon, navy, olive, purple, red, silver, teal, white, and yellow) were introduced by Microsoft and are now part of the official W3C HTML specification; the rest were introduced by Netscape. The corresponding hexadecimal code is shown next to each color name. Thus, the code **<BODY BGCOLOR="lightsteelblue">** would produce the same result as **<BODY BGCOLOR="#B0C4DE">** under any browser that supported these color names. Don't forget to use the pound symbol (#) before hexadecimal values. Color names are easier to remember than numerical codes, but may cause trouble when viewed under old or uncommon browsers. It is advisable to stick with the hexadecimal approach to colors because it is generally safer, especially since only 16 of the names are officially recognized. WebTV supports the color names but displays several colors (noted below) differently. General WebTV color support may also vary due to essential differences between computer monitors and television screens.

Hexadecimal Code	Name	RGB Equivalent	Notes
F0F8FF	aliceblue	240,248,255	The name aliceblue is not supported by Netscape.
FAEBD7	antiquewhite	250,235,215	
00FFFF	aqua	0,255,255	
7FFFD4	aquamarine	127,255,212	
F0FFFF	azure	240,255,255	
F5F5DC	beige	245,245,220	
FFE4C4	bisque	255,228,196	
000000	black	0,0,0	
FFEBCD	blanchedalmond	255,235,205	
0000FF	blue	0,0,255	
8A2BE2	blueviolet	138,43,226	WebTV displays blueviolet the same as blue (0000FF).
A52A2A	brown	165,42,42	
DEB887	burlywood	222,184,135	
5F9EA0	cadetblue	95,158,160	

Hexadecimal Code	Name	RGB Equivalent	Notes
7FFF00	chartreuse	127,255,0	
D2691E	chocolate	210,105,30	
FF7F50	coral	255,127,80	
6495ED	cornflowerblue	100,149,237	
FFF8DC	cornsilk	255,248,220	
DC143C	crimson	220,20,60	
00FFFF	cyan	0,255,255	
00008B	darkblue	0,0,139	
008B8B	darkcyan	0,139,139	
B8860B	darkgoldenrod	184,134,11	
A9A9A9	darkgray	169,169,169	
006400	darkgreen	0,100,0	
BDB76B	darkkhaki	189,183,107	
8B008B	darkmagenta	139,0,139	
556B2F	darkolivegreen	85,107,47	
FF8C00	darkorange	255,140,0	
9932CC	darkorchid	153,50,204	
8B0000	darkred	139,0,0	
E9967A	darksalmon	233,150,122	
8FBC8F	darkseagreen	143,188,143	
483D8B	darkslatebluc	72,61,139	
2F4F4F	darkslategray	47,79,79	
00CED1	darkturquoise	0,206,209	
9400D3	darkviolet	148,0,211	
FF1493	deeppink	255,20,147	
00BFFF	deepskyblue	0,191,255	
696969	dimgray	105,105,105	
1E90FF	dodgerblue	30,144,255	

Hexadecimal Code	Name	RGB Equivalent	Notes
B22222	firebrick	178,34,34	
FFFAF0	floralwhite	255,250,240	
228B22	forestgreen	34,139,34	
FF00FF	fuchsia	255,0,255	
DCDCDC	gainsboro	220,220,220	
F8F8FF	ghostwhite	248,248,255	
FFD700	gold	255,215,0	
DAA520	goldenrod	218,165,32	WebTV displays goldenrod the same as gold (FFD700).
808080	gray	127,127,127	
008000	green	0,128,0	
ADFF2F	greenyellow	173,255,47	WebTV displays greenyellow the same as green (008000).
F0FFF0	honeydew	240,255,240	
FF69B4	hotpink	255,105,180	
CD5C5C	indianred	205,92,92	
4B0082	indigo	75,0,130	
FFFFF0	ivory	255,255,240	
F0E68C	khaki	240,230,140	
E6E6FA	lavender	230,230,250	
FFF0F5	lavenderblush	255,240,245	
7CFC00	lawngreen	124,252,0	
FFFACD	lemonchiffon	255,250,205	
ADD8E6	lightblue	173,216,230	
F08080	lightcoral	240,128,128	
E0FFFF	lightcyan	224,255,255	
FAFAD2	lightgoldenrodyellow	250,250,210	
90EE90	lightgreen	144,238,144	

Hexadecimal Code	Name	RGB Equivalent	Notes
D3D3D3	lightgray	211,211,211	
FFB6C1	lightpink	255,182,193	
FFA07A	lightsalmon	255,160,122	
20B2AA	lightseagreen	32,178,170	
87CEFA	lightskyblue	135,206,250	
778899	lightslategray	119,136,153	
B0C4DE	lightsteelblue	176,196,222	
FFFFE0	lightyellow	255,255,224	
00FF00	lime	0,255,0	
32CD32	limegreen	50,205,50	WebTV displays limegreen the same as lime (00FF00).
FAF0E6	linen	250,240,230	
FF00FF	magenta	255,0,255	
800000	maroon	128,0,0	
66CDAA	mediumaquamarine	102,205,170	
0000CD	mediumblue	0,0,205	
BA55D3	mediumorchid	186,85,211	
9370DB	mediumpurple	147,112,219	
3CB371	mediumseagreen	60,179,113	
7B68EE	mediumslateblue	123,104,238	
00FA9A	mediumspringgreen	0,250,154	According to the WebTV specification, WebTV supports mediumspringgreen, but the name display does not match the numerical code display.
48D1CC	mediumturquoise	72,209,204	
C71585	mediumvioletred	199,21,133	
191970	midnightblue	25,25,112	

Hexadecimal Code	Name	RGB Equivalent	Notes
F5FFFA	mintcream	245,255,250	
FFE4E1	mistyrose	255,228,225	
FFE4B5	moccasin	255,228,181	
FFDEAD	navajowhite	255,222,173	
000080	navy	0,0,128	
9FAFDF	navyblue	159,175,223	WebTV displays navyblue the same as navy (000080).
FDF5E6	oldlace	253,245,230	
808000	olive	128,128,0	
6B8E23	olivedrab	107,142,35	WebTV displays olivedrab the same as olive (808000).
FFA500	orange	255,165,0	
FF4500	orangered	255,69,0	WebTV displays orangered the same as orange (FFA500).
DA70D6	orchid	218,112,214	
EEE8AA	palegoldenrod	238,232,170	
98FB98	palegreen	152,251,152	
AFEEEE	paleturquoise	175,238,238	
DB7093	palevioletred	219,112,147	
FFEFD5	papayawhip	255,239,213	
FFDAB9	peachpuff	255,218,185	
CD853F	peru	205,133,63	
FFC0CB	pink	255,192,203	
DDA0DD	plum	221,160,221	
B0E0E6	powderblue	176,224,230	
800080	purple	128,0,128	
FF0000	red	255,0,0	

Hexadecimal Code	Name	RGB Equivalent	Notes
BC8F8F	rosybrown	188,143,143	
4169E1	royalblue	65,105,225	
8B4513	saddlebrown	139,69,19	
FA8072	salmon	250,128,114	
F4A460	sandybrown	244,164,96	
2E8B57	seagreen	46,139,87	
FFF5EE	seashell	255,245,238	
A0522D	sienna	160,82,45	
C0C0C0	silver	192,192,192	
87CEEB	skyblue	135,206,235	
6A5ACD	slateblue	106,90,205	
708090	slategray	112,128,144	
FFFAFA	snow	255,250,250	
00FF7F	springgreen	0,255,127	
4682B4	steelblue	70,130,180	
D2B48C	tan	210,180,140	
008080	teal	0,128,128	
D8BFD8	thistle	216,191,216	
FF6347	tomato	255,99,71	
40E0D0	turquoise	64,224,208	
EE82EE	violet	238,130,238	
F5DEB3	wheat	245,222,179	
FFFFFF	white	255,255,255	
F5F5F5	whitesmoke	245,245,245	
FFFF00	yellow	255,255,0	
9ACD32	yellowgreen	139,205,50	WebTV displays yellowgreen the same as yellow (FFFF00).

Many online color references claim that further color variations can be introduced by adding the numbers 1 through 4 to color names. If this were correct, cadetblue1, cadetblue2, cadetblue3, and cadetblue4 would display as different shades of the same color, with 1 being the lightest and 4 the darkest. Some of these references also claim that gray supports up to 100 color variations (gray10, gray50, gray90, etc.). Testing reveals that this does not work under Netscape, Internet Explorer, or WebTV. It seems to almost work in Opera 3.60, however.

While the color chart presented above works in most browsers, consider that many of these named colors are not safe in the sense that they may dither on systems running 256 colors or less. See the section on browser-safe colors at the end of this appendix for more information.

HTML Color Use

In HTML, color values are used primarily with three tags: **<BODY>**, **<FONT>**, and **<TD>**. Other tags such as **<HR>** may take color attributes, but these are proprietary and should be rarely used.

Setting <BODY> Color Attributes

The **<BODY>** element takes five attributes that can be used to modify the color within a Web page. **BGCOLOR** is used to set the color for the entire page. The attribute **TEXT** is used to set default color for text in the page. **LINK** is used to set the default link colors in the page that are normally blue unless modified. **ALINK** is used to change the active link color that is usually red unless specified. An active link is a link that is in the process of being pressed. A pressed link will briefly flash the active color before it becomes visited. Finally, the **VLINK** attribute is used to specify the color of visited links that are normally purple. A complete example of the **<BODY>** element color attributes is shown here:

```
<BODY BGCOLOR="#000000" TEXT="white" LINK="#000099" ALINK="#FF0000"
VLINK="#FF0000">
```

In the preceding example, the background was set to black, the default text white, normal links a bright light blue, and active and visited links bright red.

<FONT> Color

Setting text color down to a single letter is possible using the **<FONT>** tag by setting the **COLOR** attribute to a valid color value, as shown in this short example:

```
<FONT COLOR="red">This is red.</FONT>
<FONT COLOR="#00FF00">This is green.</FONT>
```

Colored Table Cells

Setting background color for a particular region of text is most easily accomplished in HTML with colored table cells. While the **<TABLE>** tag itself may have a background color by setting the **BGCOLOR** attribute, most page authors rely on the **<TD>** element to set color. For example, to set an arbitrary region to be white text on a red background, you would use HTML markup like so:

```
<TABLE>
<TR>
<TD BGCOLOR="red">
<FONT COLOR="white">White on red.</FONT>
</TD>
</TR>
</TABLE>
```

Of course, this type of markup is extremely messy, and the use of color setting in HTML is considered deprecated under the HTML 4.01 standard. Be careful though—until your audience is using conformant browsers, you may not be able to use style sheets to set foreground and background colors.

CSS Color Values

Cascading style sheets (CSS) support the color names and values listed above, but also offer a number of other formats not available in HTML.

Three-Digit Hexadecimal Color Values

Under CSS, color values can be defined using three-digit hexadecimal color values, a concise version of the six-digit values just noted. This approach is supported by Internet Explorer 3 and higher, and Netscape Navigator 4 and higher.

```
SPAN {font-family: Helvetica; font-size: 14pt; color: #0CF}
```

RGB Color Values

Under CSS, color values can be defined using RGB values. Colors are defined by the letters *rgb*, followed by three numbers between 0 and 255, contained in parentheses and separated by commas, with no spaces between them. This approach is supported by Internet Explorer 4 and higher, and Netscape Navigator 4 and higher.

```
P {color: rgb(204,0,51)}
```

RGB Color Values Using Percentages

Under CSS, RGB color values can also be defined using percentages. The format is the same, except that the numbers are replaced by percentage values between **0%** and **100%**. This approach is supported by Internet Explorer 4 and higher, and Netscape Navigator 4 and higher.

```
P {color: rgb(75%,10%,50%)}
```

Browser-Safe Colors

While 8-bit GIF images support 256 colors, cross-platform issues leave a palette of only 216 colors that are completely safe to use on the Web. This group of Web-safe colors is often called the browser-safe palette. Use of other colors often leads to dithering. This happens when an image is remapped from a large number of colors to a smaller color palette; dithering attempts to imitate colors by placing similar colors near them, but generally creates irregularities that render the image unappealing.

The selection of the 216 safe colors is fairly obvious if you consider the additive nature of RGB color. Consider a color to be made up of varying amounts of red, green, or blue that could be set by adjusting a dial from no color to maximum color. The safe colors suggest six possible intensity settings for each value of red, green, or blue. The settings are 0%, 20%, 40%, 60%, 80%, and 100%. So, a value of 0%, 0%, 0% on the dial would be equivalent to black. A value of 100%, 100%, 100% would indicate pure white. A value of 100%, 0%, 0% pure red, and so on. The safe colors are those that only have an RGB value set at one of the safe intensity settings. The hex conversions for saturation are shown in Table D-1.

Color Intensity	Hex Value	Decimal Value
100%	FF	255
80%	CC	204
60%	99	153
40%	66	102
20%	33	51
0%	00	0

Table D-1.   *Turn the Dial to the Far Left and No Color Would Be Specified*

Setting a safe color is simply a matter of selecting a combination of safe hex values. In this case, #9966FF is a safe hex color while #9370DB is not. Most Web design tools like Macromedia Dreamweaver or Allaire HomeSite, as well as imaging tools like Macromedia Fireworks or recent versions of Adobe PhotoShop, contain safe color pickers. Designers looking for color palettes including improved color pickers and swatches should visit http://www.visibone.com/colorlab/.

Setting an unsafe color to its nearest safe color is fairly easy—just round each particular red, green, or blue value up or down to the nearest safe value. A complete conversion of hex to decimal values with the various safe values indicated in bold is shown in Table D-2.

00=00	01=01	02=02	03=03	04=04	05=05
06=06	07=07	08=08	09=09	10=0A	11=0B
12=0C	13=0D	14=0E	15=0F	16=10	17=11
18=12	19=13	20=14	21=15	22=16	23=17
24=18	25=19	26=1A	27=1B	28=1C	29=1D
30=1E	31=1F	32=20	33=21	34=22	35=23
36=24	37=25	38=26	39=27	40=28	41=29
42=2A	43=2B	44=2C	45=2D	46=2E	47=2F
48=30	49=31	50=32	**51=33**	52=34	53=35
54=36	55=37	56=38	57=39	58=3A	59=3B
60=3C	61=3D	62=3E	63=3F	64=40	65=41
66=42	67=43	68=44	69=45	70=46	71=47
72=48	73=49	74=4A	75=4B	76=4C	77=4D
78=4E	79=4F	80=50	81=51	82=52	83=53
84=54	85=55	86=56	87=57	88=58	89=59
90=5A	91=5B	92=5C	93=5D	94=5E	95=5F
96=60	97=61	98=62	99=63	100=64	101=65
102=66	103=67	104=68	105=69	106=6A	107=6B
108=6C	109=6D	110=6E	111=6F	112=70	113=71

Table D-2.   *RGB to Hexadecimal Color Conversion Chart*

114=72	115=73	116=74	117=75	118=76	119=77
120=78	121=79	122=7A	123=7B	124=7C	125=7D
126=7E	127=7F	128=80	129=81	130=82	131=83
132=84	133=85	134=86	135=87	136=88	137=89
138=8A	139=8B	140=8C	141=8D	142=8E	143=8F
144=90	145=91	146=92	147=93	148=94	149=95
150=96	151=97	152=98	**153=99**	154=9A	155=9B
156=9C	157=9D	158=9E	159=9F	160=A0	161=A1
162=A2	163=A3	164=A4	165=A5	166=A6	167=A7
168=A8	169=A9	170=AA	171=AB	172=AC	173=AD
174=AE	175=AF	176=B0	177=B1	178=B2	179=B3
180=B4	181=B5	182=B6	183=B7	184=B8	185=B9
186=BA	187=BB	188=BC	189=BD	190=BE	191=BF
192=C0	193=C1	194=C2	195=C3	196=C4	197=C5
198=C6	199=C7	200=C8	201=C9	202=CA	203=CB
204=CC	205=CD	206=CE	207=CF	208=D0	209=D1
210=D2	211=D3	212=D4	213=D5	214=D6	215=D7
216=D8	217=D9	218=DA	219=DB	220=DC	221=DD
222=DE	223=DF	224=E0	225=E1	226=E2	227=E3
228=E4	229=E5	230=E6	231=E7	232=E8	233=E9
234=EA	235=EB	236=EC	237=ED	238=EE	239=EF
240=F0	241=F1	242=F2	243=F3	244=F4	245=F5
246=F6	247=F7	248=F8	249=F9	250=FA	251=FB
252=FC	253=FD	254=FE	**255=FF**		

Table D-2.   *RGB to Hexadecimal Color Conversion Chart* (continued)

While mathematically translating to the closest browser-safe color seems appropriate, it may not look correct to many people. Consider creating a hybrid color by combining multiple safe colors together. This is done simply by creating a checkerboard effect with a GIF image, in which two or more nondithering colors are placed side by side to give the appearance of a third color. A variety of PhotoShop plug-ins, such as Colorsafe (www.boxtopsoft.com), exist for mixing colors. The site www.colormix.com is particularly interesting if you just want to see how to create a new color online.

Index

M

X

Y